Financial Engineering and Arbitrage in the Financial Markets

To Britt, Elsa, Ethan, and illy

Financial Engineering and Arbitrage in the Financial Markets

Robert Dubil

WILEY
A John Wiley & Sons, Ltd., Publication

This edition first published 2011

Registered Office
John Wiley & Sons Ltd, The Atrium, Southern Gate, Chichester, West Sussex, PO19 8SQ, United Kingdom

For details of our global editorial offices, for customer services and for information about how to apply for permission to reuse the copyright material in this book please see our website at www.wiley.com.

Library of Congress Cataloging-in-Publication Data

Dubil, Robert.
Financial engineering and arbitrage in the financial markets / Robert Dubil.
p. cm. — (The Wiley finance series)
Includes bibliographical references and index.
ISBN 978-0-470-74601-1 (cloth : alk. paper)
1. Financial engineering. 2. Arbitrage. 3. Capital market. 4. Investments—Mathematics. I. Title.
HG4523.D83 2011
332'.041—dc23

2011017543

A catalogue record for this book is available from the British Library.

ISBN 978-0-470-74601-1 (hardback) ISBN 978-1-119-95062-2 (ebk)
ISBN 978-1-119-95063-9 (ebk) ISBN 978-1-119-95064-6 (ebk)

Set in 10/12pt Times by Aptara Inc., New Delhi, India
Printed and bound by CPI Group (UK) Ltd, Croydon, CRO 4YY

Contents

Introduction

This book is an update and an improvement on my original 2004 book.

The update is the discussion of the many new things that happened in the last 10 years. Hedge funds took over the relative value strategies instead of relying on sell-side dealers pitching structured products. Credit derivatives (default swaps and collateralized debt obligations) became part of the standard tool-kit. Statistical arbitrage and tactical asset allocation edged out a lot of buy-and-hold funds. Indexing has undergone a near revolution to include new asset classes and strategies.

The improvement is in the presentation. The method of the original book was to present the difficult subjects of arbitrage, derivative pricing, and financial engineering in terms of numbers – cash flow discounting, binomial trees, tables, and diagrams – rather than differential equations. This book follows that appealing formula. All examples are worked out numerically, but they are now enhanced with flow diagrams, and are connected across the markets and chapters. Another big improvement, hopefully, is the division of the book into three parts, each offering a different perspective. If you watched three boys play with Lego, you would want to know the types of blocks (colors, the number of pegs, etc.) they are playing with, what they are building with them (a robot or a fire station), and why each boy is playing. The three parts of this book are just like that: Part I is the basic spot, futures, swap, and option transactions as building blocks; Part II illustrates examples of engineering those building blocks into CDOs or mortgage-backed securities (MBSs); and Part III relates to the players: individuals, banks, hedge funds, and private equity.

The main premise is that all financial markets are organized in the same way. All have spot (cash) transactions, forward/futures transactions and options, as well as complex swap arrangements combining all three. If you master the spot-futures cash-and-carry trade in one market (stock index arbitrage), then you can easily grasp it in another (currency-covered interest parity). If you master how delta or vega risk is hedged in equity markets, then you are likely to understand the same process in commodities or interest rates. Building a fire station with red Lego blocks is similar to building a space ship with green and blue blocks. Instead of focusing on the purpose of individual financial markets, the book focuses on the common structure. What we are building is an arbitrage or a relative value trade to profit from the real or perceived mispricing of risk. The blocks we use have the same shape, only a different color.

The building clusters in all structured products and strategies are: spot and futures trading mechanics, spot-futures linkages, option pricing, option linkages to futures, and spot, swaps, and their decomposition into bonds and forwards. The improvements in Part I consist of new chapters and easier-to-follow number and flow diagram presentations. The options discussion is split into two: options on price variables (equities, currencies, etc.) and options on non-price variables (interest rates). In the latter, we don't model prices directly – instead we model rates, derive the prices from the rates, then we price derivatives. The part includes a new chapter on credit derivatives. Part II introduces financial cash flow engineering. In addition to a survey of the perennially popular structured products, the mortgage section is substantially clearer and more complete; and the CDO section is entirely new. The analogy between prepayment and credit risk *tranching* should be very hard to miss. Part III is completely new and is mostly concerned with "why". Chapter 11, taking an individual investor perspective, is a repository of all-you-need-to-know about modern portfolio theory and its morph into statistical arbitrage methods, as well as fundamental equity valuation methods. Chapter 12 scratches the surface of hedge fund strategies and the new area of strategy indexes as a beta way of getting the alpha. Chapter 13 looks at the traditional asset-liability management for banks, which in many cases is still more useful than the newer voluminously analyzed VaR methods. Chapter 14 focuses mainly on private equity, but it also looks at liability/politics, constrained pension funds, endowments, and sovereign funds. While Part III does not answer all the *whys*, it hopefully illustrates the main motivations and quantitative techniques pursued by the key players in the financial markets.

I apologize for any mathematical errors, long sentences, or awkward grammar. I also apologize for using the royal "we" throughout the book.

Now, please find a comfortable chair, grab a pencil and a calculator, and enjoy!

1

Purpose and Structure of Financial Markets

1.1 OVERVIEW OF FINANCIAL MARKETS

Financial markets play a major role in allocating excess savings to businesses in the economy. This desirable process takes various forms. Commercial banks take depositors' money and lend it to manufacturers, service firms, or home buyers who finance new construction or improvements. Investment banks bring to market equity and debt offerings of newly formed or expanding corporations. Governments issue short- and long-term bonds to finance the construction of new roads, schools, and transportation networks. Investors (bank depositors and securities buyers) supply their funds in order to shift their consumption into the future by earning interest, dividends, and capital gains.

The process of transferring savings into investment involves various participants: individuals, pension and mutual funds, banks, governments, insurance companies, industrial corporations, stock exchanges, over-the-counter (OTC) dealer networks, and others. All these agents can, at different times, serve as demanders and suppliers of funds, or as intermediaries. Economic theorists ponder the optimal design of securities and institutions, where "optimal" implies the best outcomes – lowest cost, least disputes, fastest – for security issuers and investors, as well as for the society as a whole. Are stocks, bonds, or mortgage-backed securities, the outcomes of optimal design or happenstance? Do we need "greedy" investment bankers, securities dealers, or brokers? What role do financial exchanges play in today's economy? Why do developing nations strive to establish stock exchanges even though they often have no stocks to trade on them? Once we answer these basic questions, it will not be difficult to see why all the financial markets are organically the same. In product markets, the four-cycle radiator-cooled engine-powered car and the RAM memory-bus-hard disk personal computer have withstood the test of time. And so has the spot–futures–options, primary–secondary, risk transfer-driven design of the financial market. In the wake of the 2008 crisis we have seen very limited tweaks to the design, because it is so robust.

All markets have two separate segments: *original issue* and *resale*. These are characterized by different buyers, sellers, and different intermediaries, and they perform different timing functions. The first transfers capital from the suppliers of funds (investors) to the demanders of capital (businesses); the second transfers capital from the suppliers of capital (investors) to other suppliers of capital (investors). The two segments are:

- *Primary markets* (issuer-to-investor transactions with investment banks as intermediaries in the securities markets, and banks, insurance companies and others in the loan markets);
- *Secondary markets* (investor-to-investor transactions with broker-dealers and exchanges as intermediaries in the securities markets, and mostly banks in the loan markets).

All markets have the originators, or issuers, of the claims traded in them (the original demanders of funds) and two distinctive groups of agents operating as investors, or suppliers of funds. The two groups of funds suppliers have completely divergent motives. The first group aims to eliminate the undesirable risks of the traded assets and earn money on repackaging, the other actively seeks to take on those risks in exchange for uncertain compensation. The two groups are:

- *Hedgers* (dealers who aim to offset primary risks, be left with short-term or secondary risks, and earn spread from dealing);
- *Speculators* (investors who hold positions for longer periods without simultaneously holding positions which offset primary risks).

The claims traded in all financial markets can be delivered in three ways. The first is an immediate exchange of an asset for cash. The second is an agreement on the price to be paid with the exchange taking place at a predetermined time in the future. The last is a delivery in the future, contingent upon an outcome of a financial event, e.g. level of stock price or interest rate, with a fee paid up front for the right of delivery. The three market segments based on the delivery type are:

- *Spot* or *cash markets* (immediate delivery)
- *Forward markets* (mandatory future delivery or settlement)
- *Options markets* (contingent future delivery or settlement)

We focus on these structural distinctions to bring out the fact that all markets not only transfer funds from suppliers to users, but they also transfer risk from users to suppliers. They allow *risk transfer* or *risk sharing* between investors. The majority of the trading activity in today's market is motivated by risk transfer with the acquirer of risk receiving some form of certain or contingent compensation. The relative price of risk in the market is governed by a web of relatively simple arbitrage relationships that link all the markets. These allow market participants to assess instantaneously the relative attractiveness of various investments within each market segment or across all of them. Understanding these relationships is mandatory for anyone trying to make sense of the vast and complex web of today's markets.

1.2 RISK SHARING

All financial contracts, whether in the form of securities or not, can be viewed as bundles, or packages of unit payoff claims (mini-contracts), each for a specific date in the future and a specific set of outcomes. In financial economics, these are called *state-contingent claims*.

Let us start with the simplest illustration: an insurance contract. A 1-year life insurance policy promising to pay $1,000,000 in the event of the insured's death can be viewed as a package of 12 monthly claims (lottery tickets), each paying $1,000,000 if the holder dies during that month. The value of the policy up front (the premium) is equal to the sum of the values of all the individual tickets. As the holder of the policy goes through the year, he can discard tickets that did not pay off, and the value of the policy to him diminishes until it reaches zero at the end of the coverage period.

Let us apply the concept of state-contingent claims to known securities. Suppose you buy one share of XYZ SA stock currently trading at €45 per share and pays no dividends. You intend to hold the share for 2 years. To simplify things, we assume that the stock trades once a month and in increments of €1. The minimum price is €0 (a limited liability company cannot have a negative value) and the maximum price is €199. The share of XYZ SA can be viewed as a package of claims. Each claim represents a contingent cash flow from selling the share

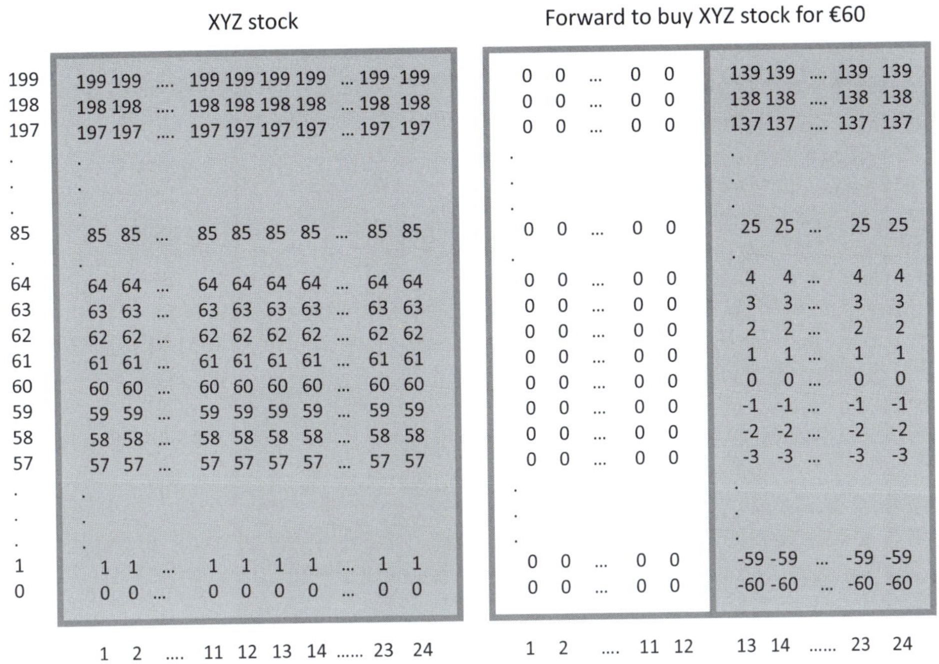

Figure 1.1 Stock and forward as packages of state-contingent claims

for a particular price in a particular month in the future. Only one of those claims will ever pay, say when we sell the stock for €78 in month 16. We can arrange the potential price levels from €0 to €199 in increments of €1 to have overall 200 possible price levels. We arrange the dates from today to 24 months from today (our holding horizon). The stock is equivalent to 200 times 24, or 480 claims. The easiest way to imagine this set of claims is as a rectangle with time on the horizontal axis and potential stock prices (states of nature) on the vertical axis. The *price* of the stock today is equal to the sum of the *values* of all the claims, i.e. all the state- and time-indexed squares of the rectangle.

Figure 1.1 shows the stock as a rectangle of 480 state-contingent claims. It also shows a forward contract on XYZ SA's stock viewed as a subset of this rectangle. Suppose we enter into a contract today to purchase the stock 13 months from today for €60. The forward can be viewed as a 200-by-24 rectangle with the first 12 months' worth of claims taken out (equal to zero, as no action can be taken). If, in month 13, the stock trades above €60, we have a gain; if the stock trades below €60, we have a loss equal to the difference between the actual stock price and the precontracted forward price.

Figure 1.2 shows a long American call option contract to buy XYZ SA's shares for €60 with an expiry 2 years from today as a 139 $\times$ 24 subset of our original rectangle, the rest zeroed out. The squares corresponding to the stock prices of €60 or below are eliminated, because they have no value. The payoff of each claim is equal to the intrinsic (exercise) value of the call. Figure 1.2 also shows a short American put struck at €60 with an expiry in 12 months.

The fundamental tenet of the option valuation methodology which applies to all securities is that if we can value each claim (one square of the rectangle) or small sets of claims (sections of the rectangle) in the package, then we can value the package as a whole sum of its parts.

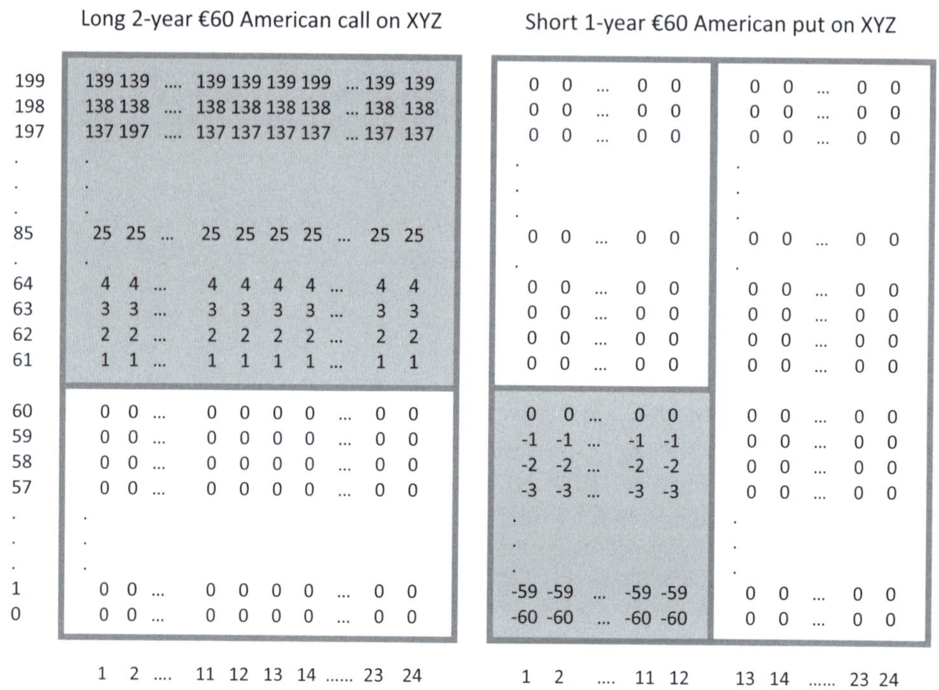

Figure 1.2 Long American call and short American put as packages of state-contingent claims.**aims**

Conversely, if we can value the package, then we are able to value subsets of claims through a subtraction of the whole minus a complement subset. Also, we may be able to combine disparate (dependent on different state variables) sets of claims (stocks on equity prices and bonds on interest rates) to form complex securities (a convertible bond). By subtracting one part (option) from the value of the combination (convertible bond), we can infer the value of a subset (straight bullet bond).

In general, the value of a contingent claim does not stay constant over time. If the holder of the life insurance becomes sick during the year and the likelihood of his death increases, then the value of all claims increases. In our stock example, the prices of the claims change as information about the company's earnings reaches the market. Not all the claims in the package have to change in value by the same amount, however. An improvement in the earnings may be only short term. The policyholder's likelihood of death may increase for the days immediately following his illness, but be less for more distant dates. As the prices of the individual claims fluctuate over time, so does the value of the entire bundle. However, at any given moment of time, the sum of the values of the claims must be equal to the value of the package, the insurance policy, or the stock. The valuation effort is restricted to here and now, and we have to repeat the exercise an instant later.

A good valuation model strives to make the claims in a package independent of each other. In our example, the payoff of the life insurance policy depends on the person *dying* during the month, not on whether the person is dead or alive. In that set-up, at most one claim of the whole set will pay. If we modeled the payoff to depend on being dead and not dying, all the claims after the morbid event would have positive prices and be contingent on each other. Sometimes, even with the best of efforts, it may be impossible to model the claims in a package as independent. If a payoff at a later date depends on whether the stock reached some level at an earlier date, the later claim's value depends on the prior one. A mortgage bond's payoff at a later date depends on whether the mortgage has not already prepaid. This is referred to as a *survival* or *path-dependence* problem. As our imaginary two-dimensional rectangles cannot handle path dependence; we ignore this dimension of risk throughout the book as it adds very little to our discussion and can usually be handled by models.

Let us turn to the definition of risk sharing.

Definition *Risk sharing is a purchase or a sale, explicit or through a side contract, of all or some of the state-contingent claims in the package to another party.*

In real life, risk sharing takes many forms. The owner of the XYZ share may decide to sell a covered call on the stock (see Chapter 5). If he sells a 2-year American call struck at €60, and gives the buyer the right to purchase the share at €60 from him even if XYZ trades higher in the market, the covered call seller is capping his stock-cum-option payoff at €60 in exchange for an up-front option premium that he receives. This corresponds to exchanging the squares corresponding to price levels above €60 for squares with a flat payoff of €60, or to subtracting, one-by-one, the payoffs in the American call package in Figure 1.2 from all the state-contingent claim payoffs in the stock package in Figure 1.1. This illustrates the important risk-sharing role of options in financial markets. Stockholders can buy or sell off parts of their holdings, and others can acquire subsets of the entire stock risk.

Another example of risk sharing is the *hedge* of a corporate bond with a risk-free government bond. A *hedge* is a sale of a package of state-contingent claims against a primary position, which eliminates all the risk of that position coming from one state variable. The sale of a security that is identical to the primary position is the only transaction that can eliminate all the risk. A *hedge* always leaves some risk *unhedged*! When a trader purchases a 10-year 5% coupon bond issued by XYZ Corp. and, in an effort to eliminate interest rate risk he simultaneously shorts a 10-year 4.5% coupon government bond – duration-matching the size of the short – he guarantees that for small parallel movements in the interest rates, the changes in the values of the two bonds are identical, but opposite in sign. If interest rates rise, the loss on the corporate bond holding will be offset by the gain on the short government bond. If interest rates decline, the gain on the corporate bond will be offset by the loss on the government bond. However, as explained in Chapters 2 and 7, the second state variable credit spread is completely unhedged. In fact, the trader speculates that the credit spread on the corporate bond declines. Irrespective of whether interest rates rise or fall, the trader gains if ever the XYZ credit spread declines since the corporate bond's price will go up more, or go down less, than that of the government bond. It is only when the credit standing of XYZ worsens and the spread rises, that the trader will suffer a loss. The corporate bond is exposed over time to two dimensions of risk: interest rates and corporate spread. In the state-contingent claim sense, the corporate bond would be represented by a large rectangular cube with time, interest rate, and credit spread as dimensions. The government bond hedge eliminates all potential payoffs along the interest rate axis, reducing the cube to a plane, with only time and credit spread as dimensions.

Almost any hedge or relative value arbitrage position discussed in this book can be thought of in the context of a multidimensional cube defined by time and risk state-variable axes. The hedge eliminates a dimension or a subspace from the cube.

1.3 TRANSACTIONAL STRUCTURE OF FINANCIAL MARKETS

Most people think of financial markets as a giant bazaar with individuals buying and selling stuff to each other for money. The "stuff" they trade is paper claims on future earnings, coupon interest, or insurance payouts. If you buy good claims and their value goes up, you can sell them for more; if you buy bad ones and their value goes down, you lose money.

Finance and economics professionals usually offer a seemingly more complete description of this process, adding detail about who buys and sells what and why in each market. They may educate us that businesses and governments need funds. They issue stock, lease- and asset-backed bonds, unsecured debentures, sell short-term commercial paper, or rely on bank loans. These issuers get their required capital and, in exchange, promise to pay interest payments or dividends in the future. The legal claims on business assets are purchased by investors, both individual and institutional, who spend cash today to get more cash tomorrow, i.e. they *invest*. Investors can leverage themselves by borrowing cash to buy more securities, and through that they themselves become issuers or users of broker margin or bank loans.

While this bazaar description of the financial transactions appears to be very comprehensive, it is actually an incomplete one-dimensional portrait of a multidimensional object. The missing dimension is the *time of delivery*.

The standard view focuses exclusively on spot markets where investors purchase securities and pay for them at the time of the purchase. To manage risk they diversify or hedge by holding shorts against longs. Most are investors (*read*: speculators) hoping to buy low and sell high. This misses the point of the risk-sharing discussion that many participants enter financial markets not to speculate/invest, but to transfer risk – and spot transactions may not be the best way to accomplish that.

Let us introduce the *time of delivery* into the picture. Let us relax the assumption that all trades of securities for cash are immediate. An equity investor may agree today to buy a stock for a certain price, but to deliver cash and receive the stock 1 year from today. The investor is entering into a *forward buy* transaction. His risk profile is drastically different from that of a spot buyer. He is exposed to the value of the stock, but his exposure does not start until 1 year from now. He does not care if the stock drops in value as long as it recovers by his delivery date. He also does not benefit from a temporary appreciation of the stock compared to the spot buyer who could sell the stock immediately. In our time-state risk rectangle with time and stock price on the axes, the forward buy looks like a spot buy, but with a subplane demarcated by today and 1 year from today taken out. Ignoring the time value of money, in Figure 1.1 the area above the forward price line corresponds to a gain, and the area below it to a loss. A forward sell would cover the same subplane, but the "good" and the "bad" areas would be reversed.

In the bazaar of finance, agents buy and sell spot, and they buy and sell forward. The forward is an important speculative and risk transfer tool. For our discussion, it does not matter if, at the future delivery time, an actual exchange of securities for cash takes place, or just a marked-to-market settlement in cash (see Chapter 3). If the stock is trading at €75 in the spot market, it is economically irrelevant whether the parties to a €60 forward transaction exchange cash (€60) for stock (share worth €75) or simply settle the difference of €15. Also, for most purposes, futures contracts can be treated as identical to forwards, even though they involve a daily settlement through a margin account. Forwards and futures attract speculators and hedgers. They first use their information to bet on the direction of the price in order to profit or risk share; the latter use their skill to arbitrage the mispricing between spot and forward transactions in the same asset.

Let us now further complicate the view of the markets by introducing the concept of *contingent delivery time*. An exchange of a security for cash, agreed upon today, is not only delayed into the future but is also made contingent upon a future event or condition. The simplest example is an insurance contract. The payment on a $1,000,000 life insurance policy takes place only upon the death of the insured person. The benefit is agreed upon and fixed up front between the policyholder and the issuing company. Hazard insurance (fire, auto, flood) is different from life in that the amount of the benefit depends on the "size" of the future event. The greater the damage, the greater the payment. An option contract is similar to a hazard insurance policy. The option payout depends on the value of the underlying financial variable in the future (see Chapters 5 and 6). A put option on the S&P 100 stock index pays the difference between the selected strike price and the value of the index at some future date times $100, but only if the index goes down below that strike price level. The buyer insures against the index going down; the more the index goes down the more benefit he obtains from the put. A *cap* on an interest rate index provides the holder with a periodic payment every time the underlying interest rate goes above a certain level. A borrower may use a cap to protect against interest rate hikes.

Options involve risk sharing, not only when buying protection, but also when selling protection. A borrower relying on revolving credit with a floating interest rate defined as spread over 3-month LIBOR can *sell* a *floor* to offset the cost of the borrowing. When the index rate goes down, he makes payments to the floor buyer. He willingly accepts that risk because when rates go down and he makes the floor payments, the interest he pays on the revolving loan also declines. In effect, the floor fixes the minimum borrowing rate in exchange for an up-front premium.

Options are not the only forms of contingent claims traded in today's markets. In fact, the contingent delivery feature, often referred to as "optionality," is quite common. Buyers of convertible bonds exchange their bonds for shares when interest rates and/or stock prices are high, making the post-conversion equity value higher than the present value of the remaining interest on the unconverted bond. Issuers call outstanding callable bonds when interest rates decline below a level at which the value of those bonds is higher than the call price. Adjustable mortgages typically contain periodic caps which prevent the interest rate, and thus the monthly payment charged to the homeowner, from changing too rapidly between periods. Many bonds have credit covenants that require the issuing company to maintain certain financial ratios; non-compliance triggers automatic repayment or default. Car lease agreements give the lessees the right to purchase the automobile at the end of the lease for a prespecified residual value, and lessees exercise those rights when the residual value is sufficiently lower than the market price of the vehicle. In many countries, including the USA, the homeowners with fixed-rate mortgages can prepay their loans partially or fully at any time without penalty. This feature allows the homeowners to refinance their loans with new ones when interest rates drop by a significant enough margin. The cash flows from the original fixed-rate loans are thus contingent upon interest rates staying high. Other examples abound.

The key to understanding complex securities is to break them down into simpler components: spot, forward, and contingent delivery. The components may trade separately in the wholesale markets, but are more likely to be bundled together for retail customers or original (primary market) acquirers. Not uncommonly, they are unbundled and rebundled several times during their lives.

All financial market evolve to have three structural components: the market for spot securities, the market for forwards and futures, and the contingent securities market which includes options and other derivatives.

Most of the activity of the last two forms is reserved for institutions, which is why most people are unaware of them. Yet their dynamic risk-sharing functions are necessary for the smooth operation of the spot markets. They constantly signal the changing price of risk to the "bundled" value of the spot securities. In some respects, the spot securities are the most complicated types from the informational content perspective. Their value reflects all available information about the financial prospects of the broad market and the entity that issued them, and is equal to the sum of the values of all state-contingent claims that can be viewed as informational units. The value of forwards and option-like contracts is tied to more narrow information subsets. These contracts have expiry dates that are short relative to the underlying security and are tailored to specific dimensions of risk. They allow the unbundling of the information contained in the spot security. This function is extremely desirable to holders of cash assets as it offers them a way to sell off undesirable risks and acquire desirable ones at various points in time. If you own a bond issued by a tobacco company, you may be worried that legal proceedings against the company may adversely affect the credit spread of the bond you hold. You could sell the bond spot and repurchase it forward with the contract date set far into the future. You could purchase an option on the yield spread or a put option on the bond, or sell calls on the bond. All of these activities would allow you to share the risks of the bond with another party and tailor the duration of the risk sharing to your needs.

1.4 ARBITRAGE: PURE VERSUS RELATIVE VALUE

We introduce the notion of *relative value arbitrage* which drives the trading behavior of financial firms irrespective of the market in which they operate. Relative arbitrage takes the concept of *pure arbitrage* beyond its technical definition of riskless profit. All primary market risks are eliminated, but some secondary market exposures are deliberately left unhedged.

Arbitrage is defined in most textbooks as riskless instantaneous profit. It occurs when the *law of one price* – which states that the same item cannot sell at two different prices at the same time – is violated. The same stock cannot trade for one price at one exchange and for a different price at another unless fees, taxes, etc., are involved, but, if it does, traders will buy it on the exchange where it sells for less and sell it on the exchange where it sells for more. Buying Czech korunas with British pounds cannot be more expensive than buying dollars with pounds and using dollars to buy korunas. If one can get more korunas for pounds by buying dollars first, no one will buy korunas for pounds directly. Anyone with access to both markets will buy korunas through dollars and immediately sell them for pounds to realize an instantaneous and riskless profit. This is a very simple example of *pure arbitrage* in the spot currency markets. Pure arbitrage can take a *static* form, where the trade is put on at the outset and liquidated once at a future date – e.g. trading Forward Rate Agreements against spot LIBORs for two different terms (see Chapter 3) – or a *dynamic* form, in which the trader commits to a series of steps that guarantee the elimination of all directional market risks and ensure riskless profit upon completion of these steps (see Chapters 4 to 7). A bond dealer may purchase a callable bond from the issuer, buy a swaption from a third party to offset the call risk, and delta-hedge the rate risk by shorting some bullet swaps. He guarantees a riskless profit provided that neither the issuer nor the swaption seller defaults. Later chapters abound in detailed examples of both static and dynamic arbitrage.

Definition *Pure arbitrage is defined as generating riskless profit today by statically or dynamically matching current and future obligations to exactly offset each other, inclusive of incurring known financing costs.*

Opportunities for pure arbitrage in today's ultra-sophisticated markets are limited. The money-making activities of most institutions rely on the principle of *relative value arbitrage*. Hedge funds and proprietary trading desks of large financial firms employ relative arbitrage techniques. Relative value arbitrage consists of a broadly defined hedge in which a close substitute for a particular risk dimension of the primary security is found, and the law of one price is applied as if the substitute was a perfect match. Typically, the position in the substitute is opposite to that in the primary security in order to offset the most significant or unwanted risk inherent in the primary security. Other risks are purposely left unhedged: if the substitute is well chosen, the risks are controllable (except in highly leveraged positions) and the acceptable risks can be precisely isolated. Like pure arbitrage, relative arbitrage can be both *static* and *dynamic*. Let us consider examples of static relative arbitrage.

Suppose you buy \$100 million of a 30-year US government bond. At the same time you sell (short) \$102 million of a 26-year bond. The amounts \$100 and \$102 are chosen through "duration matching" (Chapters 2 and 13) which ensures that when interest rates go up or down the gains on one position exactly offset the losses on the other. The only way the combined position makes or loses money is when interest rates do not change in parallel, i.e. the 30-year rates change by more or less than the 26-year rates. The combined position is not risk free. It is speculative, but only in a secondary risk factor. Investors seldom distinguish between 30- and 26-year rates; they worry more about the overall level of rates. The two rates tend to move closely together and the relative arbitrageur bets that they will diverge.

The bulk of swap trading (Chapter 4) relies on static relative arbitrage. An interest rate swap dealer agrees to pay a fixed coupon stream to a corporate customer, himself an issuer of a fixed-rate bond. The dealer hedges by buying a fixed-coupon government bond. He eliminates any exposure to interest rate movements as coupon receipts from the government bond offset the swap payments, but he is left with a swap spread risk. If the credit quality of the issuer deteriorates, the swap becomes "unfair" and the combined position has a negative present value to the dealer.

Dynamic relative arbitrage is more complicated in that the hedge must be rebalanced continuously according to very specific computable rules. A seller of a 3-year over-the-counter (OTC) equity call may hedge by buying 3- and 6-month calls on the exchange and shorting some of the stock. He then must rebalance the number of shares he is short on a daily basis as the price of those shares fluctuates. This so-called delta hedge (Chapters 5 and 6) eliminates exposure to the price risk. The unhedged exposure is to the implied volatility differences between the options sold and bought. In the preceding static swap example, the swap dealer may elect not to match the cash flows exactly on each swap he enters into. Instead, he may trade a small (duration-matched) number of "benchmark" bonds in order to offset the cash flows in bulk. The shortcut, however, will require him to dynamically rebalance the portfolio of bonds.

This book's main goal is to explain the functioning of financial markets by defining pure and relative value arbitrage linkages between different market segments. The examples appear complicated as they involve multiple futures, options and other derivatives, but they all relate to the same simple principle of profit through selective risk elimination.

Definition *Relative value arbitrage is defined as generating profit today by statically or dynamically matching current and future obligations to nearly offset each other, net of incurring closely estimable financing costs.*

To an untrained eye, the difference between relative value arbitrage and speculation is tenuous. To a professional, the two are easily discernible. An equity trading strategy called "pairs trading" is a good case in point. The strategy of buying Pfizer (PFE) stock and selling GlaxoSmithKline (GSK) is pure speculation. One can argue that both companies are in pharmaceuticals, both are large with similar R&D budgets, and both tend to move together with the pharmaceutical sector as a whole. The specific risks of the two companies, however, are quite different and they cannot be considered close substitutes. Buying Polish zlotys with British pounds and selling Czech korunas for British pounds is also speculation, not relative value arbitrage. Zlotys and korunas are not substitutes. An in-between case, but on the speculative side, is called a *basis trade*. If an airline needs to lock in the future prices of jet fuel, then instead of entering into a long-term contract with a refiner, it buys a series of crude oil futures with the idea that supply shocks that cause oil prices to rise affect jet fuel prices in the same way. When prices increase, the airline pays higher prices for jet fuel, but the profits from oil futures offset those increases, leaving the total cost of acquiring jet fuel unchanged. Buying oil futures is appealing as it allows one to liquidate the protection scheme when prices decline instead of rising, or to exit half way through an increase. This trade is not uncommon, but it exposes the airline to the *basis* risk. When the supply shocks take place at the refinery level (not the oil delivery level), spot jet fuel prices may increase more rapidly than crude oil futures.

Derivatives dealers want to make money on the bid–ask spread of their trading contracts. They rely on the relative value arbitrage principle to temporarily hedge the directional risk as they seek the other sides of the trades. When they sell options, they buy or sell the underlying stocks, bonds, or mortgages in the right proportions to exactly offset the value changes of the option and the underlying, repeating the exercise every day until the options expire or are offset. The hedge proportions change every day, depending on the changing market factors – such as the primary and secondary risks – to which the dealers are exposed. The dynamic rebalancing serves to offset the primary risks, but it does not offset all the risks. In this book, we learn how to (a) construct relative value trades with the right hedge ratios (deltas, durations) and (b) reduce the risk down to desired secondary factors (e.g. vega).

Relative value arbitrage in many markets relies on a building block of a static or dynamic *cash-and-carry* trade. The static version of the cash-and-carry trade (introduced in Chapter 3) consists typically of a spot purchase (for *cash*) and a forward sell, or the reverse. The dynamic trade (introduced in Chapters 5 and 6), as in the preceding option example, consists of a series of spot purchases or sales at different dates and a contingent payoff at the forward date. The spot and forward are tied together by the cost of financing, the *carry*, of the borrowing to buy spot or lending after a spot sale. Even the most complicated structured derivative transactions are combinations of cash-and-carry building blocks across different markets. When analyzing such trades, focusing on institutional and market structure details in each market can only cloud this basic block of arbitrage. In this book, we emphasize the common elements. We exploit the principle of arbitrage to show what motivates trades *in* each market (stock index futures vs stocks, fixed coupon stripping of bonds, triangular arbitrage in currencies) and *between* markets (simultaneous trades in currencies in money markets, hedging mortgage servicing contracts with swap options, etc.).

Many readers view the *no-arbitrage conditions* found in finance textbooks as strict mathematical constructs. They are not mathematical at all. The equations do not represent the will of God, like gravity or thermodynamics laws in physics. They are ensured by the most basic human characteristic: *greed*. Dealers tirelessly look to discover the violations of no-arbitrage, i.e. opportunities to buy an item at one price and sell a disguised version of that item for another price. By executing trades to take advantage of the temporary deviations from these paramount rules, they eliminate them by moving prices until money cannot be made and, by extension, the equations are satisfied.

In this book, all the mathematical formulas are traced back to the financial transactions that motivate them. The math serves to get the trade ratios right, but the key is to learn what to do to profit when the math is not satisfied in the markets. We overemphasize the difference between the extremes of *speculation* and *pure arbitrage* in order to bring out the relative value arbitrage (mis-called *risk arbitrage*). Apart from tiny commissions, traders earn profit from "spread" – a reward for relative value risk arbitrage. A swap trader, who fixes the borrowing rate for a corporate client, hedges by selling Treasury bonds. He engages in a relative value trade (swaps vs government bonds) that exposes him to swap spread movements. A bank, that borrows by opening new checking deposits and lends by issuing mortgages, eliminates the risk of parallel interest rate movements, but leaves itself exposed to yield curve tilts (non-parallel movements) or default risk. In all these cases, the largest risks (the exposure to interest rate changes) are hedged out, and the dealer is only exposed to secondary ones (swap spread, default).

Under our definition, most of what is conventionally labeled *investment*, qualifies as *speculation*. Over a long time, stocks should rise as the economy grows and productivity increases. Yet a stock investor, who directly or indirectly through pension and mutual funds "invests," but does not hedge or risk-share in some way, takes 100% of the price risk. He speculates, with positive odds perhaps. Financial institutions also do this: as their assets grow, they put their capital to use in new products and services. They speculate on their success.

The trading activity of many institutional dealers is *not* driven by the outright buy-low/sell-high speculation. To avoid taking primary risks by speculating on markets going up or down, traders hedge the primary risks; they leave themselves exposed only to secondary "spread" risks. Well-managed financial institutions are compensated for knowing and taking those secondary risks; poorly managed ones lose money betting on primary risks. Nearly everyone has heard of the Barings, IG Metallgesellschaft, and Orange County fiascos of the 1990s. AIG sold big bets on the default risk without knowing or hedging any of them, and lost heavily in 2008. History is filled with examples of financial institutions that were bankrupted as a result of gambling.

Institutional trading floors are designed to best take advantage of relative arbitrage within each market and between markets. Individual *trading desks*, surrounded by associated marketing and clearing teams, cover customers within a specific market segment. Trading desks that are likely to buy each other's products are placed next to each other. Special *proprietary desks* (for short called *prop* or *arb desks)* deal with many customer desks of the same firm or other firms and many outside customers in various markets. Their job is to focus on relative value trades or outright speculation across markets. The distinction between the customer vs proprietary desks is in constant flux as markets expand and shrink and desks collaborate with each other. For example, a money market desk arranges an issuance of short-term paper whose coupon depends on a stock index. It then arranges a trade between the customer and its swap desk to alter the interest rate exposure profile and between the customer and the equity derivatives desk to eliminate the customer's exposure to equity risk. The customer ends up with low cost of financing and no equity risks.

1.5 FINANCIAL INSTITUTIONS: TRANSFORMING INTERMEDIARIES VS BROKER-DEALERS

From a macroeconomic perspective, financial institutions can be broadly divided into two categories based on their *raison d'être*:

- asset transformers
- broker-dealers.

The easiest way to identify them is by examining their balance sheets. The assets of asset transformers are different from their liabilities. Broker-dealers may have different mixes, but the categories tend to be the same.

An asset transformer is an institution that invests in certain assets, but issues liabilities in a form that is designed to appeal to a particular group of customers. The best example is a commercial bank. On the asset side, a bank issues consumer (mortgage, auto) and business loans, invests in bonds, etc. The main form of liability it issues is checking accounts, saving accounts, and CDs. Customers specifically desire these vehicles as they facilitate their day-to-day transactions and often offer security of government insurance. For example, in the USA the FDIC guarantees all deposits up to $250,000 per customer per bank. The bank's retail customers do not invest directly in the bank's assets. This would be quite inconvenient as they would have to buy "bulky" assets with undesirably long maturity that entails price risk if they are sold quickly, and only offered in large denominations. In order to attract funding, the bank repackages its mortgage and business loan assets into liabilities, such as checking accounts and CDs, that have palatable characteristics – instant bankomat access, small denomination, short maturity, and deposit insurance. Another example of a "mild" asset transformer is a mutual fund (or a unit investment trust). A mutual fund invests in a diversified portfolio of stocks, bonds, or money market instruments, but issues small denomination, easily redeemable, participation shares and offers a variety of services such as daily net asset value calculation, telephone/internet fund redemption and exchange, or a check-writing ability. Other "strong" asset transformers are insurance companies. They invest in real estate, stocks, and bonds, but issue policies with payouts tied to life or hardships events (liabilities).

Because they participate in the very important cycle of capital flow between individuals and business – including money/credit creation (see later, Figure 13.1) – asset transformers are subject to special regulations and government supervision. Banks require bank charters to operate, are subject to central bank oversight, and must belong to deposit insurance schemes; the regulation of mutual funds is aimed at protecting small investors (e.g. as provided for by the Investment Company Act in the USA); and insurance company rates are often sanctioned by state insurance boards. The laws in all these cases set specific forms of legal liabilities that asset transformers may create and sound investment guidelines they must follow (e.g. percentage of assets in a particular category). Asset transformers are compensated largely for their role in repackaging their assets with undesirable features into liabilities with customer-friendly features – and that very activity automatically introduces risks into their operations. Bank liabilities have a much shorter duration (checking accounts) than their assets (fixed-rate mortgages). If interest rates do not move in parallel, the spread they earn (interest differential between rates charged on loans and rates paid on deposits) fluctuates and can be negative. They pursue relative value arbitrage in order to reduce this *duration gap*. Insurance companies deal with largely unhedgeable risks, and utilize reinsurance and securitization to share the risk.

Broker-dealers are different. They do not change the form of the securities they own and owe. They buy stocks, currencies, mortgage bonds, leases, etc., and sell the same securities. As dealers, they own them temporarily before they sell them, exposing themselves to market risks; as brokers, they match buyers and sellers.

Broker-dealers play an important role in the capital transfer from individuals to business through primary sale and secondary resale transactions, transferring securities from the original issuers to buyers as well as from existing owners to new owners. The first function is known as *investment banking* or *corporate finance*, the latter as *dealing* or *trading*. The purest forms of broker-dealers exist in the USA and Japan where the laws have historically separated them from other forms of banking. Securities firms in those two countries are pure broker-dealers (investment banking, institutional trading, and retail brokerage) with the addition of asset-transforming businesses of asset management and lending. In continental Europe, financial institutions are conglomerates, and are commonly referred to as *universal banks* as they combine both functions. In recent years, with the repeal of the Glass–Steagal Act in the USA and the wave of consolidations on both sides of the Atlantic, the US firms have converged more closely to the European model (Bank of America Merrill Lynch). Broker-dealers tend to be less regulated than asset transformers with the focus of the laws primarily on small investor protection (securities disclosure, fiduciary responsibilities of advisers, etc.). Post-2008 regulations have, however, brought them closer to banking regulations, but not fully.

Asset transformers and broker-dealers compete for each other's business. Securities firms engage in secured and unsecured lending and offer check-writing in their brokerage accounts. They also compete with mutual funds and exchange-traded funds (ETFs) by creating bundled or indexed securities designed to offer the same benefits of diversification. Commercial banks securitize credit card and mortgage loans to trade them out of their balance sheets. The trend globally has been toward *disintermediation*, i.e. securitization of previously transformed assets into standardized tradeable packages with retail customers increasingly gaining access to these new markets.

1.6 PRIMARY (ISSUANCE) AND SECONDARY (RESALE) MARKETS

From the societal welfare perspective, the primary role of financial markets has always been to transfer funds between suppliers of excess funds and their users. The users include businesses that produce goods and services in the economy, households that demand mortgage and consumer loans, governments that build roads and schools, financial institutions, and many others. All these users of capital undertake activities that are deemed economically and socially desirable. Throughout history, bankers and banks made the transfer of funds possible by accepting funds from depositors and lending them to kings and commercial ventures. The transition from feudalism to capitalism ushered in asset markets and the transfer of capital through shares of limited liability companies and bonds issued by sovereigns and corporations. Stock, bond, and commodity *exchanges* were formed to allow original investors in these securities to efficiently share the risks of these instruments with new investors. This induced many suppliers of funds to willingly become investors as the risks of holding "paper" assets were diminished. "Paper" could be sold and funds recovered. A specialized class of traders emerged who dealt only with trading "paper" on the exchanges or over-the-counter (OTC). At the same time, the role of finding productive ventures in need of capital also shifted from bankers to *investment bankers* who, instead of using their own capital to grant loans, specialized in creating new shares and bonds and selling them to investors. This requires a considerable amount of expertise. Prior to the launch of any issue, the main job of an investment banker and his *corporate finance* staff, like that of a loan banker, is to evaluate the issuing company's business and financial condition, and prepare a valuation analysis for the offered security.

Financial markets for securities are organized into two segments, defined by the parties to a securities transaction:

- Primary markets
- Secondary markets.

This segregation exists only in securities, not in private-party contracts like OTC derivatives. In private contracts, the primary market issuers also tend to be the secondary market traders, and the secondary market operates through assignments and mark-to-market settlements rather than through resale.

In *primary markets*, the suppliers of funds transfer their excess funds directly to the users of funds through a purchase of securities. An investment banker acts as an intermediary, but the paper-for-cash exchange is between the issuing company and the investor. The shares are sold either publicly, through an initial public offering (IPO) or a seasoned offering, or privately through a *private placement* with "qualified investors," typically large institutions. Securities laws of the country in which the shares are sold spell out all the steps the investment bank must take to bring the issue to market. For example, in the USA the shares must be registered with the Securities and Exchange Commission (SEC), and a prospectus must be presented to new investors prior to a sale, etc. Private placements follow different rules, the presumption being that large qualified investors need less protection than retail investors. In the USA they are governed by Rule 144-A, which allows their subsequent secondary trading through a system similar to an exchange.

In *secondary markets*, securities are traded between investors without the involvement of the issuer. Secondary markets can be organized as exchanges or as OTC networks of dealers connected by phone or computer, or a hybrid of the two. The Deutsche Börse and the New York Stock Exchange (NYSE) are examples of organized exchanges. It is worth noting, however, that exchanges differ greatly from each other. The NYSE gives access to trade flow information to human market-makers called *specialists* to ensure the continuity of the market-making in a given stock, while the Tokyo Stock Exchange is an electronic market where continuity is not guaranteed but no dealer can earn monopoly rents from private information about buying and selling. Corporate and government bond trading are the best examples of OTC markets. There, as in swap and currency markets, all participants are dealers who trade one-on-one for their own account. They maintain contact with each other over a phone and computer network, and jointly police the fair conduct rules through industry associations. For example, in the OTC derivatives markets, the International Swap Dealers Association (ISDA) standardizes the terminology used in quoting the terms and rates, and formalizes the documentation used in confirming trades for a variety of swap and credit derivative agreements. The best example of a hybrid between an exchange and an OTC market is the NASDAQ in the USA. The exchange is only virtual, as participants are connected through a computer system. Access is limited to members only and all members are dealers.

The landscape of exchange trading has seen many changes over the last 10 years. Many exchanges have merged, and human-intensive trading floors have given way to electronic platforms. The Chicago Mercantile Exchange (CME) swallowed its cross-town rivals. The Deutsche Börse made a bid for NYSE Euronext in 2011. The electronic International Securities Exchange (ISE) has wrestled half the market share of all US stock option trading from the Chicago Board of Options Exchange (CBOE). Stock trading has fragmented significantly with volume diverted from the exchanges to electronic communications networks (ECNs) and anonymity-providing "dark pools," and many brokerages internalizing retail flow. The global stock markets continue to be quite fragmented with clearing done mostly locally.

Developing countries strive to create smooth functioning secondary markets. They rush to open stock exchanges even though there may only be a few companies issuing shares. In order to improve the liquidity of trading, nascent exchanges sometimes deliberately limit access and time of trading. All these efforts are aimed at funneling all buyers and sellers into one venue. This parallels the goals of the specialist system on the NYSE. The governments in developing countries also strive to establish well-functioning government bond markets, issuing short-term obligations first and introducing longer maturities as soon as the market shows an appetite for them.

The main objective in establishing these secondary trading places is to lower the cost of raising capital by offering the primary market investors a large outlet for subsequent risk sharing. Unless investors are convinced that they can easily enter – and exit – these securities, they do not buy the equities and bonds offered by the issuers (local businesses and governments). This "tail wagging the dog" pattern of creating secondary markets first is typical not only for lesser-developed nations, but is quite common in introducing any brand new risk class into the marketplace. In the late 1980s, Michael Milken's success in selling highly speculative high-yield bonds to investors relied primarily in creating a secondary OTC market by assuring active market-making by his firm Drexel Burnham Lambert. Prior to its collapse in 2002, Enron's success in originating energy forwards and contingent contracts was driven by the company's ability to establish itself as a virtual exchange of energy derivatives (with Enron acting as the monopolist dealer, of course). In both of these cases, the firms behind the creation of these markets failed, but the primary and secondary markets they started remained strong. Newer examples of this "secondary market first" phenomenon include the expansion of trading of private placement shares in the USA, the emergence of the market in private equity secondaries, the creation of OTC and trading in synthetic collateralized debt obligations (CDOs, Chapter 10), or Goldman's floating of Facebook's and other venture-funded companies' shares prior to their registration in 2011.

1.7 MARKET PLAYERS: HEDGERS VS SPECULATORS

Without risk sharing, issuers and investors live and die with the markets. When prices increase, investors who have bought, gain; when stock prices decline, they lose. New investors "buy high" when prices rise, but "buy low" when prices decline. The decline benefits past issuers who "sold high." The rise hurts them since they received little money and now have to deliver cash flows. In this view of the markets, both sides – the issuers and the investors – *speculate* on the direction of stock prices and interest rates. The word *investment* is a euphemism for *speculation*. The logic does not change if we allow shorting of securities. The shorting allows investors to become synthetic issuers and benefit from prices going down, but they still speculate. Investors manage risk, enhance or mitigate it, by concentrating or diversifying the types of assets held. An equity investor may hold shares of companies from different industrial sectors; and a pension fund may diversify investments across domestic and foreign equities, or domestic and foreign bonds. The investor can also choose to be *long* or *short* an exposure.

It is not always clear what is safe and what is risky. It is very important to realize that the predictability of the cash flows does not imply low risk and the unpredictability does not imply high risk. Price uncertainty may be safer than future price certainty.

Sparkasse savers in Germany, postal account holders in Japan, and investors in US Treasury Bills avoid default risk and are guaranteed a positive nominal return on their savings. T-Bill and CD investors in the US lock in the rates until maturity of the instruments they hold. Are they then risk-free investors and not speculators? They certainly can calculate in advance the exact dollar amount their investment will pay at maturity. After subtraction of the original investment, the computed percentage return will always be positive; yet, by locking in the cash flows, they are forgoing the chance to make more. If, while they are holding their CD, reinvestment rates increase, they will have lost the extra *opportunity* return they could have earned. We are hinting here at the notion of *opportunity cost of capital* which is common in finance.

Let us consider another example. John Smith uses the $1,000 he got from his uncle to purchase shares in XYZ Corp. After 1 year, he sells his shares for $1,100. His annual return is 10%. Adam Jones borrows $1,000 at 5% from his broker to purchase shares in XYZ Corp. After 1 year, he sells his shares for $1,100. His annual return is 10% on XYZ shares, but he has to pay 5% or $50 interest on the loan, so his net return is 5%. Should we praise John for earning 10% on his capital and scold Adam for earning only 5%? Obviously not. Adam's cost of capital was 5%. So was John's! His was the nebulous opportunity cost of capital, or a *shadow cost*. He could have earned 5% virtually risk free by lending to the broker instead of investing in risky shares. So his relative return, or *excess return*, was only 5%. In the T-Bill or CD example, one can argue that an investor in a fixed-rate CD is a speculator as he gambles on the rates not increasing prior to the maturity of his CD. The fact that his net receipts from the CD at maturity are guaranteed to be positive is irrelevant. There is nothing special about a 0% threshold for your return objective (especially if one takes inflation into account).

In the context of this book, all investors who take a position in a risky asset, whether by borrowing or using owned funds, will be considered *speculators*. The definition is relative to the cost of capital. In this sense, both Adam and John speculate by acquiring shares whose rate of return differs from their cost of capital of 5%. An outright CD investment is speculative as the rate on the CD is not guaranteed to be the same as that obtained by leaving the investment in a variable rate money market account. A homeowner who takes out a fixed-rate mortgage to finance a house purchase is a speculator, even though he fixes his monthly payments for the next 30 years! When he refinances his loan, he cancels a prior bet on interest rates and places a new one. In contrast, an adjustable rate mortgage borrower pays the fair market rate every period equal to the short-term rate plus a fixed margin.

Most financial market participants (Chapters 11 to 14) can be divided into two categories based on whether their capital is used (a) to place bets on the direction of the market prices or rates, or (b) to finance holdings of sets of transactions which largely offset each other's primary risks:

- *Speculators* – These are economic agents who take on explicit market risks in order to earn returns in excess of their cost of capital. The risks they are exposed to through their investments are not offset by simultaneous "hedge" transactions.

- *Hedgers* – These are economic agents who enter into simultaneous transactions designed to have offsetting market risks in such a way that the net returns they earn are in addition to their cost of capital.

All arbitrageurs, whether pure or relative, are hedgers. They aim to earn nearly risk-free returns after paying all their financing costs. A pure arbitrageur's or strict hedger's returns are completely risk free. A relative arbitrageur's returns are not risk free; he is exposed to secondary market risks.

Investors use their capital to speculate. The capital is in the form of an outside endowment. Mutual funds obtain funds by shareholders sending cash; pension funds obtain capital from payroll deductions into retirement accounts; insurance companies sell life or hazard policies and invest the premiums in stocks, bonds, and real estate; while individual investors deposit cash into their brokerage accounts in order to buy, sell, or short sell stocks and bonds. In all these cases, the investors use their funds (i.e. sacrifice their cost of capital) to bet on the direction of the market they invest in. Through the fees they pay, they buy the services of broker-dealers who facilitate their investment strategies. In order to help investors improve the precision of the bets they take, broker-dealers (who, themselves, are hedgers by nature) invent new products which they "sell" to the investors. These can be new types of bonds, warrants, and other derivatives; new classes of shares, or new types of trusts and annuities. The division of players into speculators and hedgers is often replaced by alternative, less precise terms:

- *Buy-side* participants
- *Sell-side* participants.

Buy-side players are investors who do not originate the new investment vehicles. They select from a menu offered to them by the sell-side players. The sell-siders avoid gambling and use their capital to finance the hedge, i.e. to "manufacture" the new products. As soon as they "sell" them, they enter into largely offsetting trades or relative arbitrage strategies. In the latter case, the sell-siders' hedge strategies are imperfect and take time to arrange, which is when sell-siders act as speculators. The hedger/speculator is not exactly equivalent to the sell-side/buy-side division. Although sell-siders often act as both hedgers and speculators, their mindset is more tuned to that of the hedger ("to find the other side of the trade"). Buy-siders enter into transactions with sell-siders in order to become exposed to – or alter how they are exposed to – market risks ("to get in on a trade").

Geographically, the sell-side resides in global financial centers such as New York or London and is represented by the largest global banks and broker-dealers. The buy-side is dispersed and includes all smaller banks with mostly commercial business, all mutual and pension funds, university endowments, insurance companies, and all finance corporations. Larger regional banks in the USA have traditionally been buy-side institutions, but some started their own institutional trading businesses. Since the 1990s, some insurance companies established sell-side subsidiaries and used their capital strength and credit rating to compete vigorously with broker-dealers. Most of these have the phrase "Financial Products" inserted in their name, e.g. Swiss Re Financial Products or AIG Financial Products.

One type of company that can, by design, be both buy-side and sell-side is a hedge fund. Hedge funds are capitalized like typical speculators (*read*: investment companies). They are entrusted with partnership capital in order to "invest." Yet almost all hedge fund strategies are some form of relative value arbitrage, i.e. the strategies are hedges. The original capital is used only to acquire leverage and to replicate the hedge strategy as much as possible. In the early years of hedge funds (the mid-1990s), they were buy-siders. They innovated on what risks to take, but used contracts off-the-shelf from dealers. In the 2000s, hedge funds grew so large that in many markets they are now able to wrest control of the demand and supply of the information flow from the dealers and are able to sell hedges to the dealers, effectively becoming sellers of innovative strategies. Dealers and asset management companies have, however, begun to strike back with strategy index products and strategy ETFs which attempt to replicate the returns of hedge funds at lower costs (Chapter 12).

1.8 PREVIEW OF THE BOOK

Many finance textbooks are organized by market segments: stocks, money markets, bonds, real estate, currencies, commodities, etc. This is analogous to reviewing the car industry alphabetically by make, starting with Audi and BMW, and ending with Volkswagen and Volvo.

This book is arranged structurally. First, we learn the common features of all the segments: spot, forward, and option contracts, analogous to describing the car engines, body, safety features, and interior comforts. Second, we review some highly structured products (floating notes, mortgage securities, and CDOs) similar to showcasing finished cars (small Fiat 500, mid-size Honda Accord, and larger Porsche Cayenne). Last, we cover the participants in the markets and the problems they are trying to solve. This allows the reader to fully understand the internal workings of the markets, rather than learn about unimportant institutional details. The book is thus divided into three parts.

- **Part I: Relative Value Building Blocks** – Chapters 2–7 cover spot, forward/futures, options, swaps, and credit derivatives; they review the mechanics of the transactions and the arbitrage linkages within and across markets, as well as pricing methods.
- **Part II: Cash Flow Engineering** – This part is definitely not exhaustive; we devote just three chapters (Chapters 8–10) to highlight those markets that exhibit very complex cash flow diversion rules; one can legitimately claim that in many cases they are over-engineered: structured floaters with inverse, cap, and call features, mortgage-backed securities subject to sequential tranching and planned amortization schemes, and cash and synthetic CDOs with default risk tranching;
- **Part III: Players** – In Chapters 11–14, we focus on the main participant groups on the demand side: individuals planning for retirement or investing actively by valuing securities; hedge funds striving to identify relative value arbitrage alpha; banks trying to solve the perennial duration gap problem of their long assets and short liabilities; and the private markets players – pension funds, private equity, and venture capital. We omit the capital deficit agents/suppliers of securities: corporations and governments and we also omit mildly asset transforming mutual funds that engineer basket vehicles for individuals. We split the ETFs between Chapters 8, 11, and 12 – their structuring and their replication role for individuals and hedge funds.

The objective is to keep things simple. In Parts I and II we use cash flow diagrams and tables in place of equations, and we digest the complicated theory of risk–return management for the players in Part III down to concrete real-life numeric and accounting examples.

Parts I, II, and III may appeal to different audiences. Part I is a must read for those wanting to work in trading, structuring and hedge funds. It provides the fundamentals of building relative value trades and pricing. Part III is a must read for investment and derivative marketing, investment banking candidates and general economics candidates. It provides the basics of security valuation, asset-liability management and private equity processes. Part II should be of interest to both groups. While not titled "Financial Markets for Dummies," the entire book should be readable by all college graduates interested in finance, including accountants, doctors and engineers. I don't know about politicians. . .

Part I

Relative Value Building Blocks

2 Spot Markets

The art of present valuing, otherwise known as Bond Math, is the basis of all security valuation, and the majority of this chapter will be devoted to Bond Math. We abstract from the reality of the many types of borrowers in the world such as sovereign governments, corporations, and municipalities, each of which is subject to different regulations and taxes, and each has its own credit worthiness – all of which affect yield levels in each market. We assume that we are within one of these markets with one issuer and a set of bonds issued by that issuer. We introduce the most basic bond structures – zero-coupon, coupon, amortizing, and floating rate – which are going to serve as building blocks for all other concepts. We go through simple annual calculations, then introduce real-life complications: compounding more frequently than annually, day counting for interest calculations and accruals. We then arrive at the fundamental concept of the discount curve or the term structure of discount or zero-coupon rates. Using the arbitrage principle that the whole must equal the sum of its parts (in value) for all the bonds in any given market, we build one set of discount rates or factors that allow us to value any new bond in that market. The value of a bond with arbitrary cash flows is equal to the sum of all its cash flows multiplied by the correct spot discount factors. This is not because our math says so, but because the greed of financial traders will not allow the same item, repackaged under a disguised name, to trade at a different value. Any bond can be shown to be a package of positions in bonds already existing in the market, and the bond's value can be computed from the sum of these positions. In general, some of these positions can be *long* (bought) and some *short*. At the end of the chapter, when we cover equity, commodity, and currency markets, we highlight the important concept of *shorting* securities. With that, our overview of the spot transactions as the most basic building blocks in financial engineering is complete.

2.1 BONDS AND ANNUAL BOND MATH

In this book, we use the term "loan" and "bond" interchangeably. A loan is a private credit arrangement between a borrower and a lender in which the lender acquires rights to future cash flows from the borrower. A lender, subsequently, can privately resell the loan to another willing lender. A bond is a publicly traded credit arrangement. The issuer borrows money by selling the bond to a distributed group of creditors who can then resell their portion of the issued bonds to other willing creditors.

Bonds that do not contain options are easy to analyze and value. They typically come in one of four forms: zero-coupon (discount) bonds, coupon bonds, amortizing bonds, and floating rate bonds.

2.1.1 Zero-Coupon Bond

Jack lends money to the ABC Company by buying a 4-year \$1,000 face value zero-coupon bond. Let us suppose the interest rate (called the *yield-to-maturity*) Jack is going to earn is

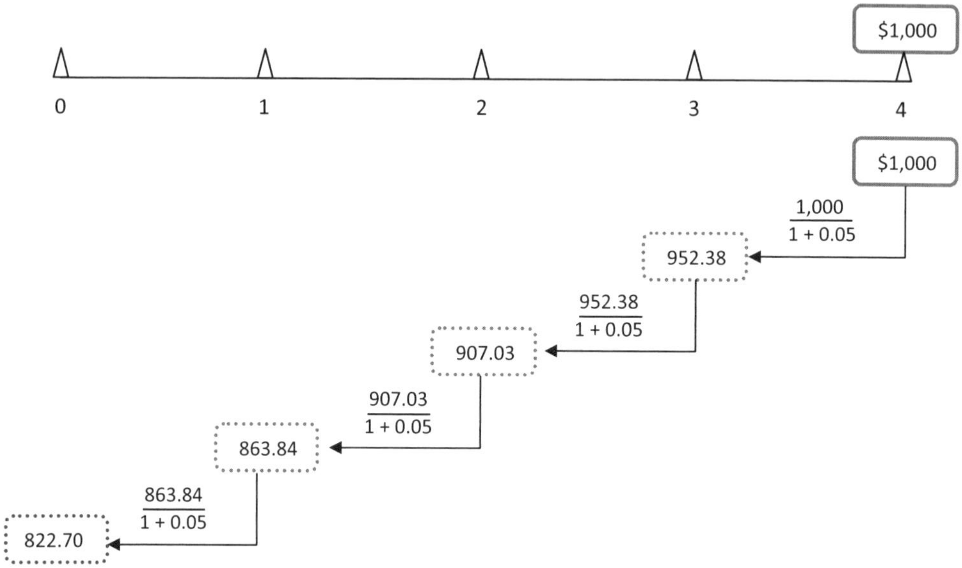

Figure 2.1 A 4-year zero-coupon bond

5%. Figure 2.1 illustrates how we can value the bond by discounting the cash flow back through time.

$$P_0 = 822.70 = \frac{\$1{,}000}{(1.05)^4} = \frac{1}{(1.05)} \times \frac{1}{(1.05)} \times \frac{1}{(1.05)} \times \frac{1}{(1.05)} \times \$1{,}000$$

In Figure 2.1 Jack is lending $822.70 to ABC today (the price he pays) and acquires a claim to receive $1,000 in 4 years' time. Jack can resell this claim later for an amount that will depend on the interest rate at the time. The buyer will perform a backward discounting calculation similar to that shown in the figure, but only using the remaining number of years to maturity. Only if the interest rate does not change and stays at 5% throughout the life of the loan will the amounts shown in the dashed boxes represent the actual future prices of the bond.

Zero-coupon bonds are typically issued with face values (par values) that are round numbers like $1,000, $5,000, or $100,000. They are bought at a discount from par and the interest is imputed in the difference between the price paid (usually not a round number) and the face value received at maturity or the price received at the time of the resale. The price is typically quoted as the percent of par. In our example, the price would be quoted as 82.27. Note that the percent price converted to a fraction 0.8227 represents the value today of $1 received 4 years from now. The number 0.8227 is called the *discount factor*.

In general, bond and loan repayment values do not have to be round numbers. Suppose Jack was willing to lend $1,035.46 to ABC. How much should he expect 4 years from now if he earns 5%? Figure 2.2 illustrates the answer. This time we sweep forward starting with the known amount of the loan, i.e., the purchase price of the bond.

In general, the price of the zero-coupon bond, expressed as a percentage of par, is equal to:

$$P_0 = \frac{100}{(1+r)^n}$$

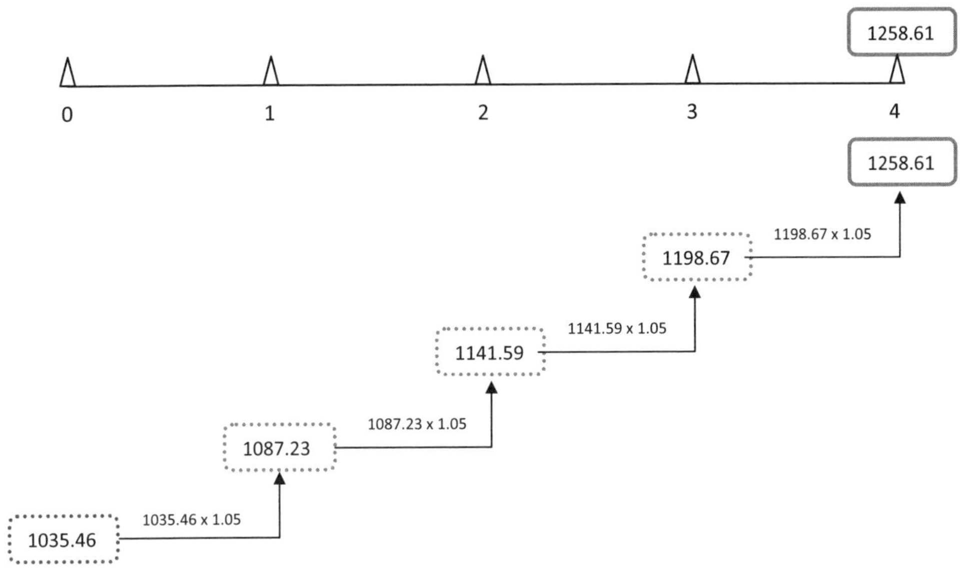

Figure 2.2 A \$1,035.46 zero-coupon loan earning 5%

where r is the interest rate and n is the number of years. The *spot discount factor* (df) is defined as:

$$df_n = \frac{1}{(1+r)^n}$$

The discount factor will prove to be extremely important when we come to value other securities. Each security will be treated as a claim on a stream of cash flows at different times. We will find the present value of those cash flows by multiplying them by their respective discount factors and summing the products to get the total value of the security. The zero-coupon bond is the only bond that has only one cash flow. All other bonds have multiple cash flows.

2.1.2 Coupon Bond

A coupon bond pays a periodic stream of identical cash flows (called *coupon interest*) and a one-time cash flow at maturity (called the *par* or *face value*). Suppose Jack buys a 4-year 6% annual coupon \$1,000 par value bond issued by the ABC Company to earn a 5% annual interest rate (yield-to-maturity) on his investment. Figure 2.3 illustrates how we can value the bond.

$$P_0 = 1{,}035.46 = \frac{1}{1.05}\left(60 + \frac{1}{1.05}\left(60 + \frac{1}{1.05}\left(60 + \frac{1}{1.05}(60 + 1{,}000)\right)\right)\right)$$

Instead of going back in time step-by-step to discount and cumulate cash flows, we can value the coupon bond as the sum of its parts. The coupon bond is a package of four zero-coupon bonds with face values of \$60, \$60, \$60, and \$1,060 and maturities 1, 2, 3, and 4 years, respectively. We do this by multiplying each coupon cash flow (face value of the component

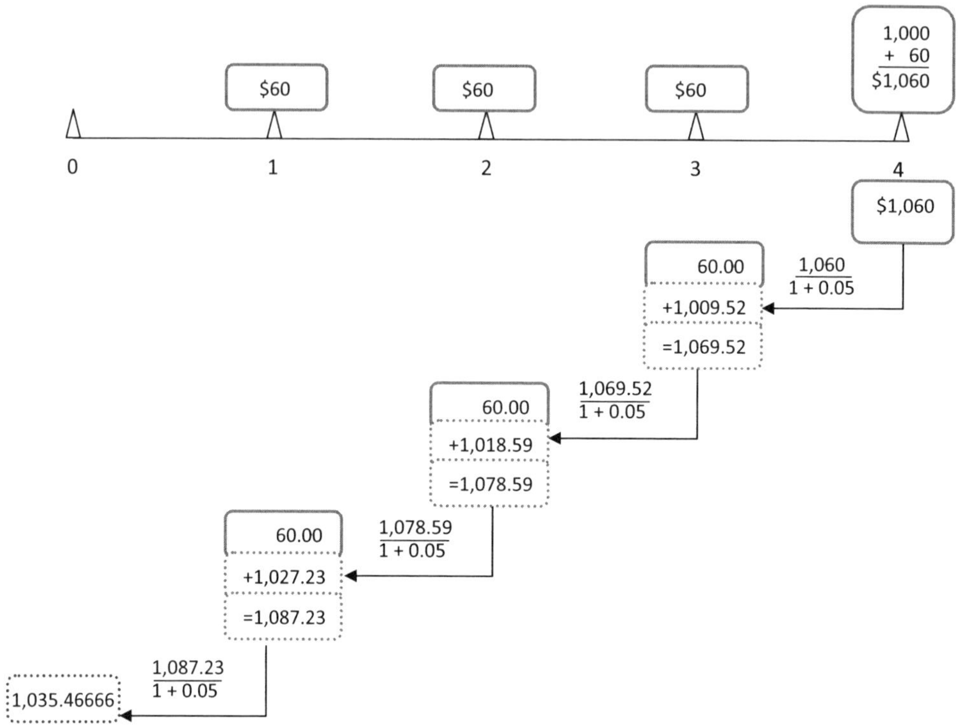

Figure 2.3 A 4-year 6% coupon bond yielding 5%: backward sweep

zero-coupon bond) by its appropriate discount factor. This factorization is illustrated in Figure 2.4.

$$P_0 = 1{,}035.46 = \frac{\$60}{(1.05)} + \frac{\$60}{(1.05)^2} + \frac{\$60}{(1.05)^3} + \frac{\$1{,}060}{(1.05)^4}$$

Also, we can factorize by separating the \$1,000 par from the rest of the cash flows:

$$P_0 = 1{,}035.46 = \$60 \times \left(\frac{1}{(1.05)} + \frac{1}{(1.05)^2} + \frac{1}{(1.05)^3} + \frac{1}{(1.05)^4}\right) + \frac{\$1{,}000}{(1.05)^4}$$

The two methods in Figures 2.3 and 2.4 – the backward step-by-step discounting sweep and the sum of the parts' present values – are equivalent and always produce the same answer. Mathematically, it makes no difference whether we multiply n times in succession by one-period (forward) discount factors

$$df_{n-1,n} = \frac{1}{(1 + r_{n-1,n})}$$

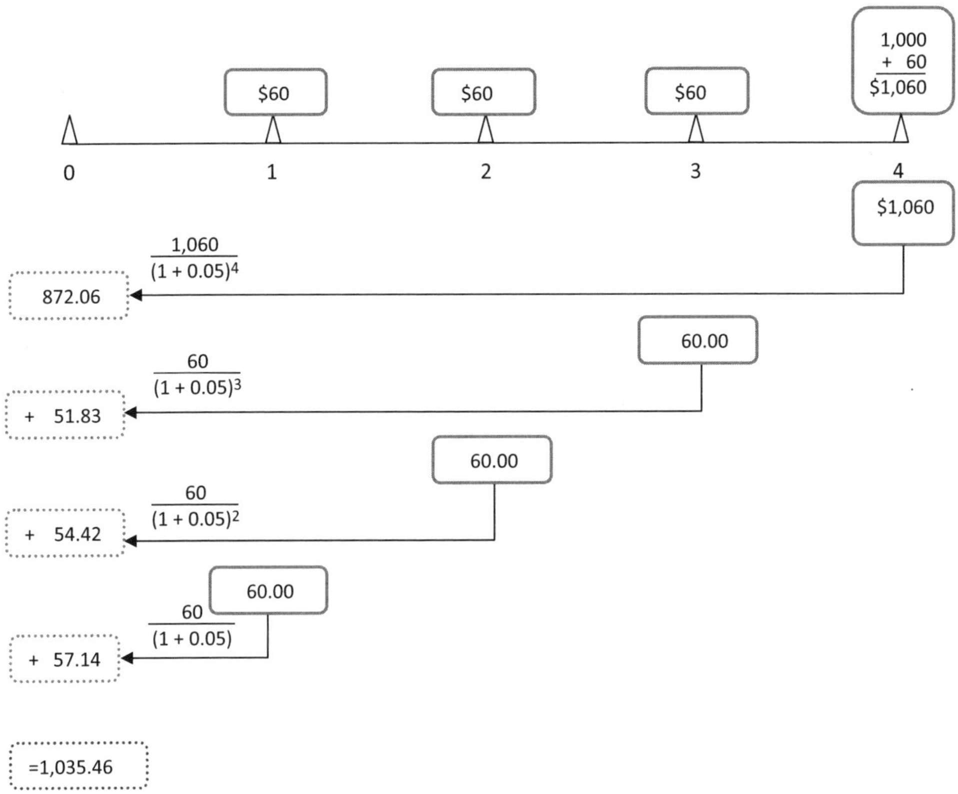

Figure 2.4 A 4-year 6% coupon bond yielding 5%: sum of the parts

or all at once by today's (spot) discount factors

$$df_n = \frac{1}{(1 + r_n)^n}$$

as long as the rates are all equal.

One has to be a bit more careful, but the two methods are still identical when interest rates for different periods are not the same. We deal with the more complicated case of changing interest rates in Section 2.3 where we call $r_{n-1,n}$ forward zero rates and r_n spot zero rates. We develop further the notion of forward rates in Chapter 3.

2.1.3 Amortizing Bond

An amortizing bond is also a multicash flow bond. Unlike the coupon bond which has an equal stream of coupon interest plus a one-time cash flow representing the return of par, the amortizing bond has a stream of equal cash flows, all of which can be thought of as partly coupon interest (on the remaining balance of the loan) and partly principal repayment. This distinction is somewhat artificial since the coupon interest of the coupon bond is generally not the same as the interest rate earned on the amount invested in the bond. The real difference between the coupon bond and the amortizing bond is the pattern of cash flows. The amortizing

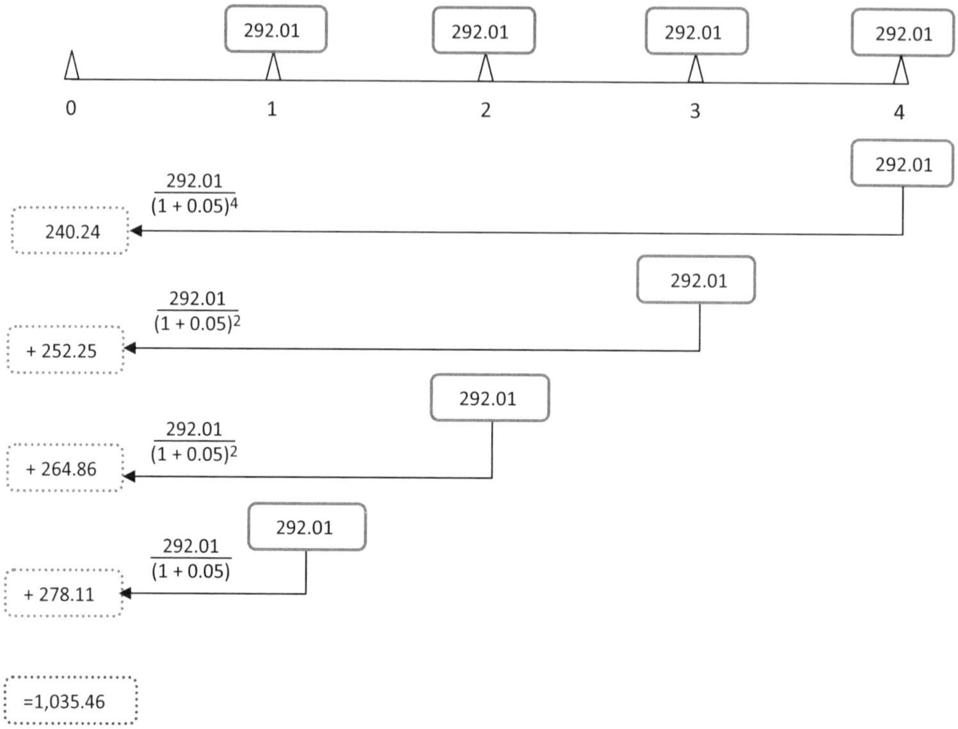

Figure 2.5 A 4-year amortizing loan yielding 5%: sum of the parts

bond's cash flows are all identical, and there is no large "balloon" payment at maturity.

$$
\begin{aligned}
P_0 = 1{,}035.46 &= \frac{\$292.01}{(1.05)} + \frac{\$292.01}{(1.05)^2} + \frac{\$292.01}{(1.05)^3} + \frac{\$292.01}{(1.05)^4} \\
&= \$292.01 \times \left(\frac{1}{(1.05)} + \frac{1}{(1.05)^2} + \frac{1}{(1.05)^3} + \frac{1}{(1.05)^4} \right)
\end{aligned}
$$

Figure 2.5 illustrates a 4-year amortizing loan of \$1,035.46 yielding a 5% interest rate. At that rate, the lender receives \$292.01 each period. (Think of a refrigerator priced at \$1,035.46 financed with a 4-year installment loan at 5%.) We value it using the sum-of-the-parts method.

2.1.4 Floating Rate Bond

The last type of bond, the floating rate bond, is also a multiple-cash flow bond. Similarly to the coupon bond, it has a stream of coupon cash flows and a large balloon cash flow equal to the par value at maturity. However, the coupon cash flows are not known up front, but are set one period in advance: next coupon payment is set today, the coupon paid 2 years from today is set 1 year from today, the coupon paid 3 years from today is set 2 years from today, etc. The idea is to reset the interest rate, as on a revolving loan, to a new "fair" rate each year, rather than holding it constant throughout of the life of the bond.

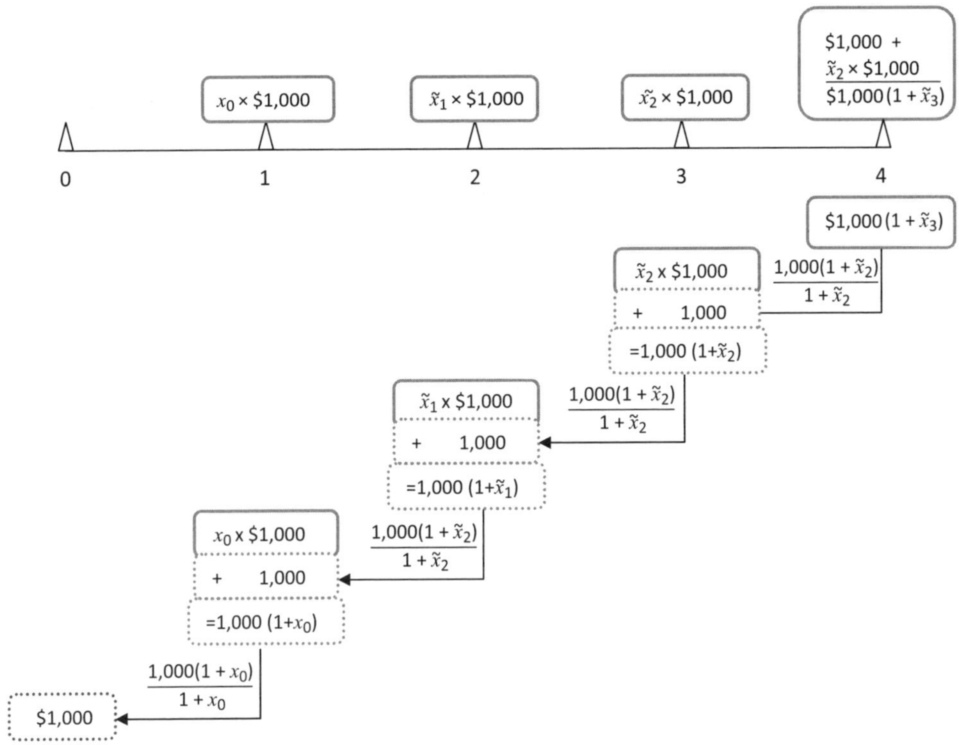

Figure 2.6 A 4-year floating-rate bond: always worth par

Since the cash flows are not known in advance (we use a tilde to denote a quantity unknown today), it may appear that the floating rate bond is impossible to value. In fact, as long as the rates set each year are flat without a margin (i.e. LIBOR plus zero), the floating rate bond is easy to value using the backward sweep method.

We illustrate that in Figure 2.6. Suppose Jack lends to the ABC Company on a floating rate basis for 4 years. The face value of the bond is \$1,000. Each year the bond's rate is set to a 1-year rate and the coupon interest is paid a year later (in arrears). At the penultimate time 3, we expect to receive 1 year later \$1,000 in principal plus the new coupon rate $\tilde{x}_3$ times \$1,000 in coupon interest. To discount from time 4 to time 3, we will multiply the cash flow \$1,000 + $\tilde{x}_3 \times$ \$1,000 to be received at time 4 by the one-step discount factor $df_{3,4} = 1/(1 + \tilde{x}_3)$. That simply produces \$1,000. This illustrates that after each coupon payment the value of the floating rate bond reverts to par. The floating rate bond is indeed equivalent to a guaranteed revolving loan without the hassle of finding a borrower and re-signing papers each year.

$$P_0 = 1{,}000 = \frac{1}{1+x_0}$$
$$\times\left(1{,}000x_0 + \frac{1}{1+\tilde{x}_1}\left(1{,}000\tilde{x}_1 + \frac{1}{1+\tilde{x}_2}\left(1{,}000\tilde{x}_0 + \frac{1}{1+\tilde{x}_3}(1{,}000\tilde{x}_3 + 1{,}000\right)\right)\right)$$

2.2 INTRA-YEAR COMPOUNDING AND DAY-COUNT

In the real world, the coupons do not accrue and interest rates do not compound over nice annual periods. We tackle things one-by-one. First, we modify our calculations to allow for semi-annual, quarterly, and monthly accrual and compounding periods. Second, we complicate our calculations with different day-counting conventions that exist in different bond markets. Last, we tackle the issue of accrued interest which is paid anytime the bond is bought between coupons, i.e. almost always.

2.2.1 Intra-Year Compounding

Interest rates are always stated on the per year basis, but interest does not have to compound annually. Suppose, for example, that a zero-coupon interest rate is stated as 5% compounded quarterly. The 5% does not mean that the borrower pays 5% of the outstanding principal in interest each quarter. The 5% rate is per annum, hence we have to divide it by 4 to get the real interest rate per quarter, which is 1.25%. Figure 2.7 shows what Jack will receive at maturity if he lends \$1,000 to ABC Company for 12 months on a zero-coupon basis (i.e. no intermediate interest receipts, all interest paid at the end, like on a bank CD) at 5% compounded quarterly.

$$1{,}000 \times \left(1 + \frac{0.05}{4}\right) \times \left(1 + \frac{0.05}{4}\right) \times \left(1 + \frac{0.05}{4}\right) \times \left(1 + \frac{0.05}{4}\right) = 1{,}050.95$$

At the end of 12 months, Jack will receive his \$1,000 back and \$50.95 in interest. A 5.095% annually compounded interest rate is economically equivalent to a 5.00% quarterly compounded interest rate. In US consumer finance and retail banking, the 5.095% annual rate is often referred to as APY or annual percentage yield (%APY), while the 5.00% quarterly rate is referred to as APR or the annual percentage rate (%APR), with annual (a) or quarterly

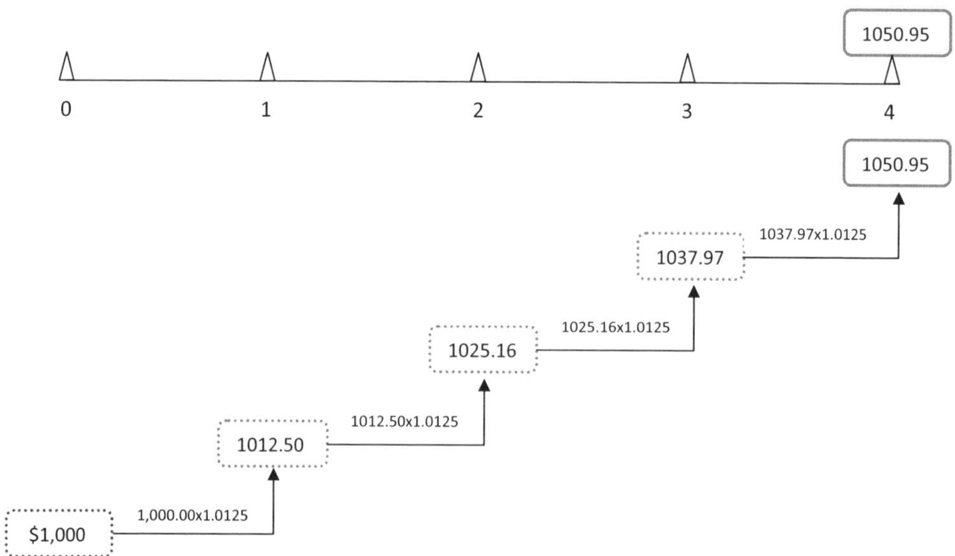

Figure 2.7 A 5% quarterly compounded rate over 1 year

(q) added after the rate. The two interest rates (%a and %q) are just different measuring units for interest in the way that miles (m) and kilometers (km) are used for distance. In general, the conversion formula for any non-annual compounded rate into annual is:

$$1 + r_a = \left(1 + \frac{r_m}{m}\right)^m$$

where r_a is the annual equivalent rate and r_m is the rate compounded m times per year. Since many bonds in the world pay interest semi-annually, it is common to actually convert non-semi-annual rates to semi-annual using the relationship:

$$\left(1 + \frac{r_s}{2}\right)^2 = \left(1 + \frac{r_m}{m}\right)^m$$

The relationship reflects the property that if the two rates are to be economically equivalent, interest earned on $1 invested must be identical over the same total interest period; in the equation, that total period is 1 year. The semi-annual rate is usually referred to as the *semi-annual bond equivalent yield* and is often added in financial tables as the last column under the heading *yield*. It allows for a quick comparison of relative value between different financial instruments.

In addition to interest rates (yields) being stated in different compounding forms, bond coupon interest is often paid more than once a year. Just like interest rates, coupon rates are stated on a per annum basis with the word quarterly or semi-annually (q or s) added afterward to warn that the stated rate needs to be decompounded to arrive at the real coupon interest amount.

Let us revisit our coupon bond example in Figures 2.3 and 2.4. Suppose that now Jack buys a 4-year $1,000 face value 6% *semi-annual coupon* issued by ABC. The bond yields 5% semi-annually. That is, the coupon interest is 3% or $30 every 6 months, and Jack earns interest at a rate of 2.5% per 6 months. Figure 2.8 illustrates the semi-annual bond using the sum-of-the-parts valuation method.

$$P_0 = 1{,}035.85 = \frac{\$30}{\left(1+\frac{0.05}{2}\right)} + \frac{\$30}{\left(1+\frac{0.05}{2}\right)^2} + \frac{\$30}{\left(1+\frac{0.05}{2}\right)^3} + \frac{\$30}{\left(1+\frac{0.05}{2}\right)^4} + \frac{\$30}{\left(1+\frac{0.05}{2}\right)^5} + \frac{\$30}{\left(1+\frac{0.05}{2}\right)^6} + \frac{\$30}{\left(1+\frac{0.05}{2}\right)^7} + \frac{\$1{,}030}{\left(1+\frac{0.05}{2}\right)^8}$$

2.2.2 Day-Count

Interest compounding is actually even more complicated, partly because the calendar years cannot be divided into equal semi-annual periods, quarters or months, and partly because of multiple day counting conventions designed to deal with that. A day-count convention prescribes two things: how to count days in the coupon accrual periods and how to count days in a year (or half-year).

Suppose that, on September 30, 2013, ABC issues a 6% semi-annual coupon $1,000 face value bond maturing on September 30, 2015. Coupon accrual periods are October 1 through March 31 and April 1 through September 30. In Figure 2.9 we review three commonly used

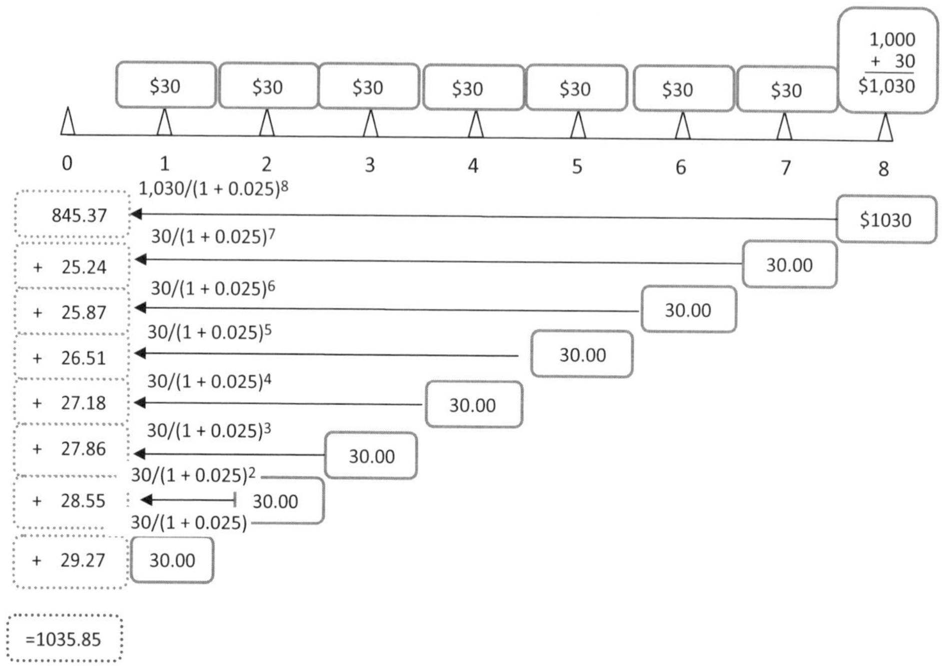

Figure 2.8 A 4-year 6% semi-annual coupon bond yielding 5%: sum of the parts

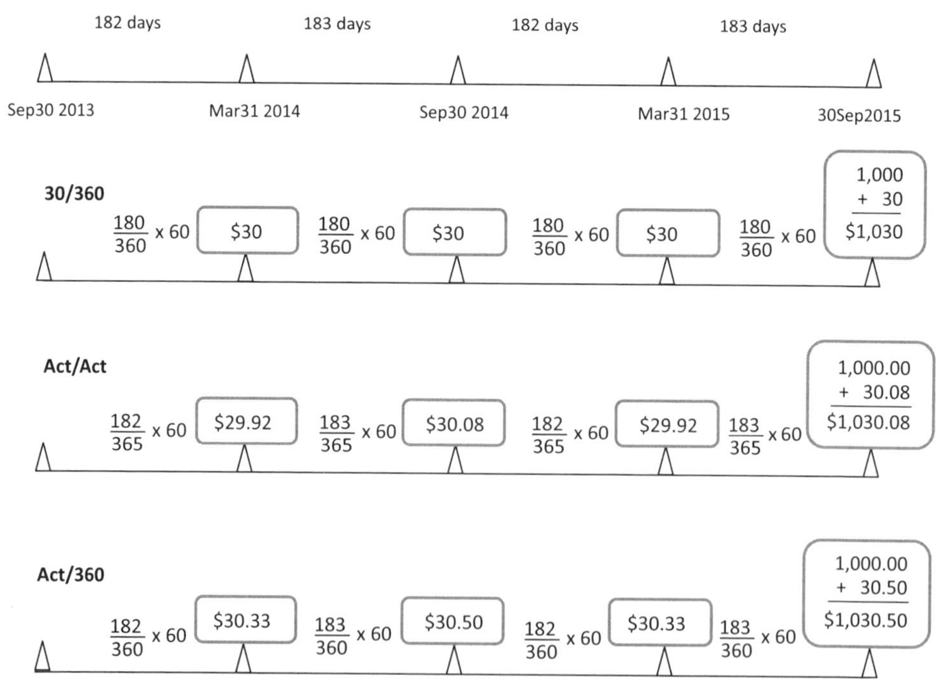

Figure 2.9 Day-count conventions

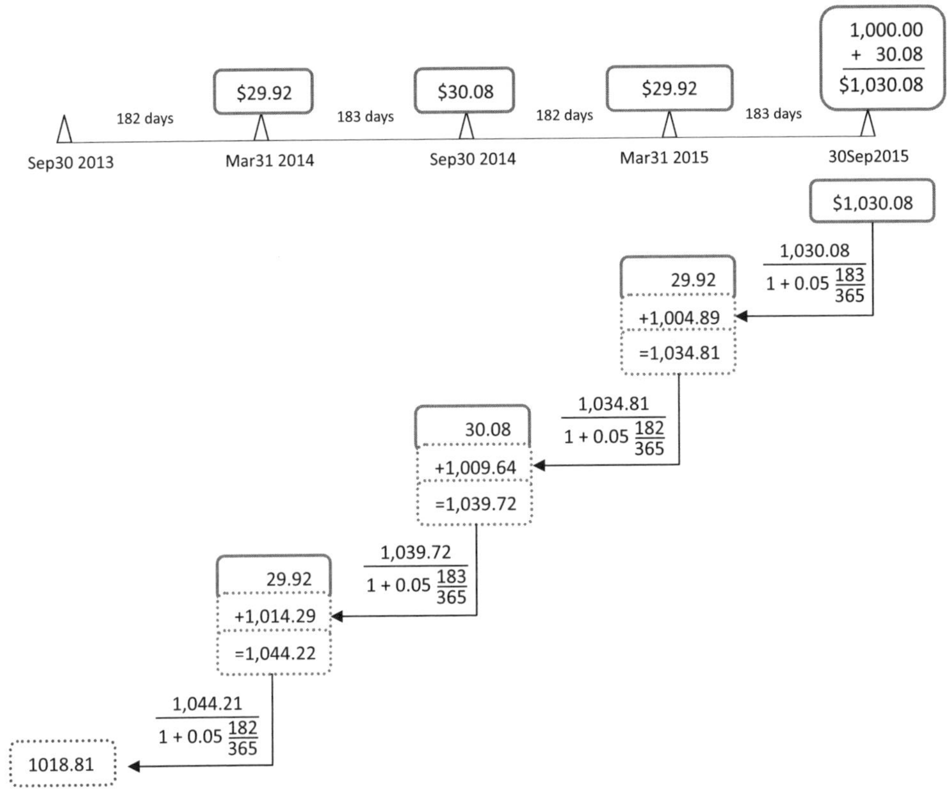

Figure 2.10 The Act/Act day-count convention

conventions: 30/360, Actual/Actual (similar to Actual/365), and Actual/360. The word Actual is usually abbreviated to Act.

US corporate bonds follow the 30/360 convention, continental Europe bonds follow a 30/360 convention modified by how month ends are treated, UK gilts follow Act/365, US Treasuries follow Act/Act using half-years, and LIBOR money markets follow Act/360. In addition to day-count conventions, different markets may have different delays ranging from zero to 3 (business) days between the end of the interest accrual period and the actual receipt of interest (and different countries have different holidays and thus business days!). The day-count convention can be followed by letters like m, mf, 2d, etc., to denote the rule on that. For example, Eurodollar (LIBOR) deposits have a 2-business-day delay, using the UK holiday calendar.

Not only the coupon accrual, but also discounting has to be modified to follow the correct convention. Let us look at the 6% semi-annual coupon bond maturing September 2015 in Figure 2.9. Let us assume that the bond follows the Act/Act day-count and that the yield is 5% on the Act/Act basis. Figure 2.10 shows the valuation using the backward discounting sweep method.

2.2.3 Accrued Interest

Except by coincidence, bonds are usually purchased between coupon dates. Once the ownership of the bond is transferred, the new owner will receive the full coupon on the next coupon

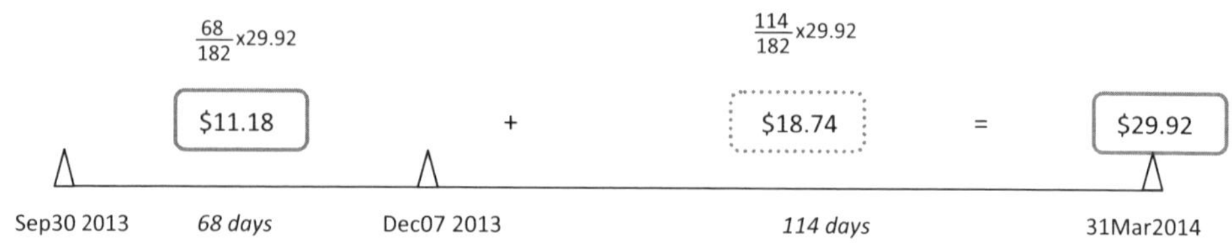

Figure 2.11 Accrued interest

payment date. Yet he will have held the bond only for the fraction of the full coupon period from the purchase date till the next coupon date. The new buyer reimburses the current one for the portion of the coupon interest accrued from the last coupon date to the date of the purchase. This reimbursement is done "in advance" at the time of the purchase of the bond through the payment of the accrued interest on top of the quoted price of the bond. The *invoice* or *dirty price* of the bond is equal to the *clean price* of the bond plus the *accrued interest*. The *clean price* is just the present value of the coupons and principal. Bonds are thus quoted clean but settled dirty.

The calculation of the accrued interest observes the day-count convention of the bond and involves prorating the current coupon between the coupon already accrued (due the current owner) and the coupon to be accrued (due the new owner). Suppose, on December 7, 2013, Jack purchases from Jill the 6% Act/Act semi-annual coupon September 2015 bond issued by ABC Company. In addition to the clean price, Jack will have to pay Jill the accrued interest for the September 30–December 7, 2013, period. The calculation is illustrated in Figure 2.11.

In the following sections, in order to keep the presentation uncluttered, we ignore the issues of day-count, intra-year compounding and accruals, and stick to even divisions by 1, 2, or 4, but the reader should at this point be able to modify all calculations to deal with the calendar.

2.3 TERM STRUCTURE OF INTEREST RATES AND THE DISCOUNT FACTOR BOOTSTRAP

Interest rates on any given day are different for different maturity instruments. A set of interest rates complete across all maturities is called the *term structure of interest rates*. This complete set can be defined using observed coupon bond rates, zero-coupon rates, or a mix of the two. The term structure implicitly defines a unique set of discount factors with which we are able to price any fixed income security in the market by present valuing its cash flows.

2.3.1 Term Structure

Jack is offered a 4.0% semi-annual $1,000 par value bond maturing in $3^1/_2$ years. How much should he pay for it? We draw a picture of the bond in Figure 2.12. We observe that the $3^1/_2$-year bond is a package of seven cash flows starting 6 months from now and ending 42 months from now, and if we knew the seven spot zero-coupon rates $r_1, r_2, \ldots, r_7$ or equivalently the seven discount factors $df_1, df_2, \cdots, df_7,$ we would know how to value the bond.

Suppose that no zero-coupon bonds are currently traded in the market from which to obtain the zero-coupon rates, but we can observe the set of coupon bond prices and rates in Figure 2.13. All the bonds have semi-annual coupons, the yields-to-maturity are stated in semi-annual

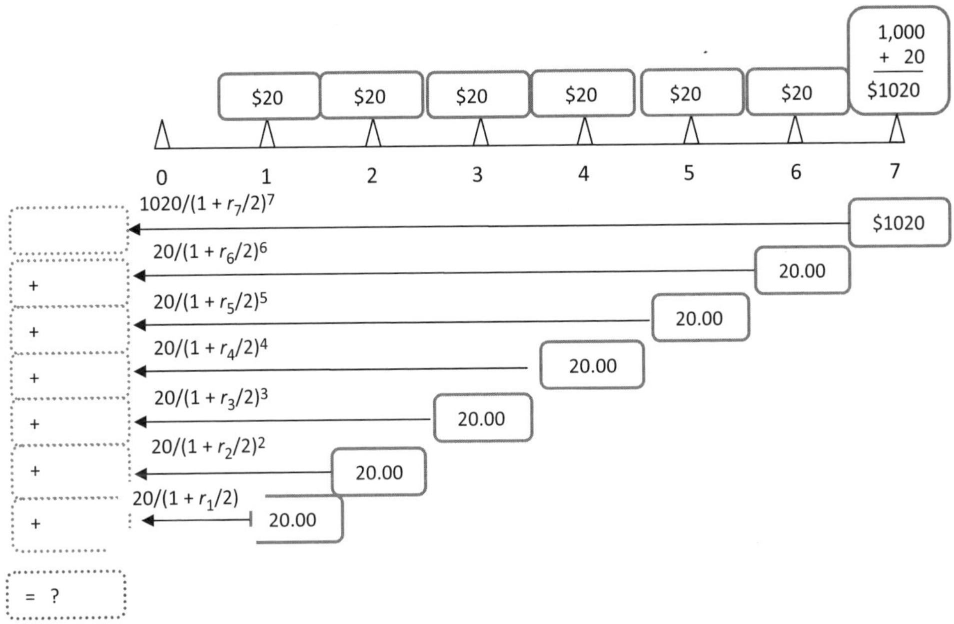

Figure 2.12 A $3^1/_2$-year coupon bond we want to value

Term	Coupon	Price	YTM
6m	2.00	100.00	**2.0000%**
1y	2.50	100.10	**2.3982%**
18m	3.00	100.25	**2.8286%**
2y	3.50	100.32	**3.3333%**
30m	3.25	99.84	**3.3172%**
3y	3.00	99.78	**3.0773%**
42m	3.25	99.89	**3.2835%**
4y	3.50	100.15	**3.4595%**

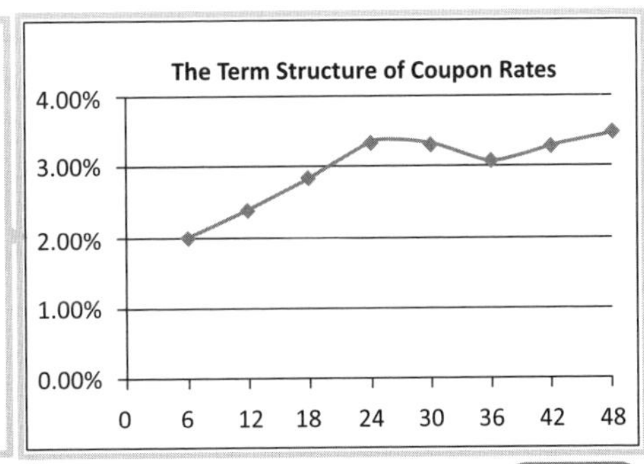

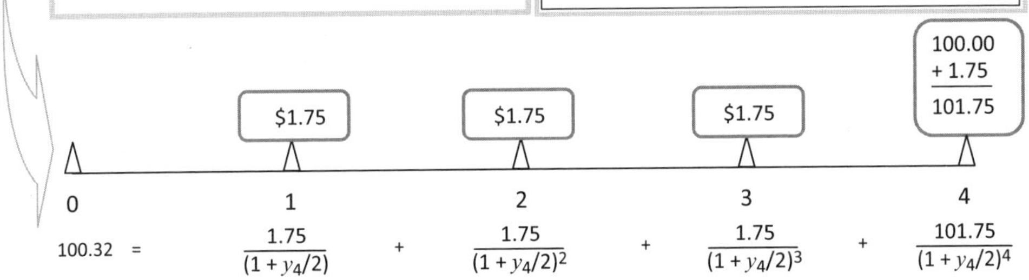

$$100.32 = \frac{1.75}{(1+y_4/2)} + \frac{1.75}{(1+y_4/2)^2} + \frac{1.75}{(1+y_4/2)^3} + \frac{101.75}{(1+y_4/2)^4}$$

ytm $y_4 = 3.3333\%$

Figure 2.13 The term structure of coupon interest rates

rates, and prices are stated per $100 par value. The yields-to-maturity are computed by solving for the discount rate for which the sum of the present values of the cash flows equals the given bond price. An example yield-to-maturity equation is shown for the 2-year 3.5% bond. The equation is solved using a trial-and-error method, a financial calculator, or an Excel function RATE. The term structure of coupon rates is a set of terms (maturities) and the corresponding yields-to-maturity. It is commonly represented as a table or graph. In Figure 2.13 we show both.

2.3.2 Discount Factor Bootstrap

The yields-to-maturity from Figure 2.13 cannot be used directly to discount the cash flows of Jack's $3^1/_2$-year bond (we need spot *zero* rates). But they contain enough information to allow us to do so. The process of obtaining spot zero rates or spot discount factors from the coupon term structure is called the yield curve bootstrap and is illustrated in Table 2.1. It proceeds step-by-step from the shortest to the longest maturity and relies on the sum-of-the parts argument. Step 1 is easy since what we labeled a 6-month 2% bond is really a 6-month zero-coupon bond with a face value of $101. So the 6-month zero rate is the same as the yield-to-maturity of the 6-month coupon bond, i.e. 2%. At Step 2, the 1-year 2.5% coupon bond is viewed as a package of two zero-coupon bonds: a 6-month $1.25 face value bond and a 12-month $101.25 face value bond. The price of the package is $100.10. Using the 6-month zero rate from Step 1, we can compute the present value of $1.25 in 6 months and subtract it from $100.10. The remainder is the present value of the 12-month $101.25 cash flow. Knowing that, we compute the 12-month zero rate and the 12-month discount factor. At each subsequent step, the coupon bond for that maturity is viewed as a package of zero-coupon bonds maturing at coupon dates and using the zero rates or discount factors from prior steps we can compute the present value of all the coupon cash flows prior to the last one. Subtracting those present values from the total value of the bond (the current price) we get the present value of the last cash flow consisting of the last coupon and principal. Again, it is easy then to solve for the zero-coupon rate or the discount factor to the date of the last cash flow.

Once we have computed all the zero rates and spot discount factors, we are also able to compute forward one-period discount factors and forward one-period zero rates. We added them in the last two columns of the last panel of Table 2.1. In valuing bonds, we use the sum-of-the parts argument similar to that in Figure 2.4 and discount cash flows directly to today (spot) using the spot zero rates or spot discount factors (instead of one yield-to-maturity). Alternatively, we can use the backward step-by-step discounting sweep argument similar to that in Figure 2.3 and discount and cumulate cash flows going back step-by-step using the forward zero rates or forward discount factors. We will return to this second method in Chapter 3 when we define the notion of forward rates. The two methods always produce identical answers.

2.3.3 Valuation of an Arbitrary Bond

Having performed the discount curve bootstrap, Jack is now ready to present-value his 4.0% semi-annual $1,000 par value bond maturing in $3^1/_2$ years. All he needs to do is to multiply his expected coupon cash flows of $2.00 and $1,000 principal by the corresponding discount factors and sum up the present values to find the total present value of the bond. Figure 2.14 presents the procedure graphically and as a simple table. This valuation method applies to any bond with fixed cash flows.

Table 2.1 The Bootstrap

n	Term	Coupon	Price	YTM	z_t	df_t
1	6m	2.00	100.00	2.0000%	?	?

$$\text{Step1} - 6\text{m}: 100.00 = \frac{101.00}{(1+z_{6m}/2)} \rightarrow z_{6m} = 0.020000, df_{6m} = \frac{1}{(1+0.02/2)} = 0.990099$$

n	Term	Coupon	Price	YTM	z_t	df_t
1	6m	2.00	100.00	2.0000%	2.0000%	0.990099
2	1y	2.50	100.10	2.3982%	?	?

$$\text{Step2} - 12\text{m}: 100.10 = \frac{1.25}{(1+0.02/2)} + \frac{101.25}{(1+z_{1y}/2)^2} \rightarrow z_{1y} = 0.024007, df_{1y} = \frac{1}{(1+0.024007/2)^2} = 0.976419$$

n	Term	Coupon	Price	YTM	z_t	df_t
1	6m	2.00	100.00	2.0000%	2.0000%	0.990099
2	1y	2.50	100.10	2.3982%	2.4007%	0.976419
3	18m	3.00	100.25	2.8286%	?	?

$$\text{Step3} - 18\text{m}: 100.25 = \frac{1.50}{(1+0.02/2)} + \frac{1.50}{(1+0.024007/2)^2} + \frac{101.50}{(1+z_{18m}/2)^3} \rightarrow z_{18m} = 0.028371, df_{18m} = \frac{1}{(1+0.028371/2)^3} = 0.976419$$

n	Term	Coupon	Price	YTM	z_t	df_t
1	6m	2.00	100.00	2.0000%	2.0000%	0.990099
2	1y	2.50	100.10	2.3982%	2.4007%	0.976419
3	18m	3.00	100.25	2.8286%	2.8371%	0.958623
4	2y	3.50	100.32	3.3333%	?	?

$$\text{Step4} - 24\text{m}: 100.32 = \frac{1.75}{(1+0.02/2)} + \frac{1.75}{(1+0.024007/2)^2} + \frac{1.75}{(1+0.028371/2)^3} + \frac{101.75}{(1+z_{2y}/2)^4} \rightarrow z_{2y}, df_{2y}$$

n	Term	Coupon	Price	YTM	z_t	df_t
1	6m	2.00	100.00	2.0000%	2.0000%	0.990099
2	1y	2.50	100.10	2.3982%	2.4007%	0.976419
3	18m	3.00	100.25	2.8286%	2.8371%	0.958623
4	2y	3.50	100.32	3.3333%	3.3542%	0.935636
5	30m	3.25	99.84	3.3172%	?	?

$$\text{Step5} - 30: 99.84 = \frac{1.625}{(1+0.02/2)} + \frac{1.625}{(1+0.024007/2)^2} + \frac{1.625}{(1+0.028371/2)^3} + \frac{1.625}{(1+0.033542/2)^4} + \frac{101.625}{(1+z_{30m}/2)^5} \rightarrow z_{30m}, df_{30m}$$

n	Term	Coupon	Price	YTM	z_t	df_t
1	6m	2.00	100.00	2.0000%	2.0000%	0.990099
2	1y	2.50	100.10	2.3982%	2.4007%	0.976419
3	18m	3.00	100.25	2.8286%	2.8371%	0.958623
4	2y	3.50	100.32	3.3333%	3.3542%	0.935636
5	30m	3.25	99.84	3.3172%	3.3323%	0.920701
6	3y	3.00	99.78	3.0773%	?	?

$$\text{Step6} - 36\text{m}: 99.78 = \frac{1.50}{(1+0.02/2)} + \frac{1.50}{(1+0.024007/2)^2} + \cdots + \frac{1.50}{(1+0.033542/2)^4} + \frac{1.50}{(1+0.033323/2)^5} + \frac{101.50}{(1+z_{3y}/2)^6} \rightarrow z_{3y}, df_{3y}$$

n	Term	Coupon	Price	YTM	z_t	df_t
1	6m	2.00	100.00	2.0000%	2.0000%	0.990099
2	1y	2.50	100.10	2.3982%	2.4007%	0.976419
3	18m	3.00	100.25	2.8286%	2.8371%	0.958623
4	2y	3.50	100.32	3.3333%	3.3542%	0.935636
5	30m	3.25	99.84	3.3172%	3.3323%	0.920701
6	3y	3.00	99.78	3.0773%	3.0797%	0.912392
7	42m	3.25	99.89	3.2835%	?	?

$$\text{Step7} - 42\text{m}: 99.89 = \frac{1.625}{(1+0.02/2)} + \frac{1.625}{(1+0.024007/2)^2} + \cdots + \frac{1.625}{(1+0.033323/2)^5} + \frac{1.625}{(1+0.030797/2)^6} + \frac{101.625}{(1+z_{42m}/2)^7} \rightarrow z_{42m}, df_{42m}$$

Table 2.1 *(Continued)*

n	Term	Coupon	Price	YTM	z_t	df_t
1	6m	2.00	100.00	2.0000%	2.0000%	0.990099
2	1y	2.50	100.10	2.3982%	2.4007%	0.976419
3	18m	3.00	100.25	2.8286%	2.8371%	0.958623
4	2y	3.50	100.32	3.3333%	3.3542%	0.935636
5	30m	3.25	99.84	3.3172%	3.3323%	0.920701
6	3y	3.00	99.78	3.0773%	3.0797%	0.912392
7	42m	3.25	99.89	3.2835%	3.2961%	0.891882
8	4y	3.50	100.15	3.4595%	?	?

$$\text{Step8} - 48\text{m} : 100.15 = \frac{1.75}{(1+0.02/2)} + \frac{1.75}{(1+0.024007/2)^2} + \cdots + \frac{1.75}{(1+0.030797/2)^6} + \frac{1.75}{(1+0.032961/2)^7} + \frac{101.75}{(1+z_{4y}/2)^8} \rightarrow z_{4y}, df_{4y}$$

n	Term	Coupon	Price	YTM	z_t	df_t	$df_{t-1,t}$	$f_{t-1,t}$
1	**6m**	2.00	100.00	2.0000%	**2.0000%**	**0.990099**	0.990099	2.0000%
2	**1y**	2.50	100.10	2.3982%	**2.4007%**	**0.976419**	0.986183	2.8022%
3	**18m**	3.00	100.25	2.8286%	**2.8371%**	**0.958623**	0.981775	3.7128%
4	**2y**	3.50	100.32	3.3333%	**3.3542%**	**0.935636**	0.976021	4.9136%
5	**30m**	3.25	99.84	3.3172%	**3.3323%**	**0.920701**	0.984037	3.2444%
6	**3y**	3.00	99.78	3.0773%	**3.0797%**	**0.912392**	0.990975	1.8214%
7	**42m**	3.25	99.89	3.2835%	**3.2961%**	**0.891882**	0.977520	4.5994%
8	**4y**	3.50	100.15	3.4595%	**3.4826%**	**0.871007**	0.976595	4.7933%

where one period forward discount factors are $df_{t-1,t} = \dfrac{df_t}{df_{t-1}}$ and forward zero rates are $f_{t-1,t} = 2(df_{t-1,t}^{-2} - 1)$

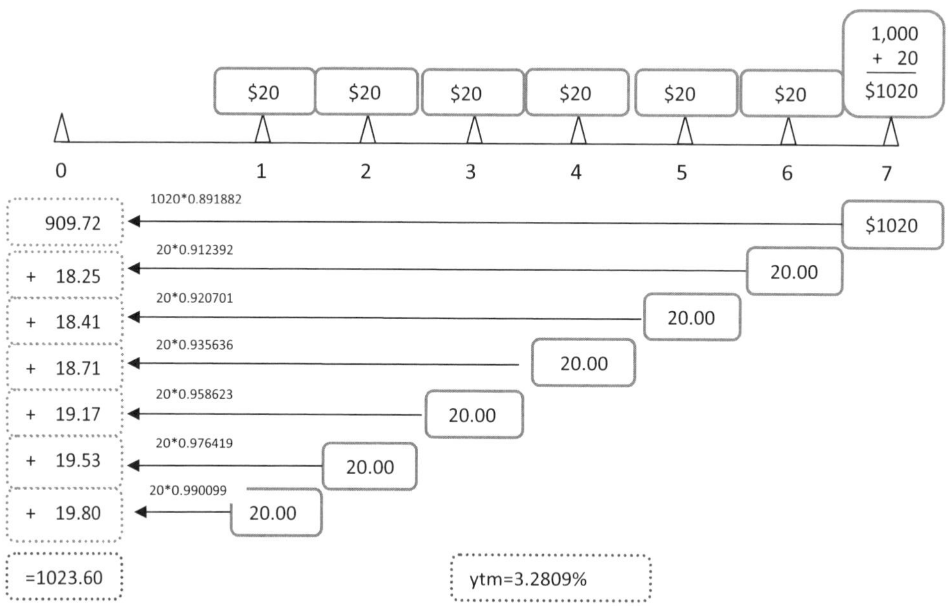

n	t	CF_t	df_t	$PV(CF_t)$
1	6m	2.00	0.990099	1.9802
2	1y	2.00	0.976419	1.9528
3	18m	2.00	0.958623	1.9172
4	2y	2.00	0.935636	1.8713
5	30m	2.00	0.920701	1.8414
6	3Y	2.00	0.912392	1.8248
7	42m	102.00	0.891882	90.9719

Figure 2.14 Valuation of the 3 1/2-year 4% semiann. coupon bond using the bootstrapped discount factors

2.4 INTEREST RATE RISK: DURATION AND CONVEXITY

There are two main risks of owning a bond. The first is the risk that the issuer may default on the bond and the promised cash flows are not paid. The second risk is that the price of the bond may go down when interest rates go up. As interest rates fluctuate over time, they affect the present value of the bond's cash flows through the discounting process. The price volatility of the bond as a result of interest rate fluctuations is referred to as the *interest rate risk* of the bond. The two main measures of the interest rate risk of the bond are the *duration* of the bond and the *price value of a basis point (PVBP)*. Both are local measures and work well for small changes in yields. For larger changes they are often corrected using the bond's *convexity*.

The price of a bond fluctuates as interest rates change. The coupon rate set at the time of issue does not change, the cash flows it defines do not change, and nor do the dates of the cash flows. But as yields demanded by investors change, so do the discounted values of those cash flows. This phenomenon is normally portrayed as a downward-sloping concave relationship between the bond's price its yield-to-maturity.

Consider a 12-year 10% semi-annual coupon bond currently yielding 10% semi-annually. The face value is \$100. The bond pays \$5 every 6 months for the next 12 years and returns the principal of \$100 12 years from today. The price of the bond today, equal to the discounted value of its cash flows, is equal to:

$$P = \frac{5}{(1+0.05)} + \frac{5}{(1+0.05)^2} + \cdots + \frac{5}{(1+0.05)^{23}} + \frac{105}{(1+0.05)^{24}} = 100$$

The bond trades at par given that the yield-to-maturity is equal to the coupon rate.

Now suppose that the market yield on the 12-year bond changes to 8% semi-annually. The new price of the 10% coupon bond is:

$$P = \frac{5}{(1+0.04)} + \frac{5}{(1+0.04)^2} + \cdots + \frac{5}{(1+0.04)^{23}} + \frac{105}{(1+0.04)^{24}} = 115.25$$

A bond paying a 10% coupon rate while investors demand 8% trades *at a premium* over par.

Conversely, if the market yield on a 12-year bond changes to 12% semi-annually, the price will drop to:

$$P = \frac{5}{(1+0.06)} + \frac{5}{(1+0.06)^2} + \cdots + \frac{5}{(1+0.06)^{23}} + \frac{105}{(1+0.06)^{24}} = 87.45$$

A bond paying a 10% coupon rate while investors demand 12% trades *at a discount*.

Plotting the relationship between the price of the bond and its yield, we get the graph shown in Figure 2.15.

Note that the maximum price for the bond is 220. If the yield drops to zero, then the value of the bond will be equal to the sum of its cash flows, or

$$P = \frac{5}{(1+0.0)} + \frac{5}{(1+0.0)^2} + \cdots + \frac{5}{(1+0.0)^{23}} + \frac{105}{(1+0.0)^{24}} = 220.00$$

The price for the bond asymptotically approaches zero as the yield goes to infinity. Most of the time, we are in between. The graph is a convex curve (bowed to below) due to interest compounding. This convexity implies that price responses are not symmetric. When the yield

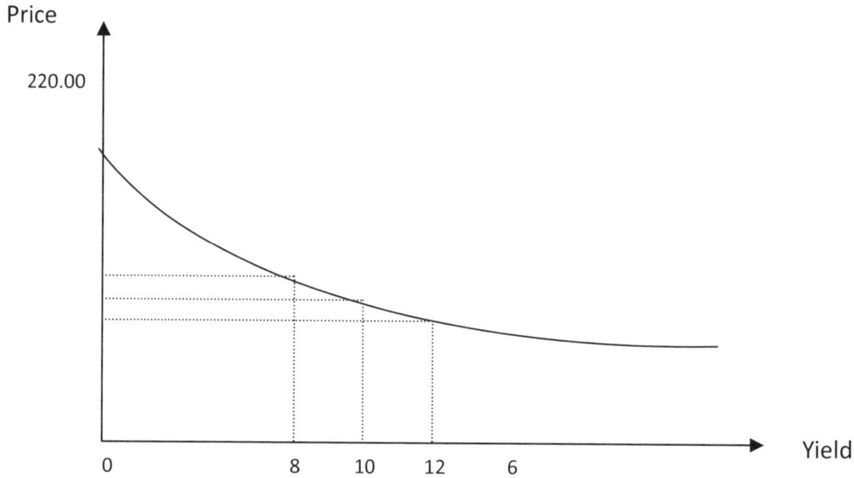

Figure 2.15 The Price–Yield Relationship of a 12-Year 10% Coupon Bond

goes down by 2%, the price goes up by 15.25, but when the yield goes up by 2%, the price goes down by 12.55. The magnitude of bond price responses to yield changes depends on three factors (in the order of importance):

- *Time to maturity* – Other thing being equal, the longer the maturity of the bond the larger are the price swings for the same change in interest rates. A 16-year 10% semi-annual coupon bond prices to par at a 10% semi-annual yield, to 117.87 at 8%, and to 85.92 at 12%. A longer bond's cash flows extend further into the future, making them more sensitive to discounting.
- *Coupon rate* – Other thing being equal, the lower the coupon rate of the bond the larger are the price swings for the same change in interest rates. Low coupon bonds derive more benefits from the principal than from coupon cash flows, and the impact of discounting is greater for later cash flows.
- *Coupon frequency* – Other thing being equal, the more frequently the coupons on the bond are paid the smaller are the price swings for the same change in interest rates, as more frequent coupons bring the cash flows closer to today, making them less sensitive to discount rate changes.

Zero-coupon bonds have the greatest interest rate risk of all bonds with the same maturity, as there is only one cash flow at maturity. Floating rate bonds have virtually no interest rate sensitivity. Their prices return to par after coupon payments and deviate from par on non-coupon dates only to the extent that the first coupon rate that has already been set is different from the discount rate for that first coupon.

The most common interest rate metrics used to compare the riskiness of bonds are *duration* and *convexity*. Both are "local" statistics describing the sensitivity of the bond's price to small changes in yields away from the current level. They do not work for large market moves: the duration of the bond when yields are 8% cannot be extrapolated from the duration of the same bond when yields are 5%.

2.4.1 Duration

The universe of bonds, even for the same issuer, can be enormous. On any given day, Jack may be considering the following set of outstanding XYZ Corporation bonds:

- a 5-year semi-annual 4% coupon bond;
- a $7^1/_4$-year annual 3% bond with next coupon due in 3 months;
- a 6-year zero coupon; or
- a 4-year step-up bond whose coupon starts at 3.5% but increases by 0.75% each year.

How does Jack choose which bond to invest in or which one to sell out of his portfolio?

Jack can compare bonds with different characteristics with the help of the notion of *duration*. In its original form, as described by Frederick Macaulay (1938), duration *(D)* is defined as the present value-weighted average time to the bond's cash flows. Macaulay duration is defined in years of time. A bond has, for example, a duration of 3.45 years, another bond has a duration of 7.29 years, and we can compare bonds based on that number.

Duration has yet another, most interesting, interpretation. *Modified duration* is the relative sensitivity of the bond price to a unit yield change. That unit can be 1%, but a preferred unit of yield change is a smaller 1 basis point (bp), or 0.01%. If a bond has a modified duration of 6.94 and the yield to maturity *increases* by 1 bp, then the price of the bond *decreases* by 6.94 bp. Modified duration is defined as the percentage change in price divided by the change in yield, or:

$$ModD = -\frac{\Delta P/P}{\Delta y}$$

Duration and modified duration are closely related through the following formula:

$$ModD = \frac{D}{1 + \frac{y}{n}}$$

where n is the number of compounding periods per year for the yield y. As the denominator is always close to 1, duration and modified duration are roughly the same. Often we speak only of one duration, quoting exclusively the modified duration number as it reflects the local riskiness of bonds, but relying on the intuitive understanding of Macaulay duration.

Consider a 6-year \$100 face value 7% semi-annual coupon bond yielding 8%. The bond pays \$3.50 every 6 months and returns the principal of \$100 in 6 years. Table 2.2 presents the logic of the Macaulay duration calculation. Columns 1 and 2 contain times and cash flows. Column 3 contains discount factors $df = \frac{1}{(1+y_n/2)^n}$, $n = 1, \ldots, 12$, for each cash flow, based on the yield of 8% (semi). Column 4 has the present value of the cash flows (cash flow times the discount factor), with the sum of the present values at the bottom. The main duration computations are in columns 5 and 6. Column 5 has the percentage that the PV of each cash flow represents in the total value of the bond. Each percentage is construed as the weight of the cash flow in today's value of the bond. Column 6 multiplies those weights by the times of the cash flows to arrive at a weighted-average time to cash flows.

Graphically, the duration is presented as the center of mass (fulcrum) of a set of blocks in Figure 2.16, each block being the percentage of present value recovered through each cash flow, the heights of the blocks taken from the rows of column 5 in Table 2.2.

The weighted average time to the cash flows, using the block heights as the weights, is equal to 4.972. (Imagine a fulcrum placed at $2 \times 4.972 = 9.944$ on the horizontal axis in Figure 2.16.

Table 2.2 Macaulay duration calculation

Maturity in years: 6

Coupon:		7.00%	semi		
Yield:		8.00%	semi		
1	2	3	4	5	6
t	*CF*	*Df*	*PV*	*%PV*	*t* × *%PV*
0.5	3.5	0.961538	3.365385	3.53%	0.0177
1	3.5	0.924556	3.235947	3.40%	0.0340
1.5	3.5	0.888996	3.111487	3.26%	0.0490
2	3.5	0.854804	2.991815	3.14%	0.0628
2.5	3.5	0.821927	2.876745	3.02%	0.0755
3	3.5	0.790315	2.766101	2.90%	0.0871
3.5	3.5	0.759918	2.659712	2.79%	0.0977
4	3.5	0.730690	2.557416	2.68%	0.1073
4.5	3.5	0.702587	2.459054	2.58%	0.1161
5	3.5	0.675564	2.364475	2.48%	0.1240
5.5	3.5	0.649581	2.273533	2.39%	0.1312
6	103.5	0.624597	64.64579	67.83%	4.0697
Total			95.30746	100.00%	**4.9720**

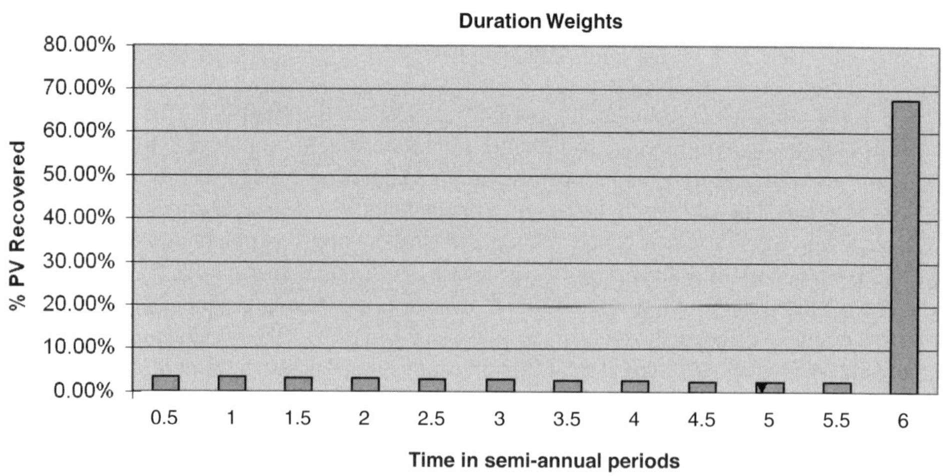

Figure 2.16 Present values of the coupons as duration calculation weights

It would make all the blocks balance.) That number is the approximate percentage change of the price corresponding to a 1% change in yield.

The Macaulay duration concept is extremely intuitive. With a little experience, one is able to guess bond durations fairly accurately. Here are some heuristics:

- The longer the maturity, the longer the duration, all other things being equal – the blocks in our graph extend further out and so the weighted time to the repayment is longer.
- The larger the coupon, the shorter the duration – the higher the coupon blocks, the less weight is assigned to the principal repayment and the smaller the weighted average.
- The greater the frequency of the coupons, the shorter the duration – as more blocks are closer to today.

  These correspond to the factors affecting the interest rate risks of bonds. Two more observations:
  - The duration of a zero-coupon bond is equal to its maturity.
  - Floating rate bonds have short durations equal to the next coupon date.

Let us now examine a more practical meaning of duration, that of the interest rate sensitivity, applied to our bond. The 6-year 7% semi-annual coupon bond yielding 8% is valued at 95.3075. We computed the Macaulay duration to be 4.9720. The modified duration is

$$ModD = \frac{4.9720}{1 + \frac{0.08}{2}} = 4.7807$$

If the yield on the bond were to increase from 8.00% to 8.15%, that is by 0.15% or 15 bp, then the price of the bond should decrease by 0.7171% (4.7807 times 0.15). Based on the starting value of 95.3075, this translates into a change to 94.6240. Mathematically this can be expressed as:

$$\begin{aligned} P_{new} &= P[1 + (-ModD)\ \Delta y] \\ &= 95.3075[1 + (-4.7807)(0.15)] = 94.6240 \end{aligned}$$

An exact calculation of the value of the bond, assuming an 8.15% yield, produces the discounted value of the bond's cash flows equal to 94.6270. For a small change in the yield, duration is a very good approximation to the exact value of the bond. This does not apply, however, if the yield change is large. In the extreme case of the yield dropping to zero, i.e. changing by minus 8%, multiplying 4.7807 by 8.00 produces the predicted change of 38.2456% of the current value, or $36.4509. Duration thus predicts the bond price rise to $131.7584 while the actual price with a zero discount rate is $142, the sum of the cash flows.

What can go wrong? As a local measure, duration is the first derivative of the price with respect to the yield. Thus, it is a linear approximation based on a straight line tangent to a polynomial curve, the true price–yield relationship. This is represented in Figure 2.17.

Later we show how the duration-based linear approximation can be improved with the use of convexity.

Most computer applications do not compute duration the way we presented it in Table 2.2. Rather they revalue the bond using two yields, one set a small number of basis points above and one set a small number of basis points below the current yield-to-maturity, and then dividing the change in the bond's value by the combined size of the yield change "blip." That is, they compute the numerical sensitivity of price to yield. If we denote the value of the bond

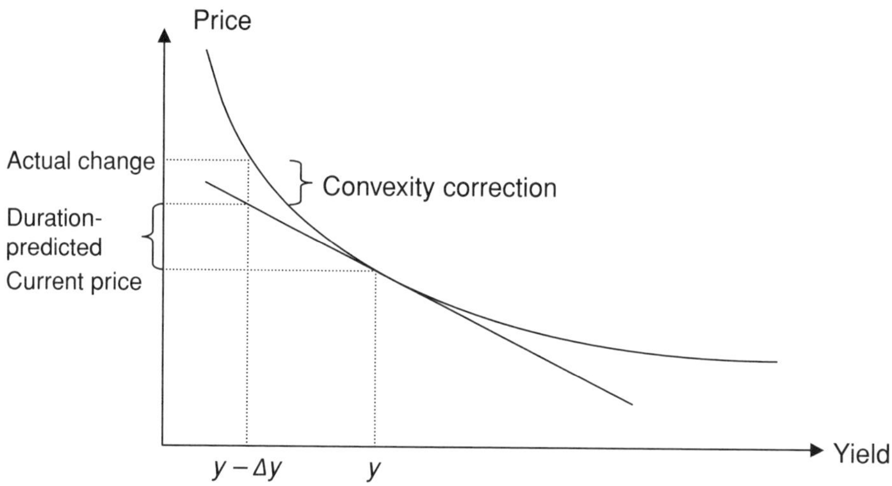

Figure 2.17 Bond price vs yield

with a yield blipped up by dy basis points as P_{+dy} and the value of the bond with a yield blipped down by dy basis points as P_{-dy}, then duration is computed numerically by dividing the percentage price change by the total change in yield:

$$ModD = -\frac{(P_{+dy} - P_{-dy})/P}{2dy}$$

The two prices can be easily found by use of a financial calculator or a spreadsheet. Doing so, at the yield of 8.02 we get $P_{+2} = 95.21639$ and at the yield of 7.98 we get $P_{-2} = 95.39864$. The duration is:

$$ModD = -\frac{(95.21639 - 95.39864)/95.30746}{2 \cdot 0.0002} = 4.7806$$

The estimate is off by 0.0001 due to the large blip of 2 bp. To improve the estimate we can use a smaller blip of 1 bp or 0.5 bp, or we can adjust the centering in the numerator.

This numerical blipping procedure of computing duration is very general and works even for the most complex bonds with embedded options, for which expected cash flows change as yields vary.

2.4.2 Portfolio Duration

Duration is very popular with managers of large bond portfolios. This is due to its one very attractive property: the duration of a portfolio is equal to the weighted average of the durations of individual bonds. The weight for each bond is simply the proportion of the portfolio invested in that bond. This property is a direct result of the fact that durations are first derivatives of the bond values with respect to yields and that first derivatives are additive. Let us look at the example in Table 2.3.

The interpretation of the portfolio duration is the same as that for individual bonds with the qualification that the duration of the portfolio is the sensitivity of the value of the

Table 2.3 The duration of the portfolio of bonds

Invested	%Invested	Coupon	Maturity	Duration
400m	20	6.50	12	9.54
900m	45	5.75	10	7.23
700m	35	5.25	6	4.85
2,000m	100			6.86

$\text{Dur} = 0.20 \times 9.54 + 0.45 \times 7.23 + 0.35 \times 4.85 = 6.859$

portfolio with respect to a *parallel shift* in yields-to-maturity. For the portfolio in Table 2.3, this translates into the following statement: *If the yield-to-maturity on each bond in the portfolio decreased by 7 basis points, then the value of the portfolio would increase by 6.859 times 7, or 48.013 basis points. In dollars, that is equal to an increase of 0.0048013 times \$2 billion, or \$9,602,600*. Conveniently, by knowing *one* statistic about the portfolio, its duration, we can predict the value of the entire portfolio very accurately for small changes in yields.

Often, bond managers engage in what is called *duration matching* or *portfolio immunization*. These terms refer to a conscious selection of bonds to be added to the portfolio in order to reduce the duration of the portfolio to zero, i.e. to eliminate all interest rate risk. This can be done by selecting the right amount of bonds to be shorted or by buying bonds with negative duration. Alternatively, managers may attempt to *shorten* or *lengthen* the duration of a portfolio by reshuffling the allocations to various bonds in order to decrease or increase the exposure to interest rate movements. Many managers of corporate bond portfolios short government bonds with the same duration to eliminate exposure to interest rates, leaving themselves with pure credit spread exposure.

If, in Table 2.3, the yields-to-maturity do not change in parallel, e.g. some change by 8 bp while others change by 6 bp, then the estimate based on portfolio duration will be somewhat inaccurate, but an estimate obtained by summing the products of the changes in yields for all bond times their individual durations will be very accurate. This is still much easier than revaluing all bonds.

2.4.3 Convexity

Convexity is used to improve the accuracy of the duration approximation to the change in the value of the bond. It is important to include it in the approximation for

- large changes in yields-to-maturity, or
- bonds whose price–yield relationship is highly non-linear (bonds with embedded options, some mortgage-backed securities, etc.).

Convexity is equal to half the second derivative of bond price with respect to the yield and as such it measures the average rate of change in the slope of the tangent duration line. Numerically it can be computed as the following difference formula:

$$C = \frac{1}{2} \cdot \frac{(P_{+dy} + P_{-dy} - 2P)/P}{(dy)^2}$$

We already have all the ingredients to compute convexity for our example bond. Let us plug the numbers into the formula to get:

$$C = \frac{1}{2} \cdot \frac{(95.21639 + 95.39864 - 2 \cdot 95.30746)/95.30746}{(0.0002)^2} = 14.4270$$

The convexity number measures the average change in the duration per dy basis points.[1] It tells us the extent to which the true price–yield curve deviates from the linear approximation. What we are mostly interested in is improving that approximation. In order to do that, we need to multiply the convexity by the relevant yield change Δy to obtain the change in duration over that entire yield change. This may explain the logic behind the following duration-cum-convexity approximation formula for the bond price change:

$$P_{new} = P[1 + (-ModD + C \cdot \Delta y)\,\Delta y]$$

The percentage price change in the bond value per unit of yield comes from two sources: the duration, which for most bonds will underestimate the magnitude of the change following a straight line, and the convexity, which will correct for that underestimation by reducing the absolute value of the duration. Using the numbers for our example bond, we get:

$$P_{new} = 95.30746[1 + (-4.7806 + 14.4270 \cdot 0.0015) \cdot 0.0015] = 95.6271$$

We have improved our estimate considerably and are almost spot on! Recall that the true value of the bond at a yield of 8.15% was 95.6270.

Convexity is used as the second summary statistic to describe large bond portfolios. Typically, durations and convexities are computed for several possible yield increments relative to today's level, e.g. –50 bp, –25 bp, 0 bp, +25 bp, +50 bp. It is important to remember, however, that convexities, unlike durations, are not additive and are computed by blipping entire portfolios and revaluing all the bonds in them. Just as with durations, managers engage in immunization strategies with respect to convexities by adding negatively convex bonds or reshuffling portfolio allocations to reduce or increase the convexity of the overall portfolio.

2.4.4 Other Risk Measures

Duration and convexity calculations assume that the underlying cash flows of the bond do not change – only the yield-to-maturity. Yet the cash flows of bonds with embedded options often change as the yields change (e.g. a 'blip' in the yield on a callable bond may trigger a call provision). In those cases, one can compute alternative measures of *effective duration* and convexity where the changed cash flows are explicitly taken into account when computing the blipped values P_{+dy} and P_{-dy}. One should, however, bear in mind, that those values are not computed through simple discounting, but, rather, with a use of an option-pricing model. As such they take into account other inputs, the most important of which is the volatility of the yield.

The volatility of the yield also enters into the analysis in a different way. Imagine a portfolio of two corporate bonds both with the same maturity and both trading at par, but one of the bonds has a much higher coupon reflecting a lower credit quality of its issuer. Is it realistic to assume

[1] Duration changes continuously between the original value P and the estimated value P_{new} corresponding to the yield change of Δy. The multiplication of the second derivative by 1/2 averages the point estimates of convexity per unit of yield over the entire range of Δy.

that the yields on the bonds will move in parallel, or is it more realistic to assume that the riskier bond's yield will fluctuate proportionately more? The volatility of the yield refers precisely to that concept. Computing portfolio durations may be of little help in this case. Rather, one may prefer to compute individual durations and scale the assumed yield movements by the respective yield volatilities to arrive at portfolio value change approximations for more realistic yield movements.

Lastly, let us define the concept of *the price value of a basis point* which is closely related to the duration. Unlike duration, which is expressed in relative terms, the price value of a basis point, or PVBP, measures the absolute value of the change in price of a bond per unit of yield change, i.e. it is defined as:

$$PVBP = -\frac{\Delta P}{\Delta y}$$

and can be approximated by:

$$PVBP = -\frac{(P_{+dy} - P_{-dy})/10000}{2dy}$$

In our bond example, it could be computed as:

$$PVBP = -\frac{(95.21639 - 95.39864)/10000}{2 \cdot 0.0002} = 0.0456$$

and is defined in dollars. The interpretation of PVBP is that one basis point change in the yield causes \$0.0456 change in the value of the bond with a face value of \$100. For par bonds, modified durations and PVBPs scaled by 1/100 are identical since percentage changes and absolute value changes are the same if $P = 100$. Modified durations or PVBPs can be used in computing hedge ratios for basis trading or portfolio immunizations.

2.5 EQUITY, COMMODITY, AND CURRENCY MATH

Stocks, like bonds, are financial assets offering a promise of future cash flows: dividends and capital gains. These cash flows are, however, much less certain. While coupon interest must be paid at the scheduled dates, cash dividends are only paid if declared by the company. Also, bond price fluctuations are constrained by the magnitude of interest rate changes and their impact on discounting; capital gains and losses on stocks can be very large, as both the cash flows (the numerator) and the discount rate (the denominator) affect the present value of the future, very uncertain, cash flows. Stock valuation is not an exact science and depends critically on the easy-to-disagree-on assumption of the rate of change (growth) in future cash flows. While we review the details of dividend and free cash flow discounting in a later chapter, we offer the basics here.

Commodities are physical assets of uniform enough quality to trade in bulk. They are purchased not for the benefit of future cash flows, but for use in production, or for a promise of price appreciation. The major groups of commodities are agricultural, metals, energy and financials. Each commodity's quality is defined very strictly in physical terms – size and quality or chemical composition – to ensure near perfect substitutability. West Texas Intermediate oil is a commodity; Brent crude is a separate commodity as it is not as light or as sweet as WTI. The price of a commodity is typically defined in currency per appropriate physical quantity: oil in dollars per barrel, corn in cents per bushel, equity index in dollars per index point.

Currencies are special commodities in that their prices are defined in currency per unit of another currency, and therefore can be inverted and are naturally traded in a triangular way, i.e. one currency traded for another, then for another, and then for another or the same.

2.5.1 Equities

Fundamentally, the price of a stock is equal to the discounted value of all the dividends/cash flows received over the expected holding horizon plus the discounted value of the final price received for the stock at the end of the holding horizon. Since, rationally, the final price that the next buyer will pay must reflect the discounted value of all the future dividends from then on, today's stock price can be viewed as the discounted value of all the dividends/cash flows received during the holding horizon and beyond. Thus, if Jack buys the stock today and expects to hold it for n years, he would value the stock as the PV of all the dividends and the PV of the sale price

$$P_0 = \frac{D_1}{1+r} + \frac{D_2}{(1+r)^2} + \cdots + \frac{D_n + P_n}{(1+r)^n}$$

Realizing that the price P_n Jill will pay him for the stock n years from today is simply the PV of all the dividends over her holding horizon plus the PV of the dividends over all subsequent holding horizon to infinity, Jack would value the stock simply as the PV of the perpetual sequence of dividends

$$P_0 = \frac{D_1}{1+r} + \frac{D_2}{(1+r)^2} + \cdots + \frac{D_n}{(1+r)^n} + \frac{D_{n+1}}{(1+r)^{n+1}} + \cdots$$

This sequence of dividends can follow several canonical patterns. If the dividends are expected to grow at a constant percentage rate g per year (which is less than the discount rate), then we can use the formula for the sum of an infinite geometric series to get the price of the stock today

$$P_0 = \frac{D_1}{r-g}$$

Stocks with a high growth rate g are called *growth* stocks; stocks with a low growth rate g are called *value* stocks (growth can even be negative). We discuss the relationship of growth rates, dividends, and earnings to price/earnings (P/E) ratios in Chapter 11. Here we point out that the assumption about g is critical in valuing a stock. Suppose both Jack and Jill are trying to evaluate a stock expected to pay at the end of the year a dividend of \$3, but Jack expects the dividends to grow at 8% per year while Jill is more optimistic and expects the dividends to grow at 9% per year. Both apply the same discount rate of 12%. They calculate the following fundamental values for the stock:

$$P_{Jack} = \frac{3}{0.12 - 0.08} = \$75 \quad p_{Jill} = \frac{3}{0.12 - 0.09} = \$100$$

In stock valuation, even a minute news release changing the forecast of the growth rate of earnings, or cash flow can lead to significant price revisions. Chapter 11 contains a thorough review of the fundamental equity valuation using discounted free cash flow.

2.5.2 Currencies

Currencies are commodities. They trade in bulk and are of uniform quality: a 20-euro note can be replaced by 20 1-euro coins without loss of value. Normally, the price of a commodity is quoted in currency per physical unit of commodity like a bushel, a barrel or a metric tonne. Currencies, also called foreign exchange (FX), are special since the priced physical unit of the commodity is also a currency. One pound sterling (the priced commodity) may cost 1.5 US dollars (pricing currency), or 1 US dollar (priced commodity) may cost 0.6667 pounds sterling (pricing currency). The price in pounds per dollar is equivalent to the reciprocal of the price in dollars per pound. Exchanging dollars for pounds can be described either as selling dollars or buying pounds.

The other feature distinguishing currencies from other commodities is that we often want to know and transact at the *cross* ratio. We rarely exchange 300 barrels of oil for bushels of wheat. However, when returning to London from Mexico, we may want to exchange the leftover 600 pesos for pounds without first selling pesos for dollars and then dollars for pounds.

Let us review quote conventions and some potential issues. In what follows, we use the easily recognizable three-letter currency codes as adopted by the transaction messaging system SWIFT. Most currencies around the world are quoted with respect to a *vehicle* currency which is one of the major hard currencies, e.g. USD, GBP, or EUR. A currency can be quoted in European terms, i.e. in currency per dollar, or American terms in dollars per currency. Most British Commonwealth currencies (AUD, NZD, etc.) and the euro (EUR) follow the American convention (US dollars per euro or pound). Most others (e.g. CHF, PLZ, JPY) follow the European convention (Swiss francs or Danish krone per US dollar). Remembering all this is important when observing quotes or percentage appreciation rates that are not labeled. This text follows the standard in which a spot exchange rate is denoted by X with the terms in square brackets or as a superscript. For example 1.5 dollars per pound sterling is:

$$X^{USD/GBP} = X\left[\frac{USD}{GBP}\right] = 1.50$$

For any two currencies, the FX rate in currency 1 per unit of currency 2 uniquely determines the FX rate in currency 2 per unit of currency 1, i.e.$X\,[Curr1/Curr2] = 1/X[Curr2/Curr1]$. In our example:

$$X\left[\frac{GBP}{USD}\right] = \frac{1}{X\left[\frac{USD}{GBP}\right]} = 0.6667$$

Most FX rates are quoted to 4 decimal places, except when the whole number is large they are quoted to 2 decimal places; for example, a JPY/USD quote may be 119.23. Often, the quotation units are assumed to follow the common (European or American) convention and are dropped. This may lead to misinterpretation of appreciation statistics. Consider Table 2.4, which you may see in the press.

Do the negative %Change numbers mean that all the listed currencies depreciated against the dollar? On the contrary, the CHF, quoted as CHF/USD, has actually appreciated as it takes 0.0030 fewer Swiss francs to buy $1 than it did yesterday, while the other two currencies, AUD and EUR, have in fact depreciated.

Table 2.4 Currency changes against the USD as of . . ./. . ./2009

	Last	Change	%Change
AUD	0.5457	–0.0014	–0.3
EUR	1.0205	–0.0020	–0.2
CHF	1.6844	–0.0030	–0.2

Confusion may also come in the percentage change statistics. If the AUD costs USD 0.5457 today and it cost 0.5471 yesterday, then we compute the percentage change as:

$$\%\Delta X^{USD/AUD} = -0.0014/0.5471 = -0.002559 = -0.2559\%$$

as shown in Table 2.4. Does this mean that the USD has appreciated by 0.2559%? Absolutely not. Today the USD costs:

$$X^{AUD/USD} = 1/X^{AUD/USD} = 1/0.5457 = 1.832509$$

Yesterday it cost:

$$X^{AUD/USD} = 1/X^{AUD/USD} = 1/0.5471 = 1.827819$$

or AUD 0.004689 more. The percentage change in the value of the USD expressed in AUD is then

$$\%\Delta X^{AUD/USD} = 0.004689/1.827819 = 0.002566 = 0.2566\%$$

The simple explanation is that the percentage change is not equal to the negative of the percentage change in the reciprocals. Over longer periods of time the differences can be great.

More complications arise when interpreting analysts' mean forecasts of currency rates. Suppose that currently

$$X^{\frac{USD}{AUD}} = 0.75, \text{ or equivalently, } X^{\frac{AUD}{USD}} = 1\frac{1}{3}$$

Half of the analysts polled predict the rate to go to $X^{\frac{USD}{AUD}} = 0.50$ ($X^{\frac{AUD}{USD}} = 2$) and the other half to $X^{\frac{USD}{AUD}} = 1.00$ ($X^{\frac{AUD}{USD}} = 1$). On average, in USD/AUD terms, they predict the rate to be 0.75 ($= \frac{1}{2}.0.5 + \frac{1}{2}.1.0$), i.e. no appreciation. At the same time, on average, the same analysts implicitly predict the rate in AUD/USD terms to be 1.5 ($= \frac{1}{2}.2 + \frac{1}{2}.1$), i.e. a USD appreciation from 1-1/3. One can find examples where, on average, both currencies may be expected to appreciate at the same time! The main lesson from these examples is that one always needs to be aware of the quotation terms being assumed when interpreting statements about appreciation or depreciation.

The main law governing spot currency trading is that of no *triangular arbitrage*. In the inter-dealer market, all spot FX rates have to be 'in line' with each other in such a way that buying one currency through a vehicle is neither cheaper nor more expensive than buying it directly. The rule, of course, does not apply to retail markets. Let us illustrate.

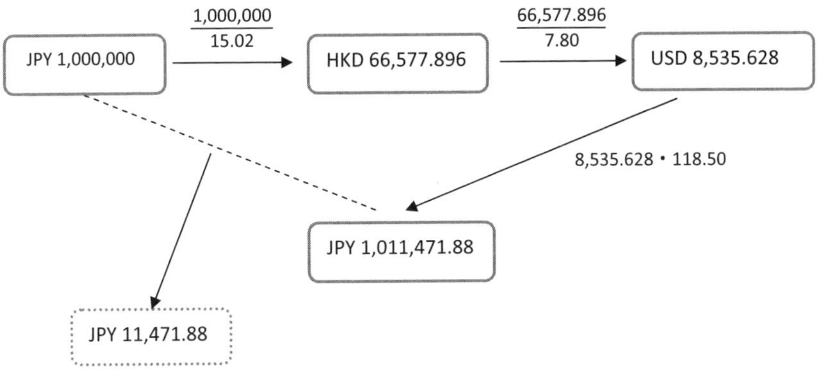

Figure 2.18 Triangular arbitrage

Suppose you observe in New York: $X\frac{JPY}{USD} = 118.50$ and $X\frac{HKD}{USD} = 7.80$. At the same moment, a dealer in Tokyo quotes $X\frac{JPY}{HKD} = 15.02$. Can you profit?

Figure 2.18 illustrates the method, assuming that you start with JPY 1 million in your pocket.

With JPY 1 million in your pocket, you purchase HKD 66,577.8961 = $[JPY]$ 1,000,000/ $[JPY/HKD]$ 15.02 in Tokyo. At the same time, in New York, you sell HKD 66,577.8961 for $[HKD]$ 66,577.8961/$[HKD/USD]$ 7.80, or USD 8,535.6277, and, with that, buy $[USD]$ 8,535.6277 $\cdot$ $[JPY/USD]$ 118.50, or JPY 1,011,471.88. You are able to make an instant profit of JPY 11,471.88 simply because HKD is cheap in the direct (**cross**) market in Tokyo relative to New York. In New York, it takes $[JPY/USD]$ 118.50/$[HKD/USD]$ 7.80 = JPY 15.19 to buy HKD 1.00, whereas, in Tokyo, HKD 1 costs only JPY 15.02.

You would not be alone in pursuing this triangle arbitrage opportunity. Dealers in New York would sell dollars for yen, convert the yen into HK dollars in Tokyo and, with HK dollars, buy back US dollars in New York (it does not matter where you start on the triangle). Every dealer around the globe would be going in the same direction. The USD-into-JPY trade would drive up the yen, the JPY-into-HKD trade would drive up HKD relative to JPY, and the HKD-into-USD trade would drive the USD up against the HKD. Likely, all three quotes would change until the yen price of HK dollars was the same in New York and Tokyo.

In the above, we ignore the transaction costs in the form of a bid-ask spread. In reality, we need to modify the computed amounts by considering that we would sell at the bid and buy at the ask. Instead of simply one FX cross rate, we need to compute its bid and ask. The principle remains the same.

The triangular arbitrage principle binds hundreds of possible currency combinations. As soon as one FX quote changes in the market, many others must follow.

2.6 SHORT SELLING

Securities – stocks and bonds – bought on behalf of their customers are held in brokerage houses in "street name," i.e. the customers' names are not identified and the brokerage simply holds the total number of shares or bonds for all its customers, collects the total amount of dividends or coupon interest from the issuer, and apportions them into the customers' accounts.

Because of that, these securities can be borrowed/lent like a generic commodity among the customers of the same brokerage house and among brokerage houses. This allows account holders to borrow securities they do not own, sell them to a third party, repurchase them from another investor, and return them to the original owner. The process of borrowing a security from a broker's pool of stocks and bonds and selling the security in the market is called *short selling*.

Just as buying a security (also referred to as going long a security) is done in the hope of profiting from its appreciation, short selling is done in a hope of being able to repurchase the security at a lower price later to profit from the reduced price. Short selling, just like buying, is an important mechanism in the process of bringing material information about the economic condition of the issuer to the market and the overall fair price discovery. Cash and margin buyers come with positive news; sellers and short sellers come with negative news.

Short selling can only take place in margin accounts. The short seller receives cash for the sold securities, but is also required to post additional cash with a broker to ensure that the securities will be returned to the original owner before he or she decides to sell them. With a large pool of similar securities to lend out, brokers rarely have to resort to calling the securities loans, but there is always a possibility. Also, if the value of the securities goes up and the short seller's liability increases, the broker will issue a *margin call* on the customer by asking for additional cash. The margin is also used to pay the original owner of the securities any intermediate cash flows due on the security while the security is sold short. The owner/lender of the security may be due dividends or coupon interest which cannot come from the issuer as these now go to the new owner, so the short seller has to compensate (through the broker) the original owner of the securities for those cash flows. Let us review the mechanics of margin accounts and buying, selling, and shorting securities.

2.6.1 Buying on Margin

Stocks and bonds can be purchases for cash, i.e. using only the buyer's own funds, or on margin, i.e. by borrowing some of the needed cash from the broker. The margin loan is collateralized by the purchased securities. Since margin loans play a larger role in money and credit creation in the economy, they are regulated by the central banks, such as the Federal Reserve in the USA, by setting the initial and maintenance margin minimums. The margin is defined as the owner's equity in the account as percentage of the value of the securities.

Suppose the broker's margin requirements are 50% initial and 40% maintenance, and Jack wants to buy 400 shares of ABC Corp. currently trading at \$50 per share. Of the \$20,000 needed, Jack puts up \$10,000 of his own cash and borrows \$10,000 from his broker. His margin is 50%. He buys the ABC stock hoping its price will go up.

Suppose he is right, and ABC's price rises by 10% to \$55. Jack sells his 400 shares for \$55 a share, or \$22,000. He pays off the margin loan of \$10,000 (we ignore the interest on the loan) and is left with \$12,000, a 20% return on his invested capital of \$10,000. His 2:1 leverage allowed him to double his profit relative to the price change. If he had purchased the stock with his own cash of \$20,000, his return would have been only 10%, the same as the rise in the price of the stock.

Suppose, instead, that Jack is wrong and ABC's stock goes down 10% to \$45. Jack sells his 400 shares for \$18,000, repays his \$10,000 margin loan and is left with \$8,000, incurring a \$2,000 or 20% loss on his investment of \$10,000. His 2:1 leverage doubled his percentage loss relative to a straight cash purchase. Margin and leverage are symmetric, they amplify gains, but they also amplify losses by the same ratio.

For a buy transaction, the margin requirement (owner's equity as percentage of security value) is defined as:

$$Margin = \frac{\text{Security value} - \$\text{ Loan}}{\text{Security value}}$$

Initially, Jack's margin was:

$$Margin = \frac{400 \times \$50 - \$10{,}000}{400 \times \$50} = 50\%$$

When ABC's stock price dropped to \$45, Jack's margin was:

$$Margin = \frac{400 \times \$45 - \$10{,}000}{400 \times \$45} = 44.44\%$$

Had the stock dropped further, Jack would have been called by the broker to post additional cash collateral. The margin call would have occurred when Jack's equity in the account dropped to 40%, i.e. when

$$0.40 = \frac{400 \times P - \$10{,}000}{400 \times P} \Rightarrow P = \$41.67$$

ABC's price dropped down to \$41.67. While an individual investor's leverage cannot in this example increase to more than 100:40 or 2.5:1, it is easy to see how a fund, if allowed to use the margined securities to collateralize additional cash loans, could obtain a much higher leverage.

2.6.2 Short Selling in a Margin Account

Suppose the broker's margin requirements are still 50% initial and 40% maintenance, and Jack wants to short sell 400 shares of ABC Corp. currently trading at \$50 per share. After borrowing the shares from the broker, Jack sells them to a third party for the \$20,000. Jack is required to leave his funds with the broker, perhaps earning interest on his balances, and he is required to post an additional \$10,000 of his own cash. The total cash balance in the account is \$30,000 and his margin is 50%. He has short sold the ABC stock hoping its price will go down.

Suppose he is right, and ABC's price drops by 20% to \$40. Jack buys back 400 shares for \$40 a share, or \$16,000. He returns the borrowed securities (we ignore any loan fees) and is left with \$14,000 in the account, a 40% return on his invested capital of \$10,000. His 2:1 leverage allowed him to double his profit relative to the price change. If he had had to post the full collateral of \$20,000 on the short sale, his return would have been only 20%, the same as the decline in the price of the stock.

Suppose instead that Jack is wrong and ABC's stock goes up 20% to \$60. Jack buys back 400 shares for \$24,000, leaving him with \$6,000 in the account, a \$4,000 or 40% loss on his investment of \$10,000. His 2:1 leverage doubled his percentage loss relative to a straight sale out of/repurchase into his own inventory. Margin and leverage are again symmetric, they amplify gains, and they amplify losses by the same ratio.

For a short sale transaction, the margin requirement (owner's equity as a percentage of security value) is defined as:

$$Margin = \frac{\$\text{ Account balance} - \text{Security value}}{\text{Security value}}$$

Initially, Jack's margin was:

$$Margin = \frac{\$30{,}000 - 400 \times \$50}{400 \times \$50} = 50\%$$

When ABC's stock price rises to \$52, Jack's margin is:

$$Margin = \frac{\$30{,}000 - 400 \times \$52}{400 \times \$52} = 44.23\%$$

If the stock were to rise further, Jack would be called by the broker to post additional cash collateral. The margin call would occur when Jack's equity in the account dropped to 40%, i.e. when

$$0.40 = \frac{\$30{,}000 - 400 \times P}{400 \times P} \Rightarrow P = \$53.57$$

ABC's price rose to \$53.57. The margin call for a short sale occurs much earlier, i.e. for a much smaller price movement, than the margin call on a buy transaction.

Short sales have been subject to some controversy, especially when the short sale is naked. Naked short selling is similar to check kiting. Because security transactions may take a few days to clear (the electronic agreement to transact is instant, but the actual delivery of securities and/or payment for them is delayed), if unchecked, it is possible for a short seller to borrow the stock, sell it, and buy it back, even before the original sale is cleared, and then roll it over into another short sale. In this way, the amount of shorted stock may exceed the total amount of stock outstanding. That is clearly not what the mechanism of short selling has been intended for.

2.6.3 Short Selling of Bonds

The above is an example of a short sale of ABC stock. If ABC happened to go ex-dividend between the time of the short sale and the time of the repurchase of the stock, Jack would have had to pay out of his account the amount of the declared dividend to the lender of the stock. The same happens when one short sells a bond (Figure 2.19).

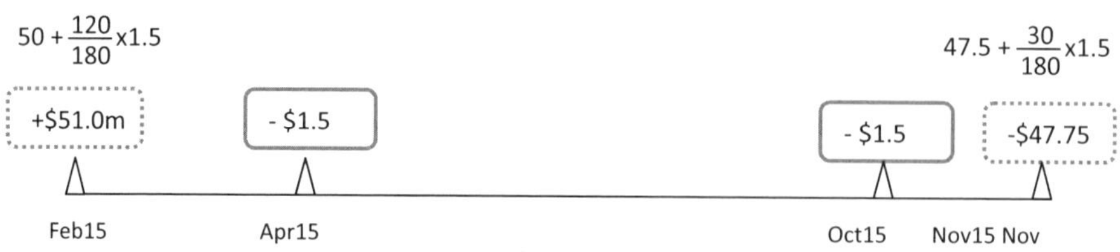

Figure 2.19 Short \$50m 6% 4/15/38 on February 15

Suppose on February 15, Jack shorts $50 million of Pfizer 6.00% April 15, 2038 bonds selling at par. On February 15, Jack borrows the bond from his broker J&R Brokerage and sells it in the open market for $50 million plus accrued interest of $1 million (120/180 of the semi-annual coupon of 3% on $50 million). On April 15, Jack has to reimburse J&R Brokerage $1.5 million for the coupon cash flow J&R would have received from Pfizer had it not lent out the bond. If the short position stays on through the next coupon date of October 15, Jack will again have to reimburse J&R $1.5 million. This will continue until Jack buys the bond back in the open market and returns it to J&R.

If the bond is trading at 95 on November 15, Jack can buy it back for $47.5 million plus the accrued interest of $250,000, or the total invoice price of $47.75 million, having in the meantime paid for two coupon cash flows of $1.5 million each on April 15 and October 15.

High grade bonds are often used in repurchase (repo) and reverse repo agreements. A repo is an overnight borrowing arrangement structured as a sale of a bond and an agreement to repurchase it the next day for a prearranged price. The difference in the sale and repurchase price is the interest paid on the borrowed funds. A repo is not a short sale, as the bonds are not borrowed but owned and delivered as collateral at the time of the repo. However, bonds obtained as collateral through a reverse repo (lending cash by buying and subsequent reselling of collateral) can be short sold to a third party. The reverse repo has to be entered into as a term agreement or rolled over daily for the duration of the short sale. A reverse repo is thus a way of borrowing bonds.

3
Futures Markets

The greatest misconception about futures and forwards is that they predict the path the spot prices will take in the future. In that view, spot prices reflect the supply and demand conditions now, and futures prices reflect the consensus about the supply and demand conditions in the future. A forecast of future drought or supply disruption leaves spot prices unchanged but raises the futures price. Yet why wouldn't a potential adverse event incentivize an enterprising trader to buy the commodity now, store it, and deliver it later, putting upward pressure on the spot price? The fact is that information about the future supply and demand conditions affects *jointly* spot and futures prices. Moreover, as discussed in this chapter, most spot and futures prices are tied to each other mathematically by a *cost-of-carry* equation which reflects the cost of financing a purchase of the commodity spot and carrying it (storing and earning a yield) to the futures expiry date. This *cash-and-carry arbitrage* allows the synthetic replication of a futures contract with a spot purchase or sale and a borrowing or lending of funds.

While futures and forwards do not predict future spot prices independently of the current spot prices, they perform a very important function in a market economy. They allow economic agents to eliminate future price risk and focus completely on product innovation and efficiency. Suppliers of commodities investing in their extraction or cultivation (corn and coffee growers, palladium miners) can lock in future sale prices today. Buyers of commodities who use them as inputs into production and innovation (coffee sellers such as Starbucks, or car company suppliers investing in lithium or cobalt batteries) can lock in future purchase prices today. The price risk transference in the futures markets would be impossible without thousands of speculators who stand ready to go long or short contracts for multiple future delivery dates. They expect to make profit over time by taking short-term positions based on the analysis of the demand and supply of the commodities, in the process establishing prices, and sending economic signals for efficient allocation of resources in the economy.

3.1 FUNDAMENTALS OF FUTURES AND FORWARDS

A spot transaction is a contract to buy or sell an asset for immediate delivery. Cash is paid and the asset is received now. A *forward* is a contract to buy or sell a specified quantity of an asset at a price agreed upon today, but for delivery at some future date called the expiry date. The seller is said to short (go short), the buyer of the asset is said to long (go long) the forward. In a *physical-settled* forward, the seller delivers the physical asset and, on the delivery date, receives the pre-agreed price for it. In a *cash-settled* forward, the seller does not deliver the asset on the delivery date. The buyer pays to the seller (or receives from the seller) the difference between the pre-agreed price and the spot price on the day of the delivery. Economically, the physical- and cash-settled forwards are the same. If, in the physical forward, the original forward price was lower (higher) than the delivery spot price, the buyer takes possession of the commodity for that lower (higher) price. In the cash forward, the buyer receives (pays) the difference between the final spot price and the original forward price, but has to pay the final spot price for the commodity. If the final spot price is higher than the forward price, he is compensated for the difference; if the final spot price is lower, he pays the difference. No matter what, his total outlay for the commodity is equal to the original forward price.

Importantly, both in physical and cash forwards, no asset or cash changes hands at the time the forward contract is established (zero entry cost), and the settlement takes place once at the end. A *futures* contract is analogous to a forward, but the settlement is piecemeal (daily) and through a clearinghouse. The buyer (going long) and the seller (going short) agree on a price and the number of contracts (quantity). Instead of waiting until expiry, each day they pay or receive cash flows equal to the movement in the price of the commodity, depending on whether the price goes up or down. These cash flows are referred to as *marking-to-market* payments or the *variation margin* settlement. On the expiry date, the futures price of the commodity is set equal to the spot price, so that the net cumulative variation margin exchanged is equal to the difference between that future spot price and the original agreed-upon futures price (times the quantity), just as in a forward contract.

The purpose of marking-to-market through a clearinghouse is twofold: credit mitigation and fungibility. Futures markets bring together buyers and sellers from all parts of the world, unfamiliar with each other or unwilling to trust each other on contract performance. Therefore, each futures trade, while entered into between two willing parties on the exchange, has the exchange's clearinghouse in the middle. The clearinghouse requires both parties to maintain a cash margin and it collects/distributes the daily variation margin settlement cash from/into the margin account. The clearinghouse can guarantee contract performance not because it has a large amount of its own capital, but because all bets are settled to their current liquidation value at the end of each day, and the clearinghouse can liquidate contracts if the next day's price movements begin to exceed the maintenance margin. Credit exposure is thus limited to one day at most, not to the entire contract period.

Having all party-to-party transactions rewritten to involve the central clearinghouse also allows for easy shorting and unwinding. Since each contract is legally with the clearinghouse (and settled at the end of each day), buys and sells between different counterparties are fungible (substitutable) and can be netted. Buys and sells can come in any order. Contracts bought by A from B can be unwound by contracts sold by A to C. Contracts sold by A to B can be unwound by contracts bought by A from C. If A bought six contracts from B at 95 on Monday and sells four contracts to C at 92 on Wednesday, the four sold contracts get settled by A paying the net variation margin of 3 each to the clearinghouse. Subsequently, A is long two, B is short six, and C is long four contracts. The clearinghouse is the other side of each position and has zero net overall exposure.

While only larger well-capitalized firms can handle the counterparty risk and unwinding difficulties of the forwards, the mark-to-market mechanism of the futures encourages smaller speculators into the market. This improves price discovery and risk sharing over time. Often the final buyers and suppliers of the commodities do not operate on the same production calendars. Agricultural crops may be reaped once or twice a year, while consumption is spread evenly. This timing-gap risk is bridged by the speculators.

In general, commodities can be divided into two main groups: financial and non-financial. The first group includes equity indexes, interest rates, and currencies. The second group includes agriculturals, metals, and energy. Some subgroups contain peculiar commodities: bond futures allowing a choice of what to deliver; Fed Funds futures settled off average effective rates over a month; electricity swap contracts on price differentials between delivery points or times; and weather contracts on cumulative temperature differentials over a month. One useful categorization of commodities is as a spectrum that runs from those subject to the strict cash-and-carry arbitrage (most financials), to one-sided cash-and-carry (easily storable agriculturals and metals), to strategic commodities (oil) with an almost broken cash-and-carry link, and to commodities with no or multiple spot markets (weather, electricity). The principle of cash-and-carry arbitrage is essential to understanding why futures prices do not arbitrarily deviate from spot prices.

Some of the newest frontiers of forward and futures markets, often referred to as *predictions markets*, are contracts on non-price events. Weather, sports, political, and macroeconomic events belong in this category. The pricing and trading of these contracts relates closely to bookmaking (varying prices to ensure that the total take is at least as great as the future payout). It may rely on scientific forecasting and actuarial science, i.e. insurance. These contracts cannot be hedged with positions in the spot commodity or any related commodities providing at least a partial hedge. These markets are truly in a category of their own. They should not be confused with contracts on events (defaults, downgrades, corporate announcements) that can be hedged with positions in related assets (corporate bonds, stocks). This last category is closely related to options with their associated hedge-based pricing methodology.

3.2 FUTURES MECHANICS

We will review the mechanics of futures trading and marking-to-market starting with physical commodities. This is an intuitive case: each contract represents a defined quantity of the commodity and the variation margin per contract settles the price change times the quantity of the commodity. Next, we move to interest rate futures where there is no "quantity," but the contract multiplier is chosen to mimic the settlement of interest payments on a principal amount. We will then cover stock indexes where the multiplier is an arbitrary number converting index points to dollars, but can be interpreted as defining the dollar amount of stocks in the cash-and-carry arbitrage. Lastly, we will cover currencies. Currencies are physical commodities; contract sizes are defined with standard quantities.

3.2.1 Physical Commodity Futures

It is Thursday, October 29, 2009. On the Chicago Board of Trade (CBT – this was acquired by the Chicago Mercantile Exchange, CME, in July 2007), corn and soybean futures trade at the prices shown in Table 3.1.

Suppose that, hoping to lock in the purchase price on 10,000 bushels of corn, we bought two corn contracts at $206\frac{1}{2}$ cents per bushel on Thursday before the close. Subsequent to that,

Table 3.1 Physical commodity contracts

	Open	High	Low	Settle	Open interest
Corn (CBT) 5000 bu; cents per bu					
Nov 2009	$201\frac{3}{4}$	$202\frac{1}{2}$	$201\frac{1}{2}$	**202**	2,429
Dec 2009	206	$207\frac{1}{2}$	$205\frac{1}{2}$	**$206\frac{1}{2}$**	211,016
Mar 2010	$218\frac{3}{4}$	$220\frac{1}{4}$	$218\frac{1}{4}$	**219**	112,379
Soybeans (CBT) 5,000 bu; cents per bu					
Nov 2009	$423\frac{1}{2}$	430	$423\frac{1}{4}$	**$428\frac{1}{4}$**	75,068
Mar 2010	$436\frac{1}{2}$	$443\frac{1}{4}$	$436\frac{1}{4}$	**$441\frac{1}{4}$**	28,917

Table 3.2 Price path for corn starting at $206^1/_2$

Date	Dec09 futures price
Fri, Oct30 2009	$207^1/_4$
Mon, Nov02 2009	$206^3/_4$
...	...
Fri, Dec18 2009	210

we observe the progression of corn futures prices for delivery in December of 2009 as in Table 3.2.

Since the price of corn is quoted in cents per bushel, and as each contract represents 5,000 bushels, each 1 cent change in the price of corn translates into a \$50 change in the total value of one contract (5,000 × \$0.01). While not commonly used with physical commodities, for continuity of exposition, we can adopt the terminology of index futures and refer to the \$50 number as the multiplier. The variation margin (MTM) amounts for each day are computed in Table 3.3.

Having bought two contracts on Thursday, we receive \$75 into our account as the price rises to $207^1/_4$ on Friday, we pay \$50 out of our account as the price drops to $206^3/_4$ on Monday, etc. As the price fluctuates we receive or pay cash daily between October 2009 and the final settlement on December 18, 2009. If, on that day, the price is 210, then the net cash gain in our account is \$350. The net (cumulative) variation margin on any day, which is the sum of daily MTM settlement amounts, can be computed as the difference between that day's (final) price minus the original price times the number of contracts times the multiplier, as all the intermediate daily prices cancel out.

If the purpose of buying two contracts at $206^1/_2$ in October was to lock in the purchase price of 10,000 bushels of corn for delivery in December, then we have accomplished our goal. The corn will cost 10,000 × \$2.10 = \$21,000 on December 18, but the \$350 gain will reduce our net cost to \$20,650, which translates to \$2.065 per bushel.

In fact, our net price will be \$2.065 no matter what the price of corn in December. Suppose the price fluctuations between October and December were as shown in Table 3.4. On December 18, 2009, we pay 10,000 × \$189.25 = \$18,925 for corn, but including the MTM loss on the futures of \$1,725, our total cost is \$20,650 or \$2.065 per bushel. It is easy to see that the futures contracts provide a cash inflow or outflow (depending on the direction of the price movement) equal to the final spot price of corn minus the original lock-in price times the desired number of bushels of corn. The futures contracts act as a two-way insurance contract, insuring the buyer against the price increase and the seller against the price decrease.

Table 3.3 MTM calculation for two contracts bought at $206^1/_2$

Date	Daily calculation	MTM (VM)	Net var. margin
Fri, Oct30 2009	2 × (207.25 – 206.50) × \$50	+ \$75.00	+ \$ 75.00
Mon, Nov02 2009	2 × (206.75 – 207.25) × \$50	– \$50.00	+ \$ 25.00
.....			
Fri, Dec18 2009	2 × (210.00 – ...) × \$50	...	+ \$350.00

Table 3.4 MTM calculation for two contracts bought at $206^1/_2$

Date	Settle price	Daily calculation	MTM (VM)	Net var. margin
Fri, Oct30 2009	$208^3/_4$	2 × (208.75 – 206.50) × $50	+ $225.00	+ $225.00
Mon, Nov02 2009	$202^1/_2$	2 × (202.50 – 208.75) × $50	– $625.00	+ $400.00
.....				
Fri, Dec18 2009	$189^1/_4$	2 × (189.25 – . . .) × $50	. . .	– $1,725.00

Of course, the original intention of going long two December contracts in October may not have been to lock in a purchase price of corn, but simply to speculate that the (futures) price will rise. In that case, the speculator has to sell the two contracts at some point to avoid taking delivery of the corn. If the price followed the path in Table 3.4, and the speculator chose to unwind at the close on December 18 (as many do), she would have lost $1,725 through MTM settlements throughout the life of her position. She also could have exited her position, wholly or partially, anytime in between. For example, she could have sold one contract earlier on Friday, October 30, as the price rose to $208^3/_4$, and the other at $189^1/_4$ on December 18. Table 3.5 shows two ways to compute her total gain/loss: one by computing the net MTM on two contracts through October 30 plus the net MTM on one contract from October 30 to December 18; and the second by computing the net MTM on one contract October 29 through October 30 plus the net MTM on one contract October 29 through December 18.

The day-by-day calculation shows the real cash flows incurred (cash accounting); the contract-by-contract calculation follows accrual accounting of closed positions.

To test the understanding of futures mechanics, let us solve the following scenario using the prices in Table 3.1. A soybean farmer wants to lock in the sale price of $441^1/_4$ cents per bushel on 30,000 bushels of soybeans in March 2010. He also thinks that March futures prices will drop to 420 by November 18, 2009, so, in addition to locking price, he wants to speculate on another 10,000 bushels. What should he do?

The strategy will be to sell eight contracts now, buy back two contracts in November, and leave the remaining six contracts short until March. One outcome of the scenario is shown in Table 3.6.

The farmer collects 30,000 × \$4.765 = \$142,950 for the corn minus the MTM loss of \$10,575 on the six contracts held to expiry, or the net of \$132,375. The latter represents 30,000 bushels at \$4.4125. In addition, the farmer made \$2,125 on two March contracts shorted in October and closed out (bought) in November.

Table 3.5 Partial unwind of one of two contracts bought at $206^1/_2$

Date	Settle price	Calculation	MTM (VM)	Net var. margin
By date				
Fri, Oct30 2009	$208^3/_4$	1 × (208.75 – 206.50) × $50	+ $225.00	
Fri, Dec18 2009	$189^1/_4$	1 × (189.25 – 208.75) × $50	– $975.00	– $750.00
By contract				
Fri, Oct30 2009	$208^3/_4$	1 × (208.75 – 206.50) × $50	+ $112.50	
Fri, Dec18 2009	$189^1/_4$	1 × (189.25 – 206.50) × $50	– $862.50	– $750.00

Table 3.6 Short soybean strategy at $441\frac{1}{4}$

Date	Settle price	Calculation	Net var. margin
Speculative part			
Wed, Nov18 2009	420	$-2 \times (420.00 - 441.25) \times \$50$	+ \$ 2,125
Lock-in part			
Fri, Mar19 2010	$476\frac{1}{2}$	$-6 \times (476.50 - 441.25) \times \$50$	− \$10,575

3.2.2 Interest Rate Futures

The mechanics of MTM settlement of interest rate futures are similar to those for physical commodity futures. The daily variation margin is equal to the number of contracts times the daily change in futures price, times the multiplier, which reflects the number of bonds in each contract. However, bonds and credit arrangements differ from stocks, currencies, and commodities in that they are rights to contractually defined future cash flows (interest and principal), thus the value of the bond can be equivalently stated in terms of price or yield-to-maturity. Yet, as the value of the commodity fluctuates, the two terms do not change one-for-one (due to convexity). Because of that, interest rate futures fall into two categories: contracts on

- long bond *prices*, and
- short-term deposit *rates*.

In bond price futures, buyers speculate on, lock in, and receive daily MTM settlements off the *price* of a bond eligible to be delivered on the expiry date. In deposit rate futures, buyers speculate on, lock in, and receive daily MTM settlements off the *interest rate* that will be earned (paid) on a deposit of fixed maturity. For consistency, futures on interest rates are constructed to settle off variables that are artificially defined to resemble bond prices, but are really linear transforms of yields. Since real prices are not linear in yields, the two categories of interest rate futures settle the variation margin differently. In addition, most bond price futures have special features granting short parties multiple delivery options (the time and type of bond to be delivered is at the short's discretion). Deposit rate futures typically are free from such complications and treat both sides equally.

3.2.2.1 Bond Price Futures

Bond price futures around the world are defined on the basis of actual or artificial bond prices, not directly on interest rates. For example, on the LIFFE (part of NYSE Euronext group, merged in 2007) in London, the long gilt contract is for GBP 100,000 face value of the long bond issued by the UK government. On the Eurex (incl. the International Securities Exchange (ISE), acquired in 2007), one 10-year Euro-Bund futures contract represents EUR 100,000 of the euro-denominated bond of the German government. Like spot, bond futures prices are quoted as a percentage of par value. On the LIFFE, the gilt contract has a tick size of 0.01% of par, so one tick is equivalent to GBP 10 (= 100,000 × 0.01/100). Similarly, on the Chicago Mercantile Exchange (CME), one Treasury bond contract represents USD 100,000 face value of a 30-year Treasury bond and the futures price is quoted as percentage of par value, but with fractions in 32nds (tick size is 1/32% of par or \$31.25, with half-tick price movements allowed). To compute the variation margin for a given day, one first translates it to a straight percentage, then proceeds the same way as with gilts – that is, divides by 100, and multiplies by the size of the contract USD 100,000. For example, if we shorted five contracts at 112-03 (= 112-3/32) and the price changed to 112-27 (= 112-27/32), we would have a loss, or a negative variation margin amount, as shown:

Calculation for price change to 112-27/32
Var. margin $= -5 \times (112\text{-}27/32 - 112\text{-}3/32)\%$
of $\$100{,}000 = -5 \times (0.75/100) \times \$100{,}000 = -\$3{,}750$

Note that the multiplier, as defined before, is in this case equal to 1,000 (× 100,000/100). For example, a 0.75% change in the price represents a $750 variation margin per contract. If one wanted to speculate directly on a specific size of an *interest rate* change and not a bond price change, one would have to base one's bet on the current duration of the underlying bond. To bet on an interest rate *increase* of 1% for $1 million face value of bonds, one would have to *short* [(1/Duration) × 10] bond contracts. As interest rates increase by 1%, the value of each of the 10 contracts representing $100,000 face value, for a total of $1 million par value, would decrease by [1 × Duration number of points], producing the desired dollar gain.

All US Treasury bond and note contracts, and many other government bond contracts, are defined not on one underlying bond but on a set satisfying certain maturity and coupon criteria (e.g. close in maturity and coupon to the 30-year 6% mark). The short party to the contract is given an option to choose which of the eligible bonds to deliver to the long party on the futures expiry date. Each eligible bond is assigned a fixed conversion factor and the short party must deliver the face value equal to $100,000 times the conversion factor. The *conversion factor*, based on relative duration, is designed to make all eligible bonds equal in value at the 6% yield. However, as it is a fixed number, the true values of the different bonds eligible to be delivered diverge, giving the short party the option to choose the *cheapest-to-deliver* alternative. Often, the identity of the cheapest-to-deliver bond changes as yields fluctuate throughout the life of the contract. The short party is also given additional timing options which complicate the analysis of these contracts. The reason behind embedding the cheapest-to-deliver and timing options in the contract is to ensure the maximum liquidity of the delivery instruments which are considered fungible.

3.2.2.2 Eurocurrency Futures

Background on Eurocurrency Deposits

A Eurodollar deposit is a non-negotiable US dollar-denominated interest-bearing loan outside the US regulators' purview. The interest rate is fixed and quoted on an *Act/360* basis and paid as add-on interest at the end. A variety of terms is available, ranging from overnight, tomorrow/next, 1-day, 1-week, all the way to 12-months; the most popular being a 3-month deposit with a 2-London-business-day settlement, followed by a 1-month term. The minimum amount is $10 million. Eurodollar lending rates are fixed daily at 4 pm GMT by a group of London banks most active in this market in the form of a London Interbank Offered Rate, or LIBOR, published by the British Bankers' Association (BBA) and widely distributed by wire services and newspapers; the bid on borrowed funds is referred to as LIBID. The LIBOR is the benchmark rate for unrestricted 3-month deposits and swap payment settlements. The Eurodollar market is the largest global money market by volume outstanding and turnover.

It swamps the within-the-US market for interbank Certificates of Deposits (CDs), regulated by the Federal Reserve and insured by the Federal Deposit Insurance Corporation (FDIC). The interest calculation on the unregulated Eurodollar deposits works as follows. Suppose on Thursday, October 25, 2012, you call a London bank to borrow dollars at the LIBOR interest rate of 2.31% for a term of 3 months. Your interest accrual period runs from October 25, 2012 to Friday, January 25, 2013, and your principal and interest payment date is due 2 business days later on Tuesday, January 29, 2013. As there are 92 days in the interest period, your total repayment per $1 million borrowed is as shown:

Calculation for a 92 day borrow at 2.31%
Repayment $\$1{,}000{,}000 \times (1 + 0.0231 \times 92/360) = \$1{,}005{,}903.33$

All major currencies have active unregulated short-term deposit markets. Given its "off-shore" location, London is the main center for borrowing and lending in Eurodollars, Euro-euros, Euroyen, Euroswiss, and several other Eurocurrencies. The prefix Euro is unrelated to the euro currency and merely reflects the historical origin of the market for unregulated interbank deposit markets (Soviet dollar balances in Paris banks in the 1960s). Day-count calculations vary from currency to currency. Most banking regulations around the world allow participation in the Eurocurrency market by domestic banks through legally segregated bank facilities.

Eurodollar Futures

The Eurodollar contract on the Chicago Mercantile Exchange (CME) is designed to allow speculating on, and locking in, the interest rate paid or received on a $1 million 3-month Eurodollar deposit starting on the futures expiry date and ending 90 days later. In order to align the bond and deposit market language conventions, where buying a bond means lending and selling a bond means borrowing, the Eurodollar contract is quoted on an artificial price basis. The futures price, rather than being a true present value of the principal to be received 3 months later equal to $100 / (1 + L/4)$, is instead defined as linear in the interest rate, but still made to look like a discount bond price:

$$F = 100 - L$$

where L is the 3-month LIBOR rate with the percentage sign dropped. Buying one futures contract at a price of 97.69 and holding it to maturity simply means locking in a LIBOR rate of 2.31% (100.00 – 97.69) on a $1 million loan. Eurodollar futures are settled in cash, and as there is no physical delivery of any deposit/loan balances, this price convention poses no problems. At the final settlement on the expiry date – while the futures price F is *not* the price of a 3-month $1 million discount bond – F is automatically set to equal 100 minus the LIBOR fixing rate for that day. Anyone speculating in Eurodollar futures is in fact betting on what the LIBOR rate will be on the expiry date, and the variation margin settlement is off the changes in anticipated LIBOR rates. Because the LIBOR rate is subtracted in constructing the futures price, speculating on the rate going up involves selling futures (to benefit from the price decline) and speculating on the rate going down involves buying futures (to benefit from the price increase), which is consistent with the direction of bond futures buying and selling. Also, because the LIBOR rate is subtracted in constructing the futures price, hedgers can always interpret $100 - F$ as being the LIBOR rate, L, that can be locked in on that day for a forward deposit starting on the futures expiry date.

The CME has two LIBOR-based Eurodollar contracts, each defined in artificial 100 – L price terms. Confusingly, the 1-month contract is referred to as the LIBOR contract and the 3-month contract is referred to as the Eurodollar contract. The CME also lists a similarly defined contract on 13-week T-Bills and 3-month yen deposits, and average price-based Fed Funds contract. The contracts can be traded electronically on the GLOBEX platform and the Eurodollar is cross-listed for floor trading on the Singapore Exchange (SGX). NYSE Euronext's LIFFE floor trades contracts on 3-month deposits denominated in euros, Swiss francs, pounds sterling, and yen, referred to as Euribor (euro LIBOR), Euroswiss, short sterling, and Euroyen contracts having, respectively, EUR 1 million, CHF 1 million, GBP 500,000, and JPY 100 million notional principals. The exchange also lists a shorter EUR 3 million Eonia contract on ECB required reserve balances. Both the CME and the LIFFE offer trading in bundles of successive month Eurocurrency futures, together with options on those futures. The mechanics of variation margin settlement are identical for Eurodollars, Euribor, and Euroswiss ($25, €25, and 25 francs per 0.01 tick); the short sterling and Euroyen requiring only size modifications (tick value being £12.5 for sterling and ¥1250 for yen). The settlement of 1-month dollar LIBOR futures and Eonia futures is identical to Eurodollars, i.e. $25 or €25 per tick, as the size compensates for shorter maturity.

Marking-to-Market Variation Margin

As the stated size of the Eurodollar contract is $1 million, and as the commodity is defined as a 90-day LIBOR deposit, the variation margin settlement has to involve a day-count fraction correction. If LIBOR were to change from 2.50% to 2.60%, which translates into a futures price change from 97.50 to 97.40, then the variation margin settlement for one long contract would be as shown:

Calculation for LIBOR change from 2.50% to 2.60%

$$\begin{aligned}\text{Var. margin} &= 1 \times (97.40 - 97.50)/100 \times (90/360) \times \$1{,}000{,}000\\ &= 1 \times (-0.10) \times \$2{,}500 = -\$250\end{aligned}$$

As the calculation shows, rather than relying on the $1 million size of the contract, the easiest way to view the mark-to-market settlement formula for Eurodollars is in terms a *multiplier* of $2,500 per 1% LIBOR change (= 1 point futures price change). The exchanges define it even more simply by designating a tick size equal to 0.01% LIBOR change, a minimum price movement currently equal to half the tick for most contracts, and a *multiplier* equal to $25 per tick. The tick is equivalent to a 1 bp change in LIBOR or 1/100 of the futures price change. For Euribor and Euroswiss contracts, substitute €25 or CHF 25 for $25 in the calculations below; for short sterling and Euroyen contracts, substitute £12.50 or ¥1,250 for $25. Table 3.7 shows the Eurodollar futures for the close of day on Thursday, October 25, 2012.[1]

The June 2013 contract closed at 97.48. That contract's underlying commodity is a $1 million deposit placed on June 19, 2013 and redeemed on September 19, 2013. The implied interest rate for that deposit is 100 – 97.48 = 2.52%. The spot 3-month LIBOR rate on October 25, 2012 is 2.31%, not reported in Table 3.7. For simplicity, we assume exactly 90 days in the June 19–September 19 period.

Suppose at the close on Thursday, we go long (buy) 1 Eurodollar contract and over the following 2 business days we observe the futures prices shown in Table 3.8.

[1] Table 3.7 contains real quotes and statistics for October 25, 2001.

Table 3.7 1- and 3-month Eurodollar futures on October 25, 2012

	Open	High	Low	Settle	Open interest
LIBOR 1-mo. (CME): \$3,000,000; pts of 100%					
Nov	97.76	97.80	97.74	**97.77**	25,544
Dec 2012	97.77	97.81	97.77	**97.80**	5,875
Jan 2013	97.91	97.92	97.91	**97.92**	3,069
Eurodollar (CME): \$1,000,000; pts of 100%					
Nov	97.79	97.83	97.78	**97.81**	41,554
Dec 2012	97.81	97.87	97.80	**97.85**	863,180
Jan 2013	97.86	97.88	97.86	**97.87**	7,080
Mar	97.71	97.80	97.80	**97.85**	628,766
Jun	97.41	97.51	97.41	**97.48**	588,920
Sep	96.98	97.12	96.98	**97.09**	396,280
Dec	96.50	96.63	96.47	**96.60**	378,297
Mar 2014	96.14	96.25	96.14	**96.24**	243,043

Table 3.9 shows that in order to compute the variation margin on one long contract using the \$25 per tick multiplier, we simply drop the decimal in the Eurodollar futures prices to convert the daily changes to basis point or tick differences.

Just as in the corn example, the net variation margin (cumulative gain/loss) of \$175 as of Monday could be computed alternatively from the difference of the Monday close and the original Thursday price:

$$1 \times (9{,}755 - 9{,}748) \times 25 = \$175$$

When the 3-month LIBOR is 3.00% on the last day of trading on June 19, 2013, the last futures price is set to $F = 100 - L = 100.00 - 3.00 = 97.00$, and the net variation margin over October through June is:

$$1 \times (9{,}700 - 9{,}748) \times 25 = -\$1{,}200$$

Table 3.8 June 2013 Eurodollar price path starting at 97.48

Date	June 2013 futures price
Fri, Oct26 2012	97.44
Mon, Oct29 2012	97.55
...	...
Wed, Jun19 2013	97.00

Table 3.9 MTM calculation for 1 Eurodollar contract bought at 97.48

Date	Daily calculation	MTM (VM)	Net var. margin
Fri, Oct26 2012	1 × (9,744 – 9,748) × \$25	– \$100	– \$ 100
Mon, Oct29 2012	1 × (9,755 – 9,744) × \$25	+ \$275	+ \$ 175
.....			
Wed, Jun19 2013	1 × (9,700 – ...) × \$25	....	– \$1,200

Locking in a Future LIBOR Rate

If the original reason we entered into the long contract at 97.48 was to lock in the rate of 2.52% on a $1 million 90-day deposit, and we deposit $1 million at 3.00% on June 19, as planned, then 3 months later we expect to receive interest on that deposit equal to:

$$1{,}000{,}000 \times 0.03 \times 90/360 = \$7{,}500$$

If we include our loss of $1,200 on the futures contract, our effective interest rate R earned can be implied from the analogous expression:

$$1{,}000{,}000 \times R \times 90/360 = \$6{,}300 = \$7{,}500 - \$1{,}200$$

which turns out to be exactly 2.52%:

$$(7{,}500 - 1{,}200)/1{,}000{,}000 \times (360/90) = (6{,}300)/1{,}000{,}000 \times (360/90) = 2.52\%$$

Suppose that instead of Eurodollar futures prices following the path in Table 3.8, LIBOR ended up at 2.00% on the last day of trading on June 19. The final settlement price would be $F = 100 - L = 100.00 - 2.00 = 98.00$. The mark-to-market calculations are shown in Table 3.10.

The net variation margin over October through June period is

$$1 \times (9{,}800 - 9{,}748) \times 25 = \$1{,}300$$

If, on June 19, we deposit $1,000,000 at 2.00%, our future interest on that deposit will be:

$$1{,}000{,}000 \times 0.02 \times 90/360 = \$5{,}000$$

Including our gain of $1,300 on the futures contract, our effective interest earned is again

$$(5{,}000 + 1{,}300)/1{,}000{,}000 \times (360/90) = (6{,}300)/1{,}000{,}000 \times (360/90) = 2.52\%$$

In fact, no matter what LIBOR is on June 19, our effective interest rate earned inclusive of the futures gain/loss is $6,300 or 2.52%. Locking in the rate of interest *to be earned* on any amount is easy with Eurodollar futures; to lock in the rate on $25 million, we buy 25 contracts. Similarly, locking in the rate *to be paid* on borrowing is easy, we only need to short the contracts.

Suppose on October 25, 2012, you want to lock in a rate on a $20 million future loan you hope to get on June 19, 2013, to be repaid on September 19, 2013. You can lock in the rate of 2.52% by shorting 20 Eurodollar contracts now and waiting to borrow spot on June 19.

Table 3.10 MTM for 1 Eurodollar contract, LIBOR ends at 2.00%

Date	Settle price	Daily calculation	MTM (VM)	Net var. margin
Fri, Oct26 2012	97.44	1 × (9,744 – 9,748) × $25	– $100	– $ 100
Mon, Oct29 2012	97.55	1 × (9,755 – 9,744) × $25	+ $275	+ $ 175
.....				
Wed, Jun19 2013	98.00	1 × (9,800 – ...) × $25	...	+ $1,300

If, on June 19, 3-month LIBOR is at 3.00% and the futures price is at 97.00, then you have a positive total cash flow from your futures contracts:

$$(-20) \times (9{,}700 - 9{,}748) \times 25 = \$24{,}000$$

You borrow \$20 million at 3.00% to incur interest cost on the loan of:

$$20{,}000{,}000 \times 0.03 \times (90/360) = \$150{,}000$$

Including your futures gain, your effective borrowing rate is:

$$(150{,}000 - 24{,}000)/20{,}000{,}000 \times (360/90) = (126{,}000)/1{,}000{,}000 \times (360/90) = 2.52\%$$

If instead of 3.00%, on June 19, LIBOR is at 2.00% and the futures price is at 98.00, then you have a negative total cash flow from your futures contracts:

$$(-20) \times (9{,}800 - 9{,}748) \times 25 = \$26{,}000$$

You borrow \$20 million at 2.00% to incur interest cost on the loan of:

$$20{,}000{,}000 \times 0.02 \times (90/360) = \$100{,}000$$

Including your futures gain, your effective borrowing rate is:

$$(100{,}000 + 26{,}000)/20{,}000{,}000 \times (360/90) = (126{,}000)/1{,}000{,}000 \times (360/90) = 2.52\%$$

You have now locked in a rate of 2.52% in October no matter where LIBOR ends up on June 19.

Let us provide another application of Eurodollar contracts, that of an extension of lending or borrowing at a guaranteed rate through a rollover or bundling strategy.

Bundling and Rollover Rate Lock

Suppose on October 25, 2012, you have excess funds of \$600 million that you want to deposit through December 19, 2013. A London bank quotes a rate of 2.31% *Act/360* through December 19, 2012. What rate of interest can you lock in on your balances over the entire 14-month period from October 2012 to December 2013 and how?

Since each successive Eurodollar contract guarantees a reinvestment rate over the 90-day period following the futures' expiry, the strategy to lock in the overall rate involves depositing the \$600 million balance for the next 2 months (until the first futures) and go long an increasing number of successive contracts to reflect the growing balance of principal and interest that needs to be rolled over. The calculation and strategy are shown in Table 3.11.

Table 3.11 Locking in rollover rates with Eurodollar bundles

Period	Days	Rate	Future value calculation	Strategy
Oct 2012–Dec 2012	55	2.31%	600,000,000 × (1+0.0231 × 55/360) = 602,117,500	Deposit \$600m
Dec 2012–Mar 2013	90	2.15%	602,117,500 × (1+0.0215 × 90/360) = 605,353,882	Long 602 Dec
Mar 2013–Jun 2013	90	2.15%	605,353,882 × (1+0.0215 × 90/360) = 608,607,659	Long 605 Mar
Jun 2013–Sep 2013	90	2.52%	608,607,659 × (1+0.0252 × 90/360) = 612,441,887	Long 609 Jun
Sep 2013–Dec 2013	90	2.91%	612,441,887 × (1+0.0215 × 90/360) = 616,897,402	Long 612 Sep

The only inaccuracy in this strategy is the rounding of the principal to the nearest million to arrive at the number of whole contracts to be bought. As successive contracts mature, we roll over the growing deposit for another 90 days using the collected/paid variation margin to offset interest cash flows. We have effectively locked in a simple rate of (16,897,402/600,000,000)(360/415) = 2.443% on an Act/360 basis for the entire period from October 25, 2012 through December 19, 2013. To lock in a borrowing rate we would have computed the same amounts but we would have shorted futures. Also, had we chosen to receive accrued interest in cash instead of reinvesting it, the number of futures contracts traded would have been a constant 600.

3.2.3 Stock Index Futures

There are two views of stock index futures. First, stock indexes are commodities. The quality is uniform, shares are perfectly substitutable, and are easily traded in bulk. Second, indexes are not real assets but simply mathematical averages; there is nothing to deliver on a futures contract. Speculating on an index level at a future date is identical to betting on the numerical outcome of a soccer match: a numerical outcome of a random event at a future date. The two views can be reconciled. Indexes are constructed so that their changes mimic one-for-one changes in the value of precisely defined diversified portfolios of stocks. Betting on the value of the index at some date in the future by buying and selling index futures can serve a useful purpose of hedging the purchase/sale price of a basket of stocks. Indexes may consist of tens or hundreds of different stocks, so to avoid actual physical delivery, index futures are settled in cash via the use of a simple multiplier.

All major stock indexes around the world have futures traded on them. The CME lists futures on all US stock averages, the Dow, S&P 500, Nasdaq, and several others, in large and mini versions (with smaller multipliers). The CME also trades Asian, emerging markets indexes, and futures on index-tracking ETFs. In Europe, NYSE Euronext's LIFFE trades futures on FTSE 100, CAC-40, and a few other continental indexes, while the Deutsche Börse's EUREX trades futures on the DAX, Swiss SMI, DJ Stoxx 50, and a few others.

All index futures specify the final settlement value of the contract equal to the index at the close of trading on the expiry date, and the multiplier that converts the point changes of the index into a cash settlement amount in a currency of denomination. The CAC-40 futures on LIFFE are defined as €10 times the index, the FTSE 100 contracts are £10 times the index, and the Mini Nasdaq 100 on the CME is $20 times the index. Some contracts are "quantoed" into an unnatural currency, such as the Nikkei 225 on the CME defined as $5 times the index (there is also a natural yen-denominated contract). While this is not really peculiar (US investors may want a pure play on the Nikkei), the multipliers of the most heavily traded contracts are always defined in the home currency of the index, reflecting the realities of stock trading and index-replicating portfolio construction (index component stocks are bought and sold in home currencies, free of artificial currency risk). The ability to replicate the index with baskets of stocks in the exact proportions of the index has important implications for the spot–futures price relationship through the cost-of-carry equation and cash-and-carry arbitrage.

The single most popular index future is the S&P 500 contract traded on the CME. The SPX's tick size is 0.10 index points and the multiplier is $250 per point or $25 per tick. It is traded open outcry on the floor of the exchange and electronically on the GLOBEX platform on the March–June–September–December cycle. Suppose on Thursday, June 24, 2010, the

Table 3.12 S&P 500 futures on Thursday, June 24, 2010

	Open	High	Low	Settle	Open interest
S&P500 (CME); $250 × index					
Sep 2010	...	...	...	**978.00**	...
Dec 2010	...	...	...	**976.10**	...
Mar 2011	...	...	...	**974.20**	...
S&P 500 index closed at 978.80; 3-month LIBOR at 1.107% *Act/360* = 1.13% cont.					

S&P 500 index closes at 978.80 (spot index) and the S&P500 futures settle at the levels shown in Table 3.12.

While the S&P 500 index is not a price of anything, but rather a capitalization-weighted average of the values of 500 US companies, it is easier to think of the index level of 978.80 as being the price of $978.80 for a basket of 500 stocks, where for each company we have some fraction of an actual share. Suppose on Thursday, June 24, 2010, we want to lock in the amount we would have to pay for 2,500 such baskets for delivery in March 2011. We buy 10 March futures contracts at 974.20. Table 3.13 shows the variation margin calculations assuming that the futures price drops to 965.50.

On March 18, 2011 we buy 2,500 baskets at $965.50 each paying $2,413,750 for all the stocks. Including the mark-to-market loss of $21,750 on the futures, the total is $2,435,500, or $974.20 per basket.

In addition to broad market indexes, Chicago exchanges trade futures on narrow indexes and ETFs. The electronic OneChicago exchange also offers futures contracts on 1,200 individual US stocks, each representing 100 shares of a stock.

3.2.4 Currency Futures and Forwards

Currency futures trade on several derivative exchanges in the USA, Europe, and Asia. The unique feature of currency trading is, however, that the market is dominated by OTC forwards, rather than standardized futures, and that a significant share of the volume of transactions (about 30% in contrast to less than 5% in other markets) is linked directly to the end-user demand from non-financial corporations managing their day-to-day FX exposure. Outright forwards represent only 7% of the total volume; forwards are packaged with spots or forwards for other dates to form short-term *currency swaps*, the main instruments traded.

Table 3.13 MTM calculation for 10 contracts bought at 974.20

Date	Settle price	Daily calculation	MTM (VM)	Net var. margin
Fri, Jun25 2010	978.60	10 × (978.60 – 974.40) × $250	+ $10,500	+ $10,500
Mon, Jun28 2010	953.70	10 × (953.70 – 978.60) × $250	– $62,250	– $51,750
.....				
Fri, Mar18 2011	965.50	10 × (965.50 – ...) × $250	...	– $21,750

Table 3.14 FX Forwards EUR/USD on August 7, 2003

Type	Expiry	Points	Bid	Ask	Time
Spot			**1.1374**	**1.1381**	19:31:00
ON	Aug08 2003	–0.36 / –0.33	1.1374	1.1381	15:49:00
TN	Aug11 2003	–1.06 / –1	1.1373	1.1380	18:42:00
SN	Aug12 2003	–0.34 / –0.31	1.1374	1.1381	04:43:00
SW	Aug18 2003	–2.3 / –2.21	1.1372	1.1379	19:31:00
2W	Aug25 2003	–4.63 / –4.48	1.1369	1.1377	19:03:00
1M	Sep11 2003	–12.5 / –7.5	**1.1361**	**1.1374**	13:41:00
2M	Oct14 2003	–23.2 / –18.2	1.1351	1.1363	15:08:00
3M	Nov12 2003	–32.3 / –27.3	**1.1342**	**1.1354**	18:19:00
4M	Dec11 2003	–41.4 / –36.4	1.1333	1.1345	19:31:00
5M	Jan12 2004	–50.5 / –45.5	1.1323	1.1336	19:12:00
6M	Feb11 2004	–58.9 / –53.9	**1.1315**	**1.1327**	19:29:00
9M	May11 2004	–82.27 / –77.27	1.1292	1.1304	19:32:00
1Y	Aug11 2004	–103.22 / –98.22	**1.1271**	**1.1283**	19:32:00
2Y	Aug11 2005	–151 / –136	1.1223	1.1245	19:30:00
3Y	Aug11 2006	–130 / –96	1.1244	1.1285	19:27:00
4Y	Aug11 2007	–53 / –7	1.1321	1.1374	19:00:00
5Y	Aug11 2008	53 / 111	1.1427	1.1492	19:12:00

FX Forwards

Spot and forward FX rates are quoted continuously in the interbank market and are reported on Bloomberg or Reuters. Normally, only forwards for standard maturities of 1, 3, 6, and 12 months are displayed, but forwards for customized expiry dates, as long as 10 years, can be easily arranged on most major currencies. Transaction sizes are large with \$10 million being a minimum lot. Table 3.14 shows quotes for the USD/EUR market found on a website of a major European bank on August 7, 2003. By convention, and despite the heading, the rate is quoted in dollars per euro.

Valid quotes go out 2 years (3-, 4-, and 5-year quotes were not updated that day) and all forwards are related to the spot quotes of USD/EUR 1.1374/81 (bid/ask) through *forward points*. These are decimals to be added to the significant digits of the spot rate. For USD/EUR, there are four significant digits after the decimal. For example, to arrive at the 9-month forward bid, we have to take the forward points of –82.27 (which are shorthand for –0.008227) and add that to the spot bid of 1.1374 to get 1.1292. Dealers shout only the forward points to each other over the phone. Just like spot, the USD/EUR forwards are quoted in American terms, with USD being the *pricing currency* of the commodity EUR. In this example, the EUR can be said to be trading at a *forward discount* as forward prices of EUR in dollars are lower than spot prices (all points are negative). Alternatively, the USD is trading at a *forward premium*. The forward premium/discount is defined as the difference between forward and spot in percentage of spot. For example, the 6-month forward discount for the euro using ask prices is equal to:

$$(1.1327 - 1.1381)/1.1381 = -0.4745\%$$

Note that the 6-month forward premium for the dollar (in euros) is not the same:

$$(1/1.1327 - 1/1.1381)/(1/1.1381) = +0.4767\%$$

Table 3.15 FX futures quotes for July 21, 2003

	Open	High	Low	Settle	Change	Lifetime high	Lifetime low	Open interest
Japanese yen (CME) – ¥12,500,000; $ per ¥100								
Sep	0.8437	0.8471	0.8432	**0.8448**	–0.0010	0.8815	0.8220	81,966
Dec	0.8478	0.8486	0.8465	**0.8471**	–0.0010	0.8915	0.8350	20,435
Est vol 8,659; vol Fri 19,005; open int 102,436, –4,422								
Euro/US dollar (CME) – €125,000; $ per €								
Sep	1.1239	1.1338	1.1226	1.1326	0.0057	1.1896	0.8780	92,581
Dec	1.1265	1.1310	1.1213	1.1299	0.0057	1.1860	0.9551	1,550
Mar 2004	1.1218	1.1270	1.1218	1.1275	0.0057	1.1795	1.0425	253
Est vol 33,046; vol Fri 41,304; open int 94,456, –2,557								

What is special for currencies is that assets underlying the forward contracts are also currencies. Quotes (but not points and the premiums/discounts) can be inverted easily to suit the viewpoint of the customer. This dual nature of FX rates also has implications for the cost-of-carry link between spot and forward FX.

FX Futures

Standardized currency futures trade on major exchanges. The CME lists G10 currencies against the dollar, several natural G10 crosses such as AUD/NZD or EUR/GBP, and several emerging market currencies against the dollar or natural crosses such as HUF/EUR. The LIFFE trades USD/EUR futures in limited volume. Except for the crosses, the CME contracts are defined in foreign currencies per dollar, irrespective of the spot quoting convention. Contract sizes are large by retail standards (e.g. €125,000), including the few half-size "mini" versions (€62,500), but are relatively small by wholesale market standards. Table 3.15 shows the settlement values of CME futures for the previous business day reported in a financial newspaper on July 22, 2003.

The mechanics of daily settlement for currency futures are identical to those for commodities with the priced currency in the denominator treated as the underlying commodity. Suppose on July 21 we entered into five long December USD/JPY contracts right at the close at 0.8471. Note that for JPY, the 0.8471 price is in dollars per 100 yen, or it is shorthand for 0.008471 in USD/JPY, which is equivalent to JPY/USD 118.05 (1/0.008471). Suppose by the next day the JPY/USD settlement rate changes to 119.25, or equivalently to USD/JPY 0.008386 or USD/100JPY 0.8386. We have a negative cash flow in the form of a variation margin settlement of:

$$5 \times 12{,}500{,}000\,(0.8386 - 0.8471)/100 = \$ - 5{,}328.48$$

The multiplier for the price as stated in the contract is thus 125,000 per yen. Note that for the USD/EUR contract, the multiplier is simply equal to the size of the contract, which is 125,000 as the price is stated in dollars per 1 euro. Since the USD/EUR rate is quoted to 4 decimal places, the multiplier can also be stated as $12.5 per pip, with 1 pip equal to €0.0001. It can be shown in a manner analogous to the commodity arguments that going long five December JPY contracts allows us to lock in an exchange rate of 118.05 on JPY 62,500,000 for the delivery on December 19, 2003. The net variation margin accumulated by that expiry date will offset any difference between the spot FX rate on that date and the original rate of 118.05 on the purchase of JPY 62,500,000.

3.3 CASH-AND-CARRY ARBITRAGE

The *cost-of-carry equation* and the *cash-and-carry arbitrage* that justifies it and are the most important links that bind the spot price of a commodity to all its forwards and futures prices. The essence of the cost-of-carry equation lies in the fact that futures and forwards are redundant derivative contracts that can be completely replicated with a spot transaction combined with financing and carrying actions. The purchase of 20,000 bushels of corn for delivery in 3 months can be replicated with borrowing money for 3 months, buying corn now, and paying for the storage of corn for 3 months. The purchase of 500 component stocks in the S&P 500 index for delivery in 6 months can be replicated with borrowing money for 6 months, buying the stocks in the right proportions now, and receiving the expected dividends on the stocks over the next 3 months, which defrays the cost of buying them now. The purchase of euros with dollars for delivery in 1 month can be replicated with borrowing dollars for 1 month, buying euros with the borrowed dollars now, and earning interest on the purchased euros over the next month. In a month, dollars are repaid with interest and euros are received with interest, but the exact amounts, and therefore the exchange ratio, are known or are locked in now, in advance. All the replicating strategies involve borrowing or lending money (financing), buying or selling a commodity now (spot), and paying for storage and/or receiving cash flows (dividends, coupon interest) from the commodity (carry). Therefore, the relationship between spot S and futures/forwards F can be written approximately as:

$$F = S + \textit{Financing} \pm \textit{Carry}$$

Or, if we define financing (paid carry) and received carry as percentages of spot, then we can write it as:

$$F = S \times (1 + \textit{Paid carry})/(1 + \textit{Received carry})$$

This equation naturally has to be corrected for the right fraction of the year or the number of years over which the commodity is carried. The (1 + rate) terms need to be modified to terms like (1 + rate × day-count) or (1 + rate) raised to the power of the number of years. We will see this equation in various guises as we discuss each commodity.

It is important to realize that the cost-of-carry equation is not as absolute as a physics equation. Distance is always equal to velocity multiplied by time; force is always equal to mass multiplied by acceleration – at least in our universe. The cost-of-carry equation holds only if there are market participants operating in unrestricted markets that force it to hold. Another way to state this is to ask: What if the cost-of-carry equation did not hold? What if the forward price of corn for delivery in 3 months was much greater than posited by the equation? We will argue that free agents motivated by profit seeking could borrow money to buy and store 20,000 bushels of corn and *at the same time* could sell four futures contracts (each for 5,000 bushels) to guarantee the future sale price on the stored corn, thus locking in a riskless profit equal to the present value of the difference between the actual (too high) futures price and the (lower) theoretical *fair value* futures price from the cost-of-carry equation. The actions of profit-seeking arbitrageurs would push the forward price down (excess supply) and spot price up (excess demand), and/or even push borrowing and lending rates, eliminating the riskless profit opportunity they were chasing. The theoretical *fair value* price is the break-even price at which no riskless profit can be generated from synthetic replication of the forward contract through cash-and-carry and simultaneous opposite transaction in the actual forward/futures. Since executing transactions takes time – although in today's electronic world, not much time – at any given moment futures and forwards may deviate from their fair values. But the existence of many speculators in the markets ensures that these deviations are speedily eliminated.

Not all commodities can be subject to cash-and-carry. Financial commodities are the easiest to arbitrage. It is easy to effect spot currency transactions and borrow and lend money in the Eurocurrency markets. Bonds (and stocks) can be easily bought or borrowed in repo markets and short-sold. But even our corn example has a flaw. It is easy to borrow money to buy corn, but what if the forward price of corn in the market fell below the fair value? The *reverse cash-and-carry* arbitrage would call for buying corn forward at the low forward price and short-selling corn now by borrowing corn and selling it spot. While borrowing stocks held in street name and shorting them is easy, short-selling corn is impossible as the market for borrowing corn is non-existent. In that case, the cost-of-carry equation has to be replaced by an inequality

$$F \leq S + \mathit{Financing} \pm \mathit{Carry}$$

Any deviation of the forward price on the up side will be arbitraged out, but deviations on the down side may not be. In this situation, we cannot argue that greed will *instantly* push prices to equality. We can only argue that, *over time*, agents, realizing that corn for future delivery is relatively cheaper while corn for immediate delivery is relatively dearer, will demand less spot and more forward corn. But this adjustment mechanism will be much slower, and may involve the actual producers/users of corn. Users of corn who have already held corn, may be inclined to reduce their holdings while increasing their long positions in forward corn. Or the adjustment mechanism may extend into riskier speculation in spot corn, something altogether different from riskless arbitrage, where users and speculators reduce their spot holdings of corn with an intent to re-acquire it later.

Commodities in general run a gamut from those subject to strict cash-and-carry (e.g. financials and gold) through approximate cash carry (e.g. corn and substitutable agriculturals) all the way to strategic non-substitutables, such as oil.

3.3.1 Commodities

Let us first consider an example of gold cash-and-carry with actual gold bullion. Suppose on December 18, 2009 we face the gold prices, financing, and carry costs in Table 3.16.

We can buy gold spot in 100-ounce bars for \$810.00 per ounce. Storing it for 3 months costs \$15 per bar, or \$0.15 per troy ounce. If we were to borrow gold to short it we would pay a borrow fee of 1.0% per annum. We can borrow or lend dollars at 1.5% per annum.

Table 3.16 Gold data on December 18, 2009

Spot gold per troy oz	\$810.00
3-month LIBOR	1.5% p.a.
Storage cost per 100 troy oz per quarter	\$15.00
Borrow fee	1.0% p.a.

Table 3.17 March 2010 gold (NYMEX) at 821.50

Fair value per oz = (S + storage) × (1 + LIBOR/4)	$F^* = (810.00 + 0.15) \times (1 + 0.015/4) = 813.19$
March futures	$F = 821.50$
Strategy:	**Cash flow:**
Borrow PV of 100 × 821.50 = 82,150/(1 + 0.015/4)	+ $81,843.09
Buy 100 oz gold spot	– $81,000.00
Pay storage	– $15.00
Sell one March contract	
Net cash at spot	**$828.09**

The fair value equation needs to reflect the cash-and-carry arbitrage we will engage. This will be somewhat different, dependent on whether the forward price of gold is higher or lower than the fair value. Table 3.17 shows the situation when the gold futures trade *above* the cost-of-carry value, computed assuming we are borrowing money to buy gold spot (cash-and-carry).

We borrow $81,843.09 today for 3 months. Of that, we spend $81,015 to buy and store 100 troy oz of gold for 3 months. We also short one gold contract at 821.50 (no cost to enter). Today, we have a net cash inflow of $828.09, which is our riskless profit. The short futures position ensures that irrespective of the price of gold by March, with the variation margin settlement (gain or loss) we will have on hand $82,150 from the sale of gold. The $82,150 will pay off the principal and interest on our 3-month borrowing of dollars, leaving us with no exposure on March 19, 2010.

Table 3.18 shows the situation when the gold futures trade *below* the cost-of-carry value computed, assuming shorting gold spot and lending money to buy gold forward (reverse cash-and-carry). Shorting gold is subject to a gold borrow fee of 1% p.a. paid in arrears.

We borrow 100 oz of gold and sell it. We collect $81,000 for it. Of that sum, we lend $80,371.11 for 3 months at 1.5%. The difference ($628.89) is our riskless arbitrage profit. We also go long one March gold contract. When the $80,371.11 deposit matures on March 19, 2010, we collect the principal and interest of $80,672.50. Of that sum, we use $202.50

Table 3.18 March 2010 gold (NYMEX) at 804.70

Fair value per oz = S × (1+LIBOR/4)/(1 + borrow/4)	$F^* = 810 \times (1 + 0.015/4)/(1 + 0.01/4) = 811.01$
March futures	$F = 804.70$
Strategy:	**Cash flow at spot:**
Borrow and short 100 oz gold spot	+ $81,000.00
Lend PV(80,470 + fee 202.50)	– $80,371.11
= (80,470 + 81,000 × 0.01/4)/(1 + 0.015/4)	
Buy one March contract	
Net cash at spot	**$628.89**
On March 19, 2010:	**Cash flow at futures expiry:**
Collect principal + interest on lending	+ $80,672.50
Pay gold borrow fee	– $202.50
Take delivery of gold (incl. var. margin)	– $80,470.00
Return gold to lender	
Net cash at futures expiry	**$0.00**

(= \$81,000 × 1%/4) to pay the fee for borrowing gold, and the remaining \$80,470, together with any variation margin settlement, to buy back 100 oz of gold to return it to the original lender. The net cash flow is zero on March 19, 2010.

3.3.2 Stock Indexes

There are several factors to consider in the fair value equation for stocks and stock indexes. Stock purchases need to be financed either *explicitly* by borrowing money in a margin account, or *implicitly* by forgoing interest that could have been earned. Holding stocks may earn a positive carry if they pay dividends. Shorting stocks may be subject to negative carry by forcing dividend reimbursement and by requiring a fee for borrowing the stocks. To keep things clear let us first consider an unrealistic case where we assume that none of the stocks in an index pays any dividends over the contract period. We then include dividends in the cost-of-carry. Lastly we consider the full case of the associated cash-and-carry arbitrage for stock index futures, often referred to as *index arbitrage*, using the data in Table 3.12.

Fair Value with No Dividends

If stocks do not pay dividends, then the only thing to consider in the cost-of-carry equation is the cost of financing the stock purchase, at least theoretically. Finance textbooks therefore show the following fair value equation:

$$F = Se^{rt}$$

where t is the time to maturity in years, e.g. $t = \frac{1}{2}$ for 6 months, and r is the continuously compounded interest rate. The expression e^{rt} is the future value factor equivalent to $(1 + r)^n$ or $(1 + r \times \text{day-count})$ in discrete time. In practice, the financing rate is likely to be LIBOR, and the fair value definition translates into the following intra-year equation:

$$F = S(1 + L \times {}^{\text{Act}}\!/\!_{360})$$

The right-hand side has two components: S the spot price, and $S \times L \times {}^{\text{Act}}\!/\!_{360}$, the interest cost on borrowing the dollar amount S until expiry. The theoretical equations need to be augmented by one practical feature of stock trading. While L is the only financing cost when borrowing money to buy stocks, it is not so when shorting stocks. In order to short stocks, they need to be borrowed first, and the borrower will pay the lender a fee. Rather than in dollar terms, that fee can be conveniently expressed as an annualized cost in basis points, similar to an interest rate (but negative). If b is the stock borrow fee on an Act/360 basis, then the corrected fair value equation is:

$$F = S \times (1 + L \times {}^{\text{Act}}\!/\!_{360})/(1 + b \times {}^{\text{Act}}\!/\!_{360})$$

The textbook continuous version of the cost-of-carry is simply

$$F = Se^{(r-b)t}$$

Note that two other practical factors can be safely omitted from the equation. First, the stock borrow fee is a real cost even if the arbitrageur uses his own to stock to sell; he gives up the revenue that could be earned by lending the stock. Second, even though stocks are shorted in margin accounts subject to initial and maintenance requirements, and the cash balances cannot be used immediately, they do earn interest and so no lending interest is lost.

Fair Value with Dividends

The fair value equation for stock index futures must be further amended to reflect the fact that some of the stocks in the index may pay dividends during the contract period. In the synthetic replication of long futures with borrowing and spot purchase, the financing cost of the spot purchase is defrayed by the amount of dividends received between the spot purchase and the futures expiry. In the synthetic replication of short futures with spot stock shorting and lending the balances, the interest earned is reduced by the amount of dividends that need to be reimbursed between the spot and the futures expiry.

There are two ways of including dividends into the fair value equation depending on how we make future dividend estimates. For shorter expiries, we can typically predict very accurately the dollar amounts and the dates of the dividends. We can present-value them up to today, subtract them from the spot price, and future-value the net amount in the cost-of-carry equation. Denoting as *D the present value* of the intervening dividends, we can write the continuous fair value equation as:

$$F = (S - D)e^{(r-b)t}$$

and the discrete one as:

$$F = (S - D) \times (1 + L \times {}^{\mathrm{Act}}\!/\!_{360})/(1 + b \times {}^{\mathrm{Act}}\!/\!_{360})$$

For longer expiries, we may feel more confident assuming that the dividend rate will be a constant, or at least a predictable, *percentage* of the stock price. So we can include dividends through a continuously compounded annualized dividend yield d and subtract it from the interest charge:

$$F = Se^{(r-d-b)t}$$

or we can express it in a similar way to the interest rate and the stock borrow fee as a discrete annualized dividend yield d and correct the discrete fair value equation with one more term in the denominator:

$$F = S \times (1 + L \times {}^{\mathrm{Act}}\!/\!_{360})/(1 + b \times {}^{\mathrm{Act}}\!/\!_{360})(1 + d \times {}^{\mathrm{Act}}\!/\!_{360})$$

There is no inconsistency between this very general expression and its previous version with the subtraction of the PV of dividends. It is simply a matter of preference of how we want to correct the amount of financing for the dividends earned or paid.

Stock Index Arbitrage

The cash-and-carry arbitrage that underlies the fair value equations is carried out through index program trading (simultaneous and instantaneous trading of all stocks in the index). Consider the data for the S&P 500 futures and LIBOR in Table 3.12 for June 24, 2010. Recall that the spot index stood at 978.80 on that day. Assume a continuous stock borrow fee of 25 bp and a dividend yield of 1.0% p.a.

Table 3.19 shows the fair value calculation (using the continuous equation) and the arbitrage for the 3-month contract period from spot on June 24 to futures expiry on September 24, 2010.

Table 3.19 Index arbitrage with September 2010 at 978.00

Fair value per contract $= F = S\, e^{(r\text{-}d\text{-}b)\, t}$	$F^* = 978.80\, e^{(0.0113-0.0025-0.01)/4} = 978.51$
September 2010 futures	$F = 978.00$
Strategy:	**Cash flow at spot:**
Borrow and short 250 S&P 500 baskets spot	+ \$244,700.00
Lend PV of 250 × 978.00 = 250 × 978.00 × $e^{-0.0113/4}$	– \$243,810.26
Pay dividends+fee 250 × 978.80 × $(1-e^{-(0.01+0.0025)/4})$	– \$763.49
Long one September 10 contract	
Net cash at spot	**\$126.25**
On September 24, 2010:	**Cash flow at futures expiry:**
Collect principal + interest on lending = 250 × 978.00	+ \$244,500
Pay for stocks (incl. var. margin) = 250 × 978.00	– \$244,500
Return stocks to lender	
Net cash at futures expiry	**\$0.00**

We assume exactly ¼ year for interest rate, borrow fee and dividend yield in the continuous equation. All resulting amounts would be identical if we were to use the discrete equation with inputs converted to 1.1070%, 0.2446%, and 0.9795%, respectively, on an Act/360 basis with 92 days. The conversion from continuous c to discrete d is $e^{c/4} = 1 + d \times 92/360$. Also note that the dividend yield of 1.0% continuous or 0.9795% discrete is equivalent to the present value of dividends, equal to \$2.44 for a stock basket costing \$978.80. The conversion from continuous yield to discrete dividend PV is $978.80 \times (1 - e^{-0.01/4})$.

If the September 2010 futures were trading above fair value, e.g. at 980, the strategy would have been the exact opposite. We would have borrowed dollars (equal to the present value of the futures) to buy stocks spot and we would have shorted futures. The difference between the borrowed dollars plus the present value of the expected dividends (and the borrow fee to be earned), net of the amount needed to purchase stocks, would have been our riskless profit.

Fair Value Equation as Arbitrage Cash Flow Equation

By rearranging the terms in the cost-of-carry equation, the equation becomes the mirror image in exact dollar amounts of the arbitrage strategy described in Table 3.19. All we need to do is to present-value the *actual* futures price rather than future-value the spot. The continuous version becomes

$$Fe^{-rt} \neq Se^{-(d+b)t}$$

and the discrete version becomes

$$F/(1 + L \times {}^{\text{Act}}\!/_{360}) \neq S/(1 + b \times {}^{\text{Act}}\!/_{360})(1 + d \times {}^{\text{Act}}\!/_{360})$$

The difference between the two sides is the profit. In the reverse cash-and-carry strategy of Table 3.19, we shorted stocks equal in value to the right-hand side, net of dividends and borrow fee (we would have to pay), and we lent out the amount equal to the (smaller) left-hand side to be able to buy the stocks back at a prearranged price. As the right-hand side was greater (receipts from shorting) in value than the left-hand side (lending), we still had some money. In a situation when the left-hand side is greater, we borrow that amount to pay for right-hand (smaller) spot purchases of stocks, net of dividends and fee to be earned.

3.3.3 Currencies

The cash-and-carry argument for currencies is similar to that for stock indexes with the dividend yield replaced by a LIBOR interest rate. Just like index futures, currency forwards are redundant contracts; they can be perfectly synthesized using a spot currency purchase/sale and two interest rate transactions, borrowing in one currency and lending in the other. With index futures, we borrow dollars (pay interest) to buy stocks, and stocks may earn a dividend while we wait. With FX forwards, we borrow dollars (pay interest) to buy euros, and we invest euros to earn interest while we wait. We match the maturity dates for borrowing and lending exactly (e.g. 3 months). On the day of maturity, we have an outflow of dollars (to pay off the borrowing) and an inflow of euros (from the investment). Today, we know what those flows are going to be. A strategy that results in a net zero cash flow today, and a known outflow in one currency and a known inflow in another currency on a future day (in 3 months), is a synthetic physical-settle (3-month) currency forward. Extending the argument, since physical and cash settle forwards are economically equivalent, and forwards and futures are almost economically equivalent (enhanced by credit mitigation and marking-to-market), the synthetic strategy essentially replicates futures and forwards and has the same value at the outset and throughout the life of the contract. This equivalence has been termed in economics as the Covered Interest Rate Parity (CIRP) and is simply another guise of the cost-of-carry equation.

Economists often talk about another parity, called (Uncovered) Interest Rate Parity, where the forward is replaced by the expected future spot FX rate. While the CIRP is a strict no-arbitrage relationship ensured by cash-and-carry arbitrageurs, the "uncovered" parity is only a macroeconomic theory.

Covered Interest Rate Parity

The CIRP principle states that a currency forward for any expiry must be at a level at which no riskless profit can be earned through cash-and-carry or reverse cash-and-carry arbitrage. For dollars (USD) and euros (EUR), that translates into the following continuous rate equation:

$$F^{\frac{USD}{EUR}} = S^{\frac{USD}{EUR}} \; e^{(r^{USD} - r^{EUR})t}$$

The FX rates, forward F and spot S, are in dollars per euro, and the exponent contains the continuous equivalents of LIBOR interest rates, with the euro LIBOR subtracted from the dollar LIBOR. Comparing this to the stock index fair value equation, we simply replace the dividend yield with an interest rate and delete the stock borrow fee, reflecting the fact that just as owned stocks earn dividends, idle cash balances of a purchased currency can be deposited to earn interest. In the discrete version of the CIRP, the interest rate terms reflect discrete present-valuing:

$$F^{\frac{USD}{EUR}} = S^{\frac{USD}{EUR}} \; \frac{\left(1 + r^{USD}\right)^t}{\left(1 + r^{EUR}\right)^t}$$

Both the numerator and denominator have to be further amended to reflect the exact way in which interest is compounded and days are counted.

Table 3.20 shows an arbitrage strategy to force the CIRP to hold. We observe the spot FX rate for JPY/EUR of 100; 1-year deposit rates are 2% in yen and 4% in euros. A dealer quotes a 1-year forward rate of JPY/EUR 98 good for up to EUR 10,000,000. According to the CIRP, a 1-year forward rate of 98.077 would be arbitrage free. Since the actual forward is lower at

Table 3.20 CIRP arbitrage: a 1-year forward example

Data: JPY/EUR Spot = 100, 1-Year Forward = 98; Rates JPY 2%, EUR 4%.	
FairValue = $S \times (1 + r^{JPY})/(1 + r^{EUR})$	$F^* = 100 \times (1 + 0.02)/(1 + 0.04) = 98.077$
1-year forward	$F = 98.00$
On spot date:	**Cash flows:**
Borrow PV of €10m = €10m/(1+0.04) at 4%	+ € 9,615,384.62
Spot FX at 100: Sell euros	− € 9,607,843.14
Buy yen	+ ¥ 960,784,313.73
Lend PV of ¥980m = ¥980m/(1 + 0.02) at 2%	− ¥ 960,784,313.73
Buy €10m at ¥/€ 98 1-year forward	
Net cash at spot	€ 7,541.48 ¥ 0.00
On forward date:	**Cash flows:**
Collect maturing ¥ deposit	+ ¥ 980,000,000.00
Complete forward FX: Sell yen	− ¥ 980,000,000.00
Buy euros	+ €10,000,000.00
Pay off borrowing	− €10,000,000.00
Net cash at forward date	€ 0.00 ¥ 0.00

98.00, the profit strategy will involve buying euros/selling yen forward. The forward-bought euros will repay a borrowing of euros, and yen deposited today will be used to acquire euros 1 year from today. We match future cash flows in yen and euros, leaving an extra spot inflow in euros as our riskless profit.

The computations of the amounts start with the forward flows that are then present-valued to establish the amount of borrowing in euros and lending in yen. The spot amount to be exchanged is computed last, based on the amount of yen we need to deposit (assuming we want our riskless profit in euros). Irrespective of the location of the arbitrageur or the desired currency of profit, the direction of the transactions would be the same. The spot and forward FX rates, and perhaps the borrowing and lending rates, would come under pressure to adjust (spot down and forward up) to such levels that the CIRP would hold, and riskless profiting would not be possible.

Note that in our example, we borrowed in a high interest rate currency and lent in a low interest rate currency. It is the relative levels of all four variables in the fair value equation that matter, not simply the interest rate differential. Another way of stating that is by rearranging the CIRP equation in terms of the forward premium/discount relative to the present value of the interest rate differential:

$$\frac{F_{\frac{JPY}{EUR}} - S_{\frac{JPY}{EUR}}}{S_{\frac{JPY}{EUR}}} = \frac{r^{JPY} - r^{EUR}}{1 + r^{EUR}}$$

According to this form of the CIRP equation, one cannot profit by borrowing in one currency and lending in another, because the loss (gain) on the forward cover will be exactly offset by the present value of the interest gain (loss).

Covered Interest Rate Parity with LIBOR Rates

The cash-and-carry arbitrage with currencies is conducted using the deposit markets of Eurocurrencies. For intra-year periods, the CIRP needs to be amended to reflect the day count for LIBOR rates. Since both dollars and euros use the *Act/360* day-count, the equation looks like this:

$$F_{\frac{USD}{EUR}} = S_{\frac{USD}{EUR}} \frac{1 + L^{USD} \times \frac{\text{Act}}{360}}{1 + L^{EUR} \frac{\text{Act}}{360}}$$

Let us apply this equation to the FX rates for August 7, 2003 in Table 3.14. The spot ask FX rate is USD/EUR 1.1374 bid and USD/EUR 1.1381 ask. The 3-month LIBOR rates on that day were 1.14% for USD and 2.1613% for EUR. Using 97 as the actual number of days between August 7 and November 12 – the stated expiry of the 3-month FX forward – we obtain the fair forward bid rate:

$$F_{\frac{USD}{EUR}} = 1.1374 \frac{1 + 0.011400 \times \frac{97}{360}}{1 + 0.021613 \times \frac{97}{360}} = 1.1343$$

and the fair ask rate:

$$F_{\frac{USD}{EUR}} = 1.1381 \frac{1 + 0.011400 \times \frac{97}{360}}{1 + 0.021613 \times \frac{97}{360}} = 1.1350$$

The actual forward bid/ask quotes of USD/EUR 1.1342/1.1354 contain a wider spread, reflecting a potential mark-up charged by the quoting dealer for unsolicited orders. Such quotes also ensure that, on August 7, 2003, one could not have picked the quoting dealer off to earn riskless profit.

3.4 FUTURES NOT SUBJECT TO CASH-AND-CARRY

Assets like stocks, fixed income instruments, and currencies are examples of *pure financial assets*. As they are claims on real assets and are held purely for investment purposes, investors are indifferent to holding these assets or claims on them. For example, stock investors are rarely interested in seeing stock certificates; what matters to them is that they receive dividends and are able to sell their holdings on demand. Bond investors want coupon and principal cash flow. Currencies are held for their purchasing power and can be substituted for by checks, debit, or credit cards. Because investors do not hold pure financial assets for their physical qualities but for their qualities as claims on income, they are held long as a store of wealth and easily substitutable by many investors. They are not subject to restrictions on short sales, and both cash-and-carry and reverse cash-and-carry strategies are executable and almost at the same cost. This is most obvious with currencies where a purchase of one currency automatically means a sale of another. For pure financial assets, the general form of the fair value equation includes the cost of financing (paid carry) net of any received carry, such as (coupon) interest or dividends.

Most agricultural, energy, and metal commodities are *convenience assets*. Holders of these commodities own them not only for investment purposes, but to be used in production, and any disruption to that production may be costly. Having a forward contract fixing the purchase price is not the same as holding the physical asset. This additional implicit value – which varies from user to user and is derived from owning the physical asset – is called a *convenience yield*. It can be most easily treated as a form of dividend, as the owner of the asset has a valuable insurance policy that his business will not be disrupted. When giving up the asset (selling or lending), the owner has to be compensated for the loss of the convenience. The reverse cash-and-carry strategy may not be executable at all or may lead to very high costs. Financial assets, such as stocks and bonds, may exhibit this convenience value, but a stock borrow fee or a *special repo* rate put a competitive market-determined dollar value on it. Gold can be argued to have some convenience aspects due to its industrial uses, but it trades mostly as a financial asset (store of wealth). It can be either directly or indirectly (through ETFs) shorted, and gold bullion is largely fungible. Some metals (such as palladium) and agriculturals (such as orange juice concentrate and soybean meal) are definitely convenience assets, and the value of the convenience has to be taken explicitly into account in the cost-of-carry equation. Using continuous notation, this can be imagined as an additional term in the exponent, similar to the dividend yield:

$$F = Se^{(r+s-cy)t}$$

where r is the interest rate, s is the storage cost as extra interest charge, and cy is the convenience yield. Again, note that the stock borrow fee is a monetized value of the convenience. For metal or agricultural commodities, the convenience value is less obvious, but not less real. In fact, we can turn the argument around to state that, by observing the futures contracts relative to the spot price, we can impute the market-determined value of the convenience (by the marginal investor) as the wedge in the cost-of-carry equation. The convenience yield can be large (positive) resulting in a decreasing pattern of futures prices on subsequent contracts, and smaller than the spot price, called *backwardation*.

There are many economic explanations for the pattern of commodity futures prices. The earliest one goes back to Keynes. In Keynes' view, most hedgers are producers of commodities (farmer selling wheat) who tend to short futures at a discount to expected future spot value (anxious to lock in price) in order to compensate speculators for accepting the risk (the difference between the expected future spot and the futures price is the reward). This results in *normal backwardation*. Note that the statement of value is relative to the expected future spot price not the fair value from the cost-of-carry equation. Figure 3.1(a) illustrates the situation. The hedgers' demand for futures is inelastic (steep) and the hedgers want to short futures. Speculators display elastic (flat) demand; they can go long or short as long as they expect

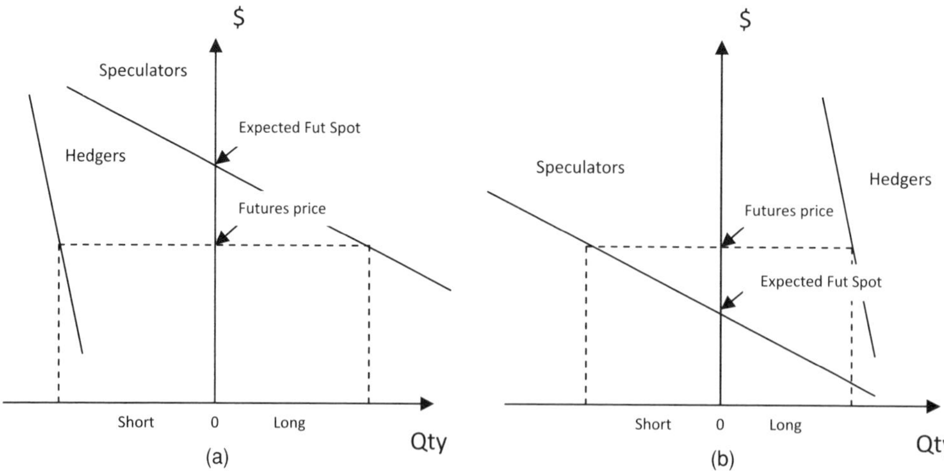

Figure 3.1 Futures not subject to cash and carry: (a) Normal backwardation (b) Contango

to make a profit on the futures price moving to the expected spot. The futures price obtains where the hedgers' demand for, and the speculators' supply of, futures are equal in absolute value.

The opposite of normal backwardation is a *contango*. Here, most hedgers are the buyers of commodities (Starbucks buying coffee) who go long futures at a premium to expected future spot value (anxious to lock in price) in order to compensate speculators for accepting the risk (the difference between the futures price and the expected future spot is the reward). This results in futures trading higher than expected spot, as shown in Figure 3.1(b). The hedgers' demand for futures is again inelastic (steep), but the hedgers now want to buy futures. The speculators' supply is elastic (flat). The futures price settles above the expected spot where the demand and supply are equal in absolute value; the speculators end up net short.

In real life, there is no way of knowing for sure whose demand (for future delivery) is stronger at any given moment of time: that of the sellers (producers) or the buyers (users). There is also no way to impute the expected future spot. The only observations we can make is futures prices relative to spot prices. Since, for most physical commodities, financing and storing are positive costs: if the convenience yield is negligible or zero, futures prices should rise with expiry. However, we also argued before that – as is the case for many physical commodities – if financing to buy spot (cash-and-carry) is easy, but shorting the commodity spot and lending money balances (reverse cash-and-carry) is not, then the cost-of-carry fair value becomes a ceiling on a futures price, i.e. we have an inequality:

$$F \leq S + Financing \pm Carry$$

We should bear these factors in mind when trying to interpret the pattern of futures prices as the normal backwardation or contango. When futures prices rise rapidly with expiry well beyond the cost-of-carry, we can construe that as a contango (and/or negative convenience yield). When they are flat or declining, we could be in the normal backwardation excess supply of futures by producers and/or we could be experiencing a large positive convenience yield of owning the asset spot. For example, after the commodity market crash in February 2009, news headlines reported large releases of oil supplies from tankers on the open sea (suggesting the unwinding of "open" cash-and-carry strategies), and the pattern of prices was increasing in expiry as in Table 3.21.

The drastic jump in price from March to April cannot be explained by financing plus storage costs and could be interpreted as a contango due to the unloading of excess supplies. Usual explanations for contangos include resolutions of wars, expectations of new supply lines, or negative convenience yields, like holding wheat just before a plentiful harvest.

Table 3.21 A sample of WTI Oil futures on February 9, 2009*

Month/year	Low	High	Last settle	Change	Open int.	Volume	Time
Mar 2009	39.58	42.43	**40.17**	+1.68	363,757	106,662	11:05am
Apr 2009	45.34	47.99	**46.15**	+1.32	134,150	51,865	11:05am
May 2009	48.15	50.47	**48.85**	+1.17	74,596	18,374	11:05am
Jun 2009	49.75	51.92	**50.39**	+1.08	120,708	13,583	11:05am

*Collected by hand from nymex.com for illustrative purposes only, accuracy not guaranteed; each contract 1,000 barrels.

Table 3.22 A sample of coffee futures on July 23, 2003*

Month/year	Low	High	Settle	Change	Open int.
Jul 2003	59.15	60.00	**59.15**	–3.15	201
Sep 2003	59.70	63.00	**60.25**	–2.95	44,656
Dec 2003	62.00	65.40	**62.85**	–2.75	13,222
Dec 2004	72.55	73.50	**72.55**	–2.25	1,490

*Collected by hand from the WSJ for illustrative purposes only, accuracy not guaranteed; each contract 37,500 lb, price in cents per lb.

On July 22, 2003, the news of the day was a substantial drop in coffee prices as expectations of frost affecting the August crop in Brazil faded. Coffee prices dropped substantially on that day, with spot prices dropping the most, resulting in a contango for the coffee prices in Table 3.22.

Assuming LIBOR of 1.13% (continuously compounded) and zero storage costs, the September–July price difference reflected the convenience yield of –9.92%. Also on July 22, 2003, NYMEX crude oil futures were reported at the prices shown in Table 3.23. The last two columns show the fair values and the convenience yields, calculated under the assumptions of LIBOR at 1.13% and storage costs of $2 per barrel per year, or 6.1% (continuously. compounded) per year given the spot price of 31.98.

The results show substantial convenience yields for the near months, much greater than the financing and storage costs. Thus, little of the futures–spot price differential is explained by the cost-of-carry argument, rendering the spot–futures and futures–futures cash-and-carry arbitrage highly speculative.

3.5 YIELD CURVE CONSTRUCTION WITH INTEREST RATE FUTURES

Eurodollar (-euro, -sterling) futures play a fundamental role in yield curve construction. Since each contract locks in the financing rate for the 3 months following the contract expiry, and as the expiries of the contracts are laid out every 3 months, the financing rate information contained in each contract can be used to calculate how much $1 would earn up to almost any date in the future using a reinvestment argument. Conversely, the present value of $1 to be received on any future date can be computed using the spot LIBOR rate and all intervening Eurodollar futures. Once the yield curve is constructed and discount factors for any future dates

Table 3.23 A sample of WTI Oil futures, fair values, and convenience yields on July 23, 2003*

Month/year	Low	High	Settle	Change	Open int.	Fair value	Conv. yield
Aug 2003	31.25	32.10	**31.78**	–0.18	45,102	31.85	
Sep 2003	30.33	31.17	**30.83**	–0.20	190,648	31.72	17.00
Oct 2003	29.95	30.64	**30.40**	–0.09	55,331	31.59	15.30
Nov 2003	29.50	30.05	**29.93**	–0.01	1,490	31.45	14.90

*Data collected by hand from the WSJ for illustrative purposes only, accuracy not guaranteed. LIBOR at 1.13% for fair value calculation.

are calculated, the value of any option-free fixed income security can be computed simply by discounting its cash flows up to today.

3.5.1 Certainty Equivalence of Eurodollar Futures

It is important to realize one fundamental feature of Eurodollar futures: they cost nothing to enter into (buy or sell). Any agent with funds available for lending/borrowing over the future period covered by the contract period has a choice: to lock in the financing rate implied by the futures price (for free) or not to lock it (for free), and wait for the future spot LIBOR to realize. Therefore, in yield curve construction, the implied futures rate can be taken to be the future spot rate for discounting purposes. Another way of stating this is that while the future spot 3-month rate almost certainly will not be equal to today's futures price covering the period in question, today's fair value of it is, and a \$100 discount bond for that period must be discounted using the futures rate. Let us illustrate.

On October 25, 2012, Jane Newbie, the Treasurer of a large financial firm facing rates in Table 3.7, overhears her CEO talking about \$100 million that her firm will have to deal with on June 19, 2013. Jane, new to her job, is unsure if the CEO said that the firm will have the \$100 million to invest or will have to borrow it; she is sure, however, that the CEO said the funds would bear interest for 3 months (till September 2013).

If the firm has \$100 million to invest, then Jane can wait till June and invest at the then prevailing LIBOR rate, bearing the risk the rate might go down, or she can lock in a rate by buying 100 Eurodollar futures. It costs her *nothing* to buy the futures and the firm has a margin account in which to settle mark-to-market amounts. If, instead, the firm has to borrow \$100 million, then Jane can wait till June and borrow at the then prevailing LIBOR rate, bearing the risk that the rate might go up, or she can lock in a rate by selling 100 Eurodollar futures. Unsure of what to do, Jane calls Smart Bank and asks for a two-way rate quote on a forward 3-month deposit and loan starting on June 19.

Smart Bank has to quote 2.52% (June futures trade at 97.48) to avoid being arbitraged.

If Smart Bank were to quote 2.64%, Jane would agree to deposit \$100 million at Smart Bank in June and would short 100 Eurodollar futures. On June 19, she would borrow \$100 million in the spot deposit market at the then prevailing LIBOR and deposit that \$100 million at Smart Bank at a rate of 2.64%. We have shown before that no matter what LIBOR is on June 19, her cost of borrowing *cum* variation market settlement is guaranteed to be 2.52%. If LIBOR is 2.00%, she would lose \$130,000 ($100 \times 52 \times 25$) on futures and pay \$500,000 in interest, making it a total of \$630,000. If LIBOR is 3.00%, she would gain \$120,000 on futures, but pay \$750,000 in interest, again making it a total of \$630,000, which is equivalent to 2.52%. At the same time, Smart Bank guaranteed to pay her $100{,}000{,}000 \times 0.0264 \times (90/360) =$ 660,000 in interest, ensuring a \$30,000 profit.

If Smart Bank were to quote 2.40%, Jane would buy 100 Eurodollar contracts and agree to borrow \$100 million in June from Smart Bank. In this arbitrage, she would use the \$100 million borrowed from Smart Bank to lend at the future spot LIBOR rate. Including the variation margin settlement, she would be guaranteed to earn 2.52%.

If Smart Bank quotes any rate different from 2.52%, between the mark-to-market on futures and the interest settlement with the bank, Jane can guarantee for her firm a positive cash flow equal to \$100 million times the interest rate deviation from 2.52% times the day-count ($\approx 1/4$). So, Smart Bank will be smart to quote 2.52%; it can then transact in futures to completely eliminate the risk of lending to or borrowing from Jane's firm.

We see that Jane and the bank have to be indifferent between the uncertain future spot rate or today's known implied futures rate, the latter's level being determined (as the balance of demand and supply of forward deposits) so that it costs nothing to convert one into the other. This observation is essential for valuing floating rate bonds, forward rate agreements, and swap contracts whose one (floating) leg contains a string of LIBOR-dependent cash flows. Although the future LIBORs are unknown today, the present value of these cash flows is computed by replacing the unknown future LIBORs with today's forward rates or implied futures rates.

3.5.2 Forward Rate Agreements

The over-the-counter forward markets trade the equivalent of the Eurocurrency futures, called *Forward Rate Agreements* (FRAs). FRAs are more flexible than futures as they can be entered into for any future dates and for any notional principal amount. The disadvantage is that there is no credit risk mitigation by a clearinghouse; they are private contracts between two private parties. In order to unwind the contracts, the two original parties have to agree on the mark-to-market value. Some of these issues are standardized by master agreements of an international industry association. These provide for credit exposure netting (cash inflows and outflows for all contracts with the same counterparty are netted in case of default, and only the net amount is exposed to default) and for using reference dealers in case the two parties cannot agree on the mark-to-market value for unwinds. While FRAs can be arranged for any future dates, standard maturities are quoted continuously by the largest dealers. These are listed for different start and end date combinations, relative to today, using the convention of "start month × end month." For example, in the quotes:

$$\begin{array}{ll} 1 \times 4 & 2.75/2.76 \\ 2 \times 5 & 2.82/2.83 \\ 3 \times 6 & 2.84/2.85 \end{array}$$

the "2 × 5" contract is bid at 2.82 and offer at 2.83. In this case, "2 × 5" means a contract with a start date of exactly 2 months from today and an end date of exactly 5 months from today. Just like Eurodollar futures, FRAs lock in a borrowing/lending rate for future 3-month periods. As the dates are defined relative to today's date, they roll every day by 1 day. In the futures markets, these are fixed in terms of actual calendar dates. Some standard 1, 6-, and 12-month forward periods are also quoted in the market, e.g. "2 × 3" or "1 × 7." The language convention for FRAs is different from the futures. Parties do not go long (buy) or short (sell), but "receive" or "pay," or "pay fixed" and "receive fixed," similar to the swap market conventions.

The main economic difference between a FRA and a Eurodollar futures contract is that the settlement of the mark-to-market takes place once at expiry, rather than daily up to the expiry date, and that the settlement amount is present-valued rather than a simple rate differential times a multiplier. To see this, let us describe the mechanics of a FRA contract.

A FRA is equivalent to a cash-settled fixed-for-floating swaplet (see Chapter 4). One party agrees to pay, and the other agrees to receive, a fixed rate of interest applied to a notional principal amount over a 3-month period in exchange for receiving (the other party paying) a floating rate equal to the spot 3-month LIBOR rate on the forward start date, applied to the same principal amount. The pay and receive amounts are netted, present-valued by the spot LIBOR on the forward start date, and settled in cash on that date. Suppose on March 19, 2013, we enter into a 3 × 6 FRA to pay 2.52% on \$20 million. The start date of the forward is June 19 and the end date is September 19. The amount the "FRA payer" will pay to the "FRA receiver" is defined as:

$$20{,}000{,}000 \times [(2.52 - L)/100] \times (\mathrm{Act}/360) \times [1/(1 + L \times \mathrm{Act}/360)]$$

The payment has the difference between the agreed-upon rate and future LIBOR applied to the notional principal, scaled by the appropriate day-count fraction, and multiplied by the present-value factor for 3 months. The payment is computed on June 19, when the LIBOR rate, L, is revealed, and remitted 2 business days later, on June 21. The cash flow can be positive or negative depending on the LIBOR rate on June 19 relative to the upfront forward rate.

Suppose that, on June 19, the 3-month LIBOR is 2.00%. The FRA payer will have to send a check to the FRA receiver for the amount of:

$$\begin{aligned} &20{,}000{,}000 \times [(2.52 - 2.00)/100] \times (92/360) \times [1/(1 + 0.02 \times 92/360)] \\ &\quad = \$26{,}442.63 \end{aligned}$$

which is close to the \$26,000 the buyer of 20 Eurodollar futures contracts would receive in the form of net variation margin by June 19.

Suppose that, on June 19, the 3-month LIBOR is 3.00%. The settlement cash flow is then computed as:

$$\begin{aligned} &20{,}000{,}000 \times [(2.52 - 3.00)/100] \times (92/360) \times [1/(1 + 0.03 \times 92/360)] \\ &\quad = \$ - 24{,}346.68 \end{aligned}$$

This time the FRA payer would receive a check for \$24,346.68 from the FRA receiver. This is almost the same as the \$24,000 that the seller of 20 Eurodollar futures contracts would receive in the form of net variation margin by June 19. The difference is that the FRA cash flow is computed for 92 days, and not for 90 days (which forces the $1{,}000{,}000 \times 90/360 \times 0.0001 =$ \$25 multiplier), it is present-valued by 3 months from the end date to the start date (the futures omit that), and it is received all at once on June 19, instead of over time in the form of daily variation margin checks. For short forward start dates, the difference between forwards and futures is negligible. For longer forward start dates, 2 years and above, the difference grows and the two zero-cost rates start to diverge. The difference between the quoted FRA and futures rates for the same dates is referred to as *futures convexity*. It is largely due to the timing and PV mismatch of the settlement flows causing futures to be price–yield convex instruments relative to forwards. (This is analogous to viewing bonds as having a convex price–yield relationship and forwards as having a straight-line relationship to forward yields.) The futures convexity charge can be quite large (in the order of several tens of basis points for 5- to 7-year futures) if the interest rate volatility between now and the expiry date is high (high interest rate volatility increases the mismatch between daily and one-time settlement).

Like Eurodollar futures contracts, FRAs allow one to lock in a net borrowing/lending rate for future periods. In a sense they do it in a more precise way. Their mark-to-market formula reflects exactly the interest exchange (LIBOR vs the lock rate) using the actual day-count and present-valuing the settlement amount to correct for an up-front (start of the interest period) cash flow instead of an arrears cash flow (end of the interest period). The FRA payer locks in a borrowing rate, while the FRA receiver locks in the lending or deposit rate. The easiest way to remember which side is which is to think of (future) *borrowing* as issuing a (forward) bond and *paying a fixed rate* on it, hence to lock in a borrowing rate one pays on a FRA, or sells futures.

The latter can be thought of as selling a forward discount bond. One can think of *lending* as buying a bond and *receiving a fixed rate* on it, hence to lock in a lending rate one receives on a FRA, or buys futures. The latter can be thought of as buying a forward discount bond.

We used the term *certainty equivalence* to mean that the market determines today a fixed rate at which agents are indifferent to exchange (at no charge) future known cash flows for future unknown cash flows based on future spot deposit rates. The *certainty equivalence of FRAs* is even more obvious than that of the Eurodollar futures. The settlement formula contains in it the exchange of the forward rate (which is known today) for a future LIBOR rate (which is not known until the start of the forward interest accrual period), applied to the desired notional principal and scaled by the appropriate day-count fraction. The present-valuing by 3 months corrects for the fact that interest is normally computed at the beginning of the accrual period but paid at the end, but the FRA settles at the beginning of the period.

3.5.3 Bootstrap Revisit: Building Spot Zeros

In Chapter 2 we showed how quotes for coupon bonds can be used sequentially to compute discount rates for present value calculations through a process called a zero curve bootstrap. We revisit the construction of the zero curve, this time with the use of futures and forwards. As previously, we will use the observed quotes in a chronological order in order to create a set of rates and discount factors that are appropriate for computing the present values of cash flows at future dates. This is a fundamental task in any valuation process.

The insight of Chapter 2 is that coupon securities are packages of zeroes (discount bonds). Assuming semi-annual coupons, the yield on a 6-month coupon bond is automatically set to the 6-month zero rate. Then, a 12-month coupon is a package of a 6-month zero with a face value equal to the 6-month coupon flow and a 12-month zero with a face value equal to the 12-month coupon flow plus the principal. If we know the 'blended' yield on the coupon security and the yield on the first (6-month) zero in the package, then we can back out the yield on the second (12-month) zero, since the price of the package (in dollars) has to equal the sum of the parts. The next step involves the price and the yield of a 18-month coupon security as package of the previously computed yields of the 6- and 12-month zeros and the to-be-determined yield on the 18-month zero. The next step is the 24-month coupon bond, etc. We continue in this way using the quoted prices on all the coupon bonds up to the longest maturity, computing along the way a set of zero-coupon yields with increasing maturities. The zero yields then allow us to discount cash flows on any future dates, and consequently allow us to value any (option-free) fixed income security.

The coupon-based bootstrap results in observations every 6 months (for UK and Canadian bonds with annual coupons, perhaps every 12 months) and is typically used in constructing the discount curve for dates past the 2-, 3-, or 5-year point, but may be too crude for shorter maturities. A forward- or futures-based bootstrap for shorter dates dovetails nicely with the coupon bootstrap for longer terms. Eurodollar futures are liquid every 3 months for 10 years, Eurosterling and Euribor futures are liquid every 3 months for 3 or 5 years. Finer observations can be obtained from 1-month LIBOR futures and FRAs. The choice of where the two methods meet, the short bootstrap based on forwards and the long one based on coupon bonds, depends on the relative liquidity of the instruments. The abundant liquidity of the futures in the short end and of the government bonds in the long end, guarantees – via the fair value arbitrage – that coupon packages can be synthetically replicated without any difficulty and that the whole process is not just a mathematical exercise but a reality ensured by potential arbitrage.

Table 3.24 Yield curve construction using Eurodollar futures

Start date	End date	Days in period	Quote	Implied rate Act/360	Forward discount factor	Spot discount factor
Spot LIBORs						
Oct15 2001	Nov21 2001	37	2.05	2.05	0.997897	**0.997897**
	Dec19 2001	65	2.12	2.12	0.996187	**0.996187**
	Jan16 2002	93	2.15	2.15	0.994477	**0.994477**
Eurodollar Futures						
Nov21 2001	Feb19 2002	90	97.81	2.19	0.994555	**0.992464**
Dec19 2001	Mar20 2002	91	97.85	2.15	0.994595	**0.990802**
Jan16 2002	Apr19 2002	93	97.87	2.13	0.994528	**0.989034**
Mar20 2002	Jun19 2002	91	97.77	2.23	0.994395	**0.985248**
Jun19 2002	Sep18 2002	91	97.48	2.52	0.993670	**0.979012**
Sep18 2002	Dec18 2002	91	97.09	2.91	0.992698	**0.971863**
Dec18 2002	Mar19 2003	91	96.60	3.40	0.991479	**0.963582**

We proceed sequentially, similarly to the coupon case. We start with a spot zero rate (1-, 2-, or 3-month LIBOR) and add forwards and/or futures with ever-increasing start and end dates to construct a discount curve of zero-coupon yields and discount factors. To avoid confusion with day-counts, it is a good practice to first compute discount factors, not zero rates. Depending on the compounding convention, there can be multiple zero rates for the same date. Discount factors are unique; they are dollar costs (present values) of \$1 face value discount bonds maturing on a given date. From the discount factors, we can recover rates based on any compounding or day-count convention.

We use spot and futures quotes for October 25, 2001. We have three spot zero rates (LIBORs) as starting points for the curve. The maturities of these deposit rates match the expiries of the first three futures contracts, i.e. November, December, and January. We use the November and January quotes merely to get fine detail for the next 6 months (i.e. to discount factors for November, January, and 3 months later for February and April). We use the December spot to compute the discount factors for December and all other dates of the quarterly futures expiry cycle (March, June, September, December). We assume that the LIBORs implied by the Eurodollar futures are for deposits spanning the 3-month periods from one expiry to the next, not the 90 days forced by the \$25 multiplier.

Table 3.24 contains the quote input information and the computed forward and spot discount factors. The first panel contains the LIBOR quotes; the second panel contains the Eurodollar futures quotes. For clarity, we show the periods spanned by the contracts and the number of days. Forward factors are intermediate calculations; they present-value \$1 from the end date to the start date. Spot discount factors present-value \$1 from the end date all the way back to the present (October 15, 2001). The whole set of the spot factors unambiguously defines the yield curve.

We observe three LIBOR rates (2.05, 2.12, and 2.15) for 1-, 2-, and 3-month deposits. We also observe a string of Eurodollar futures prices. Each locks a 3-month LIBOR for the period starting on the expiry date and ending 3 months later equal to 100 minus the futures price. Using the number of days in each period spanned by the futures expiries, we compute forward discount factors (the first three based on the spot rates are actually spot factors with the start

Table 3.25 Recovering zero rates from discount factors

Date	Days	Spot DF	Continuous yield	Simple yield Act/360
Nov21 2001	37	0.997897	2.0763	2.0500
Dec19 2001	65	0.996187	2.1453	2.1200
Jan16 2002	93	0.994477	2.1738	2.1500
Feb19 2002	127	0.992464	2.1741	2.1525
Mar20 2002	156	0.990802	2.1620	2.1423
Apr19 2002	186	0.989034	2.1637	2.1459
Jun19 2002	247	0.985248	2.1961	2.1822
Sep18 2002	338	0.979012	2.2906	2.2833
Dec18 2002	429	0.971863	2.4283	2.4295
Mar19 2003	520	0.963582	2.6040	2.6166

date of today) as $1 / (1 + r \times Act/360)$. These are present values as of the start date of \$1 received on the end date using the futures-implied yield. The logic follows from arbitrage; a \$1 face value loan for the forward period can be synthesized by locking the futures implied rate and borrowing/lending at future LIBOR. From the forward discount factors, we compute spot discount factors (present values as of today, October 25, 2001, of \$1 received on the end date) as products of forward discount factors spanning successive periods. For example, the spot discount factor of 0.979012 for September 18, 2002, is the product of the factor of 0.996187 for December, the forward factor of 0.994595 for December–March, the forward factor of 0.994395 for March–June, and the forward factor of 0.993670 for June–September. The yield curve construction could have been enriched by including liquid FRAs as substitutes for futures or used in addition for some of the in-between dates, and more spot points, or coupon instrument dates.

Once we have computed all the discount factors, we can recover discount rates according to any convention. In Table 3.25 we show the continuously compounded yields (which have the nice property that the spot continuous yield is simply an average of the forwards) and simple interest *Act/360* yields.

The yield curve for 520 days, as of October 25, 2001, is shown in Figure 3.2.

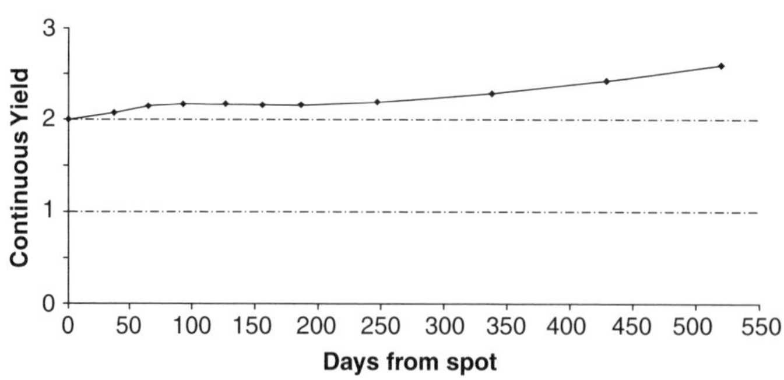

Figure 3.2 The zero-coupon curve

Since the discount factors are today's prices of future dollars, pricing fixed income securities is trivial. Suppose we are offered a structured note paying \$3,500 twice, 182 days from today and 365 days from today plus the principal of \$100,000. How much do we pay for it?

We do not have the factors for 182 days or 365 days, so we interpolate the continuous yields to obtain these two factors. Using the rates for 156 days and 186 days, we get the interpolated yield of 2.1635 and the discount factor of 0.989270 for 182 days. Using the rates for 338 days and 429 days to get the interpolated yield of 2.3314 and the discount factor of 0.976955 for 365 days. The present value of the note's cash flows is then equal to

$$3{,}500 \times 0.989270 + (3{,}500 + 100{,}000) \times 0.976955 = \$104{,}577.33$$

We pay 104.5773% of the face value for the note.

3.5.4 Recovering the Forwards

With the constructed yield curve, not only can we value securities with known (fixed) cash flows, but also those whose cash flows float with LIBOR rates (floating rate bonds, inverse floaters, leveraged floaters, etc.). We can recover forwards implied by the yield curve and substitute them for future unknown LIBORs using the certainty equivalence argument of costless conversion. The present value of an artificial security with today's forwards substituted for the unknown future LIBORs must be the same as that of the actual floating rate security.

The Valuation of a Floating Rate Bond

On October 25, 2001 we are offered a 1-year floating rate note with a face value of \$200,000 whose quarterly coupon is equal to the 3-month LIBOR. The coupon payment dates are January 25, April 25, July 25 and October 25, 2002, set 3 months prior. How much are we willing to pay for it? The valuation method is summarized in Table 3.26.

We compute the number of days from spot (today) to each rate set and interest pay date, and the number of days between the set and the pay date. We use those to interpolate the continuous discount yields and to compute discount factors to each set and pay date. From each pair of discount factors, we compute the implied forward LIBOR rate (FRA) using the arbitrage argument that discounting from the pay date to today can be synthesized by discounting from the pay date to the set date and then from the set date to today:

$$df_{PayDate} = df_{SetDate} \times \left(1 + \frac{1}{\left(1 + f_{Set \times Pay} \times \frac{Act}{360}\right)}\right)$$

For example, the Jan02 forward LIBOR, i.e. the Jan02 × Apr02 FRA, of 2.1302, is computed from:

$$0.989270 = 0.994538 \times \left(1 + \frac{1}{\left(1 + f_{Jan02 \times Apr02} \times \frac{90}{360}\right)}\right)$$

Each cash flow is set on the basis of the LIBOR forward on the set date equal to $200{,}000 \times f_{Set \times Pay} \times \frac{Act}{360}$ and paid 3 months later. We compute the PV of the cash flow by multiplying it by the discount factor to the pay date. We sum the PVs to get the price of the note which turns out to be exactly \$200,000. This is no surprise given that the floating rate note is a revolving loan always worth par.

Table 3.26 One-year floating rate bond with quarterly LIBOR sets

Set date	Pay date	Days to set	Days to pay	Days in period	Interp cont yld to pay	DF to set	DF to Pay	Implied LIBOR Set	Cash flow on pay	PV of cash flow
Oct25 2001	Jan25 2002	0	92	92	2.1728	1.000000	0.994538	2.1489	1,098.34	1,092.34
Jan25 2002	Apr25 2002	92	182	90	2.1635	0.994538	0.989270	2.1302	1,065.08	1,053.65
Apr25 2002	Jul25 2002	182	273	91	2.2231	0.989270	0.983510	2.3170	1,171.38	1,152.06
Jul25 2002	Oct25 2002	273	365	92	2.3314	0.983510	0.976955	2.6252	201,341.78	196,701.94
								Sum of PVs		200,000.00

3.5.5 Including Repo Rates in the Calculation of the Forwards

The yield curve construction process is generic to all credit markets. In one special situation, it has to be modified to take into account *special repos* which render forward replication strategies more expensive. There are times when the demand and supply forces may make a bond scarce. A lender of funds through a reverse repo (buying securities today to resell tomorrow) may lend funds at a zero interest rate just to be able to own the desired bond overnight. The resale price includes a rebate making it only minimally greater than or equal to today's purchase price. The lender earns diminished or no interest, but acquires the desired collateral (the bond). The diminished interest rate is referred to as *special repo* and is lower than the overnight or term rate implied by the yield curve.

In a simplified numerical example, assume that a 1-year zero yielding 6% enjoys general repo, while a 2-year zero yielding 6.5% is expected to be on special for the next month. We want to replicate a 1-year by 2-year forward deposit by buying the 2-year zero and shorting the 1-year zero. If neither bond were on special, then we could lock in the forward $f_{12\times 24}$ rate equal to 7.0024% implied from:

$$\frac{1}{1+0.06} \times \frac{1}{1+f_{12\times 24}} = \frac{1}{(1+0.065)^2}$$

This no-arbitrage equation states that \$1 can be received 2 years from today by spending $1/(1+0.065)^2$ on a 2-year bond or can be synthesized by spending $1/(1+0.06)(1+f_{12\times 24})$ on a 1-year bond and rolling it over into $1/(1+f_{12\times 24})$ of a 1-year by 2-year forward. However, if the 2-year bond trades special, then to own it we have to surrender interest for a month. That is like paying a higher price grossed up by 1 plus the lost interest fraction. Assuming that the 1-month rate is equal to 6%, we have

$$\frac{1}{1+0.06} \times \frac{1}{1+f_{12\times 24}} = (1+0.06)^{1/12}\frac{1}{(1+0.065)^2}$$

The forward rate we can synthesize is $f_{12\times 24} = 6.484\%$. The calculations for special repos get complicated when deriving synthetic forward prices for coupon securities. The simple discount factors in the above equations have to be replaced with PVs of coupon and principal packages. However, the principle of synthetic replication with no-arbitrage must not be violated and the mathematics must include any repo rebates earned or given up. The equations are the same for forward borrowers and lenders as the "specialness" of repo cuts both ways. The forward lender locks in a lower forward rate. The borrower also does this, and uses the hotly desired security as collateral in a repo transaction.

4 Swap Markets

Publicly traded securities – stocks and bonds – are often bought as a long-term investment. Their ownership is widely distributed among thousands of investors. Short of major corporate actions, such as tender offers, buyback programs, or bankruptcy restructurings, issuers have little leeway to change the cash flow pattern of their liabilities. This is where swap markets come in. Issuers can match the cash flows they owe on their preferred stocks or bonds while agreeing to pay completely different sets of flows to financial institutions. Fixed coupon liabilities can be swapped into floating; dollar flows can be swapped into yen or euros; callable or putable flows can be swapped into straight bullet flows. Not only can issuers change the nature and maturity of their old liabilities, but they can also take advantage of relative differences in financing costs in different markets. Bonds can be issued floating and immediately swapped into fixed, or issued in one currency and immediately swapped into another to take advantage of a low interest rate, while matching the liability to the nature and currency of the revenue stream. Nestlé can issue a Swiss franc fixed bond, swap it into floating dollars and euros, and be able to pay the coupons with revenues from global sales.

The fastest growing segments of the swap markets are interest rate swaps, cross-currency swaps, and credit default swaps with trillions of dollars of principal outstanding worldwide. We leave until later the analysis of credit default swaps which are structurally insurance arrangements, exchanging premiums for one-time event-triggered payouts. In this chapter we cover interest rate, cross-currency, equity, and commodity swaps which typically are not triggered single payouts, but have multiple predefined cash flows on both sides of the swap.

4.1 FUNDAMENTALS OF SWAPS

A swap is a private agreement between two *counterparties* to exchange two streams of cash flows. Each stream of cash flows, called a *swap leg*, resembles a coupon and principal flow on a bond. The swap agreement specifies the principals and coupon formulas for each stream, the exact dates of the cash flow exchanges and the final maturity. Coupon flows can be fixed, floating based on an interest rate reference such as LIBOR, T-Bill or gilt, or floating based on an equity index or a commodity price. The face value or the principal of a swap is referred to as a *notional principal*, as it is not necessarily the face value of any real bond, but a reference with which to easily define the coupon formula. The principals for the two sides of the swap may be unequal or defined in different currencies. In most cases, they are identical. In interest rate swaps, the notional principal for both sides is the same, therefore it is not even exchanged, and the cash flow exchange is simply fixed for floating. In cross-currency swaps, the notional principals are in two different currencies, but have the same value at the original exchange rate. Since their value is usually mismatched by the final maturity of the swap, they are exchanged to preserve the fairness of the swap agreement. Many swaps have deliberately mismatched coupon dates. The fixed side on an interest rate swap commonly pays every 6 or 12 months, while the floating side is commonly indexed off the 3-month LIBOR and pays quarterly.

4.1.1 The Dual Nature of Swaps

The fundamental property of the swaps is their *dual nature*. On one hand, a swap can be viewed as *an exchange of two fictitious bonds*. In an interest rate swap, one side – one fictitious bond – is the floating rate leg plus the notional principal, which taken together are identical to a floating rate bond. The other side – the other fictitious bond – is the fixed leg plus the notional principal, which taken together are identical to a fixed coupon bond. The cash flow formulas for each side are typically set in such a way that neither party owes anything to the other at the outset of the swap. If the fixed coupon is high, then the margin spread added to the floating LIBOR is high, so that the two legs are of equal economic value. If the floating leg is LIBOR flat (no margin), then the fixed rate is computed to ensure that the two sides have the same present value. Such a swap is called a *market swap* or an *on-market swap*. The majority of swaps originate that way, but as interest rates or currency rates change over the life of the swap, the swap legs may not have offsetting PVs, or the PVs may be mismatched from the outset. Such swaps are called *off-market swaps*. Any time the swap is unwound (cancelled) by mutual agreement of the two counterparties, a payment of the mark-to-market is exchanged to cover the off-market value of the swap. The mark-to-market value of the swap reflects the difference in the values of the two fictitious bonds exchanged through the swap.

The second nature of the swap is as *a string of forwards*. Instead of analyzing the swap one leg at a time, let us dissect the swap "horizontally," one cash flow exchange at a time. In an interest rate swap, on each date we exchange a fixed coupon for a floating one times the correct day-count fractions times the face value. Each exchange is identical to the settlement formula of a Forward Rate Agreement (FRA), and can be synthesized with a FRA or almost identically synthesized with a Eurodollar futures contract. In a cross-currency swap, we may, on each date, exchange a fixed flow in dollars for a fixed flow in euros, computed using the respective side's face value, coupon rate, and day-count fraction. Each exchange is identical to a currency forward, as it simply fixes known amounts in two different currencies, thus fixing the exchange rate between the two currencies. Viewed this way, an *on-market swap* is one where the coupon rates on both sides are set relative to each other to make the sum of the present values for all the forwards strung together in a swap equal to zero (some may be positive, some negative). An *off-market swap*'s sum of the PVs will be non-zero, and one counterparty will have to pay the other, depending on the sign of the total PV, in order to enter into a new swap or cancel an existing swap.

4.1.2 Implication for Pricing and Hedging

The dual nature of swaps profoundly simplifies the valuation and hedging analysis of swaps. We use whichever is easier and more intuitive. If a cross-currency swap is an exchange of two fixed bonds, each denominated in a different currency, we use yield curves in each currency to value each bond, and then use the spot exchange rate to find the difference in value (off-market or mark-to-market PV), or we solve for one coupon rate in order for that difference to be zero. If we know how to hedge each bond separately, then we know how to hedge the swap, since the swap is equivalent to a long position in one bond and a short position in another. Alternatively, we can value each cash flow exchange as the mark-to-market on a currency forward, and add them to find a total. The hedging then boils down to synthesizing the opposite of each forward to offset exposure. We end up in the same spot. Often we end up with an insight into alternative, economically equivalent, hedging schemes. We can hedge an interest rate swap with one duration-equivalent bond or a strip of Eurodollar futures. We can hedge a cross-currency swap with bonds or Eurocurrency positions in each currency combined with spot FX trades, or directly in spot and forward FX markets.

For larger dealers, swap hedging is done on a net basis for entire books of swaps. The cash flows of many swaps in the book may offset each other literally or in economic exposure (e.g. a 5-year bond and 4-year bond with mismatched dates are economically similar). Armed with computed net value sensitivities for the entire book to a variety of liquid hedge instruments, the dealer is in a position to choose the best overall hedge, one that is liquid, easy to alter when a new deal arrives, and easy to undo when unwinds occur. Instead of choosing exact static offsets that once and for all eliminate the risks of the swap, the dealer can save money by hedging dynamically daily changes in the net value of the portfolio, as the portfolio itself changes due to the arrival of unwinds and new deals. The dynamic approach often results in a dramatically smaller overall hedge.

4.2 INTEREST RATE SWAPS

Interest rate swap flows are defined in the same currency. They allow users to change their asset or liability flows from fixed rate to floating rate and vice versa. The floating side is in the majority of cases indexed off the LIBOR rate. In the USA, sometimes the role of LIBOR is played by the Fed Funds, Commercial Paper, T-Bill, or Cost of Funds Index (COFI) rate.

4.2.1 Definition of an Interest Rate Swap

Suppose a UK company issues a 5-year £100 million floating rate bond with an annual 12-month LIBOR coupon, but wants a fixed rate liability to match the repayment schedule to a guaranteed government contract. The floating rate bond is issued at par; each coupon rate is set at the beginning of the interest accrual period and paid at the end, making the bond equivalent to an annual revolving loan.

The company enters into a £100 million notional principal fixed-for-floating interest rate swap whereby it agrees to receive an annual floating coupon equal to LIBOR, and pay an annual 4.780222% fixed rate coupon. The pay flows are known in advance, the received LIBOR flows, except for the first one, are not. The swap cash flows summarized in Table 4.1 assume a made-up LIBOR path starting at 3.0225% and ending at 5.0625%.

The floating LIBOR receipts on the swap, whatever they happen to be, will exactly offset the coupon interest the UK company will owe on the issued bonds, leaving it with a net fixed coupon liability to the swap counterparty.

Table 4.1 A £100 million pay fixed 4.780222% interest rate swap

Year	LIBOR	Fixed	Receive £	Pay £
0	3.2256	4.780222		
1	*3.5000*	4.780222	322,560	4,780,222
2	*3.8750*	4.780222	3,500,000	4,780,222
3	*4.2500*	4.780222	3,875,000	4,780,222
4	*5.0625*	4.780222	4,250,000	4,780,222
5			5,062,500	4,780,222

We can view the swap as an exchange of two fictitious bonds by adding a receipt and a payment of £100 million in year 5; the two netting flows are skipped in Table 4.1. All the floating rate coupon receipts, plus the omitted £100 million one-time receipt in year 5, represent a bought floating rate bond (worth par today). The 4.780222% fixed coupon payments and the omitted £100 million one-time payment in year 5 represent a shorted fixed-rate bond. If the fixed rate is chosen so that the fixed-rate bond is worth par today, then no payment to or receipt from the dealer is needed today to enter into the swap (to settle the difference in present values).

The same swap, looking at each cash flow exchange in turn, can be viewed as a string of FRAs. Each exchange is an agreement to receive a floating rate, set at the beginning and paid at the end, and to pay a fixed rate at the end of the interest accrual period. This is identical to the FRA settlement formula. Even though we do not know the floating side of the exchange until the set time (FRA expiry), we know that a market FRA rate would eliminate that uncertainty at no cost. The FRA rate for each exchange is different and differs from the fixed rate of the swap, except by coincidence. Each exchange is an off-market FRA with a non-zero PV. To value the swap, we compute from the yield curve the market forward rate for each period and substitute it for the floating rate, using the certainty equivalence argument. The swap reduces to the differences between the swap fixed rate and the computed fair FRA rates. Once we compute the forward-equivalent receipts and the scheduled fixed rate payments, we discount these fixed-fixed exchanges to today. These FRA marks, some positive and some negative, represent how much would have to be paid to or received from a dealer to enter into the floating-for-fixed 4.780222% exchanges. The fixed rate on the swap would be chosen so that the sum of all the marks is zero.

Table 4.2 illustrates the principle. Given the annual spot zero rates, we recover the forward zeros, compute the floating cash flows, as if they were fixed at those forward zeros, net them against the fixed 4.780222% side, then PV the differences using the original spot rates. The fixed rate of 4.780222% is chosen so that the total mark-to-market is equal to zero at the outset.

In Table 4.2, the receipt of the floating LIBOR set 1 year from today to be paid 1 year later (2 years from today) can at the outset be locked into £4.040803 million. Netted against the £4.780222 million to be paid 2 years from today, the excess (£0.739419) can be settled today by an immediate receipt of its PV equal to £0.688493. The same logic applies to all five exchanges. In early years, these have a negative PV to the company; in the last 3 years, they have a positive PV to the company.

Fixed rate and floating rate swap flows do not have to have the same periodicity. Usually, the frequency and day-count convention of each swap leg are determined by the market. Our

Table 4.2 The PV of the £100 million pay fixed 4.780222% interest rate swap

Years	Zero rate	Float CF	Fixed CF	Equiv float CF	Difference	PV of diff
1	3.2256	$LIBOR_0$	4.780222	3.225600	−1.554622	−1.506043
2	3.6324	$LIBOR_1$	4.780222	4.040803	−0.739419	−0.688493
3	4.0400	$LIBOR_2$	4.780222	4.860016	0.079794	0.070855
4	4.4484	$LIBOR_3$	4.780222	5.683244	0.903022	0.758737
5	4.8576	$LIBOR_4$	4.780222	6.510494	1.730272	1.364944
Sum of MTMs						**0.000000**

GBP-denominated swap example would more likely have quarterly floating interest receipts and annual fixed coupons. In the USA, the fixed side is typically semi-annual with the *30/360* day-count while the floating side is quarterly with the *Act/360* day-count. Swaps following interest conventions for a given currency are labeled *plain vanilla*. They can be simply present valued using bootstrapped yield curves.

4.2.2 Valuation of Interest Rate Swaps

In order for the present value of the swap to be equal to the cost of a replicating strategy, the yield curve underlying the swap valuation must be bootstrapped from the liquid instruments that will be used to hedge the swap. The "spot zeros" reflecting swap counterparties' credits are the Eurocurrency (LIBOR) deposits that trade freely and at tight spreads in both directions, but they trade only for very short maturities. Maturities over 1 year have to be synthesized from Eurocurrency futures or FRAs. This is achievable with the use of liquid futures or forwards for up to 10 years for the US dollar, 5 years for the euro, and 2 years for the Japanese yen, the Swiss franc, and a few other currencies. Beyond 5 or 10 years, long-term government bonds can be bought and shorted at tight spreads. Since these bonds reflect the credit rating of the sovereigns (not the swap parties), they require a "plug" in the form of a swap spread which itself is continuously determined in the market.

We will illustrate the process of pricing a US interest rate swap, its execution, and the subsequent hedging involved. Suppose on September 26, 2003, a New York dealer is contacted by ABC Corp. to provide a quote on a 5-year $200 million notional principal, plain vanilla interest rate swap where ABC will pay the dealer a fixed rate semi-annually and will receive quarterly a floating rate of 3-month LIBOR. Suppose the dealer is faced with the "building blocks" rates in Table 4.3.

We assume that Eurodollar expiry dates correspond to the swap roll dates (normally we would have to interpolate). First, we determine the forward rates that can be locked in for future 3-month periods. If we had FRAs, we could use those directly, but here we do not. We need to "correct" the FRA rates implied in the Eurodollar futures prices by what is called a *futures convexity adjustment* (see Chapter 6). The correction takes into account the fact that

Table 4.3 Building blocks for the swap yield curve on September 26, 2003

Spot Money Rates	Mar 2006	96.10	Jun 2009	94.14		
3-month LIBOR	1.14%	Jun	95.87	Sep	94.07	
		Sep	95.65	Dec	94.00	
Eurodollars (CME)	Dec	95.44				
Dec 2003	98.83	Mar 2007	95.25	**US Treasury Issues**		
Mar 2004	98.75	Jun	95.08			
Jun	98.51	Sep	94.92	Maturity	Coupon	Yield
Sep	98.19	Dec	94.77			
Dec	97.77	Mar 2008	94.64	9/30/2005	1.625	1.657
Mar 2005	97.35	Jun	94.51	9/15/2008	3.125	3.030
Jun	96.96	Sep	94.41	8/15/2013	4.250	4.099
Sep	96.65	Dec	94.31	2/15/2031	5.375	5.000
Dec	96.35	Mar 2009	94.22			

Table 4.4 Building the swap yield curve

Forward period Months from today						
Start	End	100–Eurodollar	Convexity adjustment	Implied FRA	Discount rate to end date	Discount factor to end date
0	3			1.140	1.140000	0.9971581
3	6	1.17	0.000	1.170	1.155000	0.9942499
6	9	1.25	−0.008	1.242	1.183998	0.9911723
9	12	1.49	−0.016	1.474	1.256479	0.9875333
12	15	1.81	−0.024	1.786	1.362327	0.9831435
15	18	2.23	−0.032	2.198	1.501485	0.9777707
18	21	2.65	−0.040	2.610	1.659657	0.9714321
21	24	3.04	−0.048	2.992	1.825959	0.9642197
24	27	3.35	−0.056	3.294	1.988810	0.9563442
27	30	3.65	−0.064	3.586	2.148245	0.9478468
30	33	3.90	−0.072	3.828	2.300660	0.9388619
33	36	4.13	−0.080	4.050	2.446149	0.9294512
36	39	4.35	−0.088	4.262	2.585540	0.9196523
39	42	4.56	−0.096	4.464	2.719426	0.9095022
42	45	4.75	−0.104	4.646	2.847578	0.8990597
45	48	4.92	−0.112	4.808	2.969826	0.8883813
48	51	5.08	−0.120	4.960	3.086624	0.8775003
51	54	5.23	−0.128	5.102	3.198326	0.8664488
54	57	5.36	−0.136	5.224	3.304687	0.8552788
57	60	5.49	−0.144	5.346	3.406508	0.8439988

the futures settlements take place every day until the futures expiry, while the FRA settlement is one-time on the FRA start date. The longer the expiry date, the bigger is the adjustment, as it depends on the volatility of the short-term discount rate. The ultimate check if the adjustment is correct is the comparison to FRA rates, if available.

We build the zero-coupon curve from the money market rate and the convexity-adjusted implied futures. We compute the discount factors to a sequence of future dates: 3 months, 6 months, up to 60 months.

Table 4.4 shows the results. For each forward period we take 100 minus the Eurodollar futures price as the implied futures rate. We add to it the convexity adjustment to get the FRA rates (if we had some of those we could have skipped the initial steps). Then we daisy-chain today's spot LIBOR and the FRA rates to get the ever-longer spot zero rates (quarterly compounded) and discount factors. This last step reflects the cash-and-carry argument. $1 received on a future date can be synthesized by investing the dollar amount equal to the discount factor in a 3-month spot deposit and rolling it over to the final maturity by locking in the reinvestment rates implied in all intermediate futures.

Having constructed the yield curve, we are now ready to price the swap. Since the floating side of the swap (plus the principal) is worth par, in order to determine the semi-annual 5-year fixed rate, we need to price a 5-year semi-annual fixed coupon bond and find the coupon rate on the bond that prices the bond to par. We iterate on the fixed rate until we find one for which the bond's price is 100. Table 4.5 verifies that the target rate is 3.3636% semi-annually compounded.

Table 4.5 PV of the fictitious fixed rate bond with a 3.3636% semi coupon

Pay date	Cash flow	Discount factor	PV of cash flow
6 months	1.6818	0.9942499	1.6721
1 year	1.6818	0.9875185	1.6608
18 months	1.6818	0.9777220	1.6443
2 years	1.6818	0.9641191	1.6215
30 months	1.6818	0.9476774	1.5938
3 years	1.6818	0.9292022	1.5627
42 months	1.6818	0.9091777	1.5291
4 years	1.6818	0.8879853	1.4934
54 months	1.6818	0.8659856	1.4564
5 years	101.6818	0.8434727	85.7658
Sum of PVs			**100.0000**

Knowing the fair rate of 3.3636%, the dealer quotes 3.39%. ABC accepts this and the swap is done. ABC Corp. has agreed to pay a fixed rate of 3.39 (semi) and receive floating 3-month LIBOR. The dealer computes his profit relative to his estimated cost of synthetic manufacture as 2.64 bp running, which is equivalent to 12.28 bp up front, or $0.001228 \times 200{,}000{,}000 =$ \$245,639. Table 4.6 reprices the fixed rate bond using the actual agreed-upon rate of 3.39%.

The more direct way is to take the 2.64 bp difference as each cash flow, multiply by the correct discount factor, and sum the PVs to get the 12.28 bp upfront total.

4.2.3 Hedging of Interest Rate Swaps

While the profit on the swap can be calculated up front, it is not realized instantaneously, only over the life of the swap. In order for the dealer to capture this value, he will need to manufacture the swap at the estimated cost, which can be done in two ways. The first is to synthetically replicate the offset of the scheduled cash flows. Expecting to receive 3.39% fixed against floating quarterly LIBOR, the dealer can lock in a payment of 3.3636% fixed against a receipt of floating LIBOR, using Eurodollar futures or FRAs. The floating sides

Table 4.6 Dealer profit on a receive-3.39% swap

Pay date	Cash flow	Discount factor	PV of cash flow
6 months	1.6950	0.9942499	1.6853
1 year	1.6950	0.9875185	1.6738
18 months	1.6950	0.9777220	1.6572
2 years	1.6950	0.9641191	1.6342
30 months	1.6950	0.9476774	1.6063
3 years	1.6950	0.9292022	1.5750
42 months	1.6950	0.9091777	1.5411
4 years	1.6950	0.8879853	1.5051
54 months	1.6950	0.8659856	1.4678
5 years	101.6950	0.8434727	85.7770
Sum of PVs			**100.1228**
Profit			**0.1228**

would cancel and the difference in fixed sides would be the flow of profit. The second and most common is through a dynamic hedge strategy that uses the same replicating instruments. A hedge is defined as a set of positions whose values change one-for-one in opposite direction to the hedged swap. The static replication and the dynamic hedge share the same design: produce profit up front and a zero liability in the future. The difference lies in intent. In the static replication, we match the cash flows with the instruments that lock them (futures). We leave them alone, letting the cash flows offset each other as they come due. In a dynamic hedge, we blip the inputs to the yield curve construction process (futures) to compute the local sensitivity of the swap PV to each instrument's rate (local = relative to small 1 bp changes). We execute the hedge, but do not leave it alone. We recompute the set of local sensitivities and adjust the hedge after every change in the yield curve every day over the life of the swap. This by itself would produce no loss of value (zero liability) by the end of the swap, but that is not our only intention. As we enter into new unrelated swap and hedge positions, with mismatched dates and terms, or unwind the original swap, we net the hedges against those new risks, potentially resulting in a smaller net hedge. Of course, if the dealer does not "deal" – that is, pay and receive on a variety of swaps, but grows a one-sided position where he always receives but never pays fixed on new 5-year swaps – none of the hoped-for offsetting of hedges will occur. However, if the two-sided flow does occur, then the local sensitivities on the different swaps may cancel each other. That is, the swaps on the dealer's books will, with some residual hedge, balance each other and the hedging will serve a purpose of temporarily offsetting risks until the next natural hedge is found. The dynamic hedge is, in this context, mainly a solution to the new deal timing mismatch.

Normally, the dynamic hedge computation is done employing a basic blipping method as it is the most flexible. In our simplified example we assumed that the swap roll dates fall exactly on futures expiry dates. That is almost never the case and we end up interpolating the yield curve to figure out the forward rates that can be locked in and the discount factors to the pay dates. The static replication, no matter how careful, is also rarely exact. Hedging by blipping the curve simply recognizes this reality. *Blipping* consists of changing, one by one, the input rate of a spot deposit or a Eurodollar futures price, reconstructing the yield curve (discount factors), and recomputing the PV of the swap. This way, one arrives at the number of contracts of each futures that must be traded so that changes in their marks exactly offset the changes in the PV of the swap. Since blipping is performed for small rate changes (1 bp), only those small changes are perfectly hedged, the hedge has to be recomputed and readjusted frequently (perhaps once a day). That is why, even though the swap, unlike an option, can be statically replicated, the typical hedging process is dynamic and similar to delta hedging an option. Mathematically, it is equivalent to a Taylor series expansion with discretized first derivatives.

In order to determine the exact hedge for the receive-3.39% swap, we must derive the PV sensitivities of the swap to blips of the curve one instrument at a time. We start by changing the price of the first Eurodollar December 2003 contract by –0.01 to 98.82. We rebuild the zero curve and reprice the swap. The change in the present value of the swap in dollars divided by \$25 gives us the number of December contracts that need to be sold to hedge the swap. This first step is illustrated in Table 4.7 with the blipped 100 – 98.82 = 1.18 value.

In the second step, we return the December 2003 futures value back to 98.83 and change the price of the March 2004 contract by –0.01 to 98.74. We rebuild the curve and reprice the swap. The change in the present value of the swap in dollars divided by \$25 gives us the number of March 2004 contracts that need to be sold to hedge the swap. Table 4.8 illustrates the calculations. Notice the precision required to obtain the correct results.

Table 4.7 Hedging the 3.39% swap – first blip

Forward period								
Start	End	100-Eurodollar	Convexity adjust	Implied FRA	Discount rate to end date	Discount factor to end date	Cash flow	PV of cash flow
0	3			1.140	1.140000	0.9971581		
3	6	**1.18**	0.000	1.180	1.160000	0.9942251	1.6950	1.6852
6	9	1.25	−0.006	1.244	1.187998	0.9911427		
9	12	1.49	−0.012	1.478	1.260479	0.9874939	1.6950	1.6738
12	15	1.81	−0.018	1.792	1.366727	0.9830896		
15	18	2.23	−0.024	2.206	1.506484	0.9776976	1.6950	1.6572
18	21	2.65	−0.030	2.620	1.665369	0.9713354		
21	24	3.04	−0.036	3.004	1.832454	0.964095	1.6950	1.6341
24	27	3.35	−0.042	3.308	1.996137	0.9561874		
27	30	3.65	−0.048	3.602	2.156435	0.9476538	1.6950	1.6063
30	33	3.90	−0.054	3.846	2.309739	0.9386288		
33	36	4.13	−0.062	4.068	2.455968	0.9291791	1.6950	1.5750
36	39	4.35	−0.070	4.280	2.595986	0.9193421		
39	42	4.56	−0.078	4.482	2.730409	0.909155	1.6950	1.5410
42	45	4.75	−0.086	4.664	2.859027	0.8986765		
45	48	4.92	−0.094	4.826	2.981683	0.8879632	1.6950	1.5051
48	51	5.08	−0.102	4.978	3.098840	0.8770483		
51	54	5.23	−0.110	5.120	3.210862	0.865964	1.6950	1.4678
54	57	5.36	−0.118	5.242	3.317510	0.8547623		
57	60	5.49	−0.126	5.364	3.419588	0.8434516	101.6950	85.7748
PV after the blip								100.1203
– Original PV								−100.1228
Change in PV × Notional					($4,991) =	200,000,000 ×		0.0025%
	→**Dec 2003 contracts**			200 =	4,991 ÷ 25			

In the third step, we return the March 2004 futures value back to 98.75 and change the price of the June 2004 contract by –0.01. We would continue the process until we reached June 2008 futures, the last contract within the final maturity of the swap. Since the swap matures in September 2008, and September 2008 ED contract locks the rate from September to December, we don't need to blip that contract. If the swap maturity fell in between September and December 2008 and there were any interpolation involved, we would have to blip September 2008 as well.

The hedge calculation consists of perturbing each input instrument by 1 bp, rebuilding the curve, repricing the swap, and computing the change in the PV of the swap as a result of the 1 bp change in the input instrument. Since our curve-building instruments are Eurodollar futures, each with a basis point multiplier of $25, we divide the swap PV change by $25 to get the hedge ratio, or the number of contracts to be sold to offset the change in the value of the swap resulting from a 1 bp blip.

There is one other instrument that is an input to the yield curve construction: the spot 3-month LIBOR rate. Following the same procedure as illustrated in Tables 4.7 and 4.8, we blip the 3-month spot rate to obtain a swap PV change of –$4,992. Since establishing and unwinding of spot deposits every day can be costly, a substitute hedge can be put on which assumes parallel rate movements of spot deposits and the first Eurodollar futures. Normally

Table 4.8 Hedging the 3.39% swap – second blip

Forward period								
Start	End	100-Eurodollar	Convexity adjust	Implied FRA	Discount rate to end date	Discount factor to end date	Cash flow	PV of cash flow
0	3			1.140	1.140000	0.9971581		
3	6	1.17	0.000	1.170	1.155000	0.9942499	1.6950	1.6853
6	9	**1.26**	−0.006	1.254	1.187997	0.9911427		
9	12	1.49	−0.012	1.478	1.260478	0.9874939	1.6950	1.6738
12	15	1.81	−0.018	1.792	1.366726	0.9830897		
15	18	2.23	−0.024	2.206	1.506484	0.9776977	1.6950	1.6572
18	21	2.65	−0.030	2.620	1.665369	0.9713354		
21	24	3.04	−0.036	3.004	1.832454	0.9640951	1.6950	1.6341
24	27	3.35	−0.042	3.308	1.996137	0.9561874		
27	30	3.65	−0.048	3.602	2.156435	0.9476538	1.6950	1.6063
30	33	3.90	−0.054	3.846	2.309739	0.9386288		
33	36	4.13	−0.062	4.068	2.455968	0.9291791	1.6950	1.5750
36	39	4.35	−0.070	4.280	2.595986	0.9193421		
39	42	4.56	−0.078	4.482	2.730409	0.909155	1.6950	1.5410
42	45	4.75	−0.086	4.664	2.859027	0.8986765		
45	48	4.92	−0.094	4.826	2.981682	0.8879632	1.6950	1.5051
48	51	5.08	−0.102	4.978	3.098840	0.8770483		
51	54	5.23	−0.110	5.120	3.210862	0.865964	1.6950	1.4678
54	57	5.36	−0.118	5.242	3.317509	0.8547623		
57	60	5.49	−0.126	5.364	3.419588	0.8434517	101.6950	85.7748
PV after the blip								100.1204
– Original PV								−100.1228
Change in PV × Notional					($4,906) =	200,000,000 ×		0.0024%
→**Mar 2004 contracts**				196 =	4,906 ÷ 25			

this sensitivity to the spot rate can be hedged with the first available Eurodollar contract as a proxy for spot, e.g. with a serial October contract if available, stacked on top of the other Dec 2003 hedge, left unhedged, or a combination of these options. The $–4,992 change is equivalent to –200 Oct 2003 contracts.

Table 4.9 summarizes the hedge for the $200 million receive-3.9% swap. It involves short positions in 19 quarterly Eurodollar contracts and one serial front contract. Since we are receiving fixed and paying floating on the swap, the swap will gain value when interest rates decrease, and lose value when interest rates increase. The short positions in Eurodollar contracts will have a negative mark-to-market when interest rates decrease (prices increase), and a positive mark-to-market when interest rates increase (prices decrease). The offset in value changes between the swap and the hedges will be identical.

Each day after the inception of the swap, and every time interest rates change dramatically, the dealer will repeat the entire exercise, compute new hedge amounts, and trade the appropriate number of contracts to ensure that his holdings are equal to the currently required hedge. Every day the profits and losses on the futures will exactly offset the PV changes on the swap. As the swap ages and actual cash flows drop off, fewer maturities of the futures will be held. Daily adjustments to the positions will be small, and over time all hedges will be liquidated.

Table 4.9 Eurodollar hedge for \$200 million receive 3.39% Swap

Oct 2003	*−200*	Sep 2006	−179
Dec 2003	−200	Dec	−179
Mar 2004	−196	Mar 2007	−175
Jun	−196	Jun	−175
Sep	−193	Sep	−172
Dec	−192	Dec	−172
Mar 2005	−189	Mar 2008	−169
Jun	−189	Jun	−169
Sep	−185	Sep	0
Dec	−185	Dec	0
Mar 2006	−182	Mar 2009	0
Jun	−182	Jun	0

4.3 CROSS-CURRENCY SWAPS

Cross-currency swaps are exchanges of bonds denominated in two different currencies, e.g. one side is dollars and the other side is euros. The basic structure is an exchange of fixed coupon flows in one currency for fixed coupon flows in another currency, but not uncommon are exchanges of fixed-for-floating or floating-for-floating. Sometimes the coupon and the principal exchanges involve different currencies, matching flows on multicurrency bonds. Cross-currency swaps allow issuers to alter the currency of their liabilities. The valuation exploits the dual nature of these swaps, as exchanges of bonds or strings of currency forwards, and largely relies on present valuing both sides of the swap. The peculiarities are that the principal exchange must be included in the total PV and that market-structural demand/supply imbalances may cause zero-PV floating-floating exchanges to trade at non-zero values.

4.3.1 Definition of a Fixed-for-Fixed Cross-Currency Swap

A UK-based company wants to issue new debt with a maturity of 5 years to finance an expansion of its American operations. The company is unknown in the US and there is not much demand currently for its debt in the US markets. The company is expecting the funds to repay the new debt issue to come from its North American operations.

Let us assume that the current exchange rate is \$1.50/£ and the company's credit rating is AA, i.e. the same as that reflected in swap rates. The company needs to raise \$150 million now. Table 4.10 shows the yield curves at the time of the issuance, i.e. the zero-coupon rates in the US and UK (as it is usually annual in the UK and semi-annual in the USA, we show both). It also shows calculated par coupon rates. The par coupon rates are the rates that fixed coupon bonds would have to offer to price to par.

If there is no strong demand for the company's US dollar bonds, the company might have to pay investors a rate higher than the fair 4.359746% semi. To address the lack of demand, the company can issue UK bonds and swap the cash flows into dollars. If the company issues a £100 million bond with a 4.780222% annual coupon, the bonds will sell at par. The annual coupon outlay will be £4.7802222 for the next 5 years. The principal due in 5 years will be £100 million.

The proceeds of £100 million from the sale of the bonds can be exchanged into \$150 million at today's exchange rate of \$1.50/£. The company can convert the sterling-denominated coupon

Table 4.10 The yield curve faced by the UK company at the time of bond issue

Time	Semi-annual UK	Semi-annual USA	Annual UK	Annual USA
	Zero-coupon rates			
6 months	3.000000	2.200000	3.022500	2.212100
1 year	3.200000	2.450000	3.225600	2.465006
18 months	3.400000	2.700000	3.428900	2.718225
2 years	3.600000	2.950000	3.632400	2.971756
30 months	3.800000	3.200000	3.836100	3.225600
3 years	4.000000	3.450000	4.040000	3.479756
42 months	4.200000	3.700000	4.244100	3.734225
4 years	4.400000	3.950000	4.448400	3.989006
54 months	4.600000	4.200000	4.652900	4.244100
5 years	4.800000	4.450000	4.857600	4.499506
	Par coupon rates			
5 years	4.722118	4.359746	4.780222	4.409975

and principal liability all into dollars. To that end, it enters into a £100 million (=$150 million) cross-currency swap (with a bank) to receive fixed pounds and pay fixed dollars. That is, it agrees to the schedule of cash flows in Table 4.11.

The swap receipts are identical to, and will offset, the coupon and principal payments owed on the bonds, leaving the company with zero net GBP cash flows. The USD payments are equivalent to the coupon and principal payments on a $150 million face value 4.409975% coupon bond.

Except for profit markup, the dealer will not charge (or pay) anything to enter into this swap, because the present value of the USD stream is equal to $150 million (fictitious par USD bond) and the present value of the GBP stream is equal to £100 million (fictitious par GBP bond), and the two present values are equal to each other at today's exchange rate of $1.50/£.

Figure 4.1 summarizes the net flow of cash on the bond and the swap.

The receipts from the swap counterparty are passed to the bond investors. What is left is the dollar obligation in the form of a dollar coupon stream and principal payment at the end. Note that the scheduled swap flows for year 5 include the principal repayment. The company's coupon cash flow is £4.78022 million on the receive side and $6.614962 million (4.409975%

Table 4.11 5-year fixed $-for-fixed £ cross-currency swap

Years	Receive in £	Pay in $
1	4.780222	6.614962
2	4.780222	6.614962
3	4.780222	6.614962
4	4.780222	6.614962
5	104.780222	156.614962

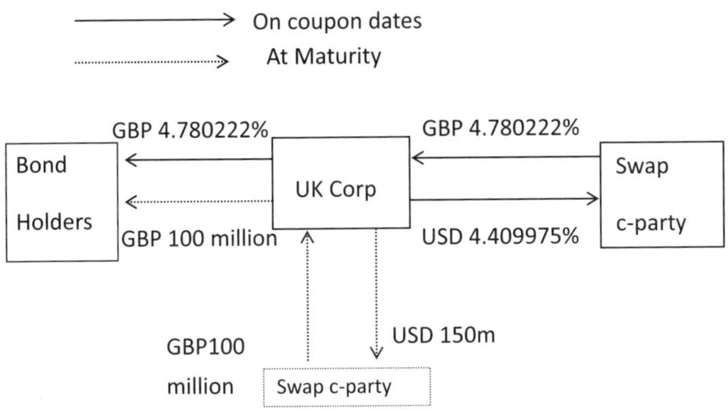

Figure 4.1 UK bond swapped into dollars

on \$150 million) on the pay side. The principal exchange is £100 million on the receive side for \$150 million on the pay side. In currency swaps, the principal exchange at the end of the swap is standard, unless specifically deleted in the swap agreement. (The exchange rate that equates the two at the outset most likely changes by the time of the exchange – the end of the swap.) In interest rate swaps, the principal exchange is defined in the same currency and, hence, not necessary.

The swap shown in Table 4.11 is non-standard. The pay side would probably pay semi-annually following the US corporate bond market conventions. For the swap to be par – i.e. with no compensating payment by either party – the swap's USD rate would be set to 4.359746% semi-annual, instead of 4.409975% annual (this is not exactly a simple EAR conversion). The company would have annual GBP cash flows on the receive side, passed on to its bondholders, and semi-annual USD cash flows on the pay side. The flows are illustrated in Table 4.12.

4.3.2 Valuation and Settlement of Cross-Currency Swaps

The hedging of cross-currency swaps is analogous to that of interest rate swaps, i.e. dynamic hedge computed by blipping the inputs to the yield curve bootstrap, except that the curve

Table 4.12 5-year fixed semi \$-for-fixed annual £ cross-currency swap

Time	Receive in £	Pay in \$
6 months		3.269809
1 year	4.780222	3.269809
18 months		3.269809
2 years	4.780222	3.269809
30 months		3.269809
3 years	4.780222	3.269809
42 months		3.269809
4 years	4.780222	3.269809
54 months		3.269809
5 years	104.780222	153.269809

blipping has to involve the yield curves in both currencies and the spot FX rate. In a fixed-fixed swap, the dealer has exposure to points on the two curves and to the currency exchange rate through the coupon exchanges and the principal exchange. The final hedge consists of Eurocurrency futures positions as in Table 4.9, but in dollar and pounds, and a spot FX position. Rather than repeating the blipping argument, let us illustrate here what happens when the swaps are off-market or are unwound.

The prior example assumed no compensatory cash flows up front. The bond issue and the swap occurred at the same time and the rates on the swap were set to the current market rates. This need not be the case. Bond issuers can come to the swap market not just at issuance, but any time they want to alter the structure of their liabilities – fixed into floating, floating into fixed, one currency for another – because their internal cash flow needs have changed or they want to speculate on the direction of currency and interest rates.

Suppose our UK company with American operations issues a 5-year £100 million 4.780222% fixed rate GBP bond. The company converts the £100 million proceeds into $150 million to invest in the project, but, expecting the widening of the interest rate differential between the UK and the USA, it leaves the bond issue unswapped. Suppose 1 year later, the FX rate is still $1.5/£ but interest rates in the UK have risen by 50 bp while interest rates in the USA have stayed the same, as in Table 4.13.

To take advantage of the interest rate differential, the company enters into a 4-year GBP/USD fixed-fixed swap. The principal is £100 million on the receive side and $150 million on the pay side. The current 4-year rate is 4.910531%, but the company asks the dealing bank to match the bond coupon rate of 4.780222% which is now *off-market*. Since the company is accepting a rate lower than the fair market rate, it will have two choices (the dealer should be indifferent). One is to pay the current on-market USD rate on the pay side of the swap, and receive a one-time payment from the dealer for the present value differential. The calculation of the upfront payment is shown in Table 4.14 and is done two ways, as the PV of the payment shortfalls (summed up) or as the shortfall PV of the 4.78022% bond which now prices to 99.532839.

Table 4.13 The yield curve faced by the UK company 1 year after the bond issue

	Semi-annual		Annual	
Time	UK	USA	UK	USA
	Zero-coupon rates			
6 months	3.500000	2.200000	3.530625	2.212100
1 year	3.700000	2.450000	3.734225	2.465006
18 months	3.900000	2.700000	3.938025	2.718225
2 years	4.100000	2.950000	4.142025	2.971756
30 months	4.300000	3.200000	4.346225	3.225600
3 years	4.500000	3.450000	4.550625	3.479756
42 months	4.700000	3.700000	4.755225	3.734225
4 years	4.900000	3.950000	4.960025	3.989006
54 months	5.100000	4.200000	5.165025	4.244100
5 years	5.300000	4.450000	5.370225	4.499506
	Par coupon rates			
4 years	4.849306	3.898814	4.910531	3.939253

Table 4.14 Upfront payment on a 4-year off-market swap

Years	Pmt diff	PV	Coupon	PV
1	0.130309	0.125618	4.780222	4.608143
2	0.130309	0.120150	4.780222	4.407538
3	0.130309	0.114024	4.780222	4.182810
4	0.130309	0.107369	104.780222	86.334348
	Sum of PVs =	**£0.467161**	**= 100 –**	**99.532839**

The second choice is to receive no payment today, but to pay a lower USD rate on the swap. We solve for the fixed USD rate which makes the PV of all the payments \$700,742 or £467,161 lower than par; the fictitious dollar bond prices to \$149.299258 million. Table 4.15 verifies that the rate 3.812193% on \$150 million produces the desired PV.

Note that the coupon rate 3.812193% is lower than the par rate of 3.939253% by 0.127060%, which is ***not*** equal to the 0.130309% UK rate differential.

4.3.3 Cross-Currency Swaps as Packages of Off-Market FX Forwards

Instead of dissecting the cross-currency swap "vertically" and viewing it as an exchange of two fixed coupon bonds in two different currencies, let us dissect it "horizontally," one cash flow exchange at a time to view it as a string of FX forwards. Let us examine the original currency swap in Table 4.11 entered into by our UK-based company with American operations, and compute the forward exchange rates locked in for each cash flow exchange. These are simply the coupon ratios for the coupon flows and the original spot \$1.50/£ rate for the final principal exchange. We separate the last exchange into the coupon and principal components.

The FX rates in the last column of Table 4.16 are not real forward rates quoted by anyone. In fact, the real forwards can be arrived at by plugging the spot rate and the zero-coupon curves shown Table 4.10 into the covered interest rate parity. Given the true FX forward quotes, we calculate in Table 4.17 the GBP equivalent of the USD payments that can be locked in today, the net GBP flow for each future date, and the mark-to-market on each forward cash flow exchange locked in the swap (net flow discounted to today). The MTM is the amount the company would have to pay (receive) up front if it were to enter into each GBP-for-USD cash flow exchange separately in the FX forward market.

The sum of all the MTMs is equal to zero. The 5-year swap can be viewed as a package of 6 forwards to sell USD forward for GBP with the amounts set by the swap cash flow schedule

Table 4.15 Pay off-market 3.812193% on a 4-year swap

Years	Coupon pmt	PV
1	5.718289	5.580724
2	5.718289	5.392993
3	5.718289	5.160597
4	155.718289	133.164944
	Sum of PVs =	**\$149.299258**

Table 4.16 5-year fixed-$-for-fixed-£ cross-currency swap

Years	Receive in £	Pay in $	FX Fwd $/£
1	4.780222	6.614962	1.383819
2	4.780222	6.614962	1.383819
3	4.780222	6.614962	1.383819
4	4.780222	6.614962	1.383819
5	4.780222	6.614962	1.383819
5	100.000000	150.000000	1.500000

and shown in Table 4.17. Each forward is off-market, i.e. it has a non-zero PV. The first five have a positive PV to the company: the GBP inflow exceeds the GBP equivalent of the USD outflow. A dealer taking the other side would have to be compensated up front with the MTM amount. For example, for year 1 the company is to receive £4.780222 million and pay $6.614962 million at today's forward FX rate equivalent to £4.442710 million, which is a net positive flow of £0.337512 million. The company would then have to compensate the dealer by paying the present value of that amount, or £0.326966 million. The same logic applies to the rest of the flows. The last cash flow exchange is a large negative PV contract – the company is to receive £100 million and pay the equivalent of £101.725158 million. To accept that, the company would have to receive up front £1.360910 million. Each cash flow exchange is an off-market FX forward with a non-zero PV. If the swap market did not exist, each could be separately arranged in the forward FX market. Yet, if the CIRP holds in FX markets, then, in today's pounds, the MTM settlements of all six off-market FX forwards sum to zero.

4.3.4 Multicurrency and Combination Cross-Currency Swaps

Depending on its needs, the UK company need not limit itself to a fixed-fixed dollar-for-sterling swap. Suppose 1 year after issuing the 5-year sterling bond, it finds itself in the situation described by Tables 4.13 to 4.15. Since the sterling rates have risen, and to offset the cash flows on the remaining 4 years of bond coupon interest, the company is in the fortunate situation of being able to be paid £467,161 for entering into an off-market receive-GBP 4.780222% 4-year swap in Table 4.15, or be paid £0 but lock in the pay-USD coupon to a low rate of 3.812193% in Table 4.15. If the company's view is that a further rate widening

Table 4.17 MTM on 5-year fixed-$-for-fixed-£ cross-currency swap

Years	Receive in £	Pay in $	FX fwd $/£	£ Equiv of $ flow	Net £ flow	MTM
1	4.780222	6.614962	1.488948	4.442710	0.337512	0.326965523
2	4.780222	6.614962	1.480936	4.466743	0.313479	0.291888597
3	4.780222	6.614962	1.475898	4.481991	0.298231	0.264820891
4	4.780222	6.614962	1.473784	4.488421	0.291801	0.245177133
5	4.780222	6.614962	1.474561	4.486054	0.294168	0.232057754
5	100.0000	150.0000	1.474561	101.725158	−1.725158	−1.360909897
				Sum of MTMs		0.000000000

between dollars and pounds is unlikely, then the company can overlay an interest rate swap on the currency swap in order to change its liability into floating USD. A receive-fixed 4-year USD fixed-for-floating interest rate swap would leave it with a floating dollar liability for the remainder of the term, or until it decided to swap again. If the company decides to take £467,161 out of the currency swap, then it can enter into an interest rate swap to receive a par rate of 3.939253% in USD and to pay LIBOR *flat*. If it did not take any money out and locked in an off-market 3.812193% in USD on the fixed-fixed currency swap, then it could enter into a USD interest rate swap to receive 3.812193% and pay LIBOR minus a large spread whose present value in today's terms is equal to $700,742. The same dealer should be able to offer a combined package of the two swaps in one *GBP fixed-USD floating currency swap*.

A fixed-floating currency swap is a combination of a fixed-fixed currency swap and an interest rate swap in one of the currencies. In practice, the cross-currency swap market convention is to treat as the principal building block a floating-floating currency swap and layer on it interest rate swaps. If we layer on one interest rate swap then one side gets converted to fixed, producing a fixed-floating currency swap; if we layer two interest rate swaps, then both sides get converted to fixed, producing a fixed-fixed currency swap. The reason for this convention is that demand and supply conditions in currency markets (typically at any given time, many corporate customers want to go the same way on the swaps, e.g. receive pounds and pay dollars) result in an unusual situation of zero PV floating-floating structures trading at non-zero PVs. A LIBOR flat-for-LIBOR flat swap in two currencies with a principal exchange at the end at the current spot FX rate should have no value. Both legs of the swap are floating rate bonds that price to par. Yet if everyone borrows in yen, but would like to pay interest in dollars, then everyone will be willing to pay a few extra basis points in dollars. Think of Japanese corporate customers with easy access to yen credit, but operations in dollars. In that case, JPY/USD cross-currency swaps will trade at yen LIBOR flat against dollar LIBOR plus spread, and that spread will vary by term. While it is easy to come up with a stylized reason for this wedge into the straight no-arbitrage present valuation, the exact reasons are not easy to explain and may involve demand and supply, transaction costs, credit differential and an imbalance in dealer and corporate customer flows. The cross-currency swap spread, although for most currency pairs is quite small, changes over time and is an additional unhedgeable source of risk for dealers.

Cross-currency swaps may involve interest and principal flows in more than two currencies. The most common *multicurrency swap* has coupon exchanges in one pair (e.g. pounds for dollars) and the final principal exchange calling for a third currency (e.g. pounds for euros). This does not engender any difficulties in pricing or hedge computation. If the principal exchange is at the current spot rate, then the swap still prices to zero; if not, it calls for an MTM settlement up front. However, the actual hedging of a long-term multicurrency swap may be more complicated. If the term of the swap is much longer than the available futures in one of the currencies, then the CIRP is unlikely to hold without a bid/ask spread. The swap's hedge has to be accomplished with coupon bonds, and the final principal exchange has to be hedged separately, perhaps with a large currency position (the principal exchange is much larger than any coupon exchange), a forward or spot plus interest rate hedges. Over time, the hedge may result in large unrealized offsetting gains and losses in multiple currencies. While theoretically this is easy to compute, practically it may result in large unwanted exposures.

There are several other variants of cross-currency swaps commonly encountered in practice. The main one is a plain vanilla two-currency swap, floating-for-floating or fixed-for-floating, but with no principal exchange at the end. Theoretically, this is easy to handle and at time zero it results in a zero PV. Practically, it involves a large FX risk at the final date of the swap. This is easy to see when considering the view of the swap as an exchange of two floating rate bonds. In static replication, the dealer would simply buy one bond and short the other to offset the flows on the swap. However, since the principal exchange is missing from the non-vanilla swap, the principal exchange on hedging bonds in this static strategy has to be undone statically through a large FX forward or a position in zero-coupon bonds. Over the life of the swap, that position may result in very large settlement balances expending dealer capital. The principal exchange in a plain vanilla cross-currency swap plays an important role in simplifying the hedge.

Coupon accrual features of swaps can cause hedging difficulties similar to the lack of principal exchange. If one side of the swap accrues but does not settle interest periodically, then large MTM balances can accumulate. This is risky even in a one-currency interest rate swap, but even more so in a cross-currency swap. A currency cocktail swap, where one side of the swap receives a single currency but the other pays multiple currencies, may exhibit hedging risks similar to accrual and no-principal swaps. The cocktail feature itself is not a source of risk. The pay side is simply dynamically hedged with strips of interest rate futures broken into component currencies. A principal exchange into the same cocktail of currencies avoids hedging pitfalls, since static replication can proceed by splitting one side into a basket of coupon bonds. If, however, the principal exchange is into just one currency, then there is a mismatch between the cocktail of coupons and the single currency of the principal.

The overall lesson of cross-currency swaps, and swaps in general, is that the more the swap looks like an exchange of two standard bonds the easier it is to hedge. As soon as there is some principal and coupon mismatch – be it in the form of a missing principal or a principal in a different currency, or a non-standard coupon – the hedging becomes more difficult. It either involves more components with offsetting but large balances, or moves away from perfect static replication to duration matching to a combination of bonds.

4.4 EQUITY, COMMODITY, AND EXOTIC SWAPS

A swap can serve the role of a flexible investment vehicle. An investment normally involves an outright purchase of a return stream earned on a risk exposure. A swap is an exchange of two streams of return flows with no outright purchase. Yet a swap structured with the receive side as the return on a risky asset and the pay side of floating LIBOR, combined with an investment in a money market account, will be equivalent to the investment in the risky asset. The floating LIBOR payments on the swap will be made with the interest earned in the money market account. The net will be the return on the risky asset. An investor can spend \$100 to buy a stock or a commodity, or he can put \$100 in a money market account and swap the LIBOR interest from the account into a return on a stock or a commodity. In general, the receive side of the swap can be structured to provide the return on any asset class combination normally not easily available to the investor, and with any degree of leverage desired.

4.4.1 Equity Swaps

Investors often desire equity exposure in a bond form. Some institutional investors are prevented by regulation from holding too much equity; others seek to obtain a merger of equity exposure with principal protection. These goals can be accomplished through structured bonds which combine equity swaps and equity options.

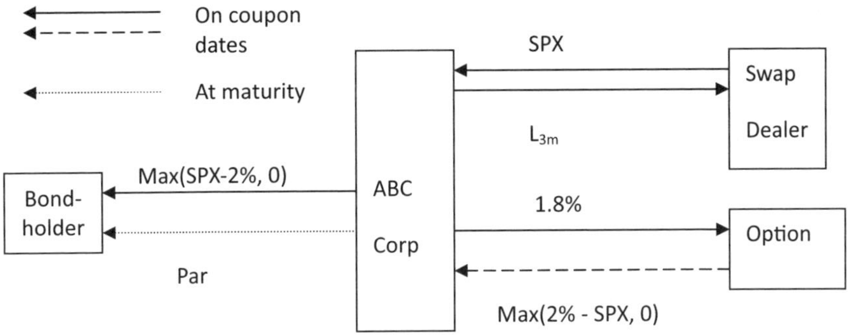

Figure 4.2 An equity swap as part of an equity-linked bond issue

A common structure defines the formula for the coupon payout as the appreciation of the stock index over the accrual period times the principal of the bond times the appropriate day-count fraction. The bondholder gets no interest unless the stock index appreciates during the coupon accrual period. The issuer of the bond (ABC Corp) desires low cost of financing that has nothing to do with equities. The dealer supplies the cash flows owed on the bond by entering into an equity swap with the issuer. The dealer pays the stock index appreciation and receives a floating interest rate. The stock return is passed on to the bondholders. The structure innately includes an at-the-money equity option as the coupon paid to the bondholder cannot be negative.

Another common equity bond structure defines the formula for the coupon payout as a small fixed coupon, paid irrespective of the index performance, plus a portion of the appreciation of the stock index over the accrual period, times the principal of the bond times the appropriate day-count fraction. Here the bondholder gets a non-zero fixed rate supplemented either by a predefined less-than-100% portion of the index appreciation, or as an excess appreciation over a certain margin (negative spread), or a combination of the two. The structure innately includes an out-of-the-money equity option as the coupon paid to the bondholder cannot be negative.

Figure 4.2 shows a diagram for an S&P 500 index-based annual coupon with no minimum fixed coupon guarantee. The investor gets 100% appreciation of the S&P 500 in excess of 2% over each annual interest period. The bond can be constructed with 2% out-of-the-money call options on S&P 500, or with equity swaps combined with 2% strike put options.[1] Assuming that the (European) 2% in-the-money put on the S&P 500 costs is 1.8% of the invested amount per year, the issuing company enters into an equity swap, paying quarterly LIBOR in exchange for S&P 500 return, and commits to buying a series of 2%-strike put options for 1.8% of the principal. In Figure 4.2, SPX stands for the percentage change in the S&P 500 during the coupon year.

Let us trace the cash flows in three scenarios. First, if SPX > 2%, e.g. SPX = 14%, the investor is entitled to the coupon equal to the excess of SPX over 2%, or 12%. The issuing company, ABC, receives 14% on the swap, pays P=1.8% for the put, but receives no payout from the put. ABC pays 12% to the bondholder and keeps 0.20%, which reduces its floating financing cost. Second, if SPX < 2%, e.g. SPX = 0.5%, the investor gets no coupon interest.

[1] This is an application of the put–call parity covered in the next chapter.

ABC receives 0.5% on the swap, pays 1.8% for the put and receives 1.5% payout from the put. ABC pays nothing to the bondholder and keeps 0.20%, which reduces its financing cost. Lastly, if SPX turns out to be negative for the year, e.g. –8%, the bondholder gets no coupon. ABC pays 8% on the swap, pays 1.8% for the put, but receives a 10% payout from the put. ABC pays nothing to the bondholder and ABC keeps 0.20% as the reduction in its financing cost. Irrespective of the S&P 500 performance, ABC financing cost turns out to be LIBOR – 20 bp.

The assumed cost 1.8% of the put in Figure 4.2 is quite low. If the 2% S&P puts cost more than the 1.8% assumed in the figure, then the issuer can raise the coupon payout threshold or reduce the coupon participation below 100%, or both.

The pricing of equity swaps is relatively easy. An equity swap can be viewed as an exchange of a fictitious floating rate bond for a fictitious par investment in the equities. The floating rate bond prices to par as long as it is equivalent to a rollover strategy. That is the case as long as LIBOR is set at the start and paid fully at the end of each interest accrual period. This forces the value of the bond to revert to par after each interest payment. Similarly, the fictitious equity investment requires that all of the equity appreciation be paid out at the end of each accrual period to force the remaining value of the equity investment to revert to the original par amount. So, while both sides of the equity swap are floating and unknown in advance, both require the same amount of investment dollars to replicate. The swap of the total return of S&P 500 for LIBOR is fair, i.e. it has a zero PV.

The dual valuation argument for the equity swap as a string of forward contracts on S&P 500 also holds directly from the cash-and-carry relationship for stock index futures. The equity swap can be viewed as a string of 1-year synthetic forward (or futures) contracts. In our case, abstracting from the quarterly/annual mismatch on the LIBOR side, the dealer views the swap's cash flows – pay SPX, receive LIBOR – as equivalent to a string of short index forwards or reverse cash-and-carry transactions. In the reverse cash-and-carry, the dealer borrows a basket of stocks, sells the stocks short, and invests the proceeds to earn LIBOR. At the end of the year, he covers the short by buying the basket in the spot market. The initial sale and subsequent repurchase of stocks are equivalent to paying out the appreciation on the basket. The interest on short sale proceeds is equivalent to receiving floating LIBOR. In order to hedge the string of short forwards packaged into the swap, the dealer has to hedge by doing the opposite. That is, he has to receive the SPX appreciation and pay LIBOR. He does that by entering each year into a 1-year cash-and-carry. He borrows the principal to pay LIBOR. He buys the stocks at the beginning of each year and liquidates them on each coupon payout date. The profits on stocks are passed to ABC to satisfy the swap obligation. The LIBOR receipt from ABC covers the borrowing cost. Each year the dealer repeats the exercise for the following year. (In reality, on the coupon pay date, the dealer liquidates only the appreciated part of the holdings, pays the proceeds to ABC, and holds the rest for the following year.)

4.4.2 Commodity Swaps

There are parallels of equity swaps that involve other asset classes. The canonical form has on one side of the swap a floating interest rate stream; the other side of the swap being a periodically paid out return stream on an asset class tailored to the needs of an investor. A common example is a commodity swap whose coupon payout is a formula based on a percentage change in the price of a commodity over the interest accrual period. Coupon

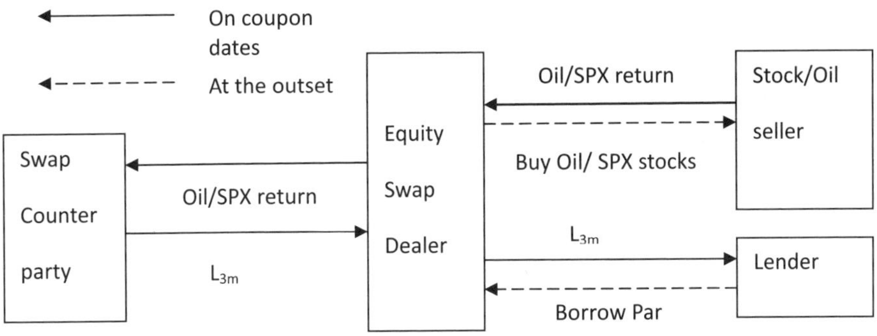

Figure 4.3 An equity/commodity swap: cash-supported

structures sold in the past have involved oil, gold, and a variety of financial assets (e.g. weather-related formulas, total-rate-of-return on a bond index).

Similar to an equity swap, a commodity swap can be engineered in two ways. First, the commodity swap can be an exchange of a fictitious floating rate bond for a par investment in commodities. The LIBOR coupon on the floating side is paid out every 3 or 6 months and the value of the floating rate bond reverts to par. The gain (loss) on the commodity over the coupon period is liquidated and paid out (received and reinvested), and the total investment in the commodity reverts to the swap par amount. Figure 4.3 shows a cash-supported oil/equity return swap. The second way of constructing the commodity side of the swap is to use the par amount to invest in a floating rate bond and enter into futures contracts (rather than spot) over the life of the swap. Using the cost-of-carry relationship, the change in the value of the futures each period plus the interest on the floating side is equivalent to the spot change in the commodity value.

The special issues of commodity swaps involve the return settlement. The cash-and-carry equations hold for swaps, but are not guaranteed to hold for commodities such as oil, and can result in a contango (see Chapter 3). The cash-supported commodity swap and the futures-supported commodity swap will not produce the same returns. This phenomenon also affects retail commodity ETNs (see Chapters 8 and 11).

4.4.3 Volatility Swaps

Increasingly, dealers push the envelope of innovation by looking to secondary and unhedgeable variables on which to write swaps. One such variable is the historical volatility of an FX rate, the interest rate, or the volatility of a price or stock index. Another is the inflation rate in an economy. The volatility index and inflation futures markets are very limited; one side of the swap cannot be easily synthetically replicated or dynamically hedged, except perhaps with the near-month S&P 500 or Oil VIX contracts. The VIX futures are based on the option-implied volatilities not historicals. If the swap is on the historical volatility or on the volatility of an asset not covered by futures, the risk management has to rely on book-matching or be part of the overall hedge for an options book. If both sides of the trade can be found, and the dealer can find two counterparties willing to take the opposite sides of swap, then the dealer can extract the bid/ask spread. If the offset cannot be found, then the only reason the dealer should enter into the volatility swap is to lay off the residual vega risk of his option portfolio (see Chapter 5).

Instead of using the realized volatility that is common in hedging FX options portfolio, the single stock and equity index options dealers prefer a variance swap to a volatility swap. The variance swap has a fixed and a floating leg applied to a fixed dollar notional principal $N_{V^2} = \$20$ million, and it is settled periodically. The fixed leg is defined as the "strike" variance level, say $K = 0.0144$, equal to 12% squared. The floating leg is defined as the annualized historical (realized) volatility of the returns on the stock index. If we settle the swap quarterly and there are 92 days in the current quarter and also assume that there are 252 (non-holiday) business days in a year, then the typical definition of the realized variance V^2 would be:

$$V^2 = \frac{252}{91} \times \sum_{n=1}^{92} \left[\ln\left(\frac{S_n}{S_{n-1}}\right) - \mu \right]$$

where S_n is the value of the index on day n and μ is the mean of the log-returns. In FX markets, the mean may be skipped, and in all markets the divisor could be 92 instead of 91. The variance is then applied to the notional principal N_{V^2} and settled against the fixed leg without any day-count adjustment. If the realized variance is equal to 15% squared or $V^2 = 0.0225$, then the cash flow exchange would pay (fixed) \$144,000 and receive (floating) \$225,000.

An options dealer long vega is a natural floating payer on the variance swap. Vega is commonly computed in dollars per 1% standard deviation change. Suppose the dealer computes his vega to be \$300,000 at the current level of volatility equal to $V_0 = 12\%$. Since the first-derivative of variance V^2 with respect to volatility V is $2V$, the first-order point conversion of vega to the variance swap principal is the division by $2 \times V_0 = 0.24$, scaled by 100. If we choose $N_{V^2} = \$125$ million as the principal, and the volatility goes up from 12% to 13%, the net payment on the variance swap will be:

$$\$125{,}000{,}000 \times \left(0.13^2 - 0.12^2\right) = \$312{,}500$$

The primary risk here is not the slight mishedge due to the second-order derivative, but the basis risk between the implied volatility driving the option portfolio vega and the realized volatility driving the variance swap hedge.

4.4.4 Index Principal Swaps

An old structure, popularized in the early 1990s – which was attractive to mortgage bond investors who wanted the enhanced yield of a prepayment-exposed investment, but wanted to limit the unpredictability of prepayments – is called an index principal swap (IPS) or index amortizing rate (IAR) swap. As is often the case, this structure is driven by this specific investor demand, while the issuer simply wants reduced floating financing. The issuer issues a bond with a formula coupon and principal to the bondholders, but reverses the cash flows of the bond by entering into an IPS with a dealer.

The swap is a fixed for floating swap, except that the notional principal of the swap changes over time. Each period one looks at the principal as of the last period times an interpolated percentage taken from an amortization table, which might look like this:

Rate	Percent notional amortized
3.00%	0%
2.00%	50%
1.00%	100%

Suppose the last period's principal was 100 and the index rate L_{3m} this period is 1.14%. We interpolate 1.14 between 1.00 and 2.00 in the table to obtain a notional percentage equal to 93%. This period, the new notional principal used to compute interest flows on both sides of the swap, is equal to the last principal times 100 minus the amortized percentage of 93, or 0.07. The new principal is thus 7.

This procedure is intended to mimic the prepayment behavior of fixed rate mortgages. As rates go down and homeowners refinance their mortgages, the principals of mortgage bonds are reduced. Similarly, the principals of IPS bonds are reduced, but based on a prespecified amortization table rather than on the actual behavior of homeowners who often do not refinance optimally.

5

Options on Prices and Hedge-Based Valuation

Options are finite-term bets on the level of prices, rates and non-financial variables. The payouts on the options are contingent upon the price/rate of an "underlying asset" being at the right level at the designated time. Option buyers have the right to receive a payout defined by a formula tied to the level of the price or rate prior to and/or at the expiry of the option if they bet right and the option is in "in-the-money," or nothing if they bet wrong and the option is "out-of-the-money." For that right they make an upfront payment called the premium. Option sellers receive the premium for the option and are obligated to make the payout on the option if the bet is in-the-money. Generally, bets on the upward movement of prices/rates are called "calls" and bets on downward movement are called "puts."

There are two types of participants in the options markets. The speculators, also called investors, spend (receive) money to buy (sell) options and wait for the desired outcome at maturity (a price rise, a rate drop). When their bets prove right, they get a payout or keep the premium; when their bets prove wrong, they get nothing or have to make a payout themselves. The hedgers – dealers and market-makers – do not take outright bets on the direction of underlying securities, but make their money from the flow of buying and selling. Often, however, they encounter imbalances in the demand for buying and selling, and when that happens they put the options on their own books – but instead of speculating, they hedge. The "delta hedging" they engage in is akin to manufacturing (synthetically replicating) the payouts of the options they bought (or sold). Their risk is not that their bets prove wrong, but only that they over- or underestimate the cost of the manufacture of the payoffs on the bets they bought at the bid or sold at the ask, the bid–ask spread being a small margin of safety relative to the cost. If they estimate the cost correctly, they always earn a profit whether prices go up or down. Dynamic delta hedging is the main principle of option valuation.

This chapter covers the basic payoff definitions of options, the main static no-arbitrage condition called the put–call parity, and the delta-hedging technique as the tool behind not only sound option trading but also all option valuation. The value of the option is the unique amount of money one needs to synthetically replicate the payoff of the option in all price scenarios, irrespective of whether the option will pay or not. The binomial model, or the Black–Scholes formula and its extensions, are the mathematical representation of the delta hedge concept.

The chapter has two central ideas. The first is that there is a big difference between options markets and insurance markets. While the options markets borrow the language and structure of insurance – premium, even-driven payout, payout dependent on the severity of the event – options dealers have one tool in their risk management tool-kit that insurance companies (and sports bookmakers) do not. They buy and sell bets whose payoffs depend on the prices or rates of instruments that themselves can be bought and sold continuously. Insurance companies and bookmakers sell their bets on the outcomes of future events (earthquake, flood, fire, soccer game). As they cannot "buy" these events, to manage the risk they adjust the odds or premiums to reflect the demand and supply of bets. In contrast, a dealer who has sold a call option on a stock can buy the stock; if the stock goes up, he can use the profit from the stock's rise to cover his liability on the option. His job is harder than that of a cash-and-carry hedger of a forward/futures contract who buys the asset and fixes financing once. The option dealer's hedge is dynamic. Every day, as the stock rises, he buys more of it; when it falls he sells some of it, expecting a lower liability. This manufacturing of the payoff liability, known as *delta hedging*, works for almost all options: calls and puts, bought and sold, linear and binary payouts, options on stocks, currencies, and interest rates. The main factor in the cost of this manufacture is the volatility of the underlying asset's price/rate. The more it moves up and down, the more it costs the dealer to adjust the hedge prior to the expiry time. The bottom line is: the dealer does not have to speculate on the direction of the price/rate, but can earn profit for the service of manufacturing the bet's payoff.

The second idea of the chapter is the contrast between speculators and delta hedgers. In order to eliminate risk, the dealer resells his option position to someone else or, for as long as necessary, delta hedges, actively trading the underlying asset and accumulating gains/losses. By the resale time or expiry date, these gains/losses are exactly equal to what he needs to liquidate the position. The speculator does not eliminate but seeks risk. Like the homeowner buying insurance in order to "profit" from a house fire, the speculator buys a directional bet and waits for the outcome to materialize. If he is right, he gets a payout formula that depends on the outcome, e.g. the excess of the stock price over some level in a call option.

These two central ideas conspire to the fact that option pricing is driven not by participants' subjective probabilities of the outcomes (expectations of the stocks going up or down), but by the dealers' estimated costs of payoff manufacture. That cost fluctuates with the perceived volatility of the underlying asset, called the *implied volatility*; sometimes bets seem cheap, sometimes dear, relative to the future payoff.

Options are *redundant* securities. Their payoffs can be manufactured through dynamic replicating strategies. The profit the dealer earns can be thought of as the fee for the convenience of preparing the payoff, so that the speculator does not have to manufacture it himself. This is like the markup for the off-the-rack clothes that you do not have to tailor yourself. Redundant does not mean useless. Options allow complicated *risk-sharing* schemes for investors. Since the primary function of securities markets is to channel savings into investment, the savers-investors (banks and funds on their behalf) must be offered liquid means of earning return for taking on various risks. Stock and credit markets offer broad access to equity and default risks, and options further that access. Through them, stock and bond investors are able to sell part of their risk by entering limited-time bets to forgo the upside or to protect the value of their investments. An analogy is the decision to buy a house for $1 million dollars. Without the ability to buy fire and flood insurance, or to borrow money against the house in case of need, surely fewer investors would buy.

5.1 CALL AND PUT PAYOFFS AT EXPIRY

Tickets sold by national lotteries around the world are bets on sets of numbers. The payoff is a fixed monetary amount if the ticket buyer guesses the right combination. Such bets are called *binary* or *digital*. It does not matter how "close" he is to the right combination, all that matters is whether he is right or wrong in guessing five or six numbers.

Most options sold in financial markets work a little differently. There is also the right and the wrong guess, but, the person who bets is right, the "more right" he is the more he gets.

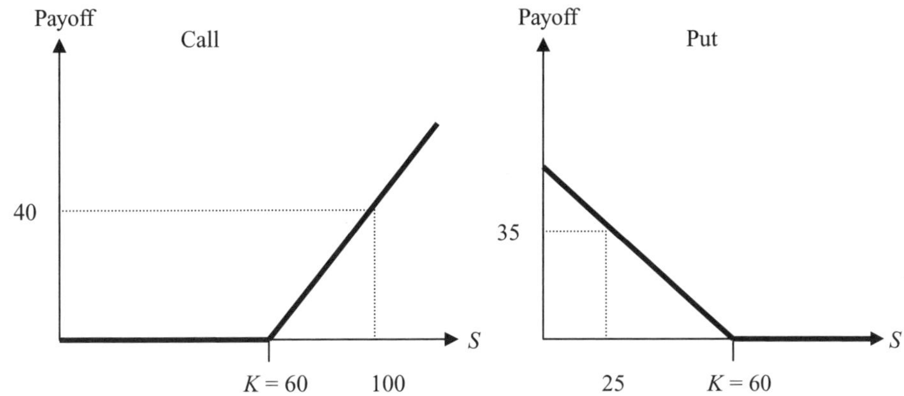

Figure 5.1 Payoff on a call and a put at expiry. K = Strike price; S = Spot price at expiry

A *call* option on a price of an asset (e.g. stock) pays on the *expiry date* the greater of zero and the difference between the asset's price and a prespecified *strike price* (bet level). If we think that the price of ABC will go over \$60 per share, we buy a call *struck* at 60. If the price on the expiry date is 67, we get \$7; if the price is 74, we get \$14. If the price ends up below 60, whether at 40 or 50, we get nothing. A *put* option on a price of an asset pays on the expiry date the greater of zero and the difference between a prespecified strike price and that asset's price. If we want to bet that the price of ABC will go under \$60 per share, we buy a put struck at 60. If the price on the expiry date is 47, we get \$13; if the price is 54, we get \$6. If the price is above 60, whether at 65 or 80, we get nothing. We graph the payoff that the buyer of the option (bet) gets as a function of the *underlying asset*'s price in the following *payoff diagrams* in Figure 5.1.

Options that pay only at expiry are called *European*. Those that pay prior to *and* on the expiry date are called *American*. Neither notion has any connection to a location.

At any given time, there may be options trading on the same underlying asset price (event), but with different strikes and expiry dates. On the exchanges, options follow a certain schedule of dates and strikes. Over the counter, they can be arranged for any payoff date and strike (bet level). The *intrinsic value* of an option is defined as the payoff the option would have if it were immediately exercisable at today's price of the underlying asset. Options with a positive intrinsic value are called *in-the-money*; options with no intrinsic value are called *out-of-the-money*; options whose strike price is equal to the asset price are called *at-the-money*. Note that options cannot have a negative intrinsic value. If the better is wrong he simply does not exercise his option and gets no payoff.

Most individual stock options and many others have a *physical settlement* provision; that is they are not pure bets, but give the holders (option buyers) the right to buy (call) or sell (put) the asset to the *option writer* (option seller) at the strike price on (or prior to) the expiry date. This is tantamount to receiving the payoffs as described above. For example, a 60 call, when the price is 67, gives the holder the right to buy the stock from the writer for 60 (exercise price). Once bought, the holder can sell the stock immediately for 67 in the spot market (open market), realizing a profit of 7. A 60 put, when the price is 47, gives the holder the right to sell the stock to the writer for 60 (exercise price). To deliver, the holder can buy the stock immediately for 47 in the spot market (open market), realizing a profit of 13. Many options written on non-price financial variables (stock indices, interest rates, etc.) are settled in cash. The settlement of options is in general similar to that of futures, cash or physical. One always needs to check contract provisions for both, as they may not follow the same rules.

5.2 COMPOSITE PAYOFFS AT EXPIRY

Long and short positions in calls and puts can be combined to achieve narrowly tailored bets on the range of the asset prices in the future. It is important to realize that speculators can both buy and sell (write) options. They can combine long and short positions. Here are some examples.

5.2.1 Straddles and Strangles

Suppose we believe that, between now and the expiry date, the price of ABC, currently 60, is going to jump dramatically but we do not know which way. Suppose we buy a put struck at 55 and a call struck at 65. This is called a 55–65 *strangle*.

If, on the expiry date, the price is very low or very high, we get a payoff; but if the price stays between 55 and 65 we get nothing. If the price is 30 at expiry, we collect 25 on the 55 put and nothing on the 65 call. If the price is 80, we collect nothing on the 55 put and 15 on the 65 call. If the price is 62, we get nothing on both options.

Because we bought both options, we incurred an upfront cost of the bet. Our profit is therefore reduced by the total price of the options. An option price is called a *premium* (as with insurance).

Next, suppose that we believe that on the expiry date the price of ABC is going to stay around 62. To give ourselves some room for error, we sell a 60–65 strangle (60 put and 65 call) and receive premiums for both options. If we are right and the price does not go below 60 or above 65, we keep the total premium and make no payoff. If we are wrong we have to make a payout on one of the options.

The payoffs on the long 55–65 strangle and short 60–65 strangle are shown in Figure 5.2.

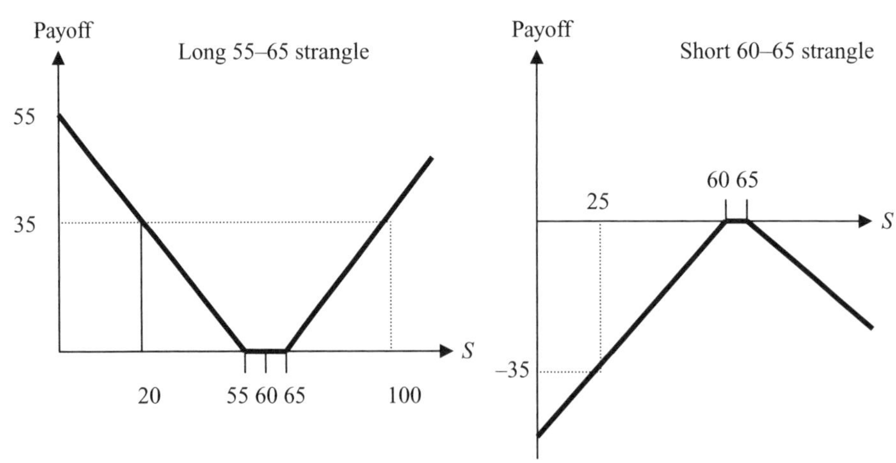

Figure 5.2 Strangle payoffs at expiry

A strangle where the call strike and the put strike are the same is called a *straddle*. Short straddles and strangles are bets that the price will not fluctuate much from some level. Long strangles and straddles are bets that the price will move away from the anticipated level.

While we are not betting on the direction of the stock price, but on whether the stock stays in or breaks out of a narrow range, straddles and strangles, as described here, are speculative bets. It is not the direction of the position, long or short, that distinguishes the speculator from the dealer, it is the actions after the bet is arranged and paid for. The speculator statically waits for the payout; the dealer manufactures his through dynamic trading.

5.2.2 Spreads and Combinations

Another set of popular speculative strategies includes call and put spreads. These combine long and short positions in options of the same type.

A long *call spread* consists of a long low strike call and a short high strike call. Suppose we believe that ABC's price will rise by expiry, but will not exceed 80. We can buy a 65 call and sell an 80 call. Any outcome between 65 and 80 will yield an increasing payoff, but we forgo any increase in payoff above 80. If the stock ends up at 76, we will collect 11 from the 65 call and we will pay nothing on the 80 call. If the stock ends up at 88, we will collect 23 from the 65 call, but we will pay 8 on the 80 call, leaving us with 15. The maximum payoff from the strategy is reached at 80. Below 65, both options are worthless.

A long *put spread* consists of a long high strike put and a short low strike put. Suppose we believe that ABC's price will drop by expiry, but not below 35. We can buy a 55 put and sell a 35 put. Any outcome between 35 and 55 will yield an increasing payoff, but we forgo any increase in payoff below 35. If the stock ends up at 46, we will collect 9 from the 55 put and pay nothing on the 35 put. If the stock ends up at 28, we will collect 27 from the 55 put, but will pay 7 on the 35 put, leaving us with 20, the maximum payoff from the strategy is reached at 35. Above 55 both options are worthless.

The payoffs on the long 65–80 call spread and long 55–35 put spread are shown in Figure 5.3.

We can package puts and calls into other combinations. If we sell a low strike put and buy a high strike call, we will have no payout over a wide intermediate range of prices (but perhaps

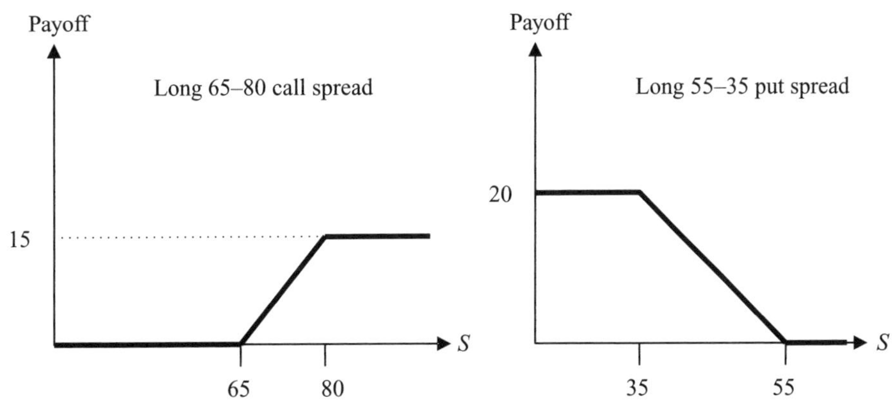

Figure 5.3 Spread payoffs at expiry

a net premium received); we will benefit on the upside, and pay out on the downside. This is called a *reverse collar*.

Options can also be combined to form *calendar spreads*. In this case, we buy an option with one expiry date and sell an option with the same (or different) strike, but with a different expiry date. For example, if we believe that ABC's price might first go up but then come down, we can buy a call with short maturity and sell one with a longer maturity. Or if we believe that neither option will ever pay, we may want to sell the more expensive (longer) one and buy the cheaper (shorter) one to pocket the difference.

Options can also be combined with long and short positions on the underlying asset and in leveraged proportions.

A *buy–write* is a strategy where we buy the stock and sell a high strike call. As the stock rises, we are exposed to the possibility that it will rise above the strike of the call. At that level, we will forgo any further appreciation in the stock as we will be forced to pay out on the call. If we believe that the stock will appreciate over time but not rapidly, we can opt to sell a string of calls with increasing strikes and maturities. We collect lots of premiums and hope that the options never pay off. This strategy is popular with asset managers (e.g. insurance companies) who naturally hold long portfolios of stocks and want to gain extra income for some extra risk. The strategy is called *covered call writing*.

In a leveraged buy–write, we buy the stock and sell two calls with the same strike and the same maturity. If the stock price rises above the bet level we may lose any of the prior appreciation we have gained.

The payoffs on a long 80-strike buy–write and a 2-to-1 leveraged version of that are shown in Figure 5.4.

We can also combine a put with a long stock position to obtain protection against the stock falling. The strategy works for holders of concentrated wealth (e.g. private stocks of wealthy families) who cannot or do not want to sell their holdings. If we are afraid that ABC's price may drop below 50, we can buy a 50 put to protect our long stock position. To reduce the cost of the protection we can sell a 40 put.

Options can help with investment timing decisions. Suppose we researched ABC's stock and consider it to be a solid long-term investment. Based on our analysis, we would like to buy

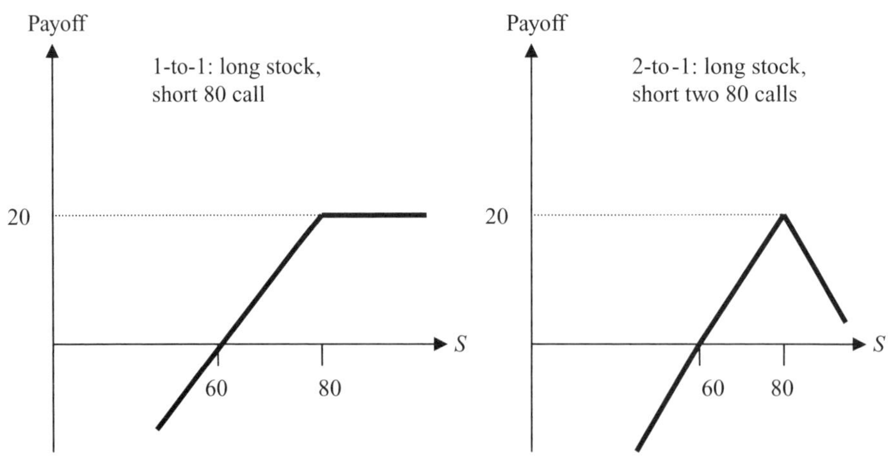

Figure 5.4 Buy–write payoffs at expiry (stock at 60)

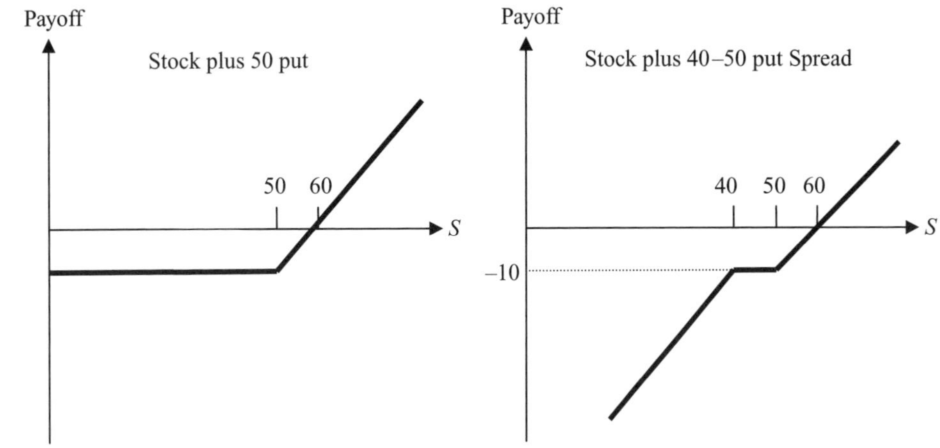

Figure 5.5 Payoffs on put-protected stock at expiry (stock at 60)

it at 56 or below, but the price has run up to 60. The stock is highly volatile in the short run. Suppose we sell (write) a 60 put for 5. If the stock continues to go up, at least we collected 5; we have to chase it up, but at least we enjoy a defrayment of cost. If the stock goes down to 57, we will be exercised against, having to pay 3. Our net profit is 2 and we can use it to buy the stock, effectively paying 55. If the stock goes down even further to 50, we pay out 10. This leaves us with a loss of 5, but we can buy the stock for 50, effectively paying 55.

The payoffs on a 50 put-protected stock and a long 40–50 put spread protected stock are shown in Figure 5.5.

Binary Options

Over the counter, one can purchase options with fixed monetary payoffs. Suppose we pay 3 to get 20 if ABC's stock goes to or above 70. Or, we pay 2 to get 20 if ABC's stock goes down to 50 but not below 40. The payoffs on these two options are shown in Figure 5.6. Binary options are more common with interest rates where a version of them is called a *range*.

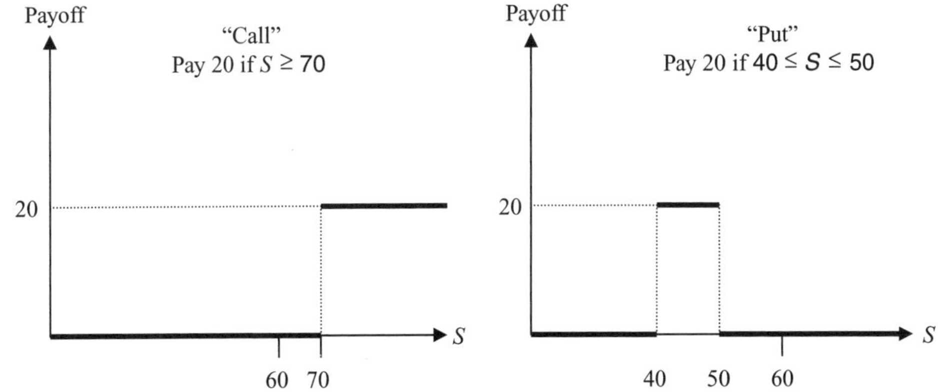

Figure 5.6 Payoffs on binary options at expiry (stock at 60)

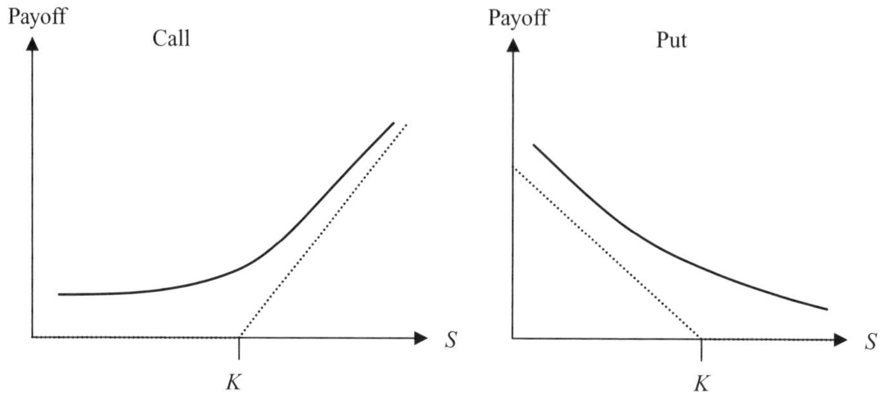

Figure 5.7 Value on a call and a put prior to expiry. K = Strike Price; S = Stop Price now

5.3 OPTION VALUES PRIOR TO EXPIRY

In all the above diagrams we showed the payoff of the options on the expiry date. Prior to expiry the option value will have to be higher than the present value of the payoff and, in most cases, even higher than the *intrinsic value* (equal to the payoff computed with today's stock price). For American options, which can be exercised immediately, this should be obvious. One can always exercise the option for its intrinsic value, so the premium cannot be lower than that. There is then the possibility of an even greater payoff. For European options, the argument is a little more subtle. For options on assets with no intermediate payouts (dividends, coupons), it can be shown that European calls should not be exercised early, and are thus equally as valuable as American calls.[1] It may be optimal to exercise American puts early and so the European options price can be lower than its American version.

In general, the value of the option prior to expiry can be represented as a line above the intrinsic value bound (Figure 5.7).

Option prices observe the following arbitrage rules.

A higher strike call will be always worth less than a lower strike call with the same expiry. If ABC's stock is at 60, then a 70 call will be worth more than an 80 call because the 70 call will always pay more than an 80 call. If the stock ends up at 75, the 70 call will pay 5 while the 80 call will pay nothing. The two will pay the same only if they both pay nothing. A lower strike put will be always worth less than a higher strike put with the same maturity. The reasoning is analogous to the call case.

An option with a longer maturity will always be worth at least as much as an otherwise identical option with a shorter maturity. If the options have the same strikes, then their intrinsic values will be the same, but the longer option will allow more time for the underlying asset to move to generate a higher payoff. The analogy is to the insurance policy comparison between short- and long-term coverage. Since long-term coverage allows for a greater possibility of a payoff, it will cost more. Insurance has asymmetric payoff. It pays nothing if the desired event does not take place, no matter how "close" to it we get; on the other side, the payoff depends on how deep into-the-money we get. With options, the longer time also offers the possibility of

[1] If the underlying stock pays no dividends, one would always prefer to sell the European call back rather than exercising it early, since the exercise confers no additional cash flow benefits.

getting deeper into the money. It is that one side of the probability distribution that determines the value of the policy.

We will discover more arbitrage rules later.

5.4 OPTIONS AND FORWARDS, RISK SHARING AND PUT–CALL PARITY

Suppose we buy a call and sell a put on the same asset. Suppose that we also search among all possible strike prices and find one strike price, K, such that the premium on the call struck at K that we buy is exactly paid for by the premium on the put struck at K that we sell. Let us examine the payoff of our strategy at expiry for physical-settle options.

If $S \geq K$, then the call option is in-the-money and we buy the stock for the amount K. If $S \leq K$, then the put option is in-the-money. We are exercised against, and we buy the stock for the amount K. By buying the call and selling the put, we are in effect agreeing to buy the stock for the amount K on the expiry date. In a cash settle case, this means that no matter whether the stock price is above or below the strike price, our payoff is $S - K$ on the expiry date.

Our strategy is equivalent to entering a long forward on the stock. Net, we pay nothing today, and on a future date we deliver the sum of money K for one share of the stock. The forward is on-market (zero PV up front).

If we were slightly less careful in our search for the perfect strike, and instead picked one at random, but made sure that the strike on the long call is the same as the strike on the short put, then we would have in effect entered into an off-market forward with the mark-to-market value (PV) equal to the difference between the premium on the call and that on the put:

$$Call - Put = Forward$$

One can think of the forward value of the stock as the median separating two possibility regions for the future stock price. The long call covers the part of the region to the right of the strike, i.e. with stock values greater than the strike. The short put covers that part of the region to the left of the strike, i.e. with stock values lower than the strike. Traders can synthesize forwards from options, or they can enter into forwards and synthesize options by selling off the undesirable probability regions. For example to synthesize a call, a dealer may enter into a forward and buy a put to offset the short put implicit in the forward. To synthesize a put, a dealer may enter into a short forward and buy a call to offset the short call implicit in the short forward.

The relationship of call and put prices to the value of the forward is known as *put–call parity*. It takes the following form for options on non-dividend-paying stocks:

Put–Call Parity

$$C - P = S - PV(K)$$

The left-hand side is the cost of the long call–short put strategy. C is the price of the call with strike K; P is the price of the put with strike K. The right-hand side is the mark-to-market (PV) of the forward contract. The forward contract to buy the stock for price K can be replicated by borrowing the present value of K and buying the stock now for the price S. If K is low, the contract to buy the stock for K at a forward date is valuable and $S - PV(K) > 0$. This also means that calls cost more than puts for low strikes. If K is high, the contract to buy the stock for K at a forward date is not desirable and $S - PV(K) < 0$. This also means that calls cost less than puts for high strikes.

There is a strike at which the prices of calls and puts must be the same, and that strike is given by the equation

$$S = PV(K)$$

This is the cost-of-carry equation in disguise. If we use the discrete form of discounting over 1 year with annual interest rate r, then the equation becomes:

$$S = \frac{K^*}{1+r}$$

The strike at which calls and puts are equally valuable is equal to the forward price of the stock. Someone should be willing to agree today to sell you a stock worth $S = \$100$ today for $K^* = \$104$ if the financing rate is $r = 4\%$. That is because they can borrow \$100 at 4% and use the money to buy the stock now; in 1 year they have to repay \$104. The put–call parity states that the long call–short put strategy is another way to replicate a forward at no cost, therefore a call struck at \$104 and a put struck at \$104 must cost the same. If you buy the call and sell the put, you guarantee yourself a \$104 purchase price for the stock in 1 year's time.

The put–call parity reflects an advanced way of risk arbitrage. The prices of calls and puts (for all strikes) have to be in line with on- and off-market forward and futures. The arbitrage is executable by combining futures and options on the same underlying asset and choosing to buy the side that is cheaper relative to the other.

This is also an advanced way of broader risk sharing. When a stock is bought in an Initial Public Offering (IPO) providing capital to a growing business, the buyer may not think much of options and forwards. He does, however, appreciate the existence of a secondary market for stocks (stock exchange), so that he can sell the stock when he no longer wants to bear its risk. The person he sells to may, however, be an option player who wants the stock, but only for a certain amount of time or only in a certain scenario. The fact that he can customize his participation in the stock may be the main reason that he purchases the stock. He does not buy another stock that does not have options trading on it, because that would force him into an all-or-nothing risk.

5.5 CURRENCY OPTIONS

Options on currency rates work the same way as options on any asset price. Because currency rates are prices of one currency in terms of another, they can be expressed with either currency as the *priced* one and the *pricing* one. We do not express the prices of other assets in such inverted terms, for example, as the number of ABC shares per dollar. With currencies, both ways – yen per dollar and dollar per yen – are natural. Due to this dual nature of FX rates, currency options, just like forwards and futures, can be viewed in two ways.

Let us consider a call option on the US dollar with a strike of 110 Japanese yen per dollar (think of the dollar as the underlying asset) with one call covering \$1,000 (think of dollars as shares and each call is on 1,000 shares). If the dollar's price rises above ¥110, the holder gets a payoff, otherwise not. The payoff, as with any call, is equal to the difference between the spot price of the underlying asset S (i.e. the spot FX rate in ¥/\$) on the expiry date minus the strike K, or nothing, times the number of units of the underlying asset (principal amount or size). That is, just like with any call, it is:

$$Call^{\frac{JPY}{USD}} = Size^{USD} \times Max\left(S^{\frac{JPY}{USD}} - K^{\frac{JPY}{USD}}, 0\right)$$

where both S and K are in ¥/\$. The payoff is denominated in ¥. If the spot FX rate at expiry is ¥117, we get ¥7 times the 1,000 unit size, or ¥7,000, equivalent to \$59.82905983 at the ¥/\$117 FX rate; if the spot FX rate at expiry is ¥102, we get nothing. A physical-settle version of this option would be the right to buy 1,000 dollars for ¥110 apiece which would be exercised only if the spot value of the dollar is greater than ¥110. But the right to buy the dollar is automatically equivalent to the right to sell the yen.

The call on the dollar struck at ¥/\$110 is also a put on the yen struck at 1/110 = \$/¥0.00909091. If the size of the call was 1,000 dollars, then the size of the put is 110,000 yen (converting, using the strike FX rate).

$$Call^{\frac{USD}{JPY}} = Size^{JPY} \times Max(K^{\frac{USD}{JPY}} - S^{\frac{USD}{JPY}}, 0)$$

When the value of the yen goes down to \$0.00854701, i.e. the spot FX rate moves to ¥/\$117, we get a payout of

$$0.00909091 - 0.00854701 = \$0.00054390$$

per unit of yen. This times the size of the option, 110,000 units of yen, gives us the total payoff of \$59.82905983, which is the same as ¥7,000 at the ¥/\$117 FX rate. When the spot FX rate goes up to \$/¥0.00980392, i.e. ¥/\$102, we get nothing. We have the following rule:

$$Call\ on\ Currency\ 1 = Put\ on\ Currency\ 2$$

with the size converted at the strike FX rate and the strike rate inverted. This rule is true for all currency options, standard or otherwise.

5.6 BINOMIAL OPTION PRICING

The option premium charged by a dealer reflects his cost of manufacturing the payoff. The dealer sells (or buys) the option, and then borrows or lends money and takes a partial position in the underlying asset. By the expiry time his hedge is worth exactly the same as the payoff on the option he owes or receives. We will illustrate the mechanics of payoff manufacturing with increasingly more revealing examples of binomial trees.[2] All examples use stocks, but are equally applicable to other traded assets.

5.6.1 One-Step Examples

We use the following assumptions for Examples 1–3. The underlying stock sells currently for $S = \$50$ a share. The expiry of the option is 1 year from today (or one period with no trading in the underlying between now and expiry). The dealer sells the option, collects the premium, and follows a set of instructions. For Examples 1, 2(a) and 3(a), we also assume that the dealer can borrow or lend money at no interest. On the expiry date, one period from today, the stock

[2] The examples follow the notation and exposition used by many option textbooks, incl. my favorites Cox and Rubinstein (1985) and Baxter and Rennie (1996).

can take on two values $S_{up} = \$70$ or $S_{dn} = \$20$. The dealer believes that the up probability is $^1\!/_4$ and the down probability is $^3\!/_4$. He takes the following steps:

1) Given the potential stock outcomes $S_{up} = \$70$ or $S_{dn} = \$20$ for the up and down states tomorrow, and given today's stock price of $S = \$50$, the dealer computes a number,

$$q = \frac{S - S_{dn}}{S_{up} - S_{dn}}$$

We will refer to q as the risk-neutral probability of the up state and to $1 - q$ as the risk-neutral probability of the down state. These are the only probability-like numbers that the dealer uses in his weighted average calculations, not his subjective beliefs $^1\!/_4$ and $^3\!/_4$ (he could easily be wrong). The risk-neutral probability, q, has no meaning outside the context of this six-step procedure, i.e. it is not a real probability of anything. In our examples, we compute q to be:

$$q = \frac{50 - 20}{70 - 20} = \frac{3}{5} = 0.60$$

2) Given the strike level K and the potential stock outcomes $S_{up} = \$70$ or $S_{dn} = \$20$ for the up and down states, he assigns the call payoffs C_{up} and C_{dn}, or put payoffs P_{up} or P_{dn}, for the corresponding states of nature in the expiry period.
3) He computes the premium on the option by taking the average of the future option outcomes weighted by the risk-neutral probabilities of the states, i.e.

$$C = qC_{up} + (1 - q)C_{dn} \quad \text{or} \quad P = qP_{up} + (1 - q)P_{dn}$$

4) He computes a hedge number

$$\Delta = \frac{C_{up} - C_{dn}}{S_{up} - S_{dn}} \quad \text{or} \quad \Delta = \frac{P_{up} - P_{dn}}{S_{up} - S_{dn}}$$

that tells him how many shares of stock he needs to hold (buy or sell) today.
5) He buys/sells the prescribed number of shares by paying/receiving $\Delta \times S$. He uses the collected premium in the purchase or sale. If necessary, he borrows/lends $\Delta \times S$ minus the option premium, so that his cash position today is zero.
6) He liquidates his hedge one period from today when the state of nature is revealed, i.e. the stock either goes up or down. He uses the proceeds to settle his borrowing/lending and to pay the agreed-upon payoff to the option buyer.

We will show that if he faithfully follows Steps 1–5, then in Step 6 he will always have on hand the exact amount of money demanded by the option holder, no matter what happens to the stock price. He will not have used his subjective beliefs to gamble on the direction of the stock.

In our illustrations, we will place all the computed numbers on nodes, as shown in Figure 5.8. Next to today's stock price of $S = 50$, we will show all the numbers from Steps 1–5, i.e. q, Δ, the option premium C or P, the cost of shares $\Delta \times S$, and the amount of borrowing/lending $\Delta \times S - C$ or $\Delta \times S - P$. Next to the potential future stock prices S_{up} and S_{dn}, we will show the corresponding value of the option C_{up} (or P_{up}) and C_{dn} (or P_{dn}), the value of the stock position held from the previous step $\Delta \times S_{up}$ and $\Delta \times S_{dn}$, and the cash position carried over from the previous step.

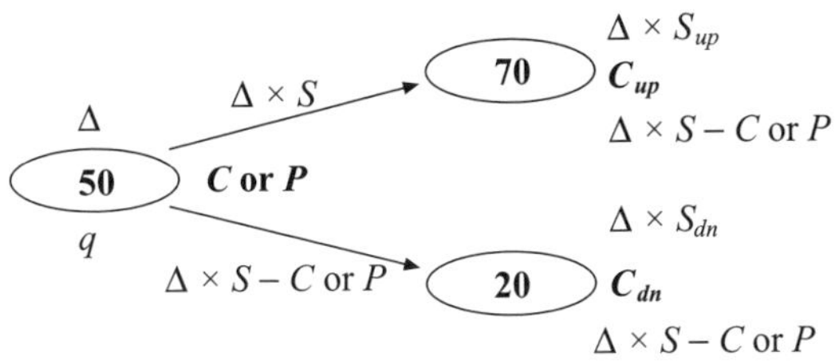

Figure 5.8

Example 1 Binary lottery, zero interest rate. John Dealer sells a binary "call" option on the stock that pays \$10 if the stock ends up at or above \$60 or nothing if it ends up below \$60 one period from today. John's calculations are as follows.

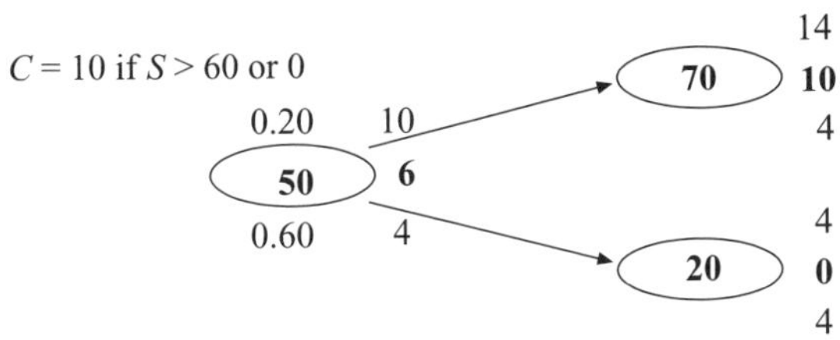

Figure 5.9 Example 1

The risk-neutral probability $q = 0.60$. The call payoffs one year from today are 10 if the stock is at 70, or 0 if the stock is at 20. So he sells the call for:

$$C = 0.60(\$10) + 0.40(\$0) = \$6$$

Given his hedge ratio

$$\Delta = \frac{10 - 0}{70 - 20} = \frac{1}{5} = 0.20$$

he buys 0.20 shares for 0.20×50 or \$10. Since he collected only \$6 for the option, he borrows $10 - 6 = \$4$.

One period later, if the stock is at \$70, his stock position is worth $0.20 \times 70 = \$14$. He liquidates it, pays \$10 on the option and repays the borrowing of \$4. If the stock is at \$20, his stock position is $0.20 \times 20 = \$4$. He liquidates it, pays nothing on the option, and repays his borrowing of \$4. Collecting the premium of \$6 on day one has allowed John to manufacture the payoff he is obligated to make irrespective of whether the stock goes up or down.

Example 2a Call struck at 55, zero interest rate. John Dealer sells a standard call option on the stock struck at \$55. At expiry, the call pays the value of the stock (i.e. S_{up} or S_{dn}) minus the strike ($K = 55$) if the stock ends up at or above \$55, or nothing if it ends up below \$55 one period from today. John's calculations are shown in Figure 5.10.

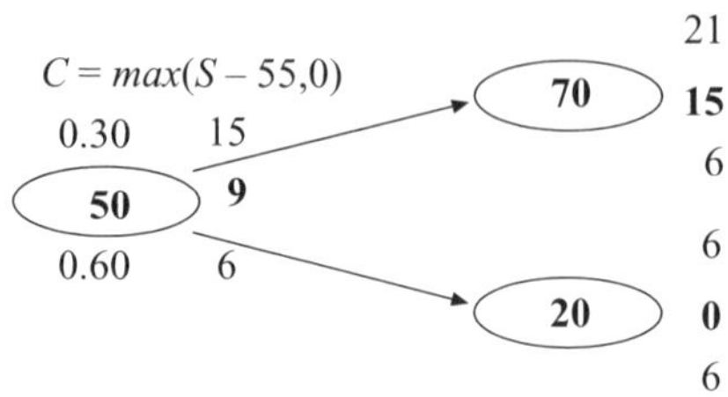

Figure 5.10 Example 2a

The call payoffs are 15 if the stock is at 70, or 0 if the stock is at 20. So he sells the call for:

$$C = 0.60(\$15) + 0.40(\$0) = \$9$$

Given his hedge ratio

$$\Delta = \frac{15 - 0}{70 - 20} = \frac{3}{10} = 0.30$$

he buys 0.30 shares for 0.30×50 or \$15. Since he collected only \$9 for the option, he borrows $15 - 9 = \$6$.

One period later, if the stock is at \$70, his stock position is worth $0.30 \times 70 = \$21$. He liquidates it, pays \$15 on the option and repays the borrowing of \$6. If the stock is at \$20, his stock position is $0.30 \times 20 = \$6$. He liquidates it, pays nothing on the option, and repays his borrowing of \$6.

Example 3a Put struck at 55, zero interest rate. John Dealer sells a standard put option on the stock struck at \$55. At expiry, the put pays the strike ($K = 55$) minus the stock value (S_{up} or S_{dn}) if the stock ends up at or below \$55, or nothing if it ends up above \$55 one period from today. John's calculations are as shown in Figure 5.11.

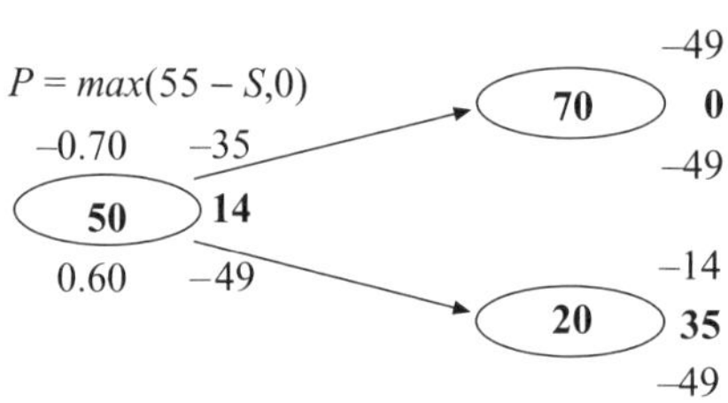

Figure 5.11 Example 3a

The put payoffs are 0 if the stock is at 70, or 35 if the stock is at 20. So he sells the put for:

$$P = 0.60(\$0) + 0.40(\$35) = \$14$$

Given his hedge ratio

$$\Delta = \frac{0 - 35}{70 - 20} = -\frac{7}{10} = -0.70$$

he shorts 0.70 shares to collect 0.70 × 50 or \$35. Since he collected \$14 for the option, he places the combined proceeds 35 + 14 = \$49 in a deposit (i.e. lends).

One period later, if the stock is at \$70, his stock position is worth –0.70 × 70 = –\$49. He liquidates it. He uses the \$49 from the deposit to buy the stock back and return it to the lender. He pays nothing on the option. If the stock is at \$20, his stock position is –0.70 × 20 = –\$14. He uses the \$49 from the deposit to liquidate the stock position (\$14) and pay \$35 on the option.

Let us make a few observations. Once the payoff on the option is defined, the rest is a mechanical adherence to a recipe. The recipe covers all potential payoff structures – binary, standard, any other exotic – as well as both puts and calls and both bought and sold options. The actions for the dealer who buys the option, instead of selling, would be analogous. They are completely determined by his hedge ratio Δ. A positive delta means long stock, a negative one means short stock. The borrowing and lending simply balances the cash position resulting from the price of the Δ amount of stock and the premium on the option.

Let us now demonstrate that the recipe works with only slight modifications when we do not make the unrealistic assumption that the financing interest rate is zero. Here are the amendments.

1) The formula for q is changed by replacing today's S with its future value equivalent, i.e. the forward. Recall that the forward is equal to the value of S multiplied by a future value factor, equal to 1 plus the interest rate r for 1 year. For fractions of a year, or special compounding and day-count conventions, it needs to be amended appropriately. For an annual period it is:

$$q = \frac{S(1+r) - S_{dn}}{S_{up} - S_{dn}}$$

In our example, we assume that $r = 10\%$ and compute q to be:

$$q = \frac{50(1.1) - 20}{70 - 20} = \frac{7}{10} = 0.70$$

2) No change.
3) We compute the premium on the option by taking the average of the future option outcomes weighted by the risk-neutral probabilities of the states, present-valued to today, i.e.

$$C = \frac{1}{1+r}\left[qC_{up} + (1-q)C_{dn}\right] \quad \text{or} \quad P = \frac{1}{1+r}\left[qP_{up} + (1-q)P_{dn}\right]$$

4) through 6) No change, but we have to remember about interest paid or earned on borrowing or lending when carrying over the cash position from the previous step.
5) Let us repeat the standard call and put example with a financing cost of 10%.

Example 2b Call struck at 55, 10% interest rate. John Dealer sells a standard call option on the stock struck at \$55. At expiry, the call pays the value of the stock (i.e. S_{up} or S_{dn}) minus the strike ($K = 55$) if the stock ends up at or above \$55, or nothing if it ends up below \$55 one period from today. John's calculations are shown in Figure 5.12.

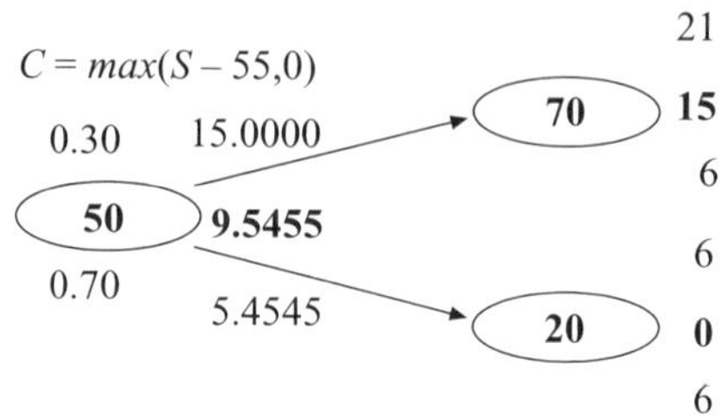

Figure 5.12 Example 2b

The call payoffs are still 15 if the stock is at 70, or 0 if the stock is at 20. But he sells the call for:

$$C = \frac{1}{1.1}\left[0.70(\$15) + 0.30(\$0)\right] = \$9\frac{6}{11} = \$9.54545$$

Given his hedge ratio

$$\Delta = \frac{15 - 0}{70 - 20} = \frac{3}{10} = 0.30$$

he buys 0.30 shares for 0.30 × 50 or \$15. Since he collected only \$9-6/11 for the option, he borrows 15 – 9-6/11 = \$5-5/11.

One period later, if the stock is at \$70, his stock position is worth 0.30 × 70 = \$21. He liquidates it, pays \$15 on the option and repays the borrowing which has by now accrued to \$6 (5-5/11 times 1.1) at the 10% interest rate. If the stock is at \$20, his stock position is 0.30 × 20 = \$6. He liquidates it, pays nothing on the option, and repays his borrowing and interest of \$6.

Example 3b Put struck at 55, 10% interest rate. John Dealer sells a standard put option on the stock struck at \$55. At expiry, the put pays the strike ($K = 55$) minus the stock value (S_{up} or S_{dn}) if the stock ends up at or below \$55, or nothing if it ends up above \$55 one period from today. John's calculations are as shown in Figure 5.13.

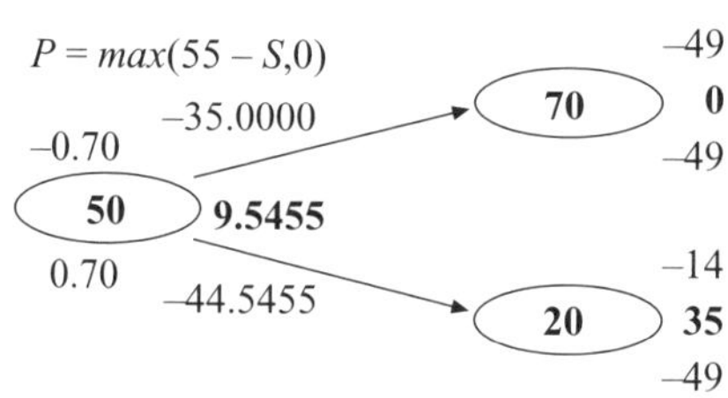

Figure 5.13 Example 3b

The put payoffs are unchanged, 0 if the stock is at 70, or 35 if the stock is at 20. He sells the put for:

$$P = \frac{1}{1.1}\left[0.70(\$0) + 0.30(\$35)\right] = \$9\frac{6}{11} = \$9.54545$$

Given his hedge ratio

$$\Delta = \frac{0-35}{70-20} = -\frac{7}{10} = -0.70$$

he shorts 0.70 shares to collect 0.70 × 50 or \$35. Since he collected \$9-6/11 for the option, he places the combined proceeds 35 + 9-6/11 = \$44-6/11 in a deposit (i.e. lends).

One period later, if the stock is at \$70, his stock position is worth –0.70 × 70 = –\$49. He liquidates it. He uses the \$49 (44-6/11 times 1.1) from the deposit, which has accrued interest in the meantime, to buy the stock back and return it to the lender. He pays nothing on the option. If the stock is at \$20, his stock position is –0.70 × 20 = –\$14. He uses the \$49 from the deposit and interest to liquidate the stock position (\$14) and to pay \$35 on the option.

Let us make a few more observations. First, the hedge ratios are the same as in the zero interest case, but the borrowing/lending grows period to period and makes a difference in the final apportioning of the proceeds at expiry.

Second, a positive interest rate raised the price of the call and lowered the price of the put (Examples 2b and 3b relative to 2a and 3a). This is because a call seller borrows money to buy stock incurring a cost, while a put seller lends money after shorting a stock accruing interest. So the cost of manufacturing the final payoff increases for the short call hedger and decreases for the short put hedger.

Thirdly, the price of the call and the put in our example was the same (Examples 2b and 3b). This was not a coincidence. The strike price on both options was equal to \$55. This is the forward price of the stock for delivery on the expiry date, equal to the spot price of the stock, \$50, times a future value factor reflecting the cost-of-carry, i.e. 50 × (1 + 0.10) = \$55.

This confirms our prior assertion, before we knew anything about option pricing, that a call and a put struck at a forward will have the same cost, so that one can manufacture the forward by buying a call and selling a put struck at the forward price.

Let us further show that the last property will hold no matter how volatile the stock is between now and expiry. Suppose that instead of potential outcomes of \$70 or \$20, the stock is perceived to have potential outcomes of S_{up} = \$80 or S_{dn} = \$15. The stock is more volatile and is thus riskier. We follow our recipe using the interest rate of 10%. The forward value of the stock is still the same \$55.

Example 2c Call struck at 55, 10% interest rate. John Dealer's calculations are shown in Figure 5.14.

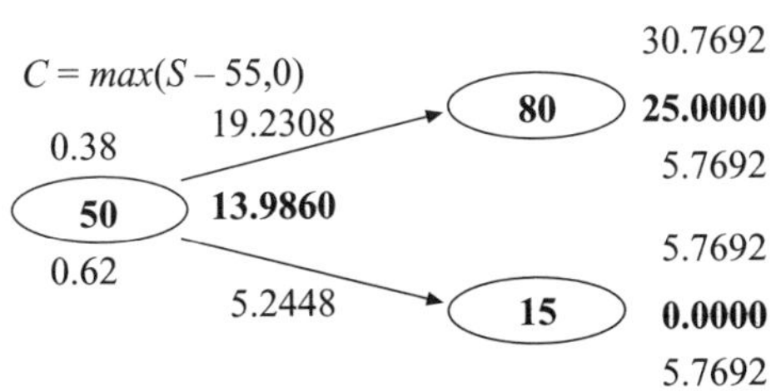

Figure 5.14 Example 2c

He sells the option for \$13.986, a lot more than before (Example 2c relative to 2b), to reflect the increased expected value of the payoff.

Example 3c **Put struck at 55, 10% interest rate.** John's calculations are shown in Figure 5.15.

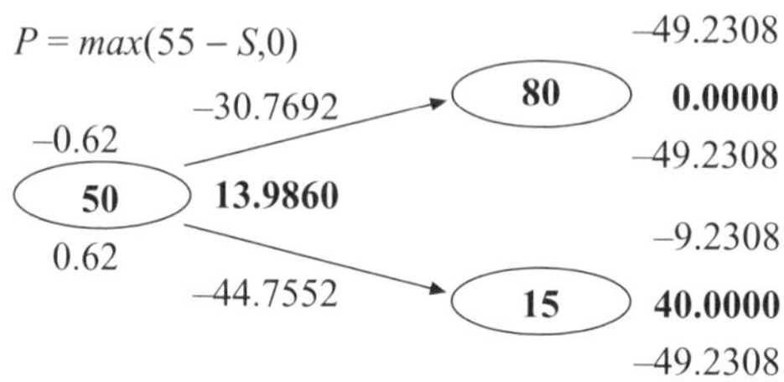

Figure 5.15 Example 3c

Again, he sells the option for \$13.986, a lot more than before (Example 3c relative to 3b), to reflect the increased expected value of the payoff.

In both cases, he sells the call for the same price as the put (Examples 2c and 3c). It will always be true that if the perceived riskiness of the underlying asset increases, both calls and puts will increase in value, but the price of a call struck at a forward will always be equal to the price of a put struck at a forward. This is because the forward does not have anything to do with the volatility of the stock, it simply reflects the cost-of-carry, and a long-call/short-put position, equivalent to the forward, must carry a net zero premium (an on-market forward costs nothing to enter into).

What we have also shown is that while the subjective probabilities of the stock outcomes are irrelevant, the volatility, or the potential dispersion of the outcomes, is not. The more volatile the stock, the higher the premiums on standard calls and puts (Examples 2c and 3c relative to 2b and 3b). This reflects the asymmetric nature of their payoffs. A more volatile stock means that when the option is in-the-money the payoff is likely to be larger, while when the option is out-of-the-money, the payoff is still the same constant zero. Thus the expected value of the payoff is higher if the volatility is higher.

Multistep Example

Let us now demonstrate the full dynamic process of hedging an option, i.e. manufacturing its payoff. We consider a put struck at $K = 54$, the interest rate $r = 2.6\%$ per period (i.e. already decompounded), the stock price currently at 50 and following the dynamics as in Figure 5.16.

For example, an option with 3 months to expiry might be divided into monthly steps. Over the first month, the stock can go up to 60 or down to 35 (the actual probability of each step is irrelevant). If the stock went down to 35 during the first month, then it can go up to 45 or down to 20 over the second month, etc. For space and clarity, we will drop the arrows in the rest of the exposition. We follow the same logic as in one-step examples for each sub-tree. We first compute the risk-neutral probability

$$q = \frac{S(1 + r) - S_{dn}}{S_{up} - S_{dn}}$$

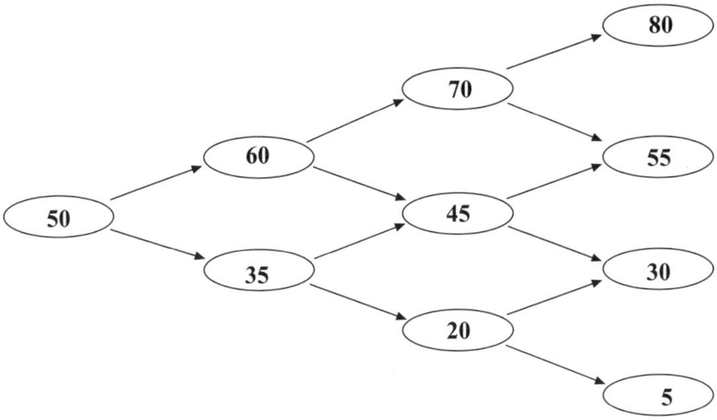

Figure 5.16 A multistep price tree

for all sub-trees. For example, for the sub-tree emanating from the 45 point, we have:

$$q = \frac{45(1 + 0.026) - 30}{55 - 30} = 0.6468$$

We also determine the payoff of the option at expiry. For example, when the stock price is 45, the payoff would be 54 − 45 = \$9. We place the qs and the final payoffs in the diagram (Figure 5.17).

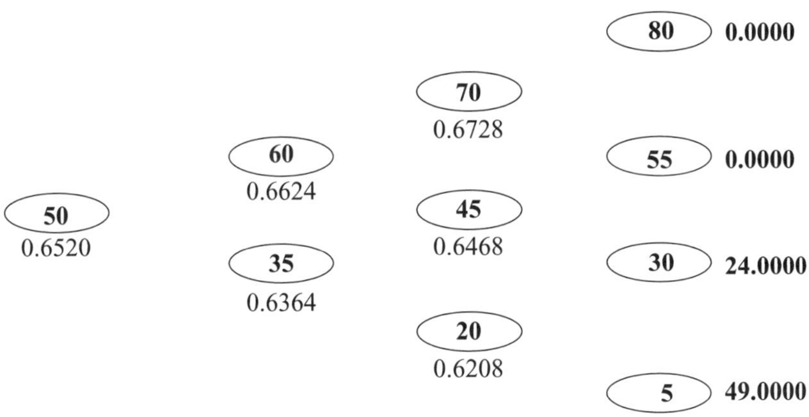

Figure 5.17 A multistep price tree with probabilities and final payoffs

As in one-step examples, we sweep through the tree backwards to determine the premium on the option today. We use the same equation as before for each node:

$$C = \frac{1}{1+r}\left[qC_{up} + (1-q)C_{dn}\right] \quad \text{or} \quad P = \frac{1}{1+r}\left[qP_{up} + (1-q)P_{dn}\right]$$

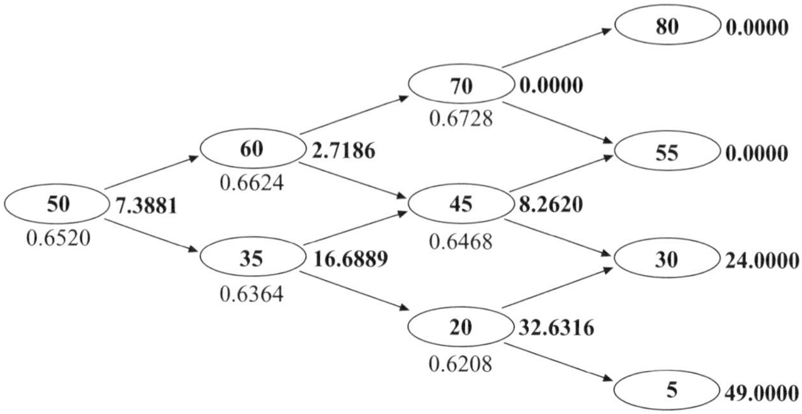

Figure 5.18 A multistep tree with option prices

We start with the second-to-last date and consider the sub-trees emanating from all three points. We compute put values for all three states: 70, 45, and 20. For the \$45 state we compute:

$$P = \frac{1}{1+0.026}[0.6468 \cdot 0 + (1-0.6468) \cdot 24] = 8.2620$$

For the \$20 state we compute:

$$P = \frac{1}{1+0.026}[0.6208 \cdot 24 + (1-0.6208) \cdot 49] = 32.6316$$

We place the values on the tree diagram (Figure 5.18). We go to one date before the one just computed, and calculate the put values for each node (60 and 35) on this date, using the same equation linking a node on a given date to two future nodes. For example, for the \$35 state we get:

$$P = \frac{1}{1+0.026}[0.6364 \cdot 8.2620 + (1-0.6364) \cdot 32.6316] = 16.6889$$

We proceed recursively like this until we obtain today's value of the put, $P = \$7.3881$.

Next, we demonstrate that no matter which route the stock price takes between today and 3 months from today, the hedge will work perfectly.

For each node, we compute the hedge number

$$\Delta = \frac{C_{up} - C_{dn}}{S_{up} - S_{dn}} \quad \text{or} \quad \Delta = \frac{P_{up} - P_{dn}}{S_{up} - S_{dn}}$$

which tells us how many shares we should hold at that node. In our put example, all deltas will be negative or zero to reflect the fact that we will short shares. For example, for the \$35 state 1 month from today the delta is:

$$\Delta = \frac{8.2620 - 32.6316}{45 - 20} = -0.9748$$

Again we place all the deltas on the diagram (Figure 5.19).

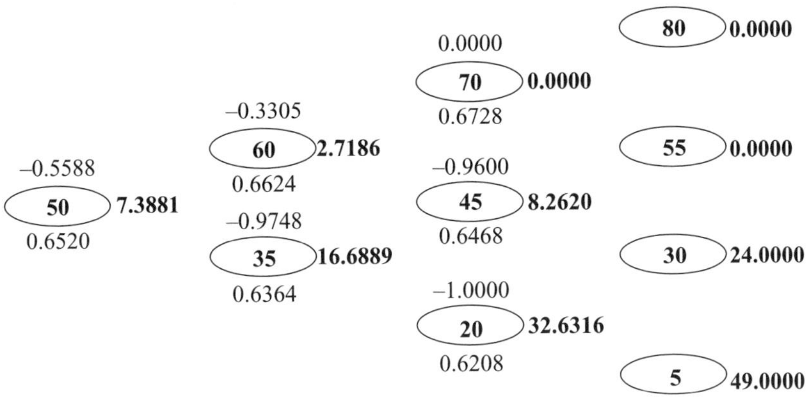

Figure 5.19 A multistep tree with deltas

Depending on the route the stock takes, all trades are now determined by the differences between deltas at subsequent nodes. The lending amounts are also determined by the cash position at each node. Let us go through the tree forward following one hypothetical path.

Suppose the stock price from today's level of \$50 goes down to \$35 1 month from today, then to \$45 2 months from today, and ends up at \$30 3 months from today. In order to hedge our position, we are required to short 0.5588 share today. This will result in proceeds of $0.5588 \times 50 = \$27.9406$. We deposit that and the premium received from selling the put, i.e. a total of $27.9406 + 7.3881 = \$35.3287$, in an account earning 2.6% per month (Figure 5.20).

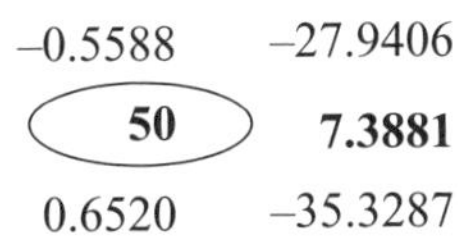

Figure 5.20

Next month the price goes down to \$35. Based on our new delta of –0.9748, we need to short additional $0.9748 - 0.5588 = 0.4159$ shares. This results in proceeds of $0.4159 \times 35 = \$14.5590$. Meanwhile, our prior lending accrued to $35.3287 \times (1 + 0.026) = \$36.2473$. We re-lend the sum of the two, i.e. $14.5590 + 36.2473 = \$50.8063$, for another month at 2.6%. (Note that the borrowing/lending amount can also be found by subtracting the put value at a node, 16.6889, from the value of the share holding, $-0.9748 \times 35 = -\$34.1174$, i.e. $-34.1174 - 16.6889 = -\$50.8063$ as in Figure 5.21.)

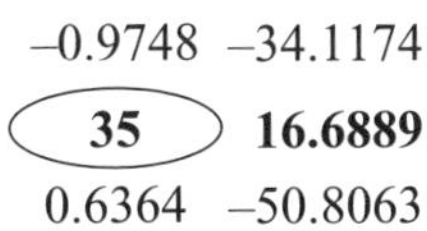

Figure 5.21

The following month, the stock price increases to \$45. Based on our new delta of –0.9600, we need to buy back $0.9748 - 0.9600 = 0.0148$ shares. This costs us $0.0148 \times 45 = \$0.6653$. We take that amount from the maturing deposit which has accrued to $50.8063 \times (1 + 0.026) = \$52.1273$. We re-lend the remainder $52.1273 - 0.6653 = \$51.4620$ for another month at 2.6%.

(Again the borrowing/lending amount can be found by subtracting the put value at a node, 8.2620, from the value of the share holding, – 0.9600 × 45 = –\$43.2000, i.e. –43.2000 – 8.2620 = –\$51.4620 – as in Figure 5.22.)

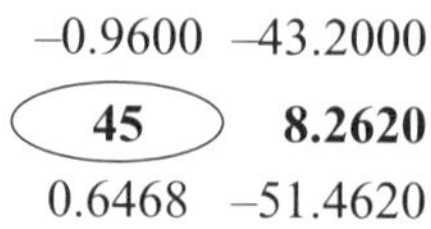

Figure 5.22

We proceed to the final step in Figure 5.23. The stock goes down to \$30. We collect the deposit with accrued interest, i.e. 51.4620 × (1 + 0.026) = \$52.8000. We buy back the shorted shares for 0.9600 × 30 = \$28.8000 and pay \$24 to the put holder. We are left with no stock position, no borrowing or lending position, and our put obligation is satisfied.

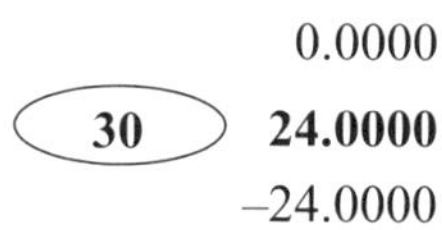

Figure 5.23

One can trace any other path through the tree to see that the result would be identical. We would end up with no stock, no cash, and we would have made a payout on the put, if any was required. The summary of all calculation is portrayed in the completed diagram (Figure 5.24).

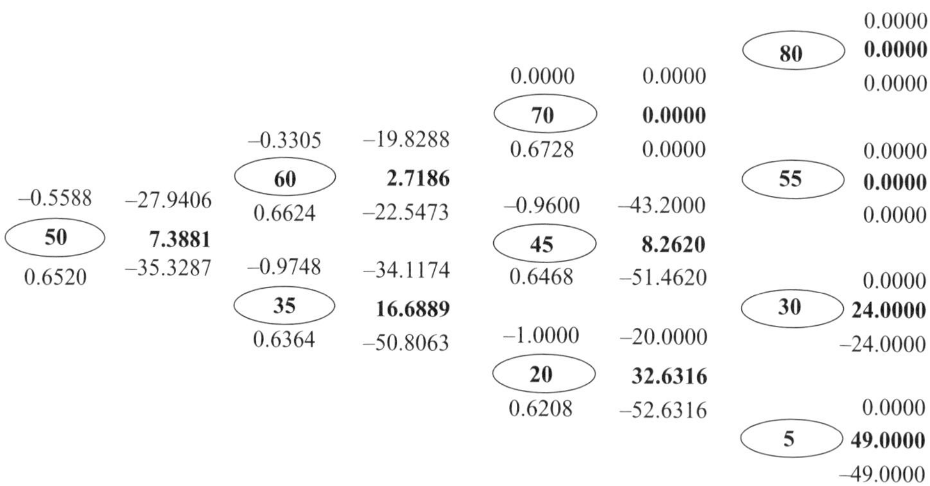

Figure 5.24

The procedure of computing the qs sweeping backwards to get the option value up front and sweeping forward to compute the required hedges and borrowing/lending positions works for all standard calls and puts, digital options, barrier options, American exercise style, and many other options. In all of these cases, the only thing that changes is the recursive computations of the option value during the backward sweep. For example, for American options that can be exercised early, one has to amend the option value for any given node to see if the immediate exercise value is not greater than the unexercised value, i.e.

$$C = Max\left\{\frac{1}{1+r}\left[qC_{up} + (1-q)C_{dn}\right], S - K\right\} \text{ or}$$

$$P = Max\left\{\frac{1}{1+r}\left[qP_{up} + (1-q)P_{dn}\right], K - S\right\}$$

This is very easy to implement in any computer code or spreadsheet.

5.7 BLACK–SCHOLES MODEL AND EXTENSIONS

The well-known Black–Scholes[3] equation for calls and puts is a continuous generalization of the binomial approach. There are at least two improvements here. First, the stock price, looking forward from one date to the next, can take on a continuum of values not just two. Second, there is a continuum of dates, not just month-to-month, or day-to-day. The equation computes the present value of a hedge strategy where the rebalancing occurs instant-by-instant and over minute price changes. The overriding principle of payoff manufacturing remains the same. An option payoff is replicated by a position in a stock combined with borrowing or lending. The stock and bond position is adjusted continuously and for infinitesimal value changes. The value of the option today is equal to the cash required to start this dynamic hedge process.

5.7.1 Black–Scholes with No Dividends

For options on a non-dividend-paying stock, the value of a call and a put option in the Black–Scholes model is equal to:

$$C = SN(d_1) - Ke^{-rT}N(d_2)$$
$$P = Ke^{-rT}N(-d_2) - SN(-d_1)$$

where $d_1 = \frac{\ln(S/K) + (r + \sigma^2/2)T}{\sigma\sqrt{T}}$, $d_2 = d_1 - \sigma\sqrt{T}$, r is a continuously compounded interest rate, and T is the time to maturity. $N(d_k)$ is the cumulative standard normal probability density function evaluated at d_k. Values of $N(d_k)$ can be found in statistical tables or in Excel by using *NORMDIST*(). The formula provides an explicit link between the annual volatility of the stock return σ and the value of the option. In Black–Scholes, the continuously compounded return on the stock over an infinitesimal interval dt is assumed to be normally distributed. What that means is that instead of the stock price taking on potentially only two values when moving from time t to time $t + dt$, the stock can take on a continuum of values such that the continuously compounded return on the stock over that interval, $\ln(S_{t+dt}/S_t)$, has a standard deviation of $\sigma\sqrt{dt}$. This is portrayed in Figure 5.25.

The probability mass curve in the graph is not the normal bell-curve but rather that of a log-normal curve. The minimal stock price is zero, the maximal price is infinity. The *percentage return is normal* and would have a bell-shaped curve.

The inclusion of price volatility in arriving at the value of the option was implicit in our binomial trees where the width of each branch depended on the variability of the stock. But,

[3] See Black and Scholes (1973). The model is also attributed to Merton (1973).

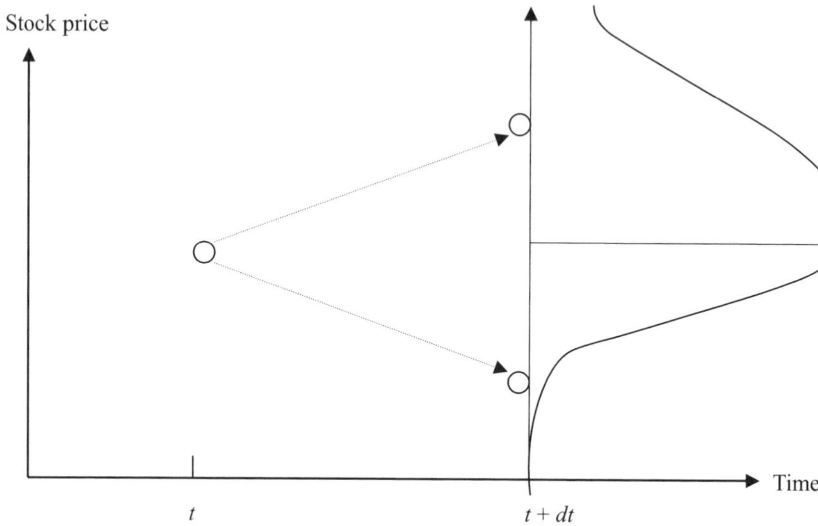

Figure 5.25

it is easy to show that if, in a binomial model with a time step of Δt, we set

$$u = e^{\sigma\sqrt{\Delta t}}, \quad d = 1/u, \quad q = \frac{e^{r\,\Delta t} - d}{u - d},$$

then the binomial model is just a discrete approximation and will converge to the Black–Scholes equation[4] as we shorten Δt, i.e. increase the number of rehedging times in the tree. That is why we chose to present the binomial approach to option pricing first here, rather than go the continuous equation route. The discrete model is intuitive and more general, as it allows us to value American exercise options; the continuous one relies on a stochastic calculus argument. The two can be made equivalent to each other, i.e. they come up with the identical answer for the premium and delta hedge ratios.

5.7.2 Dividends

The inclusion of dividends in option pricing is straightforward, assuming that dividends are a known cash payout between now and the option expiry. Their effect on option prices should be intuitive. Because they are an outflow of value from the stock, they reduce the potential future price outcomes for the stock. As such, their impact is to decrease the call values and increase the put values. This can also be argued by considering the delta hedge. The call writer buys less of the stock, and the put writer shorts more of the stock, because when they adjust the hedge the stock price will have been reduced by the amount of the dividends, whether the stock has gone up or down.

There are two ways to correct option valuation for dividends, depending on whether their amount is known in dollars or as a percentage of the stock price. Consider dividends paid

[4] This is only one of many possible ways of making the binomial tree converge to the B–S equation. For a discussion, see for example Hull (2000).

at a constant continuous rate δ. In the Black–Scholes model, the inclusion of dividends is accomplished[5] by multiplying each occurrence of the stock price S by the continuous compounding term $e^{-\delta T}$.

$$C = Se^{-\delta T} N(d_1) - Ke^{-rT} N(d_2)$$
$$P = Ke^{-rT} N(-d_2) - Se^{-\delta T} N(-d_1)$$
$$\text{with} \quad d_1 = \frac{\ln\frac{S}{K} + (r - \delta + \sigma^2/2)T}{\sigma\sqrt{T}} \quad \text{and} \quad d_2 = d_1 - \sigma\sqrt{T}$$

In the binomial model, the correction is the same. Each node's stock value is reduced by the amount of accrued dividends. We change the definitions of the upstate and the downstate to $u = e^{-\delta\Delta t + \sigma\sqrt{\Delta t}}, \quad d = e^{-\delta\Delta t - \sigma\sqrt{\Delta t}}$.

The second way to include dividends is to assume that we know the dollar amount and the exact time of their occurrence. We then present-value those dividends and subtract from the current stock price. Denoting the present value of the dividends as $PV(D)$, the corrected Black–Scholes formula looks like this:

$$C = (S - PV(D))N(d_1) - Ke^{-rT} N(d_2)$$
$$P = Ke^{-rT} N(d_2) - (S - PV(D))N(-d_1)$$
$$\text{with} \quad d_1 = \frac{\ln\frac{S-PV(D)}{K} + (r + \sigma^2/2)T}{\sigma\sqrt{T}} \quad \text{and} \quad d_2 = d_1 - \sigma\sqrt{T}$$

In the binomial model, the correction consists of superimposing the dates on the binomial grid of stock price nodes, and when the date of the dividend is reached, of subtracting the dollar amount of the dividend from the node's stock price.

5.7.3 Options on Currency Rates

Garman and Kohlhagen (1983) pointed out that options on currencies can be easily accommodated in the Black–Scholes framework by thinking of the denomination currency as a stock and the interest rate of that currency as a continuous dividend paid by that currency. The hedger of a call on the dollar/pound exchange rate will borrow dollars (and pay the dollar interest rate to finance) to buy the delta amount of pounds. Those pounds will earn an interest rate in pounds just as stock would earn a continuous dividend yield. The correction to the Black–Scholes formula to value currency options is thus the same as that for the continuous dividend yield ($\delta = r_{GBP}$). Often, however, we see in written relative to the currency forwards rather than to spots. This is how it was first proposed by Fisher Black and has become known as the *Black Model*. The formula simply includes the spot-forward cash-and-carry parity $F = Se(r_{USD} - r_{GBP})T$ and therefore looks like this:

$$C = [FN(d_1) - KN(d_2)]e^{-r_{USD}T}$$
$$P = [KN(d_2) - FN(-d_1)]e^{-r_{USD}T}$$
$$\text{with} \quad d_1 = \frac{\ln\frac{F}{K} + \left(\sigma^2/2\right)T}{\sigma\sqrt{T}} \quad \text{and} \quad d_2 = d_1 - \sigma\sqrt{T}$$

[5] See Roll (1977), Geske (1979), and Whaley (1981).

The implicit assumption in this formula is the same as in the Black–Scholes model which is that the interest rates between now and the expiry of the option are constant. Therefore the formula is most appropriate for short-term currency options.

5.7.4 Black–Scholes Delta, Gamma, and Vega

Delta is the hedge ratio that tells the hedger how many units of the stock (or currency) to buy or short over the next short time period during the dynamic hedging process. It is also the sensitivity of the option price to the stock price. Mathematically, it is the change in the value of the *option* per unit change in the value of the *stock*, and can be defined as

$$\Delta_{Call} = \frac{dC}{dS}, \ \Delta_{Put} = \frac{dP}{dS}$$

where d denotes the change in the value over an infinitesimal interval.

If the delta is equal to 0.5 then the call hedger shorts half the amount of stock. Since delta is also the dollar sensitivity of the value of the option, for each dollar movement in the price of the stock, the hedger's call value will move by 50 cents, and so by shorting half the amount the hedge is perfect.

In the Black–Scholes model, we obtain the delta by taking the first derivative of the option value with respect to the stock price. The result is simply:

$$\Delta_{Call} = e^{-\delta T} N(d_1)$$
$$\Delta_{Put} = e^{-\delta T} [N(d_1) - 1]$$

Gamma is the change in delta per unit change in the value of the stock, defined as:

$$\Gamma_{Call} = \frac{d\Delta_{Call}}{dS}, \quad \Gamma_{Put} = \frac{d\Delta_{Put}}{dS}$$

and can be computed in the Black–Scholes model by taking the second derivative of the option value with respect to the price of the stock. The result is:

$$\Gamma_{Call} = \Gamma_{Put} = {e^{-\delta T} n(d_1)}\Big/{S\sigma\sqrt{T}}$$

Vega is the sensitivity of the option value to the unit change in the assumed annual volatility. In the Black–Scholes model, it is equal to:

$$V_{Call} = V_{Put} = e^{-\delta T} n(d_1) S\sigma\sqrt{T}$$

In both equations, $n(d_1)$ is the standard normal probability density function evaluated at d_1.

The gamma of an option is an important risk measure from the standpoint of an option hedger. The higher the gamma, the higher the change in delta. A higher gamma therefore implies a more frequent rebalancing of the hedge and more price gap risk. The vega of an option is a measure of the risk relative to the assumed volatility of the stock. Both measures are typically computed using, not the continuous Black–Scholes values but by discretizing the stock space. The gamma is quoted as the change in the delta per \$1 change in the stock, and the vega as the change in the value of the option per 1% change in annual stock volatility.

5.8 RESIDUAL RISK OF OPTIONS: GAMMA, VEGA, AND VOLATILITY

Can anything go wrong with the delta hedge? If the dealer adheres strictly to the binomial algorithm, then as long as the stock follows one of the considered paths, the answer is no. Since the Black–Scholes model considers a continuum of paths, then also as long as the stock follows one of the considered paths, the answer is no. So, can anything go wrong? Unfortunately, yes.

What can go wrong is that the local and total volatility of the stock is greater than that assumed in estimating the cost of the hedge. Locally, over a small interval of time, the stock can jump, rather than move in a "smooth" fashion. The delta hedger of a call will buy at a higher price, and the put hedger will short at a lower price, than that assumed by the model. This is measured by the gamma risk. Totally, the volatility over the entire life of the option may turn out to be higher than that used up front to estimate the cost of the hedge. Some local movements may be large, but may be offset by some movements that are small. Yet if overall the stock moves more than the assumed annualized volatility, then the hedge will cost more than the model predicts. This is measured by the vega risk. Gamma and vega are closely related.

The main assumption of delta hedging is that the range of possible stock price outcomes considered is constrained by the assumed volatility of the stock. The volatility is the square root of the variance. The variance is the expected value of the squared deviations of the stock's return from the mean return over a given period. The Black–Scholes model requires volatility as an input. It then considers all the stock price paths that are within a certain range bounded by the volatility. That is, the stock price movements, period-to-period and overall, are restricted to be less than a certain number. This can be portrayed graphically as all the paths within an expanding cylinder of outcomes, with the greatest density of paths close to the center (see Figure 5.26). The edges of the cylinder are not binding, but the probability of outcomes outside, or far from the center, is minuscule. That is, we assume a bell-shaped normal curve for the path of stock returns.

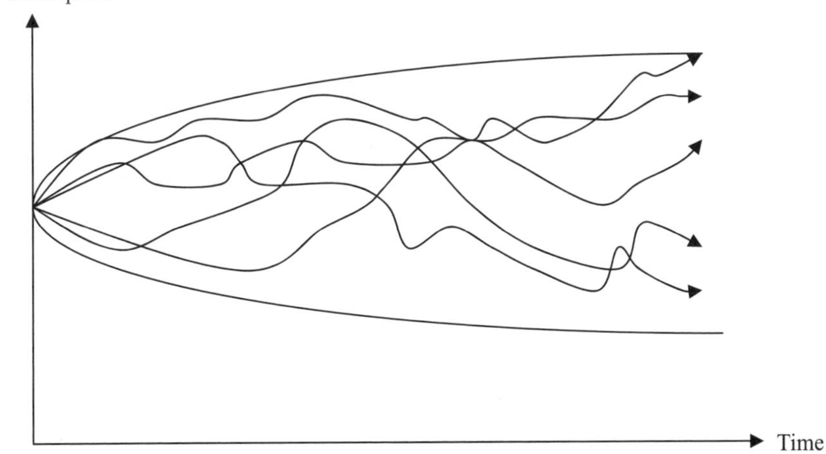

Figure 5.26 Stock price vs time

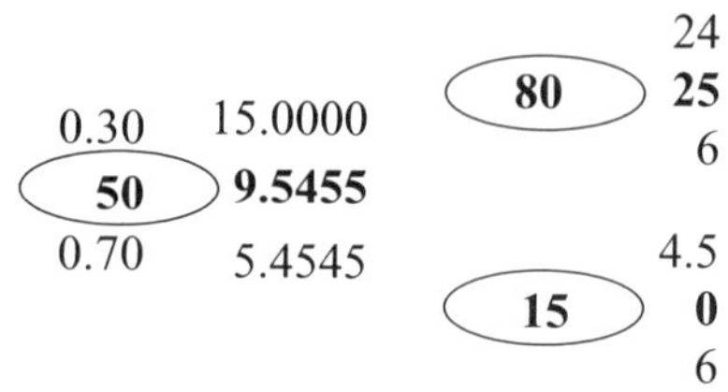

Figure 5.27 Example 2b revisited – mishedge ($C = max(S - 55{,}0)$)

In the binomial set-up, the volatility translates directly to the width of the span of potential outcomes. Thus a 30% annual volatility may translate into a 70–20 span as in Example 2b, but a 40% volatility may result in a wider span of 80–15 as in Example 2c.

If a dealer underestimates the actual volatility that the stock will experience during the life of the option, then he will discover that he has sold the option too cheaply. The premium he has charged will not cover the cost of the replicating strategy. In Black–Scholes, that means that the dealer should have used a higher volatility input. In the binomial model, the assumed span should have been wider. Note that the dealer is not asked to predict the really unpredictable, i.e. whether the stock will go up or down, but only the slightly unpredictable, i.e. whether the stock will fluctuate a lot between now and expiry.

Let us see in our binomial model what happens if the seller of a 55 call underestimates volatility. Suppose he uses the model as in Example 2b, describing potential outcomes as 70 and 20. He charges \$9-6/11 for the call and borrows \$5-5/11. With the total amount of \$15 he buys the prescribed 0.3000 shares at \$50 a share. But the stock proves more volatile, i.e. it attains either 80 or 15. The dealer will lose money whether the stock goes up or down (see Figure 5.27).

If the stock goes up to 80, the 0.3 shares are worth \$24, but the dealer owes \$25 to the option holder and \$6 on his borrowing. If the stock goes down to \$15, the 0.3 shares are worth \$4.50, but the dealer owes \$0 to the option holder and \$6 on his borrowing.

The primary risk of any option dealer is not the direction the underlying asset may take, but the exposure to the volatility of the underlying asset. A sold option results in a *short volatility position*. If the actual volatility of the underlying asset increases, the dealer loses money; if it decreases, the dealer makes money. A bought option results in a *long volatility position*. If the actual volatility of the underlying asset increases, the dealer makes money; if it decreases, the dealer loses money. The sensitivity of an option to the volatility input is called the *vega* of the option. The unit is the dollar change in the value of the option per 1% change in volatility. The vega of an option depends on the maturity of the option, the strike level relative to the current underlying asset's price (*in-the-moneyness*), and the interest rate. In general, the longer the time to expiry, the higher the vega as there is more time to lose money on mishedging. Also, the closer to at-the-money the option is, the greater the vega. Deep *in-the-money* options and deep *out-of-the-money* options have low vegas.

Option portfolios can also be described as long or short volatility. A long volatility portfolio may have bought and sold options, but the majority are bought. The "majority" here means that the net vega position in terms of net dollar sensitivity of the portfolio to a 1% change in the volatility (long vega options minus short vega options) is positive. A short volatility portfolio has a net negative vega. With many bought and sold options in the portfolio, the overall vega of the portfolio changes over time and as the price of the underlying asset fluctuates.

The vega risk of an option portfolio cannot be hedged with positions in the underlying asset, but only with option positions.

5.8.1 Implied Volatility

Running an option book is a chicken-and-egg game. To price options, we need a volatility input. To get that volatility input, we need to observe the prices of options. So which comes first?

In order to price the options we buy and sell, we need the volatility input into a pricing model (Black–Scholes, binomial, other). Different volatility assumptions will result in different hedge ratios, i.e. positions in the underlying assets. Suppose we have somehow guessed the right input, we priced all the options, computed the hedges, and bought or shorted the right net number of shares, bonds, or currency underlying the options in our portfolio. Our portfolio is now free of directional risk. Whether the underlying asset price goes up or down, we do not show any profit or loss.

But how do we guess the volatility input? We could perform a statistical analysis of the past movements in the asset's price and compute the standard deviation of the returns on the asset. This *historical volatility* could then be put into the model. However that would be tantamount to betting that the historical level of price variation will continue into the future. While we would not be betting directionally, we would be betting that the past cost of hedging would continue into the future. That is not a foolproof method.

A better way is to try to get at the market's current consensus of the future price volatility – not because the consensus will always be right, but because the consensus will determine the price of completely insuring our portfolio against the changing cost of the hedge. Where can we obtain the consensus estimate? In the option prices that we and other people charge.

Here is how this circular process works. Before we use the model to price our portfolio, we examine currently quoted option prices. Dealers who quote these prices include their estimates of future volatility as input into the same models to calculate their manufacture costs. We can back out what those estimates are by using our model to see what volatility input yields the prices they quote. This *implied volatility* can then be put into our own model to price and hedge our portfolio.

Using the implied volatility is superior to using the historical volatility as an input into an option model, because we can actually trade options that have been priced using implied volatilities. After all, we have obtained those implied volatilities from actual option quotes. And we can use those options to completely eliminate our vega risk. Suppose our portfolio is long volatility and market neutral. That is, we have bought more options than we sold, but we bought or shorted enough of the underlying asset to eliminate the directional risk. We compute the sensitivity of our portfolio to a 1% change in the volatility input, and sell new options at the quoted prices by choosing the amount sold so that those sold options have the same sensitivity to a 1% volatility change. We also neutralize the directional risk of the newly sold options through a delta hedge. Now our combined portfolio is directional risk-free and vega risk-free!

The only way for a delta-cum-vega hedger to make money from trading options is to charge more or pay less for options than the fair value of the model. The hedger's profit comes purely from the bid–ask spread and not from speculation on any explicit directional (price, rate) or implicit second-order (volatility) variable. Those primary and secondary risks are completely "sold off" by trading in the underlying assets and offsetting options.

Many dealers do not eliminate their vega risk completely and thus can be considered arbitrageurs/hedgers in first-order risk (directional) and speculators in second-order risk (volatility). They can, but choose not to, offset their volatility risk for two reasons. First, vega-hedging by buying/selling offsetting options is expensive and eats into profits. Second, the dealer's primary competence as a wholesaler of options lies in knowing the changing cost of reinsurance.

The only time one may consider using historical instead of implied volatilities as inputs into a model is the situation when there are no relevant options being quoted. By relevant options we mean options on the same underlying asset, with similar strike levels and for expiries similar to the options in our portfolio. This is typical for very long-term options. The reason for matching strikes and expiries is discussed below.

5.8.2 Volatility Smiles and Skews

An option valuation model is never perfect. It is a simplification of the potential price or rate movements. The total scope of those movements is constrained in a probability sense by the volatility input. The paths close to the mean are more likely than those away from the mean. The paths are continuous, i.e. prices do not jump discretely. Volatility is assumed constant in returns for the entire period, for sub-periods, and across price levels. In Black–Scholes, the price movements are log-normal. This means that as the price rises, the percentage changes remain on average the same, but absolute movements are assumed to grow. In currency option models, the FX rate may be assumed to fluctuate, but the interest rates are not. In interest rate option models, all rates may be assumed to move in parallel, or close to that. These are all assumptions necessary to make the math of the model tractable, but they may not all be realistic.

For these and perhaps many other reasons, it is well known that options on the same underlying asset require different volatility inputs for different strikes and expiries.

First consider the implied volatilities as published October 17, 2003 by the Federal Reserve for at-the-money currency options as of the end of the previous month (Table 5.1).

In Table 5.1, we are not shown strike levels, but for each currency the implied volatilities change with the expiry date. They tend to decrease as the time to expiry increases. This phenomenon has been alleged to have to do with the distinction between the realized or

Table 5.1 Implied volatility rates for foreign currency options* 9/30/2003

	1 week	1 month	2 months	3 months	6 months	12 months	2 years	3 years
EUR	12.6	11.8	11.6	11.4	11.4	11.3	11.2	11.2
JPY	14.3	12.5	11.6	10.8	10.3	10.1	10.0	9.9
CHF	12.7	11.9	11.7	11.5	11.5	11.5	11.5	11.4
GBP	10.3	9.8	9.6	9.4	9.3	9.3	9.4	9.4
CAD	10.1	9.7	9.5	9.4	9.1	8.9	8.9	8.8
AUD	13.2	12.3	11.9	11.4	11.1	11.0	10.9	10.8
GBP/EUR	8.3	7.8	7.7	7.6	7.6	7.5	7.5	7.3
EUR/JPY	12.8	11.6	11.11	0.7	10.5	10.3	11.6	10.3

*This release provides survey ranges of implied volatility mid rates for at the money options as of 11:00 am. The quotes are for contracts of at least $10 million with a prime counterparty.

This information is based on data collected by the Federal Reserve Bank of New York from a sample of market participants and is intended only for informational purposes. The data was obtained from sources believed to be reliable but this bank does not guarantee its accuracy, completeness, or correctness. For background information on the release, see: Page VBGROUND.FRB http://www.ny.frb.org/markets/implied.txt

Table 5.2 December: S&P 500

Strike	Implied volatility		Implied delta		Vega (ticks)
	Call	Put	Call	Put	
975	20.81	20.49	0.79	−0.2	1.24
980	20.48	20.21	0.78	−0.21	1.29
985	20.18	19.95	0.76	−0.23	1.34
990	19.91	19.72	0.75	−0.25	1.39
995	19.59	19.43	0.73	−0.26	1.44
1,000	19.36	19.16	0.71	−0.28	1.49
1,005	19.07	18.91	0.69	−0.3	1.53
1,010	18.79	18.66	0.67	−0.32	1.57
1,015	18.52	18.42	0.65	−0.34	1.61
1,020	18.19	18.12	0.63	−0.36	1.65
1,025	17.92	17.87	0.61	−0.38	1.68
1,030	17.76	17.68	0.58	−0.41	1.71
1,035	17.53	17.48	0.56	−0.43	1.73
1,040	17.29	17.27	0.53	−0.46	1.74
1,045*	17.04	17.04	0.51	−0.48	1.75
1,050	16.88	16.91	0.48	−0.51	1.75
1,055	16.65	–	0.45	* − 0.54	1.74
1,060	16.46	16.54	0.43	−0.56	1.73
1,065	16.3	–	0.4	* − 0.59	1.7
1,070	16.12	16.19	0.37	−0.62	1.67
1,075	15.91	16.02	0.34	−0.65	1.62
1,080	15.81	–	0.32	* − 0.67	1.57
1,085	15.75	–	0.29	* − 0.70	1.52
1,090	15.62	–	0.27	* − 0.72	1.45
1,095	15.53	–	0.24	* − 0.75	1.39
11,00	15.43	15.64	0.22	−0.77	1.32

Dec Fut = 1,044.50 days = 47 atmVol = 17.06% IntRate = 6.50%

The asterisk (*) indicates the closest strike to the forward (or the middle of the distribution) or at the money.
Source: http://www.pmpublishing.com/volatility/sp.html#StandardDeviations

actual volatility and "mean reversion." Short-term at-the-money options will require constant rebalancing as the hedge ratio computed between now and expiry will fluctuate. For longer-term options, the hedge ratio day-to-day is going to change much less, therefore while the actual volatility of the FX rate per day may be the same over a short period as over the long period, the dealer's "realized" volatility will be lower. The dealer will perform the buy-high/sell-low unprofitable trades less frequently. Therefore his cost of manufacture or the premium will be lower. This will result in a lower computed implied volatility. "Mean reversion" refers to the possibility that while the FX rates fluctuate unpredictably in the short run, they tend to oscillate around long-term trend lines, and the further they deviate from the trend lines the more they are pulled toward them. As option models cannot take all of these possibilities into account, they can be adjusted for them by lowering the long-term implied volatility to reflect the lower cost of manufacture.

Consider another example of the computation of implied volatilities, as of October 15, 2003, this time for options all on the same underlying asset and all with the same expiry date. Table 5.2 shows the implied volatilities on options on the S&P 500 index futures expiring

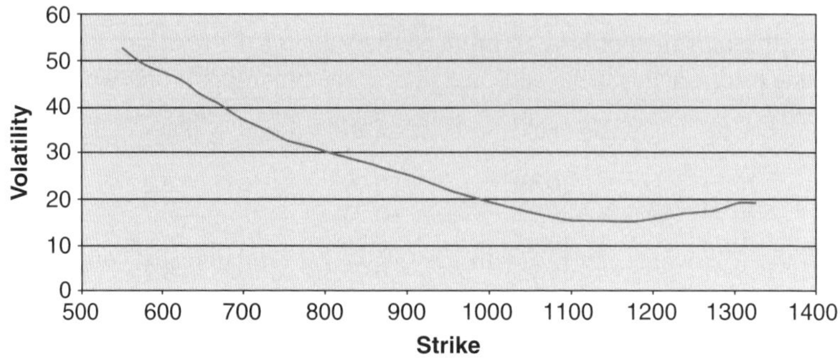

Figure 5.28 S&P 500 implied volatility skew, December 18, 2003
Puts with strikes below 1,045; Calls with strikes above 1,045

Source: http://www.pmpublishing.com/volatility/sp.html#StandardDeviations

December 18, 2003. The table also shows the delta for each option sold, in units of futures contracts to be bought/shorted per one option, as well as its vega, in ticks (index points) per 1% volatility change.

The at-the-money level is 1,044.50. Calls/puts with strikes higher/lower than that level are *out-of-the-money*, and with strikes lower/higher than that level are *in-the-money*. The table shows the implied volatilities for different strike levels. As a general rule they decrease as the strike level increases in a *half-smile* fashion as shown on the graph in Figure 5.28 (for very high strikes they start increasing again slightly).

This relationship of implied volatilities to strikes is generally referred to as a *volatility smile* or *volatility skew*. It probably reflects the fact that as prices drop, they tend to drop and fluctuate by more than assumed by the standard log-normal model, and as prices increase, they tend to increase more gradually without big jumps. There are models of the volatility skew itself that allow dealers to minimize the tertiary risk to relative volatility changes across strikes. This involves relating the different volatilities through a postulated mathematical function which is assumed not to change over time.

The significance of the volatility skew to the hedger lies in the basis risk of hedging options with one strike with options with a different strike. Even adjusting the input volatilities to compute the correct vega of the hedging instruments does not completely eliminate the risk that the skew itself may change over time. Similarly, hedging with options expiring on a different date may result in a tertiary calendar basis risk.

5.9 A REAL-LIFE OPTION PRICING EXERCISE

In this section, we put everything we have learned so far to use in one comprehensive exercise using very simple Excel models. The Black–Scholes takes five minutes to set up; the binomial takes a bit longer, but only because we have to be careful in converting the inputs consistently.

5.9.1 Consistency Checks: Put–Call Parity, Black–Scholes, and Binomial

Option models are relative value tools. We observe the implied volatility of one option and use it to price another. We observe the short-term interest rate and value the forward relative to the spot. We also use the interest rate as an input into the option valuation model. The prices of the call minus the put have to produce the value of the forward. Black–Scholes has to give the same price for European calls and puts as the binomial. If not, we are not using the models correctly.

Data

We start with the following. The 6-month LIBOR is 3% semiannually compounded (ignore Act/360). The stock index is at 1,000. The annualized volatility of the at-the-money options is 20%. The total present value of the dividends we estimate over the 6-month period is \$4.987521 on a \$1,000 investment in the index. (The dividends here could represent the interest rate differential in currencies, commodity storage fees, or stock lending fees.)

Discrete-to-Continuous Conversion

We need to make sure that we use all the variables either as discrete or as continuous. We don't want to mix them. First the interest rate conversion. We trace a \$1 investment over 6 months:

$$e^{r_c T} = 1 + \frac{r_d}{2}$$

with the discrete rate $r_d = 3\%$, time $T = 0.5$ year. We get the continuous equivalent rate $r_c = 2.9777\%$. Next we convert the dividends. Since we are given the total present value of $D = \$4.987521$, and we know the spot value of the index $S = 1{,}000$, then assuming we simply hold stocks for 6 months we get the continuous dividend yield δ from:

$$S \times e^{-\delta T} = S - D$$

The dividend yield is $\delta = 1\%$.

Futures Cash-and-Carry Parity

The fair forward in continuous time is equal to:

$$F = S \times e^{(r_C - \delta)T}$$

Plugging in we get $F = 1{,}009.938$. We verify that we would get the same in discrete time:

$$F = (S - D) \times \left(1 + \frac{r_d}{2}\right) = 995.012479 \times 1.015 = 1{,}009.938$$

Data Summary

We have:

$$\begin{aligned} S &= 1{,}000 \\ r_C &= 2.9777\% \\ \delta &= 1\% \\ \sigma &= 0.20 \\ T &= 0.5 \\ F &= 1{,}099.938 \end{aligned}$$

Table 5.3 Black–Scholes output for $K = 980$

Data		Black–Scholes pre-calc			Call	Put
		d_1	0.283490	Price	71.25126	41.75576
S	1,000	d_2	0.142069	Delta	0.608549	–0.386463
K	980	$N(d_1)$	0.611600	Gamma	0.002696	0.002696
T	182.5	$N(d_2)$	0.556487	Vega	269.6325	269.6325
r	2.98%	$N(-d_1)$	0.388400			
sig	20.00%	$N(-d_2)$	0.443513			
δ	1.00%	$sig\sqrt{T}$	0.141421			
		$e(-\delta T)$	0.995012			
		$n(d_1)$	0.383229			

Black–Scholes Prices for K = 980

First, let us price calls and puts struck at $K = 980$. We plug into the d_1 and d_2 formulas:

$$d_1 = \frac{\ln \frac{S}{K} + (r - \delta + \sigma^2/2)T}{\sigma\sqrt{T}} = \frac{\ln \frac{1{,}000}{980} + (0.029777 - 0.01 + 0.20^2/2) \times 0.5}{0.20\sqrt{0.5}} = 0.283490$$

and $d_2 = d_1 - \sigma\sqrt{T} = 0.283490 - 0.20\sqrt{0.5} = 0.142069$.

From the cumulative normal distributions, we get $N(d_1) = 0.611600$ and $N(d_2) = 0.556487$. We also get $N(-d_1) = 0.388400$ and $N(-d_2) = 0.443513$. We then plug into the Black–Scholes formula to get

$$\begin{aligned} C &= Se^{-\delta T}N(d_1) - Ke^{-rT}N(d_2) \\ &= 1{,}000 \times e^{-0.01\times 0.5} \times 0.611600 - 980 \times e^{-0.029777\times 0.5} \times 0.556487 \\ &= 71.25126 \end{aligned}$$

and

$$\begin{aligned} P &= Ke^{-rT}N(-d_2) - Se^{-\delta T}N(-d_1) \\ &= 980 \times e^{-0.029777\times 0.5} \times 0.443513 - 1{,}000 \times e^{-0.01\times 0.5} \times 0.388400 \\ &= 41.75576 \end{aligned}$$

Table 5.3 shows the Black–Scholes Excel output for the prices and the Greeks of calls and puts with $K = 980$.

Black–Scholes Prices for K = F = 1,009.938

We repeat the exercise for options with the strike price equal to the forward. Table 5.4 contains the Excel output.

Note that the price of the call and the put is the same when the strike is equal to the forward, and that irrespective of the strike the delta difference must be equal to 1. This follows from the put–call parity.

Check the Put–Call Parities for K = 980 and K = 1,009.938

We plug into the continuous version of the put–call parity with dividends:

$$C - P = Se^{-\delta T} - Ke^{-rT}$$

Table 5.4 Black–Scholes output for $K = 1{,}009.938$

Data		Black–Scholes pre-calc		Call	Put	
		d_1	0.070710	Price	56.0908	56.0908
S	1,000	d_2	−0.070711	Delta	0.525551	−0.469461
K	1,009.938	$N(d_1)$	0.528186	Gamma	0.0028	0.0028
T	182.5	$N(d_2)$	0.471814	Vega	279.9870	279.9870
r	2.98%	$N(-d_1)$	0.471814			
sig	20.00%	$N(-d_2)$	0.528186			
δ	1.00%	$sig\ \sqrt{T}$	0.141421			
		$e(-\delta T)$	0.995012			
		$n(d_1)$	0.397946			

First for the strike $K = 980$:

$$71.25126 - 41.75576 = 1{,}000 \times 0.995012 - 980 \times 0.985221 = 29.495$$

The fair value of the off-market forward to buy stock at 980 is \$29.495. To lock in the purchase price of 980 by buying calls and selling puts, one would have to spend out-of-pocket \$29.495.

Next for the strike $K = 1{,}009.938$:

$$56.0908 - 56.0908 = 1{,}000 \times 0.995012 - 1{,}009.938 \times 0.985221 = 0$$

The fair value of the on-market forward to buy stock at 1,009.938 is \$0 (costless). To lock in the purchase price of 1,009.938 by buying calls and selling puts, one would not have to spend anything out-of-pocket.

Convert the Inputs for a Binomial with N = 100 *Steps*

Using the logic of Section 5.6, but applying the continuous Black–Scholes equivalents listed in Section 5.7, we set up the binomial tree with $N = 100$ steps. Our time step is one-half year divided by 100 or $\Delta t = 1/200$. We then compute

$$u = e^{\sigma\sqrt{\Delta t}}, \quad d = 1/u, \quad q = \frac{e^{r\,\Delta t} - d}{u - d}$$

Table 5.5 shows the Excel output of the pre-calculated variables.

Table 5.5 Binomial inputs with $N = 100$ steps

Data		Set-up	100	Steps	
		Δt	0.005000	u	1.014243
S	1,000	$sig\ \sqrt{\Delta t}$	0.014142	d	0.985957
K	1,000	$r\ \Delta t$	0.000149	q	0.499961
T	182.5	$-\delta\ \Delta t$	−0.000050	$1-q$	0.500039
R	2.9778%	$e(sig)\ \sqrt{\Delta t})$	1.014243		
sig	20.00%	$e(r\ \Delta t)$	1.000149		
δ	1.00%	$e(-\delta\ \Delta t)$	0.999950		

Table 5.6 Binomial output for $K = 980$

Data		Set-up	100		Call	Put
		Δt	0.005000	Price	71.34	41.84
S	1,000	$sig\sqrt{\Delta t}$	0.014142	Delta	0.6085	−0.3866
K	980	$r\ \Delta t$	0.000149			
T	182.5	$-\delta\ \Delta t$	−0.000050	u	1.014243	
r	2.9778%	$e(sig\sqrt{\Delta t})$	1.014243	d	0.985957	
sig	20.00%	$e(r\ \Delta t)$	1.000149	q	0.499961	
δ	1.00%	$e(-\delta\ \Delta t)$	0.999950	$1-q$	0.500039	

Table 5.7 Binomial output for $K = 1{,}009.938$

Data		Set-up	100		Call	Put
		Δt	0.005000	Price	56.20	56.20
S	1,000	$sig\sqrt{\Delta t}$	0.014142	Delta	0.5255	−0.4696
K	1,009.938	$r\ \Delta t$	0.000149			
T	182.5	$-\delta\ \Delta t$	−0.000050	u	1.014243	
r	2.9778%	$e(sig)\sqrt{\Delta t}$	1.014243	d	0.985957	
sig	20.00%	$e(r\ \Delta t)$	1.000149	q	0.499961	
δ	1.00%	$e(-\delta\ \Delta t)$	0.999950	$1-q$	0.500039	

We set up the tree, assign the option values at the last time step $N = 100$ (expiry) and use the recursive algorithm for the values of the calls and puts at every node of the tree:

$$C = e^{-r\Delta t}[qC_u + (1-q)C_d]$$

Price the K = 980 *Options in the Binomial*

Table 5.6 shows the Excel output from the binomial for calls and puts struck at $K = 980$.

The prices are off by about 9 cents. To improve the accuracy, we would need to increase the number of steps or apply other error-reducing methods. One such method that is commonly used – the variance-reduction method – is to compute deviations from known continuous values instead of absolute prices. Most commercially available option-modeling software comes with plenty of tricks to eliminate pricing errors.

Price the K = 1,009.938 *Options in the Binomial*

Table 5.7 shows the Excel output from the binomial for calls and puts struck at $K = 1{,}009.938$. This time we are off by 11 cents. We would want to calibrate our model to ensure that it does not have significant pricing errors for any strikes, or any other inputs.

6
Options on Non-Price Variables

Options can be written on any variable, not just the price of some asset. Suppose we write a put option on the temperature reading in Paris on July 15, 2014, with a strike temperature of 23 °C. We need to define how the outcome of the event will be translated into a monetary payoff. With stocks or currencies, this is automatic. Once we know the size of the option, say 100 shares, the payoff is equal to the price difference per unit times the size. With options on non-price variables, we have to define a number that translates the units of the non-price variable into money. Once we specify the *multiplier* of €500 per 1 °C, the definition of our option is complete. If the temperature in Paris on the expiry date is 17 °C, our put option pays 23 – 17 = 6 times 500, or €3,000. If the temperature is 26 °C, the put pays nothing.

When valuing an option on a non-price variable, it is very important to determine whether the non-price variable is a linear or near-linear function of a price of something or whether it is not a linear function. If it is a linear function, then the valuation will rely on fairly simple modifications of the Black–Scholes model. The examples of this case include currencies and stock indexes. If the option is not a linear function of a price, then the valuation can be very complex. The examples of this second case are options on long interest rates. To hedge an option on an interest rate, one will need to buy or sell a bond. The payoff of the option is linear in the rate; the bond price is polynomial in the rate. This "convexity" of the bond price in the rate will mean that if the convexity is ignored then, even instantaneously, the hedge will be off. The goal of this chapter is to ease the reader into the complicated world of stock, currency, and interest rate options that require convexity adjusted models or full-blown interest rate models.

As a preview, we look at two easy cases. The first, common example of a non-price variable is a stock index like the S&P 500 or Nikkei 225. A stock index is not a price of anything, but a divisor-normalized number designed to track the percentage changes in a basket of stocks. The basket changes over time as some stocks come in and some are removed. Consider the Nikkei 225 index. In order to define a payoff of an option we need to translate the index points into yen. For example, we may specify that an 11,000 call will pay the difference between the index value and strike level times ¥10,000, or zero, whichever is greater. If the index hits 11,078.23 on the expiry date of the call, the holder would get

$$(11{,}078.23 - 11{,}000) \times ¥10{,}000 = ¥782{,}300$$

The second, slightly more difficult case involves the multiplier that is not be specified in what seems natural. Suppose a US investor wants exposure to the Japanese stock market, but does not want to bear currency risk. We could define the multiplier in dollars per Nikkei point, e.g. $250 per point. The holder would then get

$$(11{,}078.23 - 11{,}000) \times \$250 = \$19{,}557.50$$

The option defined in yen is easy to price and hedge; the one in dollars is not. The yen-denominated option is hedged like a stock option, by borrowing money in yen, buying the delta amount of stocks in the right proportions, and using the multiplier to define the total amount to be spent on shares. The dollar option is harder to hedge. It carries currency exposure as yen-denominated gains, and losses on the stocks have to be translated into dollars at a fictitious one-for-one fixed rate. The dollar option requires a "convexity" or "quanto" adjustment to Black–Scholes in order to price it.

A much harder non-price-based option example is an interest rate. An option on an interest rate is different from an option on a price of a bond, in which case we only need to specify the principal of the bond as the size. For options written directly on the interest rate, whether spot or forward, we cannot easily specify a "size." We can specify a multiplier, explicitly as \$25 per 1 bp of the difference between the underlying rate and the strike rate, or implicitly through a principal and day-count, e.g. \$10,000 times the quarterly 30/360 day-count of $1/4$ times the rate difference in percent. In either case, the payout is linear in the rate: we get \$25 per 1 bp rate change. Hedging such an option may be difficult. The rate cannot be bought or sold, only an instrument – a forward zero-coupon or coupon bond – whose value depends on it. The option fixes a linear yield–payout relationship; the price–yield relationship for the hedged instrument is non-linear. In some cases, this non-linearity can be ignored or handled with a "convexity" adjustment to the simple model; in many cases, however, it cannot be ignored, as it would lead to a significant mispricing and mishedging of the option. That is when we need a complicated arbitrage-free term-structure model.

There are also cases, where the "convexity" has to be taken into account in calculations that appear to have nothing to do with options. Examples of that include the *quanto* forward, analogous to the dollar Nikkei payoff, and the forward LIBOR (FRA), when constructing the yield curve using LIBOR-based Eurodollar futures.

6.1 BLACK MODELS FOR BOND PRICE OPTIONS, CAPS/FLOORS, AND EUROPEAN SWAPTIONS

In this section, we tackle the cases where most of the complications of arbitrage-free yield curve construction can be ignored. This is because these issues cause only second-order errors in the discounting and not first-order errors in the diffusion of the underlying variable. The idea is to decouple the primary driver of the value of the option – a long bond price or a swap rate – from the short-term discounting rate, and in effect treat the primary driver like the diffused stock price in the Black–Scholes, while constructing a correctly bootstrapped, but constant, discounting curve. This necessarily implies that the connection between the short and long rates in the yield curve is broken.

6.1.1 Options on Bond Prices

Options on bond prices are typically quoted over-the-counter for short expiries or are embedded in bond and swap contracts. A one-time callable or putable bond can be viewed as a package of a bullet bond and a call option held by the issuer or a put option held by the buyer. In either case, one party has the right to buy/sell the bond at a fixed strike price expressed in dollars. A European swaption is a very similar contract dressed in swap language.

The main model for dealing with short expiry options on long-term bond is the forward formulation of the Black–Scholes introduced as the Black model of Chapter 5. We assume that prior to using the model, we bootstrapped the yield curve using the methods of Chapter 2 – that is, we have a set of spot discount factors $df(0, T)$ to any date T in the future that allow us to discount any cash flows on those dates. The prices of calls and puts on bond prices are:

$$C = [FN(d_1) - KN(d_2)]df(0,T)$$
$$P = [KN(-d_2) - FN(-d_1)]df(0,T)$$
$$\text{with } d_1 = \frac{\ln\frac{K}{F} + (\sigma^2/2)T}{\sigma\sqrt{T}} \text{ and } d_2 = d_1 - \sigma\sqrt{T}$$

where F is the forward price of the bond on the option expiry date, and σ is the volatility of the price of the bond, also known as the *price volatility* of the bond to distinguish it from the *yield volatility*. The main assumption here is that the forward price (not spot price) of the bond has a constant volatility.

Consider a 6-month call option on a 5¼-year 5% semi-annual coupon bond. For simplicity assume that the yield curve out to 1 year is flat at 4% quarterly compounded. The bond currently trades at 103 and the strike is 102.50. There are three issues to consider:

- In order to compute the forward price of the bond at the expiry of the option, we need to present value the coupon cash flows between now and expiry.
- The forward bond price volatility is assumed constant; yet it is clear that the price volatility will decrease over the life of the bond to zero at maturity.
- Interest rate volatilities are often quoted in terms of yield, not price volatilities; a *yield volatility* is the standard deviation of the percentage changes in yields i.e. $\Delta y/ys$

Let us tackle each issue. First, to compute the forward price of the bond (forward to option expiry), we can present-value all the coupons that the bond will throw off between now and the option expiry to today, net the present value against the spot bond price, and then future-value the bond to the option expiry using the cash-and-carry principle.

Our semi-annual bond will pay one coupon cash flow equal to $100 \times 5\%/2 = 2.5$ one quarter from today. The PV of that is $2.5/\left(1 + \frac{0.04}{4}\right) = 2.475$. We subtract that from the spot price of the bond and then future value the net to the option expiry date. The whole expression is:

$$F = (S - CF_\tau \times df(0,\tau)) \times \frac{1}{df(0,T)}$$

or

$$F = (103 - 2.475) \times \left(1 + \frac{0.04}{4}\right)^2 = 102.545$$

We sweep the issue of the declining price volatility of the bond under the carpet. While it is true that at maturity the price volatility is zero, we are relying on the fact that the option expiry is short relative to the maturity of the bond and we can ignore this effect. Lastly, the quick and dirty conversion of yield volatilities to price volatilities is accomplished easily by multiplying the yield volatility by the modified duration of the bond and the current level of the yield. This follows from the application of Ito calculus to the derivation of the stochastic process for the bond price, given the yield process and the observation that the percentage change in the bond price is approximately equal to the modified duration times the change in yield. Hence the conversion expression is:

$$\sigma = ModD \times ytm \times \sigma_{ytm}$$

where *ModD* is the modified duration of the bond at the option expiry (forward duration), *ytm* is the yield-to-maturity on the bond at option expiry (forward yield), and σ_{ytm} is the yield volatility of the forward bond price. If the forward yield is 4.9%, the yield volatility is 25%, and the forward modified duration is 4.2, then the price volatility input into the model is:

$$\sigma = 4.2 \times 0.049 \times 25\% = 5.145\%$$

The call value using the Black formula is:

$$C = [102.545 \times N(d_1) - 102.5 \times N(d_2)]df(0, T) = 1.467$$

$$\text{with } d_1 = \frac{\ln \frac{102.545}{103} + (0.05145^2/2)0.5}{0.05145\sqrt{0.5}} = -0.1035, \quad d_2 = d_1 - 0.05145\sqrt{0.5} = -0.1399$$

$$\text{and } N(d_1) = 0.4588, \quad N(d_2) = 0.4444, \quad df(0, 0.5) = 1/\left(1 + \frac{0.04}{4}\right)^2 = 0.9803$$

The call is worth 1.47% of the principal of the bond, and in order to delta hedge the dealer will buy 45.88% of the bond's face value.

6.1.2 Cap and Floor Definitions

Many interest rate option structures are not options expiring on a single date, but rather packages of *optionlets*, each expiring on a single date. They are constructed to mimic the periodic cash flows of bonds and swaps and they borrow the language of bonds and swaps like the principal or face value and day-count applied to interest accrual calculations.

Caps and floors are packages of options, looking like calls and puts, correspondingly, on the same underlying short-term interest rate with sequential expiry dates. The vast majority of caps and floors have the 3-month LIBOR as their underlying rate. The expiry dates on the options, called *caplets* or *floorlets*, follow a quarterly or semi-annual schedule, typically matched to the maturity of the underlying rate, starting with immediate expiry and ending with the last expiry date, being one period prior to the stated maturity of the cap. For example, a 5-year cap on 3-month LIBOR struck at 4.5% consists of 20 caplets with expiries of 0 months, 3 months, 6 months, 9 months, and so on, all the way to 57 months. The payouts on the options are delayed by 3 months, i.e. made in arrears; the last payout is on the maturity date of the cap, i.e. in 60 months. The payoff on each caplet is equal to the greater of zero and the difference between the underlying LIBOR rate on the expiry date and the strike rate of 4.5%, times the day-count fraction on an Act/360 basis for the period covered by the LIBOR rate. A floor is a "put" equivalent of a cap; that is, the payoff of each floorlet is equal to the greater of zero and the difference between the strike rate of 4.5% and the underlying LIBOR rate on the expiry date, times the same day-count fraction. All these details are designed to match the swap market convention, since caps and floors are viewed as natural supplements to swaps.

Let us illustrate, in Table 6.1, a 4.5% cap and a 4.5% floor by assuming some hypothetical (unknown up front, except for the first one) LIBOR rates (in column 2) for future option expiry dates (called set dates), and day-counts for the subsequent 3-month period until the pay dates. The principal amount is $100 million.

The buyer of the cap benefits if spot LIBOR rates on future dates exceed 4.5%. The buyer of the floor benefits if spot LIBOR rates on future dates are below 4.5%. The first caplet and floorlet may be deleted, unless specifically stated to the contrary, i.e. technically we have

Table 6.1 5-year 4.5% $100 million cap and floor on 3-month LIBOR

100 million
(dates in months from today)

		Cap			Floor			
Set date	LIBOR	max($L-K$, 0)	Days	Payout	max($K-L$, 0)	Days	Payout	Pay date
0	4.50	0	91	0	0	91	0	3
3	4.20	0	91	0	0.3	91	75,833	6
6	4.81	0.31	92	79,222	0	92	0	9
9	5.20	0.7	90	175,000	0	90	0	12
12	5.40	0.9	89	222,500	0	89	0	15
15	5.55	1.05	91	265,417	0	91	0	18
18	5.83	1.33	92	339,889	0	92	0	21
21	6.21	1.71	91	432,250	0	91	0	24
24	6.43	1.93	90	482,500	0	90	0	27
27	6.11	1.61	92	411,444	0	92	0	30
30	5.73	1.23	91	310,917	0	91	0	33
33	5.32	0.82	91	207,278	0	91	0	36
36	5.17	0.67	89	165,639	0	89	0	39
39	4.85	0.35	92	89,444	0	92	0	42
42	4.62	0.12	91	30,333	0	91	0	45
45	4.33	0	91	0	0.17	91	42,972	48
48	4.02	0	89	0	0.48	89	118,667	51
51	3.78	0	92	0	0.72	92	184,000	54
54	3.66	0	91	0	0.84	91	212,333	57
57	3.21	0	90	0	1.29	90	322,500	60

19 optionlets. Bought caps can be viewed as protection against interest rate increases, while floors can be viewed as protection against interest rate declines.

The at-, in-, and out-of-the money terminology for caps and floors is a little different from stock options; there, we usually had only one option, here we have many, bought as a package. A cap or floor is said to be (struck) at-the-money if the strike price is chosen to be the swap rate of the same maturity as the maturity of the cap. Correspondingly, one can talk about in-the-money or out-of-the-money caps and floors depending on whether their strike is greater or less than the swap rate. The statement applies on an aggregate basis, not to individual optionlets. If, in our illustration, the 5-year swap rate on an Act/360 basis is 5%, then our cap would be called in-the-money (as the swap rate is higher than the strike), even though based on today's LIBOR the caplets are really at-the-money, and on a forward basis some caplets may be out-of-the-money. Our floor would be out-of-the-money as the swap rate is above the strike.

6.1.3 Relationship of Caps and Floors to FRAs and Swaps

We have shown that a swap is a package of FRAs dissected along the set dates. A 5-year quarterly swap can be viewed as a package of 20 FRAs with consecutive maturities. The start date of each FRA matches the set date of the swap, and the end date of the FRA matches the pay date of the swap corresponding to the next set date. In a 5-year quarterly swap, the first FRA is 0×3, the next 3×6, and so on. The last one is 57×60.

Instead of dissecting swaps along set and pay dates, we can dissect them along rate levels. A pay-fixed swap can be viewed as a long cap and a short floor. And each constituent FRA can be viewed as a long caplet and short floorlet position. Suppose we buy a \$100 million 5-year cap struck at 4.5% and sell a \$100 million 5-year floor struck at 4.5%. When LIBOR exceeds the strike, the payoff on the floor is zero and the payoff on the cap is equal to LIBOR minus the fixed rate of 4.5%. This is equivalent to a receipt of LIBOR and payment of fixed 4.5%. When LIBOR is below the strike, the payoff on the cap is zero and the liability on the floor is equal to the fixed rate of 4.5% minus LIBOR. This is equivalent to a receipt of LIBOR and payment of fixed 4.5%. That is, no matter where LIBOR sets, the cash flows are equivalent to those of a swap with a fixed rate of 4.5%. Table 6.2 summarizes the situation.

Each row is a dissection of an FRA into a caplet and a floorlet. The sum of the rows is equal to the swap. Each column group is a dissection of the swap into a long cap and a short floor. The net receipt on the swap is identical to the net of the cap and floor positions.

Put–Call Parity for Caps/Floors

$$\textit{Cap struck at } K - \textit{Floor struck at } K = \textit{Swap with fixed rate } K$$

Suppose that we do not pick the strike rate randomly, but instead we select it in such a way that the premium we pay on the cap is equal to the premium we receive on the floor. That is, we have no net cash flow up front. What swap would have no net cash flow up front? A *par* swap or an *on-market* swap. We can thus conclude the following.

$$\textit{Cap } (\textit{with } K = \textit{Swap rate}) - \textit{Floor } (\textit{with } K = \textit{Swap rate}) = \textit{Par swap}$$

Recall the put–call parity for stocks and the analogous relationship for stock options struck at the forward. As implied volatilities increased, the values of the calls and puts, both struck at the forward, increased by the same amount as their payoff was still equivalent to the forward. The same is true for caps and floors. In order to conform to the constraint of no-arbitrage, if prices of caps struck at the swap rate increase (due to implied volatility rise), the prices of floors struck at the swap rate must also increase by the same amount. The pricing assumptions do not change the payout on the combined position, which is still equivalent to an on-market swap. These considerations are the basis for the in-the-moneyness language for caps and floors as defined above.

One can construct swaps out of caps and floors, and vice versa. A cap can be viewed as a combination of a pay-fixed swap and a long floor position. A floor can be viewed as a combination of a long cap position and a receive-fixed swap.

6.1.4 A Cap Application

Bond issuers often combine a long over-the-counter cap position with a floating rate bond sold to investors. This ensures that the coupon payments on the bond do not exceed a certain desired level.

Suppose a company issues a 5-year bond paying quarterly floating coupons equal to LIBOR. The company also buys from a dealer a cap struck at 4.5%. If LIBOR on any coupon set date exceeds 4.5%, the company's net obligation will stay at 4.5%. If LIBOR on any coupon date is below 4.5%, the company takes advantage of the floating nature of the issue, and pays less

Table 6.2 4.5% $100 million cap, floor, and swap

5-year
(dates in months from today)

			Long cap		Short floor			Swap		
Set Date	LIBOR	Days	max($L-K$, 0)	Payout	max($K-L$, 0)	Payout	Pay date	Receive	Pay	Net
0	4.50	91	0	0	0	0	3	1,137,500	1,137,500	0
3	4.20	91	0	0	0.3	–75,833	6	1,061,667	1,137,500	–75,833
6	4.81	92	0.31	79,222	0	0	9	1,229,222	1,150,000	79,222
9	5.20	90	0.7	175,000	0	0	12	1,300,000	1,125,000	175,000
12	5.40	89	0.9	222,500	0	0	15	1,335,000	1,112,500	222,500
15	5.55	91	1.05	265,417	0	0	18	1,402,917	1,137,500	265,417
18	5.83	92	1.33	339,889	0	0	21	1,489,889	1,150,000	339,889
21	6.21	91	1.71	432,250	0	0	24	1,569,750	1,137,500	432,250
24	6.43	90	1.93	482,500	0	0	27	1,607,500	1,125,000	482,500
27	6.11	92	1.61	411,444	0	0	30	1,561,444	1,150,000	411,444
30	5.73	91	1.23	310,917	0	0	33	1,448,417	1,137,500	310,917
33	5.32	91	0.82	207,278	0	0	36	1,344,778	1,137,500	207,278
36	5.17	89	0.67	165,639	0	0	39	1,278,139	1,112,500	165,639
39	4.85	92	0.35	89,444	0	0	42	1,239,444	1,150,000	89,444
42	4.62	91	0.12	30,333	0	0	45	1,167,833	1,137,500	30,333
45	4.33	91	0	0	0.17	–42,972	48	1,094,528	1,137,500	–42,972
48	4.02	89	0	0	0.48	–118,667	51	993,833	1,112,500	–118,667
51	3.78	92	0	0	0.72	–184,000	54	966,000	1,150,000	–184,000
54	3.66	91	0	0	0.84	–212,333	57	925,167	1,137,500	–212,333
57	3.21	90	0	0	1.29	–322,500	60	802,500	1,125,000	–322,500

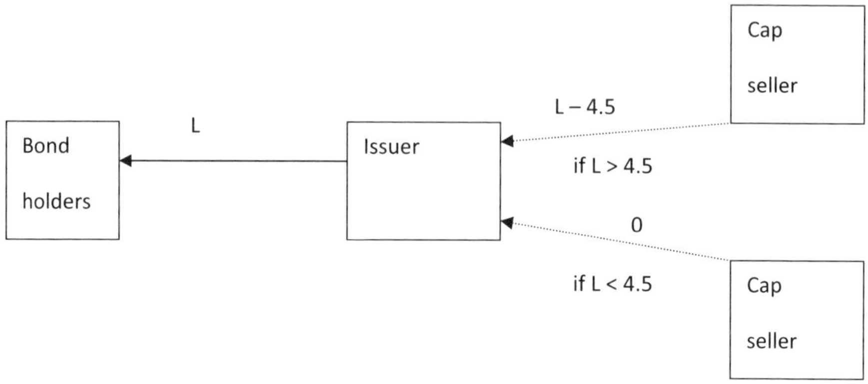

Figure 6.1 A floating-rate bond insured with a 4.5% cap

than 4.5%. Its net obligation is thus the lower of the two, LIBOR or 4.5%. The hypothetical cash flows are summarized in Table 6.3 and illustrated graphically in Figure 6.1.

For months 9 to 45, when LIBOR exceeds 4.5%, the company effectively pays 4.5% rate times the appropriate day-count.

A mirror-image application of a long floor position is on the investment side. Suppose a portfolio manager owns a floating rate bond and fears that, as rates come down, her income

Table 6.3 5-year $100 million floating rate bond and 4.5% cap

(dates in months from today)

Set date	LIBOR	Days	Long cap: max(L–K, 0)	Long cap: Payout	Floating bond Coupon	Pay date	Net
0	4.50	91	0	0	–1,137,500	3	–1,137,500
3	4.20	91	0	0	–1,061,667	6	–1,061,667
6	4.81	92	0.31	79,222	–1,229,222	9	–1,150,000
9	5.20	90	0.7	175,000	–1,300,000	12	–1,125,000
12	5.40	89	0.9	222,500	–1,335,000	15	–1,112,500
15	5.55	91	1.05	265,417	–1,402,917	18	–1,137,500
18	5.83	92	1.33	339,889	–1,489,889	21	–1,150,000
21	6.21	91	1.71	432,250	–1,569,750	24	–1,137,500
24	6.43	90	1.93	482,500	–1,607,500	27	–1,125,000
27	6.11	92	1.61	411,444	–1,561,444	30	–1,150,000
30	5.73	91	1.23	310,917	–1,448,417	33	–1,137,500
33	5.32	91	0.82	207,278	–1,344,778	36	–1,137,500
36	5.17	89	0.67	165,639	–1,278,139	39	–1,112,500
39	4.85	92	0.35	89,444	–1,239,444	42	–1,150,000
42	4.62	91	0.12	30,333	–1,167,833	45	–1,137,500
45	4.33	91	0	0	–1,094,528	48	–1,094,528
48	4.02	89	0	0	–993,833	51	–993,833
51	3.78	92	0	0	–966,000	54	–966,000
54	3.66	91	0	0	–925,167	57	–925,167
57	3.21	90	0	0	–802,500	60	–802,500

from the bond will decline. She can purchase a floor struck at the desired level to maintain her income at or above that level.

6.1.5 Pricing of Caps and Floors

The pricing of caps and floors follows the standard Black–Scholes model, or the Black version thereof, with the following enhancements:

- Prior to using the model the discounting curve has been bootstrapped and we have a set of spot discount factors $df(0, T)$ to any date T in the future that allow us to discount any cash flows on those dates.
- Each caplet/floorlet is priced separately with forward LIBOR playing the role of the forward stock/currency price in the Black model and a volatility input is applied to it.
- While the caplets/floorlets are priced separately, they all depend on the evolution of the same LIBOR rate; therefore the volatility structure input into pricing must be self-consistent and, in particular, not allow for negative forward volatilities.

The model is not arbitrage free. We have a fixed yield curve with clearly defined constant LIBOR forwards to future set dates. Yet we diffuse the LIBOR rates with a volatility input, i.e. assume that they are stochastic, while at the same time we discount the cash flows from the pay dates to today using the constant discount factors. The valuation formula for caplet setting on date T is:

$$C = Face \times [FN(d_1) - KN(d_2)] \times \frac{days}{360} \times df(0, T + 3\,months)$$

$$P = Face \times [KN(-d_2) - FN(-d_1)] \times \frac{days}{360} \times df(0, T + 3\,months)$$

$$\text{with } d_1 = \frac{\ln\frac{F}{K} + (\sigma^2/2)T}{\sigma\sqrt{T}} \quad \text{and } d_2 = d_1 - \sigma\sqrt{T}$$

where F is the forward 3-month LIBOR from set date T over the subsequent 3 months, $Face$ is the notional principal of face value of the cap/floor, *days/360* is the day-count for the interest payment period from the forward set date T to the payment date for that period 3 months later which is also the next set date, and $df(0, T + 3\,months)$ is the discount factor from today to the pay date of the caplet/floorlet which is 3 months after the set date. For example, to value the third of the 20 caplets in the 5-year cap, we would input $Face = \$100$ million, *days/360* might be equal to 91/360, if there are 91 days in the interest accrual period between 6 months and 9 months from today, and the discount factor $df(0, T + 3\ months)$ would cover the period from today to the pay date of the caplet in 9 months. The volatility input would be appropriate for diffusing LIBOR over the next 6 months and the time input would be $T = \frac{1}{2}$ to correspond to the 6 months to the LIBOR set time. The σ input is always entered on an annualized basis.

Cap/floor implied volatilities are often quoted as *flat volatilities*. A dealer may quote a 24% volatility for a 5-year cap and 27% volatility for a 3-year cap with the same strike. That is, if we apply 24% as input into each of the 20 caplet-pricing models spanning 5 years and 27% as input into each of the 12 caplet-pricing models spanning 3 years we will get the quoted price in basis points of the face value of the caps. Yet the 5-year cap is the 3-year cap plus 8 more caplets spanning years 4 and 5. A simple arbitrage rule is that a longer expiry cap or floor must be more expensive than a shorter expiry cap or floor with the same strike. So, a 5-year cap costs more than a 3-year cap. But the flat volatility quoted on the 5-year cap may be lower than that on the 3-year cap, just not arbitrarily lower.

Flat volatilities are like yields-to-maturity on coupon bonds. They are "averages" of individual caplet volatilities that produce the same overall price. By observing ever longer maturity caps and floors, we can bootstrap them to produce individual caplet volatility input called *spot volatilities*. We observe 6-month, 1-year, 2-year, etc., caps/floors and bootstrap a 3-month caplet volatility, then 6- and 9-month volatilities, then 12-, 15-, 18-, and 21-month volatilities, and so on. These spot caplet volatilities typically follow a humped pattern, first rising out to 1–2 years and then slowly declining.

The spot volatilities of caplets/floorlets must follow certain logic rules. Suppose we bootstrap the volatility for the eight caplet setting in 21 months as 29% and the volatility for the ninth caplet setting in 24 months as 18%. Let us not forget that we are diffusing the same 3-month LIBOR in each caplet-pricing model. By the simple propagation rule for a log-normal variable with a deterministic volatility schedule, we have the following relationship for the spot 24-month volatility as a function of the spot 21-month volatility and the forward volatility spanning the 3 month period from 21 to 24 months:

$$\sigma_{0-24}\sqrt{\frac{24}{12}} = \sigma_{0-21}\sqrt{\frac{21}{12}} + \sigma_{21-24}\sqrt{\frac{3}{12}}$$

Substituting $\sigma_{0-24} = 0.18$ and $\sigma_{0-21} = 0.29$, we get $\sigma_{21-24} = -0.258$. Even in the risk-neutral world, LIBOR volatility input cannot be negative. The relationship between the spot and forward caplet/floorlet volatilities which disallows negative forward volatilities puts constraints on the volatility bootstrap process. In our example, perhaps we bootstrapped the 21-month volatility from the flat volatilities to be too high at 29%, and that is why we cannot fit the price of the 24-month caplet.

6.1.6 European Swaption Definitions

Swaptions (swap options) are options to enter into a swap. Unlike a cap which consists of a series of caplets with sequential expiry dates, a swaption has one expiry date and is exercised once. Upon exercise, the holder of a swaption will enter into a swap with multiple pay and receive cash flows. Exercise can be European-style (once at expiry only), American style (once any time prior to or on the expiry date), or Bermudan style (once on any swap set date prior to or on the expiry date). For example, a 3-into-7 \$100 million European call swaption struck at 5%, gives the owner the right to receive fixed 5% against floating LIBOR, on a \$100 million 7-year swap. If the option is exercised on the expiry date, which is 3 years from today, the swap would start on that day and end 7 years later. The same swaption can be referred to as 3-year/10-year-final swaption to imply that the exercise right is in 3 years and the final maturity of the swap is in 10 years from today. A Bermudan or American version would be exercisable between today and 3 years from today, not just 3 years from today, and the swap would start immediately at exercise and end 10 years from today. The "3-into-7" language is rarely used with American and Bermudan options; the "3-year/10-year-final" language is preferable (if the option is exercised in 2 years, the swap will last 8 years).

Calls are options to receive (fixed) on the swap; puts are options to pay (fixed) on the swap. The call/put terminology corresponds to the view of swaps as exchanges of bonds. A receive-fixed swap can be thought of as a bought fixed rate bond and a sold floating rate bond,

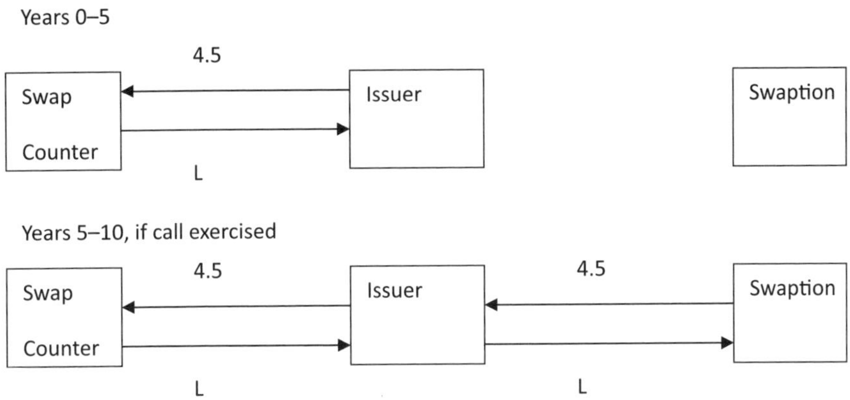

Figure 6.2 A European call swaption to cancel a swap

or a bought fixed rate bond financed by a revolving loan. So a call swaption is like an option to buy a fixed rate bond, just as a call is an option to buy a stock. A put swaption is an option to sell a fixed rate bond, i.e. the option to pay a fixed rate on an obligation, and to receive a floating financing rate.

6.1.7 Options to Cancel Swaps

A swaption can be packaged with a swap to bestow the right to cancel the swap. Suppose we pay a fixed rate of 4.5% on a 10-year quarterly swap; we receive 3-month LIBOR. If our swap counterparty sells us a 5-into-5 call swaption struck at 4.5, the call gives us the right to receive 4.5% on a 5-year swap starting 5 years from today. However, if we exercise the call, then we will exactly offset the remaining cash flows on the existing 10-year swap (Figure 6.2).

The call swaption, which we defined as the right to enter a swap to receive fixed, can also be defined as the right to cancel a pay-fixed swap. The "call" language conforms to the call provisions on fixed coupon bonds. Analogously, the "put" notion for swap options to cancel corresponds to the right of the fixed coupon bondholders to put the bonds back to the issuer at par.

6.1.8 Relationship of Swaptions to Forward Swaps

From the above construction, one should also be able to see the following put–call parity relationship:

Put–Call Parity for European Swaptions

$$\textit{Call Swaption} - \textit{Put Swaption} = \textit{Forward Swap}$$

Suppose we buy a 5-into-5 call swaption struck at 4.5% and sell a 5-into-5 put swaption struck at 4.5%. If 5-year swap rates are low in 5 years, say at 3%, then we will exercise our call right to receive fixed 4.5% (above market). The holder of the put we sold will not exercise.

Alternatively, if 5-year swap rates are high in 5 years, say at 6%, then the holder of the put we sold will exercise his right to pay fixed 4.5% (below market). We will not exercise our call. His exercise decision will force us to receive fixed 4.5%. Thus no matter what swap rates are in 5 years, we will enter into a 5-year receive-fixed swap at that time. Viewed from today, this is a forward swap agreement. It starts at a future known date (5 years) and ends at a future known date (10 years), and the fixed rate (4.5%) on it is agreed today.

In addition, if instead of 4.5% we choose the strike rate in such a way that the premium paid for the call equals that received for the put, then the sure forward swap will be arranged at no cost to either party, i.e. it will be a *par forward swap*.

This relationship will be true no matter what the level of implied volatilities used by dealers as input into their pricing models, because the static arbitrage constraint will not change.

Swaptions can be synthesized from forward swaps and other swaptions. A call is equivalent to a forward receive-fixed swap and a put swaption. A put is equivalent to a forward pay-fixed swap and a call swaption.

Swaptions can also be viewed as one-time options on long (swap) rates. Note that, in the above discussion, we decided that the call holder will exercise when future swap rates are lower than the strike. This guarantees that the present value of the swap he chooses to exercise into is positive – that is, he has a positive payoff. This is true because the LIBOR leg part of the swap (equivalent to the floating rate bond) always prices (present-values) to par, and the positive PV will come from the discounted value of the differences between the strike and the actual lower fair swap rate, i.e. the bond with a fixed coupon equal to the strike will price above par. If the fair rate were equal to the strike, the fixed bond with a coupon equal to the strike would also price to par. So the payoff of the call can be viewed as the difference between the strike and the fair swap rate times the day-count-corrected annuity factor, or sum of discount factors, for all swap payment dates.

$$\begin{aligned} Call &= max\,[0, K - Swap\ rate] \times Annuity\ factor \\ Put &= max\,[0, Swap\ rate - K] \times Annuity\ factor \end{aligned}$$

Swaptions and caps and floors are also related, but not so simply. Both types of options are ways of dissecting swaps, i.e. share the risk of the swap with other players. Caps and floors can be forward starting to make them look identical to swaptions in terms of start and end dates. But caps and floors dissect swaps on the floating side, while swaptions do so on the fixed side. Caps and floors are packages of several mini-options on each swaplet (FRA), while swaptions are one-time options on the entire swap. The two are related for the following reason. The long (forward) swap rate, which is the underlying rate for the swaption, is a package of forward starting swaplets (FRAs). That one rate can be exchanged costlessly into a series of short-term fixed rates (equal to FRA rates for the respective pay periods), or further into unknown floating rate payments (as on-market FRAs cost nothing to enter into). A long cap and short floor position is equivalent to those floating rate payments.

Because of these interrelationships between long and short rates, one can claim that the prices of swaptions and caps and floors are interrelated (as are their implied volatilities). The modeling of these relationships is extremely complex.

6.1.9 Pricing of European Swaptions

The pricing of European call and put swaptions follows the standard Black–Scholes model, or the Black version thereof, with the following enhancements:

- Prior to using the model the discounting curve has been bootstrapped and we have a set of spot discount factors $df(0, T)$ to any date T in the future that allow us to discount any cash flows on those dates.
- That same yield curve bootstrap produces all forward discount factors $df(t, T)$ that allow us to discount any cash flows from future dates T back to prior future dates t.
- That same yield curve bootstrap produces the forward swap rate $F(T, M)$ known today from the swaption expiry date T to the final swap maturity date M.
- The one-time exercise option is priced with the forward swap rate $F(T, M)$ playing the role of the forward stock/currency price in the Black model and an annual volatility input is applied to that forward swap rate

The model is not arbitrage free. We have a fixed yield curve with clearly defined constant LIBOR forwards to future set dates and constant forward swap rates from any date to any subsequent future date. Yet we diffuse the one forward swap rate $F(T, M)$ with a volatility input, i.e. assume that it is stochastic, while at the same time we discount the cash flows from the pay dates to today using the constant discount factors. The valuation formula for a European swaption expiring on date T and with a final swap date M is:

$$C = Face \times [F(T, M) \times N(d_1) - K \times N(d_2)] \times AF(T, M) \times df(0, T)$$

$$P = Face \times [K \times N(-d_2) - F(T, M) \times N(-d_1)] \times AF(T, M) \times df(0, T)$$

$$\text{with} \quad d_1 = \frac{\ln \frac{F}{K} + (\sigma^2/2)T}{\sigma\sqrt{T}} \quad \text{and} \quad d_2 = d_1 - \sigma\sqrt{T}$$

where $F(T, M)$ is the forward swap rate from the expiry date T to the final swap maturity date M, $Face$ is the notional principal of face value of the swaption, $AF(T, M)$ is the annuity factor for \$1 received/paid as the interest payment on the entire fixed leg of the forward swap from date T to date M, and $df(0, T)$ is the discount factor from today to the swaption expiry date.

Let us define all the inputs through an example and assume that the yield curve is flat at 4.5% semi-annually compounded. For a 5-into-5-year \$10 million call swaption struck at 4.5%, we set $T = 5$ and $M = 10$. From the yield curve, we compute a zero-PV forward swap rate $F(T, M) = 4.5\%$. If the swap into which the swaption is exercisable follows the standard US convention, then upon exercise in 5 years we will receive fixed 4.5% semi-annually on a 30/360 basis and pay quarterly LIBOR flat on an Act/360 basis for the next 5 years. The discount factor is

$$df(0, 5) = \frac{1}{\left(1 + \frac{0.045}{2}\right)^{10}} = 0.80051.$$

The annuity factor ignores the floating leg and is computed as the present value of \$1 on the fixed leg's interest payment dates. In general, the formula for the annuity factor is:

$$AF(T, M) = \sum_{k=n_T}^{n_{M-1}} dayfrac\,(k, k+1) \times df(T, t_{k+1})$$

We take day-count fractions for each fixed coupon period ($\approx 1/2$) and multiply them by the forward discount factors from the fixed coupon pay dates ($5^1/_2$, 6, $6^1/_2$, ..., 10 years) to the swaption expiry date (5 years).

If the convention were different from 30/360 we might need to adjust it for the fact that \$1 of interest might be multiplied by an Act/360 or Act/Act fraction not equal to $^1/_2$. Here we can use a simple textbook annuity formula divided by 2 to get

$$AF(T, M) = \frac{1}{2}\left(\frac{1}{0.045/2} - \frac{1}{(0.045/2)(1+0.045/2)^{10}}\right) = 8.8662/2 = 4.4331$$

This is a forward price value of a basis point (PVBP). The last input is the volatility which we assume we imply from other observed swaptions.

The theory of why the Black model, as opposed to a more complicated arbitrage-free interest rate model, is adequate is beyond the scope of the book. However, we state here that it can be shown that in a forward swap rate risk-neutral world relative to the fixed leg annuity, it is correct to use constant interest rates for discounting as long as we set the expected swap rate to the forward swap rate (unadjusted for convexity) and the option is exercisable into a standard swap with a fixed leg following the pay dates of the numeraire annuity. (This is not true, for example, of constant maturity swaps in which the exercise value is multiplied by a constant, *not* a future, annuity factor.)

6.1.10 Limitations of the Black Model

It is important to realize that the Black models – for bond price options, caps/floors, and European swaptions are self-consistent individually but are not consistent with each other. In particular, while all the interest rates considered, e.g. forward LIBOR rates in caps and floors, and forward swap rates in European swaptions, are related to each other through the yield curve, the different versions of the Black model treat them independently. The cap volatilities are quoted separately on a flat or per caplet basis. The European swaption volatilities have to be quoted as a matrix indexed by the expiries and final swap maturities. Also, there is nothing in the models to ensure that the pricing is logical. There is no mechanism to force 2-into-8 and 3-into-7 swaptions to have similar volatility inputs, or to force a 3-into-2 swaption and a 4-year cap to have similar volatility inputs. It is left to the user to recognize similar structures and to use appropriate inputs.

6.2 CONVEXITY-ADJUSTED MODELS FOR LIBOR FORWARDS, QUANTOS, AND CONSTANT MATURITY SWAPS

The Black model can be extended, but often requires a convexity adjustment, in order to correctly price European structures that, at first, seem to require an arbitrage-free term structure model. It can also be extended to handle structures that, at first, do not seem to require any option model, and yet they do. The first two examples of when we need a convexity adjustment are of the second variety and are the yield curve bootstrap itself and an arrears swap.

When constructing the yield curve, we want to use the most liquid instruments as their price/rate is the most reliable, and the same most liquid instruments will probably be used to hedge. To build the LIBOR/swap curve that is used to price the majority of interest rate derivatives, we typically use the combination of Eurodollar (Euroyen, Eurosterling, or Euribor) futures up to 5, 7, or 10 years and swap rates afterwards. Swaps, which can be viewed as exchanges of bonds, are convex instruments, i.e. their PV is convex in the yield. Eurodollar futures are not; they pay \$25 per basis point. When building the yield curve with longer expiring Eurodollar futures, we cannot ignore the fact that they are not identical to FRAs. The forward LIBOR cannot be simply read off the futures quotes; it must be convexity-adjusted to produce the correct value equivalent to the rate that would be quoted on an FRA.

An arrears swap – wherein the floating leg cash flows are set and paid at the beginning of each interest accrual period instead of being paid at the end – is another non-option example of requiring a convexity adjustment. The forward discount bond price is convex in LIBOR. The model is risk neutral in the forward LIBOR with respect to the forward discount factor and will price correctly the LIBOR cash flow determined on the set date, paid 3 months later, discounted back to the set date and then back to today, but will not price correctly the LIBOR cash flow paid on the set date and discounted to today.

The constant maturity swap (CMS), and options on it, are examples of where the same convexity adjustment that is present, but small, in an arrears swap becomes a big issue. In an arrears swap, the error comes from a 3-month mismatch; in the CMS options the mismatch between the set date of the swap rate (on the option expiry date) and the multiple payment dates for the fixed leg over the life of the swap is very large. The unadjusted Black model, risk neutral with respect to the numeraire annuity factor, will misprice the immediate settlement of a long swap rate.

The last case we consider below is the *quanto* case, which is very common in currency contexts. Quanto refers to assigning dollar values to non-native variables which cannot be bought and sold in dollars, like points of the Nikkei index with a multiplier defined in US dollars per index point. The hedger of a quanto structure is exposed to the cross movement of the Nikkei index and the yen/dollar exchange rate, and the forward price of the index cannot be computed using a US dollar interest rate. The Black model using dollar financing numeraire must have the index forward "convexity" adjusted.

6.2.1 Convexity Adjustment for Eurodollar Futures

Suppose we have bootstrapped discount factors out to the 3-year point and we want to use a Eurodollar futures contract on 3-month LIBOR expiring in 36 months to extend our yield curve to 39 months. Suppose the Eurodollar contract is quoted at 97.20, implying a LIBOR rate of 2.8% for the period from 36 months to 39 months. However, the 2.8% rate is not the same as the forward LIBOR rate, because the futures contract is a non-convex daily-settled arrangement. By the contract expiry date, the total mark-to-market settlement amounts will not be the same as those for settling an FRA that locks the forward 36 × 39 financing perfectly. In a short rate (normal) one-factor model (which assumes perfect correlation between the discount rates for the mark-to-market settlements and the future LIBOR rate), and ignoring the continuous-to-discrete *Act/360* conversion, the convexity adjustment formula is:

$$L_F = L_{ED} - \frac{1}{2} \times L_{ED}^2 \times \sigma^2 \times T \times (T + t)$$

where L_F is forward LIBOR (FRA equivalent), L_{ED} is LIBOR implied in the Eurodollar futures quote, σ is the log-normal volatility of the forward LIBOR rate, T is the time to the expiry of the future contract, and t is the tenor of the LIBOR rate.

In our 36 × 39 example, we set $T = 3$, $t = \frac{1}{4}$, and $L_{ED} = 2.8\%$. The last input we need is the implied volatility from Eurodollar futures options expiring in 3 years or from 3-year caplets/floorlets. Suppose the current implied volatility is $\sigma = 30\%$. Then the 36×39 forward 3-month LIBOR is computed as follows:

$$\begin{aligned} L_F &= 0.028 - \frac{1}{2} \times 0.028^2 \times 0.3^2 \times 3 \times 3\frac{1}{4} = 0.028 - 0.000344 \\ &= 2.8\% - 0.0344\% = 2.7656\% \end{aligned}$$

The convexity adjustment for short futures expiries is small. In our 3-year example, it is only 3.5 bp. However, it grows quite rapidly, roughly with the square of the time. If we compute it for a 9-year futures expiry, keeping the rest of the inputs constant, we get 29.4 bp. Tripling the time produces a nine times larger convexity wedge.

6.2.2 Convexity Adjustment for CMS Options

Constant maturity options are caps or floors with *long-term* government (Constant Maturity Treasury CMT) or Constant Maturity Swap (CMS) rates as the underlying variables, but the day-count and frequency of payoff like that of a short rate. A 5-year quarterly cap on a 10-year swap rate struck at 6% pays the greater of zero and the difference between the 10-year rate and the strike every quarter for the next 5 years. The day-count used for the payoff calculations is that of a given quarter and the payoff is made in arrears (at the end) just as for a simple caplet. The only difference between a straight cap and a CMS cap is that, instead of comparing LIBOR to the strike, we compare the 10-year swap rate to the strike.

This small difference is much bigger than it seems. With a standard LIBOR cap, the delta hedge instrument is a 3-month Eurodollar deposit, a forward or futures on it. We have learnt how to correct the yield curve to get the right number of futures in the hedge. That correction is relatively small too. With CMS caps/floors – as we compute the delta per 1 bp move in the forward swap rates, and then translate it through duration into a dollar holding of the underlying bond/swap – our hedge will always be imperfect because of the mismatch (in each caplet) between the long tenor of the forward swap and the payment settlement of the caplet only 3 months later. These hedging errors magnify the longer the hedge (on later caplets). On a 5-year maturity option, they can be very large in total. The CMT options have the added difficulty of swap spread exposure.

CMS caps/floors appear to be more similar to swaptions than to caps. A swaption is a bet on a future long-term rate with the payoff multiplied by the appropriate annuity factor reflecting the final maturity of the underlying swap. A CMS cap can be seen as a series of swaptions with increasing maturities and with payoffs multiplied by an "inappropriate" annuity factor (for 3 months). Swaptions can be hedged easily with forward swaps synthesized from long long-maturity swaps and short short-maturity swaps, because the annuity factor in their payoff matches the forward swaps. CMS caps/floors cannot.

Fortunately, the convexity correction for CMS caplets/floorlets is an easy generalization of the correction for Eurodollars, with the $(T + t)$ term replaced by the ratio of the second and first derivatives of the underlying forward bond price, i.e. roughly the ratio of the underlying bond's convexity to its duration (more precisely in price-value-of-a-basis-point terms). The ratio can be computed numerically by blipping the yield to maturity of the forward bond or closed-form for simple 30/360 fixed bonds.

For a CMS caplet/floorlet on the t-year maturity swap rate CMS_t expiring T years from now, the convexity adjustment to the forward swap rate CMS_t is:

$$-\frac{1}{2} \times CMS_t^2 \times \sigma^2 \times T \times \frac{P''_{T,T+t}}{P'_{T,T+t}}$$

where $P''_{T,T+t}$ and $P'_{T,T+t}$ are the second and first derivatives of the price of the par coupon bond starting on the forward date T and maturing t years later with respect to the yield to maturity.

Let us go through a simplified example. We are pricing a 4-year caplet on the 10-year annual swap rate. The yield curve is flat at 6%. The implied volatility on a European 4-into-10 swaption is $\sigma = 20\%$. The yield on the forward 10-year swap is the par rate on the forward 10-year fixed coupon bond and is equal to 6%. We price the forward 6% coupon bond to get its current price:

$$P = 100$$

We approximate the first and second derivative numerically by blipping the yield by 1 bp and using center difference approximations similar to the duration and convexity formulae of Chapter 2. The blips produce:

$$P_{+1bp} = 99.926434,\ P_{-1bp} = 100.073636$$

The derivatives are:

$$P' = \frac{P_{+1bp} - P_{-1bp}}{2bp} = \frac{99.9264 - 100.0736}{0.02} = -7.36$$

$$P'' = \frac{100(P_{+1bp} - 2P + P_{-1bp})}{(1bp)^2} = \frac{100(99.9264 - 200 + 100.0736)}{0.0001} = 70$$

The convexity adjustment to the CMS forward is:

$$\frac{1}{2} \times 0.06^2 \times 0.20^2 \times 4 \times \frac{70}{7.36} = 0.002739 = 0.2739\%$$

We would use the rate of 6.274% as an input into the convexity-adjusted Black model to price the 4-year caplet on the 10-year CMS rate.

6.2.3 Quanto Adjustments

Quantos are options whose payoffs are defined in non-native currencies. A seemingly standard put option on FTSE 100, whose payoff is in US dollars per point of the index, is quite a bit more complicated than that whose payoff is defined in British pounds. In the simpler pound case, the hedge is obvious. The seller of the put shorts the stocks in the index. The total change in their value in pounds dynamically produces the pound payoff at expiry. The quanto version of the option forces the dealer into an additional currency hedge as the pound payoff needs to be guaranteed in dollars, and the two hedges are interrelated. As the potential payoff in dollars rises because of the FTSE change, the underlying stock hedge pound value may over- or under-compensate for a possible FX rate change when the hedge is liquidated and the payoff made.

The *quanto* feature can be added to almost any option. A popular equity option that pays the best of several national indexes, say S&P 500, Nikkei 225, and FTSE 100, is often *quantoed* into one desired currency, say the euro. Futures are sometimes quantoed too, and require an adjustment when pricing relative to the non-quantoed cousins.

The quanto adjustment follows from the change of numeraire argument in the risk-neutral world and in continuous time it is equal to: $I_Q = I \times e^{\rho\sigma_I\sigma_{FX}T}$ where I is the spot value of the index (Nikkei), ρ is the correlation of the Nikkei returns and forward yen/dollar FX rate percentage changes, σ_I is the log-normal volatility of the Nikkei (implied from standard Nikkei options), σ_{FX} is the log-normal volatility of the forward yen/dollar FX rate, and T is the time to the quanto option expiry date in years. The result is the quanto-adjusted value of the index I_Q to be input into the Black–Scholes model. To compute the fair value of a quantoed-into-dollars Nikkei futures contract, we would further subject it to the cash-and-carry spot-forward link using the yen interest rate and Nikkei dividend yield.

Suppose the Nikkei is at 11,050, 6-month options on the Nikkei imply a volatility of $\sigma_I = 20\%$, 6-month FX options on the yen/dollar rate imply $Q_{FX} = 10\%$, and the correlation between the Nikkei and the FX rate is $\rho = 0.15$. To price 6-month quanto options on the Nikkei, we first adjust the spot index input:

$$I_Q = 11{,}050 \times e^{0.15\times0.2\times0.1\times0.5} = 11{,}066.59$$

We can compute the forward quanto-adjusted value of the index using the standard parity relationship. If the semi-annual 6-month yen LIBOR is 1.2% and the dividends are zero, then, ignoring the Act/360 convention, the forward Nikkei is equal to:

$$I_Q^F = I_Q(1 + {}^L\!/_2) = 11{,}066.59 \times 1.006 = 11{,}132.99$$

This forward Nikkei is the fair value of a quantoed futures contract and it is also the input we would use in a Black model with the dollar LIBOR rate as the risk-free rate.

6.3 ARBITRAGE-FREE INTEREST RATE MODELS

There are two good reasons for abandoning the simple Black model with convexity adjustments in favor of an arbitrage-free reduced-form model. First, it is the consistency of inputs which prevents the possibility of arbitraging oneself. The various Black model guises are often used separately, with different inputs and adjustments, to price the same or similar structures. Bond options are European swaptions in disguise. CMS optionlets on shorter rates are related to swaptions. Caps and floors are related to swaptions on short swap rates. Even very tight manual controls can sometimes fail to ensure that the models we use to price these seemingly unrelated structures produce the same prices. The second reason for using an arbitrage-free model is that options come in a variety of exotic flavors and simple adjustments may be difficult to derive. Many options, especially with American exercise features, require the modeling of the evolution of the entire yield curve and not just one main driving rate.

However, arbitrage-free modeling is not without a cost. The main cost is borne right at the start, in model calibration. These models impose a rigid structure on the evolution of interest rates allowing only for a deterministic time-dependent volatility structure. Yet we observe many caps and floors and many European swaptions with almost infinite combinations of option term and final swap term. We face an overdetermined system of too many inputs and only a few parameters to fit them with. The real world is messy and does not conform easily to a normal or log-normal reality, and exhibits skews. This necessarily implies that there is no guarantee that options not used directly in the calibration may not at times be mispriced. The second cost of arbitrage-free modeling is that because of its numeric complications, we sometimes focus on the trees and not the forest. We devote time to minutely calibrate a short-term tree, and we miss the fact that our model may only have one overriding stochastic factor that does not allow for yield curve tilts. So while we have a perfectly volatility-calibrated yield curve-fitted European swaption model, the model still misprices multiple American exercise features or options on the difference between the 10-year point and the 2-year point. In this last case, the simpler, non-arbitrage-free model may actually be better!

In this section, we review a few popular short rate models, and their most common numerical implementation through the use of trinomial trees, the general one-factor Heath–Jarrow–Morton framework which subsumes most short rate models, and we finish with a two-factor approach of the LIBOR market model to addressing yield curve tilts.

6.3.1 Short Rate Models

We skip the discussion of early equilibrium models of Vasicek (1977), Rendleman and Bartter (1980), and Cox, Ingersoll, and Ross (1985), which attempt to endogenize how interest rates are formed from underlying economic activity, and focus on reduced-form no-arbitrage models. Reduced-form models take the yield curve as a given and price derivatives relative to it. Short rate models focus on describing the stochastic evolution of the instantaneous discount rate as moves through time. They have a non-stochastic mean, or drift, component, and a stochastic (random) component.

They are usually identified by the underlying evolution equation written in continuous time, where discrete changes Δ are replaced by instantaneous changes denoted with a small letter d. This is similar to standard calculus where, for example, we model the position of a train relative to the departure point as a variable $s = s(t)$, which is a function of time t. If the train is traveling at a constant speed ν then the function is simply $s = \nu \cdot t$. The change in the train's position, or the distance from the departure point, can be written in the form of a differential equation, as $ds = \nu \cdot dt$. In differential calculus, the position equation $s = \nu \cdot t$ is referred to as a general solution to the differential equation $ds = \nu \cdot dt$, which is also known as the equation of motion. We can then identify the constant parameters and impose some initial conditions, e.g. $\nu = 60\,\text{km}/h$ and $t_o = 0:00\,\text{am}$. If the train traveled for $dt = 1$ h then the position is $s = 60 \cdot 1 = 60\,\text{km}$ away from the departure point. So the typical set-up is: define the instantaneous equation of motion for a variable of interest as a function of dependent variables; obtain the general solution for the current position of the dependent variable; and solve for the current position numerically relative to the starting point. In cases where we cannot obtain the general solution, we mimic the instantaneous equation of motion with a numerical tree or grid (e.g. a trinomial explicit tree) and obtain the solution numerically. That is, we have a computerized algorithm, instead of a neat mathematical function, to compute the dependent variable for any level of independent variables.

In stochastic calculus, the set-up is the same as in the standard differential calculus, except that in addition to the deterministic independent time variable t, we add a stochastic independent variable z. All dependent variables of interest to us, and changes in them, depend on one of these (time or random variable only) or both. Depending on the form of the equation of motion for an interest rate, we may or may not be able to obtain the general solution for the interest rate itself or derivatives on it. The models differ in the form of dependence on time and on the stochastic variable.

In the Ho–Lee model (Ho and Lee, 1986), the instantaneous short rate changes are given a normal form:

$$dr = \mu(t)dt + \sigma dz$$

In this continuous time notation, the instantaneous change in the (instantaneous) short rate r has a general time-dependent mean component $\mu(t)$ and a normal random component. In the latter, we have a constant volatility parameter σ multiplying the normal variable dz which is distributed, $N(0, dt)$. So, if the current super-short ("overnight") discount rate is at 5% and the annual volatility is $\sigma = 0.1$, then we are postulating that, in the absence of any drift, the short rate 1 month later at $t = 1/12$ is normally distributed with a mean of 5% and standard deviation of $0.1.\frac{1}{12} = 0.8333\%$. This necessarily means that interest rates in the model can be negative, although with very low probabilities. As written, the Ho–Lee model also imposes a rigid drift along the instantaneous forward curve on the evolution of the short rate ($\mu(t)$ can be derived analytically as a forward at t plus $\sigma^2 t$). The advantages of the model are that zero-coupon bond prices have an analytical solution simplifying the numerical implementation of the model.

Hull and White (1990) improve the model by introducing mean reversion into the drift structure $\mu(t)$. The differential equation is:

$$dr = [\theta(t) - \alpha r]dt + \sigma dz$$

As written, the equation postulates that the short rate r drifts along the variable $\theta(t)/\alpha$ and if it moves away from that level as a result of a random shock, it reverts to that mean level with speed α. The mean reverting level is equal to the initial forward yield curve plus a small term. The Hull–White specification restricts the short rate away from extreme values and yields analytic formulas for bond prices, but still does not prevent negative interest rate values.

The Black and Karasinski (1991) model does exactly that. The short rate is log-normal, rather than normal, and it is subject to mean reversion. The functional form is:

$$dr = [\theta(t) - \alpha(t) lnr]dt + \sigma(t)dz$$

The model is most appealing from the perspective of allowable interest rate movements – mean reversion, no negative values, and a time-dependent volatility structure – but completely loses analytic tractability. The only way to use it is through a numeric implementation. Most commonly, this is done with the use of a trinomial tree.

6.3.2 Trinomial Trees and Calibration

Trinomial trees are discretized representations of continuous equations of motions. They are equivalent to explicit methods of numerical analysis in mathematics. Instead of an instantaneous time movement dt of an interest rate starting at the initial position $r_0 = 5\%$ at time $t_0 = 0$ along a continuous straight line representing time along the horizontal axis, we introduce a small discrete step Δt of segment-by-segment jumps of the rate r along the horizontal axis. That is, time changes discretely, not continuously. The stochastic (random) nature of the movement of the interest rate is accomplished by splitting the movement along the horizontal line (originally flat at 5%) into three discrete nodes in which the line can jump (up, middle, and down). The movement can then continue from each node (say 5.10%, 5%, 4.9%) separately along the time-segmentized line, with new jumps allowed on each new horizontal line. We therefore measure the level of the interest rate vertically, and time horizontally, and the interest

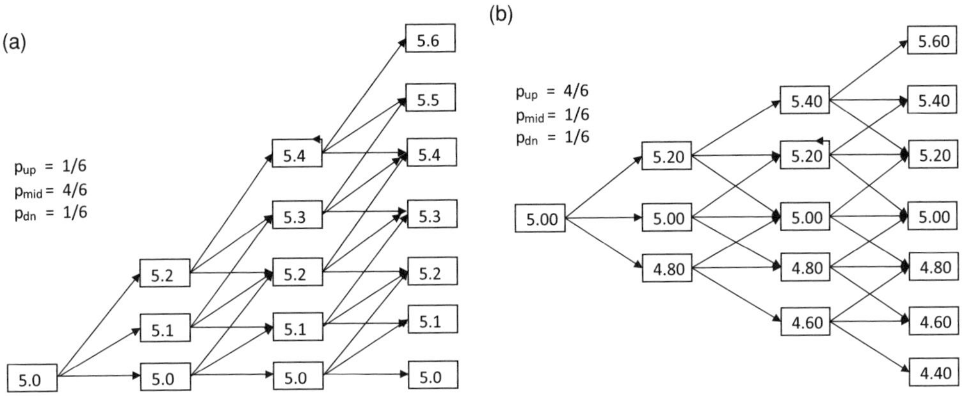

Figure 6.3 Examples of recombinant trinomial trees

rates are discretized in both dimensions. The discretization along the vertical axis is equivalent to converting the assumed continuous normal or log-normal distribution to a trinomial and relying on the central limit theorem, with some stochastic calculus corrections, that with ever smaller Δt steps the discrete and the continuous are going to be the same. If we construct a dense enough tree, the algorithm will produce the same prices as the original equations would if they were solvable.

The typical trinomial tree is recombinant. Subsequent nodes of a node are the same as some of the subsequent nodes of another node, and there are multiple ways to get to any interior node. The recombinant feature reduces the number of calculation as it reduces the overall number of nodes, and allows the algorithm to handle American exercise options. The drift and mean reversion of interest rates are controlled jointly by assigning the interest rate levels for the nodes and the probabilities of jumping to those nodes. Parts (a) and (b) in Figures 6.3 show simple recombinant trinomial trees, both with instantaneous forward short-rate drifting up.

In both trees, the up-jump followed by a middle-jump is the same as the middle-jump followed by an up-jump, and the same for down-middle sequences, i.e. either way the interest rate ends up at the same level along the vertical axis after two time steps. That need not be the set-up of a trinomial tree. While tree (a) in Figure 6.3, does not allow any nodes with interest rates decreasing from 5% at time t_0 and appears to be drifting up, tree (b) has the same drift up, owing to the way in which the probabilities of the nodes are assigned. Let us compute the mean for the next time period t_1. In tree (a), the mean is:

$$\bar{r}_1 = \frac{1}{6} \cdot 5.20 + \frac{4}{6} + \cdot 5.10 + \frac{1}{6} \cdot 5.00 = 5.10$$

In tree (b) the mean is:

$$\bar{r}_1 = \frac{4}{6} \cdot 5.20 + \frac{1}{6} + \cdot 5.00 + \frac{1}{6} \cdot 4.80 = 5.10$$

In the last time period t_3, the mean for tree (a) is:

$$\bar{r}_3 = \left(\frac{1}{6}\right)^3 \cdot 5.60 + 3\left(\frac{1}{6}\right)^2\left(\frac{4}{6}\right) \cdot 5.50 + \cdots + 3\left(\frac{1}{6}\right)^2\left(\frac{4}{6}\right) \cdot 5.10 + \left(\frac{1}{6}\right)^3 \cdot 5.00 = 5.30$$

and for tree (b) is:

$$\bar{r}_3 = \left(\frac{4}{6}\right)^3 \cdot 5.60 + 3\left(\frac{4}{6}\right)^2\left(\frac{1}{6}\right) \cdot 5.40 + \cdots + 3\left(\frac{1}{6}\right)^2\left(\frac{4}{6}\right) \cdot 4.60 + \left(\frac{1}{6}\right)^3 \cdot 4.40 = 5.30$$

We compute these by observing that in each tree there are multiple ways to get to a given node at time t_3. To compute the unconditional probabilities of each node, we cumulate the conditional probabilities across paths. For example, in tree (a), there are three ways to get to node 5.50% at time t_3: up-up-mid, up-mid-up, and mid-up-up, each path with probability $\left(\frac{1}{6}\right)^2\left(\frac{4}{6}\right)$.

We could similarly compute the unconditional variances for each time slice t_n by taking square deviations from the mean and weighting them by probabilities. At this point, the reader should be sensing how these variances may be related to the implied volatilities on caps and floors and how the reverse calibration process may proceed. Good examples of building trinomial trees for the Hull–White model are given in Hull and White (1996).

We do not cover the details of the tree calibration process here except to point out the main restricting conditions that the tree algorithm must meet:

- The tree must price all zero-coupon bonds correctly: \$100 to be received at time t_n assigned to each node at time slice t_n discounted and probability-weighted backwards along the tree branches must produce the price of a zero-coupon bond maturing at time t_n.
- The tree must price a target set of liquid caplets/floorlets and European swaptions; e.g. in order to set the drift and volatility inputs, we consider a 1-year caplet on 3-month LIBOR; we build the tree out to time slice $t_n = 1$ year; for each final node, we recover the 3-month LIBOR analytically, or by continuing the tree for another 3 months, from the conditional 3-month discount bonds; we search for a volatility input which, combined with the drift inputs, will produce the correct price of the caplet when discounted and probability-weighted from the pay time of the caplet backward in the tree all the way back to time t_o; we repeat the procedure for caplet/floorlets with ever increasing expiry dates.

Since the drift and volatility input parameters are time-dependent constants, there are only so many inputs with which to match the traded prices of all the caps/floors and swaptions. The calibration process is in most cases overdetermined, and not all options prices can be matched exactly.

6.3.3 The Heath–Jarrow–Morton Model and the LIBOR Market Model

The HJM model (Heath, Jarrow, and Morton, 1992) is often referred to as the best no-arbitrage interest model. In fact, it is simply a generalized framework of no-arbitrage conditions that interest rate models must satisfy. The HJM argument starts by postulating a general process for the set of all instantaneous forward rates maturing at time τ for periods $(\tau, \tau + 1)$. It then derives the link between the drift term and the general volatility term that all models must satisfy. In the most general form of the model, the short rates are non-Markov, i.e. they are path dependent, which means that recombinant trees cannot be built for them. However, one can impose restrictions on the general form to reduce the general HJM framework to Markov forms, and one can show that all no-arbitrage short-term models are special cases of it.

The subtle point about the HJM frameworks is that when modeling the forward rates, rather than short rates, the solution for the drift term in the risk-neutral world depends only on the volatility parameters and does not include the unknown equilibrium price of risk. That is often not so in short rate models unless one skips directly to the risk-neutral world, but that then renders the interpretation of volatility and drift parameters difficult (e.g. not directly translatable to Black–Scholes volatilities).

Here is the general idea of the HJM framework in a three-step numerical example. The simplifying assumptions and the notation are as follows.

- We use a binomial tree with annual steps $\Delta t = 1$ from time $t = 0$ to time $t = 3$ years from now.
- We denote by $f_t(\tau, \tau + 1)$ the continuously compounded forward rate at time t for year τ, e.g. $f_0(0, 1)$ is the forward rate today for the period from today to 1 year from today, i.e. the 1-year spot rate, and $f_0(1, 2)$ is today's forward rate for the period from 1 year to 2 years from today. We use superscripts u and d repeatedly to denote the up and down steps.
- The model is normal, rather than log-normal. We take the starting yield curve at time t and we add the drift and the volatility, $f_t(\tau, \tau + 1) + \theta_t(\tau, \tau + 1)\Delta t \pm \sigma(\tau, \tau + 1)\Delta t$, instead of multiplying it to get expressions like $f_t(\tau, \tau + 1)e^{\theta(\tau)\Delta t \pm \sigma(\tau)\Delta t}$.
- To get a recombinant tree we set the probability of the up state equal to the probability of the down state and equal to ½, i.e. $q = 1 - q = \frac{1}{2}$, and we set the volatility to be constant for each forward maturity τ, i.e. σ only has a $\tau, \tau + 1$ index, but does not have a time t subscript.
- We assume that initially at time $t = 0$, the forward 1-year rates for years 0, 1, and 2 are $f_0(0, 1) = 4.8\%$, $f_0(1, 2) = 5.0\%$ and $f_0(2, 3) = 5.2\%$, respectively. The volatility of the 1×2 forward rate is $\sigma(1, 2) = 0.02$ (equivalent to 40% log-normal, $0.02 = 0.05 \times 0.40$) and the volatility of the 2×3 forward rate is $\sigma(2, 3) = 0.03$.

The set-up is depicted in Figure 6.4. It follows the Black–Scholes set-up of Chapter 5, the only exception being the issue of fixing the drift terms for the diffusion in the tree through a bootstrap. To do this, we use the no-arbitrage restriction that the tree must price each successive maturity zero-coupon bond correctly.

$$f_2^{uu}(2, 3)$$

$$\begin{matrix} f_1^u(1,2) \\ f_1^u(2,3) \end{matrix} = \begin{matrix} f_0(1,2) \\ f_0(2,3) \end{matrix} + \begin{matrix} \theta_0(1,2) \\ \theta_0(2,3) \end{matrix} + \begin{matrix} \sigma(1,2) \\ \sigma(2,3) \end{matrix} = \begin{matrix} 0.050 + \theta_0(1,2) + 0.02 \\ 0.052 + \theta_0(2,3) + 0.03 \end{matrix}$$

$$\begin{matrix} f_0(0,1) = 4.8\% \\ f_0(1,2) = 5.0\% \\ f_0(2,3) = 5.2\% \end{matrix} \qquad f_2^{ud}(2, 3)$$

$$\begin{matrix} f_1^d(1,2) \\ f_1^d(2,3) \end{matrix} = \begin{matrix} f_0(1,2) \\ f_0(2,3) \end{matrix} + \begin{matrix} \theta_0(1,2) \\ \theta_0(2,3) \end{matrix} + \begin{matrix} \sigma(1,2) \\ \sigma(2,3) \end{matrix} = \begin{matrix} 0.050 + \theta_0(1,2) - 0.02 \\ 0.052 + \theta_0(2,3) - 0.03 \end{matrix}$$

$$f_2^{dd}(2, 3)$$

Figure 6.4 A one-factor three-step HJM model

$$f_2^{uu}(2,3) = f_1^u(2,3) + \theta_1(2,3) + \sigma(2,3) = 0.1130495 + \theta_1(2,3)$$

$$\begin{matrix} f_1^u(1,2) \\ f_1^u(2,3) \end{matrix} = \begin{matrix} 7.02000\% \\ 8.30495\% \end{matrix}$$

$$\begin{matrix} f_0(0,1) = 4.8\% \\ f_0(1,2) = 5.0\% \\ f_0(2,3) = 5.2\% \end{matrix} \qquad f_2^{ud}(2,3) = \begin{matrix} f_1^u(2,3) + \theta_1(2,3) - \sigma(2,3) \\ f_1^d(2,3) + \theta_1(2,3) + \sigma(2,3) \end{matrix} = 0.0530495 + \theta_1(2,3)$$

$$\begin{matrix} f_1^d(1,2) \\ f_1^d(2,3) \end{matrix} = \begin{matrix} 3.02000\% \\ 2.30495\% \end{matrix}$$

$$f_2^{dd}(2,3) = f_1^d(2,3) + \theta_1(2,3) + \sigma(2,3) = -0.006951 + \theta_1(2,3)$$

Figure 6.5 A one-factor three-step HJM model continued

To fix the drift term $\theta_0(1,2)$, we price the 2-year \$100 zero-coupon bond. We sweep backwards through the tree, probability weighting the values of 1-year discount bonds in the up and down states at time $t = 1$, and discounting them by 1 year to time $t = 0$:

$$P_0(0,2) = e^{-0.048} \times \left(\frac{1}{2}e^{-0.07-\theta_0(1,2)} \times 100 + \frac{1}{2}e - 0.03 - \theta_0(1,2) \times 100\right)$$

From today's yield curve, we know that the 2-year zero-coupon bond is worth:

$$P_0(0,2) = 100 \times e^{-0.048} \times e^{-0.05} = 90.665$$

Setting the two equations equal, we get $\theta_0(1,2) = 0.00020$. We also get the two 1×2 forward rates in the up and down states at time $t = 1$:

$$f_1^u(1,2) = 7.02\% \quad \text{and} \quad f_1^d(1,2) = 3.02\%$$

Next we can fix the $\theta_0(2,3)$ drift term by pricing the 3-year zero-coupon bond and setting its value equal to:

$$P_0(0,3) = 100 \times e^{-0.048} \times e^{-0.05} \times e^{-0.052} = 86.071$$

We use the newly computed $f_1(1,2)$ values at time $t = 1$ to probability weight the values of discount bonds with 2 years left to maturity in the up and down states at time $t = 1$; we discount them by 1 year to time $t = 0$:

$$P_0(0,3) = e^{-0.048} \times \left(\frac{1}{2}e^{-0.0702)} \times e - 0.082 - \theta_0(2,3) \times 100 + \frac{1}{2}e^{-0.0302} \times e^{-0.022-\theta_0(2,3)} \times 100\right)$$

Setting this equal to 86.071, we get $\theta_0(2,3) = 0.001049$ and the two 2×3 forward rates in the up and down states at time $t = 1$:

$$f_1^u(2,3) = 8.30495\% \quad \text{and} \quad f_1^d(2,3) = 2.30495\%$$

The next step is to go to time $t = 2$ and, again, given the volatility $\sigma(2,3) = 0.03$ and today's price of the 3-year zero-coupon bond, to fix the drift term $\theta_1(2,3)$.

$f_2^{uu}(2,3) = 11.35\%$

$\begin{matrix} f_1^u(1,2) \\ f_1^u(2,3) \end{matrix} = \begin{matrix} 7.02000\% \\ 8.30495\% \end{matrix}$

$f_0(0,1) = 4.8\%$
$f_0(1,2) = 5.0\%$
$f_0(2,3) = 5.2\%$

$f_2^{ud}(2,3) = 5.35\%$

$\begin{matrix} f_1^d(1,2) \\ f_1^d(2,3) \end{matrix} = \begin{matrix} 3.02000\% \\ 2.30495\% \end{matrix}$

$f_2^{dd}(2,3) = -0.65\%$

Figure 6.6 A one-factor three-step HJM model solved

We use the price of the 3-year zero-coupon bond to fix the last drift term:

$$P_0(0,3) = e^{-0.048} \times \left[\begin{matrix} \frac{1}{2} \times e^{-0.0702} \times \left(\frac{1}{2} e^{-0.1130495-\theta_1(2,3)} \times 100 + \frac{1}{2} e^{-0.0530495-\theta_1(2,3)} \times 100 \right) + \\ +\frac{1}{2} \times e^{-0.0302} \times \left(\frac{1}{2} e^{-0.0530495-\theta_1(2,3)} \times 100 + \frac{1}{2} e^{+0.006951-\theta_1(2,3)} \times 100 \right) \end{matrix} \right]$$

We set this value equal to 86.071, to get $\theta_1(2,3) = 0.00045$ and the final forward rates:

$$f_2^{uu}(2,3) = 11.35\%,\ f_2^{ud}(2,3) = 5.35\%,\ \text{and}\ f_2^{dd}(2,3) = -0.65\%$$

Figure 6.6 shows the final tree for the evolution of the forward curve. Here is the summary of the important points about our HJM exercise:

- We have chosen $\sigma(1,2) = 0.02$ and $\sigma(2,3) = 0.03$ first. In reality, these two would have to be bootstrapped from the prices of caplets setting 1 and 2 years from today, and paying 2 and 3 years from today. Thus, we would end up with a joint or nested bootstraps in the following order:
  - fit the volatility $\sigma(1,2)$ and the drift $\theta_0(1,2)$ to hit the first caplet and the 2-year zero; then
  - fit the volatility $\sigma(2,3)$ and the drifts $\theta_0(2,3)$ and $\theta_1(2,3)$ to hit the second caplet and the 3-year zero.
- We have some degree of freedom (three drifts and two volatilities) on the structure of the drifts and volatilities, so we can either impose restrictions (smoothness), or fit additional securities, like a 1-into-2 European swaption.
- Changing to a log-normal forward model is quite easy. Replace the additive drift and diffusion (volatility) terms with exponential terms. This would preclude our negative rate in the down–down node of the time $t = 2$ step.
- All non-option bonds will be priced perfectly in our tree. All calibrating options will be priced correctly. And the model is arbitrage free overall and step-by-step.
- The model as described is still one factor with maturity-dependent volatility structure.

While the HJM framework can be extended to many factors, the numerical complexity of it and calibration issues make even two-factor extensions very difficult. To accommodate two factors in our tree set-up, we would have to introduce in the diffusion equations at least one additional volatility term for the second factor (and perhaps one more drift term). This alone would necessitate at least a trinomial. It would also significantly complicate the calibration to caplets. What other security would we have to choose at the first step of the bootstrap to fix the drift term and two volatility terms? It would have to be an option whose value was sensitive to more than one factor. In our model a caplet setting in one year and a 1-into-1 swaption are identical. If the tree was more finely sliced into shorter time steps, we could try to fit caplets/floorlets and longer swaptions at the same time, but even that most likely would not help. Caps and short European swaptions are not multifactor sensitive options. Their values depend mostly on the volatility of the entire yield curve and not so much on the correlation structure which drives tilts and non-parallel moves. To properly calibrate the model, we would need to introduce multiple-exercise options (like Bermudans) or yield curve options.

As a more tractable extension of HJM, Brace, Gatarek, and Musiela (1997), and others, have proposed a non-arbitrage-free framework of modeling directly discrete LIBOR forwards instead of instantaneous forwards from which all other rates have to be recovered. This approach simplifies implementation and calibration since the nodes have LIBOR forwards, very much like in our example implementation in Figures 6.4 to 6.6. The HJM actually models instantaneous forward from which actual LIBOR forward have to be recovered. BGM models LIBORs directly. This makes hitting cap prices trivial, but at the expense of delinking rates of different maturities from each other under the same risk-neutral measure. It does, however, allow an easy introduction of additional volatility factors. The numerical procedure is often a non-recombinant tree or Monte Carlo.

6.3.4 Bermudan Swaptions and Multifactor Models

The HJM and BGM model frameworks can both be extended to more than one stochastic factor. To appreciate the importance of having such a model, consider a Bermudan swaption. Suppose the yield curve is flat at 5% and you purchase the right to enter into a pay-fixed 5% interest rate swap. Your right is exercisable every 6 months for the next 5 years. Upon exercise, the swap you will enter into will have a final maturity of 10 years from today. The structure described would be referred to as a 5-into-5 Bermudan put swaption. The equivalent European swaption would have only one exercise time in 5 years and upon exercise, the swap we would enter into would have another 5 years left to maturity. The Bermudan swaption gives us the multiple exercise rights. Today we can exercise into a 10-year swap, in 6 months we can exercise into a 9.5-year swap, in one year we can exercise into a 9-year swap, etc. If the yield curve is not flat, but upward sloping from 3% to 5%, then the most likely exercise point is 5 years from today. If the yield curve is flat at 5%, then exercising today, in 5 years and anywhere in between is approximately equally likely. In a one-factor model, the yield curve moves in parallel with today's entire curve, up or down. This is not a problem in valuing a one-time exercise European swaption. In fact, we have shown that we can do that in a Black–Scholes model just as well as in a complicated term-structure model with the use of simple convexity adjustments. Suppose, however that, we use a short rate term structure model to value the Bermudan. The exercise right will be evaluated correctly at each node by comparing the discounted value of future exercise to the immediate exercise value. Yet what will be missing is any allowance for non-parallel yield curve moves. In a short-term model, the allowable yield curve moves do not include tilting and inversion. An inversion from a flat yield curve at 5% would clearly favor early exercise of the put swaption. The unfortunate fact is that a one-factor model cannot even tell how much that extra "volatility" of the yield curve is worth, because tilts cannot be accommodated in it. On the flip side, a two-factor model would have to be calibrated to curve tilt-sensitive options, like other Bermudans or spread options, through one or more correlation inputs.

6.4 EXOTIC INTEREST RATE OPTIONS

The term "exotic options" applies to all options traded over-the-counter whose payoffs do not follow the standard over or under the strike call/put blueprint. Exotic options include digital (binary) options (fixed payoffs irrespective of how far in the money the option is), barrier options, e.g. knock-ins or knock-outs (the underlying price/rate has to hit/not hit a barrier prior to expiry for the payoff formula to apply), as well as a whole variety of options that are difficult to price because their primary risk is not easily hedged. We do not attempt a complete list of the exotics; instead, we focus on two very popular structures that appear to be deceivingly simple. In reality, they are anything but simple.

6.4.1 Periodic Caps

Consider a fairly standard provision of an adjustable rate mortgage. The interest rate changes once a year on the basis of some floating index. The mortgagee has in effect issued a floating rate bond to finance a house purchase. Every year, the interest rate he pays is based on the cost of funds for that year (set at the beginning of the year based on some 1-year money rate). Next year the rate adjusts up or down, but the rate is guaranteed not to go up by more than 2% year-to-year or 6% total over the lifetime. So if the index changes from 3% to 6%, the homeowner's rate increases only by 2% instead of 3%. The option the homeowner holds is not a standard call option on a rate or a cap. The strike on the option changes every year and is based on last year's rate and last year's strike. If the index changes from 6% to 9% the following year, the mortgage rate again only goes up only by 2%, and only from the already "unfairly" low previous year's level that did not reflect a full index increase at that time. Mortgage banks that want to protect themselves against income lost due to these imbedded options purchase periodic caps from dealers. *Periodic caps* pay the difference between the mortgage rate (with the options) and the fully indexed floating rate (without the options). The resetting strike feature changes the probability of payoff relative to a straight call. It also changes how the payoff can be manufactured. The dealer-hedger cannot compute the delta on the option until he knows the strike. Thus, it is not the implied volatility over the entire life of the option that determines the cost of manufacturing, but the sequence of future implied volatilities on shorter one-year options. This is true with a caveat that previous strikes also carry over, as in our example. The cost of payoff manufacturing has thus a known component (stickiness of the strike) and some unknown component (future annual rate differences). The premium quoted will reflect the subjective bet on the future path of implied volatilities (or the volatility of volatility).

6.4.2 Digitals and Ranges

A *digital option* is an option with a fixed monetary payoff if a price or rate breaches a certain strike level. A *range* is a compound version of a digital option where the underlying price or rate has to breach one level but not go over or under another level, i.e. it has to end up within a predetermined range. These structures are popular in commodity, FX, and interest rate markets. In interest rate markets, they are typically packaged into cap- of floor-like serial forms with short-term LIBOR rates as the underlyings and range levels changing period-to-period. These options are not difficult to price theoretically, but they pose a risk of low-probability events with highly uncertain hedge outcomes.

Suppose we sold an FX range that pays \$1 if the USD/EUR rate is within 1.30 and 1.50. We price the option using a binomial tree and have followed the hedge recipe. At 1 day prior to expiry, the spot USD/EUR FX rate stands at 1.50. If it ticks up by tomorrow, we will owe nothing to the option holder. If it ticks down we will owe \$1 (everything). There is no effective hedge strategy that will produce the desired payoff, \$0 or \$1. We have to gamble. At the time the option was sold, this knife-edge event had effectively a zero probability. In a standard call or put, these events do not occur because the size of the payoff changes monotonically with the level of the rate, allowing us to adjust the hedge. Here it jumps from zero to everything over an almost non-existent move in the underlying.

7 Default Risk and Credit Derivatives

As of 2011, while currency trading still dominates the daily turnover and interest rate swaps dominate the total principal outstanding, credit derivatives form one of the fastest growing segments of the global financial over-the-counter markets. Rightly or wrongly, they also received bad press and blame for the 2008 financial crisis and the 2010 European debt crisis. Credit derivatives are insurance-like contracts between two counterparties where protection buyers make periodic premium payments to protection sellers who promise to make potentially large one-time payouts contingent on adverse corporate events, particularly defaults in corporate bonds. The demand for such insurance should not be surprising. In all asset markets, investors make risk management decisions. Equity investors and insurance companies tend to diversify their risks. Concentrated investors tend to hedge: insurers reinsure, real estate owners buy hazard insurance, large equity holders buy puts or collars. Corporate bond investors and lenders seek credit derivatives as a way to eliminate (hedge) their exposure to defaults on individual corporate bonds or entire portfolios of corporate bonds and loans. The role of credit derivatives in the 2008 financial crisis perhaps lies not in their function as enablers of speculation on adverse events, but mainly in the massive defaults of two large protection sellers, Lehman and AIG, and the systemic consequences of that.

Standard Bond Math techniques based on cash flow discounting do not tackle explicitly the possibility of default. In Bond Math, coupon and principal cash flows are assumed to be known with certainty. Prices of securities are computed as the present values of the known cash flows discounted by given discount rates. These discount rates implicitly account for the uncertainty about the cash flows. In Bond Math, the discount rates used are either the yields-to-maturity or the zero-coupon rates bootstrapped from the yields-to-maturity. If the issuer of the priced bond is not a sovereign entity that prints money, but a corporate (or municipal) entity that could default on its obligations, then the yields-to-maturity or zero-coupon rates used to discount cash flows are adjusted up by what is loosely termed *corporate spread*, and the resulting present value or the price of the bond is lower than that on an otherwise similar sovereign bond. Conversely, given the price of a corporate bond, investors often compute the yield-to-maturity as the internal rate of return on the bond's cash flows, i.e. the discount rate which, when used to discount the bond's cash flows, produces the present value equal to the bond's price. The computed yield-to-maturity can then be compared to the yield on a similar sovereign bond (same term and coupon level) to make return vs risk investment decisions.

In this chapter, standard Bond Math (yield curve construction) is paired with probabilistic models of corporate default. There are two main approaches to modeling defaults: structural models of the firm asset value and its debt/equity financing, and reduced-form models of corporate yield curve bootstrapping (e.g. Poisson model). Structural models are the basis for what is known as corporate arbitrage (the cheapness/richness of the company's debt relative to its equity, including the hybrids), convertibles, and preferred. The reduced-form models are the basis of most credit derivative pricing, the way Black–Scholes is for stock options. They rely on survival (non-default) probability calibrations to sets of increasing-maturity corporate bonds for a single issuer (similar to the yield curve bootstrap), and may include assumptions about the correlation of the reference issuer's default and the protection seller's default. We limit our discussion to reduced-form models.

We start with the definition of the most common credit derivative structure, the credit-default swap (CDS), and its basic no-arbitrage relationship to the corporate spread. We proceed with a simple binomial default probability model in order to put structure on the relationship of default probabilities to corporate spreads. We assume no value recovery following the default, but show extensions of the basic model to a richer credit migration framework. We then come back to the binomial enhanced with the standard Poisson process of single issuer default under the assumption of a known recovery rate and no correlation between the bond issuer and the default swap writer. We end the chapter with a simplified Bernoulli framework for including the correlation of the issuer and swap seller defaults.

We defer the broader discussion of correlations, basket credit derivatives and collateralized debt obligations (CDOs) to Chapter 10. Basket credit derivatives are multiple-default insurance arrangements on more than one issuer name. They are written in the form of first-to-default, last-to-default, or multiple-default payouts. The pricing of basket credit defaults relies on the modeling of the multivariate probability distributions in a way that is consistent with the single issuer modeling of the marginal distributions, while allowing for a default correlation structure among many issuers. The standard approach involves using a *copula* function which, in mathematical probability theory, is defined as a multivariate function of correlated uniform random variables whose transforms have known marginal probability density functions.

7.1 CREDIT DEFAULT SWAPS

More than two-thirds of all credit derivatives trading in the world are credit default swaps which insure the risk of default of a single bond issue or issuer. In this section, we describe the basic transaction, and relate it structurally to the floating rate bond in order to derive the fundamental no-arbitrage relationship for credit derivatives. We then show some common variants of the structure of the credit default swap.

7.1.1 Credit Default Swap

A credit default swap (CDS) is a default insurance arrangement between two counterparties dressed in a language of swaps. The protection contract is most commonly written on a single bond issue, called the reference issue. The buyer of the default protection, called the *buyer*, makes periodic payments, called the *spreads*, on the premium leg of the swap until default or maturity of the reference issue, whichever comes earlier. The *seller* of the protection pays a lump-sum payment only once if and when the default occurs, but nothing otherwise. The swap is typically physically settled to avoid disputes over the post-default value of the reference bond and has no embedded delivery options. Upon the default, the seller of the protection pays the principal and the accrued interest in exchange for the receipt of the defaulted bond. On rare occasions, the two parties may settle the swap in cash with the protection seller paying the difference between the principal plus the accrued interest and the recovery value of the bond – the recovery value being defined as the after-market price of the defaulted bond.

Figure 7.1 shows the cash flows of a 3-year credit default swap under two alternative scenarios, one that the reference issuer defaults on the reference bond in year 2 and the other that the bond does not default during the life of the swap.

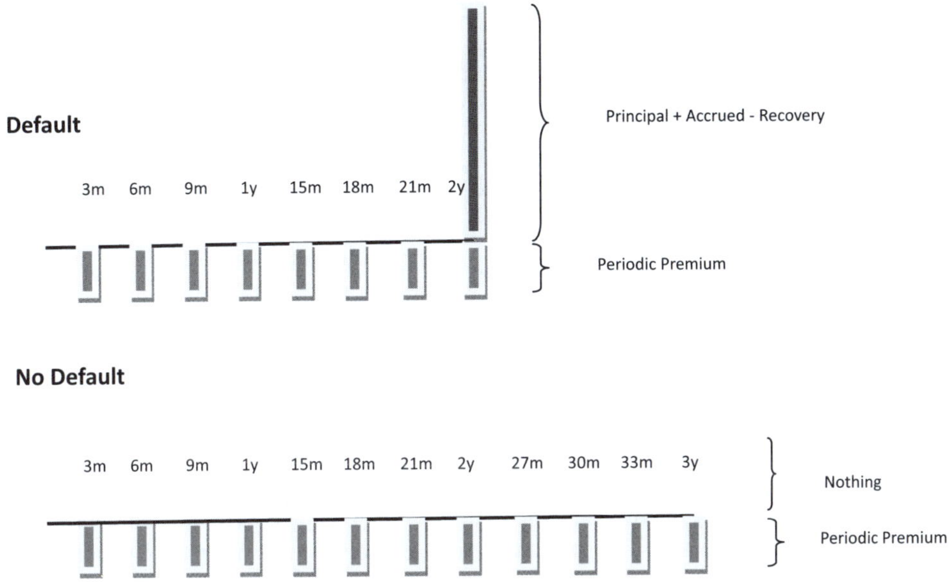

Figure 7.1 The credit default swap

If the reference issuer defaults on the bond 2 years into the credit default swap, then the protection seller pays to the protection buyer the value lost on the bond. At that time, the protection buyer stops making the periodic premium payments. Typically, the premium payments are quarterly, and quoted on a per annum Act/360 basis for dollar bonds (to correspond to a LIBOR-plus-margin convention).

7.1.2 No Arbitrage: CDS vs Corporate Bond Spread

Under the assumption of no counterparty risk, i.e. no possibility that the protection seller himself may default on the credit default swap, the swap is a perfect hedge for a corresponding par floating rate bond and the premium amounts must be equal to the corporate spread the reference issuer would pay on a floating rate bond with a maturity equal to the maturity of the credit default swap. This is the fundamental no-arbitrage principle of credit derivatives.

To see this, consider the following strategy. An investor purchases a par floater that pays LIBOR plus a spread, and finances the purchase by borrowing at LIBOR. At the same time, the investor buys a default swap. The premium on the default swap must be equal to the corporate spread paid by the issuer to prevent arbitrage, because the strategy is equivalent to buying a par floater paying LIBOR and financing it at LIBOR. If we substitute the term "risk-free rate" for "LIBOR" in this argument and add a condition that the protection seller is a default-free sovereign, then the strategy is equivalent to purchasing a default-free par floater and financing it at a risk-free rate.

Figure 7.2 shows the cash flows of the strategy under the default and no-default scenarios, excluding the LIBOR financing cost (and repayment of the borrowing) of buying the floater.

The investor pays the spread on the default swap. He receives LIBOR plus the spread from the bond. Net, his periodic cash flow is equal to LIBOR. If the default occurs, he stops paying the spread, and stops receiving LIBOR plus spread. His principal is also returned. In cash

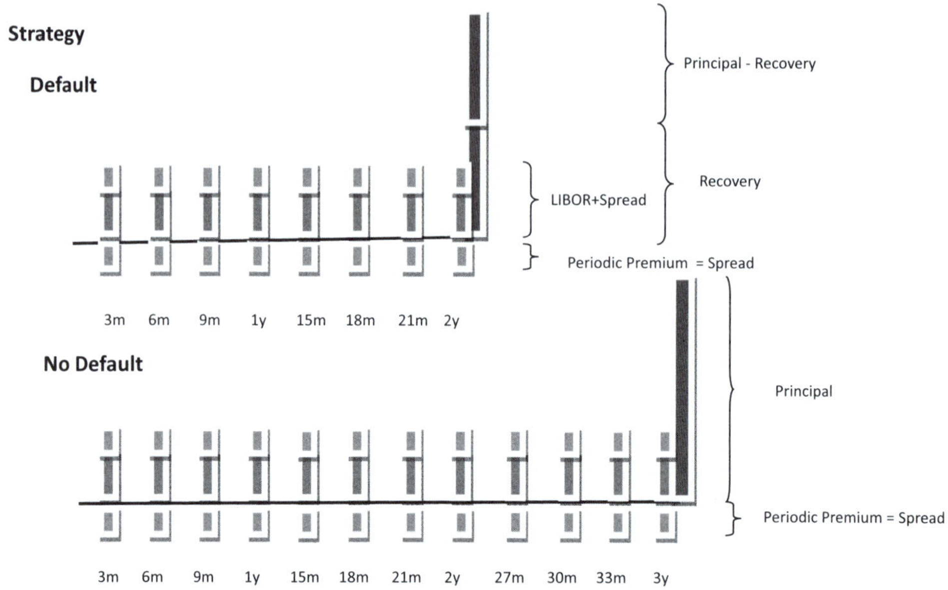

Figure 7.2 A par floater replication

settlement, he receives the principal minus the recovery value from the protection seller plus the recovery value in the after-market. In the physical settlement, he exchanges the defaulted bond for the principal from the protection seller. The total principal is used to pay off his borrowing. The investor gained or lost nothing.

If the bond does not default, then the investor receives all the scheduled LIBOR plus the spread payments, spends the spread on protection and LIBOR on financing, and uses the final principal of the bond to pay off his borrowing.

The argument holds if there are no day-count and payment date discrepancies between floating coupons and swap premium payments, and if defaults occur only on (i.e. right after) the payment dates. If they occur in between, then the interest accruals may make the swap settlement amount slightly different from the amount needed to pay off the borrowing.

In reality, the credit default premium will be different from the par floater spread to the extent that there is a difference in the credit quality of the reference issuer and the protection seller. If the reference issuer is an AA-rated corporate entity, but the protection seller is a single A-rated broker-dealer, then the credit default premium will be lower than the corporate spread on the floater to compensate for the fact that the guaranteeing counterparty is of a lower credit quality. Actually, the exact pricing of this disparity requires modeling the correlation of the default probabilities of the corporate issuer and the protection seller, covered intuitively at the end of this chapter. The exact valuation relies on the default correlation models of first-to-default baskets tackled in Chapter 10.

7.1.3 Bundled Single-Name Credit Derivatives

In addition to the credit default swap, holders of corporate bonds or loans have one other way to manage the default risk of their assets. They can enter into a total rate of return swap with a dealer whereby they give up the fixed rate of return on the asset in exchange for a floating rate coupon quoted as LIBOR plus (or minus) a spread. The total rate of return swap is a vehicle for synthetically creating floating rate bonds with default risk. This asset swap spread should in theory be equal to the CDS premium. Often it is not, because the asset swap spread bundles the cost of the protection contract with a repo-financed purchase of the asset. The CDS basis is defined as the difference between the cost of pure insurance and the asset swap margin, or

$$CDS\ basis = CDS\ premium - Asset\ swap\ spread$$

The basis can be positive or negative. The main factor determining the basis is how far from par the bond trades, as that drives the financing cost of buying the asset.

7.1.3.1 The Total Rate of Return Swap

A total rate of return swap is an off-market interest rate swap in which one counterparty, who typically holds a corporate bond or loan, pays a fixed rate related to, or equal to, the fixed coupon rate of the corporate bond or loan to another counterparty in exchange for a floating rate coupon expressed as LIBOR plus, or minus, an asset swap spread. The maturity of the swap is equal to the maturity of the underlying bond or loan. In the par-in par-out version of the swap, the notional principal on both legs of the swap is equal to the principal of the bond/loan. In the market-in market-out version, the floating leg's notional principal is equal to the current price of the bond/loan. The objective of the fixed rate payer is to retain the credit exposure of the underlying bond, but swap the interest rate risk of the fixed leg into a near-zero interest rate risk of the floating leg.

In Figure 7.3, the Kool Kredit Bank has a loan out to ABC on which it receives a fixed rate of return. It enters into a total return swap with a dealer in which it transfers the fixed coupon on the ABC loan to the dealer in exchange for a floating coupon. Kool Kredit does not have to involve ABC in the transaction. The dealer agrees to pay Kool Kredit LIBOR plus a spread. The spread level depends on the current value of the loan.

In the par structure of this asset swap, the floating leg's notional principal is set to be equal to the fixed leg's principal. Yet if the bond does not currently trade at par, then the present values of the two legs, including the principal exchanges at the end, are not equal. The floating leg's PV is equal to par, while the fixed leg's PV is equal to the value of the bond. The spread over LIBOR is determined to make the two PVs balance. In the market structure of this asset swap, the floating leg's notional principal is set to equal the current value of the underlying bond or loan which, in turn, is equal to the present value of the fixed leg. The mismatch of

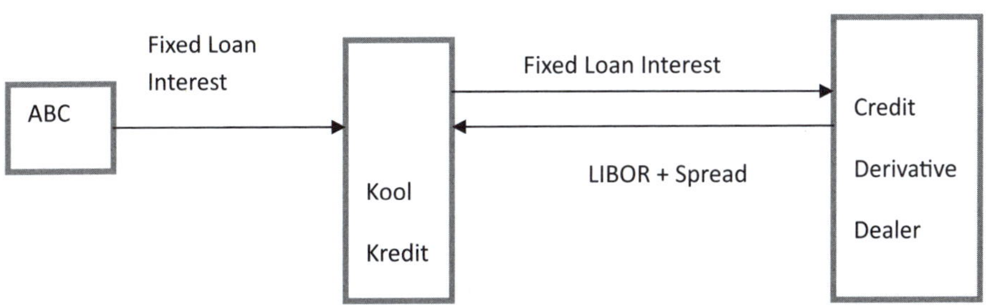

Figure 7.3 The total rate of return

the principals results in a net payment at maturity to settle the principal exchange (similar to currency swaps).

7.1.3.2 CDS Basis and No Arbitrage between CDSs and Asset Swaps

Credit default swap spreads and asset swap spreads are tied together through a no-arbitrage condition. The CDS exposure can be replicated synthetically with the use of a total rate of return asset swap and a repo purchase of the underlying bond. To see this, let the coupon on the underlying bond or loan be denoted as the equivalent maturity Treasury plus a corporate bond spread, or $T + c$. Let the interest rate swap spread be denoted by s. Thus a zero-PV (on-market) interest rate swap is quoted as fixed $T + s$ against a floating LIBOR L flat (no spread). The repo rate on purchasing the corporate bond is quoted as LIBOR minus the repo premium, or $L - \rho$. Let us assume that there is no haircut on the repo (i.e. no difference between the value of the securities purchased in the repo and the money received). We will consider the following numerical values for our example. The underlying bond has 5 years left to maturity and 5-year Treasuries trade at $T = 4\%$ yields. Five-year swap spreads are at $s = 0.5\%$, and swaps are quoted at $T + s = 4.5\%$. The underlying bond is a BBB+-rated bond with a coupon and the yield to maturity equal to $T + c = 5\%$. Consider the following simultaneous transactions:

- Term repo: Borrow 100 at a floating rate $L - \rho$ and buy the BBB+ bond for 100. When the bond matures, it will be redeemed for par and the borrowing will be repaid.
- Pay fixed $T + s = 4.5\%$ on an interest rate swap to receive floating L.

The cash inflows are: $T + c = 5\%$ from the bond and L from the swap. The cash outflows are: $L - \rho$ on the repo financing and $T + s = 4.5\%$ on the swap. Net the cash inflow is:

$$T + c + L - (L - \rho) - (T + s) = c - s + \rho$$

which is equal to a fixed periodic spread of 0.5% if the repo is non-special and $\rho = 0$.

If the bond defaults and trades at the recovery rate R, the funds borrowed on the repo (100) are immediately repaid. The net cash outflow at the time is $100 - R$. The synthetic exposure of the two transactions is the same as that of a protection seller in a CDS: a receipt of a fixed periodic premium for a one-time payment of $100 - R$ if and when the bond defaults. Therefore the CDS swap should trade close to $c - s + \rho$. The forces that cause deviations from the no-arbitrage condition include to a lesser extent special repo conditions and primarily funding cost differentials between protection buyers and sellers. Highly creditworthy entities that can fund themselves at sub-LIBOR levels can use their funding cost advantage to hold assets to swap out of them, or in conjunction with protection purchases.

7.1.3.3 Credit-Linked Notes

A credit-linked note is a debt security whose principal repayment depends on the value of a third-party reference security. In case of third party default, the defaulted security recovery value is passed on to the investor in lieu of principal. The enhanced interest rate of the credit-linked note reflects the implicit sale of credit protection by the investor. The issuer of the note is typically a trust set up by a bank arranging the sale of the note. The trust receives premiums for the sale of the protection to the bank. The premiums subsidize the coupon of the note issued to the investors. The trust uses the proceeds from the sale of the note to invest in

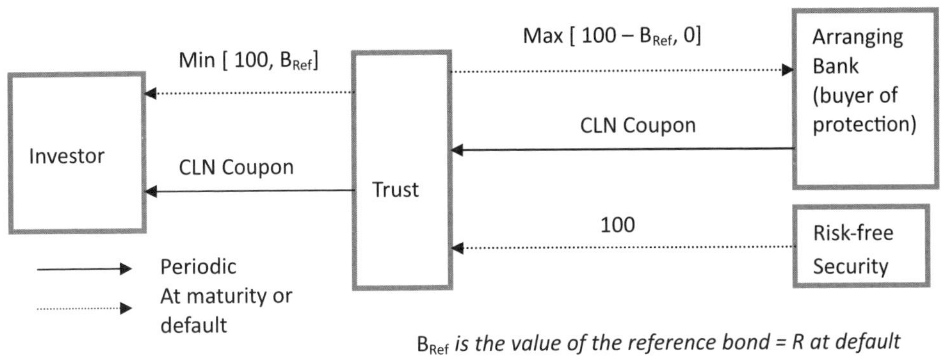

Figure 7.4 A credit-linked note

risk-free securities to guarantee the principal of the note. If the third party does not default, that principal is returned to the credit-linked note holder. If the third party defaults, the principal is exchanged for the recovery value of the reference security with the protection buyer, and only the recovery value is returned (early) to the credit-linked note holder.

The investor gains a much enhanced interest rate, but bears all the risk of default. The arranging bank acquires protection for its loan or bond portfolio. In the case of default of the underlying issuer, the bank receives the excess of the value of the securities held by the trust over the recovery value of the reference security.

The credit-linked note bundles a credit default swap with a standard bond obligation. The credit protection premium paid by the arranging bank in Figure 7.4 is passed on to the investor in the form of an enhanced coupon. The protection payout is passed from investors to the bank at redemption. If there are no credit events associated with the reference security, the investor gets a periodic coupon and par at maturity. A synthetic collateralized debt obligation (CDO) tranche certificate is an example of a credit-linked note.

7.1.3.4 Credit Spread Options

Credit spread options pay out the yield differential between defaultable securities and reference benchmarks. The payout is not contingent on a credit event. Most credit spread options are structured as put options on the price. The holder of a credit spread option has the right to sell a particular corporate bond at a contingent strike price. The strike price is computed to be the value the corporate bond would need on the expiry date so that its yield to maturity would equal the yield to maturity on the reference default-free security plus a spread strike. For example, the buyer of a spread option on ABC's 5-year note struck at a spread strike of 50 bp over the 5-year US Treasury note will face either of two possibilities on the expiration date. If the spread between the yield to maturity on the ABC bond and the Treasury note is less than 50 bp, the option expires worthless. If the spread exceeds 50 bp, the ABC bond is sold to the option writer. The price he receives is equal to the present value of the cash flows from the ABC bond discounted at the yield equal to the 5-year Treasury yield plus 50 bp.

To illustrate this numerically, suppose 1 year ago we purchased a 1-year European option on the spread between ABC's 6-year bond paying a 5% coupon semi-annually and the 5-year US Treasury struck at 55 bp. The face amount of the option was \$100 million. At that time, the

ABC bond yielded 5.75% (semi) to price at 96.2392. The reference Treasury from which we were going to calculate the yield spread between the two bonds had not been issued. The then current 5-year Treasury paying a 5.25% semi-annual coupon, yielded 5.23% and was priced at 100.1019. The option was described as 3 bp out-of-the-money since the spread at the time of the option purchase was 52 bp. Recently, the US Treasury auctioned off a new 5-year note with a coupon of 5.125%. This note will be used to determine the payoff on the spread option.

Suppose the now 5-year ABC bond is yielding 5.68%. The current market price is 97.0759. The new 5-year Treasury is yielding 5.04% and is priced at 100.3716. The yield spread between the two bonds at 64 bp is higher than the strike spread of 55 bp. We will exercise our option to sell the bond at 55 bp over Treasuries, that is, at a yield of 5.59%. Computing the price of the ABC bond at that yield we obtain 97.4571. Since we can buy the bond for 97.0759 on the open market, the payoff on the option to us is:

$$(97.4571 - 97.0759)/100 \times \$100{,}000{,}000 = \$381{,}153$$

Suppose instead that the now 5-year ABC bond is yielding 6.23%. The current market price is 94.7846. The new 5-year Treasury is yielding 5.59% and prices to 97.9958. The yield spread between the two bonds again at 64 bp is higher than the strike spread of 55 bp. We will exercise our option to sell the bond at 55 bp over Treasuries, that is, at a yield of 6.14%. Computing the price of the ABC bond at that yield, we obtain 95.1551. Since we can buy the bond for 94.7846 on the open market, the payoff on the option to us is:

$$(95.1551 - 94.7846)/100 \times \$100{,}000{,}000 = \$370{,}528$$

The option payout in the two scenarios is not identical, but is almost the same. This is because it can be viewed as purely a bet on the spread between the two bonds grossed up by the duration of the bond under consideration. For the last scenario, the duration of the bond computed by blipping the yield from 6.14 to 6.15 is 4.1254. The payout on the option is based on 9 bp (64 – 55). So using the duration approximation, the total payout is:

$$0.041254 \times 9 \times \$100{,}000{,}000 = \$371{,}289$$

Nowhere in the calculations did we use the actual price of the Treasury. Comparing the two examples, we can see that the payout is independent of whether interest rates in general go up or down. The relevant factor is the yield spread between the bond and the reference risk-free security. Spread options are sometimes written by fixing the duration multiplier and defining the payout explicitly as the difference in yields.

The fundamental difference between credit spread options and other credit derivatives is that credit events do not explicitly drive the payout, but are implicitly incorporated in the payout through a spread differential which, in turn, depends on the probability of default of the underlying bond.

7.2 A CONSTANT DEFAULT PROBABILITY MODEL

Suppose we want to price a 3-year 5% annual coupon bond issued by the ABC Corp. ABC is a US corporation and the bond's principal and interest are to be paid in US dollars. We observe that 1-, 2-, and 3-year US Treasury notes with coupon rates equal to 2.500000%, 2.623305%, and 2.745279%, respectively, trade at par. For simplicity, we assume annual 30/360 interest calculations. From the Treasury par curve, using the techniques of Chapter 2, we bootstrap the following default-free term structure of interest rates in Table 7.1.

Table 7.1 Default-free yield curve

Year	Forward yield	Year	Zero-coupon yield	Year	Par coupon yield
0 × 1	2.50	0 × 1	2.500000	1	2.500000
1 × 2	2.75	0 × 2	2.624924	2	2.623305
2 × 3	3.00	0 × 3	2.749797	3	2.745279

The usual Bond Math no-arbitrage relationships apply to the computed zero-coupon yields which discount cash flows from a point in the future to today and to the computed forward (zero) yields which discount cash flows one year at a time.

Suppose we assume that the probability that ABC will go bankrupt or default on its bond over the first year is $0.0011 = 0.11\%$. If ABC goes bankrupt during the first year, then not only will it *not* pay the 5% coupon due in 1 year, but it will also *fail* to pay any coupons after that. For now, we assume no recovery of any value following the default. If ABC survives the first year, then the probability that it will go bankrupt in the second year will again be 0.11%. If ABC fails in year 2, then it will fail to pay the coupon in year 2 and the coupon and principal in year 3. If it survives year 2, then it will again face the probability of default of 0.11% for year 3.

Rather than thinking about the probability of default, it helps to think in terms of the probability of survival. The constant default probability model is then the same as the constant survival model. Since we assume a Bernoulli (binomial) set-up with only two possibilities – default or survival – the survival probability is equal to 1 minus the default probability. For each year, we set the survival probability to a constant 0.9989. Figure 7.5 captures the evolution of outcomes over time. The tree is truncated in the down states since, if there is default, the subsequent cash flows are zero.

One way to price the ABC bond would be to sweep backwards through the tree, adding the coupon cash flows at every step. We would start at time $t = 2$. We would take the discounted expected value of the cash flows at time $t = 3$ and add the current cash flow. That is, at time $t = 2$, right after the coupon payment, the bond would have a value of:

$$B_2 = \frac{1}{1 + 0.0300}\left[0.9989 \times (\$100.0000 + \$5) + 0.0011 \times \$0\right] = 101.8296$$

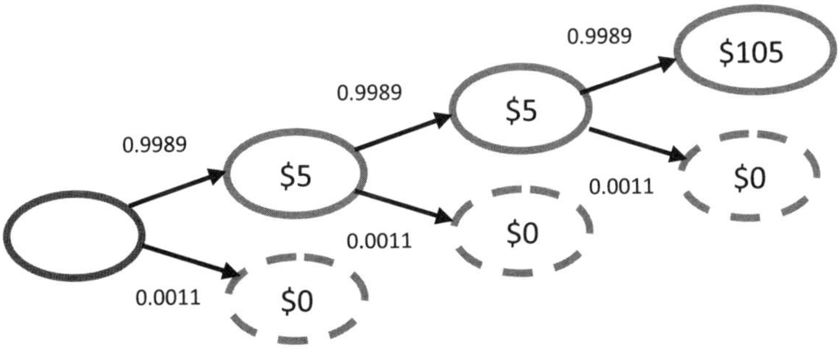

Figure 7.5 Constant probability of default

Table 7.2 Bond valuation using the cumulative survival probability

Year	CF	Prob/Year	Cumulative survival prob.	Risk-free zero rate	Risk-free DF	PV
1	5	0.0011	0.99890	2.5000%	0.975610	4.8727
2	5	0.0011	0.99780	2.6249%	0.949499	4.7371
3	105	0.0011	0.99670	2.7498%	0.921843	96.4745
					Sum PV =	106.0842
					Yield =	2.8550%

At time $t = 1$, right after the coupon payment, the bond would have a value of:

$$B_1 = \frac{1}{1 + 0.0275}\left[0.9989 \times (\$101.8296 + \$5) + 0.0011 \times \$0\right] = 103.8561$$

Finally, at time $t = 0$, we would compute the price of the bond as the probability-weighted present value of the bond's cash flows, equal to

$$B_0 = \frac{1}{1 + 0.0250}\left[0.9989 \times (\$103.8561 + \$5) + 0.0011 \times \$0\right] = 106.0842$$

There is a simpler way. Since the tree is truncated in the down nodes, all we have to worry about is the *cumulative* survival probability up to any given time (or year) n, which is equal to 0.9989^n. What follows is that the expected present value of any coupon payment is equal to the cumulative survival probability times the promised cash flow times a discount factor, where the discount factor is computed using default-free rates. In the backward sweep, we used the one-step default-free forward rates, but since each cash flow is discounted to today, we can simply use the spot discount factors based on spot zero rates. These simplified calculations are:

$$B_0 = \frac{0.9989 \times \$5}{1.02500000} + \frac{0.9989^2 \times \$5}{1.02624924^2} + \frac{0.9989^3 \times \$105}{1.02749797^3} = 106.0842$$

as summarized in Table 7.2.

Table 7.2 also shows the yield to maturity on the ABC bond implied from the formula:

$$\frac{\$5}{1 + y} + \frac{\$5}{(1 + y)^2} + \frac{\$105}{(1 + y)^3} = 106.0842$$

which turns out to be 2.855. Given the risk-free par coupon rate of 2.745% for a 3-year maturity, the corporate credit spread on the ABC bond would be quoted as 11 bp.

We use our simple default valuation method to compute, in Table 7.3, what would happen to the same 3-year 5% ABC bond if ABC drops to a "junk" rating as the perceived probability of default changes to 10% per year.

The promised cash flows do not change, but their probability-weighted discounted value does. The price of the bond drops to 78.7982, and the yield-to-maturity increases to 14.156%. The credit spread is now 11.411% over the same maturity Treasury.

The deterministic default probability model is easy to calibrate. Just as in a standard yield curve construction, we need to observe the default-free yield curve and an array of bonds of the same issuer with increasing maturities. We can then bootstrap the implied probability of default for each forward period starting with 6-month or 1-year bonds and ending with the

Table 7.3 The ABC bond with a 10% default probability

Year	CF	Prob/Year	Cumulative survival prob	Risk-free zero rate	Risk-free DF	PV
1	5	0.1000	0.90000	2.5000%	0.975610	4.3902
2	5	0.1000	0.81000	2.6249%	0.949499	3.8455
3	105	0.1000	0.72900	2.7498%	0.921843	70.5625
					Sum PV =	78.7982
					Yield =	14.1562%

longest maturity bonds. Once that is done, we can use the term structure of default probabilities to price any cash flow structure offered by the same issuer.

7.3 A DETERMINISTIC CREDIT MIGRATION MODEL

The constant default probability model can incorporate a deterministic scenario of changing credit quality. Suppose we believe that the probability of default for year 1 is 0.11%, but 6% in year 2 and 8% in year 3. Table 7.4 shows that all we need to do is recompute the cumulative survival probabilities; the rest proceeds as before.

The corporate credit spread on the bond is now 4.979%.

Perhaps a better, or at least a richer, way of dealing with a deterministically changing default rate is a credit migration model. The term "credit migration" refers in general to the path dependence of the probability of default. More narrowly, it refers to the possibility that the probability of default for a future period depends on the default risk of the bond during the previous period.

If a bond is currently rated single A and we assign some probability to the possibility that the bond will be upgraded from A to AA and also some probabilities that the bond will remain A-rated or be downgraded from A to BBB over the next year, then the unconditional probability of default for the following year will depend on the current rating of the bond, the conditional probabilities in the up, down, and any middle states, and on the transitional probabilities of migrating from the current state to a different default rating category. In this approach, we consider the probabilities not only of default, but of more gradual changes to the bond's credit rating, and the path of those changes. We can also take into account the changing nature of the subsequent probabilities of upgrades and downgrades. The model can be made as rich as necessary, as long as there are enough observable bonds of the same issuer with different maturities to calibrate it (here we may need more than one bond per

Table 7.4 The ABC bond with a deterministic non-constant default probability

Year	CF	Prob/Year	Cumulative survival prob.	Risk-free zero rate	Risk-free DF	PV
1	5	0.11%	0.99890	2.5000%	0.975610	4.8727
2	5	6.00%	0.93897	2.6249%	0.949499	4.4577
3	105	8.00%	0.86385	2.7498%	0.921843	83.6150
					Sum PV =	92.9454
					Yield =	7.7238%

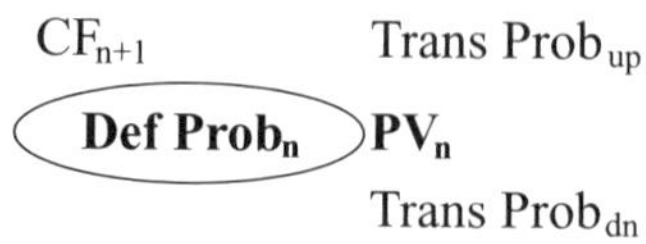

Figure 7.6 One node of a credit migration model

maturity). Effectively, we are replacing the assumption of temporal independence with a model of conditional probabilities.

Let us examine the following scenario. ABC has the probability of default over the next year of 0.20%. We postulate that the annual default probability for year 2 will change to 0.10% with the probability of 30%, or to 0.70% with the probability of 70%. The 30–70 probabilities of period-to-period changes in the issuer's credit rating are referred to as *transitional* probabilities. Now, depending on where we end up in year 2, we will assume different transition probabilities for years 2–3 and different default probabilities for year 3. If we end up at 0.10% for year 2, then we postulate that the annual default probability for year 2 will change to 0.05% with the probability of 25%, or to 0.30% with the probability of 75%. If we end up at 0.70% for year 2, then we postulate that the annual default probability for year 2 will change to 0.30% with the probability of 30%, or to 3.00% with the probability of 70%. This way we can model a non-linear path toward credit trouble and a migration from one credit category to the next over time.

We use a decision tree similar to the binomial tree for options to depict our scenario (our tree is recombinant, but that is not essential). On each node, we mark the probability of default for the year starting at that node and ending next year. We show transitional probabilities of going up or down. We also show the scheduled cash flow for the *next* period. The present value displayed at each node is the discounted expected value of the cash flow to be received next period, cumulated with the expected value of the subsequent period's cash flow which is probability-weighted and discounted. Graphically each node n is represented as in Figure 7.6.

To compute the present value of future cash flows, we cannot ignore the down nodes as we did in Figure 7.5. We also have to "disassemble" the discounting into one-step forward rates. At each, the probability-weighted discounted value of future cash flows is equal to

$$\begin{aligned} PV_n &= (1 - DefProb_n) \\ &\quad \times [CF_{n+1} + (TransProb_{Up} \cdot PV_{Up} + TransProb_{Dn} \cdot PV_{Dn})]/(1 + r_{n,n+1}) \end{aligned}$$

To value the 5% 3-year bond issued by ABC, we sweep backwards through the tree, taking into account our transitional and survival assumptions. Today's price of the ABC bond turns out to be 104.14 and the yield-to-maturity is 3.5217%. The result is shown in Figure 7.7.

Note that our tree does not rely on a hedging argument. It is a convenient graphical tool for computing probability-weighted averages given the conditional default and transition probabilities. It only coincidentally resembles option-pricing trees which are risk-neutral discretized price dynamics. Also note the large number of inputs into the model. Observing 1-, 2-, and 3-year bonds issued by ABC would not be enough to calibrate the model. A reasonable simplification might involve fixing the default probabilities at each note (e.g. set them equal to historic default rates for different rating categories) and calibrating only on the transition probabilities.

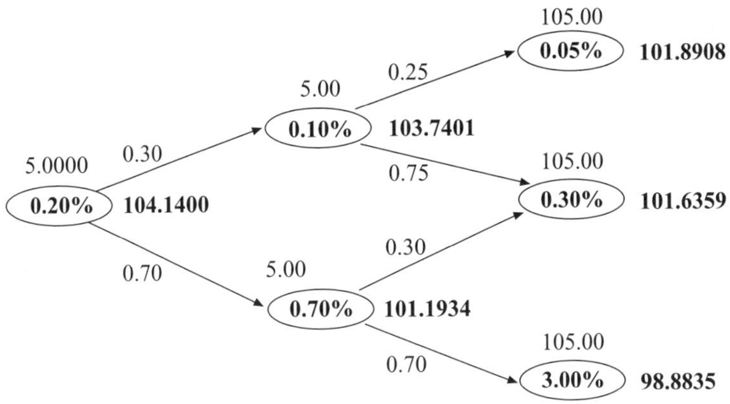

Figure 7.7 A binomial credit migration model with deterministic conditional default and transition probabilities

7.4 A POISSON MODEL OF SINGLE ISSUER DEFAULT

As in Section 7.2, we adopt a reduced-form pricing approach and model default as an exogenous process. Following Jarrow and Turnbull (1995), Duffie and Singleton (1999), and Hull (2010), we assume that defaults follow a Poisson process, i.e. occur as unexpected jumps of a continuous variable. The defaults are defined in a risk-neutral setting so that we can first probability-weight and then discount cash flows using a risk-free rate as we did in Section 7.2. We start by reviewing the assumptions of Poisson processes and distributions, following Hogg and Craig (1978). In their context, we define the default intensity and survival probability per unit of time. We then propose a Poisson model of single issuer default with risk-free and risky discounting, and a fixed recovery percentage. This model can be easily calibrated and used to price credit derivatives. We also offer some thoughts on extending the modeling to include the correlation between the default of the reference security issuer and the protection seller.

7.4.1 Poisson Distribution

Poisson distributions are common in modeling life expectancies, earthquake probabilities, or product failures. All these cases have the following common characteristics:

- The modeled "events" are discrete jumps.
- The probability of an event occurring over a small time interval is small and proportional to the waiting time.
- The probability of more than one event occurring in a small time interval is zero or minuscule.
- The number of events in non-overlapping time intervals is stochastically independent.

A typical set-up in Poisson modeling calls for defining a failure intensity parameter λ, say $\lambda = 1/5{,}000$ chance that we will find a flaw in 1 ton of a material or $\lambda = 1/5{,}000$ mortality rate per year, and a time or quantity parameter ω, say $\omega = 10$ tons of material or $\omega = 10$ years of life. From those two parameters, coupled with the assumption of independence over time (or quantity batches), we can derive failure and survival probabilities over non-cumulative and cumulative periods of time.

Suppose for a given category of bond issuer we define a "failure" or default intensity parameter λ and a time interval ω over which we observe the failure. For example, suppose we think that $\lambda = 0.5\% = 0.005$ of triple-CCC credits default per year based on $\omega = 10$ years of observation. We can then define the Poisson distribution of the number of failures by defining its mean as $\mu = \lambda\omega = 0.05$ and the probability density function as:

$$f(x) = \frac{\mu^x e^{-\mu}}{x!}$$

where x is the number of failures in the interval ω and $f(x)$ is the probability of x failures. In particular, we are interested in the probability of no default, i.e.

$$f(x = 0) = \frac{\mu^0 e^{-0.05}}{0!} = 0.9512$$

The probability of no default is called the survival probability and we will denote it as $P(\omega)$, where

$$P(\omega = 10) = 0.9512$$

Let us note the similarities to the Bernoulli set-up of Figure 7.5. As in that diagram, we will be able to represent the survival of the bond on a tree, as each time interval is independent. Also, the cumulative probability of survival will be the product of the survival probabilities of the intervening intervals, but here we impose a time proportional structure of those probabilities. Everything in the Poisson set-up depends on a single intensity parameter. In practical terms, this ensures the simplicity of the calibration process.

7.4.2 A Single Issuer Default Model

Our model is very simple. We assume a *risk-neutral* default intensity $\lambda = 0.5\%$ and thus a 1-year risk-neutral survival probability $P(\omega = 1) = 0.9950$. We give up any pretense of trying to calibrate our model to historical defaults of the issuer, the rating category, or any default forecast based on the financial statement analysis. The default intensity parameter or the 1-year survival probability must come from another corporate bond by the same issuer or another credit derivative on the reference issuer. It is, by definition, an implied input. It is backed out of the same model with the same underlying risk-free yield curve.

We use the same default-free yield curve as in Table 7.1. Under time independence, nothing is different, and we can proceed exactly as in Figure 7.5 and Table 7.2; the only change being the new per-year probability of default of 0.995. The price of the bond is

$$B_0 = \frac{0.995 \times \$5}{1.02500000} + \frac{0.995^2 \times \$5}{1.02624924^2} + \frac{0.995^3 \times \$105}{1.02749797^3} = 104.9027$$

The yield-to-maturity is 3.258% and the corporate spread is 0.513%.

Incorporating the recovery rate into the model is pretty straightforward. Suppose we assume that whenever the bond defaults the owner is able to recover $R = 60\%$ of the face value of the bond. First, we alter Figure 7.5 to provide us with Figure 7.8.

We then sweep back through the tree adding the coupon cash flows at every step. We start at $t = 2$ and compute the discounted expected value of the cash flows at $t = 3$, right after the

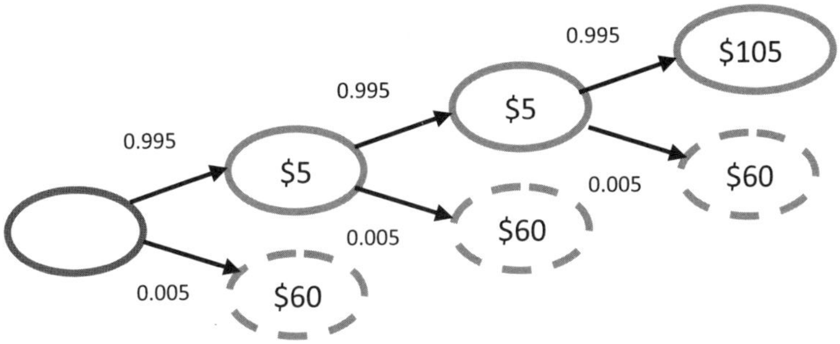

Figure 7.8 Constant probability of default with recovery

coupon payment at $t = 2$:

$$B_2 = \frac{1}{1 + 0.0300}\left[0.995 \times (\$100.0000 + \$5) + 0.005 \times \$60\right] = 101.7233$$

At $t = 1$, immediately after the coupon payment, we have the value of the bond:

$$B_1 = \frac{1}{1 + 0.0275}\left[0.995 \times (\$101.7233 + \$5) + 0.005 \times \$60\right] = 103.6396$$

Finally, at $t = 0$, we would compute the price of the bond as the probability-weighted present value of the bond's cash flows equal to

$$B_0 = \frac{1}{1 + 0.0250}\left[0.995 \times (\$103.6396 + \$5) + 0.005 \times \$60\right] = 105.7526$$

The recovery values are non-zero and do not drop out of the calculation, but we can separate their probability weighting and discounting from the probability weighting and discounting of the stated bond cash flows. As before, this will allow us to discount directly to today using spot zeros, instead of step-by-step using forwards. Table 7.5 summarizes the calculation procedure.

Note that the cumulative probabilities of recovery values are 0.005, 0.995×0.005, and $0.995^2 \times 0.005$. Also note that the inclusion of the recovery value in the valuation changes the model price (by 0.85%) and the yield-to-maturity quite significantly (2.968% vs 3.258%). The corporate spread is equal to 0.223%. Recovery values are rarely zero, and a 60% recovery assumption is not uncommon in credit derivative valuation.

Table 7.5 Corporate bond valuation in a default probability model with recovery

Year	Def prob. per year	Risk-free zero rate	Risk-free DF	Cum survival prob	CF	PV	Cum Prob. of recov.	CF	PV
1	0.005	2.5000%	0.975610	0.99890	5	4.8727	0.005000	60	0.2927
2	0.005	2.6249%	0.949499	0.99780	5	4.7371	0.004975	60	0.2834
3	0.005	2.7498%	0.921843	0.99670	105	96.4745	0.004950	60	0.2738
	Sum PV		105.7526	=		104.9027	+		0.8499
	Ytm		2.9676%						

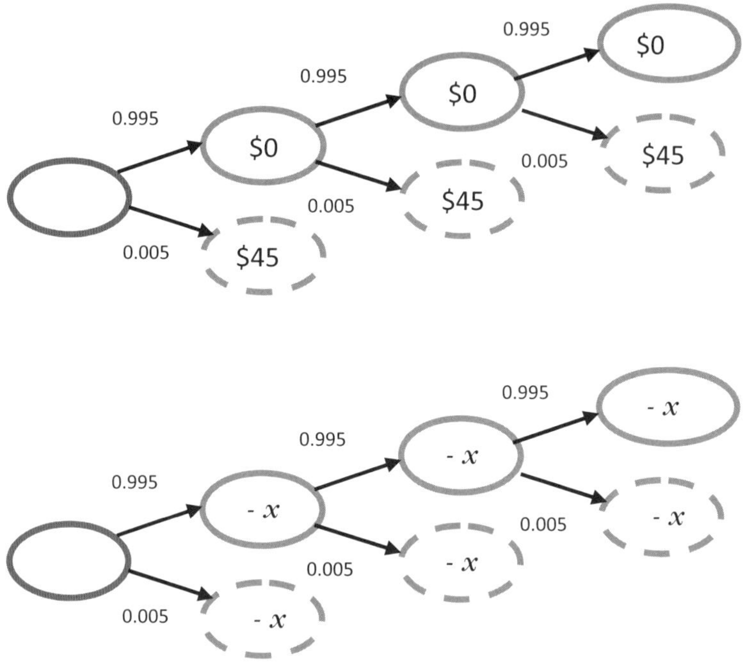

Figure 7.9 Cash flows of a credit default swap

7.4.3 Pricing a Credit Default Swap in a Single Issuer Default Model

Let us now price a credit default swap on the ABC bond of Section 7.4.2 with the *risk-neutral* default intensity $\lambda = 0.5\%$ and thus a 1-year risk-neutral survival probability $P(\omega = 1) = 0.9950$. We assume a 60% recovery. We denote the premium paid for the default protection as x. Figure 7.9 portrays the cash flows paid and received by the protection buyer.

In order to determine the premium charged on the swap, we need to set the probability-weighted discounted value of the receipts on the swap, equal to the face value plus accrued interest minus the recovery (i.e. $100 + 5 - 60 = 45$) to the probability-weighted discounted value of the payments on the swap. Table 7.6 shows the computation of the premium. In the table we verify that $x = 0.224$ is the solution to this PV matching exercise.

The premium charged for CDS protection on a fixed rate bond in a non-flat yield curve is approximately equal to the observed corporate spread. We argued earlier in this chapter that for floating rate bonds the premium is identical to the corporate margin over LIBOR.

Table 7.6 Pricing the credit default swap

Year	Def prob per year	Risk-free zero rate	Risk-free DF	Cum prob of receipt	CF	PV = CF × DF × Pr	CF	PV = CF × DF
1	0.005	2.5000%	0.975610	0.005000	45	0.2195	0.2239	0.2184
2	0.005	2.6249%	0.949499	0.004975	45	0.2126	0.2239	0.2126
3	0.005	2.7498%	0.921843	0.004950	45	0.2053	0.2239	0.2064
	Ytm					0.6374		0.6374

Table 7.7 The joint probability of default of the reference issuer and protection seller

PS		No default $X_{ABC} = 0$	Default $X_{ABC} = 1$	Marginal PS
No default	$X_{PS} = 0$	0.80	0.10	0.90
Default	$X_{PS} = 1$	0.05	0.05	0.10
Marginal ABC		0.85	0.15	1.00

7.5 THE DEFAULT CORRELATION OF THE REFERENCE ISSUER AND THE PROTECTION SELLER

The arbitrage argument of Section 7.1.2 breaks down in the presence of the possibility of default by the protection seller. Financing the purchase of a corporate bond at LIBOR and buying CDS protection on the bond do not produce a risk-free bond if the protection seller can default. The arbitrage argument turns into an inequality. The premium charged can be *at most* equal to the LIBOR margin, equal if the protection seller were a default-free sovereign, and strictly lower otherwise.[1] Intuitively, the higher the credit quality of the protection seller, the closer the CDS premium can get to the corporate spread of the issuer. In general, what matters is the joint distribution of defaults of the reference issuer and the protection seller. Modeling this joint distribution parametrically is generally quite difficult. Only marginal normal distributions can be naturally combined into multivariate normals. Fitting a univariate Poisson to obtain a term structure of intensity parameters λ for a given corporate does not easily combine with a separate marginal Poisson fitting for the protection seller. However, one way to do it is to specify the correlation of defaults implicitly through joint and conditional probabilities.

Following the logic of Chen and Sopranzetti (2002), let us assume a joint Bernoulli set-up for defaults of the reference issuer ABC and the protection seller PS. We denote the random variables

$$X_{ABC} = \begin{cases} 0, & \text{if no default} \\ 1, & \text{if default} \end{cases} \quad \text{and} \quad X_{PS} = \begin{cases} 0, & \text{if no default} \\ 1, & \text{if default} \end{cases}$$

and the joint probability of defaults as in Table 7.7.

The marginal probability of default of the reference issuer ABC is $P(X_{ABC} = 1) = p_{ABC} = 0.15$ and the marginal probability of default of the protection seller PS is $P\,(X_{PS} = 1) = p_{PS} = 0.1$. Using the basic mathematical probability definitions in Hogg and Craig (1978), the means and variances of the two Bernoulli random variables are:

$$\mu_{ABC} = p_{ABC} = 0.15, \quad \sigma^2_{ABC} = p_{ABC}\,(1 - p_{ABC}) = 0.1275,$$

and

$$\mu_{PS} = p_{PS} = 0.10, \quad \sigma^2_{PS} = p_{PS}\,(1 - p_{PS}) = 0.09$$

[1] We ignore here the issues of TED spread, i.e. the difference between LIBOR financing and risk-free financing.

Dropping the zero terms, we can compute the covariance of defaults

$$E[(X_{ABC} - \mu_{ABC})(X_{PS} - \mu_{PS})] = E[X_{ABC}X_{PS}] - \mu_{ABC}\mu_{PS}$$
$$= 1 \times 1 \times 0.05 - 0.15 \times 0.1 = 0.035$$

and, finally, the unconditional correlation coefficient

$$\rho = \frac{0.035}{\sqrt{0.1275} \times \sqrt{0.09}} = 0.3267$$

The unconditional correlation coefficient is rather unintuitive. The more relevant quantity from the perspective of the protection buyer may be the conditional probability of the protection seller's default, given that the reference issue has defaulted, that is

$$P(X_{PS} = 1 | X_{ABC} = 1) = \frac{P(X_{PS} = 1 \cap X_{ABC} = 1)}{P(X_{ABC} = 1)} = \frac{0.05}{0.15} = \frac{1}{3}$$

The probability that the protection buyer will not receive the payment when it is due – that is, the insurer will default when the insurance is needed – is 1/3.

The pricing of the CDS in this set-up follows the logic of Figure 7.9, i.e. of matching the probability-weighted discounted payoff to the probability-weighted discounted premium, but in a multinomial set-up. We don't show it here, as this set-up is rarely used for the following two reasons. First, suppose that the protection seller and the protection buyer are both large institutional CDS dealers – both defaultable entities. Therefore, the seller in setting the premium would have to take into account that the buyer may also default on the premium payments. In theory, we then have to take into account the joint distribution of three parties: the reference issuer, the protection seller, and the protection buyer. However, the positions of the seller and buyer in the CDS contract are not the same. The protection buyer will only default if he is not due any payoff. The seller then should ignore the probability of the default by the buyer and should charge a full premium assuming there will be no buyer default. However, this argument also breaks down since the ISDA master documents provide for the netting of the derivative contracts. This argues in favor of ignoring both buyer and seller defaults in the calculation of the CDS spreads as long as there is no large imbalance of the supply and demand of the contracts, i.e. they are not all sold by the same dealer. In that case, the buyers face the average credit quality of the entire dealer community, similar to swap pricing at LIBOR flat, irrespective of the relative credit quality among the participating dealers. The only argument that survives is whether the CDS premiums should be equal to or lower than the corporate spread on the reference issue.

The second reason why the correlation model proposed in this section is not strictly followed is that, given the reality of the CDS market, it is much more important for the dealers to try to model the joint multivariate distribution of corporate credits in their bond, loan and CDS portfolios. The marginal λ fitting and Poisson pricing of single-issuer CDSs is a boundary condition, but the joint distribution modeling allows the pricing of basket credit derivatives and the risk management of the entire portfolios of the credit derivative contracts. We defer the multivariate copula-based modeling till Chapter 10.

Part II

Cash Flow Engineering

8

Structured Finance

Structured finance is a very broad term encompassing any complicated cash flow arrangement between two or more parties. The arrangement often involves contingent payouts that may be event-driven or at the discretion of one the parties involved. In corporate securities, a callable or a convertible bond, and convertible preferred or hybrid debt, might peripherally fall under this description. Many lease and swap arrangements would also fit this description. However, we will apply the term structured finance in a narrower sense.

A structured security typically takes the form of debt. It is issued as a note or a bond and has a non-standard coupon or principal redemption definition. Often the coupon is fixed and the principal formula is tied to the performance of another asset, the principal is fixed and the coupon is tied to the performance of another asset, or both. The formula of the bond's coupon or principal can depend on the performance of a stock index, commodity, currency, or the movement of interest rates. The performance of the reference asset can be directly part of the formula, e.g. coupon of 3% plus 70% of the appreciation in the S&P 500 index, or the payment may be contingent on the asset reaching a level or being in the range, e.g. daily coupon of 5% p.a. but accrued only for days when LIBOR is between 1% and 3.5%. The payout formula may also be tied to the performance of non-asset economic or event variables, e.g. inflation, GDP, or catastrophic events like hurricane damage. In general, one sees three types of structured securities in terms of design intent: capital (principal) protected (where the holder will get at least the full principal back), yield enhanced (where the coupon formula offer "additions" tied to other assets), and income structures. While common, this is not a very good classification, since the designer of the security can easily shift cash flows between coupon and principal. Legally, principal and coupon may be distinct, but practically they are just arbitrarily defined cash flows. We will attempt a different classification in the next section.

Structured notes have traditionally been put together by large broker-dealers and banks and sold to institutional investors. The issuers have been either sovereigns and corporates, or special purpose vehicle (SPV) trusts. In either case, the structuring dealers would enter into a set of derivative (swap plus option) transactions with the issuer. The purpose of these derivatives would be to pay to the sovereign, corporate, or the SPV the coupon or principal formula which would then be passed on to the investor. More recently, structured notes entered the retail market through two channels: electronically traded notes (ETNs) and structured bank deposits. An ETN is a structured note that trades on a stock exchange like a regular stock. The main advantage of an ETN form is its liquidity. While the ETN has all the features of a structured bond (periodic cash flow tied to the performance of an equity index or a commodity, and may have a stated maturity or be a rollover structure), the retail investor can trade in and out of it with much more ease. Many banks have also started offering deposit accounts whose interest accrual calculation is tied to the performance of equities, currencies, or commodities. Usually these are renewable term deposits (like CDs with stated maturities) or the interest formula is applied at regular calendar intervals (pay the percentage interest equal to the S&P 500 appreciation for the calendar quarter).

Structured finance is the subject of this and the next two chapters. The latter cover specialized areas of mortgage-backed securities (MBSs) and collateralized debt obligations (CDOs). The special features there are the pooling of credit risk and the tranching of cash flows. Other markets that share the credit risk pooling feature are generally all asset-backed securities (ABSs), like bonds backed by consumer credit card receipts, car and student loans, etc. All ABSs, including MBSs and CDOs, are structured with the use of an SPV trust that holds the underlying risky loans or bonds, and issues *pass-through* certificates entitling the holder to the proportional share of the coupon cash flow (similar to a mutual fund design) which is fixed and equal to the weighted average of all the coupon flows received by the trust. Those pass-through certificates can then be pooled and, with the use of another SPV, be spliced (tranched) into several classes of certificates with unequal rights to the cash flows.

In this chapter, we focus on the rest of structured notes trading in the financial markets, most of which are not tranched, and whose coupon and principal are often not simple weighted average pass-through quantities, but are specifically designed to depend on other economic variables to meet the investors' demand for risk. We start with a general consideration of the purpose of structured finance, followed by the examples of the main three types and a discussion of the design and valuation issues.

8.1 A SIMPLE CLASSIFICATION OF STRUCTURED NOTES

According to Wikipedia, the US Securities and Exchange Commission (SEC) Rule 434 defines structured securities as "securities whose cash flow characteristics depend upon one or more indices or that have embedded forwards or options or securities where an investor's investment return and the issuer's payment obligations are contingent on, or highly sensitive to, changes in the value of underlying assets, indices, interest rates, or cash flows." The main characteristic of structured products is that they are created to meet specific needs that cannot be met from the standardized financial instruments available in the markets (like stocks and bonds). Many structured notes have implicit options embedded in them (contingent payout that depends on market movements). Yet while retail brokerage customers in the USA have to go through a stringent option-trading approval process, they can buy structured notes in their accounts as easily as any other bonds. Also, some structured notes or deposits are advertised with a "principal protected" label. The "protected" label refers to the fact that the payout formula may affect only the coupon, not the fact that the issuer or deposit holding bank may not default.

The main appeal of structured notes to investors is access to risk. Investors receive compensation in the form of coupon or principal enhancement for risks not easily embedded in standard securities. The main disadvantages are: the credit risk of the issuer (an investor may want a currency bet, but not a bet on the Kingdom of Belgium issuing the unsecured note), the lack of daily pricing and liquidity, and the complexity of the terms which often hides the dealer fees.

When attempting to classify structured notes, we often focus on how the risk comes into play in defining cash flows. A currency – or equity-linked note – where the issuer takes the \$100 principal paid by the investor, buys a zero-coupon bond \$82, and spends the remaining \$18 minus the fees on an at- or out-of-the-money currency/equity call option expiring at maturity of the note – might be classified as principal-protected. The \$82 spent on the zero coupon guarantees \$100 at maturity. Instead, we could also have sold currency/equity puts expiring at maturity of the note (or entered into a forward), saving the \$18 to acquire some derivatives paying on coupon dates. We also could have simply used the entire \$100 to buy a bullet bond and enter into an equity swap. The bullet bonds coupon cash flows could be exchanged for equity-related flows. We would thus structure currency- or equity-linked coupon flows, principal-unprotected with the puts or forward and principal-protected with the swap. In all cases, we are trying to be compensated for bearing equity risk in the form of a bond.

We adopt a different classification of structured products based on the type of risk to which the bond or note is exposed. This has great implications for who the issuers are, who the investors are, and how the structure is priced. Here are the main three categories of structured products:

- Interest rate and yield curve-based structured notes: the examples include capped/floored floaters, inverse floaters, range collars, callables, leveraged floaters, amortizing bonds
- Asset class-linked notes: the examples include non-interest rate asset classes: equity-, currency- and commodity-linked notes and deposits, rainbow (best of, horse race, lookback) and hybrid-linked notes and deposits; credit-linked notes and quanto variations; both with coupon and principal-embedded payout formulas
- Economic variable and insurance risk transfer notes: the examples include inflation; GDP and corporate event-driven bonds as well as reinsurance aimed bonds like catastrophe (CAT) bonds linked to earthquake or hurricane risk; or pooled reinsurance notes

The first category is investor-demand driven. Investors seek income or yield enhancement through inverse floaters when interest rates are low; they want ranges when interest rates are low and volatile; they want fixed coupons or callables when the yield curve is steep. The issuer is irrelevant to the success of the bond here: a sovereign or an SPV as long as the coupon formula is attractive. The valuation relies on standard interest rate modeling and pricing interest rate options.

The second category is driven by customized access to an asset class. An equity participation rate of less than 100% may mean a less-volatile exposure to equity. Spot currency trading is volatile and cheapest at the wholesale bank level. A quarterly-reset currency-linked structured note with averaging features may be more appealing. Commodity markets in general exhibit the greatest liquidity in futures contracts and may be inaccessible for spot trading; structured notes offer exposure to the commodity price movements without trading spot, complicated with quality and supply characteristics, or futures in margin accounts. The cash flow formula suppliers may be the structuring dealers, but can often be commodity (energy, chemical) companies and commodity funds looking to offload risk. The pricing can become complex as it may cut across asset classes, involve basis (correlation) risk, and be subject to non-hedgeable risk (contango or backwardation in futures, basis swaps).

The third category is driven by agents seeking to diminish economic and business risks. They can be both sellers and buyers of cash flows. Inflation-linked note buyers want to hedge the inflation risk. Insurers who lack reinsurance outlets sell catastrophe bonds in financial markets to transfer some of the largest concentrated risks (hurricanes in Florida, California earthquake, shipping through the Gulf of Aden) to investors. They also sell notes that act as outright shares in their entire portfolio of risk. The pricing of the third category of structured notes is the most difficult and crosses over from financial option modeling into actuarial science, meteorological and seismic sciences, and economic forecasting. That crossover from financial options to physical science modeling implies almost complete unhedgeability and actuarial (historic) calibration rather than market price (implied) calibration.

8.2 INTEREST RATE AND YIELD CURVE-BASED STRUCTURED PRODUCTS

Swaps combined with interest rate options (caps/floors and swaptions) are the main building blocks for structured bonds. In Chapter 4, we showed how corporations issue straight bonds and then use swaps to turn fixed bond liabilities into floating, or one currency into another. Sometimes they issue a highly structured bond and use a dealer to strip it of all complication to leave the company with a simple fixed or floating liability. The driver is often the investor demand for a customized interest rate exposure scenario. The issuer's objective is a lower cost of funding.

In this section, we go over the cash flow engineering of several popular yield curve structures. We use flow diagrams as the exposition tool with all flows shown in per annum percent-of-principal terms (i.e. to convert to dollars they need to be multiplied by a quarterly or semi-annual day-count).

A sovereign, corporate, or trust issuer sells structured notes to investors. The notes carry coupon interest subject to a formula. The floating coupon formula reflects the investor's view of the likely future yield curve scenario. If the investor is right, he will receive more interest dollars than on a straight bullet bond. If he is wrong and his interest rate path prediction proves wrong, he will receive less. The investor may also be simply trading later cash flows for earlier ones. The issuer enters into a series of derivative and option agreements with the structuring dealer. The derivatives are designed to exactly replicate the coupon formula minus the profit to the dealer minus the funding subsidy to the issuer. The dealer's benefit may also be selling out of an interest rate risk.

We start with inverse floaters that pay high interest in low interest rate scenarios and low interest in high interest rate scenarios. We show a capped floater where the cap on the coupon is traded for a yield enhancement. We look at a callable where a short swaption is traded for a yield enhancement. We end with periodically used designs like range floaters and index amortizing swaps.

For our examples, we use as a starting point, the hypothetical US LIBOR and Treasury rates as of September 26, 2013 (Table 8.1).

We use the Bond Math of Chapter 2 and curve building methods of Chapter 3 to give us the forward curve in Table 8.2.

Using the swap valuation methods of Chapter 4, we present-value (Table 8.3) a 5-year swap to show that the zero-PV semi-annual rate on a 5-year swap against floating 3-month LIBOR is 3.3636%.

In order to understand the economics of the deals, the reader should also review the discussion of floating rate note pricing. A floating rate bond (with no margin) is always worth par on coupon dates and its duration is less than the next coupon reset date.

8.2.1 An Inverse Floater

An inverse floater is a bond whose coupon payout is equal to a fixed rate minus a short-term floating rate. Such a coupon structure is often demanded during the times of low rate volatility, a steep yield curve, and when investors expect the short-term rates to remain (and be low) or to decrease. The pricing is then attractive as forwards increase with maturity.

Using the rate inputs as of September 26, 2013, with a 5-year par swap at 3.3636% semi-annual, equivalent to 3.3496% quarterly, rounded to 3.35%, an investor may be offered a

Table 8.1 US spot yield curve on September 26, 2013

Eurodollar (CME)		US Treasury issues Maturity	Coupon	Yield
Dec13	98.83			
Mar14	98.75			
Jun	98.51			
Sep	98.19	9/30/2015	1.625	1.657
Dec	97.77	9/15/2018	3.125	3.030
Mar15	97.35	8/15/2023	4.250	4.099
Jun	96.96	2/15/2041	5.375	5.000
Sep	96.65			
Dec	96.35	Money rates		
Mar16	96.10			
Jun	95.87	3-mo LIBOR	1.1400%	
Sep	95.65			
Dec	95.44			
Mar17	95.25			
Jun	95.08			
Sep	94.92			
Dec	94.77			
Mar18	94.64			
Jun	94.51			
Sep	94.41			
Dec	94.31			
Mar19	94.22			
Jun	94.14			
Sep	94.07			
Dec	94.00			

5-year structured bond whose quarterly coupon is equal to

$$6.50 - L_{3m}$$

We explain this structure in the diagram of Figure 8.1. To show the reduced cost of funding to ABC Corp., we separate the issuing entity from the company's operations. The two are often the same.

On the issue date ABC Capital Corp. sells the inverse floater bonds with a quarterly coupon of 6.50 – 3-month LIBOR (L_{3m}) for 100. It transfers the proceeds to its operations unit. It enters into a swap with a notional principal of 200 to receive 3.34 and pay L_{3m} (times the appropriate day-count) on the same dates as the coupon dates. It buys a cap for which it pays 37.4 bp up front or over time the equivalent of 8 bp p.a. running (0.374 is equal to 0.08/2 times the sum of the discount factors from Table 8.2). The cap provides protection for the scenario that L_{3m} is above 6.50 on any coupon date. In those cases, the option dealer who sold the cap will compensate ABC Capital for the difference. If L_{3m} stays below 6.50, ABC Capital will receive nothing. ABC nets 10 bp running which reduces its cost of funding to L_{3m} – 10. The swap dealer makes a profit on the swap (paying 3.34 while the fair rate is 3.35); the option dealer's profit is in the price of the cap. The investor gets a desired coupon formula, today paying 6.50 – 1.14 = 5.36% well above today's LIBOR of 1.14%. To make the economics of cash flows clear, let us examine two scenarios.

Table 8.2 US forward curve on September 26, 2013

Forward period time (months from today)						
Start	End	100-Eurodollars	Convexity adjustment	FRA rate	Zero rate (to end time)	Discount factors (to end time)
0	3			1.140	1.140000	0.9971581
3	6	1.17	0.000	1.170	1.155000	0.9942499
6	9	1.25	−0.008	1.242	1.183998	0.9911723
9	12	1.49	−0.016	1.474	1.256479	0.9875333
12	15	1.81	−0.024	1.786	1.362327	0.9831435
15	18	2.23	−0.032	2.198	1.501485	0.9777707
18	21	2.65	−0.040	2.610	1.659657	0.9714321
21	24	3.04	−0.048	2.992	1.825959	0.9642197
24	27	3.35	−0.056	3.294	1.988810	0.9563442
27	30	3.65	−0.064	3.586	2.148245	0.9478468
30	33	3.90	−0.072	3.828	2.300660	0.9388619
33	36	4.13	−0.080	4.050	2.446149	0.9294512
36	39	4.35	−0.088	4.262	2.585540	0.9196523
39	42	4.56	−0.096	4.464	2.719426	0.9095022
42	45	4.75	−0.104	4.646	2.847578	0.8990597
45	48	4.92	−0.112	4.808	2.969826	0.8883813
48	51	5.08	−0.120	4.960	3.086624	0.8775003
51	54	5.23	−0.128	5.102	3.198326	0.8664488
54	57	5.36	−0.136	5.224	3.304687	0.8552788
57	60	5.49	−0.144	5.346	3.406508	0.8439988

Table 8.3 The present value of a 5-year par swap on September 26, 2013

		Par swap rate = 3.3636	
Zero rate (to end time)	Discount factors (to end time)	Cash flow	PV of cash flow
1.140000	0.9971581		
1.155000	0.9942499	1.6818	1.6721
1.184664	0.9911674		
1.257978	0.9875185	1.6818	1.6608
1.364726	0.9831142		
1.504816	0.9777220	1.6818	1.6443
1.663938	0.9713596		
1.831202	0.9641191	1.6818	1.6215
1.995023	0.9562112		
2.155433	0.9476774	1.6818	1.5938
2.308828	0.9386522		
2.455132	0.9292022	1.6818	1.5627
2.595214	0.9193650		
2.729692	0.9091777	1.6818	1.5291
2.858358	0.8986989		
2.981055	0.8879853	1.6818	1.4934
3.098249	0.8770702		
3.210303	0.8659856	1.6818	1.4564
3.316980	0.8547836		
3.419085	0.8434727	101.6818	85.7658
		Sum =	100.0000

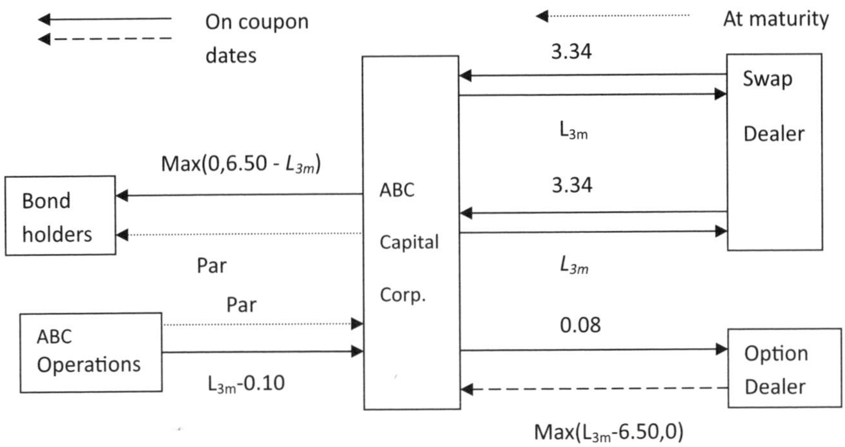

Figure 8.1 A 5-year 6.50% minus 3-month LIBOR inverse floater

First assume that on some coupon date L_{3m} is 2.00%, i.e. lower than 6.50. The bondholder's coupon is 4.50%. ABC Capital Corp. receives 3.34 on the two swaps, i.e. a total of 6.68. It pays 0.08 out of that for the cap and receives nothing from the cap. The remainder, equal to 6.60, plus the $L_{3m} - 0.10 = 1.90$ it receives from ABC Operations as the cost of using the principal funds, gives it a total of 8.50. From that it pays $2 \times 2.00 = 4.00\%$ on the floating legs of the two swaps and 4.50 to the bondholders.

Next assume that L_{3m} is 7.50, i.e. higher than 6.50, on some coupon date. The bondholder's coupon is zero. ABC Capital Corp. receives 3.34 on the two swaps, i.e. a total of 6.68. It pays 0.08 for the cap, and receives $7.50 - 6.50 = 1\%$ as the cap payoff. It also receives $L_{3m} - 0.10 = 7.40$ from ABC Operations as the cost of using the principal funds. Out of the total of $6.68 - 0.08 + 1.00 + 7.40 = 15\%$, ABC Capital pays $2 \times 7.50 = 15\%$ on the floating legs of the two swaps and zero to the bondholders.

On the maturity date, ABC Operations pay back the principal $100 which is forwarded to the bondholders. The net cost for using those funds to ABC Operations is L_{3m} minus 0.10 irrespective of the level of L_{3m} on any coupon date. The coupon on the bond looks attractive to the investors who do not believe that short-term rates will go up from the currently low level. The fixed portion of the coupon reflects double the current term swap rate net of the cost of the cap. The cap protection tends to be cheap as it has a high strike price. In most cases, the swap and the option dealer are the same, providing the issuer with a competitive quote on the entire behind-the-scenes part of the deal.

8.2.2 A Leveraged Inverse Floater

The leveraged inverse floater combines three or more swaps and a cap into a single bond. Consider the following quarterly coupon formula offered by ABC Capital to its investors:

$$9.60 - 2 \times L_{3m}$$

It is easy to see that, compared to the standard inverse floater, all we need to do is add another swap to triple the principal on the swap, lower the strike on the cap, and double the principal on the cap. The summary diagram is shown in Figure 8.2.

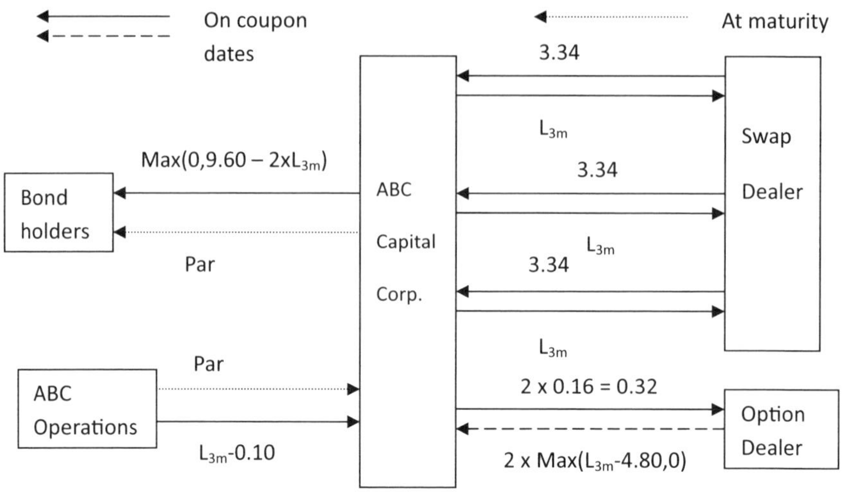

Figure 8.2 A 5-year 9.60% minus 2 times 3-month LIBOR inverse floater

The structure looks attractive for everyone involved. The investors' coupon on day 1 is $9.60 - 2 \times 1.14 = 7.32$, which is very attractive compared to the alternatives of 3.34% fixed or $L_{3m} = 1.14\%$ floating. The dealer makes a profit on two caps and pays bid on three swaps. The cost of each cap is 16 bp running or 74.8 bp up front, but the principal is 200. The issuer gets L_{3m} – 10 bp financing. The investors bear the risk in this structure that short rates may increase rapidly, which would sharply reduce or potentially eliminate the coupon payout.[1]

Let us verify that the structure works by examining two scenarios: one with LIBOR below 4.80% and one with LIBOR above 4.80% (all amounts are in percent of the bond principal (100), and per annum, i.e. before multiplication by a day-count fraction). If LIBOR is 2% on a coupon date, then ABC Capital receives 11.92:

$$3 \times 3.4 = 10.02 \text{ on the three swaps}$$
$$2.00 - 0.10 = 1.90 \text{ from ABC Operations}$$

and it pays 11.92:

$$2 \times 0.16 = 0.32 \text{ for the caps}$$
$$3 \times 2.00\% = 6.00 \text{ on the floating legs of the three swaps}$$
$$9.60 - 2 \times 2.00\% = 5.60 \text{ to the bondholders}$$

If LIBOR is 5.5% on a coupon date, then ABC Capital receives 16.82:

$$3 \times 3.4 = 10.02 \text{ on the three swaps}$$
$$5.50 - 0.10 = 5.40 \text{ from ABC Operations}$$
$$2 \times (5.50 - 4.80) = 1.407 \text{ payout on the cap}$$

[1] Consider the duration and convexity of a leveraged inverse floater. A small rate increase may render the PV of future coupons zero.

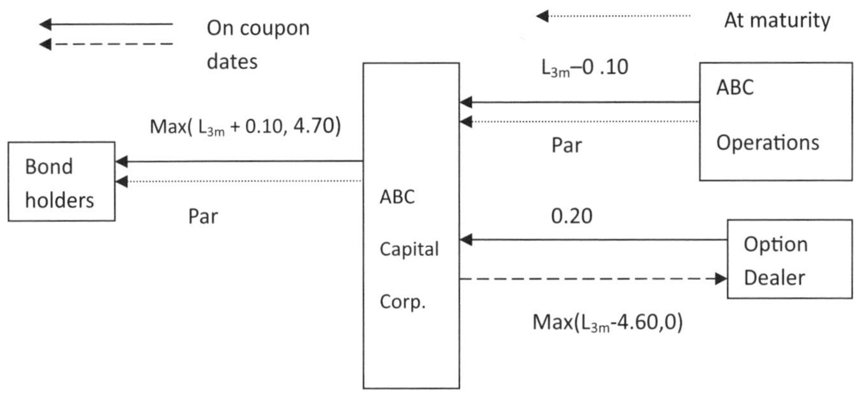

Figure 8.3 A 5-year capped floater

and it pays 16.82:

$$2 \times 0.16 = 0.32 \text{ for the caps}$$
$$3 \times 5.50\% = 16.50 \text{ on the floating legs of the three swaps}$$
$$0.00\% \text{ to the bondholders}$$

8.2.3 A Capped Floater

A capped floater is a bond whose coupon is floating, but it is capped. The investor forgoes the upside above the cap for a larger coupon now. The larger coupon comes in the form of extra margin on top of LIBOR. The issuer gets the reduced cost of financing. This structure is much simpler than an inverse floater.

To structure the deal, ABC Capital Corp. sells the cap embedded in the coupon formula to the dealer and uses the annuitized proceeds to enhance the bond coupon. The diagram in Figure 8.3 shows the structure in which investors in the bond receive the 3-month LIBOR plus 10 bp up to 4.7%. They trade off the unlikely future scenarios of LIBOR above 4.6% for the extra 0.10% now.

The investor's coupon is L_{3m} + 10 bp, but no more than 4.70. ABC get funding at L_{3m} – 10 bp. The option dealer buys the 4.60 strike cap for 0.935% up front or 0.20% quarterly premium. If LIBOR on any coupon date is below 4.60, the cap does not pay. ABC Capital Corp. passes the (L_{3m} – 10) interest its affiliates pay for using the proceeds of the bond, enhanced by the 20 bp premium it receives for the short cap, to the bondholders. If LIBOR on a coupon date is greater than 4.60, say 5.50, ABC Capital receives 5.40 from its affiliate (the company as a whole pays for using the funds) and 0.20 as the premium for the cap. From the total 5.60, it pays the bondholders 4.70 and pays back 0.90 to the dealer as the payoff on the cap.

8.2.4 A Callable

Fixed rate bonds, floating rate bonds, and all the structured bonds can be issued in a callable form. In such case, ABC Capital would have the right to call the bonds from the bondholders at par or at a price specified in advance in a call schedule. The bond may be sold as a 5-year issue callable in or after one year. The call feature is more convenient than a tender offer to repurchase bonds when the issuer wants to refinance the bonds prior to maturity. If ABC Capital chooses to retain the right to call the bonds, it will bear the cost of a higher coupon demanded by the investors. ABC Capital can also choose to sell that right to a dealer for an upfront fee, or to annuitize it. In that case, the annuitized premium the dealer pays covers that extra cost, leaving ABC with a straight fixed rate liability. The choice depends on ABC's needs and on the deal's pricing. If interest rate implied volatilities are currently high, the dealer might be willing to pay a lot for the call right, potentially reducing ABC's fixed financing cost well below the fair fixed swap rate. Similar to the capped floater, the premium for the swaption pays for the excess coupon paid to the bondholders and for the funding subsidy to the company.

The 5-year bond callable in 1 year can be viewed two different ways. One is a 5-year bullet bond with a call option to buy the bond at par. The other is a 1-year bond with a 1 year right sell for par a 4-year bond with the same coupon. When selling the call right to the dealer, the issuer usually sells a call swaption, and sometimes enters into a swap to receive fixed in order to convert the bond to a floating rate liability at a LIBOR minus the margin level.

8.2.5 A Range Floater

A range bond pays a coupon that depends on how many days during the interest accrual period a floating rate stayed within a prespecified range. The issuer desires the low cost of floating financing. It offers investors an enhanced floating (LIBOR plus spread) or fixed coupon rate for each day the floating rate does not leave the range bounds. Investors get no interest rate accrual for days when the rate is outside the range. They are betting that the rate will not jump up and/or down. The range can have upper (range cap) or lower (range floor) bounds or both (range collar). The coupon formula for any interest period might read the following:

$$L_{3m} + 100\,\text{bp} \times \text{Number of days where } 0.75 < L_{3m} < 2.75, \text{ divided by } 365$$

The range option embedded in the coupon is sold to an option dealer in exchange for the spread and some extra margin which reduces the issuer's financing (e.g. for 110 bp). The structure resembles a capped and floored floater, but it is not the same. In the capped/floored floater, the reference LIBOR rate is checked against the bounds only once at the set time of the interest accrual period. The net premium on the sold cap minus the bought floor that the issuer arranges with the dealer pays for the margin. Either none or one of the options gets triggered on the set date. In the range floater, the coupon rate may be fixed (4%) or floating ($L_{3m} + 100$), but we check against the bounds every day during the interest accrual period. If, out of 92 days in the interest period, the reference rate has remained within the bounds for 46 days, then we multiply the stated coupon rate by 46/365. That is equivalent to losing half the coupon for the period. The range option can be quite complicated to price and hedge from the dealer's perspective. It is composed of a series of daily digital options. The shorter those are to expiry and the closer to the bound (strike), the more difficult they are to hedge (high gamma).

8.2.6 An Index Principal Swap

A structure attractive to mortgage bond investors who want the enhanced yield of a prepayment-exposed investment, but want to limit the unpredictability of prepayments is called an index principal (IPS) or index amortizing swap (IAR). As is often the case, the design is driven by the specific investor demand for a callable-like yield enhancement, while the issuer simply wants reduced floating financing. The issuer issues a bond with a formula coupon and principal to the bondholders, but reverses the cash flows of the bond by entering into an IPS with a dealer.

The swap is a fixed for floating swap, except the notional principal of the swap changes over time. Each period one looks at the principal as of the last period times one minus a percentage taken from an amortization table which might look like this:

Rate	*Percent Notional Amortized*
3	0%
2	50%
1	100%

Suppose last period's principal was 100 and the index rate, L_{3m}, this period is 1.14%. We use 1.14 to interpolate between 1 and 2 in the table to obtain the notional percentage equal to 93%. This period, the new notional principal used to compute interest flows on both sides of the swap is equal to the last principal times 100 minus the amortized percentage of 93, or 0.07. The new principal is thus 7.

This procedure is intended to mimic the prepayment behavior of fixed rate mortgages. As rates go down, homeowners refinance their mortgages. The principals of the mortgage bonds are reduced. Similarly, the principals of the IPS bonds will be reduced, but based on a prespecified amortization table rather than the actual behavior of homeowners who often do not refinance optimally.

The IPS was first popularized in the mid-1990s in the US where over 50% of mortgages are fixed with no prepayment penalties and a large securitized mortgage market exists. Most reference rates used were LIBOR rather than long rates (like the 10-year Treasury) providing for another interesting play on the yield curve and the relative volatility of swaptions and caps.

8.3 ASSET CLASS-LINKED NOTES

Structured notes often have coupon or principal payoffs linked to the performance of equities, currencies, or commodities. The most popular are equity-linked notes and the most common design is a principal-protected equity participation note (EPN). The design typically relies on using the proceeds (100) from selling the note to purchase a zero-coupon bond (PV of 100) with the face value equal to the principal of the note (100) and using the remainder of the proceeds minus fees to buy equity call options on the desired index. In the standard EPN the options are struck at the money, but there is not enough money to purchase the same principal amount as that of a bond. This results in less than 100% participation to the investor. To reach fuller participation, the options have to be cheaper, and so they can be purchased out-of-the-money, have barrier knock-out features, or otherwise the principal cannot be fully guaranteed. The same exact EPN design can be applied to currencies or commodities. These notes can also be offered in the form of bank CDs and ETNs.

8.3.1 Principal-Protected Equity-Linked Notes

The basic design is very simple. Suppose the principal of the note is \$100 and the note is sold to investors at par. Five-year zero-coupon rates are at 4%. The issuing trust sponsored by the selling dealer splits the received \$100 into three parts, as depicted in Figure 8.4. The first is a 5-year zero bought for the PV of \$100 discounted by 5 years; the second is the underwriting fee and dealer profit; the third is the equity option.

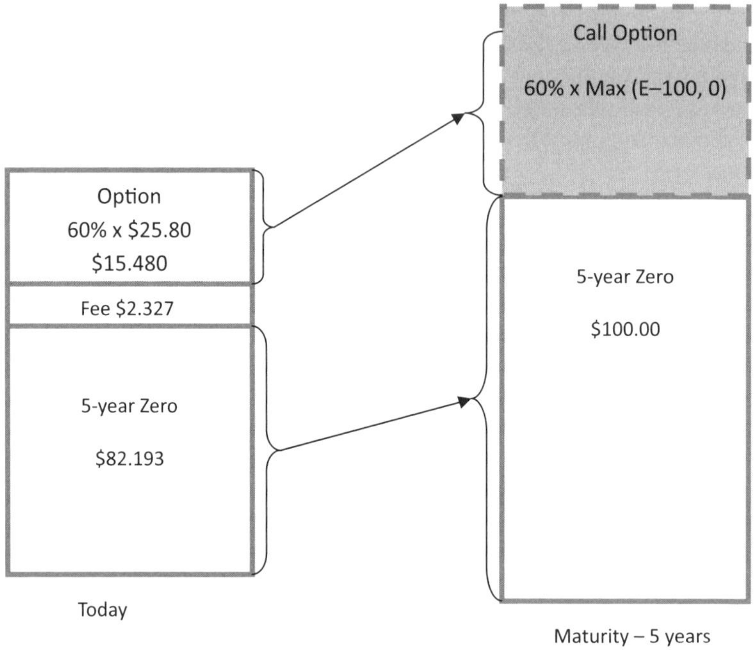

Figure 8.4 A 5-year 60% equity participation note

The PV of $100 at 4% is $82.193. We assume that a 5-year at-the-money option on the index costs $25.80 per $100 principal. We buy index options on $60 principal. At maturity, the investor gets $100 plus 60% of any appreciation of the equity index over the initial level of the index on the issue date of the note. If the index is the S&P 500 and we start at the 1,300 level and the index moves up 74% over the 5-year period to 2262, the investor will get an additional $44.40. The total redemption value of the note will be $144.40.

Of course, the option embedded in the EPN need not be a straight call. Analogous to the capped floater, we can cap the level of equity appreciation in exchange for a kicker up to that level. Instead of a margin, the easiest way is to boost the participation. The cap is accomplished with the use of an equity call spread. The trust buys at-the-money calls and sells deep out-of-the money calls. Suppose 50% out-of-the-money calls at the time of the issuance trade at 5.20. The call spread costs 25.80 – 5.20 = 20.60. For $15.48 we can buy call spreads on 75.1% of the principal. We could thus structure a note with a 75% participation rate up to the cap of 37.50%. The 37.50% cap translates into a 50% out-of-the-money call on 75% of the principal. If the index goes up by 74%, the investor would only get $137.50 upon redemption. The capped structure has an advantage over the straight one at lower levels of equity appreciation. At a 50% index rise, the investor gets $137.50, while the straight 60% participation note investor gets $130. Figure 8.5 shows a capped structure with a higher participation rate.

Yet another way to increase the participation rate is through a leveraged equity-linked note. Instead of buying calls on 60% or 75% of the principal, we buy two or three calls. To be able to afford those, they need to be packaged into a tight spread, ranged or subject to barriers. Figure 8.6 shows a structure with two return barriers set at –5% and 10%. The leverage is a factor of two, and the total return cap is set at 20. The investor only gets the equity return

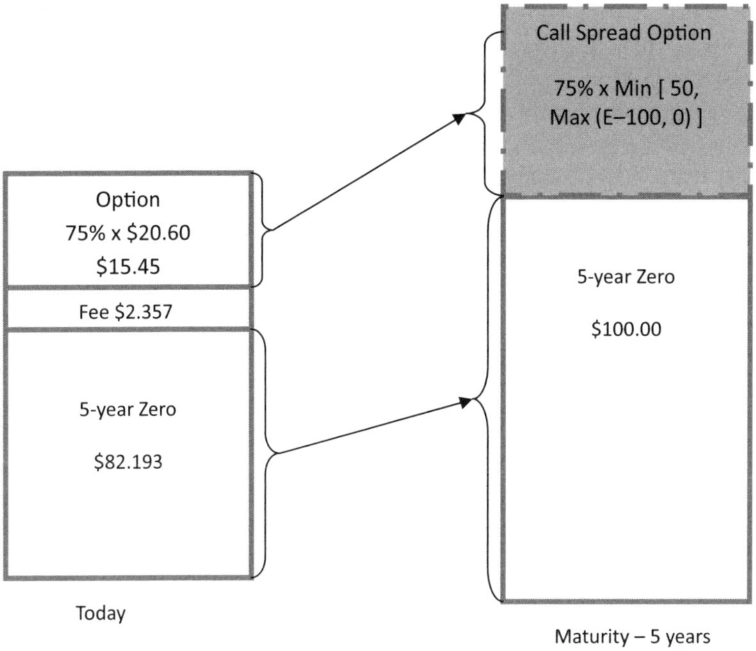

Figure 8.5 A 5-year 75% equity participation note: trade a cap for a higher participation rate

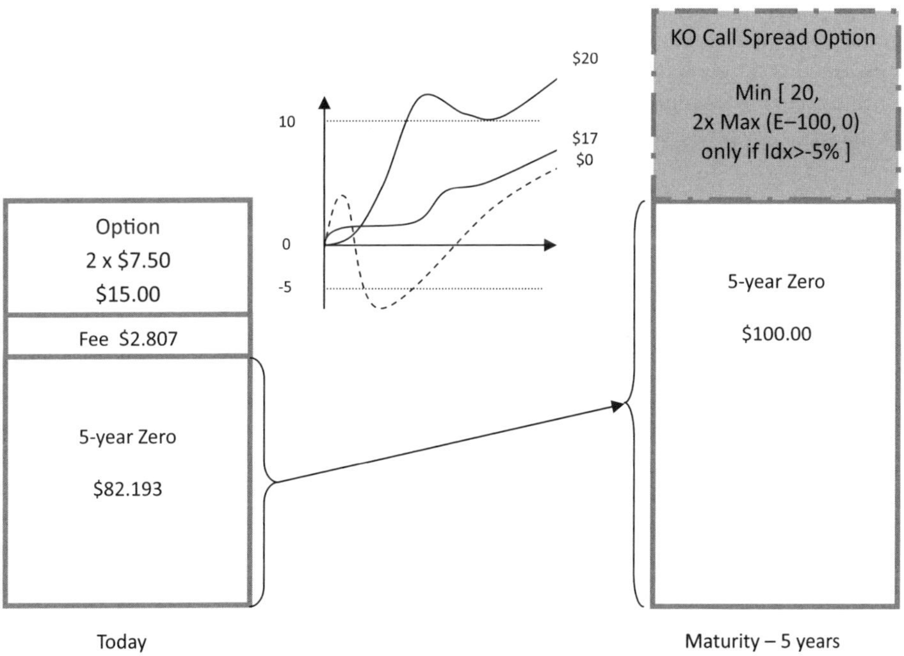

Figure 8.6 A 5-year 2 × leveraged equity linked note: barrier at −5%, cap at 20%

if the index during the life of the note never drops below 5% of the original level. If the index stays above the −5% lower barrier, the investor gets double the return on the index, but only up to the maximum of 20%. Implicitly, the equity option premium is spent on two at-the-money down-and-out call spreads. Each call spread (long at-the-money call and short 10% out-of-the-money call) has a maximum payout of 10, and is subject to a down-and-out knock-out barrier at −5%. We assume that each call spread is worth $7.50. We spend the total of $15 on the equity kicker; the dealer's fee is $2.807.

Other variations include lookback or Asian features. In a lookback, the investor may be able to lock in the highest level that the index has reached over the life of the note. Lookbacks are quite expensive, so the participation rate achieved may be low. In an Asian option structure, the investor gets the average of the index levels over the life of the option rather than the final value. Asian options are often cheaper than straight calls.

8.3.2 A (Rainbow) Multi-Asset-Linked Note

The basic design is similar to the above described equity-linked notes, except the asset return-kicker on top of the guaranteed principal is either a best-of-many option or a basket. In the best-of-many case, the investor may get a 60% participation in the best performing asset class over the life. Typically, the choices are several equity indexes (e.g. FTSE 100, S&P 500 and Nikkei 225) or disparate asset categories (equity, currency, commodity). The choices may be currency-translated or quantoed. If the note is sold to the Japanese investors, then the FTSE 100 and S&P 500 may be translated into yen, i.e. raw index returns corrected for the currency fluctuation, or quantoed, i.e. raw pound and dollar returns taken as straight percentages and paid in yen.

In the rainbow basket case, each asset in the basket may have its own participation rate defined, and the return kicker is defined as the percentage change in the entire basket over the life of the note. For example, the basket may be:

$$(20\% \times \text{S\&P 500}) + (10\% \times \text{FTSE 100}) + (10\% \times \text{DAX}) + (10\% \times \text{CAC40})$$

A more expensive version of the rainbow case is to define the percentages for each index, and then buy those percentages worth of call options, that is, to buy a basket of options on each index rather than one option on the basket. While dealers are more likely to have the expertise in multi-equity index rainbows housed in one equity department, the disparate asset class versions of rainbows, e.g. combining commodities with equities, may be harder to handle. The delta hedging by itself may not be hard as long as all indexes and assets have futures traded on them. The long-term volatility and the correlation exposure are the real risks of the structures on asset baskets.

8.3.3 Principal-At-Risk Notes and Commodity-Tracking ETNs

Putting all or some principal at risk is accomplished by having the issuing trust not only buy calls but also sell puts or put spreads. Just as in the previous call spread example, the objective is to boost the participation rate. The other use of the principal-at-risk design is the commodity-tracking ETN.

Suppose, as before, the principal of the note is $100 and the note is sold to investors at par. Five-year zero-coupon rates are at 4%. The issuing trust splits the received $100 into three parts. The first is a 5-year zero bought for $82.193 equal to the PV of $100 discounted

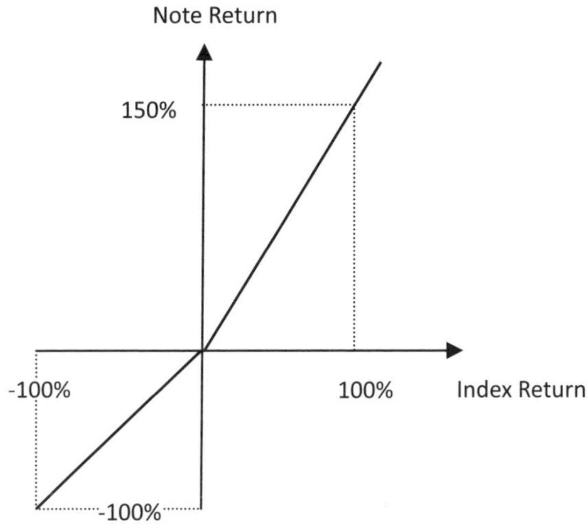

Figure 8.7 A 5-year 1.5 leveraged principal-at-risk index-linked note

by 5 years; the second is the underwriting fee and dealer profit of \$2.357; the third is the equity kicker worth \$15.45. The option money is spent on at-the-money calls on 150% of the principal which cost 1.5 × \$25.8; the trust also sells an at-the-money put for \$23.25. The investor has a 1.5 times leveraged position on the way up and unleveraged downside exposure. The investor's payoff diagram is shown in Figure 8.7.

A common variation on this design is to put a floor under the principal loss. Instead of selling a straight put, the issuing trust sells an at-the-money put, but also buys an out-of-the-money put, say 15%. In an upward-sloping yield curve environment, the 15% out-of-the-money European put can typically be bought cheaply, resulting in little participation loss on the upside.

The long call–short put position is equivalent to the long forward position. Most commodity-tracking ETNs are designed as a combination of a money-market account and a long futures position. At the time of the issuance, investors pay \$100 for the commodity-linked fund. The proceeds are invested in a futures margin account paying a money market interest rate. The fund also takes a long position in the most liquid futures contract with the shortest expiry. Each month or quarter, the ETN is rolled into the new near futures position. The futures gain or loss is added to/subtracted from the account. In this way the ETNs track the performance of the commodity over time. The fund manager's fee is taken out of the interest earned on the margin account. In effect, the ETN is a principal-at-risk floating rate note or a rollover structure where the principal expands or shrinks as the commodity moves up or down. In this design, it is easy to have a short-commodity ETN (sell futures), or a leveraged long and short tracking fund (buy or short futures on twice the principal), since the invested proceeds fully support a margin account, and no money has to be taken out to spend on options.

Figure 8.8 portrays the idea behind a commodity-tracking ETN assuming the gains or losses on the futures are credited once a quarter. At the start, investors put \$100 into the fund. Over the quarter, the money market account earns 4% per annum interest or \$1. The fund manager gets a fee of \$0.50. The remainder \$0.50 pays for fund expenses or is paid out to the investors. Meanwhile the futures position has a gain or loss. If the commodity's return over the quarter was 10%, the marking to market produces \$10. The fund's net asset value is \$110, and the

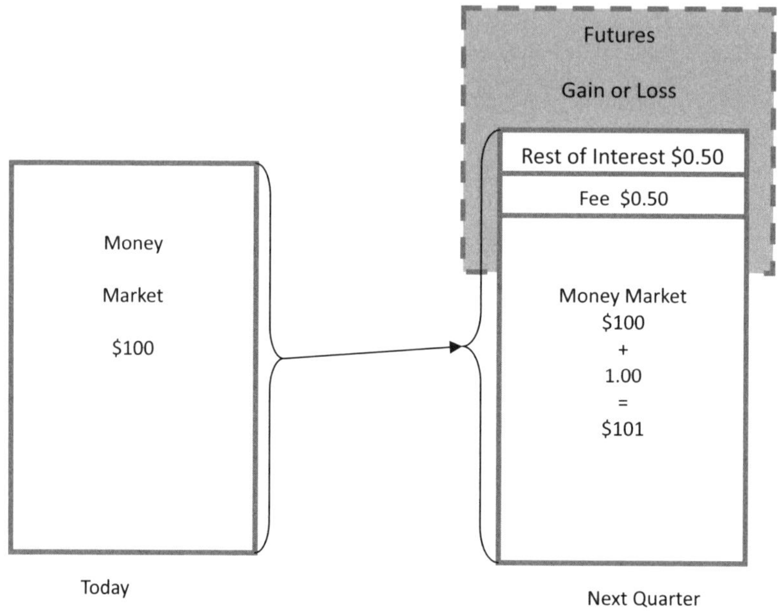

Figure 8.8 A commodity-tracking ETN

process starts again with $110 principal. The funds trade on the stock exchange at a discount or premium to the net asset value as a closed-end fund or ETF.

Equity index ETNs may offer advantages over ETFs. An ETF takes money in and buys the underlying stocks in the index. As such, an ETF is likely to accumulate at least some tracking error due to the cost of maintaining the index composition by buying/selling individual stocks. In theory, the ETN can avoid that by simply taking a long futures position. Also, ETFs typically pay out dividends as they come, while ETNs may be able to roll over the dividends into an increased principal position, perhaps taxed at a lower capital gains tax rate.

The main problem with the commodity-tracking ETN design is that tracking the first futures contract is not the same as tracking the spot commodity. This may be especially true for commodities for which the cost-of-carry arbitrage equation does not hold, and these commodities may often be subject to a contango or backwardation. In a contango, the next futures trades at a price higher than the front futures. As the ETN manager rolls into the next contract, he incurs a cost of selling the expiring futures and buying the next at a higher price, which then drifts down relative to the spot price movements. Since their introduction in 2006, there are several examples of commodity-tracking ETNs posting negative returns despite increasing commodity prices. Regulators, such as FINRA, have written guidelines directing sponsoring institutions to include warnings about the tracking errors associated with futures rollover strategies in the offering materials. Another drawback of an ETN is the credit exposure to the sponsoring bank that backs the money market account.

The real advantage of the ETN design lies in its flexibility, since the invested funds simply sit in a margin account. The supported futures strategy can be anything and fairly active. Thus ETNs can be designed to track hedge fund strategies like momentum reallocation, long-short or global macro.

8.4 INSURANCE RISK STRUCTURED PRODUCTS

Since the beginning of time, the main ideas behind insurance have been pooling and diversification. Pooling is the idea that, among people buying insurance, some will make claims, many will not. Those who will not in effect subsidize those who will. This works as long as the percentage of claimants is small, which keeps the premiums low for everyone. Diversification comes into play, because insurers cannot hedge the risks of natural or man-made but unpredictable disasters. Selling insurance to a variety of people, and selling a variety of insurance types, sometimes does not reduce risk enough when disasters result in large, concentrated claims. For centuries, insurers have turned to reinsurance markets to share risks. Reinsurance works through syndication. A large concentrated risk is parceled out into smaller pro-rata pieces and large institutions (reinsurance companies) or wealthy individuals (Lloyd's of London "names"), who normally compete with one another, take unlimited liability risks in the concentrated pool of policies. A "quota-share reinsurance" arrangement involves transferring the risk of a percentage of a "book of business" to a reinsurer.

The ideas of securitizing insurance risks have floated around since the beginning of the 1990s, with first transactions occurring in the mid-1990s, but it is only in the last decade that the market for the alternative risk transfer (ART), reinsurance sidecars and catastrophe (CAT) bonds has finally arrived. The issuance reached $4 billion in 2006. It stalled as large insurers and reinsurers faced financial headwinds in the 2008 credit crisis. According to the Bermuda-based ARTemis website, the issuance picked up again and topped $5 billion in 2010.

The design of reinsurance sidecars or CAT bonds follows the path of the loan-backed credit-linked notes. The natural or physical risks to which the CAT bond investor is exposed are often not referenced directly. The bond's exposure is to the payouts on a pool of individual insurance contracts. The contracts' payouts are exposed to the physical risks, but could also be affected by litigation and other factors. Sometimes, the bond's payout is based on modeled rather than actual payouts; and sometimes the bond's payout is linked to the natural disaster directly, via a set of parameters mimicking potential payouts.

The typical chronology is as follows. An insurer sells hurricane policies to individuals or industrial clients along the Gulf of Mexico. The policy pool becomes large and concentrated in a small geographical area. Instead of turning to a reinsurer, the insurer contacts a special purpose reinsurance trust or company domiciled in the Cayman Islands or Bermuda. The reinsurance vehicle issues the CAT notes to investors. The notes promise to pay a floating interest rate equal to LIBOR plus a very large margin up to 20%. The notes are rated by the rating agencies as junk, perhaps B or B+. (It is hard to see how S&P or Moody's can evaluate the risks without the help of the insurer...) The proceeds are received by the reinsurance vehicle and can be invested to earn interest; also, the insurer (the cedant) pays into the vehicle company, and for that money the reinsurance company either writes a derivative or a reinsurance contract (often more than one). According to that reinsurance contract, if the disaster covered by the policies takes place, then the trust and the investors lose the principal on the bonds, and the insurer uses the money in the trust to pay the individual policy claims. If the contract is a derivative, then the loss of principal is triggered by prespecified narrowly defined index or event parameters rather than actual claim payouts. Figure 8.9 illustrates a non-derivative structure of a CAT bond. The issuer holds the pool of principal money. If the disaster does not occur, the money is returned to the investor. If the disaster does occur, the money is used to pay the claims on a segregated sub-portfolio of the insurer's policies. The investors in the CAT bonds are hedge funds and specialized catastrophe funds, as well as (life and other) insurers, reinsurers, and pension funds.

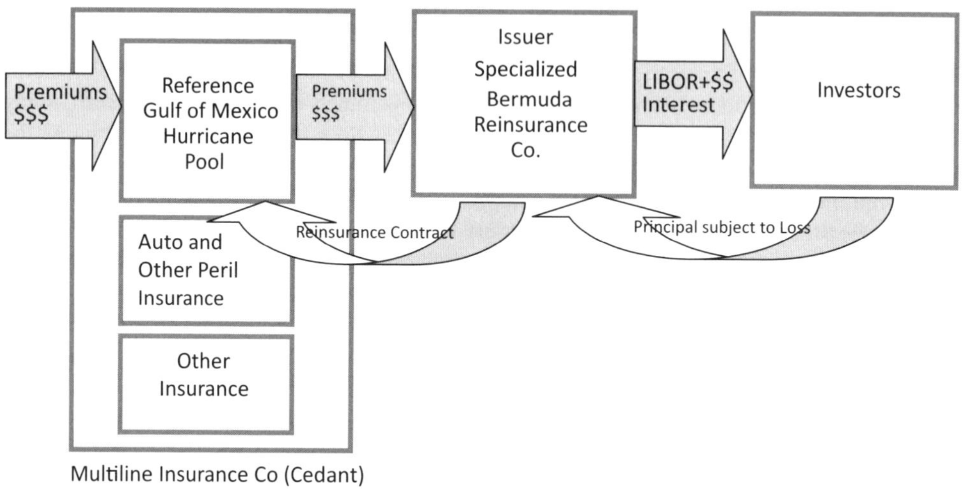

Figure 8.9 A CAT bond

In a derivative-based structure of the CAT bond, the loss of principal is triggered by modeled losses or events. The principal lost may then not be equal to the actual payouts with the insurer bearing the basis risk. The typical triggers involve:

- excess indemnity
- total industry loss
- modeled loss
- parameter index.

The excess indemnity simply means a large deductible. The loss of principal is triggered only if the actual claims exceed a certain minimum threshold (e.g. the first $250 million). Instead of using the insurer's claim losses, one can use total industry losses. The potential for verification or disputes is diminished as the issuing reinsurer can use the services of a large independent data company. For property-casualty claims, one such source may be the Insurance Service Office, Inc. (ISO).

Instead of the actual individual insurer or industry losses, the modeled loss CAT bond involves the use of a catastrophe modeling algorithm based on physical parameters of the actual event (e.g. wind speed). The modeled loss CAT bond allows a faster transfer of the principal money before the claims are paid over time. To minimize the risk of using the wrong parameters (e.g. gathered over or more heavily weighted by different weather station locations, or time-average speed instead of top speed) that may not correlate well with the actual losses on the geographically spread insured properties, the index-parametric CAT bond uses an index developed by a specialized analytic company. The advantage of the latter is independence and transparency of the index calculating agent.

Catastrophe modeling has developed as a new field of actuarial science that draws on the science fields of engineering, seismology and meteorology. The objective is to identify the many aspects of physical (and human-induced) peril phenomena that can be measured (wind speed change, ground displacement, hail size, etc.), combine them with the data about the insured properties (construction standards, age of structures, building height), and match them to many aspects of the potential damage (roof collapse, HVAC system damage, sprinkler damage). Similar to actuarial science approaches to life insurance, where many factors are identified that influence conditional life expectancy, the objective is to identify the peril factors and to develop often non-linear deterministic or multivariate probabilistic algorithms that combine them into a predictive model. Similarly on the output side, instead of using the total dollar amount of the loss, the objective is to identify the types of damage that a peril may cause, model them individually or jointly first, and then combine them into loss estimates by adding the information about the terms of the insurance covering the losses. Besides natural catastrophes (hurricanes, tornados, earthquakes, floods, fire), the modeling can include human-made ones (terrorism, war, shipping piracy, work accidents, product defects). The advantage of catastrophe modeling is that the models can produce the entire loss distributions from which one can compute other statistics, e.g. averages over time, maximums, etc. CAT modeling is used by the reinsuring CAT bond issuers, the rating agencies, and the investing funds. The insurance industry works on coordinating the standards for data collection and data sharing.

9
Mortgage-Backed Securities

Mortgage loans provide financing for residential and commercial real estate. The primary feature of a mortgage is the first lien (mortgage note, encumbrance) right of the lender to foreclose on (liquidate) the property. The lender has the most senior claim in case the borrower defaults. The appetite for mortgage financing around the world is huge. Commercial banks that issue mortgage loans do not have an unlimited amount of capital. In order to replenish the loaned funds, they turn to the mortgage-backed securities (MBS) market.

In Continental Europe, banks take in deposits and issue unsecured bonds to finance their overall loan activity. They also segregate pools of mortgages on the asset side of the balance sheet and issue covered bonds securitized by these mortgages. In Germany, such a structure is called a Hypothekenpfandbrief. The mortgage loans stay on the balance sheet of the bank; the Pfandbrief is a liability of the bank. Currently the Pfandbrief market is reaching a EUR 1 trillion mark in terms of total outstanding. This form of covered debt refinancing of real estate loans is popular in Germany, but to a lesser extent in Denmark, Spain, and France.

In the USA most mortgage loans are moved off the balance sheets of the originating banks through the securitization process. Loans are sold in an arm's length transaction to government sponsored agencies (GSEs) or privately-sponsored trusts ("private label" sponsors are banks or Real Estate Investment Trusts, REITs). The GSEs – GNMA, FNMA, FHMC, known by their nicknames Ginnie Mae, Fannie Mae, Freddie Mac, as well as the Federal Home Loan Banks, FHLBs – dominate the market due to their explicit or implicit government guarantee and the implicit cost of funding subsidy (they are perceived as risk free). Through a variety of securitization programs (e.g. GNMA Platinum or FNMA CL pool prefix) these agencies form pools of purchased mortgages separated into trust vehicles. To be included in the various pools, the mortgages have to be "conforming," i.e. they have to satisfy certain conditions, such as maximum size, loan-to-value ratio, or type of property; otherwise they are placed in special non-conforming pools, such as "jumbo" or "5/1/ Hybrid." FNMA assigns a prefix to each pool's ID number to identify the type of mortgages in the pool. Once the pool of mortgages with similar characteristics is formed, the pool trust issues "pass-through" certificates to investors. These pass-through bonds entitle holders to the proportional share of all cash flows (principal plus interest minus insurance and servicing fees) coming out of the pool. The pass-through certificates can be securitized again into collateralized mortgage obligations (CMOs). The pass-throughs are placed into a new trust that issues CMO certificates that are not proportional, but rather divert the interest, principal, and prepayment cash flows unequally among several classes of investors. The primary objective of CMOs is the separation of the total pool cash flow into senior bonds with limited interest and credit risk, mezzanine and junior ("equity") bond classes subject to a great risk of default, and, even in the absence of default, the risk of the timing of the cash flows. The cash flow timing risk is due to the fact that, in the USA, most residential mortgage loans can be prepaid by the borrower at no penalty. The "prepayment risk" is a form of call risk. Similar to corporate issuers, homeowners often choose to refinance their loans when interest rates decrease. When the homeowner refinances, the old loan is paid off and drops out of the pool. Some prepayments are not interest rate driven, e.g. when homes are sold.

The MBS market in the USA is gigantic. According to the Securities Industry and Financial Markets Association (SIFMA), as of the end of 2009, there were \$9.1 trillion in MBS bonds outstanding. By comparison, the US Treasury bonds, notes and bills outstanding were \$7.6 trillion, the corporate bonds were \$6.8 trillion, and the municipals were \$2.8 trillion. The total cap of the US stock market was \$13.4 trillion as of December 2010.

Our discussion proceeds in three stages: the basics of mortgage financing, the prepayment measurement and risk, and the discussion of the three basic of CMO structures (sequential tranching, planned amortization classes, PACs, and interest-only/principal-only, IO/PO, split). The CMO tranche design is common across many asset-backed securities, including CDOs and CLOs covered in detail in Chapter 10.

9.1 MORTGAGE FINANCING BASICS

Mortgage loans that are used to finance the purchase of a piece of real estate are recorded in municipal property registers. The record includes the name of the bank granting the loan (or the subsequent assignees) and the lender's first (lien) right to liquidate the property or to the funds obtained from the future sale of the property by the owner. Mortgage loans are thus strongly collateralized.

Mortgage "originators" like banks or mortgage brokers (UK: building societies, credit unions, and banks) use several criteria in evaluating the mortgage loan application. In the USA they may use the "FICO score" (after the Fair Isaac model) contained in a credit risk evaluation report compiled by a credit-reporting firm such as Experian, Equifax, or TransUnion. They may use the information about the income sources provided by the buyer on his loan application form ("documentation"). They use the information about the property regarding ownership or "title" and evaluate the loan-to-value (LTV) ratio. Since the loan is likely to be immediately sold, the originators make sure that the loan fits into one of the "conforming" categories defined by the GSE that will buy the loan. If the LTV is high, the mortgagee may be forced to take out private mortgage insurance (PMI) or a second-line loan to increase the down payment (equity part). In the 1990s–2000s, documentation standards were sloppy (often falsified) as originators were eager to classify any loan as conforming to get it ready for an instant sale.

The underwriting process of a mortgage lender moves the loan through the application, appraisal, and documentation stages. Once the loan is approved, the lending bank or credit union commits funds until the closing date. On that date, the funds are paid out and the ownership of the property is transferred, including the recording of the transfer and the loan in the town or county records. Almost immediately, the loan is sold. The originating bank or broker earns the origination fee, which is a percentage of the face value of the loan. The sale of the loan does not change the fact that the payments on the loan will have to be collected over the following years, also taxes and hazard insurance on the property will have to be paid quarterly or annually. The work of collecting loan payments and maintaining the associated escrow accounts to cover the disbursements is called "servicing." The institution that provides the servicing of the loan is compensated for it in the form of a "base" servicing fee, 0.25–0.4% per annum of the outstanding balance. Often excess servicing is also retained. Before the mortgage is securitized and placed in the pool it may also be insured. The total of these payments is referred to as "servicing fee." Very large banks and specialty servicing banks offer servicing to other lenders. Sometimes the originating bank retains the servicing.

Mortgage loans can have a variety of terms. Maturities are 10, 15, 20, or 30 years. The interest rates can be fixed, floating, or a combination of the two. Payments are typically monthly, but can be biweekly. They include interest and principal portions in the fully amortizing (UK: repayment mortgage) or adjustable (UK: standard variable) case, or only interest in the interest-only balloon case. The most popular mortgage loans are a 30-year level-payment fully-amortizing fixed rate monthly loan, a 30-year fully amortizing annually or monthly adjustable rate mortgage (ARM) tied to T-Bills or LIBOR plus a margin (sometimes the Fed Funds, Prime rate, or the COFI index are used), and the hybrid fixed-floating structure wherein the rate is fixed for 3–7 years and then floats. Each of these structures provides different prepayment incentives to the borrower. Generally the greatest interest rate risk (duration and convexity) is associated with the 30-year fixed structure. The interest rate on the mortgage is stated as an annual percentage rate APR (e.g. 6%), but is compounded monthly (i.e. is really $6\%/12 = 0.5\%$ per month), resulting in an effective annual rate (EAR) higher than the APR. Mortgage interest accrues over a calendar month and is paid in arrears (at the end of the month) with a slight (up to 2-week) grace period. The servicer collects the mandatory interest and principal portion plus any partial prepayment amount, sometimes also escrow amounts for taxes and insurance if the homeowner prefers that method. The interest, principal, and prepayment portion minus the servicing fee are then forwarded to the pool trust entity that owns the mortgage.

Mortgage loans come in a variety of forms and sizes. A "conventional" loan, as defined by Fannie Mae, is no bigger than $300,000 to $900,000 depending on the geographic location; a larger size is called "jumbo." Residential mortgages cover single family detached homes, 1–4 family homes, multifamily homes, condominiums, co-ops, etc. "Conventional" can also referred to fixed rate. Mortgages can also be divided into "prime" (high FICO), further divided into A-paper and Alt-A, and "sub-prime" (low FICO score and high LTV).

Table 9.1 shows the amortization for a standard 30-year monthly level pay 6.5% mortgage loan. The monthly payment of $1,896.20 is determined up front as the annuity cash flow whose present value, discounted over 360 periods (months) at the rate of $6.5\%/12 = 0.5416667\%$ per

Table 9.1 The Amortization table for a 30-year 6.5% fixed rate mortgage loan

Month	Beginning principal	Payment	Interest	Principal	Scheduled end principal
1	300,000.00	1,896.20	1,625.00	271.20	299,728.80
2	299,728.80	1,896.20	1,623.53	272.67	299,456.12
3	299,456.12	1,896.20	1,622.05	274.15	299,181.97
4	299,181.97	1,896.20	1,620.57	275.64	298,906.34
5	298,906.34	1,896.20	1,619.08	277.13	298,629.21
6	298,629.21	1,896.20	1,617.57	278.63	298,350.58
...	...				...
100	264,596.02	1,896.20	1,433.23	462.98	264,133.04
101	264,133.04	1,896.20	1,430.72	465.48	263,667.56
102	263,667.56	1,896.20	1,428.20	468.00	263,199.55
...	...				...
206	198,534.29	1,896.20	1,075.39	820.81	197,713.48
207	197,713.48	1,896.20	1,070.95	825.26	196,888.22
208	196,888.22	1,896.20	1,066.48	829.73	196,058.50
...	...				...
357	7,483.21	1,896.20	40.53	1,855.67	5,627.54
358	5,627.54	1,896.20	30.48	1,865.72	3,761.82
359	3,761.82	1,896.20	20.38	1,875.83	1,885.99
360	1,885.99	1,896.20	10.22	1,885.99	0.00

period, equals the borrowed principal balance of \$300,000. The interest portion of the monthly payment is always 0.5416667% of the outstanding principal at the beginning of the month. The principal reduction portion is the remainder of the monthly payment.

The mortgage holder can send extra payments sporadically or each month at his/her discretion. These are applied to the principal and reduce the ending principal balance for the month in which they are sent. Since the total scheduled monthly payment stays the same, the interest part of subsequent months' scheduled payments shrinks, leaving room for a faster repayment of the principal.

9.2 PREPAYMENT RISK

Residential mortgage loans in the USA can be prepaid by the borrowers without any penalty (in the UK they may incur a redemption penalty or a tie-in). In contrast, commercial real estate loans are often subject to lock-out periods and varying penalties for an early repayment. This no-penalty feature makes residential mortgages easy to refinance with an entirely new loan (some home purchases are refinanced many times), partially prepay ("curtail") with extra monthly checks, pay off at the time of the sale. Generally, all of these cases are termed "prepayments." However, some prepayments are interest rate-sensitive and some are not. Refinancings are driven by the difference between the current level of interest rates and the fixed rate on the mortgage, and by the speed of decline in the interest rates. Prepayments due to curtailments, home sales, property destruction, or defaults, are generally driven by the life factors of the homeowner, not interest rates. There are other factors that affect the prepayment behavior of homeowners, such as the year the owner bought the house, the geographic location, and the general economy and employment.

The standard unit of prepayment speed is the PSA (Public Securities Association) benchmark, developed a long time ago on the basis of prepayment statistics for GNMA loans. Instead of quoting directly the percentage of the principal prepaid during the month (called the single monthly mortality rate, SMM) or the annualized equivalent of SMM (called the conditional prepayment rate, CPR), traders quote the percentage PSA. "100% PSA" or "100 PSA" means that for mortgages under 30 months old we use a CPR equal to $n \times 0.2\%$, where n is the seasoning (age) of the mortgage, and for mortgages 30 months and older we use a 6% CPR. "140 PSA" means that they multiply these numbers by 1.4. The idea is that newly originated mortgages are less likely to be paid off or refinanced (as the homeowner is settling or interest rates have not had a chance to move), so it is necessary to have an upward sliding scale ("ramp") of the rate of prepayments relative to the age of the mortgage. At $2\frac{1}{2}$ years of age or older, all mortgages are roughly equally likely to prepay at 6% CPR. Figure 9.1 shows the PSA ramp.

The information about the prepayment rate of a mortgage or a pool of mortgages is interpreted in the following stages. We are given the PSA rate as 175, $PSA = 175\% = 1.75$. Together with the age of the mortgage n in months, we translate the PSA into the CPR. If the mortgage is $n = 7$ months old, then:

$$CPR = 1.75 \times 1.4\% = 2.45\%$$

If the mortgage is $n = 101$ months old ("fully seasoned"), then:

$$CPR = 1.75 \times 6\% = 10.5\%$$

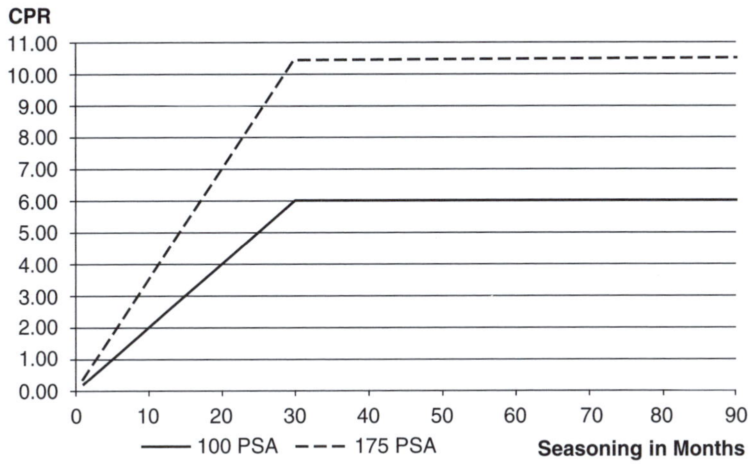

Figure 9.1 The PSA Curve.

We then de-annualize the CPR into the SMM following the monthly compounding rule:

$$1 - CPR = (1 - SMM)^{12}$$

to get

$$SMM = 0.9202\%$$

The SMM is then applied to the ending scheduled principal for the month. That is the prepayment represents the additional decrement of the principal on top of the scheduled amortization as part of the scheduled monthly payment. In the individual mortgage example of Table 8.1, the scheduled ending principal in month 101 would be reduced by 0.9202%, i.e.

$$\begin{aligned} End\ Principal &= SchedEnd\ Principal \times (1 - \text{SMM}) \\ &= 263{,}667.56 \times (1 - 0.009202) \\ &= 261{,}241.29 \end{aligned}$$

9.3 MORTGAGE PASS-THROUGH SECURITIES

When individual mortgages are combined into pools, one generally needs to know the following information about the pool:

- the principal: $Princ = \$300{,}000{,}000$
- the weighted average coupon: $WAC = 6.5\%$
- the pass-through rate, or net coupon: $R = 6.0\%$
- the weighted average maturity: $WAM = 349$ months, or the seasoning: $Age = 11$ months
- the current PSA: $PSA = 175$.

The difference between the *WAC* coming into the pool from the homeowners and the pass-through rate, *R* is the servicing fee. The *WAM* and the *Age* add up to 360 months.

Once pools are formed and separated into trusts, the sponsoring agency issues trust certificates. These are called pass-through certificates or pass-throughs, because the owners are entitled to the proportional share of all the cash flow coming into the pool net of the servicing, irrespective of whether the cash flow is from interest, scheduled principal payment, or (any type of) prepayment (e.g. due to curtailment, sale of property, refinancing). The pools are usually assembled from mortgages issued within a few months of each other, with similar sizes and interest rates.

Trading in mortgage pools, and the pass-through certificates on them, has its own quirks. In specified pool trades, we usually know the pool ID, say Fannie Mae CL201107B4, and the original principal balance on the pool, say \$325,000,000. In to-be-announced and stipulated trades, the agency and the pass-through rate are known, but the pool IDs are not known by the buyer in advance, but are subject to established rules and value adjustments.

Once we know the basic statistics of the pool, we can project the pool's cash flows based on the current PSA estimate. Table 9.2 shows the projected cash flows for a hypothetical CL201107B4 pool. Note two fundamental differences from an individual mortgage behavior. Even when the pool is newly formed, some mortgages may already be a few months old; some may have prepaid. More importantly, since prepayments are largely the result of entire mortgages paying off and falling out of the pool due to sale or refinancing, the scheduled cash flow coming into the pool drops every month. The new scheduled cash flow is computed on the basis of the principal balance outstanding at the beginning of the month. We show that the *WAC* interest, the net interest coming out of the pool, is 0.5%/12 lower.

Table 9.3 shows the same mortgage pool assuming faster prepayments at the rate of 240 PSA. At this rate of prepayment, the total interest paid by the homeowners into the pool drops significantly. The total principal returned is still \$300 million, but it is returned more quickly. By month 102, only \$75 million is still owed; previously over \$107 million was still owed.

The buyer of a pass-through certificate is entitled to the (proportion of the) total cash flow of the pool: interest, scheduled principal payment, and principal prepayment. To price the pass-through, the buyer discounts the total cash flow by an interest rate. That discounting is done under some positive PSA assumption, e.g. 200 PSA. What happens if our assumption is wrong? If interest rates don't change, but prepayments speed up (slow down), the cash flow returned will be smaller (greater) but faster (slower). The PV outcome depends on the shape of the yield curve. Often the question is posed differently, mixing the change in the interest rate with the likely response of prepayments.

Assuming a fairly flat yield curve, what happens to the value of a pass-through when interest rates change? This is a duration-convexity question applied to a security that has an option (a call option) to prepay built into it.

A corporate bullet bond's response to an interest rate change is predictable. The bond increases (decreases) in value in percentage terms approximately by the amount equal to the modified duration times the decrease (increase) in the interest rates (yield to maturity). Actually, the bond increases (decreases) in value more (less) than the duration-predicted move when interest rates decrease (increase). In both cases – interest rate increases and decreases – the holder of the bond undervalues the bond using the duration method (gains more or loses less). This is known as the "positive convexity" of the price–yield relationship. An amortizing bond not subject to prepayments is less convex than a bullet (interest-only) structure with a large balloon principal at the end, but it is still convex.

A mortgage pass-through subject to prepayment behaves differently. As interest rates drop, the bond's duration shortens as prepayments speed up making the bond behave like a shorter-maturity bond ("contraction risk"). The drop in the interest rates increases the PV of each

Table 9.2 \$300 million pool CL201107B4 pass-through with WAC = 6.5%, WAM = 349, 175 PSA

Month	Beg princ	Pmt	WAC int	Pass int	Princ.	SchedEndPrinc	SMM	PrepayPrinc	EndPrinc
1	**300,000,000.00**	\$1,915,779.30	1,625,000.00	1,500,000.00	290,779.30	299,709,220.70	0.3569	1,069,734.18	298,639,486.52
2	298,639,486.52	1,908,941.42	1,617,630.55	1,493,197.43	291,310.87	298,348,175.64	0.3873	1,155,537.21	297,192,638.44
3	297,192,638.44	1,901,547.87	1,609,793.46	1,485,963.19	291,754.41	296,900,884.02	0.4178	1,240,456.57	295,660,427.46
4	295,660,427.46	1,893,603.18	1,601,493.98	1,478,302.14	292,109.19	295,368,318.26	0.4484	1,324,415.43	294,043,902.83
5	294,043,902.83	1,885,112.36	1,592,737.81	1,470,219.51	292,374.55	293,751,528.28	0.4791	1,407,337.97	292,344,190.30
6	292,344,190.30	1,876,080.95	1,583,531.03	1,461,720.95	292,549.92	292,051,640.38	0.5099	1,489,149.50	290,562,490.88
...						...			...
100	110,801,799.59	810,072.17	600,176.41	554,009.00	209,895.76	110,591,903.83	0.9202	1,017,633.47	109,574,270.36
101	109,574,270.36	802,618.13	593,527.30	547,871.35	209,090.84	109,365,179.52	0.9202	1,006,345.53	108,358,834.00
102	108,358,834.00	795,232.68	586,943.68	541,794.17	208,289.00	108,150,545.00	0.9202	995,168.82	107,155,376.18
...						...			...
206	30,347,785.72	304,060.86	164,383.84	151,738.93	139,677.03	30,208,108.70	0.9202	277,965.94	29,930,142.75
207	29,930,142.75	301,262.99	162,121.61	149,650.71	139,141.38	29,791,001.37	0.9202	274,127.84	29,516,873.53
208	29,516,873.53	298,490.86	159,883.06	147,584.37	138,607.79	29,378,265.74	0.9202	270,329.98	29,107,935.76
...						...			...
346	328,926.34	83,348.14	1,781.68	1,644.63	81,566.46	247,359.88	0.9202	2,276.13	245,083.75
347	245,083.75	82,581.20	1,327.54	1,225.42	81,253.66	163,830.08	0.9202	1,507.52	162,322.57
348	162,322.57	81,821.31	879.25	811.61	80,942.07	81,380.50	0.9202	748.84	80,631.66
349	80,631.66	81,068.42	436.75	403.16	80,631.66	–	0.9202	–	–

Table 9.3 $300 million pool CL201107B4 pass-through with WAC = 6.5%, WAM = 349, 240 PSA

Month	Beg princ	Pmt	WAC int	Pass int	Princ	Sched end princ	SMM	Prepay princ	EndPrinc
1	**300,000,000.00**	$1,915,779.30	1,625,000.00	1,500,000.00	290,779.30	299,709,220.70	0.4932	1,478,042.53	298,231,178.17
2	298,231,178.17	1,906,331.47	1,615,418.88	1,491,155.89	290,912.58	297,940,265.59	0.5355	1,595,450.05	296,344,815.54
3	296,344,815.54	1,896,123.19	1,605,201.08	1,481,724.08	290,922.10	296,053,893.43	0.5780	1,711,270.91	294,342,622.52
4	294,342,622.52	1,885,163.09	1,594,355.87	1,471,713.11	290,807.22	294,051,815.31	0.6208	1,825,360.41	292,226,454.90
5	292,226,454.90	1,873,460.72	1,582,893.30	1,461,132.27	290,567.42	291,935,887.47	0.6637	1,937,576.29	289,998,311.18
6	289,998,311.18	1,861,026.58	1,570,824.19	1,449,991.56	290,202.39	289,708,108.79	0.7068	2,047,779.02	287,660,329.77
...						...			...
100	78,494,400.14	573,872.71	425,178.00	392,472.00	148,694.71	78,345,705.43	1.2873	1,008,582.95	77,337,122.48
101	77,337,122.48	566,484.97	418,909.41	386,685.61	147,575.55	77,189,546.93	1.2873	993,699.15	76,195,847.78
102	76,195,847.78	559,192.33	412,727.51	380,979.24	146,464.82	76,049,382.96	1.2873	979,021.25	75,070,361.71
...						...			...
206	14,504,418.18	145,322.82	78,565.60	72,522.09	66,757.23	14,437,660.95	1.2873	185,863.14	14,251,797.82
207	14,251,797.82	143,452.01	77,197.24	71,258.99	66,254.77	14,185,543.04	1.2873	182,617.50	14,002,925.54
208	14,002,925.54	141,605.28	75,849.18	70,014.63	65,756.10	13,937,169.44	1.2873	179,420.06	13,757,749.38
...						...			...
346	93,482.53	23,687.96	506.36	467.41	23,181.60	70,300.93	1.2873	905.02	69,395.91
347	69,395.91	23,383.02	375.89	346.98	23,007.12	46,388.79	1.2873	597.19	45,791.60
348	45,791.60	23,082.00	248.04	228.96	22,833.96	22,957.64	1.2873	295.55	22,662.10
349	22,662.10	22,784.85	122.75	113.31	22,662.10	–	1.2873	–	–

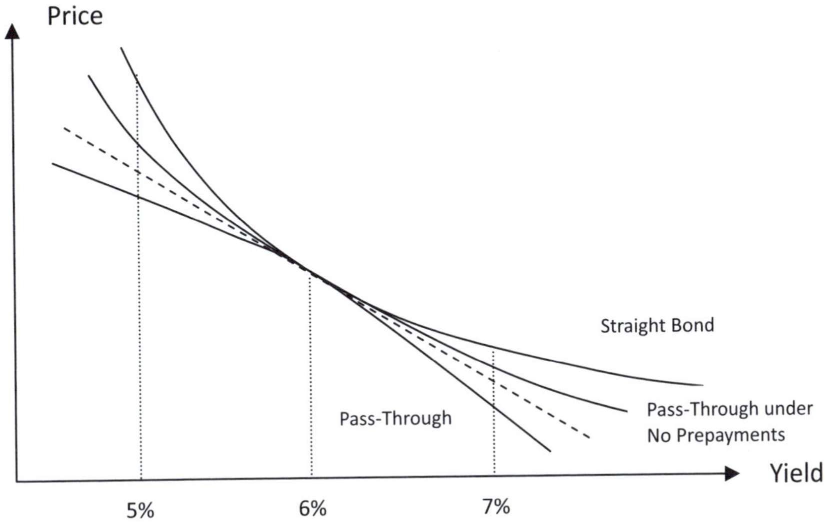

Figure 9.2 The negative convexity of a mortgage pass-through

individual cash flow *ceteris paribus*, but the total cash flows decrease. The net effect is that the bond's value goes up less than predicted by the modified duration.

As interest rates increase, the bond's duration lengthens as prepayments slow down, making the bond behave like a longer-maturity bond ("extension risk"). As interest rates increase, we lose the present value due to discounting alone. We also lose the present value because the actual cash flows will occur later.

This phenomenon of underperformance relative to the straight-line duration response is known as the "negative convexity" of mortgage bonds (the same holds for corporate callable bonds). Often, instead of, or in addition to, the duration and stated maturity of the mortgage bond, one needs to know the weighted average life (WAL) of the pass-through. The WAL is computed as the principal-weighted time average given the PSA assumption. What is really helpful is the schedule of WALs given different PSA assumptions.

Figure 9.2 shows the intuitive meaning of negative convexity. The dashed straight tangent line is the trajectory of the present value (price) using the duration approximation. The convex line above is the price–yield function of an amortizing bond assuming no change in prepayments from the current level. The more convex line above that is the price–yield function of a straight bullet bond. The concave line below the straight dashed duration approximation line is the price–yield function of an amortizing (pass-through) bond subject to prepayment (call) risk. The distance between the actual and the duration-projected price line is the convexity. It is positive in up and down scenarios for a bullet/amortizing bond with no prepayments. It is negative in up and down scenarios for a mortgage pass-through. In our illustration, the duration is the same for both bonds. The tangent line is downward-sloping, reflecting the negative price–yield relationship.

Let us also illustrate the negative convexity numerically. We discount the projected cash flows of the mortgage pass-through in Table 9.3 at 240 PSA using the yield to maturity of 6.0% monthly. The total dollar amount is $300 million. We blip the yield up and down by 1 bp to estimate the PVBP and the modified duration of the pass-through to be

$$ModD = -\frac{299,861,602.97 - 300,138,512.88}{300,000,000 \times (0.0601 - 0.0599)} = 4.615$$

If the yield to maturity moves down to 5.5%, and the prepayments stay at the same 240 PSA speed, then the PV of the cash flows will be \$307,070,471. The duration-predicted new price will be:

$$P = 300,000,000 \times (1 - ModD \times \Delta y) = 300,000,000(1 + 4.615 \times 0.005) = 306,922,747$$

However, if, at the same time as the yield drops from 6% to 5.5%, the prepayment speed increases from 240 PSA to 300 PSA, then the price of the pass-through (the PV of its cash flows) will increase only to \$306,101,402 (we rerun the cash flow projections and discount the total flow by 5.5%/12).

9.4 COLLATERALIZED MORTGAGE OBLIGATIONS

Collateralized mortgage obligations (CMOs) are created by unbundling the interest, scheduled principal and prepaid principal flows of pass-throughs and rebundling them back into new streams of cash flows, called "tranches," according to strict priority rules. Pooling can only go so far in diversifying risk. The objective of the tranche design is to create senior classes of securities with stable cash flows that are safer than the underlying pool. The senior classes have cash flow priority. As a consequence, we end up with very risky companion "equity" classes to which the risk is transferred.

There are several ways to slice loan cash flows. We cover the three most common designs:

- The sequential class CMO, with several classes ordered by priority and labeled A, B, C, D, etc. Each class receives the stated interest as it comes, but principal is sent first to A, then to B, then to C, etc.
- The PAC CMO (the planned amortization class CMO) is a variant of the sequential CMO with a principal amortization schedule based on lower and upper bands on prepayments.
- The IO/PO classes, where interest is sent to the IO class and all principal is sent to the PO class. This can be combined with a PAC design.

Each design divides the total risk of the pool differently. In the sequential structure, no matter how risky the pool, class A always gets paid first. This insulates it from almost all default risk and a lot of prepayment risk. The PAC structure artificially restricts the prepayment risk even further by not sending too much principal flow when prepayments are very high, and sending extra flow when prepayments are very slow. A senior PAC class's cash flows are very predictable. The IO/PO structure exposes the IO holders to the risk of fast prepayments and the PO holders to the risk of slow prepayments. This design focuses primarily on interest rate risk.

9.4.1 Sequential-Pay CMO

We take our hypothetical pool CL201107B4 defined in Tables 8.2 and 8.3 and divide its cash flows into three sequential tranches. The total principal outstanding at the outset is \$300 million; the underlying pool is already seasoned by 11 months; the WAC is 6.5% and the pass-through coupon is 6.0%. We create three tranches: A, with a principal of \$125 million; B, with \$100 million; and C, with \$75 million. Each tranche has a stated pass-through coupon of

6.0%. Each tranche also has a stated maturity, A being the shortest, but the actual maturity is unknown. The stated maturity on A is 7 years. We then project the cash flows of the tranches.

Table 9.4 shows the cash flows at 175 PSA. In the early months, all scheduled and prepaid principal flows go to tranche A paying down its principal. Meanwhile B and C receive only interest cash flows. Once A's principal is returned and all cash flows to the A certificate holder stop in month 57, tranche B begins to receive scheduled and prepaid principal flows. When B is paid in month 134, C receives the principal flows.

Table 9.5 shows the cash flows for the same CMO at 240 PSA. Again, all scheduled and prepaid principal flows go first to tranche A, then to B, then to C. Since the prepayments come in faster at 240 PSA, all classes pay down the principal sooner. Tranche A gets paid off in month 44 instead of month 57 at 175 PSA. Tranche B gets paid off in month 103 instead of month 134 at 175 PSA.

Tranche C carries the greatest prepayment risk. We know that the total amount principal it will receive is \$75 million. We don't know when its principal is going to be paid. At 175 PSA it starts being paid down in month 134; at 240 PSA it starts being paid down in month 103. We don't know up front how much total interest the tranche will receive. Both interest and principal stretch out to 349 months with the very uncertain principal flows coming in later months. The cash flows are back-loaded more like those of a long-duration balloon bond. This makes present-valuing the cash flows very sensitive to the PSA assumption.

In contrast, tranche A holders know that, under most reasonable interest rate scenarios and PSA assumptions, they will be paid off before the certificate's stated maturity of 84 months. At medium 175 PSA speed, the final cash flows are in 57 months; at a faster 240 PSA speed, in 44 months. At a high speed, the total cash flow is slightly smaller as the total amount of interest shrinks, but it comes back sooner. The present value of the total does not vary much, making class A certificates behave like a very short maturity bond.

9.4.2 Planned Amortization Class CMO

The senior class of the sequential-pay CMO is well protected from default risk, and quite well isolated from the prepayment risk, due to its priority status to the principal flow. Yet to some investors, the cash flow, while exhibiting very short duration risk, may still be too variable. In our example above, the change in the prepayment speed from 175 to 240 PSA shortened the maturity of the class A certificate by 13 months. The PAC design further restricts the range of the principal flow by fixing an artificial schedule of prepayments which is likely to be adhered to.

Let us start with a very simple exercise of structuring a two-tranche PAC CMO. Class A will have a planned amortization schedule. The "supporting" or "companion" tranche K's role will be to absorb the excess prepayment risk. Suppose we project the prepayments to the pool to run at 175 PSA. We set the minimum prepayment schedule for tranche A to be 80 PSA, and the maximum prepayment speed to be 275 PSA. This is the "initial PAC collar band." The actual future prepayment speed is unknown and can be slower or faster than the 80–275 PSA band; it can also be variable, running very fast and slowing down, and vice versa. The objective of the PAC design is not simply to "sell the wings" and divert the prepayments in excess of 275 PSA to the companion class or somehow supplement the prepayments slower than 80 PSA with the flow from the companion class. The objective is to try to fix the prepayment schedule completely. This will not always succeed, as we have no control over the prepayment decisions.

Table 9.4 A sequential-pay CMO based on CL201107B4 with three classes at 175 PSA

Month	Tranche A				Tranche B				Tranche C			
	BegPrinc	Princ	Int	End Princ	Beg princ	Princ	Int	End princ	BegPrinc	Princ	Int	EndPrinc
1	125,000,000.00	1,360,513.48	625,000.00	123,639,486.52	100,000,000.00	–	500,000.00	100,000,000.00	75,000,000.00	–	375,000.00	75,000,000.00
2	123,639,486.52	1,446,848.08	618,197.43	122,192,638.44	100,000,000.00	–	500,000.00	100,000,000.00	75,000,000.00	–	375,000.00	75,000,000.00
3	122,192,638.44	1,532,210.98	610,963.19	120,660,427.46	100,000,000.00	–	500,000.00	100,000,000.00	75,000,000.00	–	375,000.00	75,000,000.00
4	120,660,427.46	1,616,524.62	603,302.14	119,043,902.83	100,000,000.00	–	500,000.00	100,000,000.00	75,000,000.00	–	375,000.00	75,000,000.00
5	119,043,902.83	1,699,712.53	595,219.51	117,344,190.30	100,000,000.00	–	500,000.00	100,000,000.00	75,000,000.00	–	375,000.00	75,000,000.00
6	117,344,190.30	1,781,699.42	586,720.95	115,562,490.88	100,000,000.00	–	500,000.00	100,000,000.00	75,000,000.00	–	375,000.00	75,000,000.00
...	...			...	...			...	...			...
55	5,637,941.04	1,909,393.40	28,189.71	3,728,547.64	100,000,000.00	–	500,000.00	100,000,000.00	75,000,000.00	–	375,000.00	75,000,000.00
56	3,728,547.64	1,890,875.69	18,642.74	1,837,671.95	100,000,000.00	–	500,000.00	100,000,000.00	75,000,000.00	–	375,000.00	75,000,000.00
57	1,837,671.95	1,837,671.95	9,188.36	–	100,000,000.00	34,860.06	500,000.00	99,965,139.94	75,000,000.00	–	375,000.00	75,000,000.00
58	–	–	–	–	99,965,139.94	1,854,360.74	499,825.70	98,110,779.19	75,000,000.00	–	375,000.00	75,000,000.00
59	–	–	–	–	98,110,779.19	1,836,360.29	490,553.90	96,274,418.90	75,000,000.00	–	375,000.00	75,000,000.00
60	–	–	–	–	96,274,418.90	1,818,529.07	481,372.09	94,455,889.84	75,000,000.00	–	375,000.00	75,000,000.00
...	...			...	...			...	...			...
132	–	–	–	–	1,988,188.50	892,326.35	9,940.94	1,095,862.15	75,000,000.00	–	375,000.00	75,000,000.00
133	–	–	–	–	1,095,862.15	883,410.18	5,479.31	212,451.97	75,000,000.00	–	375,000.00	75,000,000.00
134	–	–	–	–	212,451.97	212,451.97	1,062.26	–	75,000,000.00	662,126.80	375,000.00	74,337,873.20
135	–	–	–	–	–	–	–	–	74,337,873.20	865,831.30	371,689.37	73,472,041.90
136	–	–	–	–	–	–	–	–	73,472,041.90	857,167.02	367,360.21	72,614,874.89
137	–	–	–	–	–	–	–	–	72,614,874.89	848,585.13	363,074.37	71,766,289.76
138	–	–	–	–	–	–	–	–	71,766,289.76	840,084.87	358,831.45	70,926,204.89
...	...			...	...			...	...			...
345	–	–	–	–	–	–	–	–	413,861.59	84,935.25	2,069.31	328,926.34
346	–	–	–	–	–	–	–	–	328,926.34	83,842.59	1,644.63	245,083.75
347	–	–	–	–	–	–	–	–	245,083.75	82,761.18	1,225.42	162,322.57
348	–	–	–	–	–	–	–	–	162,322.57	81,690.90	811.61	80,631.66
349	–	–	–	–	–	–	–	–	80,631.66	80,631.66	403.16	–

Table 9.5 A sequential-pay CMO based on CL201107B4 with three tranches at 240 PSA

	Tranche A				Tranche B				Tranche C			
Month	Beg princ	Princ	Int	End princ	BegPrinc	Princ	Int	EndPrinc	BegPrinc	Princ	Int	EndPrinc
1	125,000,000.00	1,768,821.83	625,000.00	123,231,178.17	100,000,000.00	–	500,000.00	100,000,000.00	75,000,000.00	–	375,000.00	75,000,000.00
2	123,231,178.17	1,886,362.64	616,155.89	121,344,815.54	100,000,000.00	–	500,000.00	100,000,000.00	75,000,000.00	–	375,000.00	75,000,000.00
3	121,344,815.54	2,002,193.01	606,724.08	119,342,622.52	100,000,000.00	–	500,000.00	100,000,000.00	75,000,000.00	–	375,000.00	75,000,000.00
4	119,342,622.52	2,116,167.63	596,713.11	117,226,454.90	100,000,000.00	–	500,000.00	100,000,000.00	75,000,000.00	–	375,000.00	75,000,000.00
5	117,226,454.90	2,228,143.72	586,132.27	114,998,311.18	100,000,000.00	–	500,000.00	100,000,000.00	75,000,000.00	–	375,000.00	75,000,000.00
6	114,998,311.18	2,337,981.41	574,991.56	112,660,329.77	100,000,000.00	–	500,000.00	100,000,000.00	75,000,000.00	–	375,000.00	75,000,000.00
...	...			...	...			...	...			...
42	7,079,261.60	2,571,491.56	35,396.31	4,507,770.03	100,000,000.00	–	500,000.00	100,000,000.00	75,000,000.00	–	375,000.00	75,000,000.00
43	4,507,770.03	2,536,675.23	22,538.85	1,971,094.81	100,000,000.00	–	500,000.00	100,000,000.00	75,000,000.00	–	375,000.00	75,000,000.00
44	1,971,094.81	1,971,094.81	9,855.47	–	100,000,000.00	531,225.18	500,000.00	99,468,774.82	75,000,000.00	–	375,000.00	75,000,000.00
45	–	–	–	–	99,468,774.82	2,468,419.80	497,343.87	97,000,355.02	75,000,000.00	–	375,000.00	75,000,000.00
46	–	–	–	–	97,000,355.02	2,434,968.73	485,001.78	94,565,386.28	75,000,000.00	–	375,000.00	75,000,000.00
47	–	–	–	–	94,565,386.28	2,401,960.89	472,826.93	92,163,425.39	75,000,000.00	–	375,000.00	75,000,000.00
...	...			...	...			...	...			...
101	–	–	–	–	2,337,122.48	1,141,274.70	11,685.61	1,195,847.78	75,000,000.00	–	375,000.00	75,000,000.00
102	–	–	–	–	1,195,847.78	1,125,486.07	5,979.24	70,361.71	75,000,000.00	–	375,000.00	75,000,000.00
103	–	–	–	–	70,361.71	70,361.71	351.81	–	75,000,000.00	1,039,547.24	375,000.00	73,960,452.76
104	–	–	–	–	–	–	–	–	73,960,452.76	1,094,540.55	369,802.26	72,865,912.21
105	–	–	–	–	–	–	–	–	72,865,912.21	1,079,378.12	364,329.56	71,786,534.09
106	–	–	–	–	–	–	–	–	71,786,534.09	1,064,418.96	358,932.67	70,722,115.13
107	–	–	–	–	–	–	–	–	70,722,115.13	1,049,660.37	353,610.58	69,672,454.76
...	...			...	...			...	...			...
345	–	–	–	–	–	–	–	–	118,059.07	24,576.54	590.30	93,482.53
346	–	–	–	–	–	–	–	–	93,482.53	24,086.62	467.41	69,395.91
347	–	–	–	–	–	–	–	–	69,395.91	23,604.31	346.98	45,791.60
348	–	–	–	–	–	–	–	–	45,791.60	23,129.50	228.96	22,662.10
349	–	–	–	–	–	–	–	–	22,662.10	22,662.10	113.31	–

Table 9.6 The design of a 80–275 band PAC tranche A

Month	80 PSA	275 PSA	PAC Sched	Cum Princ
1	774,586.46	1,991,253.46	774,586.46	774,586.46
2	815,040.24	2,125,533.49	815,040.24	1,589,626.70
3	855,232.10	2,257,617.26	855,232.10	2,444,858.80
4	895,145.28	2,387,313.98	895,145.28	3,340,004.08
5	934,763.16	2,514,436.59	934,763.16	4,274,767.24
6	974,069.28	2,638,802.27	974,069.28	5,248,836.52
...				
55	1,264,249.08	2,229,911.37	1,264,249.08	69,989,402.37
56	1,259,492.07	2,194,867.32	1,259,492.07	71,248,894.44
57	1,254,755.06	2,160,363.04	1,254,755.06	72,503,649.50
58	1,250,037.97	2,126,390.32	1,250,037.97	73,753,687.48
59	1,245,340.72	2,092,941.07	1,245,340.72	74,999,028.20
60	1,240,663.23	2,060,007.32	1,240,663.23	76,239,691.43
...				
132	1,076,797.07	1,122,734.72	1,076,797.07	120,106,211.93
133	1,072,830.79	1,104,809.01	1,072,830.79	121,179,042.72
134	1,068,881.31	1,087,161.96	1,068,881.31	122,247,924.03
135	1,064,948.55	1,069,789.31	1,064,948.55	123,312,872.59
136	1,061,032.46	1,052,686.86	1,052,686.86	124,365,559.45
137	1,057,132.96	1,035,850.48	1,035,850.48	125,401,409.93
138	1,053,249.99	1,019,276.08	1,019,276.08	126,420,686.01
...				
345	473,856.37	12,311.99	12,311.99	185,895,986.80
346	472,523.13	12,018.81	4,013.20	185,900,000.00
347	471,196.13	11,731.05		
348	469,875.35	11,448.63		
349	468,560.76	11,171.44		

Given the desired initial PAC collar of 80–275, we first compute the principal cash flow that can be delivered to class A if the prepayment speed stays within the band, and the principal of tranche A that can be supported by the band. Table 9.6 shows the design blueprint. We look at the entire $300 million CL201107B4 pool, compute the total principal flow at 80 and 275 PSA, and take the lesser of the two for each month. There is a crossover point. For early months, we take the flow under the 80 PSA assumption and, for later months, under the 275 PSA assumption. This is because when prepayments are fast, they pay down the principal so rapidly that at some point there is not much of it left to pay even at a high speed, and the slower speed results in a higher flow. The PAC schedule is set as the month-by-month lesser of the two bands' principal flows.

We determine the principal for tranche A by cumulating the principal under the PAC schedule. Toward the end of the schedule we set a cut-off point beyond which the balance is so small that, for practical reasons, it is paid off. We would like the starting principal balance for tranche A to be large in order to create the largest possible protected class. However, we have to balance that goal against the strength of the companion class. If the companion is too small, and the actual prepayments run in excess of the upper band, the companion might be extinguished very quickly and no longer be able to support the PAC tranche. This would result in a "broken" or "busted" PAC. In Table 9.6, the total PAC schedule flow could be \$185,942,356.73. We set the principal for tranche A at \$185,900,000. Under the PAC schedule, this will repay the principal in month 346. The companion tranche K's principal is set at \$114,100,000. The pass-through coupon rates for both tranches are set at 6.0%.

The PAC structure works perfectly for any prepayment speed within the initial collar. Prepayments are always in excess of the PAC schedule (which is set to the minimum), and are sent to the supporting tranche K. Tranche A is completely insulated from the actual prepayments and follows the set PAC schedule. The PAC tranche A's weighted-average life (WAL) is constant if the prepayment speed stays within the band, irrespective of what it actually is. Tranche A behaves like a fixed cash flow security. Table 9.7 shows the cash flows to the two tranches for 175 PSA. The principal cash flow to tranche A is equal to the PAC schedule every month; tranche K absorbs the excess.

Next we show two examples of broken PACs. In Table 9.8, prepayments come in at 350 PSA. The companion tranche K absorbs so much excess principal flow that it gets paid off in month 48 and is no longer available to support the PAC tranche A. Its WAL is under 3 years. Tranche A's WAL also shrinks. As soon as K is extinguished, the principal flow to A accelerates; A now has to take in all prepayments irrespective of its PAC schedule.

Table 9.9 shows the opposite case. Prepayments are slow at 60 PSA. In the early months, all the principal flow goes to A, but there is not enough flow to meet the PAC schedule. Tranche K receives no principal flow. In month 108, at the 60 PSA speed, the total principal flow from the pool starts to exceed the required PAC schedule. Tranche A receives the scheduled flow; tranche K gets the excess. However, since A did not amortize enough at the beginning, its principal balance extends much further into the future, while K gets paid off first. The WAL of tranche A is longer than the PAC design's goal. Tranche K's WAL is actually even longer as the excess prepayments it receives are very small until the final few years.

9.4.3 Interest-only (IO) and Principal-only (PO) Classes

Instead of organizing tranches according to priority over cash flows, interest and principal flows can simply be separated into two distinct classes: the interest-only (IO) tranche and the principal-only (PO) tranche. The idea is quite simple. What is interesting is the interest rate and prepayment speed sensitivity of the two tranches.

Table 9.10 shows the PVs of the IO and PO tranches of the CL201107B4 pool for different PSA speeds. The cash flows are discounted at 5.5%. The total PV of the pool pass-through is not super-sensitive to the PSA assumptions, but the PVs of the interest-only and principal-only tranches are. They also move in the opposite way. The IO's value decreases with an increase in the prepayment speed as the total amount of interest over the lifetime of the pool declines. The PO value increases as prepayments speed up as the total is returned more quickly. The total cash flow that the PO holders receive is \$300 million no matter what the speed. If the prepayments run fast, the PO holders get their cash sooner. The numerator effect for IOs and POs swamps any countervailing discounting effect when considering joint interest rate and prepayment movements.

Imagine an investor buying an IO strip when prepayments run at 175 PSA and interest rates are at 5.5%. If interest rates drop and prepayments speed up, the investor gains because the discount rate is lower, but the gain is likely to be completely offset and turned into a loss since the total cash flow to be received over time decreases. If interest rates rise and prepayments slow down, the investor loses because the discount rate is higher, but the loss is more than

Table 9.7 The two-tranche 80–275 PSA PAC CMO at 175 PSA

	Tranche A: $185,900,000				Tranche K: $114,100,000			
Month	Beg Princ	Princ	Int	End Princ	Beg Princ	Princ	Int	End Princ
1	185,900,000.00	774,586.46	929,500.00	185,125,413.54	114,100,000.00	585,927.02	570,500.00	113,514,072.98
2	185,125,413.54	815,040.24	925,627.07	184,310,373.30	113,514,072.98	631,807.84	567,570.36	112,882,265.14
3	184,310,373.30	855,232.10	921,551.87	183,455,141.20	112,882,265.14	676,978.88	564,411.33	112,205,286.26
4	183,455,141.20	895,145.28	917,275.71	182,559,995.92	112,205,286.26	721,379.35	561,026.43	111,483,906.91
5	182,559,995.92	934,763.16	912,799.98	181,625,232.76	111,483,906.91	764,949.37	557,419.53	110,718,957.54
6	181,625,232.76	974,069.28	908,126.16	180,651,163.48	110,718,957.54	807,630.15	553,594.79	109,911,327.40
...	...			...	...			...
55	117,174,846.71	1,264,249.08	585,874.23	115,910,597.63	63,463,094.33	645,144.32	317,315.47	62,817,950.01
56	115,910,597.63	1,259,492.07	579,552.99	114,651,105.56	62,817,950.01	631,383.62	314,089.75	62,186,566.39
57	114,651,105.56	1,254,755.06	573,255.53	113,396,350.50	62,186,566.39	617,776.95	310,932.83	61,568,789.44
58	113,396,350.50	1,250,037.97	566,981.75	112,146,312.52	61,568,789.44	604,322.77	307,843.95	60,964,466.67
59	112,146,312.52	1,245,340.72	560,731.56	110,900,971.80	60,964,466.67	591,019.57	304,822.33	60,373,447.10
60	110,900,971.80	1,240,663.23	554,504.86	109,660,308.57	60,373,447.10	577,865.83	301,867.24	59,795,581.27
...	...			...	...			...
98	66,870,585.14	1,076,797.07	334,352.93	65,793,788.07	46,423,014.25	175,265.21	232,115.07	46,247,749.04
99	65,793,788.07	1,072,830.79	328,968.94	64,720,957.28	46,247,749.04	166,906.72	231,238.75	46,080,842.32
100	64,720,957.28	1,068,881.31	323,604.79	63,652,075.97	46,080,842.32	158,647.93	230,404.21	45,922,194.39
101	63,652,075.97	1,064,948.55	318,260.38	62,587,127.41	45,922,194.39	150,487.81	229,610.97	45,771,706.58
102	62,587,127.41	1,052,686.86	312,935.64	61,534,440.55	45,771,706.58	150,770.96	228,858.53	45,620,935.63
103	61,534,440.55	1,035,850.48	307,672.20	60,498,590.07	45,620,935.63	155,742.08	228,104.68	45,465,193.55
104	60,498,590.07	1,019,276.08	302,492.95	59,479,313.99	45,465,193.55	160,563.42	227,325.97	45,304,630.13
...	...			...	...			...
345	16,325.19	12,311.99	81.63	4,013.20	397,536.40	72,623.27	1,987.68	324,913.13
346	4,013.20	4,013.20	20.07	(0.00)	324,913.13	79,829.39	1,624.57	245,083.75
347					245,083.75	82,761.18	1,225.42	162,322.57
348					162,322.57	81,690.90	811.61	80,631.66
349					80,631.66	80,631.66	403.16	0.00

Table 9.8 The two-tranche 80–275 PSA broken PAC CMO at 350 PSA

Month	Tranche A: $185,900,000				Tranche K: $114,100,000			
	BegPrinc	Princ	Int	EndPrinc	BegPrinc	Princ	Int	EndPrinc
1	185,900,000.00	774,586.46	929,500.00	185,125,413.54	114,100,000.00	1,699,548.03	570,500.00	112,400,451.97
2	185,125,413.54	815,040.24	925,627.07	184,310,373.30	112,400,451.97	1,829,089.78	562,002.26	110,571,362.18
3	184,310,373.30	855,232.10	921,551.87	183,455,141.20	110,571,362.18	1,955,442.31	552,856.81	108,615,919.88
4	183,455,141.20	895,145.28	917,275.71	182,559,995.92	108,615,919.88	2,078,312.55	543,079.60	106,537,607.33
5	182,559,995.92	934,763.16	912,799.98	181,625,232.76	106,537,607.33	2,197,414.73	532,688.04	104,340,192.59
6	181,625,232.76	974,069.28	908,126.16	180,651,163.48	104,340,192.59	2,312,471.30	521,700.96	102,027,721.29
...	...			...	...			...
46	128,770,494.56	1,307,975.75	643,852.47	127,462,518.81	4,077,999.65	1,445,517.99	20,390.00	2,632,481.66
47	127,462,518.81	1,303,035.03	637,312.59	126,159,483.79	2,632,481.66	1,394,503.54	13,162.41	1,237,978.13
48	126,159,483.79	1,404,727.55	630,797.42	124,754,756.23	1,237,978.13	1,237,978.13	6,189.89	–
49	124,754,756.23	2,588,972.78	623,773.78	122,165,783.45	–	–	–	–
50	122,165,783.45	2,536,318.00	610,828.92	119,629,465.46	–	–	–	–
51	119,629,465.46	2,484,719.89	598,147.33	117,144,745.57	–	–	–	–
...	...			...	...			...
98	44,111,025.62	938,792.80	220,555.13	43,172,232.82	–	–	–	–
99	43,172,232.82	919,389.66	215,861.16	42,252,843.16	–	–	–	–
100	42,252,843.16	900,380.11	211,264.22	41,352,463.05	–	–	–	–
101	41,352,463.05	881,756.24	206,762.32	40,470,706.81	–	–	–	–
102	40,470,706.81	863,510.33	202,353.53	39,607,196.48	–	–	–	–
103	39,607,196.48	845,634.82	198,035.98	38,761,561.66	–	–	–	–
104	38,761,561.66	828,122.26	193,807.81	37,933,439.40	–	–	–	–
...	...			...	...			...
345	12,349.91	2,636.07	61.75	9,713.84	–	–	–	–
346	9,713.84	2,550.91	48.57	7,162.93	–	–	–	–
347	7,162.93	2,467.89	35.81	4,695.03	–	–	–	–
348	4,695.03	2,386.96	23.48	2,308.07	–	–	–	–
349	2,308.07	2,308.07	11.54	(0.00)	–	–	–	–

Table 9.9 The two-tranche 80–275 PSA broken PAC CMO at 60 PSA

	Tranche A: $185,900,000				Tranche K: $114,100,000			
Month	BegPrinc	Princ	Int	EndPrinc	BegPrinc	Princ	Int	EndPrinc
1	185,900,000.00	652,826.13	929,500.00	185,247,173.87	114,100,000.00	–	570,500.00	114,100,000.00
2	185,247,173.87	683,580.66	926,235.87	184,563,593.21	114,100,000.00	–	570,500.00	114,100,000.00
3	184,563,593.21	714,168.39	922,817.97	183,849,424.82	114,100,000.00	–	570,500.00	114,100,000.00
4	183,849,424.82	744,579.68	919,247.12	183,104,845.14	114,100,000.00	–	570,500.00	114,100,000.00
5	183,104,845.14	774,804.97	915,524.23	182,330,040.17	114,100,000.00	–	570,500.00	114,100,000.00
6	182,330,040.17	804,834.75	911,650.20	181,525,205.42	114,100,000.00	–	570,500.00	114,100,000.00
...	...			...	...			...
105	78,136,789.61	963,046.41	390,683.95	77,173,743.20	114,100,000.00	–	570,500.00	114,100,000.00
106	77,173,743.20	960,993.28	385,868.72	76,212,749.92	114,100,000.00	–	570,500.00	114,100,000.00
107	76,212,749.92	958,948.48	381,063.75	75,253,801.44	114,100,000.00	–	570,500.00	114,100,000.00
108	75,253,801.44	955,519.06	376,269.01	74,298,282.38	114,100,000.00	1,392.95	570,500.00	114,098,607.05
109	74,298,282.38	940,195.64	371,491.41	73,358,086.74	114,098,607.05	14,688.21	570,493.04	114,083,918.84
110	73,358,086.74	925,111.03	366,790.43	72,432,975.72	114,083,918.84	27,752.93	570,419.59	114,056,165.91
...	...			...	...			...
318	19,217,572.09	22,653.51	96,087.86	19,194,918.58	2,476,387.61	664,336.03	12,381.94	1,812,051.58
319	19,194,918.58	22,173.58	95,974.59	19,172,745.00	1,812,051.58	664,178.75	9,060.26	1,147,872.83
320	19,172,745.00	21,702.17	95,863.72	19,151,042.83	1,147,872.83	664,018.33	5,739.36	483,854.50
321	19,151,042.83	201,239.53	95,755.21	18,949,803.30	483,854.50	483,854.50	2,419.27	–
322	18,949,803.30	684,472.91	94,749.02	18,265,330.39	–	–	–	–
323	18,265,330.39	683,857.14	91,326.65	17,581,473.25	–	–	–	–
324	17,581,473.25	683,246.70	87,907.37	16,898,226.55	–	–	–	–
...	...			...	...			...
345	3,353,334.35	671,646.54	16,766.67	2,681,687.82	–	–	–	–
346	2,681,687.82	671,151.55	13,408.44	2,010,536.27	–	–	–	–
347	2,010,536.27	670,661.72	10,052.68	1,339,874.55	–	–	–	–
348	1,339,874.55	670,177.04	6,699.37	669,697.51	–	–	–	–
349	669,697.51	669,697.51	3,348.49	(0.00)	–	–	–	–

Table 9.10 The PV of IO and PO at yield = 5.5%

PSA	IO	PO	IO + PO
80	141,374,397.20	170,406,802.56	311,781,199.77
175	101,956,411.58	206,539,956.06	308,496,367.63
240	84,845,652.15	222,224,818.86	307,070,471.01

made up for by the increase in the total cash flow to be received over time. An IO holder has a negative duration instrument.

Imagine an investor buying a PO strip when prepayments run at 175 PSA and interest rates are at 5.5%. If interest rates drop and prepayments speed up, the investor gains twice: the discount rate is lower and the principal is returned faster. If interest rates rise and prepayments slow down, the investor loses twice because the discount rate is higher and the principal is returned more slowly. A PO holder has a high positive duration instrument.

Besides custom-designed servicing hedge swap arrangements, POs and short IOs are the main hedging instrument for mortgage servicing companies. A mortgage servicer loses revenue when interest rates drop and prepayments speed up. While the change in the PV of a PO may not offset the lost revenue exactly, its PV in general increases when interest rates drop. A short IO is an even closer hedge, since the servicer's cash flow is defined as a constant spread fee times the remaining principal.

9.5 MULTICLASS AND NON-VANILLA CMOs

Many CMOs have multiple classes of securities and combine PACs, IO/POs, floaters, etc., into one deal. Some classes naturally fit together, some do not. We examine briefly some common combinations.

9.5.1 A Multiclass PAC Structure with a PAC I/O and a Floater/Inverse Coupon Split

We take our CL201107B4 pool and create several PAC classes, some with sequential dependence, some with different initial collars. We also provide supporting tranches and attach IO and floating interest tranches. Let us look at a hypothetical structure.

Table 9.11 A multiclass collateralized mortgage obligation participation tranches

Tranche	Principal	Description	PSA band	WAL
PAC-A	45,000,000	Level I PAC 4.00%	80–375	1.7
PAC-B	30,000,000	Level I PAC 4.375%	80–325	2.7
PAC-C	20,000,000	Level I PAC 4.625%	80–275	3.6
PAC-D	25,000,000	Level I PAC 5.75%	80–250	4.6
PAC-KA	25,000,000	Level II PAC 5.5%	80–375	3.5
PAC-KB	30,000,000	Level II PAC 5.5%	80–325	4.0
TAC-E	15,000,000	Level I TAC 5.5%	240	2.3
PAC-IO	20,000,000	PAC I/O 5.5%	80–275	6.8
PAC-SF	50,000,000	Support tranche – floating		19.5
PAC-SI	45,000,000	Support tranche – inverse floating		19.5

Table 9.12 A multiclass sequential-pay CMO

Tranche	Principal	Description	Features
A	115,000,000	Senior sequential 6.0%	Very short WAL
B	45,000,000	Sequential 6.0%	
C-PO	25,000,000	Sequential P/O 0.0%	Concurrent with D
D-IO	25,000,000	Sequential I/O 6.0%	Concurrent with C
E	55,000,000	Sequential junior 6.0%	
Z	35,000,000	Accrual – Support of A only	

The CMO in Table 9.11 offers four PAC tranches. Two of the most senior PAC tranches – classes A and B – have support PAC tranches, KA and KB, which are essentially sequential tranches that pay after A and B. There is one TAC (targeted amortization class) tranche which is a one-sided PAC. There is one PAC I/O class which is entitled to interest only and is applied to the PAC schedule with its rules on excess and insufficient prepayments. The last two classes are true support tranches, absorbing excess prepayments from all the others. They are structured as a floater and an inverse floater. The attraction of the floating structure is the elimination of the interest rate sensitivity (in exchange for refinance/liquidity risk). The attraction of the inverse floating structure is most often a high initial coupon in a low interest rate environment.

9.5.2 Non-Accelerating Senior and Accrual Tranches in Sequential CMOs

There are two common improvements on the sequential-pay design, both of which aim at increasing the stability of the cash flows of the senior classes. The non-accelerating senior (NAS) class is subject to a prepayment lockout, followed by a step-up prepayment participation. In a sequential design, this means that class A does not receive prepayments for a specified period of 0–3 years, then the prepayments are phased in gradually, all the time with class A retaining priority to the principal cash flows. While this may extend the WAL of class A, it narrows down the prepayment scenarios. The objective is to define an almost fixed coupon-like bond, with all the principal coming back during a very narrow time window. This mitigates or eliminates the negative convexity of the prepayment risk.

Sequential and NAS designs often include an "accrual tranche," also called a "Z bond." In addition to the principal flow of the pool, the interest that would have been paid on the Z bond's principal is diverted to prepay the senior sequential tranches. The "missing" interest is accrued to (increases) the starting principal of the Z bond until the Z bond starts paying down. Table 9.12 shows an example of a sequential structure including a Z bond.

Other variants include NAS sequential CMOs with several NAS tranches each with its own lockout. These are usually supported by the "relatively unstable" sequential classes rather than Z bonds.

Accrual bonds, instead of companion classes, are used to support "very accurately defined maturity" (VADM) bonds. These are PAC-like with two PSA bands. The Z bond support offers tighter contraction and extension protection than a support class can. It provides interest cash flow to replenish missing prepayment flow (reducing extension risk). The increased principal is able to absorb many prepayments.

10
Collateralized Debt Obligations and Basket Credit Derivatives

In April 2010, Goldman Sachs was accused by the Securities and Exchange Commission (SEC) of misleading investors into buying designed-to-fail synthetic collateralized debt obligations (CDOs) in 2007. Goldman's executives were grilled by a US Senate subcommittee. The senators' lack of understanding of the basics of securitization and appreciation for the mix of market-making and supporting principal trading that dealers routinely perform was evident. Goldman officers struggled not to offend the law makers.

CDOs are bond instruments backed by debt assets held by a special purpose trust or an asset manager. The debt assets backing the CDOs can be corporate loans, corporate bonds, or mortgage securities. These can be static, i.e. selected once when the CDO is structured and placed in the trust, or actively managed by a designated asset manager. The cash flows accruing from the assets can be passed through to the CDO investors, but most often are *tranched* into several categories of CDO certificates, according to their seniority or stated maturity. The objective of the CDO issuance is for one bank or fund entity to pass the risk of the underlying securities to another entity. For example, a holder of mortgage securities or corporate bonds, instead of selling them outright, can put them into a trust and sell partial or tranched interest in them to others. The buyer usually seeks to gain exposure to risks to which he normally has no easy access. By their nature, the CDOs are investment conduits to assets and risks carefully selected by someone trying to get rid of them, and carefully chosen by someone to buy into. This exposure can also be created synthetically through a combination of Treasuries and short default swaps.

We start the chapter with the definition of the most common structure, the static cash CDO. We go through the cash flow mechanics of synthetic CDOs and basket credit derivatives with exposures to multiple credits through first-to-default, last-to-default, or multiple-default payouts. We delve into the pricing of CDOs and credit baskets which relies on the modeling of multivariate defaults, consistent with the single issuer default modeling of the marginal distributions, but allowing for a default correlation structure of many issuers. The standard approach is to use a *copula* function, which is a multivariate function of correlated uniform random variables whose transforms have known marginal probability density functions. The objective is to have a parsimonious correlation parameterization that fits the observed market prices of basket and single-issuer credit derivatives and corporate bond spreads. We then cover the issues of CDO cash flow tranching, and the difficulties of rating tranched CDOs. We briefly discuss the role of CDOs in the financial crisis of 2007–2008 and their general role in risk trading.

10.1 COLLATERALIZED DEBT OBLIGATIONS

CDO issuance grew from less than \$150 billion in 2003 to \$520 billion in 2006 and \$481 billion in 2007, then collapsing to just \$61 billion in 2008. The vast majority of CDOs, about 80%, are cash CDOs. CDOs transfer the risks of corporate bonds, loans, or mortgage pass-throughs from one entity to another. This is done on a cash basis with the actual underlying securities put in a trust, or on a synthetic basis with high-quality collateral (e.g. Treasuries) put in the trust and the trust selling default protection to the originator of the CDO.

10.1.1 Cash CDO

In a cash CDO, several similar assets called the CDO collateral are placed in a special purpose vehicle (SPV) created by the sponsor-originator of the CDO and administered by a trustee. Sponsors are investment banks earning fees by underwriting the CDO. By 2008, the top underwriters were Bear Stearns, Merrill Lynch, Wachovia, Citigroup, Deutsche Bank, and Bank of America.

The SPV receives all the cash flows from the underlying assets, including interest and principal payments. The originator distributes to the buyers CDO certificates which are claims on the cash flows coming into the SPV minus the expenses associated with running the SPV. Those are retained by the trustee and the manager of the CDO. An institution like the Bank of New York, State Street Bank, Wells Fargo, BNP Paribas, or Deutsche Bank holds title to the assets on behalf of the investors. CDOs are often actively managed by a CDO manager. In that case the collateral changes over time at the discretion of the manager and the cash flows distributed to the CDO investor include the sales of the collateral. In 2009 there were approximately 300 CDO managers. Some of the top managers were Trust Company of the West (TCW), BlackRock, C-BASS Investment, Duke Funding or Ellington Management in the USA and Deutsche, Credit Suisse, West LB, and Rabobank in Europe. The role of the manager is to maintain the credit quality of the collateral throughout of the life of the CDO. But even before that, following issuance, the manager acquires the assets for the CDO during the *ramp-up* period by making capital calls to the senior tranche investors and buying the underlying assets into the SPV. The ramp-up period lasts several months. In the subsequent reinvestment or revolver period, the manager may make additional purchases of the collateral as specified in the transaction documents. The manager earns senior and subordinated fees for his services. Many CDOs are passively managed with the role of the manager limited simply to maintaining the portfolio. In these *static cash* CDOs investors know with certainty the composition of the collateral.

While there are many motivations for sponsors and investors to participate in CDO deals, e.g. sponsors wanting to reduce their balance sheet credit exposure or investors wanting access to certain risks, the main motivation is almost always arbitrage – that is, the creation of a wide spread between the high yield on the equity part of the deal and the relatively lower yield on the highly rated portion of the deal. The main goal is to be able to offer senior certificates that are of higher credit quality than the underlying assets themselves. To that end, the CDO is typically tranched into senior, mezzanine, and subordinated (equity) tranches.

Figure 10.1 shows an example of a static cash CDO in which \$100 million junk-rated BB+ assets with a weighted average coupon of 7.5% are placed in the SPV. The rates on risk-free and AAA-rated bonds are at 5%. The cash flow from the BB+ collateral is tranched into three sets of CDO certificates. The senior tranche has a face value of \$80 million, carries a coupon of 5.5%, and is rated AAA. The mezzanine tranche has a face value of \$15 million, carries a coupon of 9.17%, and is rated BBB. The equity tranche has a face value of \$5 million, carries a coupon of 24.5%, and is unrated. The custody and asset management fees are 0.5%.

If no defaults occur during the life of the CDO, then the \$7,500,000 annual coupon flow will cover the fees and the stated coupon rates of the different tranches: 5.5% × \$80 million

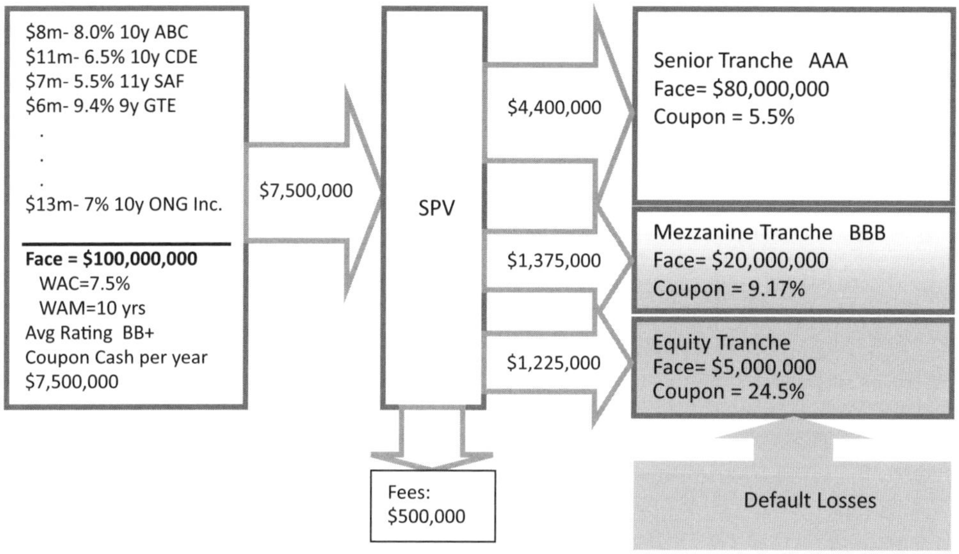

Figure 10.1 A cash CDO

= \$4.4 million; 9.17% × \$15 million = \$1.375 million; and 24.5% × \$5 million = \$1.225 million. If all tranche holders purchase their certificates at par, then the senior tranche holders will make a return of 5.5%, the mezzanine holders will make a return of 9.17%, and the equity holders will make a return of 24.5%.

If the bonds held by the SPV begin to default, then the returns on the equity and mezzanine tranches will be drastically different, while the senior tranche will enjoy a cushion of protection, because initially all default losses will be allocated to the equity tranche. If more than \$5 million bonds default, then the losses will start to be allocated to the mezzanine tranche. More than 20% of the underlying collateral has to default before the senior tranche is affected.

Let us consider a scenario where \$2.5 million bonds default in year 3 and another \$7.5 million bonds default in year 4. The actual return to equity holders (IRR) will be −23.01% as they will receive the first two coupons, only half the coupon in year 3, and no principal back. The return to mezzanine holders will be 4.45%. They will receive full first three coupons, as the loss in year 3 is fully absorbed by the equity holders. Of the default in year 4, \$2.5 million will be absorbed by the equity holders, but the remainder \$5 million will reduce the mezzanine holders' cash flow by one-third. At maturity, they will also only receive \$10 million of their principal. The IRR on their investment will be 4.45%. If there are no additional defaults, then the senior tranche holders will be unaffected and will have earned 5.5%, a 0.5% premium over comparable AAA investments. However, it is very likely that by year 3 or 4, the mezzanine tranche will be downgraded to junk, and the senior tranche perhaps to a single A, or lower. By then, the equity tranche is wiped out offering no protection to the mezzanine tranche, while the collateral is only BB+ and some securities in it are rated even lower than that. Also, by then, the protection cushion offered by the mezzanine tranche to the senior tranche will be severely depleted.

Two important refinements are commonly found in cash CDO structures. First, there need not be only three tranches, as laid out in Figure 10.1. In fact, most CDOs created in the first

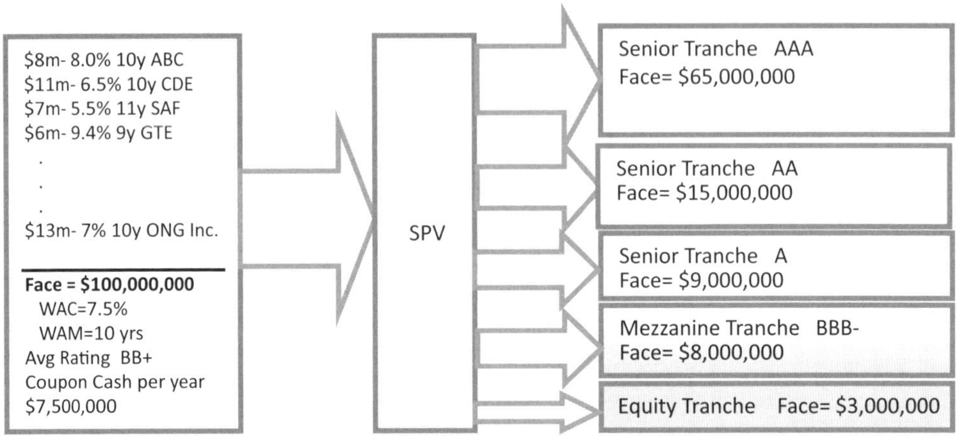

Figure 10.2 A cash CDO with multiple senior tranches

decade of 2000s had several investment-grade tranches, and the mezzanine and equity tranches were typically much thinner. Figure 10.2 illustrates how the same collateral could have been used to create five different tranches.

The second common feature is the layering of securitization. The most senior and the mezzanine tranches could be put into new SPVs and then tranched even more finely. This creates a more skewed default protection structure and can produce even more senior tranches. Figure 10.3 shows an example of a CDO of a CDO.

Two new SPVs are created, one from the most senior tranches and one from the mezzanine tranche. The first issues what would be called a high-grade CDO-backed CDO. The second issues a mezzanine CDO-backed CDO. Each has one or more AAA-rated tranches. The objective is to break up the proportional flow of default losses shared equally by all certificate holders of a given class into an ordinal flow with junior tranches being the first to absorb the losses. This second layer of securitization (and one can easily envision a third layer) allows the creation of a larger total principal of AAA-rated CDO certificates.

For the senior AAA tranche holders of the high-grade CDO to suffer losses, the original collateral not only has to wipe out the original CDO's $3 million equity tranche and the $8 million mezzanine tranche, but also the subordinated classes of the new high-grade CDO. In the mezzanine CDO, the senior AAA tranche holders are insulated from default losses by the original $3 million equity tranche and by the $5.5 million worth of all the subordinated tranches of the new CDO, from the $0.5 million equity class all the way up to the $2 million junior AAA class. While the original $8 million of mezzanine was rated BBB, now $3.5 million of it is re-rated senior AAA, and another $2 million is rated junior AAA. The two would not carry the same yield, as the second is riskier than the first, but both may still qualify for an AAA rating based on their low expected default rate. Note that the model default rate critically depends on the speed and the correlation of defaults of all the credits in the original CDO.

10.1.2 Synthetic CDO

The objectives of a cash CDO, i.e. spread compensation for bearing the risk of default of one credit or a basket of credits, can be replicated synthetically through the use of credit

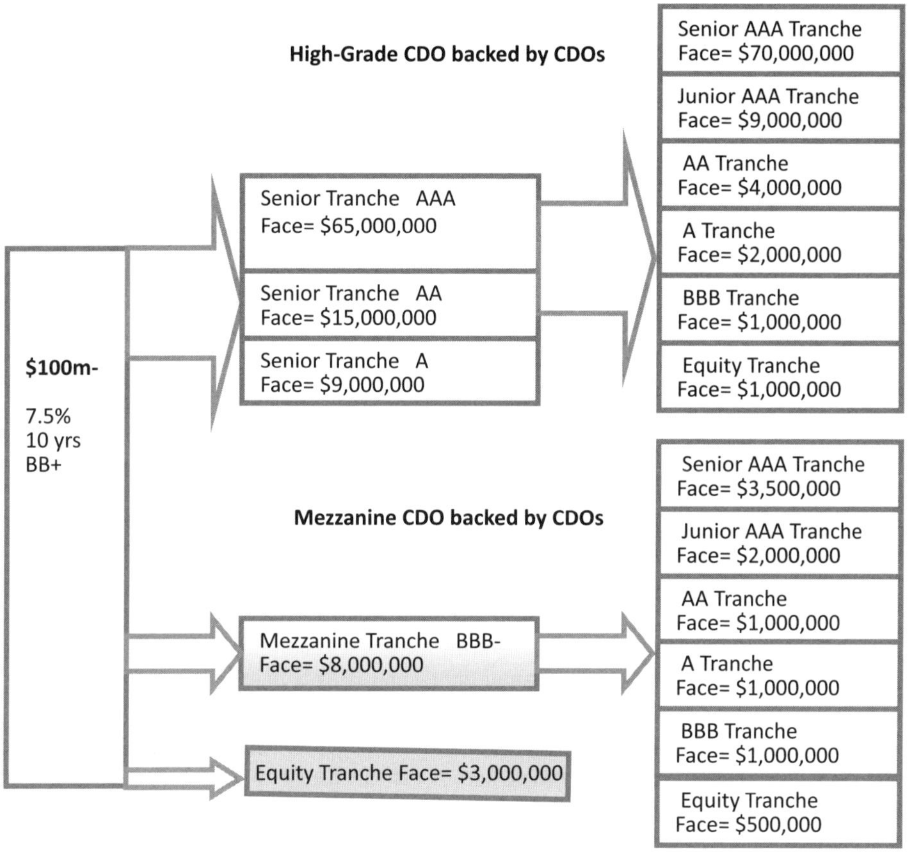

Figure 10.3 A CDO of a CDO

default swaps (CDSs) or basket credit swaps. The 2.0% coupon differential between the 7.5% weighted average coupon of the collateral minus the fees of 0.5% and the risk-free rate of 5% can be earned by the SPV by selling credit default protection to an unrelated third party. The $100 million proceeds from selling the CDO certificates can be used to purchase risk-free Treasuries yielding 5%.

Let us suppose that, as in the previous example (Figures 10.1 to 10.3), the underlying collateral is a single 7.5% 10-year bond issued by the XYZ Corporation. In Chapter 7 we argued that the premium for the CDS on a corporate bond should be approximately equal to the difference between the corporate bond's yield and the yield of a comparable maturity Treasury bond. If the 10-year default-free rate is 5%, then the XYZ bond can be insured by paying 2.5% per annum in exchange for par minus the recovery rate if, or when, the bond defaults.

Figure 10.4 shows how a synthetic CDO on the XYZ bond would work. Here the XYZ bond serves as a reference collateral on a CDS sold by the SPV, rather than actual collateral being purchased by the SPV. The reference collateral is chosen by an asset selection agent (a credit analysis and sponsoring asset manager). The CDS is sold by the SPV to a third party, typically the sponsoring investment bank arranging the transaction. The SPV holds Treasuries yielding 5% and collects an additional 2.5% in premiums on the CDS. The $7.5 million cash

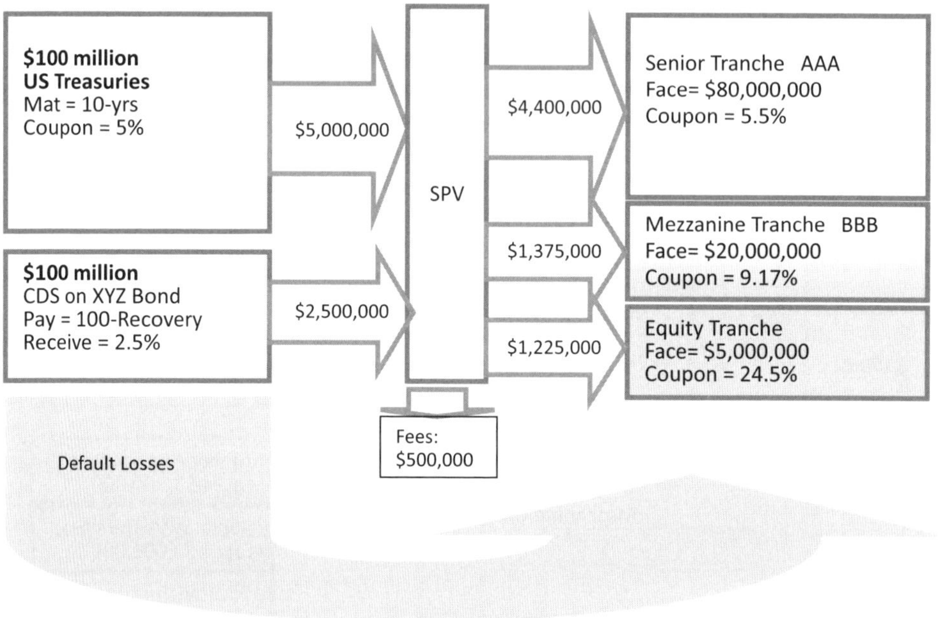

Figure 10.4 A Synthetic CDO

flow is then tranched into the same classes of CDO certificates as in our cash CDO example. If defaults occur, the SPV has to liquidate some of its Treasury holdings to pay claims on the CDO. The equity and mezzanine tranches are first to absorb these losses.

If the collateral consists of a basket of credits (ABC, CDE, SAF, etc.) as in our original example, then the CDS on a single XYZ bond is replaced by a basket of CDSs each with the correct notional principal on each of the bonds in the basket ($8 million, $11 million, $7 million, etc.); the total notional principal is equal to $100 million.

A cash CDO is almost self-managing. As bonds begin to default, the principal losses get fully allocated first to the equity and then to the mezzanine tranches, reducing their outstanding principal amount. The coupon rate does not have to be changed, but the subsequent dollar coupon flow is diminished proportionately to the face value reduction. In a synthetic CDO, the manager of the CDO has to sell Treasuries out of the SPV to make payments to the CDS counterparty. This reduces the subsequent coupon flow and the principal amount of collateral, with the principal reduction again fully allocated first to equity and then to mezzanine holders.

The *raison d'être* of synthetic CDOs is the fact that neither the sponsor nor the manager of the CDO requires access to the reference collateral. In the cash CDO, the collateral securities must actually exist and be available for purchase into the SPV. In the synthetic CDO, the reference assets theoretically don't even have to exist or be easily tradeable. As long as a payout formula for the backing CDSs can be established, the CDO can be created and investors in it can receive coupon spread compensation for the default exposure to the reference collateral. The slightly negative aspect of the synthetic CDO is the additional credit exposure to the CDS counterparty for the CDS premium receipts.

In May 2010, Goldman Sachs executives were grilled by US congressmen over the synthetic Abacus 2007-AC1 CDO referenced with sub-prime mortgage loans. According to the US lawmakers, Goldman was at fault at having not informed the buyer of the CDO (the German bank IKB) that a hedge fund manager, John Paulson, was going short the mortgage loans. The congressmen failed to grasp that in a synthetic CDO, the SPV always sells a credit default swap to a third party in order to generate the spread income for the buyer of the CDO, so the fact that Goldman owned protection on ("was massively short") a portfolio of sub-prime mortgages was not a surprise. The congressmen drilled into the fact that something was not right if the 90 mortgage securities underlying the CDO had not been chosen by an independent portfolio selection agent or asset manager, ACA Management, but had been allegedly hand-picked by Paulson to fail. Goldman's pitch book touted ACA's expertise in credit evaluation and CDO collateral management to the investors. ACA decided to sue Goldman for "fraud and unjust enrichment" in 2011.

10.2 BASKET CREDIT DERIVATIVES

The term "basket credit derivative" sometimes refers to a CDS on a portfolio of defaultable securities. The protection buyer pays a fixed dollar premium per quarter, expressed as per annum basis points on the total principal of all the securities in the basket, and receives losses from default events. Such a structure, which typically underlies a synthetic CDO, is simply a basket of individual CDSs written on each bond or loan in the portfolio. For example, a $200 million basket CDS written on four bonds, each with $50 million principal, is really four $50 million CDSs. If each premium is 50 bp, then the basket CDS premium is initially 200 bp, and it is reduced every time an underlying bond matures or defaults. The pricing of the simple basket CDS is easy as the sum of the separable components. In this section, we describe more complicated variants of the true basket structures in which there is a payout interaction of the component bonds or loans.

10.2.1 First-to-Default Basket

The most popular basket credit derivative on the market is the *first-to-default basket*. The underlying portfolio (cash or synthetic) typically contains three or more different corporate names. Similar to a one-name CDS, the contract is structured as a swap with one leg being the premium for default insurance paid to the protection seller, and the other leg being a one-time protection payout settlement (cash or physical exchange) if and when the default occurs. The main difference is the definition of default as the first default on any (reference) bond in the portfolio. Upon default, the premium payments stop and a one-time protection payout is made by the protection seller. In the cash settlement formula, the payout is equal to 100% minus the percent recovery value on the defaulted bond times the principal amount of the basket. In the physical settlement formula, the protection seller pays the principal amount of the swap and receives the principal amount of the defaulted bond. At the time of the first default, the protection on all the subsequent defaults is discontinued.

Figure 10.5 shows an example of a first-to-default basket derivative. The basket contains three reference bonds issued by ABC Corp., XYZ Corp, and SAF Corp. The total notional principal on the swap of $100 million, the maturity of 5 years and the premium of 2% are agreed upon. As soon as the first default occurs, the buyer of the protection stops the premium payments and receives from the seller of the protection the principal amount plus the accrued interest minus the recovery value of the defaulted bond. Since the total principal of the basket is $100 million and the premium is 2.0% quarterly, then assuming it is stated on a 30/360

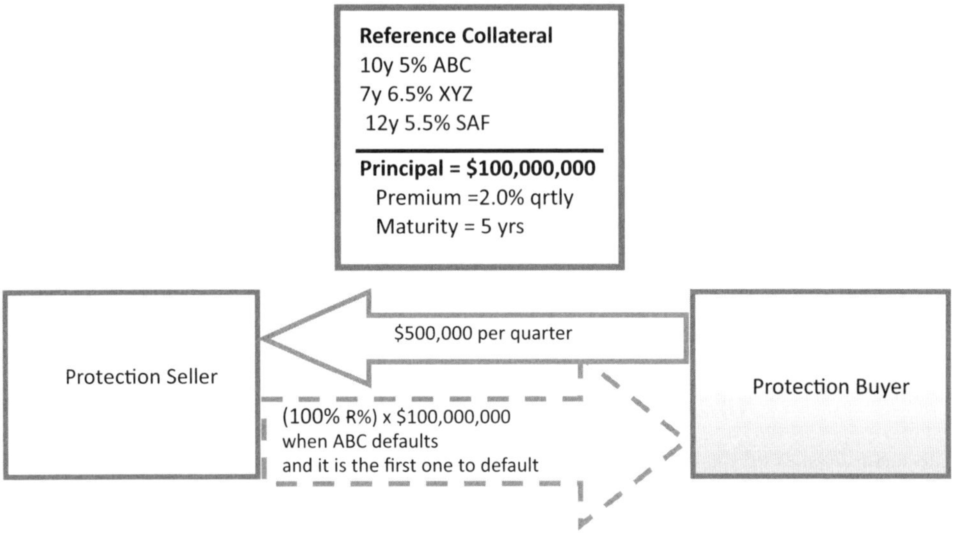

Figure 10.5 A first-to-default basket derivative

basis (normally it is not and matches the LIBOR convention, e.g. *Act/360* in the USA), the protection buyer pays a 2.0% / 4 × $100 million = $500,000 premium to the protection seller every quarter. If, 2 years into the 5-year swap, ABC Corp.'s bond defaults and it trades in the aftermarket at 60 cents on the dollar, the protection seller will make a one-time payment of 100% – 60% times $100 million (= $40 million) to the protection buyer, and the arrangement will be terminated. The seller will not receive any premiums after that, and the buyer will not receive any payments even if XYZ and/or SAF bonds default over the subsequent 3-year period.

The pricing of basket derivatives is quite difficult and depends critically on the correlation of defaults of the reference names. The minimum price of the first-to-default basket is the price of the highest single-name CDS, i.e. CDS on the riskiest bond. The maximum price is the sum of three single-name CDSs. If the correlation is high, and the bonds will tend to default together, the price of the first-to-default structure will be low, but always at least as much as that of the riskiest bond. As the correlation diminishes from one (bonds default together) to zero (bonds default in different scenarios), and further, the probability that one of the many bonds will default increases, and the price goes up all the way to the sum of all single-name CDSs. From the seller's perspective, the attraction of the first-to-default basket lies in the fact that typically the price charged will be much higher than that of the riskiest single-name CDS, to compensate for the increased probability of default relative to the single-name CDS, yet the total loss exposure is limited to the same amount as on the single-name CDS. From the buyer's perspective, the first-to-default is a cheaper way to hedge exposure of the entire portfolio of bonds than buying all the individual CDSs. Of course, the hedge is not perfect, it protects against the "most likely" default, and the buyer is exposed to the risk of multiple defaults.

It is not only the correlation, but also the statistical dependence (or directional causality) of the defaults that drives the price of the basket derivative. To see this, consider the case where ABC is a major airline like Lufthansa or Delta, and SAF is a regional airline like Augsburg Air or Skywest, the latter two deriving most of their revenue by contracting to operate short-distance flights for the big airlines. Clearly a default by a small airline will not necessarily cause a default by a major one, but a default by Delta/Lufthansa will ruin Skywest/Augsburg. In this case, the price of the basket derivative will be close to the higher of the two: the cost of the CDS on the major airline or the cost of the CDS on the regional airline. Since either default triggers the swap, the cost will depend on the riskier of the two.

Now consider the case of no dependence and negative default correlation. Suppose the basket consists of Glaxo, a UK pharmaceutical company, and Best Buy, a US electronics retail company. BestBuy is a highly cyclical consumer discretionary retailer; Glaxo is a global countercyclical staples company. The two are unrelated business entities. The cost of the basket security is likely to be near the cost of purchasing two separate single-name CDSs on the two companies as either default will trigger the swap, and the defaults are likely to occur under different economic conditions. As the two companies' defaults are most likely not *perfectly* negatively correlated, the total price of the basket derivative is likely to be lower than the sum of the two CDSs.

10.2.2 *N*th-to-Default Basket, Arbitrage Conditions, and Hedging

Theoretically, other basket structures, such as second-, third-, or last-to-default derivatives, can easily be structured, but as of this writing they have not proved to be very popular.

Let us understand the workings of the last-to-default basket structure. The derivative pays only if all the reference bonds default. The minimum price can be lower than the lowest of the individual name CDSs; that is, it can be close to zero. The maximum price is the price of the highest of all the individual CDSs on the riskiest bond. The obvious arbitrage bound is that the price of the second-, third-, or last-to-default basket must be lower than the price of the first-to-default basket (assuming the same recovery rate for all the bonds) as the latter structures always pay later, and the payout is applied to the same total notional principal. The second arbitrage condition is that the purchase of all the ordered derivatives, i.e. the first-, second, ..., last-to-default baskets is identical to the purchase of all the individual name CDSs. So, while the price of the first may be higher than the highest individual CDS and the price of the last-to-default may be lower than that of the least risky CDS, the sums of the prices must be the same.

The exact price of the last-to-default depends on the individual securities default probabilities (marginal distributions), on the default correlation structure, and on the directional dependence (causality) structure. High correlation, which means a higher probability of joint losses, tends to increase the price of the last-to-default. Lower correlation, which implies a lower probability of multiple defaults, tends to decrease the price of the last-to-default.

The interaction of the correlation and the directional causality also plays a role. In the Delta/Skywest example, the correlation is high (implying a high price for the last-to-default) and the causality runs from the bigger airline (Delta) to the smaller one (Skywest). In the last-to-default case, the basket only pays if both names default, so the probability structure of Delta dominates (the price of the basket is close to the price of the individual CDS on Delta) irrespective of whether Delta's marginal probability of default is lower or higher than Skywest's. Even if Skywest's marginal probability of default is much higher than Delta's, since Skywest's default does not cause Delta to default, the price of the last-to-default basket will be closer to the individual CDS on Delta, the lower of the two.

In the low correlation, low causality Glaxo–Best Buy case, the price is driven by the joint probability distribution. The probability of two defaults is likely to be lower than the probability of the default of the riskier of the two. If the correlation is zero or negative, then the probability of two defaults drops to zero.

10.2.3 Hedging of Basket Derivatives

The standard technique for hedging basket credit derivatives is to take positions in delta amounts of individual CDSs. A default correlation is calibrated using the term structure of individual name CDSs. The correlations are taken as constants and the exposures of the basket structure to the individual CDSs are computed. The best comparison would be to an option on a small portfolio of equities priced in a Gaussian fixed correlation structure model with exposures computed to the individual stocks. The dealer is left with the residual risk to the changing correlation structure. The hedge is also subject to high rebalancing costs as the underlying hedge instruments are individual CDSs, not cash bonds.

Consider the hedge for a dealer buying of a 5-year first-to-default credit derivative defined in Figure 10.5. The hedge illustrated in Figure 10.6 consists of selling three individual CDSs on ABC, XYZ, and SAF. Suppose we use a Gaussian copula model with an average correlation input of 0.5 and compute the price for the basket of 200 bp. Suppose also that the delta, i.e. the hedge ratio, for each CDS turns out to be 0.7 and each CDS is quoted at 100 bp.

Initially, for each $100 million of the first-to-default the dealer buys, he sells $70 million of each individual CDS. He spends 200 bp on premium and receives 210 bp in premium. That is, each quarter he pays $500,000 and receives $525,000. The dealer is typically a net premium receiver and has exposure to time decay. The dealer is also "long gamma." Every time the cost of the underlying individual CDSs change and the dealer has to rebalance the hedge, he "buys low and sells high." When the cost of insuring ABC credit rises and the CDS spread on ABC widens from 100 bp to 120 bp, the delta increases. Conversely, when the cost of insuring SAF credit declines from 100 bp to 80 bp, the delta decreases.

Figure 10.6 shows the hedge rebalancing for a long first-to-default position. When the spread on the ABC credit widens (ABC becomes riskier) and the spread on the SAF credit narrows (SAF becomes safer), the dealer sells another $10 million of the ABC CDS receiving additional 1.2% on a $10 million notional, and unwinds at a profit or buys $10 million of the SAF CDS paying 0.8% on a $10 million notional. Net, the dealer has a positive cash flow on the rebalance. If the SAF credit were to subsequently widen back to 100 bp or more, the dealer would sell more of the SAF CDS. In this way, the dealer sells more at a higher spread and buys back at a lower spread. Meanwhile, if none of the credits defaults, the value of the first-to-default basket insurance slowly decays.

10.3 COPULAS AND THE MODELING OF DEFAULT CORRELATION

Since the bulk of the credit derivatives business is in individual name CDSs, and for each name multiple maturity CDSs trade at the same time, calibrating marginal default probability distributions and simple univariate default models – like those in Chapter 7 – is quite easy. However, the individual CDSs contain no information about the default correlation structure among different names. These have to be extracted from basket structures or CDOs. The main problem in modeling default correlation is the simple fact that, in mathematical statistics, very few distributions generalize easily from univariate to multivariate functions. While the multivariate normal distribution consists of correlated marginal univariate normals, the same

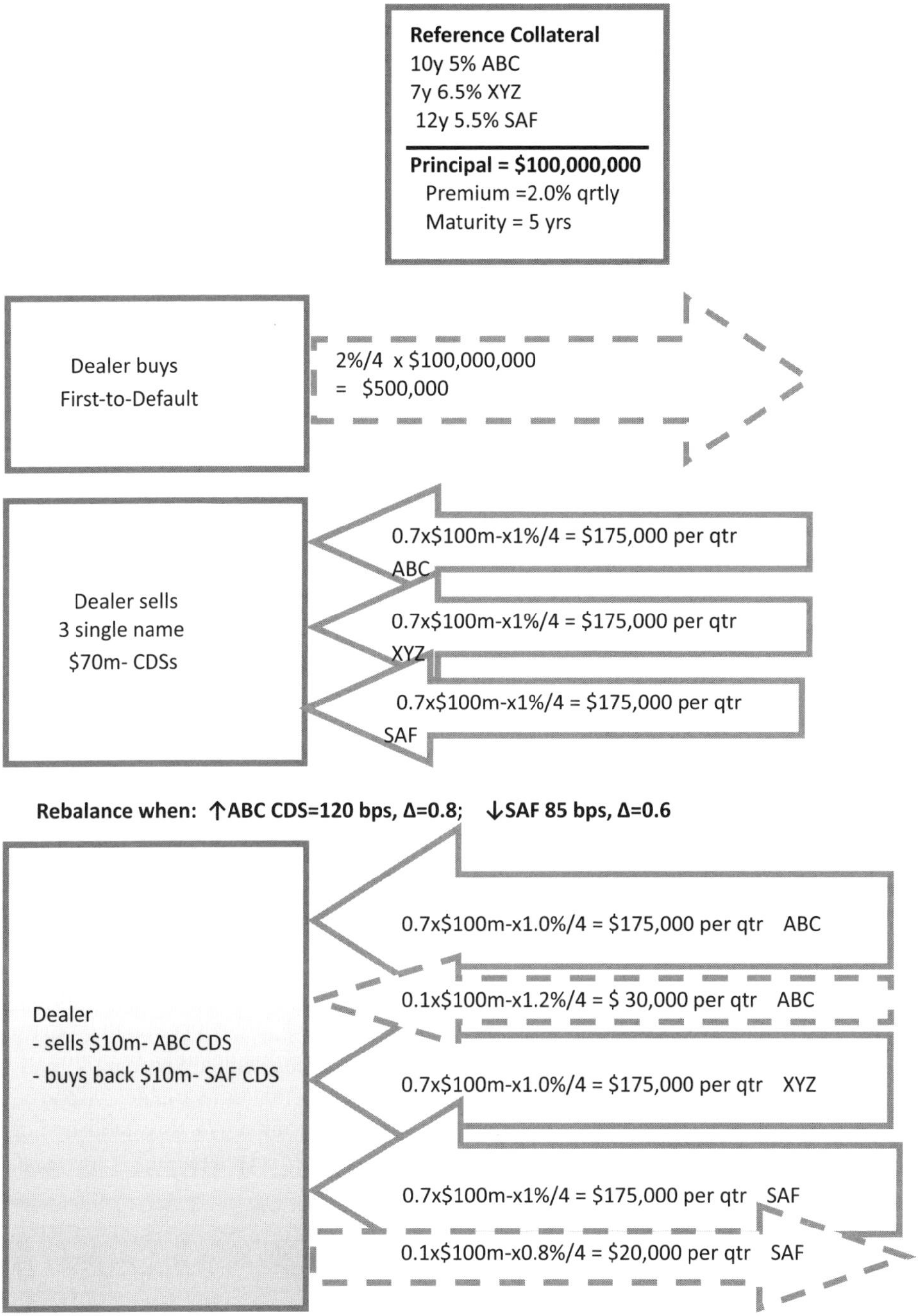

Figure 10.6 Hedging a long position in the first-to-default basket

is not generally true of other distributions with non-independent marginals or transforms of known distributions. Defaults are binary events that are most naturally handled with Poisson or Gamma processes, not continuous normals. The main way of dealing with the problem of generalizing univariates to correlated multivariates is through the use of copula functions.

The essence of the copula method is to start with known marginal probability distributions and, since they may not generalize easily to a tractable multivariate distribution, to map them one-by-one into new marginal probability distributions, on which to impose a correlation structure and a tractable multivariate distribution. The transformation mappings are called copula functions. Thus we do not model directly the correlation of defaults; instead we define correlations for random variables that are one-for-one transforms of individual defaults, and then fit the model to observed prices. We start with a numerical example of a Gaussian copula and then discuss extensions and calibration issues.

10.3.1 A Gaussian Copula

Recall from Chapter 7 the Poisson model of the default probability of an individual credit. It takes as input a "failure" intensity parameter λ observed over a period ω. A credit may default with a probability of $\lambda = 0.005$ over the period of $\omega = 10$ years. These two parameters define the mean $\mu = \lambda\omega = 0.05$ of the Poisson probability density function $f(x)$ of a discrete random variable x, which is the number of "failures" (defaults) over the interval ω. In the pricing of CDSs, we are not interested in more than one default for the same issuer. We are mostly interested in the probability of survival $f(0)$, i.e. the probability of no failure. This univariate set-up easily extends to the case of λ changing over time deterministically and we can calibrate the vector of input parameters μ if we observe sequential CDS prices for longer maturities.

Suppose, by observing CDS spread levels, we have fitted constant μs for two credits. ABC is a C-rated company with $\lambda = 0.03$, $\omega = 10$, and $\mu = \lambda\omega = 0.3$. SAF is a DD-rated company with $\lambda = 0.05$, $\omega = 10$, and $\mu = \lambda\omega = 0.5$. We let x_1 denote the number of ABC defaults and x_2 denote the number of SAF defaults. We transform the variables x_1 and x_2 into two new standard normal variables y_1 and y_2. We do this by computing the cumulative Poisson distribution values for x_1 and x_2 and finding the standard normal values y_1 and y_2 that correspond to the same cumulative probabilities. Because the new variables are normal or Gaussian, we call this mapping a Gaussian copula. Table 10.1 shows the Poisson density and cumulative probability values for x_1 and x_2 and the corresponding standard normals y_1 and y_2.

We then postulate that the correlation between the two new random variables y_1 and y_2 is equal to $\rho = 0.5$. With the copula correspondences $x_1 \leftrightarrow y_1$ and $x_2 \leftrightarrow y_2$ established, it is

Table 10.1 A Gaussian copula of two Poisson variables

x_1	Poisson p.d.f.	Poisson c.d.f.	y_1	x_2	Poisson p.d.f.	Poisson c.d.f.	y_2
0	0.740818	0.740818	0.6459	0	0.606531	0.606531	0.2703
1	0.222245	0.963064	1.7874	1	0.303265	0.909796	1.3395
2	0.033337	0.996401	2.6875	2	0.075816	0.985612	2.1866
3	0.003334	0.999734	3.4643	3	0.012636	0.998248	2.9197
4	0.000250	0.999984	4.1618	4	0.001580	0.999828	3.5795
5	0.000015	0.999999	4.8025	5	0.000158	0.999986	4.1865

Table 10.2 Cumulative joint probability of x_1 and x_2

	$x_2 =$			
x_1	0	1	2	3
0	0.5163	0.7058	0.7374	0.7406
1	0.6000	0.8872	0.9527	0.9620
2	0.6062	0.9083	0.9828	0.9948
3	0.6065	0.9097	0.9854	0.9980

easy to construct a two-dimensional table of the cumulative probability density values of the default variables x_1 and x_2. Table 10.2 shows these numbers for x_1 and x_2 running from 0 to 3.

10.3.2 General Copula Models

The Gaussian copula generalizes easily to many random variables. Once the default random variables are transformed into univariate normals, the marginal normals form a multivariate normal distribution have known properties, with the inputs limited to the correlation matrix.

While the copula method solves the issue of generalizing marginal univariate distributions, it is not without its own problems. First, the correlation inputs are not the correlations of defaults, but the correlations of artificially created random variables with one-to-one correspondences to the default random variables. The issue is compounded by the fact that derivative valuation imposes no-arbitrage conditions which result in risk-neutral pricing. Thus the correlation structure we impose is not only *not* directly that of the defaults themselves, but is also the risk-neutral correlation, making it even harder to interpret. All this necessitates another layer of model calibration with potentially irresolvable pricing inconsistencies. For any model to be useful, the inputs have to be intuitive and easily extracted from securities priced in liquid markets. In a credit derivative model, an intuitive input would be the default correlation. This could, for example, be checked against historical evidence for similar names or credit categories. In order to use a copula model, one can start with default correlations and then try to fit the correlation structure of the copula-transformed variables to produce the desired default variable correlation structure, or basket derivative prices, in the market. As in calibration, the problem may be under- or overdetermined. We may observe too few or too many basket prices to fit the model. In the first case, we may have to simplify the correlation matrix through parameterization. In the second case, we may not be able to match all the observed prices.

The under-determined case is often treated with a factor model. Suppose we try to model the correlation structure for hundreds of credits in a portfolio. There is hardly any chance to precisely fit each pairwise correlation by observing basket structures containing those pairs. Similar to the method used in modeling the risk of equity baskets, we can impose an index structure on the default correlations. Instead of transforming xs into ys individually, we impose a common-factor structure:

$$y_1 = \theta_1 I + \sqrt{1 - \theta_1} z_1$$
$$y_2 = \theta_2 I + \sqrt{1 - \theta_2} z_2$$

where the common factor I is of a desirable form, normal in the Gaussian case, and the θs are the correlations of each transformed default variable y with the index. This simplification reduces the number of inputs from $n(n-1)/2$ for the entire pairwise correlation matrix to n in a diagonal form of factor-credit correlations (like betas in the equity model).

Finally, defaults are low-probability tail events. In the example above, we deliberately used risky credits with fairly high default probabilities to generate cumulative probabilities distinguishably less than 1 in Table 10.2. When dealing with investment-grade credits, the individual default probabilities are extremely low. Therefore, credit modeling is, by definition, confined to the modeling of the tails of distributions. In the multivariate case, this is even harder since the cumulative densities have to be computed numerically and with some error. One way to deal with it is by the use of a Student t-copula instead of a Gaussian copula. The t-distribution is much more fat-tailed, and the factor model still works if we assume that I is Student t-distributed and the zs are standard normal. The other way to deal with it is to abandon the modeling of the entire distributions and focus on multivariate modeling and parameterization of the tails alone. Some successes have been reported with the use of Pareto functions as tail approximations, but multivariate tail modeling remains a challenge. The interested reader may want to look into the Extreme Value Theory research initially applied to VaR modeling.

10.4 SYNTHETIC CDO TRANCHE PRICING AND LOSS ANALYSIS

The first decade of 2000s ushered in an explosive growth of synthetic CDOs. The search for yield and risk diversification drove investors to accept exposure to new assets. For example, European banks sought exposure to US mortgage assets. The credit derivative market was mature enough to absorb this and make markets in a variety of credits and structures. The demand for exposure drove the CDS spreads often higher than the credit spreads in corporate and sovereign bond markets. Synthetics also allowed the customization of credits and cash flows. The one thing that was not predicted by the yield-hungry investors was the risk of the rising correlation of defaults due to systemic risk. It is very instructive to analyze a typical set-up of a synthetic CDO, its initial pricing, and the change in tranche pricing and loss exposure as CDS spreads widened.

10.4.1 Synthetic CDO Revisited

Figure 10.7 shows an example of a \$500 million synthetic CDO structure with a \$415 million super-senior unfunded tranche and six investment tranches totaling \$85 million principal and ranging from AAA rating all the way down to the unrated equity tranche. The tranches are issued as credit-linked notes (CLNs).

The CDO-issuing SPV enters into a \$500 million cash-settled CDS agreement with a third party (typically a sponsoring investment bank) selling it credit protection on a portfolio of 100 credits (equivalent to 100 individual CDS). The periodic premium received is to serve as the spread on the coupons paid to the CDO tranche holders. This spread is what the investors are seeking. Presumably, it is higher than what they could obtain in the corporate bond market on equivalent credits.

The SPV receives \$85 million for the CLN tranches. This principal money is not used to buy the underlying corporate bonds or loans as in the cash CDO, but it is deposited into a credit support account invested in US Treasuries. It is to be used to absorb any losses coming from defaults. The CLN tranches are hit in the reverse order of seniority, with the first default losses reducing and then wiping out the equity tranche (first 2% of the collateral defaulting), then the

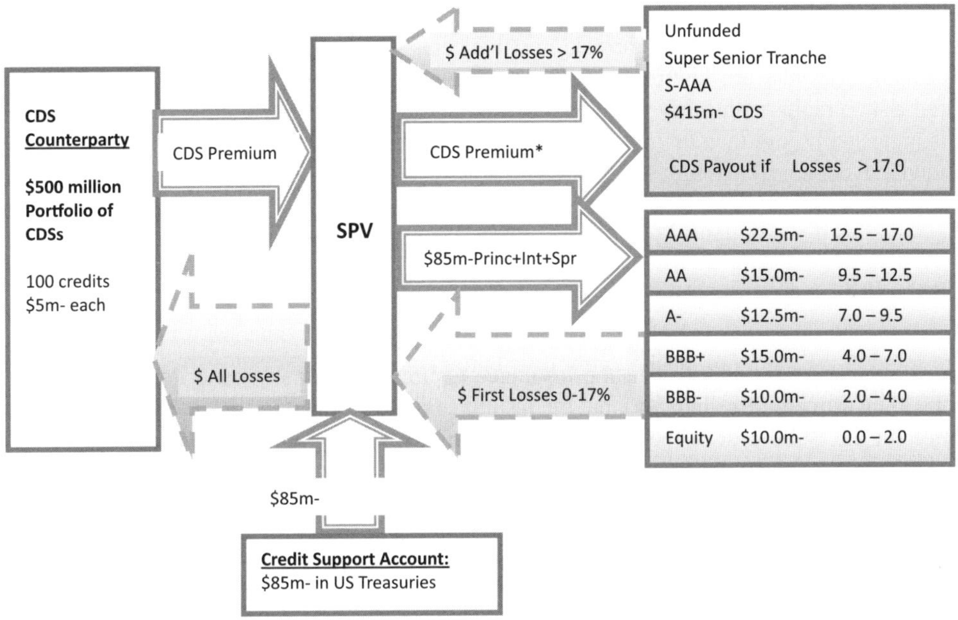

Figure 10.7 A super-senior synthetic **CDO**

mezzanine (BBB-) tranche (the next 2% defaulting), and then investment grade tranches (the next 13% defaulting). The super-senior tranche holders are the most protected. They have not put any money into the structure, they simply collect some of the CDS premium, and fully $85 million of losses (17% of the collateral principal) have to occur before they start making payments on their CDS. Their main risk is the exposure to losses in excess of $85 million in exchange for the CDS premium per $1 of insured collateral that is lower than the original CDS premium received by the SPV. This is due to their "better-than-AAA" status delivered by the protection cushion of the junior tranches.

10.4.2 Synthetic CDO Pricing and Expected Loss

To understand the pricing of the synthetic CDO, let us consider the simple constant probability of default model introduced in Section 7.2 of Chapter 7. Let $p = 0.08$ be the one-period (conditional) probability of default and $q = 1 - p = 0.92$ be the one-period (conditional) survival probability. Let us also posit a constant recovery rate $R = 0.4$. Figure 10.8 shows the last step of a pricing tree for a credit sensitive discount bond.

Consider that last step portrayed by solid lines. If we assume no discounting, then the price of the discount bond is equal to the expected value of the payoff, $100 with probability 0.92 and $40 with probability 0.08:

$$P = \$100 \times (q + R \times p) = \$100 \times (0.92 + 0.4 \times 0.08) = \$95.20$$

By arbitrage, the price of a 1-year CDS on the discount bond must be $4.80. To replicate a riskless discount bond paying off $100 for certain, one can buy the risky discount bond for $95.20 and spend $4.80 to insure it. If the risky bond does not default, then the $95.20

Figure 10.8 A discount bond subject to constant probability of default

investment turns into \$100, and the insurance expires. If the risky bond defaults, then the \$95.20 investment turns into \$40, but the insurance pays $\$100 \times (1 - R) = \$60$. We can thus interpret the \$4.80 cost of the insurance equal to 4.8% of the face value as the risk-neutral credit spread on the bond (here in discount yield terms). It is important to note that the credit spread is also equal to the expected risk-neutral loss on the bond. If we define the loss as the loss of principal, then it is equal to zero in the survival state with probability $q = 0.92$, and equal to $\$100 \times (1 - R) = \$60$ with probability $p = 0.08$. In general,

$$E\,[Loss] = \$100 \times p \times (1 - R)$$

In order to extend the expected loss discussion to a multi-period pricing tree, let us distinguish between the conditional and the cumulative probabilities of default. The conditional probability of default over period n, denoted $p(n-1, n)$, is defined as the probability of default in period n conditional on surviving (not defaulting) in previous $n-1$ periods. The cumulative probability of default over n periods, denoted $p(0, n)$, is the probability of default between now, time zero, and the end of period n. Consider the dashed lines in Figure 10.8 representing the second-to-last step of a multi-period tree. In the Figure, both conditional default probabilities are the same and equal to 8%, or

$$p\,(0, 1) = p\,(1, 2) = 0.08$$

The cumulative probability of default over two periods between now and the end of period 2 is:

$$p\,(0, 2) = p\,(0, 1) + [1 - p\,(0, 1)] \times p\,(1, 2) = 0.08 + 0.92 \times 0.08 = 0.1536$$

In a general multi-period model, we are typically able to bootstrap the term structure of corporate spreads for any given credit (from corporate bonds or CDSs). As with interest rates, we can recover "zero" spreads or forward spreads, i.e. those charged on a CDS between now and n periods from now, and those for each forward period. Let us denote the former, which is how CDSs are normally quoted, by $s(0, n)$. Assuming a constant recovery R, we can generalize our one-step example to the following formula for the cumulative default probability:

$$p\,(0, n) = \frac{1 - \dfrac{1}{[1 + s\,(0, n)]^n}}{1 - R}$$

For example, using this formula, an annualized spread of 0.5% with a recovery rate of 40 cents on the dollar translates into the cumulative probability of default over 5 years of 4.1%.

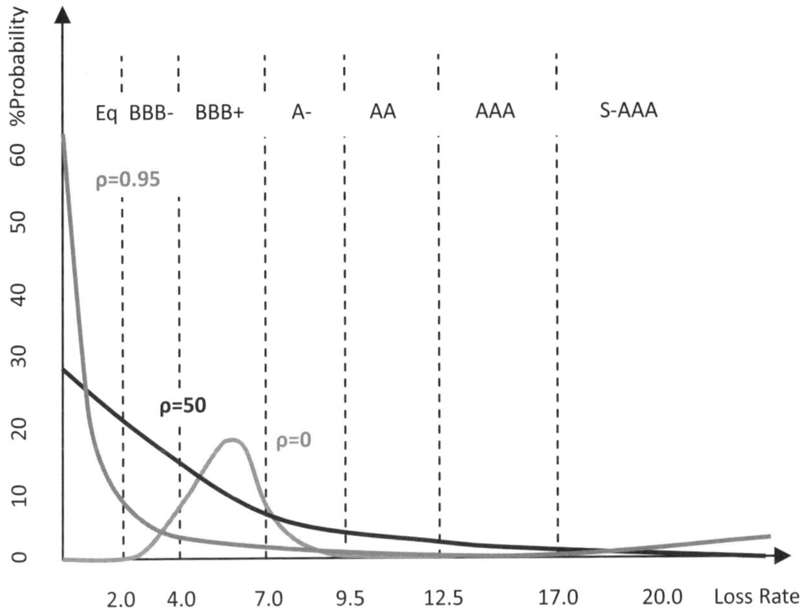

Figure 10.9 Loss rate distribution for $\rho = 0$, 0.5 and 0.95

Given the cumulative probabilities, we can recursively back out the conditional probabilities using the equation for our two-step example and solving for $p\,(1, 2)$. Once we have the entire conditional probability tree, we can compute the expected loss assuming a deterministic recovery rate.

10.4.3 Synthetic CDO – Loss Rates, Ratings and the Crisis of 2008

With a little bit of work, one can extend the constant probability of default model for one credit to a Gaussian copula approach with multiple credits. After all, what determines default losses is imply the cumulative joint probability distribution. The default loss behavior of the CDO collateral depends critically on the correlation of defaults.

Figure 10.9 shows the distribution of loss rates under correlation assumptions of 0.0, 0.50, and 0.95. The loss rate is defined as the total loss over a 5-year period as a percentage of the total CDO principal. We superimpose the loss absorption thresholds for the different CDO tranches.

When the correlation is zero, the loss distribution centers around its mean and losses higher than 10% are unlikely (tail probability less than 0.005). As the correlation increases, multiple defaults become more likely and so do higher total losses (fatter right tail). Small losses also become more likely (fatter left tail). When the correlation is very high, the distribution becomes almost binomial, either all assets default together or none defaults. The distribution is dictated by the lowest probability assets. The probability of a zero loss is about 2/3, but there is a non-zero probability of very high losses over 50%. What this implies for the different tranches is that, at zero correlation, even the BBB+ tranche has a high cumulative probability of principal losses, while the S-AAA tranche may remain intact. However, as the correlation increases, the loss on the mezzanine tranches BBB– and BBB+ becomes less likely, but the probability of losses for the super-senior tranche increases from near zero to above 5% and close to 10%.

This last observation is the crux of the 2008 crisis of defaults of senior sub-prime mortgage-backed CDOs. They had been structured with a view of low correlation of defaults: some homeowners were supposed to default while some were not. This would have created the situation where the junior tranches would have absorbed all the losses from the least creditworthy homeowners. However, as correlations increased dramatically and all homeowners started to default at the same time (or at least the perception of that likelihood increased), the losses spread to the super-senior tranches of the CDOs. Instead of accepting near zero spread on their tranches, the senior holders should have demanded spreads in excess of 50 bp per annum to compensate them for the loss of market value due to higher correlation of defaults.

Most rating models of CDOs tranches have been inadequate. From the pronouncements by the S&P one could guess that their approach was based on the riskiest-credit-in-the-basket principle. This implies that the first-to-default baskets and the junior tranches of a CDO are assigned the credit rating of the weakest names in the pool. This also implies a view that weakest credits always default first. Clearly that has to understate the total cumulative probability of default. Moody's approach was to not only include the probability of default but also to run all structures through expected loss scenarios. While this may have appeared to be an improvement, since one added to the probability analysis the dimension of the severity of the loss, in reality it was not. If the recovery rates and default losses were simulated to match observed spreads or historical levels, then they also severely underestimated the cumulative defaults.

10.5 CREDIT DERIVATIVE INDEXES

In 2011 there were two main credit derivative indexes. In Europe, the iTraxx CDS Europe index tracks 125 investment grade corporate credits, changed every 6 months. The index is owned by the International Index Company, a subsidiary of the Markit Group. The IIC licenses the index to over 30 market makers for over-the-counter trading. Markit.com provides daily pricing information on the index. It also offers several sub-group indexes, but the trading in these indexes is very thin.

In North America, the dominant index is the CDX or the CDX.NA, also referencing 125 investment grade corporate credits. The index is owned by the CDS Index Company, a subsidiary of the Markit Group. There is also a CDX.EM index covering fewer than 15 emerging market credits.

The indexes provide a good way of tracking the overall level of prices in the CDS market. However, they suffer from the same drawbacks as any insurance cost index. Insurance is purchased on an individualized basis to insure the loss on a specific portfolio of risks. An index often covers risks that may not be of interest to the buyer of the insurance. That is why, while the volume of CDS trading continues to grow rapidly, the CDS index trading lags.

This issue is important to understand. After 2010, as part of the gigantic Dodd–Frank Reform Act, there was an effort in the USA to move the settlement of the CDS trading from over-the-counter to a clearing house. Presumably, the rationale is that the volume of CDS trading is a multiple of the total outstanding of the insured credits, therefore there is undue counterparty risk. It remains to be seen to what degree this effort will succeed. First of all, netting alleviates the counterparty risk; but since CDS trading is customized party-to-party insurance-like in character, it is not obvious how it can be efficiently cleared by a centralized agent on a fully standardized and collateralized basis. To define an index and trade it, is one thing. To trade thousands of different customized contracts off the exchange, but to clear them through an exchange, is another. The documentation issue alone could put the clearing agent at legal risk. The law drafters should probably have put a little more thought into this before enacting it.

Part III

The Players

11

Individual Investors: A Survey of Modern Investment Theory

In this first chapter on the players in the financial markets, we consider the tiniest economic agent: you and me. Individuals supply funds to business by investing in securities directly, with the help of pooling funds, or through complex intermediated arrangements. Figure 11.1 shows a simplified graph of those flows and is a subpart of the full flow of funds diagram in Chapter 13 (Figure 13.1), where we tackle the capital transformation role of banks in the economy and their long asset–short liability dilemma.

How individuals should select their investments has been a subject of serious financial economics research for the last 80 years. The subject is complicated as it blends the characteristics of investments with the goals of individuals. The latter are often referred to as the optimal consumption-investment bundle. The main characteristics of individuals taken into account include age/longevity (investment horizon) and bequest (estate planning), consumption/cash flow constraints (including housing needs), and the investor's natural attitude toward risk. The latter is most often represented by "risk aversion," but may include other behavioral and psychological factors.

In general, the approach to investment can be divided into two kinds: active and passive. An active investor seeks to analyze each investment on its own merits, and to value it in some way in order to uncover the value (positive or negative) that is not reflected in the investment's current price. The active investor relies on his superior knowledge of the investment, his superior analysis method, or the speed of analysis and execution. The active investor takes a relatively short perspective. He takes a position (buys, sells, shorts, or enters into derivatives) on the investment as soon as he discovers the mispriced value, and liquidates the position as soon as the assets price returns to the value he places on it. The active investor uses what we call *fundamental valuation* methods. A passive investor believes in the wisdom of the markets or that active investors through their actions force the prices of assets to be at their fair fundamental value or the deviations are very short. The passive investor focuses on the long-term objectives of achieving the highest return compatible with his attitude toward risk and consumption needs. He does not attempt to value investments in order to uncover mispricing. Rather he uses the information in the prices of assets to construct the best portfolio for himself that trades off expected return against risk over time. He uses tools like *portfolio optimization* and makes decisions on *asset allocation* among many alternatives which often result in diversified portfolios of many assets. Passive asset allocators subscribe to the *two-fund separation* principle and pursue indexing in the risky part of their portfolio. Recently, the indexing trend has expanded beyond simple diversified portfolios of developed country stocks and into global stock and bond portfolios and commodities. Also recently, a new blended breed of investors has emerged. These *tactical allocation* investors are neither active nor passive. They believe that value discovery through fundamental valuation is difficult. But they also believe that long-term asset allocations based on broad indexing lead to inferior results. So they pursue monthly or quarterly rebalancing strategies, shifting in and out of

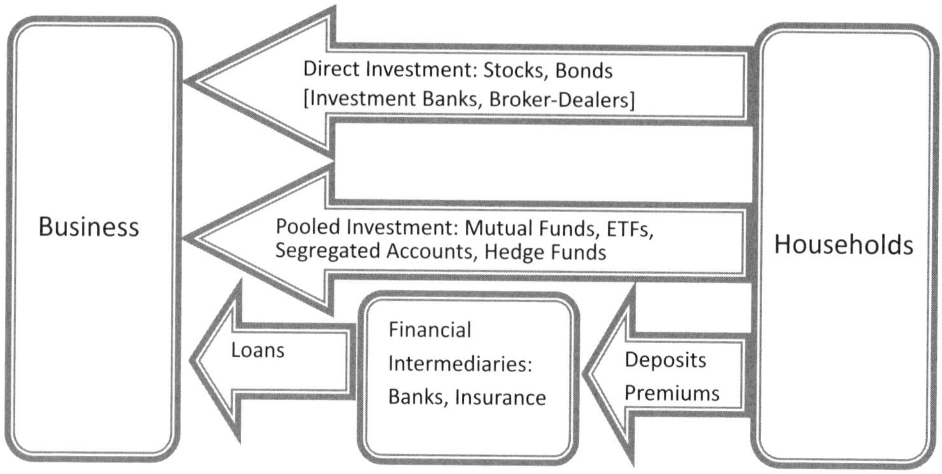

Figure 11.1 Direct and intermediated flow of investment capital in the economy

sectors, geographies, or asset classes. Their decision algorithms blend technical trends with economic fundamentals. The newest super-active investment strategy is *algorithmic trading*. Here the investors do not perform fundamental cash flow valuation analysis, but rely on statistical within-asset-class co-movement modeling of all the stocks within a stock market or individual currencies/commodities within the entire currency/commodity market. They attempt to discover very short termed deviations (hourly, daily) of the prices from the overall movement of assets within the class. An example here is *momentum investing*. The model may be purely statistical or blend in economic or accounting data. The last case in some sense amounts to relative rather than absolute fundamental asset valuation.

This chapter outlines the current state of thinking in both the active and passive approach to investing in the following order. We start with a historical perspective on the evolution of investment thought. We go through the basics of free cash flow discounting in stock valuation – something any entrant into investment banking must know, and should have learnt in college, and then switch to the Modern Portfolio Theory of stock diversification. We end with "post-modern" multifactor index and algorithmic models, and defer the discussion of alpha (reward for active skill) vs. beta (reward for factor risk) to Chapter 12 on hedge funds. Hedge funds span passive and active investing. They often aim for alpha, but end up with beta.

11.1 A BRIEF HISTORY OF INVESTMENT THOUGHT

In February 1637, a single bulb of a tulip sold for 10 times the annual wage of a skilled artisan. In 1720, investors in the South Sea Company – a chartered monopolist in the trade with the Western Hemisphere – lost huge amounts amount of money as the company failed. Japanese investors bought the Rockefeller Center in New York for $1 billion in 1990. In 1995, the Rockefeller Center went bankrupt and sold for $0.5 billion. Apple Computer traded at $13 in 1996, got up to $101.25 and split 2-for-1 at the height of the tech bubble in June 2000, then dropped back to $14 in 2002. Then the near dead company reinvented itself with its revolutionary iPhone, iPad, on-line music, and video delivery. The stock closed at $348.48 on January 14, 2011.

The first exposition of a rational investment philosophy is Benjamin Graham's *Security Analysis* (Graham, with Dodd, 1934, 2008) followed by *The Intelligent Investor* (Graham, with Dodd, 1948, 2003). Graham, the father of value investing, attempted to define what an investment is, provided the first reference to the active and passive style, and drew distinction between the short-term fluctuation and fundamental value. A worthwhile investment was one whose price was lower than the "intrinsic value" providing a "margin of safety." The investor's job was to do the right analysis to come up with this intrinsic value, ignore "Mr. Market" offering to buy or sell shares at irrational prices, and wait to buy it at the right price. Graham excoriated corporations for the opacity of the financial reporting and non-dividend payment.

The challenge to Graham's somewhat active value investing came first with Harry Markowitz's (Modern) Portfolio Theory (Markowitz, 1952), later morphed into the Treynor–Sharpe–Lintner Capital Asset Pricing Model (CAPM) of the early 1960s (see Treynor, 1961). According to Markowitz, active investing made no sense. Stock markets were efficient valuation machines. Investors had no chance to uncover mispricing or the mispricing has been taken out by the active investors. The best strategy was to rely on the correlation effect to form portfolios of stocks and, better still, to choose only from the portfolios on the *efficient frontier*. The efficient frontier drawn in the mean-standard deviation space offered the best combinations of risk and return to a risk-averse investor. The CAPM extended this thought by showing that under certain utility and distribution assumptions, investors will do best by allocating their investment dollars between a money market fund and the cap-weighted portfolio of the entire market (rather than other portfolios on the efficient frontier). This has become known as the *two-fund separation* theorem. Furthermore, if all investors choose to diversify and index, the specific risk has no value. The way stocks are priced in the market is by their degree of *systematic risk*. It is not total risk (standard deviation), but systematic risk (*beta*) that enters the expected return that investors demand on the stock and therefore the price they pay for it.

While the theory was extremely appealing, the practice was not. Tests showed very low R^2s in explaining the stock markets variation; the theory had no time dimension for estimation. Violations of the efficient market hypothesis (EMH), which effectively ruled out active investing as foolish, did not help. Why would you index if you could make money on Mondays or in January? Improvements ranged from theoretical (e.g. include consumption in the definition of the market portfolio) to practical (e.g. time-changing betas, leverage-adjusted betas). Ross (1976) published his arbitrage pricing theory (APT) which introduced the notion of stock portfolios as additional priced systematic risk factors, but more than anything started the search for the missing systematic factors. A California company, BARRA, started providing factor data and portfolio optimization services. Yet the inclusion of observable macroeconomic variables (GDP, inflation, yield curve shape) as risk factors in the models largely failed. It was not until Fama and French (1996) introduced their three-factor model that non-theoretical index modeling took off. In addition, to the market portfolio Fama and French included two firm-specific characteristics: size and book-to-market value. The loadings (betas) on these factors proved to be persistent components of a stock's expected rate of return. Carhart (1997) added one more cross-sectional common factor: momentum. These three- and four-factor specifications delivered super-high R^2s in the regression tests of the models. At the same time, researchers embarked on adding higher moments (co-variance, co-skewness, co-kurtosis) instead of additional factors to the asset-pricing models with some success.

However, the bigger parallel thought revolution started back in the late 1970s and the 1980s. The salvos came from experimental psychology. The very basic assumptions of investor rationality began to be questioned. And investors were not rational, but diverse, the representative agent models that allowed generalizing microeconomic behavior and choices to the entire market, started to collapse. Kahneman and Tversky (1979) offered that investors were not risk-averse, but loss-averse. Did mean-variance modeling make sense then? Thaler documented many behavioral inconsistencies with the rationality assumptions throughout the 1980s, and eventually put them into summary books (Thaler, 1991, 1992). The irrationalities came in two streams: common errors people make when processing information and in behavioral biases affecting decision making. Many behavioral finance irrationalities were consistent with the stock market behavior and provided alternative explanations of observed phenomena. Earnings announcement drifts and reversals perhaps had to do with small sample representativeness bias and not information leakage. Underperformance of high P/E stocks could be explained by forecasting errors. Value stock risk premium could be explained by regret avoidance combined with mental accounting as investors shunned unpopular stocks, focused on individual stocks not portfolios, became more risk-averse, and applied higher discount rates to recently underperforming stocks.

The 1980s also saw a revival of active investing. Value Line continued to be a popular and widely studied source of stock picks. In 1989, Peter Lynch, Fidelity Magellan's manager, published his book in which he espoused a very simple philosophy of "investing in what you know" (Lynch, with Rothchild, 1989). He also posed that well-informed observant individuals may be better stock pickers than Wall Street fund managers. They go through their personal lives and business lives and can spot good investments before optimization obsessed fund managers. Lynch's favorite stock picking metric was the PEG (price earnings growth) ratio. The idea is that if a firm is growing, its P/E ratio will grow.

Many of the behaviors identified by the behaviorists have practical life implications. Framing can lead to the wrong asset allocation or unconsciously opting out of tax-advantaged accounts. Overconfidence can lead to high turnover and poor returns. Yet it is not clear that if a certain percentage of the population is afflicted with these failings and biases, then the marginal investor who dictates the prices is subject to them. The counter-revolution in behavioral economics started almost as soon as the behavioral explanations of market phenomena started multiplying, e.g. to include the gloominess of the Nordics due to the lack of sun. Rationality got a second look. Expanded models based on rationality countered many behavioral claims. Perhaps it is not behavior, but market frictions, taxes, leverage and regulation that dictate price behavior.

Whether one subscribes to the behavioral critique or not, the main trend in investment modeling that can certainly be identified is the move away from theory-based models toward statistical models. Factor and index models do not have to justify utility assumptions; all they need to do is show out-of-sample strategy profits. Momentum can simply be accepted as a fact of life, whether as an informational/microstructure phenomenon, or an outcome of behavioral irrationality. The second trend in developing trading algorithms is the use of accounting data (asset growth, capital expenditure, etc.) superimposed on a three- or four-factor model to extract the extra "alpha." The last trend is in "black box" tactical allocation modeling. One overarching development is that of model engines that allow one to combine historical information with some distributional priors or implied inputs and customizing the optimization to one's need. This is not a neural network – that idea has largely failed too – but rather a simpler philosophy that some things are easier estimated (risk) than others (mean returns). The idea goes back to the Black–Litterman model developed at Goldman Sachs (Black and Litterman, 1992). The objective is to combine the historical estimation of the inputs to the portfolio optimization with the realization that the world is changing. In Bayesian statistics that means starting with a prior, superimposing a view and developing a posterior. Asset classes are selected as inputs, and many customized constraints can be imposed. The outcome is an optimized portfolio suited to the client's needs.

11.2 FREE CASH FLOW VALUATION OF COMPANIES

The value of any security is equal to the present value of its cash flows. The value of the bond is the PV of the coupon annuity plus the PV of the principal. The value of the option is the PV of the contingent payout it might pay. The value of a real estate investment is the PV of the rent we may get minus expenses plus the PV of the future price we may sell for net of the initial price plus costs.

The value[1] of the stock (company) is equal to the discounted value of its cash flows. But there are problems with this definition:

- What are the cash flows for a stock? Dividends, earnings, cash position?
- How do we handle the perpetual nature of the stock, no principal and unending uneven cash flow?
- At what rate do we discount?
- Is there an extra value to the voting right?

A good way to proceed is to draw a contrast to bonds. In bonds, the numerator variables are known: coupons and face. In stocks, they are unknown (literally, they depend on the success of the company) and undefined (dividends? What if the company does not pay dividends, but reinvests?). First, we solve the second problem. We have three potential definitions of the numerator cash flows:

- Dividends paid to equity holders only
- FCFE – Free cash flow to equity holders only
- FCFF – Free cash flow to the firm's claimants, both debt and equity.

We will come back to the precise definitions of these. Each of these could grow, decline, or go up and down, over time. To each of these variables, we attach a variable that describes their changing nature. For convenience, we assume geometric growth; so we will start with the best estimate for the current year, denoted with the subscript 1, and then we assume a percentage change per year, g. If the growth pattern is uneven, we can handle it by dividing the future into life stages and discounting those separately. That is an easy problem.

What about the perpetual nature of the stock? The company may last forever, or fold, or be sold in a few years. How many cash flows are we going to get? No problem. Let's think like a real estate investor. If I buy the apartment to hold for 5 years, I will get rent for 5 years and then sell the apartment. Conditional on today's information about real estate, how much should I expect for the apartment in 5 years? The next investor will buy it from me, improve it, and hold it for 7 years and then sell to the next one. In effect, when I buy today, I am buying my cash flows, the next investor's cash flows, and the next's. Then in 5 years, I sell the PV of the rest of the cash flows to the next investor; then in 7 years, he sells the PV of the remaining cash flows. It does not matter what holding horizon we assume, 5 years, 10, or perpetual. The discounting should produce the same value today equal to the PV of the cash flows to infinity.

[1] We will use the term fundamental value or intrinsic value interchangeably.

At what rate do we discount? That depends on what we discount. Dividends and FCFEs are paid to equity holders, so they should be discounted with the cost of equity. Dividends are paid only if the management declares them; FCFE is defined irrespective of that as the cash flow before any reinvestment/dividend decision. We will discount them at the same rate, in effect giving the right to vote a zero value. We will rely on the argument that the price per share is the same to the controlling and small stock holders, and the controlling ones act in the interest of all.

FCFFs are paid to both debt and equity holders. They include interest paid on the debt, any repayment of debt, dividend and any stock repurchases. They should be discounted by the WACC – the weighted-average cost of capital. If the company has preferred stock, we include their cost in the WACC calculation.

The cost of debt is relatively easy to figure out. Look up the yield currently paid by the company on all its outstanding debt. The interest rate the company pays has to do with the default-free level of interest rates (government curve) plus the default premium related to the company's credit standing. The total is relatively easy to observe. The concept of the cost of equity sounds a bit more nebulous, but need not be. It is equal to the cost of equity for the entire stock market plus the risk premium for our company based on its sensitivity to the systematic risk factors. We cover the details in the next section. The main thing we need to be conscious of at all times is the old Miller–Modigliani argument of no free tradeoffs of the leverage changes. The company could load up on relatively cheap short-term debt. Should we use a lower WACC rate to discount FCFFs? Miller and Modigliani say no. The increased leverage makes the cost of equity (and long-term debt) go up and the average cost stays the same, tax considerations excluded. So, before we proceed with the actual valuation techniques, the last word of caution is: beware of false precision. The cost of capital is an estimate. The numerator cash flows are estimates. Stock valuation is not a relative value, but an absolute value technique, therefore it involves:

- the voodoo art of predicting the future prospects of the company: g;
- the inexact accounting science of defining the cash flow, D, $FCFE$ or $FCFF$;
- the inexact science of modeling the cost of equity, r_E, and by extension $WACC$; and
- the exact science of doing the discounting right.

11.2.1 Free Cash Flow Definitions

In order to understand deeply the cash flow definitions, we review the construction of the company's accounting statements. We focus primarily on the flow statements: the income statement (I/S) and the cash flow statement, also known as the "sources and uses" statement. Even for a small or an upstart company, where we simply try to estimate future cash profits, it pays to run things through the accounting logic to make sure we don't miss any tax, accrual, or reinvestment variables. Let us take the perspective of a manufacturing or service company, not a financial one.

Consider the I/S for ABC Corp for the ending fiscal year 2011 in Table 11.1. The top half of the I/S deals with ongoing operations. We subtract direct and indirect costs from sales revenue, then we subtract the depreciation allowance for the deteriorating production capacity. EBIT represents our first estimate of the health of our operations. Bear in mind that a lot of accrual thinking goes into the seemingly innocuous variables like revenue or costs. What do we do with a 5-year sales contract that combines manufactured product delivery with consulting services

Table 11.1 The income statement of ABC Corp. for 2011. Amounts in $ millions

Revenue	$10,000
– Cost of goods sold (CoGS)	– 4,000
– Administrative and selling expenses	– 1,000
Earnings before interest, taxes and depreciation (EBITDA)	5,000
– Depreciation expense (DEP)	– 1,000
Earnings before interest and taxes (EBIT)	4,000
– Interest expense (INT)	– 1,000
Earnings before taxes (EBT) = Taxable income	3,000
– Tax	– 900
Net income (NI) = Earnings	$2,100

that is paid for over a 7-year period with partial money-back guarantee? The product took 3 years to develop. Accountants have capitalized some of the costs, expensed some others, and booked some revenue before it was actually received.

The bottom half of the I/S has to do with the financing and tax costs to non-equity claimants: interest expense and taxes; the latter computed independently according to cash accrual rules of the tax code. The net income number is a blend of some real and accrued revenues and expenses, a non-cash arbitrary depreciation allowance and some financing cost. Omitted financing cost includes any repayment of debt or new refinancing. There is no accounting for new investments on the I/S.

The simplified sources and uses statement in Table 11.2 attempts to provide the missing information. It takes a decidedly cash as opposed to accrual perspective. It is divided into three sections seeking to explain the cash from operations, investment and financing.

The purpose of the first section is the same as of the top of the income statement, but on the cash basis. So we add back the unreal depreciation expense and make adjustments for short-term trade financing we provided or enjoyed, financing for inventories and work-in-progress. In Table 11.2, the ABC Corp freed cash by liquidating $500 worth of inventory or accounts receivable, but it used cash to pay off additional $1,000 of accounts payable perhaps because its suppliers tightened their payment terms. The combined increase in current assets minus the increase in current liabilities is called the change in the net working capital (ΔNWC). For ABC, it is equal to +$500 for 2010.

Table 11.2 The cash flow statement of ABC Corp for 2011. Amounts in $ millions

Net income (NI)		$ 2,100
+ Depreciation expense (*DEP*)		+ 1,000
– Increases in current assets		+ 500
+ Increases in current liabilities		– 1,000
Cash flow from operations	$ 2,600	
– Increases in gross fixed assets (*CAPEX*)		– 1,000
– Investments		– 500
Cash flow from investments	– 1,500	
+ Increases in long-term liabilities ($\Delta DEBT$)		+ 1,000
– Dividends (D)		– 700
Cash flow from financing	+ 300	
Net cash	$ 1,400	

The second section covers investments in capital (fixed) assets (*CAPEX*), or their disposal, and investments in other companies. ABC bought \$1,000 worth of new plant equipment and made a \$500 investment in a joint venture in China in 2011. The additions and subtractions in this section are made irrespective of how these purchases were financed. The *CAPEX* variable should in principle include only the maintenance portion and not new growth-oriented capital expenditures (often not separated out in the statements).

The third section deals with long-term financing. Interest had already been subtracted to arrive at net income. Here we add new financing obtained or subtract any debt repaid. We also subtract the dividends paid or stock repurchases. In 2011, ABC issued \$1,000 of new lease bonds (to finance equipment?) and paid \$700 in dividends. The bottom line of the cash flow statement corresponds to the change in the cash position reported on ABC's balance sheet for the end of 2011 relative to the beginning balance.

The FCFF and FCFE definitions share the philosophy of the cash flow statement. For FCFF, we start with the net income number and make adjustments to it to arrive at the best estimate of the cash flow available to the debt and equity claimants from operations, after making operations-related investments decisions, and before we make any strategic growth-related reinvestment and financing decisions. For FCFE, we further adjust the estimate by taking into account changes in the company's long-term financing position. For FCFF, since we add back interest, we make an adjustment for the lost tax shield (if we were to not incur interest, we would not save on the tax deduction).

Here is the formal definition of the FCFF.

$$FCFF = EBIT(1-\tau) + DEP - CAPEX - NWC$$

Assuming the tax rate of $\tau = 30\%$, the FCFF for ABC for 2011 was:

$$FCFF_0 = \$2,800 + 1,000 - 1,000 - 500 = \$2,300$$

The formal definition of the FCFE contains the additional subtraction of long-term debt-related expenditures, interest and principal changes, net of the tax shield.

$$FCFE = FCFF - INT(1-\tau) + \Delta DEBT$$

The FCFE for ABC for 2011 was:

$$FCFE_0 = \$2,300 - 700 + 1,000 = \$2,600$$

Another way to get at the FCFE is to start with net income which nets the first terms of the two definitions, *EBIT* and *INT*, and subtracts taxes. That is, we can also write:

$$FCFE = NI + DEP - CAPEX - \Delta NWC + \Delta DEBT$$

Plugging into the equation the amounts for 2011, we get:

$$FCFE_0 = \$2,100 + 1,000 - 1,000 - 500 + 1,000 = \$2,600$$

We have computed three cash flow variables for ABC for 2010:

- $D_0 = \$700$ million
- $FCFE_0 = \$2,600$ million
- $FCFF_0 = \$2,300$ million

We have denoted them all with the time subscript zero, since they all referred to the currently ending accounting period. Note that the $FCFE_0$ for 2011 exceeds the $FCFF_0$ due to the significant increase in the company's long-term debt, hardly a sustainable situation.

Suppose we develop pro-forma income cash flow statements for 2012. We think that in the coming year, 2012, the capital expenditures (*CAPEX*) will drop to the long-term level of \$500 and the new issuance of debt ($\Delta DEBT$) will drop even further to the long-term annual refinance level of \$300. All the other variables will stay the same. The company will embark on an ambitious growth plan, but will finance most of the growth with retained earnings. In 2012 ABC plans to raise the total dividends paid to shareholders to \$750. We are forecasting for 2012:

- $D_1 = \$750$ million
- $FCFE_1 = \$2,400$ million
- $FCFF_1 = \$2,800$ million

11.2.2 Growth and the Discounting of the Cash Flows

We start with the discounting of the equity cash flows. As the next section will show, we can use the CAPM or a multifactor model to estimate the cost of equity for ABC by adding to the risk-free rate the risk premiums for the priced market factors. Suppose we use the CAPM with the inputs of the risk-free rate $r_F = 3\%$, the market $\beta = 1.25$, zero additional factor loadings, and the market risk premium $r_M - r_F = 8\%$. The equity cost of capital is:

$$r_E = r_F + \beta\,(r_M - r_F) = 3\% + 1.25 \times 8\% = 13\%$$

We are projecting the long-term growth in FCFE to average $g = 3\%$ per year. ABC has 200 million shares outstanding. Using the geometric growth assumption, the total value of the company's equity in \$ millions is:

$$EQ_0 = \frac{FCFE_1}{r_E - g} = \frac{2,400}{0.13 - 0.03} = 24,000$$

The price per share is:

$$P_0 = \$120$$

We can also approach the valuation from the dividend side. Here is how we may proceed. The company expects the total earnings for 2012 of \$2,100 million and will pay \$750 million or 35.7% out as dividends. Its *earnings retention* or *plowback ratio* can be defined as:

$$b = 64.3\%$$

It hopes to earn a long-term return on these retained earnings of $ROI = 15.5\%$. If that is the case, then it will be able to grow its dividend at an annual rate of:

$$g = b \times ROI = 0.643 \times 15.5\% = 9.964\%$$

The total value of the company's equity in \$ millions is:

$$EQ_0 = \frac{D_1}{r_E - g} = \frac{750}{0.13 - 0.09964} = 24,706$$

The price per share is:

$$P_0 = \$123.53$$

We now turn to the slightly more complicated method of pricing the total enterprise value of the company (market value of the assets as a going concern) by discounting FCFFs, and then subtracting the market value of the long-term debt to get the total value of the equity.

After some research, we estimate that the total market value of the long-term debt is \$12,500 million, most of the debt is fairly recent and trades close to par, and the average interest rate ABC pays on its long-term debt is about $r_D = 8\%$. This corresponds to the annual interest expense of \$1,000 reported on the income statement. The average stock price over the last three months has been \$125. The total equity value is about \$125 times 200 million or \$25,000 million. The company has no preferred. The company is financed with one-third debt and two-thirds equity. We estimate the after-tax weighted-average cost of capital to be:

$$WACC = \frac{DEBT}{DEBT + EQ}(1 - \tau) \times r_D + \frac{EQ}{DEBT + EQ} \times r_E$$

$$WACC = \frac{12{,}500}{12{,}500 + 25{,}000}(1 - 0.30) \times 8\% + \frac{25{,}000}{12{,}500 + 25{,}000} \times 13\% = 10.53\%$$

We estimate the long-term growth rate in FCFF to be $g = 2.75\%$. The total value of the firm's assets is:

$$V_0 = \frac{FCFF_1}{WACC - g} = \frac{2{,}800}{0.1053 - 0.0275} = 35{,}989.72$$

Subtracting the value of the debt, we get the total value the company's equity in \$ millions:

$$EQ_0 = V_0 - DEBT_0 = 35{,}989.72 - 12{,}500 = 23{,}489.72$$

The price per share is:

$$P_0 = \$117.45$$

We got three different estimates of the fundamental price of the stock: \$120, \$123.53, and \$117.45. If only we could ever get this close! Anyone involved in valuation is aware of the hours spent on reconciling accounting data, growth assumptions, and price estimates. Small changes in the growth inputs produce vastly different price estimates. The income and cash flow statements of real-life companies are never as easy to read as those of the ABC Corp. Usually they are full of extraordinary adjustments, negative earnings, one-time charges, and lots of confusing footnotes. However, giving up and simply pricing the company based on an earnings multiple is not right, or is it?

Suppose we price the value of the equity as 10 times the earnings. We assume the fair P/E multiple to be 10. The earnings are \$2,100. The total equity value is \$21,000 million and the per-share price of the stock is \$105. Using a simple P/E multiple implies using a no-growth perpetuity assumption. If we price the stock this way at \$105 and Mr. Market discounts is one day to \$85, wouldn't Benjamin Graham say that we have the required "margin of error" over the "intrinsic value"? Private equity shops that routinely quote X-times-earnings (with X usually 4 or 6) must think so.

11.2.3 Terminal Multiple Models of Cash Flow Discounting

We end with a brief review of two-stage models that avoid the difficult task of guessing the sustainable growth rate g. In the above discussion, g was given. In reality, g drives the results.

In the preceding FCFE example, changing g from 3% to 4% changes the stock price from \$120 to \$133.34. That is a big difference.

Suppose, as is common in investment banking, we are working on the pro-forma accounting statements for an acquisition/merger target. We use a percentage-of-revenue forecasting model with financing adjustments. We estimate next year's FCFE to be $FCFE_1 = \$2{,}400$ million. We project the FCFEs for the following 2 years to be $FCFE_2 = \$2{,}520$ and $FCFE_3 = \$2{,}615$. What we need is the estimate of the equity value in year 3. If we had that, we could use the following two-stage model:

$$EQ_0 = \frac{FCFE_1}{1 + r_E} + \frac{FCFE_2}{(1 + r_E)^2} + \frac{FCFE_3}{(1 + r_E)^3} + \frac{EQ_3}{(1 + r_E)^3}$$

The first three terms represent the discounted value of the cash flows that come out of our pro-forma projections. The last term represents the plug for the terminal value of the company. That terminal value represents what we think the company could trade at or be sold for 3 years from now. If we don't want to make a cash flow growth assumption beyond year 3, we can use the terminal value multiple approach. Two multiples are commonly used in investment banking. Both use the *enterprise value* as the numerator. The enterprise value, EV, is defined as:

$$EV = EQ + DEBT + PREF + MINT - CASH$$

where *PREF* is the value of the preferred, if any, *MINT* is the value of the minority interest, if any, and *CASH* is the amount of cash on the balance sheet. The two multiples are:

- *EV/REVENUE*
- *EV/EBITDA*

The latter comes with some modifications for different industries; the logic being that the denominator is supposed to be the purest measure of operating profit, free of future growth and distribution outlays, and related only to core operations. Instead of *EBITDA*, we may want to use *EBITDAR*. For pharma companies, the *R* may represent R&D (future growth investment); for airlines the *R* may represent airplane leasing revenue (side business). The "correct" multiple may be taken from "precedent transactions."

Suppose, for 2014 (3 years from now), we project the partial income statement in Table 11.3. We also estimate the *DEBT* to be \$12,865 million and $FCFE_3 = \$2{,}615$ million.

We estimate that in the last year similar companies' enterprise values were valued at 6 times the *EBITDA*. We use the multiple of 6 to estimate that

$$EV_3 = EQ_3 + DEBT_3 - CASH_3 = 6 \times EBITDA_3$$

Table 11.3 The pro-forma income statement of ABC Corp for 2014. Amounts in \$ millions

Revenue	\$ 11,600
– Cost of goods sold (CoGS)	– 4,200
– Administrative and selling expenses	– 1,000
Earnings before interest, taxes and depreciation (EBITDA)	6,400
– Depreciation expense (DEP)	– 1,200
Earnings before interest and taxes (EBIT)	5,400

Our assumptions are

$$CASH_3 = FCFE_3 = \$2615, DEBT_3 = \$12{,}865, EBITDA_3 = \$6{,}400$$

therefore:

$$EQ_3 = \$28{,}150$$

We plug into the two-stage model to get the total equity value:

$$EQ_0 = \frac{2{,}400}{1.13} + \frac{2{,}520}{1.13^2} + \frac{2{,}615}{1.13^3} + \frac{28{,}150}{1.13^3} = \$25{,}419.11$$

and the price per share:

$$P_0 = \$127.10$$

We can repeat the exercise using the $EV/REVENUE$ multiple; we can repeat the exercise using the FCFF method with WACC; we can also dig deeper into the pro-forma projections.

11.3 THE MODERN PORTFOLIO THEORY AND THE CAPM

The original modern portfolio theory (MPT), as laid out by Markowitz, and the CAPM have no time dimension. There is now, time prior to investment, and tomorrow, when we know how the investment turns out. Now the investor can work only with a probability distribution, best described by its first two moments. The mean, or expected return, measures the reward. The variance, or its cousin standard deviation, measures the risk. In MPT, standard deviation is synonymous with total risk. A stock whose price appreciates, but swings wildly up and down in the process, is considered risky. A stock whose price goes down, and swings wildly up and down in the process, is also considered risky, perhaps less risky if its standard deviation is lower.

The way to think about the time dimension is to consider a repeated gambling process. Investors choose their stocks at the beginning of each month based on their probability assessments. A month later, the future reveals itself, and the investors settle their winnings or losings. Then they place new bets for the next month. In this set-up, it still makes sense to think in terms of probabilities, means, and standard deviations. The only potential trouble is that weekly, monthly, and quarterly data will produce different samples and different relative estimates of means and standard deviations.

11.3.1 Diversification and the Efficient Frontier

We perform a simple experiment. In Table 11.4, we have collected monthly stock returns[2] for Cisco (CSCO) and Exxon Mobil (XOM) for 19 months from January 2005 to July 2006. We have added a column labeled "TBill" with a constant return of 0.2% per month. We have also added two portfolio columns. The first labeled "70/30" contains the returns on a risky–risky portfolio invested 70% in CSCO and 30% in XOM. The second labeled "60/40" contains the returns on a riskless–risky portfolio invested 40% in TBill and 60% in XOM. We compute the means and standard deviations for all investment strategies. The CSCO-XOM correlation coefficient for the period is 0.08.

[2] The table contains continuously compounded total returns including dividends.

Table 11.4 Risky–risky and riskless–risky portfolio returns

Month	CSCO	XOM	**70/30**	"TBill"	XOM	**40/60**
Jul 2006	–8.83%	9.91%	–3.21%	0.20%	9.91%	6.02%
Jun 2006	–0.77%	0.72%	–0.32%	0.20%	0.72%	0.51%
May 2006	–6.25%	–2.99%	–5.27%	0.20%	–2.99%	–1.71%
Apr 2006	–3.38%	3.57%	–1.29%	0.20%	3.57%	2.22%
Mar 2006	6.83%	2.49%	5.52%	0.20%	2.49%	1.57%
Feb 2006	8.61%	–5.01%	4.53%	0.20%	–5.01%	–2.93%
Jan 2006	8.13%	11.07%	9.01%	0.20%	11.07%	6.72%
Dec 2005	–2.42%	–3.25%	–2.67%	0.20%	–3.25%	–1.87%
Nov 2005	0.51%	3.82%	1.50%	0.20%	3.82%	2.37%
Oct 2005	–2.66%	–12.38%	–5.57%	0.20%	–12.38%	–7.35%
Sep 2005	1.69%	5.90%	2.95%	0.20%	5.90%	3.62%
Aug 2005	–8.33%	2.43%	–5.10%	0.20%	2.43%	1.54%
Jul 2005	0.37%	2.19%	0.91%	0.20%	2.19%	1.39%
Jun 2005	–1.66%	2.24%	–0.49%	0.20%	2.24%	1.42%
May 2005	11.63%	–0.94%	7.86%	0.20%	–0.94%	–0.49%
Apr 2005	–3.53%	–4.42%	–3.79%	0.20%	–4.42%	–2.57%
Mar 2005	2.66%	–6.04%	0.05%	0.20%	–6.04%	–3.54%
Feb 2005	–3.50%	20.94%	3.84%	0.20%	20.94%	12.65%
Jan 2005	–6.85%	0.66%	–4.60%	0.20%	0.66%	0.48%
Avg.	–0.41%	1.63%	0.20%	0.20%	1.63%	1.06%
St. Dev	5.85%	7.26%	4.47%	0.00%	7.26%	4.36%

Figure 11.2 shows the information graphically. In the first graph, what stands out is that, while the mean of the 70/30 portfolio is simply the average of the means, the standard the standard deviation of the 70/30 portfolio is lower than the standard deviation of either CSCO or XOM. Because of the imperfect correlation between the two stocks, we achieve risk reduction. In the second graph, both the mean and the standard deviation of the 40/60 portfolio are the averages of the individual means and standard deviations.

In MPT, the efficient frontier is a generalization of the left-hand graph in Figure 11.2 and the line we added to show where all the combinations of CSCO and XOM with varying

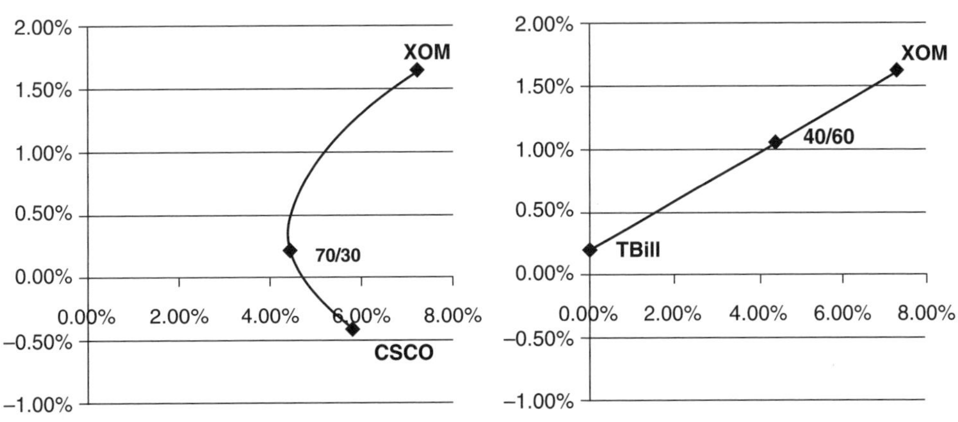

Figure 11.2 Y = mean vs X = st. deviation for risky–risky and riskless–risky portfolios

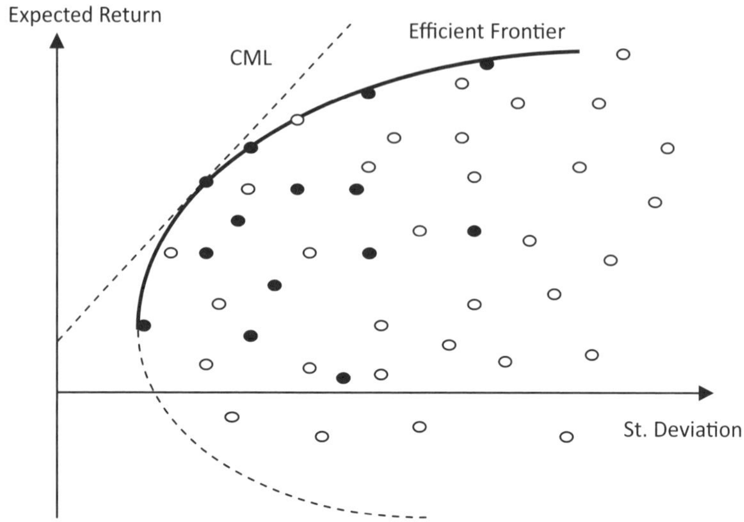

Figure 11.3 The efficient frontier of risky assets and portfolios

investment proportions would be. The efficient frontier is the locus of all the "best" stocks and all the "best" portfolios consisting of the stocks (including all combinations of stocks and all weight combinations) in the mean–standard deviation space. Because few stocks are perfectly positively correlated, we achieve diversification effects with many portfolios, moving them to the left relative to the component stocks while getting the average return. The "best" here means the lowest standard deviation for a given level of expected return and/or the highest expected return for a given level of standard deviation. Conversely, it also means that horizontally there is no combination of stocks with a lower risk for a given level of expected return than that on the frontier. Figure 11.3 shows the efficient frontier of the best risky–risky combinations drawn in the mean–standard deviation space. Stocks are portrayed as white dots, portfolios as black dots. The efficient frontier traces out the northwestern contour of the cloud containing stocks and their combinations. No rational investor chooses to put all of his money into any dot in the interior of the cloud. Rational investors choose only from the efficient frontier menu. Risk-averse investors choose the portfolios on the lower part of the frontier (lower risk), less risk-averse on the upper part (higher risk).

11.3.2 Two-Fund Separation

In Figure 11.3, we also show the locus of portfolios that are even better than those on the efficient frontier. These are labeled "CML" for the capital market line. The CML portfolios lie to the northwest of the efficient frontier. They offer even better reward-to-risk tradeoffs: lower risk for a given return or higher return for a given level of risk. However, these combinations are not risky–risky of stocks alone. These are the combinations of the risk-free asset (the T-Bill), which has zero risk and lies on the vertical axis, and of the tangent portfolio, one very special portfolio lying on the efficient frontier. The CML is the generalization of the right-hand graph of Figure 11.2 with a riskless–risky combinations lying on a straight line.

In order to achieve the best reward-to-risk tradeoff, investors must divide their money between the T-Bill and the tangent portfolio. *What is the tangent portfolio?* If all investors are risk-averse and think in mean-variance terms and all choose to diversify, then no investors choose the portfolios on the efficient frontier except for the tangent one. They combine it with the risk-free asset. All investors compute the same weights for the stocks in the preferred risky–risky part of their portfolio. If they compute the same weights, they all own a part of the same portfolio – just as if there was only one investor in the whole market called the representative agent. The agent owns a portfolio of stocks, and all the stocks are owned by someone. But there is only one investor, so that investor owns all the stocks. This simple accounting argument leads to the identification of the tangent portfolio as the capitalization-weighted portfolio of all the stocks in the market. The weights in the portfolio are simply the total dollar numbers it would take to buy all the stocks in the entire economy.

The two-fund separation theorem states that the best portfolio choices for a mean-variance investor lie on the CML and the investor does not have consider all the combinations of assets (including riskless), but can divide his job into two stages. First, based on his risk aversion he must decide where on the CML he wants to be, lower left or upper right. This decision on how many dollars to allocate to the risk-free asset and how many to the risky assets is called the asset allocation decision. Second, the investor must invest the allocated risky dollars to the cap-weighted market portfolio, and not to try to beat the market in some way. In modern financial advising, that second stage means choosing an index fund and supplementing it with non-equity asset classes to represent the entire universe of risky assets.

11.3.3 Systematic Risk and the CAPM

If all investors engage in indexing with their risky dollars, then no investors ever hold stocks individually. If they never hold stocks individually, they never experience the standard deviation risk of a stock. Investors are never exposed to the total "wiggliness" of the stock's price as this total risk is muted in their diversified portfolios. The total risk is not priced in the market, but only the portion of risk that contributes to the wiggliness of the market portfolio (which is what all investors own). In statistics we use ANOVA to break down the total variance into the explained variance and the residual variance. The total risk of the individual stock can be broken into systematic risk (explained variance) and specific risk (residual variance). The systematic portion can be thought of as coming from the common market factors; the specific portion comes from any unique risk posed by the stock's individual characteristics. If investors always form diversified portfolios, and always end up with the same overall market portfolio, then the systematic risk can further be identified as that pertaining to market portfolio risk. Since we are optimizing in mean-variance terms – which is what a regression process does (minimize sum of squared deviations from the characteristic line) – the systematic portion of the stock risk can also be precisely defined as the slope coefficient of the regression of a security's excess returns on the market portfolio's excess return. The excess return, or the risk premium, is defined as the difference between the return and the risk-free return. Statistically, the total return (variance) can be broken into two parts:

$$\sigma_i^2 = \beta_i^2 \times \sigma_m^2 + \sigma_e^2$$

where β_i is the slope of the regression, σ_i^2 is stock i's variance, σ_m^2 is the market (portfolio) variance, and σ_e^2 is the residual variance. If we divide both sides by the total σ_i^2, then we get the breakdown in percentage terms. The R^2 of a regression is the percentage of explained variation.

The CAPM model is the representation of the two-fund separation principle and the ANOVA logic applied to stock pricing. It relates the random variables r_i, the individual stock returns to the risk-free rate, and the random variable r_m, the market portfolio return. It states that the expected excess returns on the individual stocks in the markets are not driven by the total risks of the stocks, but are proportional to the systematic risk β_i only. The proportionality factor is the expected excess return on the overall market portfolio, also known as the market risk premium.

The CAPM equation is:

$$E[r_i] = r_F + \beta_i \times (E[r_M] - r_F)$$

The best way to think about this equation is that it is a relative value statement about the investors' confluence of beliefs about the long-term expected return on each stock or portfolio of stocks. That long-term mean return is proportional to the response parameter β_i which multiplies the overall return on the total stock market. Diversifying investors do not expect that a stock will return 600% annually if it is highly correlated with the stock index and only mildly more volatile, and they expect the market to return 10%. Instead they use the regression slope coefficient:

$$\beta_i = \rho_i \times \frac{\sigma_i^2}{\sigma_M^2}$$

to relate individual stock returns to the overall market returns. ρ_i denotes the correlation of the individual stock returns to the market portfolio return. The CAPM equation also states that investors expect a zero alpha over time – that is, in the rearranged equation,

$$E[r_i] - r_F = \beta_i \times (E[r_M] - r_F)$$

there is no intercept term on the right-hand side.

Figure 11.4 shows the CAPM graphically. In the mean-beta space, the CAPM equation is represented by the straight Security Market Line (SML). Ex ante, prior to investing, all stocks and risky portfolios lie on the CML. Stocks do not have a positive alpha and lie above the line, or have negative alpha and lie below the line. Stocks with low betas are defensive. As the market moves up and down, they wiggle very little. Stocks with high betas are aggressive. As the market moves up and down, they wiggle a lot.

11.3.4 Using the CAPM as a Stock Screen to Discover Alpha

While the CAPM is the result of a neat theory of diversification, it can be used as a simple screen of under- or overpriced individual stocks. We compute the CAPM-expected returns on stocks and compare them to the implied rates of return based on some fundamental analysis of cash flows. We are looking for Benjamin Graham's "margin of error" on top of a "fair return."

Suppose we are looking at three stocks with the following characteristics in the first four columns of Table 11.5.

The risk-free rate is 3% and the market risk premium is 6.5%. In column 5, we compute the CAPM-"warranted" returns. In column 6, we compute the expected return based on the constant-growth fundamental valuation model of Section 11.2.2 using the recent prices in

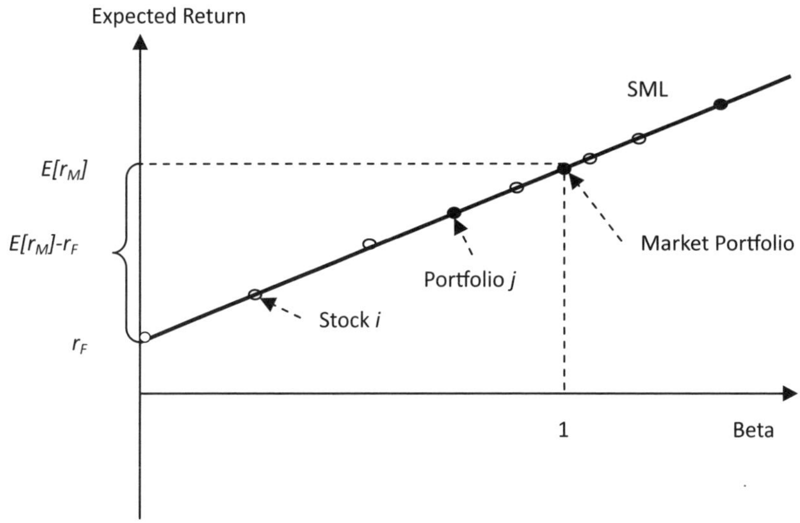

Figure 11.4 The CAPM security market line (SML)

column 7. Column 8 contains the "fair" price based on the fundamental discounting of FCFE using the CAPM discount rate. Column 9 contains a proxy for the price/earnings ratio.

Stock A's recent price is very low relative to the cash flow and the growth rate we estimate for the stock. The implied return on the stock, given the recent price, is high. The stock is "underpriced." Stock B's recent price is high relative to the cash flow and growth rate; the resulting implied return is lower than that appropriate for the level of risk. Stock C appears to be mildly underpriced with CAPM and cash flow-implied returns close to each other. Note also that the traditional value investing based on P/E ratios would produce a similar screen favoring A over C. However, in our analysis A is a high growth stock, and B is a low growth stock.

Figure 11.5 shows graphically our stock selection analysis.

Admittedly, our analysis is a bit naïve and relies heavily on the estimates of earnings, cash flows, and growth rates. Philosophically, it is, however, identical to the many "rigorous" analyses advertised by financial advisers and asset managers. Theirs is perhaps strengthened by the use of a multifactor systematic model paired with additional fundamental selection parameters (revenue growth, R&D expenditure, CAPEX, etc.) which further support the cash flow and growth estimates. It is certainly not less rigorous than the blind P/E ratio-based selection.

Table 11.5 CAPM-based stock screen

1 Stock	2 Beta	3 FCFE/shr	4 Growth	5 CAPM ret	6 Implied ret	7 Recent price	8 Fair price	9 P/FCFE
A	1.10	$ 4.50	5%	10.15%	14.00%	$ 50.00	$ 87.38	11
B	0.93	$ 2.45	3%	9.05%	8.16%	$ 47.50	$ 40.50	19
C	1.33	$ 11.20	6%	11.65%	11.79%	$ 193.25	$ 198.23	17

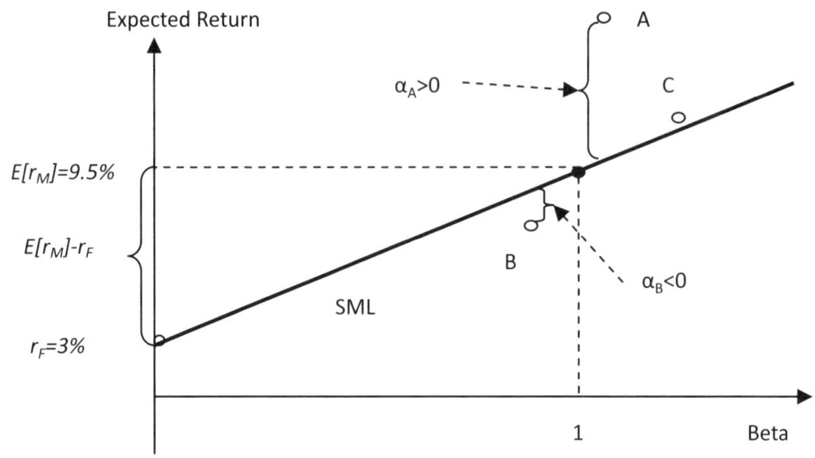

Figure 11.5 A stock screen using the CAPM

11.4 MULTIFACTOR INDEX MODELS

The CAPM model is very elegant, but untestable as it is an *ex ante* statement about the means of stock returns based on tight utility (risk aversion) and/or distributional (normality) assumptions. If we are not interested in a general equilibrium theory, but simply want to discover what works statistically, then why not just regress stock returns on a bunch of variables to see what works? That is exactly what index modeling is.

In the 1970s, researchers ran tests of the CAPM and generally became dissatisfied with the low explanatory power of the model and persistent positive intercepts. Broadening the definition of the market portfolio to include other assets and consumption, and allowing for time-changing betas did not help much. In 1975, BARRA launched its equity analysis platform allowing users to use a multifactor framework to decompose stock returns. However, the addition of macroeconomic factors (GDP, yield curve, inflation) did not lead to significantly improved results. One last attempt at elegant theory came in 1986 from Stephen Ross in the form of the arbitrage pricing theory (APT) that relied on the spanning principle of factor analysis. The intuition goes as follows. If we have 8,000 stocks then at most we have 8,000 risk factors. What if we form various portfolios of those stocks and discover that a few of these portfolios, when used as independent regression variables, explain most of the stock variation? Ross was able to show that a three-factor specification

$$r_i - r_f = \alpha_i + \beta_{i1}(f_1 - r_f) + \beta_{i2}(f_2 - r_f) + \beta_{i3}(f_3 - r_f) + \tilde{e}$$

could explain close to 95% of the variance. The β_{in}'s are the risk loadings for stock i on factor n. Each stock's excess return is decomposed into the risk premiums on three common factors. The main trouble with the APT which doomed it from the beginning was the fact that the factors were not identified as some macro variables, but were portfolios of stocks that did not resemble anything intuitive.

11.4.1 The Fama–French Three-Factor Model

Fama and French (1996) proposed the following index model for US stock returns:

$$r_i - r_f = \alpha_i + \beta_{i1}(r_M - r_f) + \beta_{i2}(r_{small} - r_{big}) + \beta_{i3}(r_{highB/V} - r_{lowB/V}) + \tilde{e}$$

The model exhibits R^2's above 90% for a variety of historical periods. What is new is the identification of the factors. It is somewhat surprising that the factors are not macroeconomic variables, but relate to innate characteristics of the stocks (which perhaps subsume macroeconomics?). The first factor is the cap-weighted market index; factors 2 and 3 are long/short-sorted portfolios. They are built by sorting all the stocks from the first to the last, dividing them into deciles (top 10%, second 10%, . . ., tenth 10%), forming cap-weighted portfolios for the top and bottom 10%, and subtracting the bottom (shorting) from the top (long). The sorting criterion for factor 1 is the size of the company defined by total capitalization and we sort from the smallest to the largest. The sorting criterion for factor 2 is the book-to-market value ratio, and we sort from the highest to the lowest. Once the portfolios are formed for any given historical period (say last 5 years of monthly data), we regress individual excess stock returns on the three factors to estimate the factor loadings (betas).

Fama and French publish the data for the factors and distribute the factor realizations through the CRSP database widely used in academia. On French's website, as of the end of April 2011, one could find the following factor realizations for the trailing 12 months:

$$\begin{aligned} r_M - r_f &= 18.82\% \\ r_{small} - r_{big} &= 4.36\% \\ r_{highB/V} - r_{lowB/V} &= -8.73\% \end{aligned}$$

The market excess return was 18.82%. The smallest stocks outperformed the biggest by 4.36% and the high book-to-market companies trailed the low book-to-market companies by 8.73%. Fama and French have an association with Dimensional Fund Advisors of Austin, Texas.

There is no solid theory as to why size or book value should be priced systematic factors. One story sometimes told in support of alternative weighting is that cap-weighting overweights large caps and underweights growth, and the two additional factors correct for that. An alternative story told from the perspective of the reward for risk is that small size and high book value pose additional risks to survivability and additional value creation.

11.4.2 The Carhart Fourth Factor: the Momentum

Carhart (1997) added the fourth systematic factor related to the momentum. "Momentum" intuitively refers to the increased likelihood of a positive return following a positive return and a negative following a negative return. In the popularly used factor database available from Kenneth French, the momentum factor is defined as follows. Form six portfolios as the intersection of two metrics: two sorted size groups (Big and Small, demarcated by the median NYSE size) and three sorted return groups (past 12 month) portfolios (High, Mid, and Low, demarcated by the 30th and 70th percentiles). Then average the good recent returns across Big and Small and average the poor recent performance across Big and Small to compute, for each month, the difference of the two:

$$r_{MOM} = (r_{Small\,High} + r_{Big\,High})/2 - (r_{Small\,Low} + r_{Big\,Low})/2$$

Then regress individual returns to obtain individual stock loadings on r_{MOM}. Note that each month the formed portfolios will contain different stocks. The factor loading for a stock can be interpreted as a response function to recent winners minus losers, irrespective of which stocks they are.

11.4.3 International Index Factors

Fama and French make available factor data for international stocks that belong to the MSCI EAFE index. For each country, they construct risk factor value-weighted portfolios based on book-to-market, earnings-to-price, cash earnings-to-price, and dividend-to-price ratios. They also construct international index portfolios where the factor portfolios are weighted by the country EAFE weights.

While the CAPM theory is a bit thorny for several reasons (like the definition of risk-free and monetary numeraire), there is nothing stopping anyone from constructing optimal global stock portfolios based on one factor – global market index – or many factors. There are some hurdles to overcome when dealing with international data, like dual shareholding classes and float-to-total cap, which complicate the definitions of the universe of risky assets. Also, generally speaking, the availability of trustworthy clean data outside of the USA and Europe, and a few other countries, is quite poor, but improving.

11.5 FUNDAMENTAL INDEXING

The last 10 years have ushered in a new trend in indexing. Instead of the traditional self-rebalancing cap weighting model, several funds shifted to alternatives in designing their diversified portfolios. In general, the use of any stock-weighting method other than cap-weighting is called fundamental indexing. The two most popular of these schemes are equal weighting and dividend weighting, followed by earnings, revenues, free cash flows, book equity, and composites thereof. Why is there such an interest?

In the CAPM theory, one of the critical assumptions is that every investor (if he or she is mean-variance "rational" or subject to certain "rational" utility function) will choose the market portfolio. This uniform behavior will dictate that the best portfolio is a cap-weighted set of all risky securities. The world isn't so neat. Some asset classes are illiquid; riskless assets are different for investors in different part of the globe. Not everyone indexes; perhaps there is value to be discovered. According to Rob Arnott of Research Affiliates, a firm that offers several fundamental index ETFs, cap-weighting overweights overpriced stocks and underweights underpriced stocks. The three- and four-factor index models seem to state that in addition to the cap market portfolio, size, book value, and momentum matter. Simple cap weighting may not be the optimal method for a passive investor trying to capture reward for systematic risk. To index properly, a passive investor would have holdings of portfolios mimicking all systematic factors. Is fundamental indexing an attempt to build such investable vehicles in one fell swoop? While there is no convincing research to show how fundamental indexing relates to the priced risk factors, the intuition points to the possibility that fundamental indexing is related to capturing, in a haphazard way, the exposure to the other factors. Or perhaps the index model's factors are haphazard (only imperfectly rotated from the true factors), and fundamental indexing captures the true factors better.

11.5.1 A Brief History of Fundamental Indexing

Burton Malkiel and John Bogle, the founder of Vanguard, have not budged one bit in their strong support of cap indexing since the 1970s (see Malkiel, 1973). The self-maintaining cap weighting is the cheapest way to replicate the performance of the entire stock market. Stocks that go up increase their weight in the index; stocks that go down decrease their weight in the index. Theoretically, the portfolio manager offering an index fund has to do nothing beyond administer the fund, collect dividends and update the shareholding for splits. The only maintenance and turnover come from constructing a narrower index (only 500 stocks) and cost optimization by not holding all the required stocks and incurring a tracking error. However, if all the stocks represent all the systematic risks in the economy, then one should hold all the stocks.

In 2003, Rydex/SGI offered to investors the first equal-weighted index of S&P 500 stocks under the ticker RSP. The same year, iShares (originally owned by Barclays, currently owned by BlackRock) launched the first dividend-weighted index ETF of top 100 US stocks under the ticker DVY. In 2005 and 2006, Research Affiliates offered several fundamentally-weighted indexes of US stocks under the PowerShares family. Wisdom Tree launched their fundamental-weighted ETFs in 2006. Since then, all of these providers have created or are working on funds and ETFs reweighting international markets, country indexes and sub-indexes, and industrial sectors. For example, in the global stock space, DEM is an ETF tracking a dividend yield rank-weighted index of emerging market stocks. It covers stocks from Asia, Eastern Europe, and Latin America with weights based on their dividends. In the US space, DLS is small-cap dividend weighted, DIM is mid-cap dividend weighted, and DLN is large-cap dividend weighted. The innovation in the ways indexing can be done efficiently continues apace.

One potential drawback of alternative indexing is portfolio turnover. The general expense ratios for equal and fundamental-indexed funds hover around 0.4–0.5%, while cap indexing is generally under 0.2% for most of the developed country stock markets. However, because this way of indexing is not self-sustaining (cap weighting is), the fundamental-indexed ETFs have double the turnover and potentially higher cap gains distributions than cap-weighted ones.

11.5.2 Fundamental Indexing and Rebalancing

One important feature of the fundamental-indexed funds is their scheduled rebalancing. In defining a cap-weighting index, no one asks how often the fund manager rebalances to maintain the composition of the portfolio. It does not matter; the fund rebalances itself except for unusual situations of stocks merging, dropping out of the index, etc. This is not so with equal or fundamental-indexed funds. The frequency of rebalancing is dictated by the compromise between the desire to maintain the index weights and to avoid transaction costs and turnover. Most of the time, the funds are rebalanced quarterly.

Consider SPY, the SPDR cap-weighted index of the top 500 US stocks, and RSP, the Rydex equal-weighted index of the same universe of stocks. To start with, RSP overweights in smaller stocks and underweights in the largest stocks relative to SPY. As some stocks go up, and some go down, SPY does nothing, while RSP sells the winners and buys the (relative or absolute) losers.

Two facts, well documented by the US stock research, jump to mind. First, small stocks outperform large over time; small stocks have higher standard deviations. Second, stocks exhibit short-term momentum and long-term reversals. The automatic rebalancing built into

Table 11.6 Fundamentally indexed and narrow sector ETFs in the USA as of March 31, 2011

Fund Name	Ticker	Category	Size ($mil)
Rydex S&P Equal Weight	RSP	S&P 500 Equal Weight	3,002
Rydex Russell 1,000 Equal Weight	EWRI	Russell 1,000 Equal Weight	8
WisdomTree Earnings 500	EPS	S&P 500 Earnings Weighted	5
WisdomTree LargeCap Dividend	DLN	Dividend Weight	594
RevenueShares LargeCap	RWL	Revenue Weight	221
PowerShares FTSE RAFI US1,000	PRF	Book, Cash Flow, Sales, Divs Idx	1,110
WisdomTree Intnl SmallCap Dividend Idx	DLS	Intnational Sm Dividend-Weight	476
WisdomTree Intnl MidCap Dividend Idx	FDSFX	Intnational Mid Dividend-Weight	158
Guggenheim China Small Cap	HAO	China Small Cap	377
Market Vectors Junior Gold Miners	GDXJ	Narrow Sector	2,340
United States Commodity Idx	USCI	14 of 27 Commodity Futures	324
iShares Dow Jones Select Dividend	DVY	100 Top US Dividend	5,960

the equal-weight fund can potentially be a way to bet on these statistics and take advantage of reversals. The overweighting in small caps (actually small large caps) can also contribute to the relative outperformance of these indexes. We may not be overperforming, but rather being compensated for increased risk.

EWRI is a US stock ETF equally weighted in sectors. It is well documented that it is not small-vs-large or value-vs-growth, but actually the industrial sector variation that accounts for most over- or underperformance of a portfolio relative to the index. The appeal of the EWRI is the sector rebalancing. EPS is an earnings-weighted ETF of US stocks. Earnings and cap weightings are closely related reflecting the earnings discounting philosophy of stock valuation. PRF is based on a composite of Research Affiliates fundamental metrics. Let us hope they have picked the right ones.

11.5.3 Tactical Asset Allocation

This section is deliberately one paragraph long. Tactical asset allocation is active investing with passive (sector, country, asset class) ETF vehicles relying on a black-box allocation tool. It is a religion: if you believe in the statistical or man-biased crystal ball inside the black-box because it performed miracles in the past, or an adviser talks you into it, you go for it. The fundamental indexing crystal ball is mechanical and 100% transparent. The real unanswered question is: are both the result of statistical data mining into the past to see what worked and offer no guidance for the future? And how different is that from a four-factor index model?

11.5.4 Fundamentally Indexed US Funds

Here is a sample of retail fundamentally indexed funds trading on US exchanges as of March 2011. They are in no particular order, just what I found interesting scouring press coverage; some funds are not fundamentally indexed but offer strangely narrow market focus. Table 11.6 contains the list with the size of the fund. Table 12.3, at the end of Chapter 12, contains a similar random list of retail funds attempting hedge fund replication. Buyer beware!

12

Hedge Funds: Alpha, Beta, and Strategy Indexes

Hedge funds are investment funds that are lightly regulated, open only to institutional or qualified (satisfying minimum wealth requirements) investors, with limited liquidity (quarterly or annual redemptions), and charging performance fees. The fee structure is typically 2% plus 20%, meaning 2% of assets under management plus 20% of profits. Both numbers can be higher or lower. The 20% performance incentive fee may be subject to high *water marking*, i.e. requiring the fund to make up losses first. As of 2010, the hedge fund industry is estimated to have over \$1.5 trillion in assets under management with perhaps as many as 8,000 funds in operation. The largest operators of hedge funds include J.P. Morgan Chase, Bridgewater Associates, Paulson & Co., Soros Fund Management, and D.E. Shaw Group, each in the \$25–55 billion range.

Hedge funds are said to be a type of alternative investment. The definition of what constitutes an alternative investment asset class is unclear and combines some legal, access, and strategy aspects of investing. Retail mutual funds are regulated. They must satisfy strict disclosure, redemption, and investment rules; and their behavior is largely constrained to long investments in stocks, bonds, and ETFs. Hedge funds can easily pursue short or neutral strategies, can use derivatives extensively to express their value views, can change strategies over time, and have limited redemption privileges. Institutions, rather than individuals, are the natural investors in hedge funds. Other alternative investments share these characteristics. Figure 12.1 shows a recent approximate breakdown of alternative investments out of the total investment dollars.

Hedge funds pursue a great variety of investment strategies. These can be classified according to the style (macro, directional, event-driven, managed futures), market (equity, fixed income, commodity, currency), industry (technology, pharma, emerging markets), instrument vehicles (long/short, options, futures, swaps), stated exposure (directional, neutral), or selection method (discretionary, quant, statistical). No matter how you slice it, none of the promised return from a hedge fund can come without risk. The principle is always relative value with the big question of how relative. A global macro fund buying German bonds and selling British gilts may call itself non-directional market neutral. Of course, it is anything but neutral. By comparison, a credit fund trading CDS against hedged corporate bonds to arbitrage "mispricing" has much less directional risk, or at least narrower in scope, as does a statistical arbitrage equity fund pursuing a momentum strategy or a managed futures fund.

We will attempt our own classification of hedge funds, based on the subjective criterion of how the relative value that the fund tries to unlock is pursued. Broadly, we can group funds into four blocks, from general bets on asset classes groups, all the way down to technical mispricing:

- Relative Asset Value (Directional) Funds – global macro, emerging markets, short bias, long/short equity, high yield convertible, managed futures.

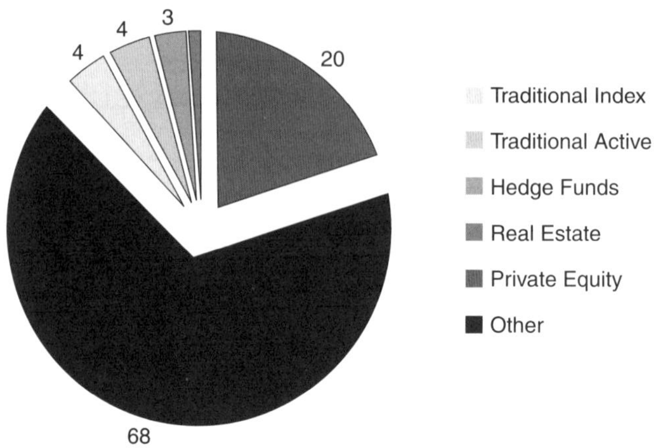

Figure 12.1 Alternative investments

Sources: Compiled by the author from various public domain sources, blending 2009–2010 data. The percentage of assets in the various categories is approximate and unconfirmed.

- Relative Corporate/Credit Structure – capital structure, emerging market and corporate credit arbitrage, event-driven merger or distressed.
- Relative Value (Theoretical Arbitrage) – fixed income arbitrage, managed futures, convertible arbitrage.
- Relative Value (Statistical Arbitrage) – momentum, pairs, quantitative directional.

The biggest attraction and risk of a hedge fund is an almost unlimited discretion afforded the fund manager. This engenders two negative aspects of hedge fund investing. Those are *style drift* and *clustering*. Since hedge funds are unregulated and their prospectuses are very vague, there is nothing stopping the manager from pursuing currency ideas one year and fixed income or equity ideas in the next, or to go from technical mispricing strategies to event-driven ones. This is referred to as style drift. The investor here has to truly believe in the manager's skill (alpha). Also, it has been well documented that at any given moment of time many managers pursue the same ideas and may be on the same end of a trade. This is clustering. Often they hold illiquid securities and cannot quickly get out of their strategies. In an important study by Hasanhodzic and Lo (2007), the authors find significant serial correlation in hedge fund returns. They suggest that hedge fund outperformance alphas may not be coming from managers' investment acumen but may simply be reward for illiquidity that public market investors cannot gain exposure to. The Sharpe ratios may be artificially lowered as the reported returns are necessarily smoothed in the process of marking to market illiquid holdings, resulting in artificially low computed standard deviations. All this leads to the fundamental question of whether the oft-claimed superior hedge funds returns are due to the superior managers and strategies, or whether they are due to access and illiquidity factors. This then begs the question of whether they can be synthetically replicated by exposure to a number of macro factors. While hedge funds claim economic and technical sophistication, or alpha, it is likely that the return on a group of similar strategy funds, or even each individual fund, can be attributed to the exposure to economic factors, preferably with investable vehicles proxying them. Because the funds do not have to disclose their holdings the way mutual funds do, perhaps we currently have no way to easily determine the complete set of factors.

In the mutual fund industry, several studies have shown that active management does not lead to superior returns at all, and most returns can be decomposed into a set of three or four systematic factors explaining 95% of the variation of the returns. Mutual funds also exhibit style drift (in the USA funds change their locus in the Morningstar matrix in order to earn more stars), but to a much more limited extent as their behavior is constrained by the objectives defined in the fund prospectus. More than two-thirds of the active mutual funds underperform their benchmark when taking into account the fees they charge. What if we find that hedge fund returns can also be decomposed into a set of factors, and factor loadings for each fund or group of funds can be easily computed? If so, are the alphas really alphas, or are they betas coming from the exposure to the factors, and can one avoid paying the 2+20 fee structure with the use of "indexing"? Perhaps with a little bit of empirical research, we may soon be able to enhance the standard index models applicable to more traditional long-only investments, such as mutual funds, with additional investable factors to be able to replicate hedge fund returns. We will come back to this question when discussing strategy indexes.

12.1 HEDGE FUND STRATEGIES

While global macro, fixed income and event-driven funds have often attracted press coverage, more than 50% of all hedge funds employ strategies focused on equities. Figure 12.2 shows a breakdown compiled from various sources as of the end of the first quarter of 2010.

In this section, we go through examples of some common strategies to get the flavor of hedge fund operations. We definitely do not cover all of them.

12.1.1 Relative Asset Value Funds

As a starting point, let us consider an example of a *130/30 long-short* equity fund. The fund goes long 130% of the invested funds, using the leverage from shorting 30% of the invested funds. This is a strategy pursued by some mutual funds that try to compete with hedge funds.

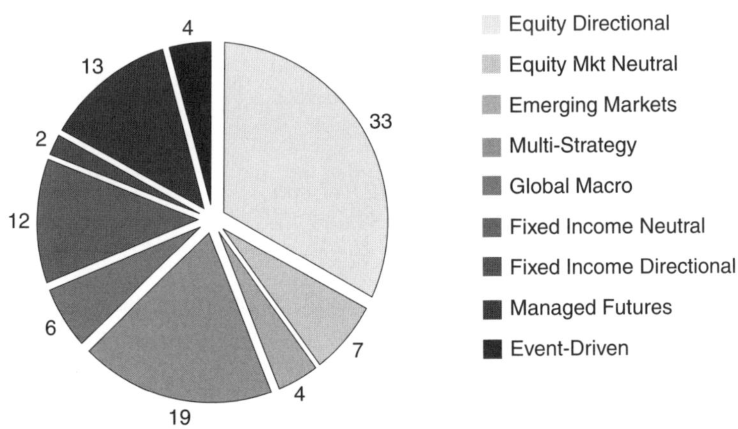

Figure 12.2 Hedge fund strategies

Source: Various public domains. Breakdown of assets under management as of Q1 2010. Approximate and unconfirmed.

Of course, there is nothing constraining a hedge fund from using a much higher leverage and ratio of longs to shorts, or by using invested funds to create a short bias.

Suppose it is December 2010 and we are starting a $100 million fund. We have expertise in US financials, tech, and pharma. In each sector, we like one stock in particular: J.P. Morgan Chase (JPM), currently trading at $38 in financials, Cisco (CSCO) trading at $20 in tech, and Merck (MRK) trading at $34.50 in pharma. The stock market has had a 10% pullback recently and we want to have a positive bias on the market in general. In addition, we think that, in the market upturn, on a relative basis, CSCO is going to outperform Oracle (ORCL) trading at $27, and MRK is going to outperform Pfizer (PFE) trading at $16, but while we like JPM in financials, we think that Citigroup (C) – which is currently trading at $4.20, having recently gone through a significant restructuring – is going to outperform JPM.

We allocate 40% to financials, 30% to tech, and 30% to pharma. Our strategy is to short:

- 315,800 shares of JPM at $38 to receive $12,000,400
- 333,300 shares of ORCL at $27 to receive $8,999,100
- 562,500 shares of PFE at $16 to receive $9,000,000

and to use the $29,999,500 received from the shorts, together, with the $100 million of invested funds, to buy:

- 12,381,000 shares of C at $4.20 for $52,000,200
- 1,950,000 shares of CSCO at $20 for $39,000,000
- 1,130,400 shares of MRK at $34.50 for $38,998,800.

We are assuming that our prime broker allows us to treat the longs in our account as sufficient margin for the shorts with no haircut. Net we have spent $99,999,500.

Suppose over the next quarter the stock market overall, and each sector separately, goes up 10%. In a simple long fund, we would get a return of 10% on $100 million, or $10 million. Suppose, as we had hoped, C in financials goes up by 14.3% to $4.80 while JPM goes up 7.9% to $41; CSCO in tech goes up by 12.5% to $22.50 while ORCL goes up 7.4% to $29, and MRK in pharma goes up by 11.6% to $38.50 while PFE goes up 9.4% to $17.50. Our longs are worth $146,824,200:

- 12,381,000 shares of C at $4.80 for $59,428,800
- 1,950,000 shares of CSCO at $22.50 for $43,875,000
- 1,130,400 shares of MRK at $38.50 for $43,520,400.

We cover our shorts with $32,457,250:

- 315,800 shares of JPM at $41 to receive $12,947,800
- 333,300 shares of ORCL at $29 to receive $9,665,700
- 562,500 shares of PFE at $17.50 to receive $9,843,750.

The net value of the fund is $114,366,950, or a 14.4% return. In this example, the 130/30 ratio acts like a specific security selection tilt in the construction of the equity portfolio. Most mutual funds, because they are always long-invested assets, are restricted from pursuing stronger tilts. Hedge funds are not.

The more extreme version of the long/short strategy is *pairs trading*. Imagine all the same before and after assumptions for our six stocks. This time, however, let us assume a 50% margin requirement for shorting. We assume that the margin balance is all in cash, and long stock positions cannot be used as margin, i.e. are subject to a 100% haircut. (In reality, the longs are likely to be marginable too, so we could increase our positions.) The fund uses the $100 million in invested cash as margin to allow it to short $200 million worth of stocks. So the strategy will be to go long $200 million in stocks and go short $200 million in stocks. It is market-neutral on paper: without the pairs selection, we would expect a 0% return irrespective of whether the stock market goes up or down. We retain the same 40/30/30 industry allocation and buy

- 19,047,700 shares of C at $4.20 for $80,000,340
- 3,000,000 shares of CSCO at $20 for $60,000,000
- 1,739,100 shares of MRK at $34.50 for $59,998,950;

and short

- 2,105,300 shares of JPM at $38 to receive $80,001,400
- 2,222,200 shares of ORCL at $27 to receive $59,999,400
- 3,750,000 shares of PFE at $16 to receive $60,000,000.

Our receipt from the short is $200,000,800. We have $100,000,000 of our own cash in the account. We spend $199,999,290 on stock purchases, and thus we have minimally more than the $100,000,400 in the account required to support the short position. Three months later our long stock holdings are worth $225,884,310:

- 19,047,700 shares of C at $4.80 for $91,428,960
- 3,000,000 shares of CSCO at $22.50 for $67,500,000
- 1,739,100 shares of MRK at $38.50 for $66,955,350.

Subtracting the shorts (worth $216,386,100):

- 2,105,300 shares of JPM at $41 to receive $86,317,300
- 2,222,200 shares of ORCL at $29 to receive $64,443,800
- 3,750,000 shares of PFE at $17.50 to receive $65,625,000,

we have a gain of $9,498,210, or a 9.5% return, not including the interest that we could have earned on the $100 million cash balance in the account. The key here is that even if the overall market had gone down, but our pair had been correctly chosen, we would have had a positive return.

The next variation in the long/short genre is a *short bias* fund. Without going through a numerical example, we intuitively believe that, in this case, the market overall is going down and so we short more stock than we buy, i.e. we pursue a 30/130 ratio or even 0/100, using the invested cash as short-supporting margin.

Structurally, a *global macro* fund is not very different. To a large extent, we use the invested cash to support margin buying and selling in the account. The philosophy and the covered markets are, of course, different. We go long and short the entire asset classes, e.g. long emerging markets stocks and short US stocks, or long German bonds and short UK bonds. The positions have residual currency exposures, and we can choose to leave them unhedged, or we can partially hedge them using currency swaps or forwards. A global macro fund can lever up even more by eschewing buying and shorting cash instruments in favor of futures or OTC derivatives. Buying German bond futures and shorting UK gilt futures might eat up much less cash for margin than the same position in cash bonds. That is not always necessarily the case, and the proper comparison between the two strategies actually requires a cash-and-carry calculation involving the repo financing cost/benefit on both sides.

12.1.2 Relative Corporate/Credit Structure

In this space, let us consider two distinct strategies: merger arbitrage and credit structure arbitrage. The first is a play on the prospects of a merger or a break-up of a company with profit coming from the correct assessment of the probability of the corporate event. The second is a play on the relative value of equity, preferred and debt in a company's structure, the relative values of the different forms of debt, or the price of debt in the corporate bond market and CDS market.

Suppose Big Kahuna Corp. with 500 million shares outstanding, and currently trading at \$50 per share, announces a hostile takeover of Target Corp. through a tender offer on all 100 million shares of Target, currently trading at \$40. The final date for the tender is 1 month away and Big Kahuna is offering a 25% premium for Target's price, or \$50 per share. Target's management promises to fight the hostile takeover.

Prior to the tender announcement, Big Kahuna was worth \$25 billion and Target was worth \$4 billion. Big Kahuna's management claims that post-merger synergies will slash several hundred million in annual costs off the combined company, so that the present value of the combined company's free cash flows will be \$30 billion and the new Super Kahuna Corp. will be able to compete more effectively. After the tender is announced, big Kahuna's stock drops to \$48 while Target's stock increases to \$48. The market is thus skeptical about the synergy claims and is valuing the combined company at \$28.8 billion.

The managers at the Happy River Merger Fund decide that perhaps the \$48 that Target is trading at is not about the cost savings, but more likely reflects the market's assessment of the probability that the merger will actually close. Target's management is very opposed to the idea and is contemplating strong defensive measures. The Happy River traders think all these will fail and the merger will close on time. They have several options: they can

- buy Target shares for \$48 and short Big Kahuna's shares at \$48 if they think the merger will close on time, but the synergies are unlikely;
- buy Target shares for \$48 and Big Kahuna shares for \$48 if they think the merger will close on time and the synergies are real and the drop in Big Kahuna's price reflect the market's unwarranted pessimism; or.
- just buy Target shares at \$48.

The managers at the Dark Ocean Merger Fund see things differently. They decide that Target's management will be able to convince their local government to help to thwart the merger on the grounds of devastating job losses. They think that either the merger attempt will fail, or at least the perceived probability of it happening will diminish. This would drive the current \$48 price for Target down toward \$40 or even below if the company is weakened in the battle. They also think that Big Kahuna will suffer as it will not be able to acquire Target's businesses that fit neatly into its business strategy. The Dark Ocean traders can:

- short Target shares at \$48 to unwind them prior to the merger's closing as the event's probability decreases, or after the failed closing date;
- short Target at \$48 and Big Kahuna at \$48 if they think the merger will not close at all;
- short Big Kahuna at \$48 if they are unsure if the merger will happen, but the business outcome will be unhappy for the acquirer anyway.

In December 2010, major US newspapers (see the *WSJ* on December 3) reported that the US regulators launched an insider-trading investigation into the pre-merger buying of shares by several hedge funds. The trading activity concerned three prior mergers in the pharma sector: AstraZeneca's April 23, 2007, announcement of the takeover of MedImmune, Pfizer's January 26, 2009, announcement of the takeover of Wyeth, and Merck's March 9, 2009, announcement of the takeover of Schering–Plough. In each case, based on the hedge fund's own insider-trading filings with the SEC, their holdings of the target companies went from zero or insignificant to hundreds of thousands of shares *prior to* the announcements. The interesting question here is whether the buying of the shares prior to the takeover was due to insider trading, and potential leaking of the information by the investment banks advising the acquiring and target companies, or due to a legitimate strategy on betting that the mergers will be successful and the target company's price will increase to the tender offer level as the merger solidifies. The increases in the stock prices prior to earnings and merger the announcements had been well documented in event study articles researching the informational efficiency of market prices. The new issues here are related to the involvement of large well-capitalized and well-informed players like the hedge funds: insider cheating or superior analysis?

Let us turn to credit (structure) arbitrage. This is a play on the relative seniority of the different claims on a company's assets and their relative pricing. We start with the general option-theoretic approach. We consider the simplified balance sheet of the Green Diamond Corp. Green Diamond is a commercial stage renewable energy spin-off of Black Diamond Energy, a utility company. Green Diamond specializes in wind turbines. At the time of the spin-off, it was financed with a transfer of the face value of \$163.9 million of cheap Black Diamond debt and an equity IPO. The debt is currently worth \$146 million, and the total market cap of equity is about \$54 million. Free cash flow valuation produces about \$200 million as the value of the company's assets. The average maturity of debt is 3 years.

The option theory comes in here in the following way. If we denote as $\tilde{V}$ the total value of the company's assets and treat it as random, and we denote as K the face value of the debt, then the equity value E is a call option on $\tilde{V}$ with a strike price of K. The equity holders will get the discounted risk-neutral expected value ($\boldsymbol{E}^*$) of the excess of the company's enterprise value over the face value of debt, or:

$$E = df \times E^* max\left[\tilde{V} - K, 0\right]$$

To apply the Black–Scholes model we need a volatility input. We observe the options on equity-financed competitors Wind Resources and Air Energy trading at 40% and 42% implied volatilities. Green Diamond's business is a bit more mature and we choose $\sigma = 20\%$ as our input. We assume a continuously compounded risk-free interest rate $r = 3\%$. Using software with a Black–Scholes $BS(\cdot)$ function, we get the value of the equity:

$$E = BS_{Call}\,(S = 200, K = 163.90, \sigma = 20\%, r = 3, T = 3) = 56.93$$

A simple conclusion might be that the equity is undervalued by about \$2.93 million. Of course, this is a chicken-and-egg situation. We don't know if the equity is undervalued, debt overvalued, or perhaps the value of the assets is misvalued. To further gain insight, we use the put–call parity to break down the total enterprise value of the firm into equity plus debt:

$$\tilde{V} = E + D = C + PV(K) - P;$$
$$E = C \text{ and } D = PV(K) - P$$

The value of the equity is the value of the call on $\tilde{V}$ with the strike K. The value of the debt is the present value of the strike minus the value of the put on $\tilde{V}$ with the strike K. The debt holders' forward position is not simply K. If the value of the enterprise falls below the face value of the debt, they will not get the full principal back. Implicitly, they have written a put option on the value of the firm. Thus if the equity is fairly priced, what is the value of debt including the Black–Scholes model put value? We solve:

$$\begin{aligned} D &= PV(K) - BS_{Put}(S = 200, K = 163.90, \sigma = 20\%, r = 3, T = 3) \\ &= 163.90 \times e^{-3\times 0.03} - 6.72 = 149.79 - 6.72 = 143.07 \end{aligned}$$

We cannot be sure that our numbers are exactly right. We do know, however, that at higher volatility numbers, we would get an even greater undervaluation of equity given debt, and overvaluation of debt given equity. We zero in on the following relative value "hedge" strategy:

- short Green Diamond's debt (perhaps hedged with long Treasuries)
- buy Green Diamond's stock.

This is not an arbitrage trade, but a bet that the relative values of debt and equity will converge to their true values. We are computing a call value not fully priced into the value of the equity (\$56.93 vs \$54 million) and/or a put value embedded in debt that is not fully reflected in the yield-to-maturity on debt. We are implying the risk-adjusted yield-to-maturity of

$$4.5\% = 1/3 \times \ln(163.90/143.07).$$

instead of the current

$$3.85\% = 1/3 \times \ln(163.90/146).$$

This option-theoretic approach can be pushed further to break up the different levels of debt. Suppose we believe that, as we computed, the total value of debt is overpriced by about \$2.97 million. Green Diamond has a \$123.90 million face of senior debt and \$40 million of subordinated debt. The senior debt trades at 110.88, implying a yield to maturity of 3.7%; the subordinated debt trades at 35.12, implying a yield to maturity of 4.33%. We have two ways to evaluate the relative pricing of the two kinds of debt. *Spread analysis*: is the extra 63 bp in yield enough to cover the relative default risk of the two debt tranches? Or *option-theoretic*: assume little or no default risk on the senior debt and price the junior debt. Define $\tilde{V} - 110.88$ as an asset with a strike of 40. Adjust the volatility of the new asset and price in an Asian option model. Asian options on prices of assets averaged over the time of the options have a component that has already been set (prices already observed) and a component that has not been set (the remaining asset prices to be observed till expiry). Here part of the asset is assumed to be known: the value of the senior debt. The rest is unknown and has the most optionality. The volatility adjustment is down and is proportional to the square root of the ratio of the unknown component to the total.

12.1.3 Theoretical Relative Value

In this space, the logic of most strategies is decomposition of securities into the sum of its pieces. In fixed income, coupon bonds are stripped into principal and coupon strips and some parts of them sold off. In asset classes, convertibles are divided into bullet bonds and options to convert into equity. In managed futures, the cash-and-carry is used to put together a convergence trade. Let us dissect the basics of each strategy.

Let us start with *fixed income arbitrage*. It is most often posed as some kind of rich/cheap yield curve pricing inefficiency, but the essence of the trade is always long a package of cash flows, and short a package of identical (or nearly identical) cash flows with the residual risk being a forward interest rate, volatility, or swap spread.

In *swap spread arbitrage*, we take a long or short position on the swap spread:

- If we think the swap spread for maturity τ is going to narrow, we receive fixed a swap rate S against floating LIBOR $\tilde{L}$, we short the corresponding maturity Treasury yielding the rate T, and we earn the repo rate $\tilde{R}$ in the margin account. Effectively, we lock in the swap spread $S - T$ against uncertain difference $\tilde{R} - \tilde{L}$. If the swap spread narrows in the market, the locked-in difference has a positive PV.
- If we think the swap spread for maturity τ is going to widen, we pay fixed a swap rate S against floating LIBOR $\tilde{L}$, and we buy the corresponding maturity Treasury yielding the rate T, financing the purchase at the repo rate $\tilde{R}$ in the margin account. Effectively, we lock in to pay the swap spread $S - T$ against receiving the uncertain difference $\tilde{L} - \tilde{R}$. If the swap spread widens in the market, then what we locked in to pay has a positive PV.

In *yield curve arbitrage*, the strategies are close substitutes – long/shorts, butterflies, or steepeners/flatteners:

- If we think the 29-year Treasury yielding 5.15% is very cheap relative to the on-the-run 30-year Treasury yielding 4.9%, and the relative pricing is going to persist even after the 30-year goes off-the-run and loses its liquidity, then we can buy the 29-year and short the 30-year as long as neither is subject to special repo.
- If we think the curve is too humped in the middle, we can pursue a duration-matched butterfly: buy the 5-year and short the 2-year and the 10-year Treasury or agency, all price-value-of-a-basis-point matched to create a parallel rate move neutral trade.
- If we think the curve is about to flatten/steepen, we go short/long the short end and long/short the long end, again all PVBP matched.

Volatility arbitrage can take various forms. Two regularities in volatility products are often examined:

- More often than not, short-term volatilities are higher than long-term volatilities – this is true in bond, caps, or swaption volatilities that are often in equities and currencies. There are many potential explanations, such as mean reversion, with the trade being on the relative point on the volatility curve.
- Implied volatilities tend to be higher than subsequently realized volatilities. This could be an artifact of the demand for the liquidity or convenience of risk insurance, rather than self-insurance. The trade is to go long volatility and to delta hedge the exposure.

The sources of profit in *convertible bond arbitrage* include:

- The (option model) theoretical underpricing of the conversion option included in the bond. The arbitrage trade is to buy the bond, short the stock, and short a bullet bond on the same company. The riskier version involving corporate spread risk is to buy several convertibles and short Treasuries or note/bond futures to establish an aggregate hedge. The long convert/short stock/bullet strategy allows the hedger to acquire a cheap equity option on the

company. The relative value can also be monetized by not shorting stock, but instead selling call options matching the embedded options. The main risks are that the stripping of the convert of the interest rate risk is imperfect as most converts have long-term conversion rights during which interest rates, and therefore effective strike prices, change.
- The severe underpricing of the conversion feature when the relative value is hard to monetize. If not enough liquid calls are traded on the stock and/or shares cannot be easily/cheaply borrowed for shorting, then the conversion right underpricing can persist. Buying the convert and shorting bullets may be possible, but locking in the equity side of the trade may not.

Managed futures strategies, to a large extent, rely less on theory and more on technical analysis, but often blend both. Some common strategies involve:

- Trend following – Moving average and similar indicators signal the start or end of a short-term trend. This is the most popular strategy.
- Countertrend trades – Identifying trend reversals.
- Spread trading – When implied volatility is high, write out-of-the-money calls and puts and take a residual position in futures to profit from range trading. The main risk for an investor here is to define the risk properly for funds that have experienced positive returns in the past.
- Basis trading – Trade subsequent expiry futures against each other, based on the cost-of-carry and convergence criteria.

12.1.4 Statistical Relative Value Arbitrage

Statistical arbitrage is often driven by large computerized models relying on the historical individual security return data. The trade signals are not at the market or sector level, and thus cannot be easily replicated by a small unsophisticated player. Let us give a somewhat contrived index model example.

Suppose we use the historical database of US stocks and we are convinced that individual stocks exhibit short-term (daily) momentum. That is, we believe in first-order autocorrelation. While our intuition may be right in some sense, a naive strategy of buying a stock at the end of the day on which it is going to profit from the subsequent upward likelihood of more than $^1/_2$, is subject to directional risk that may swamp any momentum profits. We need an index model for two reasons:

- to separate the systematic beta factors from the idiosyncratic factors, to dissect the returns down to the "pure" momentum signals which may not be market but individual security level;
- to properly identify the market-neutral long/short set-up we will pursue to strip the returns down to the momentum factors.

Let us assume that we have read the academic literature on the three-factor Fama and French (1992) model; and we have not found much appeal in the Carhart (1997) four-factor model with the market-wide momentum factor. So, for each stock we intend to trade, we proceed by computing the factor loadings for the three factors: first beta on the market index return, second beta on the high/low book value sorted long/short portfolios factor, and the third beta on the small/large sorted long/short portfolios factor. We identify the factor trading vehicles: an index fund/futures and two sorted long/short portfolios. The factor loadings (betas) we have computed will serve as hedge ratios for all stocks relative to the factors. We analyze the index model and compute the residuals of realized stock returns minus model returns. For example, if we found that GE's factor loadings are constants 1.25, 0.4, and –0.3, then for GE returns we compute:

$$X_t^{GE} = r_{GE} - \left[r_F + 1.25\,(r_{Mkt} - r_F) + 0.4\left(r_{HiBV/MV} - r_{LoBV/MV}\right) - 0.3\left(r_{Sm} - r_{Lg}\right)\right]$$

The first term in the model is the excess return on S&P 500 or Russell 2000, our chosen market index proxy; the second is the difference in returns between high and low book-to-market sorted portfolios (highest decile minus the lowest decile); and the third is the small minus large cap sorted portfolios return differential. We compute these residuals for every stock. The real work begins now.

We dig into the data to discover statistical momentum or reversal relationship. These are searched for on an aggregate basis by imposing some joint dependence form on the residuals, with autoregressive (AR), moving average (MA), variance, etc., terms. For ease of exposition, we follow an example where we dissect the residuals for each stock independently.

We choose to perform an ARMA(2, 2) time series statistical analysis of the individual stock residuals and discover a momentum "signal" for each stock in the first and second AR terms. The strength of the signal is measured by the first and second AR coefficients in the ARMA specification. The direction will be indicated by the realizations of past residuals; since we did not find significance in the MA terms, the error terms will not contribute. To summarize, we have estimated the coefficients γ, α_1, α_2, β_1, and β_2 in:

$$X_t^{GE} = \gamma + \varepsilon_t + \alpha_1 X_{t-1}^{GE} + \alpha_2 X_{t-2}^{GE} + \beta_1 \varepsilon_{t-1} + \beta_2 \varepsilon_{t-2}$$

We are ready to trade. We buy stocks with long momentum signals; we short stocks with sell momentum signals. The signals are X_{t-1}^{GE} and X_{t-2}^{GE}. If the strength coefficients α_1 and α_2 are positive, and the last 2 days (weeks) show positive residuals X_{t-1}^{GE} and X_{t-2}^{GE}, we buy GE. We do this for all our stocks. On any given day, some get included in the long portfolio, some get included in the short portfolio. Since we have computed the stock exposures to the factors, we can compute the net exposure to the factors and hedge the directional risk by trading in the factor vehicles. The expected net excess return we hope to generate from all the longs and shorts over time is our model alpha.

If we employ Carhart's four-factor model, then we have to include the market-wide momentum factor in the loadings calculations before computing the residuals. After the residual analysis, we may have to modify our individual momentum signals to include the momentum beta. The excess return generated from individual stock trades over time, in addition to the four-factor-hedged return, is our model alpha.

The preceding discussion serves to show the amount of data and model sophistication required to investigate a statistical arbitrage idea. We need as much stock history as possible with all the details of dividends, splits, delistings, etc. Once a regularity is discovered, the model needs to be converted into a trading platform that updates the data, re-estimates factors and coefficients, and translates the signals into trade orders. It also must not fail at any given time in computing the rebalancing orders. We are not engaging in a one-time gamble, but hope to earn a positive alpha over time, with many negative days along the way. After all, we are relying on the past repeating itself over a large number of short gamble experiments. We just trust that our decomposition of the past is much better than what others have attempted before.

12.2 PORTABLE ALPHA AND MARKET-NEUTRAL PLAYS

Many market-neutral funds are designed to appeal to a broad set of investors who make their own asset allocation decisions and seek to find skilled managers to generate excess returns. Imagine a large US pension fund that follows a core-satellite approach to investment. For the first half of 2012, it allocates (core: beta) 30% of its portfolio into US equities, 25% into European equities, 25% into emerging markets, 10% into global commodities, and has (satellite: alpha) 10% of its investment dollars left to allocate to other asset classes. It comes across the Clever Alpha Fund that specializes in identifying mispricing in the US ETF market. The fund's manager Joe Saxon has developed an algorithm that signals when an ETF is underpriced relative to the underlying basket of stocks it holds. Saxon has a great track record in three US sectors – financial, tech, and biotech – in identifying these discounts when they occur, but his algorithm does not work for overpricing situations. The pension fund decides to allocate 5% of its investment dollars to Clever Alpha, but while they admire Saxon for his mispricing skills, they do not want him to take the general exposure to US equities. What if the underpricings happen before the general market drops? So while we buy a relatively cheap ETF full of US industrial or financial stocks at a discount to the net asset value, and while the fund's price "corrects up" to the full NAV, the US market corrects down. Clever Alpha has a *portable alpha* solution for that. It offers a market-neutral Clever Alpha ETF Neutral Arbitrage Fund in which it hedges its overall exposure to US equities with short S&P 500 futures. The pension fund can then manage its asset allocation independent of its specific security selection. In the middle of 2012 it can decide to reduce the allocation to US equities from 30% to 20% or even to zero, but still retain the same 5% in Clever Alpha. The process of separating the asset class exposure from specific risk plays is called *alpha transfer*.

Let us explain the design of the Clever Alpha ETF Neutral Arb Fund with the use of an index model. The sectors where the mispricings occur are cyclical, and so the overall beta of the portfolio is $\beta = 1.25$. The excess return on Clever Alpha can then be decomposed as follows:

$$r_{CAlpha} - r_F = \alpha + \beta\,(r_{S\&P500} - r_F) + \tilde{e}$$

where α is the anticipated return due to the ETF mispricing discovery, r_F is the risk-free or short-term financing rate, and $\tilde{e}$ is the residual reflecting unanticipated specific sector or component company risk. The residual risk could be not insignificant if the chosen ETFs are very narrow, and one out of 10 stocks in an ETF explodes. In our case, the specific stock component of it is relatively small; it is more likely related to sector underperformance risk and could further be decomposed into, and mitigated by, short positions in sector index funds. If Clever Alpha employs \$10 million dollars to buy underpriced ETFs and S&P 500 futures currently trade at 1,250, we compute the right hedge ratio using the beta of the fund as $10{,}000{,}000 \times 1.25/1250 \times 250 = 40$ futures contracts. The hedging strategy is dynamic. If, in September of 2012, the Clever Alpha algorithm signal is not strong and it wants to reduce the amount of purchased ETFs to only \$8 million, it will reduce its futures hedge to 32 contracts. Also, if it reallocates among sectors and more of its underpriced ETFs come from tech increasing the overall beta of the fund to $\beta = 1.50$, then on \$10 million invested the futures hedge will increase to 48 contracts.

The portable alpha is delivered to the investor through the process of dynamically hedging the changing nature of the underlying portfolio to offset the systematic beta risk of an asset class. The objective of the portfolio remains unlocking the value due to specific risk, structural design, or relative value mispricing within that asset class. The investor can independently decide on the allocation of beta risks.

12.3 HEDGE FUND REPLICATION AND STRATEGY INDEXES

The oft-quoted statistics of superior returns of the hedge funds over traditional investments suffer from two related problems. First, the number of funds launched and liquidated each year is very large. Fung and Hsieh (2009) point out that when hedge funds migrate from one database to another, or databases are merged, performance has to be supplied for early years (backfill) or the fund has to be deleted (survivorship). In 2008 about 1,500 funds were liquidated and 500 launched; in 2009 about 1,000 were liquidated and more than 500 new ones launched. While the average return may be higher than a passive index strategy, extreme positive and negative surprises abound. How would an investor know in advance which fund to choose to be at or above average? The survivorship bias implies that each year many failed funds are excluded from the average calculation. We have no way of knowing what the average would be if we could include failures. And what if the high fees charged by the funds eat away any alpha over time? Arnott and West (2008) explore the erosion of gross returns of funds of funds by fees (asset-based plus carry). Bollen and Pool (2009) find evidence that funds use discretion in valuing illiquid securities to temporarily overstate their returns. Bollen and Whaley (2009) show the errors produced trying to estimate alpha, when the benchmark constantly moves (shift in asset classes, strategies and leverage). Hedge fund investors have to face the lack of transparency, high net worth requirements, lack of liquidity, and being shut out of many funds with good records as they close to new investors. There are also questions about the persistence of hedge fund returns. Brown et al. (1999) found no evidence of year-to-year persistence when controlling for survivorship bias. Agarwal and Naik (2000) found persistence in the 1982–98 period, attributing it to superior mutual fund managers opening new hedge funds. Agarwal et al. (2009) further suggested that funds with generous managerial option-like incentives and discretion delivered better performance. Yet, similar to mutual funds, large size and fund inflows seem to negatively affect subsequent performance. Boyson (2009) finds strongest persistence in younger and smaller funds, as a group outperforming older, larger ones by over 10%. Most surveys show that investors shrug off these questions; the surveys cite high fees and illiquidity topping the concern list. Other research into hedge fund performance has also documented a very high correlation of their returns with passive index strategies (with the exception of some long/short and most inflation focused funds). Could it be that hedge fund investors get no superior returns, get no benefits of diversification, and suffer high fees?

A better question is whether hedge fund strategies can be replicated more cheaply. In the last 3 years, a new industry has come to life: creation of strategy indexes and offering those indexes in the form of cheap passive funds. "Passive" comes with a caveat: the replication strategy may be very intense requiring ultrafrequent rebalancing, but it is algorithmic and precisely defined by the index creator. The players in this business are Credit Suisse, State Street Global Advisors and Goldman Sachs on the institutional/wealth management side, and IndexIQ, WisdomTree and AdvisorShares on the retail side. The business is slowly moving from the institutional space to retail. As of the end of 2010, a handful of ETFs are offering passive hedge fund replication. A performance report found on Indexlq website (see Table 12.1) lists the indexes tracking the performance of "primitive strategy" indexes that have come to be known as "alternative beta" factors, as of November 2010.

Table 12.1 IndexIQ hedge fund replication beta indexes

	1 month	3 months	YTD	1 year	3 years
IQ Hedge Global Macro Beta Index IQHGGMB	–2.18%	–2.73%	4.62%	0.68%	0.03%
IQ Hedge Long/Short Beta Index IQHGLSB	–2.80%	4.27%	7.22%	0.90%	–5.27%
IQ Hedge Event-Driven Beta Index IQHGEDB	–1.03%	3.83%	9.62%	6.50%	3.38%
IQ Hedge Market Neutral Beta Index IQHGMNB	–0.71%	1.16%	3.47%	1.61%	2.46%
IQ Hedge Emerging Markets Beta Index IQHGEMB	–1.31%	5.71%	7.96%	6.46%	7.95%
IQ Hedge Fixed Income Arbitrage Beta Index IQHGFIB	0.45%	3.22%	5.56%	6.68%	2.64%
IQ Hedge Composite Beta Index IQHGCOB	–1.26%	2.57%	5.35%	3.87%	2.35%

Source: http://www.indexiq.com/media.html

The same IndexIQ report lists the ETFs aimed at replicating specific hedge fund categories (see Table 12.2).

Replication strategies are commonly classified into three groups: factor-based, rule-based, and distribution replication. Hasanhodzic and Lo (2007) is the first paper to test the linear factor-based replication models. They explain the serial correlation in hedge fund returns not with managers' investment acumen (alpha), but as extra reward for illiquidity (on top of standard beta models) that public market investors cannot gain exposure to. Sadka (2010) adds that the loading on the covariation with aggregate liquidity as a significant determinant of a fund's return, irrespective of the fund's strategy. Amenc et al. (2010) test non-linear replication strategies. Their main findings are that non-linear and conditional models do not improve replication; choosing better economic factors does. However, the replication strategies systematically underperform the actual hedge funds. Brooks et al. (2007) shows how incentive fees obscure the true beta exposure of hedge funds. Net returns tend to understate beta exposure contribution by 60 bp per year. Replication should thus be based on gross returns.

Fung and Hsieh (2007) review the rule-based replication. Fung and Hsieh (1997) identified five strategies as accounting for 45% of the variation of hedge fund returns. They labeled them "trend following" one and two, "value", "global/macro", and "distressed securities". Fung and Hsieh (2001 and 2004) advanced the concepts of rule-based replication building blocks they labeled "primitive trading strategies" applied to trend following, long-short equity, and credit arbitrage. Others added them for merger arbitrage, convertible arbitrage, and general equity and emerging markets funds. Thus diversified hedge fund portfolios could be described in terms of these "alternative beta" factors, the remainder being "alternative alpha". Jaeger (2008) estimates that with factor-based, rule-based and distributional replication, beta can account for up to 90% of hedge fund returns. He reviews the entire spectrum of techniques. He and Roncalli

Table 12.2 IndexIQ hedge fund replication ETFs

Fund Name	Ticker	Category
IQ Alpha Hedge Strategy Fund	IQHIX, IQHOX	Long/Short
IQ Hedge Multi-Strategy Tracker	QAI	Multi-strategy
IQ Global Resources	GRES	Global resources
IQ Merger Arbitrage	MNA	Merger arbitrage
IQ Hedge Macro Tracker	MCRO	Global Macro/Emerging Markets
IQ Real Return	CPI	Real return/Inflation

Source: http://www.indexiq.com/media.html

and Weisang (2008) propose the core-satellite approach to overcoming the lack of access to the alpha of hedge funds. The approach stresses traditional long asset class allocation for the bulk of investment dollars, supplemented with satellite alpha-focused investments. There is another way to classify hedge fund replication techniques:

- Regression models estimating factor loadings on traditional economic and alternative indexes
- Active formulaic replication of current fads

The first is technically relatively simple. We pose a linear regression model of hedge fund returns on a set of factors, look for significance of factors, and estimate factor loadings (betas). The main problem is that of factor identification. While this may seem impossible at first, a little bit of clever thinking leads in the following directions.

- Can other people's aggregate long/short selections be deduced from the exchange reported short interest as percentage of total float of a stock?
- Can a put-to-call open interest ratio tell us anything? If so, we have a replication strategy.
- Is liquidity risk related to the change in the implied volatilities? If so, we gain exposure to it through volatility futures, options or swaps.
- Can inflation be stripped out of nominal rate and real rate Treasuries? If so, we can create real rate of return vehicles.
- Can some merger activity be induced by the relative cost of financing, relative P/E within the industry, percentage premium offered in the tender, etc.? If so, perhaps it can be modeled.

The second, harder, approach to hedge fund replication involves active research into the current trade ideas. If we can observe the clustering of the hedge fund positions and their flows, we can replicate their relative exposure to various factors without knowing the exact purpose of the strategy. Some strategy styles, such as market-neutral or merger-driven ones, may be impossible to replicate this way. In market-neutral strategies with close substitutes, the arbitrage is over a few basis points and the two substitutes may be difficult to distinguish by the replicator. In merger arbitrage, the replicator may simply always be too late to the game. However, many global macro and some credit arbitrage strategies take several weeks or months to establish and unwind, and the clustering of the trades may be easily detectable.

Table 12.3 presents a sample of retail alternative investment and strategy index funds trading on US exchanges, or as mutual funds (five-letter ticker) in the USA, as of March 2011. They

Table 12.3 Other alternative and hedge fund replication ETFs as of March 31, 2011

Fund name	Ticker	Category	Size ($mil)
iShares Diversified Alternative	ALT	Long/short multiasset	118
CreditSuisse Long/Short Liquid ETN	CSLS	Long/short equity index	25
PowerShares Nasdaq100 BuyWrite	PQBW	Stock-covered call	5
GreenHaven Continuous Commodity	GCC	Long commodity futures	689
Claymore/Delta Global Shipping	SEA	Shipping stock index	16
WisdomTree Dreyfus Emerging Currency	CEW	Em currency MM basket	380
CreditSuisse Merger Arbitrage Liquid Idx ETN	CSMA	Long/short merger	50
Frost Diversified Strategies*	FDSFX	Fund of funds index + alternative	15
Natixis ASG Global Alternatives*	GAFYX	Long/short stock + bond	731

*Mutual funds; all others are ETFs.

Table 12.4 Dow Jones Credit Suisse Hedge Fund Indexes

Name	Ticker	Currency
Dow Jones Credit Suisse Core Hedge Fund Index (USD)	CORHI	USD
Dow Jones Credit Suisse Core Hedge Fund Net Index (USD)	CORHIUSD	USD
Dow Jones Credit Suisse Core Hedge Fund Net Index Euro Hedged	CORHIEUR	EUR
Dow Jones Credit Suisse Core Hedge Fund Net Index Swiss Franc Hedged	CORHICHF	CHF
Dow Jones Credit Suisse Core Hedge Fund Net Index Pound Sterling Hedged	CORHIGBP	GBP
Dow Jones Credit Suisse Core Hedge Fund Net Index Yen Hedged	CORHIJPY	JPY
Dow Jones Credit Suisse Core Convertible Arbitrage Hedge Fund Index (USD)	CORHICA	USD
Dow Jones Credit Suisse Core Emerging Markets Hedge Fund Index (USD)	CORHIEM	USD
Dow Jones Credit Suisse Core Event Driven Hedge Fund Index (USD)	CORHIED	USD
Dow Jones Credit Suisse Core Fixed Income Arbitrage Hedge Fund Index (USD)	CORHIFI	USD
Dow Jones Credit Suisse Core Global Macro Hedge Fund Index (USD)	CORHIGM	USD
Dow Jones Credit Suisse Core Long/Short Equity Hedge Fund Index (USD)	CORHILS	USD
Dow Jones Credit Suisse Core Managed Futures Hedge Fund Index (USD)	CORHIMF	USD

are in no particular order, just what could be found while scouring the press announcement of newly launched funds. The table contains the list and the size of the fund. Buyers beware!

Lastly, a lot of time in hedge fund replication, it is not clear what it is that we are trying to track? Specific fund or specific strategy? If it is the broad asset-weighted indexes of liquid, investable hedge funds, then, in April 2011, Dow Jones launched a series of Credit Suisse hedge fund indexes normalized to 100 as of 12/31/2010. Table 12.4 shows the list of the indexes, their tickers and currency of denomination.

13

Banks: Asset–Liability Management

Banks play a very important role in the flow of funds in the economy. Capital received by households in the form of wages and investment returns is recycled back to business entities either through financial markets or through financial institutions. Consider the simplified model of the capital flow for the US economy in Figure 13.1.

The relative size of the arrows varies across countries. Taxes are 24% of GDP in the USA, but 49% in Denmark and 42% in France. Wages in the USA have historically been 60–64% of the GDP, but have fallen to 58.5% by Q3 of 2010.

Chapters 11 and 12 dealt primarily with the first channel of the capital flow back from households to business. There, individuals bought stocks and bonds issued by corporations directly, or mutual and hedge fund shares. The latter served as pooling vehicles and invested the received funds in bonds and stocks. In this chapter, we deal with the second channel of capital transfer through one type of a financial intermediary: the commercial bank. What is special about this channel is the capital transformation function performed by the intermediary. Banks do not simply pool capital. They take in deposits in the form of checking, savings, or CD accounts, and make real estate, consumer, and business loans. The deposits are mostly short term up to 1 year, very liquid and often accessible through an ATM or Internet transfer, and small in size up to $100,000. The loans are long term up to 30 years, illiquid (rarely callable and with individualized terms), and come in large chunk sizes from a few thousand to a few billion dollars. (Insurance companies have similar asset–liability mismatches.) The second important role of the banks is the money and credit creation. Since the capital loaned to businesses by the banks is often redeposited (perhaps even many times) in the banking system, banks can create more than $1 loans out of $1 in deposits. This money multiplier effect depends on the reserve and capitalization requirements for banks as well as the velocity of money in the economy.

The last 20 years have ushered in dramatic changes in the risk management of banks. Two factors are of note. First, certain national government and central bank policies have contributed to the rapid increase in leverage in the banking system, and moved away from the traditional deposit-driven banking to market financing and service fee revenue models. In the USA, home ownership financing and tax subsidies by the federal government, low interest rates, and the accelerated developments in securitization have pushed the role of the banks from market and credit risk bearing more into payment services and loan origination and resale. This decreased risk taking allowed them to lever up and reduce their capital base. Similar developments – real estate booms and loan origination and repackaging sophistication – took place in many European countries, and are making their way to emerging markets. The second factor is the evolution of bank regulation rules under Basel accords, starting with the original flawed agreement in 1988, market risk amendments in 1996, the move to internal models in Basel II (2004–6), updated in Basel III (2010). While the Basel accords emphasize several "pillars" of sound bank management, they tend to emphasize the Value at Risk (VaR) methodology for market and credit risk. There are, however, several issues with that approach. The move to quantitative methods in credit risk management makes sense, given

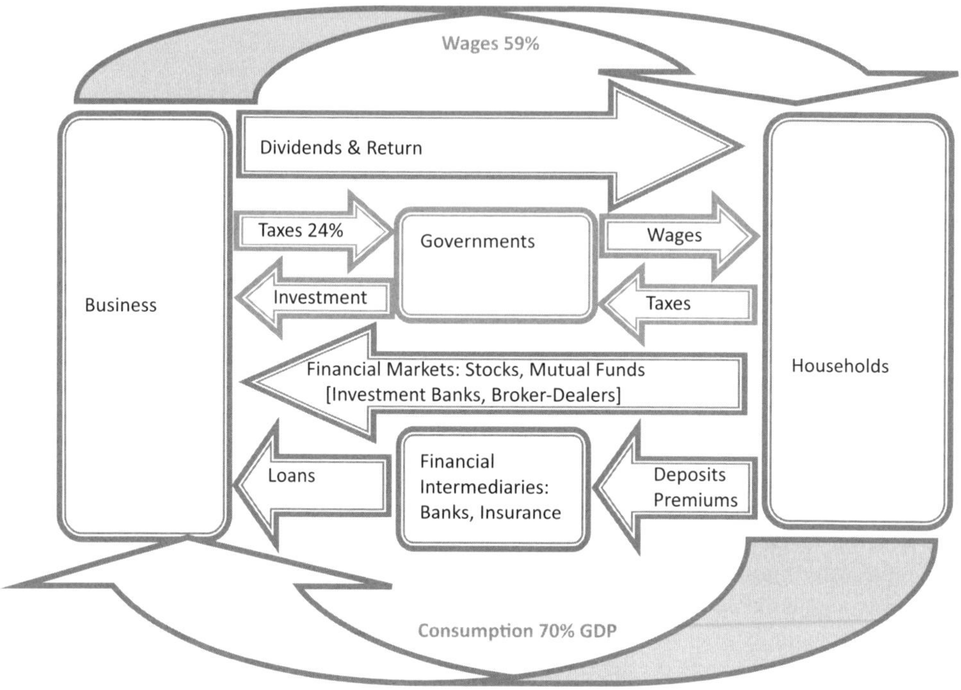

Figure 13.1 The flow of capital in the economy

the scale and volume of credit markets. The methodologies and their usages are not perfect. FICO scores, used in the consumer loan business, shift attention away from the qualitative factors that affect repayment prospects. Credit VaR necessarily relies on correlation assumptions which change in times of crises. Yet both of these techniques allow the quantification of credit exposure which, by itself, is a good thing. The main problems with the VaR methods come on the market and liquidity side. The commercial bank cannot be conceptually reduced to a set of market factors and sensitivities to those factors in the way that a mutual fund can. This has to do with the capital transformation role of the banks. As the 2008 financial crisis made clear, banks are not retail funds or hedge funds with liquid assets. While their funding can evaporate very quickly, their assets cannot be liquidated with the same speed. Also, their incomes depend not only on the exposure to market price factors (interest rates and currencies), but on compensation for liquidity, credit, and maturity gap risk. Only belatedly, and prompted by the 2008 crisis, the regulators around the world started paying attention to the issues of leverage, capital, and liquidity sources. Yet all along, these have been covered in banking textbooks and bank examiner manuals. This chapter reintroduces the basic techniques of bank asset–liability management. We start with Interest-Sensitive (Maturity) Gap Management as the main tool for managing future profit risk (income statement focus). We present the Duration Gap Management as the main tool for equity capital risk (balance sheet). We contrast how VaR tools fit in with the latter for the largest financial institutions to enhance the risk management beyond yield curve factors to equities, commodities, etc., and to integrate it with credit risk. It is important to realize that the universal banks (i.e. those combining investment banking and broker-dealing) are the only institutions that benefit from the VaR methods. The vast majority of banks around the world that offer traditional loan – deposit services (regional banks in the USA, mutual bank systems in Europe, postal and regional bank savings institutions around the world) should eschew VaR almost completely and focus on sound gap and credit management.

13.1 BANK BALANCE SHEETS AND INCOME STATEMENTS

Financial statements of banking institutions are not easy to read, because most of us grew up on accounting textbooks devoting much space to manufacturing categories like cost of goods sold, property plant and equipment, and depreciation. Let us start by looking at two very different US banks. The first is J.P. Morgan, a global bank headquartered in New York with over 230,000 employees around the world, and with large investment banking, asset management, private equity, and institutional trading businesses. In the USA, such a bank is referred to as a money-center bank. The Federal Reserve subjects money center banks with large trading books to Basel rules. In continental Europe, J.P. Morgan would be classified as a universal bank similar to Deutsche Bank or UBS. The second bank we look at is Zions Bancorporation, a fairly large regional bank based in Salt Lake City, Utah, with over 10,000 employees, and geographically covering the southwestern and intermountain region of the USA from Texas in the south through Arizona, Nevada, and California, up to Washington in the northwest. The equivalent profile banks in Europe would be "La Caixa," the third largest bank in Spain with 27,000 employees, or Raiffaisen Bank co-op with 55,000 employees in central Europe (Austria and beyond). The difference for the European banks is their multicountry/currency structure. However, the main business is similar: payment services, savings and deposit accumulation and consumer business, and real estate credit extension.

First, we look at the income statement and the (average) balance sheet of J.P. Morgan Chase as of Q3 of 2010 in Tables 13.1 and 13.2, found in the November 9, 2010, Form 10-Q filing with the Securities and Exchange Commission (SEC). In Table 13.1, of the total $23.8 billion revenue in Q3 2010, $11.3 billion or 47% comes from fees, and $12.5 billion or 53% comes from Net Interest Income. The fee revenue components are investment banking, principal trading, custody, asset management, credit cards, and others. Roughly then, in a broad sense, J.P. Morgan's income is a little more than half traditional bank and a little less than half investment bank. A typical investment bank, like Goldman Sachs or Morgan Stanley, combines pure investment banking with principal/institutional trading and asset management. A look at the assets and liabilities in Table 13.2 confirms this assessment. Long-term loans represent 34% and all interest-bearing assets including loans, deposits, fed funds, and debt tradeables represent 81% of all the assets. Interest- and non-interest-bearing deposits represent 47% of total liabilities. Other main sources of funding include fed funds, general long-term debt, and trading liabilities.

When trying to evaluate J.P. Morgan's financial health, one needs to look at threats/opportunities to its revenue/income stream and at the net worth position equal to the value of assets minus the value of liabilities. For the former, we can use the traditional maturity gap analysis and credit management methods to analyze the 53% coming from net interest income. We would need other methods to evaluate the quality of the earnings on the investment banking, custody, or asset management side. Market VaR methods can only help with characterizing the principal trading revenue, and, to a limited extent, some of the other areas.

Table 13.1 The income statement of J.P. Morgan Chase & Co. for September 30, 2010

JP MORGAN CHASE & CO.
Consolidated statements of income (unaudited)

(In millions, except per share data)	Three months ended Sept 30		Nine months ended Sept 30	
Revenue	2010	2009	2010	2009
Investment banking fees	$ 1,476	$ 1,679	$ 4,358	$ 5,171
Principal transactions	2,341	3,860	8,979	8,958
Lending- and deposit-related fees	1,563	1,826	4,795	5,280
Asset management, administration and commissions	3,188	3,158	9,802	9,179
Securities gains	102	184	1,712	729
Mortgage fees and related income	707	843	2,253	3,228
Credit card income	1,477	1,710	4,333	5,266
Other income	468	625	1,465	685
Non-interest revenue	11,322	13,885	37,697	38,496
Interest income	15,606	16,260	48,170	50,735
Interest expense	3,104	3,523	9,271	11,961
Net interest income	12,502	12,737	38,899	38,774
Total net revenue	23,824	26,622	76,596	77,270
Provision for credit losses	3,223	8,104	13,596	24,731
Non-interest expense:				
Compensation expense	6,661	7,311	21,553	21,816
Occupancy expense	884	923	2,636	2,722
Technology, communications and equipment expense	1,184	1,140	3,486	3,442
Professional and outside services	1,718	1,517	4,978	4,550
Marketing	651	440	1,862	1,241
Other expense	3,082	1,767	9,942	5,332
Amortization of intangibles	218	254	696	794
Merger costs	–	103	–	451
Total non-interest expense	14,398	13,455	45,153	40,348
Income before income tax expense and extraordinary gain	6,203	5,063	17,847	12,191
Income tax expense	1,785	1,551	5,308	3,817
Income before extraordinary gain	4,418	3,512	12,539	8,374
Extraordinary gain	–	76	–	76
Net income	$ 4,418	$ 3,588	$ 12,539	$ 8,450
Net income applicable to common stockholders	$ 4,019	$ 3,240	$ 11,353	$ 5,825
Per common share data:				
Basic earnings per share				
Income before extraordinary gain	$ 1.02	$ 0.80	$ 2.86	$ 1.50
Net income	1.02	0.82	2.86	1.52
Diluted earnings per share				
Income before extraordinary gain	1.01	0.80	2.84	1.50
Net income	1.01	0.82	2.84	1.51
Weighted-average basic shares	3,954.30	3,937.90	3,969.40	3,835.00
Weighted-average diluted shares	3,971.90	3,962.00	3,990.70	3,848.30
Cash dividends declared per common share	$ 0.05	$ 0.05	$ 0.15	$ 0.15

Source: Public website of jpm.com

Table 13.2 The consolidated average balance sheet of JP Morgan Chase & Co. for September 30, 2010

JPMORGAN CHASE & CO.
Consolidated average balance sheets, interest and rates (a)
(Taxable-Equivalent Interest and Rates; in millions, except rates)

(In millions, except rates)	Three months ended Sept 30 2010			Three months ended Sept 30 2009		
Assets	Average balance	Interest amount	Rate in % ann.	Average	Interest	Rate in % ann.
Deposits with banks	$ 38,747	$ 82	0.85	$ 62,248	$ 130	0.83
Fed funds sold & securities purchased under resale agreements	192,099	448	0.92	151,705	368	0.96
Securities borrowed	121,302	66	0.22	129,301	(30)	(0.09)
Trading assets – debt instruments	251,790	2,775	4.37	250,148	3,017	4.78
Securities (e)	327,798	2,207	2.67	359,451	3,281	3.62
Loans	693,791	9,978	5.71	665,386	9,450	5.64
Other assets(b)	36,912	146	1.57	24,155	133	2.18
Total interest-earning assets	$1,662,439	15,702	3.75	1,642,394	16,349	3.95
Allowance for loan losses	(35,562)			(29,319)		
Cash and due from banks	29,963			21,256		
Trading assets – equity instruments	96,200			66,790		
Trading assets –derivative receivables	92,857			99,807		
Goodwill	48,745			48,328		
Other intangible assets:						
Mortgage servicing rights	10,807			14,384		
Purchased credit card relationships	1,013			1,389		
Other intangibles	3,081			3,595		
Other assets	131,570			130,552		
Total assets	$2,041,113			$1,999,176		
Liabilities						
Interest-bearing deposits	$ 659,027	$ 846	0.51	$ 660,998	$ 1,086	0.65
Fed funds purchased & sec's loaned/sold – repurchase agreements (d)	281,171	(199)	(0.28)	303,175	150	0.20
Commercial paper	34,523	18	0.20	42,728	24	0.23
Trading liabilities – debt instruments	73,278	487	2.64	47,467	539	4.50
Other borrowings and liabilities (c)	130,191	176	0.54	131,518	228	0.69
Beneficial interests issued by consolidated VIEs	83,928	287	1.36	19,351	70	1.43
Long-term debt	252,097	1,489	2.34	271,281	1,426	2.09
Total interest-bearing liabilities	1,514,215	3,104	0.81	1,476,518	3,523	0.95
Non-interest-bearing deposits	213,700			191,821		

(Continued)

Table 13.2 (Continued)

JPMORGAN CHASE & CO.
Consolidated average balance sheets, interest and rates (a)
(Taxable-Equivalent Interest and Rates; in millions, except rates)

(In millions, except rates)	Three months ended Sept 30 2010			Three months ended Sept 30 2009		
Assets	Average balance	Interest amount	Rate in % ann.	Average	Interest	Rate in % ann.
Trading liabilities – equity instruments	6,560			12,376		
Trading liabilities – derivative payables	69,350			75,458		
All other liabilities, incl. the allowance for lending-related commitments	65,335			85,383		
Total liabilities	1,869,160			1,841,556		
Stockholders' equity						
Preferred stock	7,991			8,152		
Common stockholders' equity	163,962			149,468		
Total stockholders' equity	171,953			157,620		
Total liabilities and stockholders' equity	$2,041,113			$1,999,176		
Interest rate spread			2.94%			3.00%
Net interest income and net yield on interest-earning assets		$12,598	3.01%		$12,826	3.10%

(a) Effective January 1, 2010, the Firm adopted new guidance that amended the accounting for the transfer of financial assets and the consolidation of VIEs.
For further details regarding the Firm's application and impact of the new guidance, see Note 15 on pages 155–167 of this Form 10-Q.
(b) Includes margin loans.
(c) Includes brokerage customer payables and advances from Federal Home Loan Banks.
(d) Reflects a benefit from the favorable market environments for dollar-roll financings in the third quarter of 2010.
(e) For the quarters ended September 30, 2010 and 2009, the annualized rates for AFS securities, based on amortized cost, were 2.74% and 3.64%, respectively.
Source: Public website of jpm.com

Looking at the balance sheet side, we find that about 81% of the assets are yield curve sensitive. Here, traditional duration gap and market VaR methods would seem to be close cousins. Both focus on defining the yield curve hedge exposures in interest-sensitive assets and liabilities. Market VaR can be used to extend the hedge approach to cover equity positions and derivatives.

The financial statements for Zions in Tables 13.3 and 13.4 reveal a different business mix. The main contributor to revenue/profit is net interest income, aided by deposit account fees and service charges. Employee expenses, and derivative and securities losses offset all the income resulting in small net losses for the reporting periods. The trading account is minuscule. The balance sheet confirms the picture of Zions as a traditional deposit-and-loan

Table 13.3 The income statement of Zions Bancorporation for September 30, 2010

ZIONS BANCORPORATION AND SUBSIDIARIES
CONSOLIDATED STATEMENTS OF INCOME (Unaudited)

	Three Months Ended Sept 30		Nine Months Ended Sept 30	
(In thousands, except per share amounts)	2010	2009	2010	2009
Interest income:				
Interest and fees on loans	543,478	586,246	1,625,096	1,749,688
Interest on loans held for sale	2,223	2,434	6,523	8,272
Lease financing	4,788	5,125	14,168	14,453
Interest on money market investments	3,487	1,195	7,527	6,114
Interest on securities:				
Held-to-maturity – taxable	1,000	4,864	9,569	33,139
Held-to-maturity – nontaxable	5,063	5,806	15,687	17,867
Available-for-sale – taxable	19,782	23,460	60,571	72,145
Available-for-sale – nontaxable	1,571	1,830	4,992	5,286
Trading account	542	842	1,674	2,236
Total interest income	$ 581,934	$ 631,802	$ 1,745,807	$ 1,909,200
Interest expense:				
Interest on savings and money market deposits	29,900	54,554	100,413	194,056
Interest on time and foreign deposits	16,468	42,780	54,784	158,036
Interest on short-term borrowings	3,566	2,325	10,119	12,006
Interest on long-term borrowings	80,125	59,963	259,970	104,459
Total interest expense	$ 130,059	$ 159,622	$ 425,286	$ 468,557
Net interest income	$ 451,875	$ 472,180	$ 1,320,521	$ 1,440,643
Provision for loan losses	184,668	565,930	678,896	1,626,208
Net interest income after provision for loan losses	**$ 267,207**	**$ (93,750)**	**$ 641,625**	**$ (185,565)**
Non-interest income:				
Service charges and fees on deposit accounts	49,733	54,466	153,250	159,087
Other service charges, commissions and fees	41,780	39,227	124,217	117,745
Trust and wealth management income	6,310	8,209	20,940	24,124
Capital markets and foreign exchange	13,154	12,106	32,426	41,621
Dividends and other investment income	8,874	2,597	25,453	13,689
Loan sales and servicing income	8,390	2,359	20,439	15,250
Fair value and nonhedge derivative income (loss)	(21,854)	58,092	(21,218)	82,412
Equity securities gains (losses), net	(1,082)	(1,805)	(5,747)	339
Fixed income securities gains, net	8,428	1,900	10,214	3,539
Impairment losses on investment securities:				
Impairment losses on investment securities	(73,082)	(198,378)	(141,209)	(435,509)
Noncredit-related losses on sec's not exp to be sold	49,370	141,863	68,174	254,352
Net impairment losses on investment securities	(23,712)	(56,515)	(73,035)	(181,157)
Valuation losses on securities purchased	–	–	–	(212,092)
Gain on subordinated debt modification	–	–	–	493,725
Gain on subordinated debt exchange	–	–	14,471	–

(Continued)

Table 13.3 (*Continued*)

ZIONS BANCORPORATION AND SUBSIDIARIES
CONSOLIDATED STATEMENTS OF INCOME (Unaudited)

	Three Months Ended Sept 30		Nine Months Ended Sept 30	
(In thousands, except per share amounts)	2010	2009	2010	2009
Acquisition related gains	–	146,153	–	169,130
Other	20,179	3,951	25,813	10,802
Total non-interest income	$ 110,200	$ 270,740	$ 327,223	$ 738,214
Non-interest expense:				
Salaries and employee benefits	207,947	205,433	618,056	612,014
Occupancy, net	29,292	28,556	85,602	83,534
Furniture and equipment	25,591	25,320	76,290	75,189
Other real estate expense	44,256	30,419	119,348	72,510
Credit related expense	17,438	11,793	51,921	28,632
Provision for unfunded lending commitments	1,104	36,537	(18,546)	46,291
Legal and professional services	9,305	9,076	28,168	27,116
Advertising	5,575	4,418	17,721	17,244
FDIC premiums	25,706	19,820	76,354	76,320
Amortization of core deposit and other intangibles	6,296	7,575	19,287	21,539
Other	83,534	55,760	201,324	169,992
Total non-interest expense	$ 456,044	$ 434,707	$ 1,275,525	$ 1,230,381
Impairment loss on goodwill	–	–	–	633,992
Income (loss) before income taxes	$ (78,637)	$ (257,717)	$ (306,677)	(1,311,724)
Income taxes (benefit)	(31,180)	(100,046)	(82,722)	(275,534)
Net income (loss)	$ (47,457)	$ (157,671)	$ (223,955)	(1,036,190)
Net income (loss) applicable to noncontrolling interests	(132)	(2,394)	(3,427)	(4,143)
Net income (loss) applicable to controlling interest	$ (47,325)	$ (155,277)	$ (220,528)	$(1,032,047)
Preferred stock dividends	(33,144)	(26,603)	(84,797)	(78,336)
Preferred stock redemption	–	–	3,107	52,418
Net earnings (loss) applicable to common shareholders	$ (80,469)	$ (181,880)	$ (302,218)	$(1,057,965)
Weighted average common shares outstanding during the period:				
Basic shares and Diluted shares	172,865	127,581	161,996	119,248
Net earnings (loss) per common share:				
Basic and Diluted	$ (0.47)	$ (1.43)	$ (1.87)	$ (8.87)

Sources: Public websites of zionsbank.com, yahoo.com, edgar-online.com

bank with some derivative hedging overlays. Loans represent 91% of total assets. Interest-bearing deposits represent 61.5% and non-interest-bearing deposits another 30.4% of the total liabilities. Borrowed funds are relatively small; most are fed funds and repos. In September 2010, Zions, like many regional banks in the USA, had still not repaid the government bailout (TARP) funds showing on the balance sheet as preferred shares, and was still working through

Table 13.4 The consolidated average balance sheet of Zions Bancorporation for September 30, 2010

ZIONS BANCORPORATION AND SUBSIDIARIES
CONSOLIDATED AVERAGE BALANCE SHEETS, YIELDS AND RATES (Unaudited)

	Three months ended Sept 30 2010			Three months ended Sept 30 2009		
(In thousands)	Average balance	Amount of interest[1]	Average rate %	Average balance	Amount of interest[1]	Average rate %
ASSETS						
Money market investments	$5,192,847	$3,487	0.27	$1,861,523	$1,195	0.25
Securities:						
Held-to-maturity	843,268	8,789	4.14	914,648	13,797	5.98
Available-for-sale	3,282,056	22,199	2.68	3,749,566	26,275	2.78
Trading account	59,216	542	3.63	94,658	842	3.53
Total securities	4,184,540	31,530	2.99	4,758,872	40,914	3.41
Loans held for sale	188,794	2,223	4.67	194,596	2,434	4.96
Loans:						
Net loans and leases excluding FDIC-supported loans[2]	36,525,416	515,419	5.6	40,246,789	570,652	5.63
FDIC-supported loans	1,149,976	34,572	11.93	1,494,857	22,562	5.99
Total loans and leases	37,675,392	549,991	5.79	41,741,646	593,214	5.64
Total interest-earning assets	47,241,573	587,231	4.93	48,556,637	637,757	5.21
Cash and due from banks	1,063,000			1,187,594		
Allowance for loan losses	(1,556,558)			(1,317,078)		
Goodwill	1,015,161			1,017,387		
Core deposit and other intangibles	97,741			126,614		
Other assets	3,917,955			3,923,371		
Total assets	$51,778,872			$53,494,525		
LIABILITIES						
Interest-bearing deposits:						
Savings and NOW	$6,186,704	5,060	0.32	$5,162,852	5,262	0.4
Money market	15,584,312	24,840	0.63	17,538,319	49,292	1.12
Time under $100,000	2,103,818	6,623	1.25	2,954,680	16,612	2.23
Time $100,000 and over	2,462,904	7,495	1.21	4,363,017	22,690	2.06
Foreign	1,563,090	2,350	0.6	1,901,789	3,478	0.73
Total interest-bearing deposits	27,900,828	46,368	0.66	31,920,657	97,334	1.21
Borrowed funds:						
Securities sold, not yet purchased	38,789	423	4.33	45,866	590	5.1
Fed funds purchased and security repurchase agreements	873,954	315	0.14	1,708,888	1,207	0.28
FHLB advances and other borrowings:						
One year or less	210,235	2,828	5.34	47,965	528	4.37
Over one year	18,415	220	4.74	18,854	228	4.8
Long-term debt	1,927,360	79,905	16.45	1,955,725	59,735	12.12
Total borrowed funds	3,068,753	83,691	10.82	3,777,298	62,288	6.54

(Continued)

Table 13.4 (*Continued*)

ZIONS BANCORPORATION AND SUBSIDIARIES
CONSOLIDATED AVERAGE BALANCE SHEETS, YIELDS AND RATES (Unaudited)

	Three months ended Sept 30 2010			Three months ended Sept 30 2009		
(In thousands)	Average balance	Amount of interest[1]	Average rate %	Average balance	Amount of interest[1]	Average rate %
Total interest-bearing liabilities	30,969,581	130,059	1.67	35,697,955	159,622	1.77
Non-interest-bearing deposits	13,786,784			11,428,774		
Other liabilities	601,439			517,200		
Total liabilities	$45,357,804			$47,643,929		
Shareholders' equity:						
Preferred equity	1,819,889			1,518,289		
Common equity	4,601,920			4,309,497		
Controlling interest shareholders' equity	6,421,809			5,827,786		
Non-controlling interest	(741)			22,810		
Total shareholders' equity	6,421,068			5,850,596		
Total liabilities and shareholders' equity	$51,778,872			$53,494,525		
Spread on average interest-bearing funds			3.26			3.44
Taxable-equiv net int income & net yld on int-earning assets		$457,172	3.84		$478,135	3.91

[1] Taxable-equivalent rates used where applicable.
[2] Net of unearned income and fees, net of related costs. Loans include nonaccrual and restructured loans.
Sources: Public websites of zionsbank.com, yahoo.com, edgar-online.com

its troubled real estate loan portfolio. The TARP funds strengthened its liquidity, increasing its money market position. Net interest margin (the difference between the rates earned on invested assets minus the rates paid on the liabilities) remained very healthy, above 3.5%.

The vast majority of commercial banks around the developed world have a profile similar to that of Zions or J.P. Morgan, or in between. The more global ones may show more investment banking, trading, custody, or asset management income. Specialty banks would have revenues concentrated on particular areas. Smaller Swiss banks may have more asset management and private banking fee revenues. Bank of New York or State Street Bank in the USA may show more custody and commission income. The world's more regional- or savings-oriented banks would show mostly deposits and loans and majority interest and service fee income similar to Zions. In either case, the interest-rate sensitive portfolio would probably represent more than three-quarters of all balance sheet assets.

The next two sections cover two main methods of assessing a financial institution's investment value, profitability, and risk relative to changing market interest rates, each focusing on one key variable:

- Interest-Sensitive (Maturity) Gap Management:
  Net interest margin = (Interest revenue – Interest cost) / Total earning assets
- Duration Gap Management:
  Net worth = Market value of assets – Market value of liabilities

The objective of Asset–Liability Management (ALM), often conducted through the asset-liability committee (ALCO) of a firm, is not simply to arrive at a final number, but to have a firm grasp of the details. In particular, we want to understand the breakdown of the income or net worth exposure to interest risk organized into maturity/duration buckets.

13.2 INTEREST-SENSITIVE GAP MANAGEMENT

Let us step back and think broadly about analyzing the future prospects of any company. If we were looking at Apple, we would want to know the product development mix: new phones, music, and video players. The same would apply to any drug company or industrial manufacturing company, like Siemens. We would want to know not only Siemens' new equipment line-up, but also the long-term contract pipeline for power plant construction and large industrial installations. What about a bank such as Zions? The main drivers of future revenue, besides fees charged on deposit and loan servicing, would be the ability to generate new loans and the interest rates earned on those new loans. The aim of the Interest-Sensitive (Maturity) Gap methods is to quantify the number of loans that come due in the near future, break them down by maturity, and assess the amount of revenue at risk.

Let us introduce some terminology. First let us define the Net Interest Margin (NIM) and compute it for Zions (amounts in \$ millions, we multiply by 4 to annualize):

$$NIM = \frac{Interest\ income - Interest\ expense}{Total\ earning\ assets}$$

$$NIM = \frac{581.9 - 130.1}{472,41.6} \times 4 = 3.83\%$$

Conceptually, the bank as a whole can be viewed as earning the Net Interest Margin on the difference between loans and deposits, supplemented with fee income, with which to cover loan loss provisions and employee expenses. We see from Zions' statements that elevated post-2008 crisis loss provisions in 2010 continued to eat away at NIM and employee/operating expenses took the rest. Despite the healthy NIM the management had very little room for error in managing interest rate risk. In late 2010, the US yield curve was upward sloping, resulting in a positive *maturity gap* for the bank: loans had longer maturities than deposits, and earned higher interest rates. But what if the yield curve were to flatten, or the cost of deposits rose due to another liquidity shock? To maintain the same NIM, the bank would have to significantly increase the amount of loans to deposits, taking on more liquidity and business risk. What if the yield curve steepened? New loans would earn higher rates, but old loans would lose market value.

To examine the new business (revenue) tradeoffs, we turn attention to the maturities and the repricing opportunities on interest-bearing assets and liabilities. What we want to know is the difference between the dollar amount of repriceable assets and the dollar amount of the repriceable liabilities for each future time period. Repriceable assets are loans about to mature or to be renewed–short-term securities, variable-rate loans. Repriceable liabilities are maturing certificates of deposit (CDs), floating rate deposits, and short-term money market

Table 13.5 Zion's debt securities by maturity (final balance)

	Held-to-maturity		Available-for-sale	
(In thousands)	Amortized cost	Estimated fair value	Amortized cost	Estimated fair value
Due in 1 year or less	$ 64,315	$ 65,087	$ 357,285	$ 349,824
Due after 1 year through five years	217,101	218,377	821,946	788,892
Due after 5 years through ten years	204,229	185,345	820,345	694,681
Due after 10 years	385,433	314,553	1,861,449	1,307,022
	$871,078	$783,362	$3,861,025	$3,140,419

Source: 10-Q Report for Q3 2010 on the public website of zionsbank.com.

instruments. Instead of repriceable, we will call them interest sensitive. Non-repriceable assets are cash and reserves, long-term loans, and long-term securities. Non-repriceable liabilities are non-interest-bearing demand deposits, long-term savings accounts, and equity.

We define the Dollar Interest-Sensitive Gap (*ISGap*) as:

$$ISGap = ISAssets - ISLiab$$

The *ISGap* can be positive or negative. A bank with the positive gap is called asset sensitive; a bank with the negative gap is called liability sensitive. If interest rates rise, an asset-sensitive bank's net interest margin will rise and a liability-sensitive bank's net interest margin will decline. If interest rates decline, an asset-sensitive bank's net interest margin will decline and a liability-sensitive bank's net interest margin will rise. We define the Interest Sensitivity Ratio (*ISRatio*) as:

$$ISRatio = ISAssets/ISLiab$$

We can also define the gap relative to some measure of the bank's size, e.g. total assets, in order to compare it with other banks. We can define the Relative Interest-Sensitive Gap as:

$$Relative\ ISGap = ISGap/TotalAssets$$

Let us try to define these terms for Zions. We gather additional information contained in Zions' 10-Q Report for Q3 2010 filed with the SEC, and the management's presentations to various investors' groups. We find the information about the maturity of the securities shown on the balance sheet. We are forced to make some assumptions about the maturities of the various types of loans. Clearly, the details would be available to the management of the bank. The analysis here is for illustrative purposes only, and may not be reflective of the true position of Zions as of September 30, 2010.

Nearly 80% of the bank's portfolio is commercial lending; 17.5% are consumer loans. Commercial lending consists of general commercial and industrial business loans, owner-occupied loans, and commercial real estate loans. Business loans can be term or revolving; real estate loans tend to be term and intended either for new construction or for tenant rental or owner-occupied existing properties. In consumer loans, home equity and bank card loans tend to be revolving adjustable; the remainder are short (construction) or very long maturity residential real estate loans.

Based on the management discussion and the notes to the financial statements contained in the 10-Q Report, as well as from the management presentations to the investors' groups

Table 13.6 Zion's loan portfolio by type of loan (average balance)

	Sept 30 2010		Dec 31 2009		Sept 30 2009	
		% of		% of		% of
(In millions)	Amount	total	Amount	total	Amount	total
Commercial lending:						
Commercial and industrial	$ 9,402	25.0%	9,922	24.6%	10,124	24.5%
Leasing	402	1.1%	466	1.2%	449	1.1%
Owner occupied	8,345	22.1%	8,752	21.7%	8,745	21.1%
Total commercial lending	18,149		19,140		19,318	
Commercial real estate:						
Construction and land development	4,206	11.2%	5,552	13.8%	6,087	14.7%
Term	7,550	20.0%	7,255	18.0%	7,279	17.6%
Total commercial real estate	11,756			12,807		13,366
Consumer:						
Home equity credit line	2,157	5.7%	2,135	5.3%	2,114	5.1%
1-4 family residential	3,509	9.3%	3,642	9.0%	3,698	8.9%
Construction and other consumer real estate	366	1.0%	459	1.1%	537	1.3%
Bankcard and other revolving plans	287	0.8%	341	0.8%	333	0.8%
Other	271	0.7%	293	0.7%	343	0.8%
Total consumer		6,590		6,870		7,025
Foreign loans	84	0.2%	65	0.2%	74	0.2%
FDIC-supported loans	1,090	2.9%	1,445	3.6%	1,607	3.9%
Total loans	$37,669	100.0%	$40,327	100.0%	$41,390	100.0%

Source: 10-Q Report for Q3 2010 on the public website of zionsbank.com.

posted on the bank's website, we make the following assumptions about the maturity of the various types of loans contained in Table 13.7:

Admittedly, our assumptions may not be perfect. The investor presentations contain detailed information about the commercial real estate portfolio, but not about the other categories. In consumer loans nearly half are revolving home equity lines, the rest are longer-term primary mortgage loans. In commercial lending, about half are general business loans, the other half

Table 13.7 Zion's loan portfolio by maturity of loan (our guess)

Maturity	Comm real estate	Commercial lending	Consumer
1 year or less	8%	20%	50%
1–5 years	42%	60%	10%
5 years and longer	50%	20%	40%

Source: The investor relations/presentation section of the public website of zionsbank.com

Table 13.8 The estimate of Zion's interest-sensitive assets and liabilities

In thousands		
Money market investments		$ 5,192,847
Securities:		
Held to maturity	7.383% × $ 843,268	62,262
Available for sale	9.254% × $3,282,056	303,709
Trading account		59,216
Loans:		
Commercial/ind	20% × $ 18,149,000	3,629,800
Comm real estate	8% × $ 11,756,000	940,480
Consumer	50% × $ 6,590,000	3,295,000
Allowance for loan losses est.	15% × $ 1,556,558	(233,484)
Total IS Assets		$13,249,830
Savings and NOW		$6,186,704
Money market		15,584,312
Time under $100,000	80% × $2,103,818	1,683,054
Time over $100,000	80% × $2,462,904	1,970,323
Foreign		1,563,090
Borrowed funds:		
Securities sold, not yet purchased	38,789	
Fed funds purchased and security repurchase agreements	873,954	
FHLB advances and other borrowings: ≤ 1 yr	210,235	
Total IS Liabilities		$28,110,461

are owner-occupied loans. We guess the first type might be shorter/riskier, none as long as mortgage loans.

Let us compute the *ISAssets* as those assets that are repriceable within 1 year. Using the balance sheet quantities supplemented with the securities and loan maturity information, we have the following categories. To account for the fact that the supplemental securities information is for the final balance, and the loan estimates are based on prior quarters, while we have the average balance sheet we use the percentages (1-year maturity relative to total) from the supporting information and multiply those by the dollar amounts in the average balance sheet.

In computing *ISLiab* we assume (no information) that 80% of retail (<$100,000) and wholesale (>$100,000) time deposits, and 100% of savings/NOW and foreign deposit accounts are repriceable within 1 year. Table 13.8 shows the computation of interest-sensitive assets and liabilities.

The dollar *ISGap*, the *ISRatio*, and the *Relative ISGap* for Zions are:

$$ISGap = 13{,}249{,}830 - 28{,}110{,}461 = -\$14{,}860{,}631$$

$$ISRatio = \frac{13{,}249{,}830}{28{,}110{,}461} = 0.47$$

$$Relative\ ISGap = \frac{-14{,}860{,}631}{51{,}778{,}872} = -0.29$$

As of September 30, 2010, Zions is a *liability-sensitive* bank. A rise in interest rates will raise the cost of liabilities and erode the Net Interest Margin. The management discussion contained in the 10-Q Report and the main three near term goals in the investor presentations show the management's clear awareness of the bank's situation. They emphasize the efforts to maintain liquidity and the GAAP and Core Net Interest Margin (GAPP and Core NIM) by working through the loan portfolio of troubled credits to reduce existing loans, generate new loans especially in government-guaranteed programs and commercial and industrial lending (shorter term), and reduce excess cash balances.

Regional banks have a variety of derivative-hedging techniques available to them. The most widely used and flexible are interest rate swaps. Unfortunately, they do not solve the problems of bad credits in the portfolio or the lack of growth of new loans. One stopgap solution for a liability-sensitive bank like Zions would be to pay fixed on a short-maturity interest rate swap. The floating rate receive side on the swap would offset the floating cost of the money-market-indexed liabilities. The fixed pay leg of the swap would fix the financing rate on short-term liabilities. On the asset side, the solution is not so simple. If interest rates rise and new loans cannot be generated, which is the main risk, the bank will not have repricing opportunities. This lack of new loan repricing can be supplemented by a program of receive fixed swaps put on over time. The fixed receive legs will act like the new loans. However, a significant part of the bank's interest margin comes from the credit spread earned on the new loans. The swaps would surely earn much lower rates eroding the margin.

The gap analysis in Table 13.8 is crude and only for one maturity. While we don't have the information, the bank can most likely perform a much more detailed breakdown of repricing maturities. For example, we could arrange all assets and liabilities in the increasing order of coming due in order to compute the intermediate gaps, net interest margins, and income risks. An illustration of the complete Interest-Sensitivity Gap Analysis for Zions, all with made-up intermediate numbers, is shown in Table 13.9.

The objectives of the gap analysis in Table 13.9 are many. We break down the ISGap for 1-year and under into several finer maturity buckets. We see that while we have a positive gap for the first week, months 4 through 12 contribute most to the large negative gap. We see the categories that contribute most to the overall gap. Money market-indexed liabilities with maturities of 4 to 12 months greatly outweigh the loans maturing or repriceable during that period. We see that the first week presents an important repricing opportunity for money market investments.

While we are not showing that in the table, the detailed gap analysis of Table 13.9 allows one other important view of the bank's position. We can take the asset and liability amounts for each maturity bucket and multiply them by the average interest rates earned on them to produce the differences in the interest amounts earned for each maturity. Thus we can have a breakdown of the Net Interest Margin by the maturity buckets.

The main drawback of the ISGap analysis comes not so much from the methodology itself, but the implicit philosophy of parallel interest rate movements. Since most of the risk for a typical bank comes from short-term liabilities, and the interest rates on the various types of liabilities often move independently of each other (some are stickier than others), lumping all the categories into uniform maturity buckets may produce a distorted picture. One way to deal with that is to allow for interest sensitivity weights attached to the actual asset and liability categories. For example, many of the depositors' savings and money market accounts' interest rates do not adjust as fast as the rates on fed funds or marketable securities. This may be written into the accounts' rules, for customer relationship reasons, or at the discretion of the bank. Those accounts would thus be assigned weights less than 1. Many of the money market investments on the asset side might be assigned weights greater than 1 as their rates might

Table 13.9 The interest-sensitive gap analysis for Zions for September 30, 2010

ZIONS BANCORPORATION AND SUBSIDIARIES
Assets and liabilities maturing or subject to repricing in the following maturity buckets:

(In millions)	One day	Day 2–7	Day 8–30	Day 31–90	Day 91–365	Over One Year	Balance 30 Sep 10	Ave % rate
Assets								
Money market investments	115	1,201	1,107	1,975	795	–	$5,193	0.27
Securities:								
Held to-maturity		–	–	12	50	781	843	4.14
Available-for-sale	–	52	115	98	38	2,979	3,282	2.68
Trading account	–	7	52	–	–	–	59	3.63
Total securities	–	59	167	110	88	3,760	4,185	2.99
Loans held for sale	–	–	–	–	–	189	189	4.67
Loans:								
Net loans/leases excl. FDIC	12	163	948	1,878	4,445	29,079	36,525	5.60
FDIC-supported loans	–	–	12	87	320	419	1,150	11.93
Total loans and leases	12	163	960	1,965	4,765	29,810	37,675	5.79
Total interest-earning assets	127	1,423	2,234	4,050	5,648	33,759	47,241	4.93
Cash and due from banks	–	–	–	–	–	1,063	1,063	
Allowance for loan losses	(2)	(25)	(32)	(76)	(98)	(1,323)	(1,556)	
Goodwill	–	–	–	–	–	1,015	1,015	
Core deposit and intangibles	–	–	–	–	–	97	97	
Other assets	–	–	–	–	–	3,917	3,917	
Total assets	$ 125	$ 1,398	$ 2,202	$ 3,974	$ 5,550	$38,528	$51,778	

LIABILITIES AND EQUITY								
Interest-bearing deposits:								
Savings and NOW	–	–	216	1,293	4,678	–	$6,187	0.32
Money market	10	117	1,097	3,239	11,121	–	15,584	0.63
Time under $100,000	–	–	365	621	696	422	2,103	1.25
Time $100,000 and over	–	–	286	694	990	492	2,462	1.21
Foreign	–	77	178	11	1,297	–	1,563	0.6
Total interest-bearing deposits	10	194	2,142	5,858	18,782	914	27,900	0.66
Borrowed funds:								
Securities sold, not yet purchased	18	20	–	–	–	–	38	4.33
Fed funds and security repos	296	288	290	–	–	–	874	0.14
FHLB advances and other borrow:	–	–	–	100	110	18	238	5.34/4.74
Long-term debt	–	–	–	–	–	1,927	1,927	16.45
Total borrowed funds	314	308	290	100	110	1,945	3,068	10.82
Total interest-bearing liabilities	324	503	2,432	5,959	18,892	2,859	30,969	1.67
Non-interest-bearing deposits	–	–	–	–	–	13,787	13,787	
Other liabilities	–	–	–	–	–	601	601	
Total liabilities	324	503	2,432	5,959	18,892	17,247	$ 45,357	
Shareholders' equity:								
Preferred equity	–	–	–	–	–	1,819	1,819	
Common equity	–	–	–	–	–	4,601	4,601	
Total shareholders' equity	–	–	–	–	–	6,421	6,421	
Total liabilities and equity	$ 324	$ 503	$ 2,432	$ 5,959	$18,892	$23,668	$51,778	
ISGap	–$ 199	$ 895	–$ 230	–$1,985	–$13,342	$14,861		
Cumulative ISGap	–$ 199	$ 696	$ 466	–$1,519	**–$14,861**	$ 0		
ISRatio	0.39	2.78	0.91	0.67	0.29	1.63		

move more instantly and by disproportionately larger amount. In Zions' case, overall, this would result in the lower computed, weighted ISGap.

13.3 DURATION GAP MANAGEMENT

The Duration Gap Management serves a very different purpose of the ISGap analysis. Instead of focusing on the repricing risk of the different asset and liability categories, we attempt to describe the interest rate exposure of the existing asset and liabilities in order to assess the risk to the net worth of the bank. We assign durations to all asset and liability categories and we compute the weighted average duration of all assets and liabilities. The duration analysis is mathematically equivalent to the first-order Taylor expansion. The effect on the net worth is equal to the sum of the asset durations times interest rate changes minus the sum of the liability durations times the interest rate changes.

The Duration Gap analysis is similar in spirit to the market VaR factorization, but instead of multiple yield curve point exposures, we have one duration number describing each asset and liability category. Conceptually, by producing a composite duration for the whole asset portfolio and a composite duration for the whole liability portfolio, we are assuming parallel yield curve movements. The advantage is the relative simplicity and yet, at the same time, the completeness of the picture. Each balance sheet category's one duration number has a hedge interpretation. And we have the picture of the overall potential effect of interest rate changes on the bank's equity value.

Let us apply the Duration Gap Management method to Zions' balance sheet. We should be using the market values (many of which are contained in the bank's 10-Q), but in Table 13.10 we are using the accounting numbers to get the relative weights of the different categories. We are making up the intermediate duration numbers.

We start by computing the weight $w_i^A = A_i/TA$ of each asset line item in the total assets, and the weight $w_i^L = L_i/TL$ of each liability line item in the total liabilities. We perform a detailed analysis of each line item to determine the modified duration for that item, not shown here. For example, available-for-sale securities could be further broken down into US Treasuries, agencies, corporates, and municipals. One-to-four family residential real estate loans could be broken down into fixed and adjustable, and fixed further into 15-year and 30-year fixed. Each subcategory would be characterized by its own modified duration. The numbers in our table—D_i^A for asset categories and D_i^L for liability categories—are already weighted averages of these subcategories. We compute the weighted modified duration of all the assets and the weighted duration of all the liabilities:

$$D_A = \sum_i w_i^A \times D_i^A = 2.2254$$

$$D_L = \sum_i w_i^L \times D_i^L = 0.6469$$

The raw Duration Gap is equal to the difference of the durations:

$$DG = D_A - D_L = 2.2254 - 0.6469 = 1.5785$$

From this number, we see that the bank should strive to lengthen the duration of its liabilities or shorten the duration of its assets in order to achieve the neutral net worth position. In the absence of any repricing, interest rate changes alone will change the equity value of the bank.

Table 13.10 The duration gap analysis for Zions for September 30, 2010

ZIONS BANCORPORATION AND SUBSIDIARIES
Duration of assets and liabilities

(in millions)	Balance Sept 30 2010	Ave % rate	Weight %	Duration	Weight × Duration
Assets					
Money market investments	$5,193	0.27	10.03	0.22	*0.0221*
Securities:					
Held-to-maturity	843	4.14	1.63	9.62	*0.1568*
Available-for-sale	3,282	2.68	6.34	3.87	*0.2454*
Trading account	59	3.63	0.11	6.62	*0.0073*
Total securities	4,185	2.99	8.08		
Loans held for sale	189	4.67	0.37	2.20	*0.0081*
Commercial loans:					
Commercial & industrial	9,402		18.16	1.10	*0.1998*
Owner occupied & leasing	8,741		16.88	2.27	*0.3832*
Commercial real estate loans:					
Construction & land development	4,206		8.12	0.98	*0.0796*
Term	7,535		14.55	2.86	*0.4161*
Consumer loans:					
Home equity credit line	2,157		4.17	0.77	*0.0321*
1-4 Family residential	3,504		6.77	7.88	*0.5335*
Construction & other RE	366		0.71	1.12	*0.0080*
Bankcard, revolving, other	558		1.08	0.36	*0.0039*
Foreign loans:	56		0.11	0.26	*0.0003*
Net loans/leases excl. FDIC	36,525	5.60	70.54		
FDIC-supported loans	1,150	11.93	2.22	8.23	*0.1827*
Total loans and leases	37,675	5.79	72.76		
Total interest-earning assets	47,241	4.93	91.24		
Cash and due from banks	1,063		2.05	0.00	*0.0000*
Allowance for loan losses	(1,556)		(3.01)	1.77	*−0.0533*
Goodwill, core, other	5,029		9.71	0.00	*0.0000*
Total assets	$51,778		100.00		**2.2254**
LIABILITIES AND EQUITY					
Interest-bearing deposits:					
Savings and NOW	$6,187	0.32	13.64	0.66	*0.0900*
Money market	15,584	0.63	34.36	0.51	*0.1752*
Time under $100,000	2,103	1.25	4.64	1.08	*0.0501*
Time $100,000 and over	2,462	1.21	5.43	0.96	*0.0521*
Foreign	1,563	0.6	3.45	1.16	*0.0400*
Total interest-bearing deposits	27,900	0.66	61.51		
Borrowed funds:					
Securities sold, not yet purchased	38	4.33	0.08	3.22	*0.0026*
Fed funds and security repos	874	0.14	1.93	0.18	*0.0035*
FHLB advances and other borrow:	238	5.34/4.74	0.52	0.65	*0.0034*
Long-term debt	1,927	16.45	4.25	5.34	*0.2270*
Total borrowed funds	3,068	10.82	6.76		
Total interest-bearing liabilities	30,969	1.67	68.28		
Non-interest-bearing deposits	13,787		30.40	0.01	*0.0030*
Other liabilities	601		1.33	0.00	*0.0000*
Total liabilities	$ 45,357		100.00		**0.6469**
Total shareholders' equity	6,421				
Total liabilities and equity	$51,778				

Duration Gap 2.2254 − 0.6469 = **1.5785**

Leverage-Adjusted Duration Gap 2.2254 − 0.6469 × 45,357 / 51,778 = **1.6587**

A rise in the interest rates will reduce the value of the assets disproportionately more that the value of its liabilities.

Since the objective of the Duration Gap analysis is to provide a meaningful hedge recommendation, and as the dollar assets normally exceed the dollar liabilities, we are often interested in the Leverage-Adjusted Duration Gap:

$$LADGap = D_A - D_L \times \frac{TL}{TA} = 2.2254 - 0.6469 \times \frac{45{,}357}{51{,}778} = 1.6587$$

The interpretation of the Leverage-Adjusted Duration Gap is that the duration of the liabilities must change by more than that indicated by the raw gap in order to immunize the net worth of the bank.

Note the different emphasis of the Duration Gap from the Maturity Gap analysis. While the bank may not be able to adjust the relative composition of its loan and deposit portfolios and repricing may take time, it may choose to focus on the durations of each category, or focus on financial hedging. Suppose the management of the bank anticipates a 0.75% average rise in the interest rates over the next year. The effect of that interest rate rise on the bank's net worth would be:

$$\Delta E = (-D_A) \times \Delta r \times TA - (-D_L) \times \Delta r \times TL$$
$$\Delta E = (-2.2254) \times 0.0075 \times 51{,}778 - (-0.6469) \times 0.0075 \times 45{,}357$$
$$\Delta E = -864.20 + 220.06 = -\$644.14\,\text{million}$$

In the above calculation, we could have assumed different interest rate changes for total assets and total liabilities, or even for the different categories. For a parallel move in the interest rates assets and liabilities, the calculation can be performed more simply using the Leverage-Adjusted Duration Gap:

$$\Delta E = (-LADGap) \times \Delta r \times TA$$
$$\Delta E = (-1.6587) \times 0.0075 \times 51{,}778 = -\$644.14\,\text{million}$$

Relating this number to the bank's Income Statement, we see that this size change in the equity value represents roughly 2–6 months' worth of net interest income. The risk is thus not insignificant. The bank would have to generate that much more in income in order to maintain the current equity value. The alternative is financial hedging in the form of shorting long-term securities, shorting bond futures, or paying fixed on long-term swaps. The choice is often dictated by liquidity considerations, cost, and the fit with the income and repricing strategy. If the largest contributors to the gap–the commercial and residential real estate loans can be reduced or their duration shortened relatively quickly, then bond or note futures could be the best choice, if any hedging is to be undertaken. On the deposit side, Eurodollar, LIBOR or TBill futures could be used to hedge the cost of money market-indexed deposits.

13.4 VALUE AT RISK

The objective of the Market Value-at-Risk (VaR) analysis is to factorize the present value of assets and liabilities of a financial company and compute the loss that the present value would suffer if the factors fall into a 5% or 1% probability adverse "tail" event. There are two general distributional approaches in the banking industry used to define the tail event: historical non-parametric or normal (or log-normal) with a given volatility and correlation structure of the factors. The factors can be any variables (preferably observable and tradeable) that affect the institution's portfolio of assets and liabilities: equity indexes and individual stock prices, currency rates, and commodity prices, points on the government yield curve, swap spreads, other credit spreads, implied volatilities of interest rates, and equities.

For a bank like Zions, the market VaR method boils down to extending our duration factorization to the moves in more yield curve points (3 month, 6 month, 1 year, 2 year, 3 year, 5 year, 10 year, 30 year), credit spreads/rates (TED, Fed funds, Prime, COFI), perhaps one or two currency rates (Mexican peso, Canadian dollar). The main extension is in all the yield curve points, the TED spread (LIBOR minus TBill), and a few swap spread variables. All the other factors are much less significant to the value of assets and liabilities. And the way we will proceed is very similar to our duration analysis. We will take the line items on the balance sheet and, instead of describing them with one duration sensitivity to parallel interest rate movements, we will describe each with several finer sensitivities to the movements along the specific yield curve points and spreads. (Roughly, the sensitivities have to add up to the duration.)

Let us first go through some VaR definitions. In general, *VaR*, at a confidence level c, over a given horizon period d, is defined as the critical value PV^*, such that the probability that the profit $\widetilde{PV}$ will be lower or equal to PV^* is equal to $1 - c$. That is,

$$1 - c = \text{Prob}\left(\widetilde{PV} \leq PV^*\right)$$

There are two givens: the confidence level c, equal to 95% or 99%, and the time horizon d in years, e.g. 1 day (1/252), 1 week (1/52), or 2 weeks (1/26). At some stage, the BIS explicitly required publishing 10-day 99% *VaR* with minimum 6 months of data. We will use *VaR* and PV^* interchangeably.

VaR is expressed in dollars and leads to statements like: "The change in the firm portfolio's *PV* is likely to be above PV^* dollars with c percent probability", or "The *PV* loss will exceed $|PV^*|$ million dollars only $1 - c$ percent of the time."

In practice, we posit that the change in the PV of the institution's portfolio is a function of J factors and we compute the dollar sensitivities $\beta_1, \ldots, \beta_J$ of the PV to those factors, just as the duration gap was sensitive to interest rate moves. We modify the VaR definition in terms of the probability region for the factors:

$$1 - c = \text{Prob}\left[PV\left(\tilde{F}_1, \ldots, \tilde{F}_J\right) \leq PV^*\right]$$

This is the leanest specification for the non-parametric case. Here is the numerical procedure for the simplest VaR implementation, a historical bootstrap:

- Collect N weeks' worth of factor change data; N weeks, each with J factor change observations
- Given the sensitivities of the PV to the factors, for each week compute the gain/loss to the portfolio's PV, if the factors moved by the observed amount, denoted by PV_n, $n = 1, \ldots, N$
- Order the gains PV_n from the lowest (high negative) to the highest (positive)
- Pick the 5% lowest as your critical loss PV^* and as your 95% weekly *VaR*.

The main burden is in identifying all the factors that affect the portfolio's PV and computing the PV's sensitivities to those factors. That is, the main burden is in defining completely the first (or higher) order Taylor expansion of the PV function. If the factorization is linear, then the simplest form of the PV change function is:

$$PV\left(\tilde{F}_1, \ldots, \tilde{F}_J\right) = \beta_1 \times \tilde{F}_1 + \beta_2 \times \tilde{F}_2 + \cdots + \beta_J \times \tilde{F}_J$$

A historical simulation is a scrambled bootstrap where we randomly choose with replacement (simulate) factor histories from the observed N weeks of data in order to increase the sample size. In either case bootstrap or simulation, we do not know the form of the joint distribution function of all the factors.

Many industry implementations of VaR are parametric. In this case, we observe N weeks of factor data and compute the volatilities of the factors and the correlation structure of the factors. We then assume the multivariate distribution $\Phi(\cdot)$ and density function $\varphi(\cdot)$ of the continuous factors (or their logs) to be Gaussian (normal). *VaR* is then the cutoff PV change PV^* corresponding to the $1-c$ tail of the multivariate normal:

$$1 - c = \int \ldots \int_{PV(\tilde{F}_1,\ldots,\tilde{F}_J)\leq PV^*} \varphi\left(\tilde{F}_1, \ldots, \tilde{F}_J\right) d\tilde{F}_1 \ldots d\tilde{F}_J$$

This form is the general specification for the Monte Carlo simulation:

- Collect N weeks' worth of factor change data.
- Compute the variance–covariance matrix Σ of the factor changes where the diagonals and individual factor volatilities squared, or volatilities and correlations which define Σ
- Generate $\eta \geq 10{,}000$ vectors of factor samples $\tilde{F}_1, \ldots, \tilde{F}_J$.
- Given the sensitivities of the PV to the factors, for each sample compute the gain/loss to the portfolio's PV if the factors moved by the amount observed in the sample, denoted by $PV_n, n = 1, \ldots, \eta$.
- Order the gains PV_n from the lowest (high negative) to the highest (positive).
- Pick the 5% lowest as your critical loss PV^* and as your 95% weekly *VaR*.

The main feature of the VaR definition is its local focus and one-sidedness. Even though we reconstruct the entire distribution of PV changes, the VaR statistic is taken from its extreme left tail and ignores the rest of the information. For the complete discussion of the VaR methods' evolution, theoretical and implementation issues, see Dubil (2009) or Jorion (2009).

Let us get back to Zions' portfolio. Again, we use balance sheet numbers as market values and make up intermediate sensitivity numbers. Suppose instead of simple durations, we identify four points on the US Treasury yield curve – 3-month, 1-year, 5-year and 10-year – the TED spread (Libor minus TBill) and the 10-year swap spread as the main factors affecting the value of the portfolio. We characterize each asset and liability item on the balance sheet by the dollar exposure to those six factors. That is, we specify the dollar change in the PV of the bank's portfolio as a result of a 1 basis point change in the underlying rate. (Recall the definition of the PVBP in Chapter 2.) This step alone is difficult for any bank to implement. The bank would have to recompute the value of each loan or security on its books with the blipped rates. (Recall the understandable resistance of many European banks to the original EU-wide 2006 VaR Directives 2006/48/EC and 2006/49/EC, subsequently enhanced with 2010/76/EU.) Even more complicated might be computations of the exposure to convexity or to volatility for derivatives.

Table 13.11 shows the six factor sensitivities for Zions expressed in dollars per basis point move up. The minuses in front of the numbers for assets come from the fixed rate nature of most assets. We show the totals for interest rates for each balance sheet category. We also show totals for each factor for the entire bank. Given these sensitivities

Table 13.11 The VaR factor sensitivities for Zions for September 30, 2010

(Balance in millions, PVBPs in dollars)	Balance Sept 10	PVBPs FOR YIELD CURVE POINTS AND SPREADS						
		3-mo	1-yr	5-yr	10-yr	TED	10-yr Swp Sp	Total Yld Curve
ASSETS								
Money market investments	$5,193	–87,634	–26,612			–26,395		–114,246
Securities:								
Held-to-maturity	843				–810,966			–810,966
Available-for-sale	3,282		–342,875	–795,433	–131,826			–1,270,134
Trading account	59			–14,722	–24,336			–39,058
Total securities	4,185							
Loans held for sale	189	–1,433	–20,672	–17,475	–2,000	–1,433	–5,233	–41,580
Commercial Loans:								
Commercial & Industrial	9,402	–288,293	–592,110	–153,817		–124,199		–1,034,220
Owner Occupied & Leasing	8,741	–302,448	–725,239	–932,746	–23,774	–143,840	–23,774	–1,984,207
Commercial real estate loans:								
Construction & Land Development	4,206	–286,266	–125,922			–112,322		–412,188
Term	7,535	–299,143	–714,278	–1,024,193	–117,396	–143,228	–22,845	–2,155,010
Consumer loans:								
Home equity credit line	2,157	–93,467	–72,622			–21,010		–166,089
1-4 Family Residential	3,504		–241,842	–478,193	–2,041,117		–322,192	–2,761,152
Construction & other RE	366	–22,351	–18,641			–6,219		–40,992
Bankcard, Revolving, Other	558	–16,218	–3,870			–3,227		–20,088
Foreign loans:	56	–1,456				–1,456		–1,456
Net loans/leases excl. FDIC	36,525							
FDIC-supported loans	1,150			–18,039	–928,411		–201,771	–946,450
Total loans and leases	37,675							
Total interest-earning assets	47,241							
Cash and due from banks	1,063							–
Allowance for loan losses	(1,556)		154,221	121,191				275,412
Goodwill, Core, other	5,029							–
Total assets	$51,778	–1,398,709	–2,730,462	–3,313,427	–4,079,826	–583,329	–575,815	–11,522,424

(Continued)

Table 13.11 *(Continued)*

(Balance in millions, PVBPs in dollars)	Balance Sept 10	PVBPs FOR YIELD CURVE POINTS AND SPREADS						
		3-mo	1-yr	5-yr	10-yr	TED	10-yr Swp Sp	Total Yld Curve
LIABILITIES AND EQUITY								
Interest-bearing deposits:								
Savings and NOW	$6,187	243,283	165,059			148,933		408,342
Money market	15,584	311,992	482,792			266,119		794,784
Time under $100,000	2,103	20,906	176,335	29,883		36,229		227,124
Time $100,000 and over	2,462	56,013	169,337	11,002		102,337		236,352
Foreign	1,563		166,534	14,774		188,992		181,308
Total interest-bearing deposits	27,900							–
Borrowed funds:								
Securities sold, not yet purchased	38		2,354	9,882				12,236
Fed funds and security repos	874	12,614	3,118			1,133		15,732
FHLB advances and other borrow:	238	8,442	7,028			2,001		15,470
Long-term debt	1,927		95,701	277,329	655,988			1,029,018
Total borrowed funds	3,068							–
Total interest-bearing liabilities	30,969							–
Non-interest-bearing deposits	13,787	13,787						13,787
Other liabilities	601							–
Total liabilities	$45,357	667,037	1,268,258	342,870	655,988	745,744	–	2,934,153
Total shareholders' equity	6,421							
Total liabilities and equity	$51,778							
Total VaR Factor Sensitivities		**−731,672**	**−1,462,204**	**−2,970,557**	**−3,423,838**	**162,415**	**−575,815**	**−8,588,271**

$\beta_1 = -731{,}672, \ldots, \beta_6 = -575{,}815$, the rest of the VaR analysis relies on using a relatively simple stand-alone procedure of using simulated samples for the factor changes, multiplying them out to compute the PV changes $PV_n, n = 1, \ldots, \eta$, and picking off the lower 99- or 95-percentile PV number.

Suppose that Scenario No. 233 is a parallel yield curve shift up of 75 basis points, i.e. the factor realizations for that sample are:

$$F_1 = F_2 = F_3 = F_4 = 75, \quad F_5 = F_6 = 0$$

Then the PV change for that sample is:

$$PV_{233} = -731{,}672 \times 75 - 1{,}462{,}204 \times 75 - 2{,}970{,}557 \times 75 - 3{,}423{,}838 \times 75$$
$$PV_{233} = -644{,}120{,}325$$

The bank would lose \$644.1 million in that scenario. Of course, a parallel move of 75 bp in 1 week is most unlikely, so that scenario would have to be an extreme left-tail event. We would more likely have samples like the yield curve steepening Scenario 7256.

$$F_1 = 7,\ F_2 = 9,\ F_3 = 12,\ F_4 = 15,\ F_5 = 2,\ F_6 = 4$$

Then the PV change for that sample is:

$$\begin{aligned} PV_{7256} &= -731{,}672 \times 7 - 1{,}462{,}204 \times 9 \\ &\quad - 2{,}970{,}557 \times 12 - 3{,}423{,}838 \times 15 \\ &\quad + 162{,}415 \times 2 - 575{,}815 \times 4 \\ PV_{7256} &= -107{,}264{,}224 \end{aligned}$$

If we have 10,000 samples, we arrange the sampled PV changes from the lowest to the highest and pick the 500th one to obtain the 95-percentile weekly *VaR*.

The VaR analysis makes more sense for a global bank like J.P. Morgan. The large derivative portfolio would have to be described in terms of sensitivities to swap spreads, cap and swaption volatilities, detailed equity indexes and perhaps individual stocks, their volatilities, currencies, and their volatilities. We might even have esoteric variables like volatility skews, credit default swap rates, etc. During the author's tenure in the corporate risk management of Merrill Lynch, the bank collected data from 3,000 trading units for hundreds of factors, excluding individual equities. What may make sense for both Zions and J.P. Morgan is the enhancement of the market VaR with credit VaR. In credit VaR, the banks would attempt to factorize the credit exposure of their securities and loan portfolios. Again, the guiding mathematical principle would be a Taylor series expansion with first-order derivatives. The factors might be key credit indexes or spreads, like average sovereign spread, spread for top investment grade, bottom investment grade, and a few junk categories, etc. The methodological difficulty might come from trying to adequately parameterize these variables with their volatilities and correlations. And as the 2008 crisis showed, all of these methods may fail if they do not account for liquidity factors or as correlations dramatically increase in times of severe market dislocations.

14

Private Equity, Pension, and Sovereign Funds

Like banks and insurance companies, pension funds and private equity firms play a very important role in recycling excess savings back to business entities. Defined benefit pension funds invest the pension contributions they receive monthly into public and private markets in order to be able to meet very large future pension liabilities. Sovereign funds and private equity funds seek public and private investments in order to maximize intermediate term returns. The common feature of these intermediaries is that they often seek returns not only from taking on systematic (general macroeconomic) risk of the public stock markets (like mutual funds or individual investors), but also rents earned on bearing illiquidity risk, corporate reorganizations, and distressed turnarounds. This by itself forces an intermediate 2- to 10-year horizon. Also, unlike most hedge funds, they use their capital, often enhanced with leverage or pooled with other contributors, to "invest" (buy and hold) rather than to support (margin) a relative value arbitrage strategy. That is, they take long positions in companies and engage in providing important management services aimed at "unlocking value" (reorganizing underperforming managements, demerging and selling off, guiding through the venture capital stages). This human capital injection is an important part of their strategy for success.

Private equity firms do not aim to arbitrage generic asset classes against each other, US interest rate vs US stocks, or US interest rates vs Australian interest rates. The financial engineering and arbitrage here takes place at the corporate level and is individualized. Each case is different. Some firms need the entrenched management to be removed, some need to be split up, and some need production methods rationalized; early-stage venture firms have product development strategies, but need corporate finance expertise. In short-term-obsessed public markets, these goals are often impossible to accomplish. Private equity firms serve as organizing clusters. They form funds in which they invest their own capital, but invite pension funds, sovereign funds, investment companies, and "qualified" (wealthy) individuals to contribute the bulk of the capital. The purchased businesses are guided to success, or failure. The investments are sold off, funds liquidated, and the capital is returned to all the contributors. The process takes up to 10 years.

The objective of the chapter is to overview this investment process and its quantification language. We start at the private equity firm level: the formation of the limited partnership fund, the investments in a leverage buyout or a venture start-up, and the exit strategy through an IPO or a secondary market sale. We then go on to the investing firms' level to discuss the risk-budgeting process. Risk-budgeting is an alternative to asset allocation; the focus is on risk rather than expected return weighting.

14.1 PRIVATE EQUITY

Private equity firms have generally two ways to raise funds when acquiring a company. One, common in taking a publicly traded company private, is to have the acquired

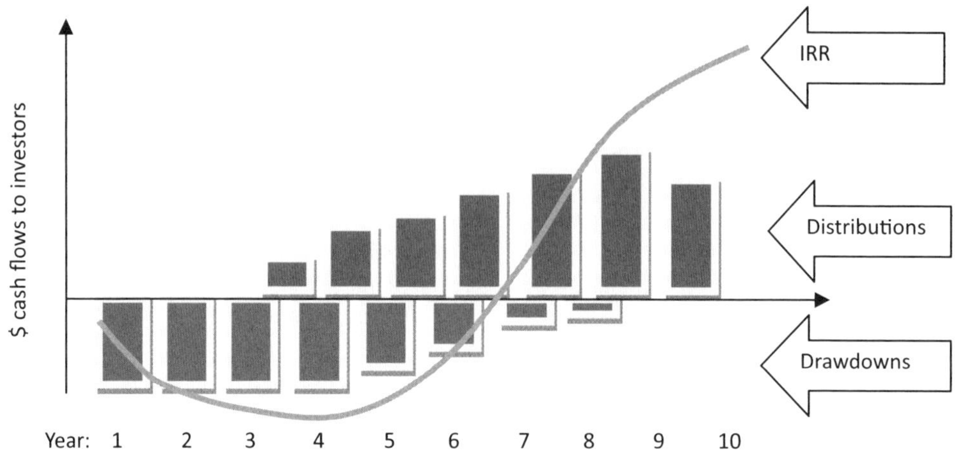

Figure 14.1 Private equity fund life cycle
Graph idea adapted from en.wikipedia.org/wiki/J_curve

company issue debt. The other, common in venture start-ups, is to form a partnership fund, capitalized mostly by other investors, that makes equity investments in one or many companies.

14.1.1 Investment in Private Equity – Limited Partnership Funds

ABC Capital forms ABC Explorer Fund, a limited partnership (LLP). ABC becomes a general partner (GP). ABC turns to several investors (pension funds, endowments, other private equity firms) to become limited partners (LPs) in the new fund. LPs first agree to commit capital over a specified period of time (up to 2–5 years). ABC Explorer Fund plans to make equity investments over that period. The GP calls capital from the LPs (drawdowns) when the investments become available. In the process, the potential investors (with capital call liability) become real (LP) investors in the Fund. They are issued limited partnership shares. Not all the committed capital is always called. Sometimes capital is called, but not immediately used. Over the following several years, the Fund finishes making investments and returns the capital back to the limited partners. For tax purposes, the returns can be in the form of interest, dividends, or partnership capital returns. Often there is an overlap period over which capital is still being called while some returns are already made.

Figure 14.1 illustrates the typical process. As the Fund is formed, capital is drawn down over the first 3 years while very few investments are made. In the second phase, the majority of the capital is called and most investments are made. Some investments start paying. In the third phase, investments are liquidated and capital is returned; some additional capital may still be called if opportunities arise.

Figure 14.1 also shows the so-called "J-curve." If we compute the net asset value (NAV) and the return on investment in the Fund, in the early years it is negative and increasingly so, as expenses are incurred and no return is made. In the early years, the fund spends capital on new investments and on human capital it injects into the acquired firms. Later in life, returns turn positive, as appreciated investments are liquidated, the NAV increases, and the cash is returned to the investors.

14.1.2 Leverage Buyouts

The most common way of taking a public company private is a leverage buyout (LBO). An interesting feature of the LBO is that the debt used to acquire the target company becomes the target company's liability with non-recourse to the acquiring private equity limited partnership. An LBO is typically of a large established company generating large operating cash flows. Those cash flows are used to pay off the debt in order to increase the equity portion of the company.

The best way to understand a leverage buyout is to see it in the following stages:

- A private equity firm identifies XYZ Corp. as a target company. XYZ is a consumer staples company and generates large operating cash flows. Its debt is $50, equity is $45, and it generates $12 in EBITDA (earnings before interest, taxes, and depreciation).
- The private equity firm ABC Capital forms ABC Raider Fund, a limited partnership (funded by its own capital or with contributions by others). ABC Raider raises $16.
- ABC Raider Fund obtains a $64 loan commitment from Granite Bank. Granite Bank's loan will become the senior debt of XYZ after the acquisition. The coupon is 6.625% or $4.
- ABC Raider Fund also obtains mezzanine (subordinated) debt financing from Shark Bank. Shark will lend $20 at 10%.
- ABC Raider makes a tender offer to the shareholders of XYZ at $50 total, i.e. at an 11% premium to the current stock price to acquire the company and to pay off its existing $50 debt.
- XYZ's stock is delisted from the stock exchange and ABC Raider becomes its sole shareholder. ABC installs its own management.
- XYZ's liabilities are $64 to Granite Bank and $20 to Shark Bank. Its equity is valued at $16.

The acquisition process is complete. The annual operating cash flow (EBITDA = $12) of XYZ (the acquired company) is said to cover seven "turns of debt" ($84). The process of improving efficiency, liquidating assets, or turning the company around starts as soon as the acquisition is complete. A new management is installed. The explicit objective is to pay off all the debt. Let us assume that we are able to increase EBITDA by about $1–3 each year. Here is what happens in the first few years.

- Year 1: EBITDA of $14 covers $6 in interest ($4 to Granite and $2 to Shark) and pays off $8 of Granite Bank's debt. The remaining balance is $56.
- Year 2: EBITDA of $16.71 covers $5.71 in interest ($3.71 to Granite and $2 to Shark) and pays off $11 of Granite Bank's debt. The remaining balance is $45.
- Year 3: EBITDA of $18.98 covers $4.98 in interest ($2.98 to Granite and $2 to Shark) and pays off $14 of Granite Bank's debt. The remaining balance is $31.
- Year 4: EBITDA of $22.05 covers $4.05 in interest ($2.05 to Granite and $2 to Shark) and pays off $18 of Granite Bank's debt. The remaining balance is $13.
- Year 5: EBITDA of $24.86 covers $2.86 in interest ($0.86 to Granite and $2 to Shark) and pays off the remaining $13 of Granite Bank's debt and $9 of Shark Bank's debt.
- Year 6: EBITDA of $25.90 covers $0.90 in interest (to Shark) and pays off the remaining $9 of Shark Bank's debt. The remaining EBITDA is split between taxes $6 and a $10 dividend to ABC Raider Fund.
- Also in Year 6: XYZ goes through an IPO and the company is sold to the public. If the economic value-to-EBITDA multiple remains the same as prior to the buyout, i.e. 95/12 = 7.927, then XYZ is sold for $25.90 × 7.927, or $205.04. Including the $10 dividend in Year 6, ABC Raider has earned a 54.19% annual compound return on its $16 investment over the 6-year period!

Clearly, the risk is leverage and the interest liability burden. The success depends on increasing the EBITDA through efficiency gains or on asset sales. Also, ABC Raider Fund, and its investors, may not want to wait until Year 6 to see the first dividend. Splitting some of the EBITDA between debt relief and dividends would lengthen the repayment process, but reduce the risk for the fund. On the other hand, ABC Raider does not have to wait till Year 6 to sell its equity stake. The company could be sold back to the public with debt on its books.

14.1.3 Private Equity Lending – Mezzanine Capital and Distressed Loans

Instead of leading the LBO with a leveraged equity investment, the private equity firm can provide capital in the form of debt. Typically, senior debt carrying a relatively low interest rate is provided by banks. Junior, subordinated, debt is provided by private equity firms. In this case, the firm or a partnership formed by it is the supplier of leverage to the lead buyout firm. The capital is provided either in the form of high interest debt or preferred shares. In either case, in the capital structure of the firm that is being taken private, it sits between the senior debt and the equity stake, hence the "mezzanine" label. The buyout firm has every incentive to repay this debt before it can realize its own return on equity. The US government used the high coupon preferred structure in its 2008–9 bailouts of the banking and auto industries. The banks providing senior financing to the LBO may require some mezzanine financing to be used. On the other hand, the advantage of using some mezzanine debt by the LBO firm may be the ability to renegotiate the terms. This is not always easy with regulated banks that must satisfy capital ratio requirements and must report any impairment on the debt they hold. The private equity firm supplying the mezzanine debt can act more freely and simply agree to increase the interest rate when the newly privatized company's financial ratios fall outside specified ranges and it struggles to repay. The debt may carry conversion rights or equity warrants. In our example above, Shark Bank was the provider of mezzanine debt.

Another way for a private equity firm to provide debt is "distressed financing." In the USA, companies can file for bankruptcy with the objective of liquidation or restructuring. In the latter case, the bankruptcy judge works with the company's management on reducing the liabilities of the company by voiding labor and supplier contracts and restructuring bond and bank debt. In the process, the shareholders are wiped out and the equity is delisted, while current debt holders may be bought off with equity ownership. Private equity firms or limited partnerships can step in during this process and buy up the existing debt in the hope of owning the company when it re-emerges from bankruptcy. They can also provide new "turnaround" or "special situations" financing with the same objective.

14.1.4 Other Forms of Private Equity – PIPEs

An LBO takes a healthy public company private. Sometimes public companies need additional capital to grow or face temporary distress. In these cases, they can turn to private equity firms or sovereign funds for injections of private equity "growth capital" in the form of a minority stake in the company. What distinguishes these private investments in public equities (PIPEs) from simply buying up the company's stock above the 5% control threshold is that it is a seasoned new capital offering going directly to the company which is dilutive to other shareholders, and it is often a private offering unregistered for 2 to 3 years or sold as a "registered direct" offering placed with a specific buyer. At the time of the capital injection, the public company issues either a convertible debt security or a preferred security. Its conversion feature is structured to be attractive to the investing fund (low conversion price) and thus potentially highly dilutive.

14.1.5 Venture Capital

The venture capital industry provides equity capital and management services to newly formed business. Its *raison d'être* is the fact that in some industries the time and capital required to bring a new product to market is long/large. The product is past its fundamental research stage (done at universities, government, or private labs), but still in its commercial infancy. The capital needed is very large: drug testing or large software development. The time to commercialization is long and the adoption is fraught with uncertainty. This risk cannot be borne by banks or lenders. The risk cannot be financed by public equity capital with its insistence on short-term returns. Venture capital bridges that gap.

The venture capital legal structure parallels private equity. Venture capital firms form limited partnerships in which they put some of their own capital and invite other investors to participate through capital commitments. The objective is different. Rather than taking cash-rich public companies private, injecting human capital to squeeze synergies out of them and reselling them in the public markets, venture capital firms help to form companies starting with a handful of employees/owners, supply management expertise, and guide them through several capital and product milestones. The final goal is still a sale in the public market or a resale to a large public company. Private equity is often viewed as ruthless and destructive, while venture capital is viewed as building companies. Yet there is an element of ruthlessness in both; the difference is the stage at which they take over the companies. Private equity takes already operating companies, but perhaps with entrenched managements or with faltering strategies. Venture capital takes new companies that perhaps lack large company management expertise or simply need large amounts of capital and patience. The equity money is not free. Often the owner-entrepreneurs end up with small stakes or lose control of their companies altogether.

The venture capital process proceeds in several financing stages and frequently involves an employee option plan. Each stage dilutes the previous owner's stakes, but is necessary for the ultimate success of the company. To save money on operating expenses, employees are offered a "venture" stake of their own. Instead of full cash compensation, they are paid in long-term options on the company's stock, or less commonly in restricted stock. Options carry 5- to 10-year expiries and may be subject to vesting. Management expertise can also be purchased with options when talented individuals are given upfront allocations.

It is often overlooked that the venture capital process starts with the entrepreneur first drawing on his or her own funds. The "seed stage" or the "proof of concept" stage involves angel investors who put in up to $500,000 to enable the entrepreneur/inventor to file for patents, finish the first code or produce a product prototype. The angels are found through informal networking, or through a public or private incubator. The angel investors and the entrepreneur become the founders of the company. Their investment is made through common stock or a convertible note; the latter converted into common at the same price as the next funding stage's investors minus a small discount up to 20%. The seed stage investment is very risky; there is no product yet, nor is there an organization to develop a product. The expected return at this point is 20–30 times the investment.

At the next "start-up" or "early stage" venture round, a consortium of angels or an early stage venture fund make investments of $1–5 million in the form of common stock or most often in the form of preferred shares Series A with dividend, liquidation, and anti-dilution rights as well as first refusal on the sales of the shares by the owners/angels. The capital is used to develop the product, code, or drug, and to start marketing it. At this point, first critical employees are hired, and offices are opened. The employees participate in the stock option plan as part of their compensation. The investors in this stage look for 5–10 times returns.

After the early stage round, there may be one or more "growth" or "expansion" stage venture rounds with investments ranging from $5 to $25 million. During this time, the product is developed and the effort is placed on commercialization, marketing, and reaping network benefits if it is software or hardware. The product may not be profitable at this phase, but the plan to make it profitable must be clear. Investors receive common or preferred Series B or C with superior rights to the previous round. Of course, they pay more for those privileges. The investors look for 2–5 times returns. Sometimes when the growing company burns through cash from the previous round, but is not ready for the next, it may seek "bridge" or "mezzanine" capital in the form of convertible debt or debt with warrants that automatically convert to preferred or common at the next round at a small discount.

Before the company can be sold to a big corporate buyer or the public, sometimes it needs to go through one more "buyout capital" round. It raises capital to buy smaller related or critical knowledge (software, hardware, drug delivery patents) companies and merge them into one organization fully able to achieve its product strategy objectives. It may also seek additional "bridge" financing before it is sold. Often at this point, the management of the company is replaced as the next public stage will require a different skill set.

14.1.6 Exit Strategies – IPOs and Secondary Sales

The best exit scenario is an initial public offering (IPO) on a public stock exchange. The venture capital investors are able to liquidate their holdings; founders may be subject to a partial lockout, but also generally can cash in on some of their holdings. The objective is a large P/E multiple and an oversubscribed offering. The second best exit is a sale to a large public corporation. The standalone start-up firm may not have the requisite distribution or brand recognition. Putting a large pharma firm's name and sales force to work can help.

The third often forgotten exit is through a secondary sale to other private equity investors. In the 1990s, this exit channel mostly covered distressed sales. In the 2000s, secondary intermediaries emerged sometimes set up by major investment banks, and private equity funds not interested in early stage investing begun entering investments in smaller chunks and at later stages. This allowed them to diversify their private equity holding across stages and shorten the time to cash-out. As more buyers and sellers entered, the pricing improved and the transactions were no longer distress sale-driven. The 2008–9 crisis period saw a temporary price depression with liquidity-driven sales, but by 2010 the market returned to normal.

In the secondaries market, what are traded are often the limited partner's holdings in the entire private equity fund. That is, the market is not trading in stakes in individual start-up firms, but in stakes in private equity limited partnerships, each perhaps funding 20–30 different start-ups in different stages of commercialization. The secondary sale can proceed in two ways. First, the selling limited partner can approach the general partner to assist in the sale, in finding an interested buyer or already having a buyer in mind. The second way is to conduct an auction. The auction can be an "open auction" to several interested buyers conducted by the limiter partner, or it can be a "targeted auction" conducted by a secondary intermediary. The auction itself can have two stages, with the first narrowing down the list of buyers to two to three. The main motivation of the sellers in the secondaries market is liquidity. The private equity partnership life may be quite long, with capital calls preceding any distributions by several years, tying up the capital for a long time (the "J-curve effect"). Another motivation may be the so-called "denominator effect." When the total holding of a pension fund or a sovereign fund decline, and the fund is committed to maintain a certain percentage of investment in a particular asset class, it may happen that public holdings marked-to-market may decline in value faster than private holdings forcing the liquidation of the latter. The buyers' motivations are typically portfolio reallocation and diversification, early stage into later stage (moving along the J curve), large stakes into smaller stakes, and across industries. Sometimes it is to get in with preferred general partners.

The total amount of secondary transaction in private equity reached $82 billion. The amount of capital raised for dedicated secondaries-only funds was over $20 billion. Secondaries are attractive to funds-of-funds; they account for 30–40% of all purchases in any given year.

14.2 RISK ALLOCATION FOR PENSION FUNDS AND SOVEREIGN FUNDS

Pension funds and sovereign funds, while subject to guidelines set by their governing bodies, enjoy great discretion in allocating their investment dollars, and often do not shy from alternative investments. These include commercial real estate and land development, hedge funds and private equity. In addition to investment (asset) management, pension funds and endowments often have extensive disbursement obligations on the liability side. Pension fund assets must be liquidated to satisfy monthly disbursements to pensioners; endowments provide specific dollar amounts or guaranteed rates of return to the universities, cultural institutions, or charities they support. Sovereign funds in particular, but pension funds and endowments too, may be subject to political pressures to allocate funds in a particular way or provide extraordinary disbursements. Table 14.1 shows the largest six pension and sovereign funds in the world.

14.2.1 Defined Benefit Pension Funds and Endowments

The management of the defined benefit pension plans and endowments is of special interest as it shares some features of insurance companies. Defined benefit plans often give the employees

Table 14.1 Top 6 Pension and Sovereign Funds in the World

Pension Fund	**Dec 2009 Assets in $ bn**
Government Pension Investment Fund, Japan	$1,315
Government Pension Fund, Norway	$476
Stichting Pensioenfonds ABP, Netherlands	$300
Korea's National Pension Corp	$235
Federal Retirement Thrift, USA	$234
California Public Employees' Retirement System, USA	$199
Sovereign Fund	**Dec 2010 Assets in $ bn**
Abu Dhabi Investment Authority	$627
SAMA Foreign Holdings, Saudi Arabia	$415
SAFE Investment Company, China	$347
China Investment Corporation	$289
Government of Singapore Investment Corporation	$248
Hong Kong Monetary Authority Investment Portfolio	$228

they cover a specified retirement formula. In the USA, a popular plan is 2% per number of years worked times the last year's or last 5 years' average salary. There may be a kicker where the percentage gradually increases from 2% to 3% if the number of years exceeds 25 or 30, and there is a specified minimum retirement age. University endowments guarantee to disburse a dollar amount equal to a guaranteed interest rate. Both these arrangements are similar to life insurance policies which credit cash accounts with a declared interest rate and offer a guaranteed life benefit. The attitudes to funding life insurance vary around the world with British companies carrying more equity in their investment portfolios, and their American counterparts carrying hardly any. After all, the liability here is quite fixed. Many scholars question the practice of incurring fixed liabilities and funding them with an equity portfolio. Often the liabilities end up being grossly underfunded as the discount rates assumed to present-value the future obligations are quite high (based on long-term equity returns). Several researchers have suggested funding them with high-grade fixed income investments, perhaps enhanced with some equity options. Few of these serious suggestions have been taken seriously by the plan sponsors – governments, workers' unions, or private corporations.

Given that state of affairs, pension plans and endowments have to aggressively pursue risk in order to maximize return. The standard allocation method is the same as for individuals except that it includes alternative illiquid asset classes. The total dollars coming in to be invested are divided among the different classes dependent on the duration of the liabilities. The total investment portfolio, governed by the plan's investment committee, is rebalanced quarterly or semi-annually, with the objective to meet the statutory return rate with the lowest amount of risk (classic mean variance approach enhanced with some VaR tools). In the last 10 years, another approach called "risk-budgeting" has gained some traction. The approach has been pitched by many advisers at various conferences and specialized training programs. The approach is not revolutionary, but offers some interesting insights. The next section describes its main principles.

14.2.2 The Risk Budget Allocation Process

The central idea in risk-budgeting is to allocate a specific percentage of risk rather than investment dollars to a specific asset class. This necessitates the definition of risk and the specification of the overall risk tolerance for the fund. This does not avoid making standard decisions on active–passive split and specific active manager allocations. However, it leads to interestingly different emphasis from the traditional investment amount allocation.

We present the ideas using the mean-variance risk framework, but everything that follows could be translated into the VaR framework.

Consider a US-based pension fund allocating its portfolio to three risky assets: US stocks, developed country non-US stocks, and emerging markets stocks. We label them: US, EAFE, and EM. Let us start with a 40%/40%/20% allocation, as in Table 14.2, and show the volatility and correlation assumptions.

The US and EAFE parts of the portfolio are highly correlated. The sum of the weights times the volatilities is equal to 24%. The total volatility of the portfolio, 19.86%, is computed using the individual weights, volatilities, and correlations. The difference is due to (correlation) diversification. Table 14.3 shows the same portfolio through a lens of risk attribution.

The unit Marginal risk contribution (MRC) is computed by blipping the weight by 0.1%, recomputing the total volatility of the portfolio and scaling it by 10. The interpretation is that a 1% increase in the volatility of the US part of the portfolio would lead to a 0.15%

Table 14.2 The volatilities and correlations for the US/EAFE/EM portfolio

	Weight	Volatility	Correlation matrix			
				US	EAFE	EM
US	40%	18.0%	US	1.00	0.85	0.20
EAFE	40%	22.0%	EAFE	0.85	1.00	0.50
EM	20%	40.0%	EM	0.20	0.50	1.00
Total	**100%**	**19.9%**				

increase in the total volatility. The next column multiplies that number by weight, and the last column represents the result in percentages of the total volatility. While the US may have the lowest unit MRC, because it is 40% of the portfolio, a unit change in volatility leads to roughly the same change in risk as a unit change in EM volatility even though EM is only 20% of the portfolio. The interesting result portrayed in Table 14.3 is that EAFE's and EM's contributions to risk are larger than their investment weights while the US's contribution is disproportionately smaller. This is due to the lower volatility of the US returns and higher correlation of EAFE with EM than US with EM. The main objective of the risk attribution is to see these not always intuitive co-dependencies of volatilities and correlations.

The lesson here is that we are overweighted in the US and underweighted in the EM in terms of return contributions; we are grossly underweighted in the US and overweighted in the EAFE and EM in terms of risk! That may be a completely unintended consequence of the asset allocation percentages for this US-based pension fund.

Let us perform a simple experiment. Suppose we wanted to limit to 20% the allocation of risk to the EM. Table 14.4 shows one such possible scenario.

The upshot is that we need to reallocate 4.63% of the portfolio from the EM to the US part. Note that we may further desire to reallocate some of the EAFE investment to the US to reduce its contribution to risk, too.

The risk-budgeting process includes the following steps:

- Set an overall target volatility level – absolute for a defined contribution plan, incremental in excess of guaranteed return for a defined benefit plan.
- Allocate to passive and active management – assume zero correlation between the two if active is managed as a portable alpha; passive presumably has the lion's share of the % risk attribution.
- Allocate within the passive part not to exceed the allocated risk ceiling.
- Select active asset classes and active managers.

Table 14.3 Marginal (MRC) and total risk contribution (TRC)

	MRC		% Risk attribution
	Unit	× Weight	
US	0.15%	5.9%	29.7%
EAFE	0.21%	8.4%	42.2%
EM	0.28%	5.6%	28.1%
Total		**19.9%**	**100.0%**

Table 14.4 Weights, MRC and TRC with a 20% limit on EM risk

		MRC		% Risk
		Unit	× Weight	attribution
US	44.63%	0.16%	7.0%	36.0%
EAFE	40.00%	0.21%	8.5%	44.0%
EM	15.37%	0.25%	3.9%	20.0%
Total	**100.00%**		**19.3%**	**100.0%**

Suppose we decide on the overall risk not to exceed 8% volatility. Suppose we think the passive benchmark can be tracked with a mixed asset portfolio subject to 10% volatility, and an active portfolio subject to 4% volatility. Then we must allocate 79.6% of the investment dollars to passive and 20.4% to active management. This comes from the simple act of solving for the weights of a two non-correlated asset portfolio.

We then repeat the process for the passive and active parts by solving for the investment dollars allocated to each asset category within the passive and active parts of the portfolio. The calculation includes our assumptions about the individual volatilities and pairwise correlations, similar to our experiment in Table 14.4 but with 7% and 4% targets. In the active part, many correlations should, but need not, be assumed zero. In the passive part, they are computed from market data or can be input.

The risk budget imposes a different discipline on the fund sponsors from standard asset allocation. In the classic approach, everything is return-driven. To stick to the prescribed asset allocation, the quarterly or annual rebalancing implies selling a winner and buying underperformers. In the risk-budgeting approach, it is the market volatility that drives the rebalancing not relative performance. Another implication is that since our allocation was based on risk, less risky areas (fixed income) will tend to be overweighted relative to riskier classes (commodities, equities).

The most obvious criticism of the risk-budgeting approach is that the initial allocation is based on risk calculations of historical volatility and correlation estimates. Yet risk changes over time and in extreme tail events correlations dramatically increase. The answer to this criticism is that standard allocation is implicitly based on realized return histories which may be just as unreliable. After all, we tend to allocate to equities and emerging markets because we expect higher returns there. What if they don't materialize?

ACKNOWLEDGMENT

Special thanks to two of my undergrad students at the University of Utah: Kyle Poulin for entertaining conversations on LBOs and investment banking, and Huan Yuan for her research into private equity secondary sales. Some data in this chapter is taken from her April 2010 thesis defense and is unconfirmed. The section on risk-budgeting is based on my own understanding and interpretation of the subject and may diverge from the industry practice and language, as my objective was to simplify the concepts down to an easy-to-follow numerical example.

References

Agarwal, V. and Naik, N.Y. (2000) Multiperiod performance persistence analysis of hedge funds. *Journal of Financial and Quantitative Analysis* **35**(3), 327–342.

Agarwal, V., Daniel, N.D. and Naik, N.Y. (2009) Role of Managerial Incentives and Discretion in Hedge Fund Performance. *The Journal of Finance* **64**(5), 2221–2256.

Amenc, N., Martellini, L., Meyfredi, J.-C. and Ziemann, V. (2010) Passive Hedge Fund Replication – Beyond the Linear Case. *European Financial Management* **16**(2), 191–210.

Arnott, R. and West, J. (2008) Liquid Alternatives: More Then Hedge Funds. *IndexUniverse.com.*

Baxter, M. and Rennie, A. (1996) *Financial Calculus.* Cambridge University Press.

Black, F. and Karasinski, P. (1991) Bond and option pricing when short rates are lognormal. *Financial Analysts Journal* (July/August), 52–59.

Black, F. and Litterman, R. (1992) Global portfolio optimization. *Financial Analysts Journal* (September), pp. 28–43. http://www.blacklitterman.org/

Black, F. and Scholes, M. (1973) The pricing of options and corporate liabilities. *Journal of Political Economy* **81** (May–June), 637–659.

Bollen, N.P.B. and Whaley, R.E. (2009) Hedge Fund Risk Dynamics: Implications for Performance Appraisal. *The Journal of Finance* **64**(2), 985–1035.

Bollen, N.P.B. and Pool, V.K. (2009) Do Hedge Fund Managers Misreport Returns? Evidence from the Pooled Distribution. *The Journal of Finance* **64**(5), 2257–2288.

Boyson, N.M. (2008) Hedge Fund Performance Persistence: A New Approach. *Financial Analysts Journal* **64**(6), 27–44.

Brace, A., Gatarek, D. and Musiela, M. (1997) The market model of interest rate dynamics. *Mathematical Finance* **7**(2), 127–155.

Brooks, C., Clare, A. and Motson, N. (2008) The Gross Truth About Hedge Fund Performance and Risk: The Impact of Incentive Fees. *Journal of Financial Transformation* **24**, 33–42.

Brown S.J., Goetzmann, W.N. and Ibbotson, R.G. (1999) Offshore hedge funds: survival and performance 1989–1995. *Journal of Business* **72**(1), 91–117.

Carhart, M. (1997) On persistence of mutual fund performance. *Journal of Finance* **52**, 57–82.

Chen, R.-R. and Sopranzetti, B.J. (2002) *The valuation of default-triggered credit derivatives.* Rutgers University Working Paper.

Cox, J.C. and Rubinstein, M. (1985) *Option Markets.* Prentice-Hall.

Dubil, R. (2009) A practitioner's critique of value-at-risk models. In Greg N. Gregoriou (ed.), *The VaR Implementation Handbook* (Chapter 7, pp. 147–181). McGraw-Hill.

Duffie, D. and Singleton, K. (1999) Econometric modeling of term structure of defaultable bonds. *Review of Financial Studies* **12** (4), 687–720.

Fama, E. and French, K. (1992). The Cross-Section of Expected Stock Returns. *Journal of Finance* **47**(2), 427–465.

Fama, E. and French, K. (1993) Common risk factors in the returns on stocks and bonds. *Journal of Financial Economics* **33**, 3–56.

Fama, E. and French, K. (1996) Multifactor explanations of asset pricing anomalies. *Journal of Finance* **51**, 55–84.

French, K.: Link to data: http://mba.tuck.dartmouth.edu/pages/faculty/ken.french/data_library.html#International

Fung, W. and Hsieh, D.A. (1997) Empirical characteristics of dynamic trading strategies. The case of hedge funds. *Review of Financial Studies* **10**(2), 275–302.

Fung, W. and Hsieh, D.A. (2001) The risk in hedge fund strategies. Theory and evidence from trend followers. *Review of Financial Studies* **14**(2), 313–341.

Fung, W. and Hsieh, D.A. (2004) The risk in hedge fund strategies. Theory and evidence from long/short equity funds. Working paper. Revised version in *Journal of Empirical Finance* in 2011.

Fung, W. and Hsieh, D.A. (2007) Hedge fund replication strategies: implications for investors and regulators. Banque de France *Financial Stability Review* **10**, 55–66.

Fung, W. and Hsieh, D.A. (2009) Perspectives: Measurement Biases in Hedge Fund Performance Data: An Update. *Financial Analyst Journal* **65**(3).

Garman, S. and M. Kohlhagen, M. (1983) Foreign currency option values. *Journal of International Money and Finance* **2**, 231–237.

Geske, R. (1979) A note on an analytic valuation formula for unprotected American call options on stocks with known dividends. *Journal of Financial Economics* **7**, 375–380.

Graham, B. with Dodd, D. (1934) *Security Analysis* (1st edition). Whittlesey House.

Graham, B. with Dodd, D. (1949) *The Intelligent Investor* (1st edition). HarperCollins.

Graham, B. with Dodd, D. (2003) *The Intelligent Investor* (4th edition). HarperCollins.

Graham, B. with Dodd, D. (2008) *Security Analysis* (6th edition). McGraw-Hill.

Griffin, J.M. and Xu, J. (2009) How Smart Are the Smart Guys? A Unique View from Hedge Fund Stock Holdings. *The Review of Financial Studies* **22**(7), 2531–2570.

Hasanhodzic, J. and Lo, A.W. (2007) Can Hedge Fund Returns Be Replicated? The Linear Case. *Journal of Investment Management* **5**, 5–45.

Heath, D., Jarrow, R.A. and Morton, A. (1992) Bond pricing and the term structure of interest rates: a new methodology. *Econometrica* **60** (1), 77–105.

Ho, T.S.Y. and Lee, S.-B. (1986) Term structure movements and pricing interest rate contingent claims. *Journal of Finance* **41**, 1011–1029.

Hogg, R.V. and Craig, A.T. (1978) *Introduction to Mathematical Statistics* (4th edition). Macmillan, New York and Collier Macmillan, London.

Hull, J. (2000) *Options, Futures, and Other Derivatives* (4th edition). Prentice Hall.

Hull, J. (2010) *Risk Management and Financial Institutions* (2nd edition). Prentice Hall.

Hull, J. and White, A. (1990) Pricing interest rate derivatives. *Review of Financial Studies* **3** (4), 573–592.

Hull, J. and White, A. (1996) Using Hull–White interest rate trees. *Journal of Derivatives* (Spring), pp. 26–36.

IndexUniverse.com offers a variety of free educational resources, including past webinar replay at: http://www.indexuniverse.com/webinars/on-demand-webinar-playback.html.

Jaeger, L. (2008) Alternative Beta Strategies and Hedge Fund Replication. John Wiley & Sons, Ltd.

Jarrow, R. and Turnbull, S. (1995) Pricing options on financial securities subject to default risk. *Journal of Finance* **50** (1), 53–86.

Jorion, P. (2007) *Value at Risk: The New Benchmark for Managing Financial Risk* (3rd edition). McGraw-Hill Irwin Professional Publishing.

Kahneman, D. and Tversky, A. (1979) Prospect theory: an analysis of decision under risk. *Econometrica* **47**, 263–291.

Lintner, J. (1965) Security prices, risk, and maximal gains from diversification. *Journal of Finance* **20**, 587–615.

Lintner, J. (1965) The valuation of risk assets and the selection of risky investments in stock portfolios and capital budgets. *Review of Economics and Statistics* **47** (1), 13–37.

Lynch, P. with Rothchild, J. (1989) *One Up On Wall Street* (revised 2000). Simon & Schuster.

Macaulay, F. (1938) *Some Theoretical Problems Suggested by the Movement of Interest Rates, Bond Yields, and Stock Prices in the US Since 1856*. National Bureau of Economic Research, New York.

Malkiel, B.G. (1973) *A Random Walk Down Wall Street* (revised 2003). W.W. Norton & Company, New York and London.

Markowitz, H.M. (1952) Portfolio selection. *The Journal of Finance* **7** (1), 77–91.

Merton, R.C. (1973), Theory of rational option pricing. *Bell Journal of Economics and Management Science* **4** (Spring), 141–183.

Roll, R. (1977) An analytic formula for unprotected American call options on stocks with known dividends. *Journal of Financial Economics* **5**, 251–258.

Roncalli, T. and Weisang, G. (2009) Tracking Problems, Hedge Fund Replication and Alternative Beta. SSRN Working Paper.

Ross, S. (1976) The arbitrage theory of capital asset pricing. *Journal of Economic Theory* **13**, 341–360.

Sadka, R. (2010) Liquidity risk and the cross-section of hedge fund returns. *Journal of Financial Economics* **98**, 54–71.

Sharpe, W.F. (1964) Capital asset prices: a theory of market equilibrium under conditions of risk. *Journal of Finance* **19**(3), 425–442.

Thaler, R.H. (1991) *Quasi Rational Economics*. Russell Sage Foundation. New York.

Thaler, R.H. (1992) *The Winner's Curse: Paradoxes and Anomalies of Economic Life*. Princeton University Press, Princeton, NJ.

Treynor, J.L. (1961) *Market value, time, and risk*. Unpublished manuscript.

Whaley, R. (1981) On the valuation of American call options on stocks with known dividends. *Journal of Financial Economics* **9**, 207–211.

Index

Index compiled by Terry Halliday